DISCOVERING CALCULUS

A Preliminary Version
I Single Variable

Alan L. Levine
George M. Rosenstein, Jr.
Franklin and Marshall College

McGraw-Hill, Inc.
College Custom Series

New York St. Louis San Francisco Auckland Bogotá
Caracas Lisbon London Madrid Mexico Milan Montreal
New Delhi Paris San Juan Singapore Sydney Tokyo Toronto

DISCOVERING CALCULUS: A Preliminary Version
I Single Variable

 4 5 6 7 8 9 0 PCP PCP 9 0 9 8 7 6 5 4

ISBN 0-07-037555-0

Editor: Margaret A. Hollander

Cover Design: Mark Anderson

Printer/Binder: Port City Press

TABLE OF CONTENTS

PREFACE TO THE STUDENT

"What is mathematics?"

Ponder that question for a moment. You've taken something called "math" throughout most of your elementary and high school careers, so you ought to have a pretty good idea of what mathematics is, right? Maybe. You can list subjects--arithmetic, algebra, geometry, trigonometry--that you covered in your math courses, but can you identify some unifying theme, some reason that they are all called "math"?

What do these courses have in common? Think about the kinds of tasks you had to perform in these courses. Certainly, a major activity in all math courses--either in class, on exams or homework--is solving problems. The problems may be routine exercises involving nothing more than straightforward calculations. They may be more complicated, multi-step problems. They may involve applications or they may be proofs, as in geometry. Since learning to solve problems is a desired outcome of all math courses, then maybe mathematics is problem solving.

That's not a bad answer but it's a bit too simple. Why is problem solving important? Certainly, the application of mathematics to other disciplines has led to many important discoveries and theories, but there's more to it. Problem solving is the process by which mathematics itself is created!

Perhaps you've never thought about mathematics being "created" or "discovered". Maybe you thought that it just appeared on earth one day (a sort of Big Bang theory of mathematics) or that it is part of the Old Testament (in the Book of Numbers?). In fact, new mathematics is constantly being discovered, just like any science, through experimentation, through conjecture, through problem solving.

It is this idea of discovery that we emphasize throughout this book; hence, we've chosen the title, "Discovering Calculus". We want to take you on a journey, starting with some very simple numerical and geometrical concepts and building upon them until we develop the subject of calculus. Along the way, we'll stop to see some interesting applications. And we'll give you the opportunity to explore some things on your own. Of course, in order to enjoy the trip, you have to want to enjoy it. We realize that you may have found mathematics in the past to be difficult, boring or generally not a pleasant experience. While there may be many reasons for this, we hope you can put the past behind you and approach calculus with a fresh attitude.

In order to truly appreciate this journey, you have to be an active participant. You may be accustomed to learning mathematics as a spectator, with an instructor lecturing and you practicing what the instructor shows you how to do. If you use this approach, you are really missing a lot of the discovery. It's like getting a guided tour of a foreign country without ever stopping to meet the people or sample the local food or see the sights up close. Years later, you may vaguely remember being there but the memories will be far more intense and lasting if you actually have "hands-on" experience.

Perhaps you also have discovered clever ways to avoid the "sights" that your teacher has wanted you to see. One way all of us (including the authors of this book) have done this is, when faced with a problem, looked back in the text for an example like the problem that we've been assigned. When we can find such an example (and in most texts, that's not too difficult) we simply follow the steps, applying them to our problem. That way, we don't have to think too carefully about what we're doing and we miss the attraction that our instructor wanted us to see.

If you've used this technique and others like it frequently, you may have learned that you didn't have to read the text in order to do your assignments. In fact, you may have discovered that, if your teacher was helpful, you could get good grades without ever reading the text. Perhaps that's fine as far as it goes, but you will not always have a teacher available and — surprise! — you may have to learn some mathematics on your own.

We've written a book for you to read. We suggest that you read the book before your instructor covers the material in class. That way, it will seem familiar and you will have some idea what to expect. This, in turn, makes the class easier to follow and makes you a better prepared participant in the discussion. Even if you don't understand everything that you read, at least you'll recognize some of the words and basic concepts. It's somewhat like reading a travel guide before going on vacation--you know what to look for when you get there. At the very least, you should read the book shortly after the lecture (not the night before the exam) to reinforce the ideas and give you a different perspective. It's much easier to understand something when you see it from several points of view.

Here are a few pointers for reading our book. First, reading a math book is not like reading a novel. Mathematics is much more structured and much denser (and, quite honestly, despite our efforts to use picturesque language, a bit blander) than ordinary prose. There are not many extra words thrown in for color. You cannot try to scan one paragraph at a time; you must read each sentence and equation and make sure you understand it before you go on to the next. While we've tried to provide as much detail as possible, we occasionally skip some algebraic steps. Keep a paper and pencil handy to fill in details if you cannot follow what we've done.

A section of the book probably contains several different ideas. It's often difficult to see a new idea coming, so we've put a marker, ¤, at the beginning of the development of a new subsection. When really big changes in direction are made, we introduce subsections with their own titles. Of course, definitions and theorems are important, so we've used bold-faced type to make them stand out. So, you have a variety of clues as to when something important has happened or will happen.

To help you decide whether you really understand a concept, we've interspersed questions, called Test Your Understanding (TYU for short), throughout the text. When you reach one, stop and do it to make sure you understand the concept before going on. The answers to the TYU's are found at the end of the section but you must resist the temptation to look at the answers before you really try the question. If you are stuck, try reading the preceding paragraphs again. Only as a last resort should you look at the answers. The key to understanding mathematics is being able to do a problem from start to finish, not watching someone else do it or working backwards from the answers. This point cannot be emphasized too strongly.

There is an analogy to foreign languages: It is much easier to learn to read a language or understand when someone else speaks it than to actually speak or write the language coherently yourself. We want you speaking and writing mathematics. Only in this way will calculus become a useful tool for you.

At the end of each section is a set of Exercises and a set of Problems. The Exercises are fairly routine and mechanical, much like the TYU's. We don't have as many exercises as some other books. We believe it is better to concentrate on a few exercises and really understand the underlying concepts than to practice superficially. Again resist the temptation to work backwards. You will discover that often the exercises are not merely examples from the text with new numbers. We'd like you to understand the ideas of the section and we hope the exercises help that understanding.

The Problems are not as straightforward as the Exercises and will require even more thought. You may find them frustrating at first but if you persevere, we think you'll find them easier as you get further into the course. Perhaps your instructor can teach you some problem solving strategies if you find that you have difficulty getting started.

Finally, at the end of each chapter is a set of questions called Questions to Think About. These review the main points of the chapter and ask you to discuss the concepts.

Well, that's enough advice from the authors. Just sit back, relax and begin "Discovering Calculus".

PREFACE TO INSTRUCTORS

In recent years, a nationwide movement ("Lean and Lively Calculus") has called for a change in the way calculus is taught. Many schools have responded to the challenge by experimenting with revised calculus courses. While the revised courses vary widely in nature, most concentrate on making calculus more applied, teaching more problem solving skills and incorporating modern computer/calculator technology into the courses. Many revised courses use existing texts with home-grown supplementary material. This retro-fit approach carries all of the disadvantages of the old materials along with the new ideas.

We felt that no meaningful revision could take place within the framework of an existing text. We decided to restructure the calculus course from the ground up and write a book that fit the course as we envisioned it.

The biggest problem students face when learning calculus is that they confuse "doing" with "understanding". The reason for this confusion is that their entire mathematical education has focused on learning mechanical procedures, not concepts--that is, on the "how", not the "what" and "why" of mathematics. Combatting this requires a change in pedagogy. Students must become more active in the learning process. Teachers must do more than just lecture. Assessment procedures must focus on important ideas rather than easy-to-grade procedures.

Our book addresses these issues from several points of view. First comes the question of content. We have selected a set of topics that we feel are central to the understanding of calculus; these form the core of the text. There are many topics (such as techniques of integration) ordinarily found in texts that are largely mechanical and do not enhance the underlying concepts. These have either been de-emphasized, been omitted entirely or placed in the set of projects at the end of each chapter.

We also believe that students will show more interest in mathematics if they can see its applications. Consequently, we have included sections illustrating the application of calculus to fluid dynamics, biology, physics, chemistry, engineering, economics and astronomy. Other applications are included in the projects, as well.

Many of the applications involve differential equations, a topic not normally given much emphasis in beginning calculus courses. We introduce first-order differential equations in Chapter 5 and use them to motivate exponential and logarithmic functions. Second-order equations are introduced in Chapter 7 and used to motivate trigonometric functions. Chapter 11 on infinite series is motivated by the problem of determining power series solutions of differential equations.

Traditionally, calculus has been taught in a lecture/recitation format with little input from the students. One of the reasons for this is that the texts are, for the most part, unreadable by the average student. Our book is written in a way that allows other teaching styles to be used. The language used is less formal and we have eliminated much of the rigor and technical jargon that makes the standard texts so formidable. We have found that, with a little encouragement, students can read our book in advance of class and come prepared to discuss the material. To help the students with their reading, we have interspersed "Test Your Understanding" questions throughout the text so that students can check whether they really understand what they have read before going on to the next topic.

Most existing texts advertise 5000 exercises, many of which can now be done by computer. Students believe these represent what calculus is about and what they must learn. We have only a fraction of that amount. In addition, we ask different types of questions--some exercises, some more conceptual problems and some essay questions. Many of our exercises and problems are unlike any example in the text. While students, used to seeking "templates" for homework problems among the examples, may find this frustrating, this encourages them to think about what they are doing, rather than just changing numbers and plugging into an equation.

As we said earlier, one of the motivating factors behind the calculus reform movement is the appearance of computers and calculators that take the drudgery out of doing calculus and allow for changing the emphasis in teaching to concepts. Our book does not require any specific technology, although there are many places where the classroom presentation of a topic will be enhanced by a computer or graphing calculator. Some of the exercises, problems and projects require or are made easier by the use of technology. We'll give some strategies for incorporating technology into a calculus course in our instructor's manual.

Finally, we'd like to hear your reactions to this text. While we've been encouraged by our colleagues at Franklin and Marshall and by reviewers, we've learned that there are many ways of looking at the pedagogical problems we've tackled. Please do no hesitate to share your insights with us.

ACKNOWLEDGMENTS

Many individuals and institutions have helped and supported us throughout the development of this book.

The Howard Hughes Medical Institute provided Franklin and Marshall College with a grant that supported the development of this text for several years. We are grateful that we have been part of this effort to improve science education at the college.

Brad Rathbone has been a part of this project since the beginning. He created many of the graphs in the text and suggested numerous exercises and problems. By serving as a teaching assistant for the first two years in which we class-tested this book, he was able to observe and report student reactions from a student's perspective. As a result, he was able to suggest many areas of the book that needed clarification.

Brad and Beth Rosenstein have contributed to the solution manual for the book. Ali Salahuddin prepared the index.

The students at Franklin and Marshall College who were taught from earlier versions of this book deserve thanks for their tolerance. Their responses to the book, not always positive, have encouraged us and pointed us in better directions.

The individual and collective support of our departmental colleagues has been invaluable. They allowed us to undertake this project, and then agreed to adopt the text for all calculus sections starting in the 1991-92 school year. Each one of them has contributed to the text.

We'd like to thank Arnold Feldman and Gene Johnson for being brave enough to try teaching from this text during the 1990-91 school year. Their suggestions have been most valuable. William Tyndall has proven to be a proof reader without peer. His eagle eyes have saved us from any number of gaffes and inconsistencies. Timothy Hesterberg has also been a careful and helpful reader. Bernard Jacobson has contributed the wisdom of his years of experience teaching calculus to an accurate and even-handed appraisal of our work. Robert Gethner's enthusiasm for the project, his many helpful suggestions and his thoughtful reflections on teaching have strongly influenced this book. Robert Lubarsky suggested the term "direction" as a collective noun for "increasing or decreasing". Barbara Nimershiem and Annalisa Crannell, who joined the department in 1992, have provided a fresh look at the materials.

We'd like to acknowledge the many reviews we received from unnamed colleagues at other institutions. This project certainly would not have come to this point without their support. We have gloried in their praise and have acknowledged ruefully the validity of their criticisms. Their comments have been most helpful as we prepared this revision.

We also acknowledge conversations with many teachers of calculus. These conversations have taken place both at meetings of the calculus reform network and informally and privately. The stimulation of colleagues who are worrying about similar problems has sharpened our own sense of our objectives.

Many of the historical comments are the result of conversations with historians of mathematics, particularly V. Frederick Rickey of Bowling Green State University.

Finally, we would like to thank the McGraw-Hill Publishing Company and in particular, our current editor, Jack Shira, and our former editor, Richard Wallis, for believing enough in this project to offer us a contract to publish it.

Alan Levine
George M. Rosenstein, Jr.

CHAPTER 1

FUNCTIONS

1.1 SOME DEFINITIONS AND MOTIVATIONAL EXAMPLES

There are many real-world situations in which some quantity depends on one or more other quantities. The area of a rectangle depends on the length and width; the distance travelled by a car in one hour depends on its speed; the average daily temperature in a city depends on its location and the time of year.

In this chapter, we will study **functions**, which are one way of expressing the dependence of one quantity, the **dependent variable**, on one or more other quantities, the **independent variables**. Arguably, the concept of function is one of the most important in all of mathematics and a large part of calculus is devoted to the study of the behavior of functions.

The key idea is that a function associates a (unique) value of the dependent variable with each value of the independent variable or variables. It may be convenient to think of a function as a machine: You feed in values of the independent variable(s) and the function spits out the corresponding value of the dependent variable. Throughout the first 11 chapters of this book, all functions will have one independent variable. In Chapters 12 through 14, we'll deal with functions with more than one independent variable.

Functions can be represented in several different ways--graphically, in a table of values, or by a formula. One of the goals of this chapter is to become adept at working with functions, no matter how they are represented.

Usually, functions are denoted by letters such as f, g, h, etc. Specifically, if the dependent variable, y, is related to the independent variable, x, by the function f, we will write $y = f(x)$. The symbol "$f(x)$" represents the value of y associated with the given value of x. For example, $f(2)$ is the y-value when $x = 2$. It can be determined from a graph (by reading the y-coordinate of the point whose x-coordinate is 2), from a table (by reading the y-value corresponding to $x = 2$) or from a formula (by plugging in $x = 2$).

Figure 1.1 shows the graph of a function f. To determine $f(6)$, we draw a vertical line from $x = 6$ on the x-axis to the graph and then draw a horizontal line to the y-axis. Hence, $f(6) = 4$.

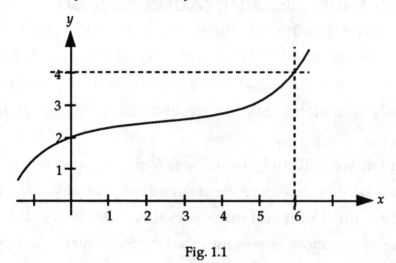

Fig. 1.1

The table below gives the values of a function g for various x-values.

x	0	1	2	3	4	5	6
$g(x)$	8	6	4	7	1	2	5

So, $g(0) = 8, g(1) = 6$, etc. Figure 1.2 is a graph of this function, at least for the x-values given in the table. We don't know what happens in between, so we can't "connect the dots".

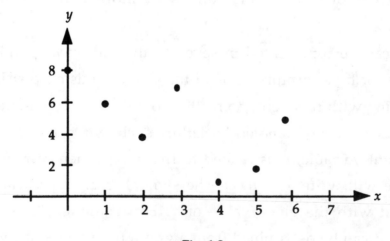

Fig. 1.2

Finally, suppose the function h takes a number, squares it and adds 1. We can denote this by the formula $h(x) := x^2 + 1$. Note the use of the ":=" when defining the function. (Many computer languages use the same symbol to define functions.) Then $h(2) = 2^2 + 1 = 5, h(4) = 4^2 + 1 = 17$, etc. Figure 1.3 shows a graph of this function. Note that h is defined for all x, so the graph is a connected curve, as opposed to the discrete set of points in Figure 1.2.

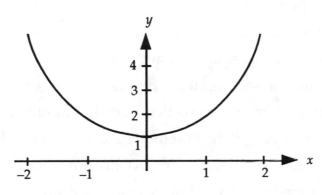

Fig. 1.3

TEST YOUR UNDERSTANDING

1. Write a statement indicating that the dependent variable s is related to the independent variable t by the function g.

2. Write a statement indicating that the volume of a gas is a function of its pressure. How would you represent the volume of a gas whose pressure is 20 pounds per square inch?

3. For the function in Figure 1.1, what is $f(0)$? For what value of x is $f(x) = 3$?

4. Let $g(x) := x^3 - x$. (a) Determine $g(2)$ and $g(-2)$. (b) For what x-values is $g(x) = 0$?

◻ The set of values of the independent variable (inputs) is called the **domain** of the function. The set of values of the dependent variable (outputs) is called the **range**. If the variables involved in the function have no particular physical interpretation, then the domain will consist of those inputs for which it is algebraically possible to compute the corresponding output.

For instance, suppose $f(x) := \dfrac{1}{x-4}$. It is possible to compute a value for $f(x)$ for every x except 4 (since doing so would entail division by 0). Hence, the domain is $\{x \mid x \neq 4\}$. Similarly if $q(x) := \sqrt{x^2 - 4}$, then q is defined for all x for which $x^2 - 4 \geq 0$. Thus, the domain of q is $\{x \mid x \geq 2 \text{ or } x \leq -2\}$.

On the other hand, if the variables represent actual physical quantities, then the domain may be restricted so that both the inputs and outputs make sense physically. For instance, the volume of a cube is related to the length of the side by the function $v = f(s) := s^3$. Although v can be computed for any value of s, side lengths and volumes must be positive quantities. Thus, the domain must be restricted to $\{s \mid s \geq 0\}$.

◻ We'll now look at some specific examples of situations that can be conveniently described by functions. For some examples, we'll use our intuition to develop a sense of how the dependent variable changes when the independent variable changes. For instance, does increasing the independent variable cause an increase or decrease in the dependent variable? In other examples, we'll either do some calculations or collect actual data and make a table of values. For others, we may actually derive a formula relating the dependent and independent variables. In all cases, we'll draw a graph of the function with the dependent variable on the vertical axis and the independent variable on the horizontal axis. The key idea is to be able to translate from one representation to another.

EXAMPLE 1.1:

You throw a ball into the air from an initial height of 8 feet off the ground and let it fall back to the ground. How does the height of the ball depend on the time elapsed since you let go of it?

We'll let t represent the elapsed time (the independent variable), h represent the height of the ball (the dependent variable) and call the function f; that is, $h = f(t)$. Intuitively, the ball should go up for awhile, then turn around and come back down. Since the initial height (i.e. when $t = 0$) is 8 feet, then $f(0) = 8$. In other words, the graph should pass through the point (0, 8). Figure 1.4 below has these properties. It is not the only graph we could have drawn; indeed, we would need more information, such as the speed at which you threw the ball, to determine the graph more accurately. We will look at this problem in more detail in Chapter 3.

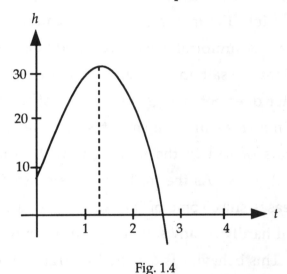

Fig. 1.4

Notice that the ball attains a maximum height of approximately 33 feet when $t = 1.25$ and that the ball hits the ground at $t \approx 2.6$. Since nothing interesting happens after the ball hits the ground, we could say that the domain is the set $\{t \mid 0 \le t \le 2.6\}$. The range is $\{h \mid 0 \le h \le 33\}$. ♦

- -

TEST YOUR UNDERSTANDING

5. (a) In the graph above, at what time(s) is the ball 20 feet off the ground?

   (b) At what time does the ball return to its initial height?

6. How would the graph change if the ball were thrown with a greater initial speed?

- -

EXAMPLE 1.2:

A 10 gallon tank is filled with water into which 3 lbs. of salt is dissolved. Fresh water is poured into the tank at a rate of 2 gal./min; the tank is well-stirred so that the salt is uniformly dissolved and the overflow drains off. How does the amount of salt in the tank depend on time? (Note that dissolving salt in water does not change the volume of water signficantly.)

Let t represent time (measured in minutes) and let $p = g(t)$ represent the number of pounds of salt in the tank at time t. Initially, there are 3 pounds of salt, so $g(0) = 3$. As the fresh water is poured in, the amount of salt in the tank decreases since some of it drains off with the overflow. After a long time, there will hardly be any salt at all. In other words, $g(t)$ gets close to 0 as t gets bigger. This behavior is depicted in Figure 1.5 below. Since this process can go on forever, the domain of this function is $\{t \mid t \geq 0\}$. Since the amount of salt never exceeds 3 pounds, then the range is $\{p \mid 0 < p \leq 3\}$.

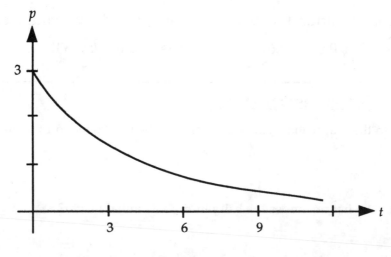

Fig. 1.5

It is possible to approximate the values of $g(t)$. For instance, after 1 minute, we've replaced 2 gallons of the original solution with fresh water. Since 2 gallons is $\frac{1}{5}$ the capacity of the tank, then we've removed approximately $\frac{1}{5}$ of the original amount of salt. In other words, $g(1) \approx 3 - 3\left(\frac{1}{5}\right) = 2.4$ lbs. After another minute, we will have removed approximately $\frac{1}{5}$ of the remaining salt; hence, $g(2) \approx 2.4 - 2.4\left(\frac{1}{5}\right) = 1.92$ lbs.

The reason that these are approximations is that once we start adding the fresh water, the amount of salt immediately starts to decrease. At any instant, we are removing $\frac{1}{5}$ of the salt in the tank at that moment. Hence we are actually removing somewhat less than $3\left(\frac{1}{5}\right)$ lbs. of salt during the first minute so $g(1)$ will actually be a little bigger than 2.4 lbs. This idea of approximating the values of a function is a central concept in the study of calculus and we shall see it many times throughout this book. ♦

TEST YOUR UNDERSTANDING

7. Compute an approximate value of $g(3)$.

8. How would the graph change if the fresh water were added at a rate of 4 gal./min.? Compute approximate values of $g(1)$ and $g(2)$ in this case. Do these values confirm your answer to the question?

EXAMPLE 1.3:

In colder climates during the winter, meteorologists often describe how cold it feels on windy days in terms of a "wind chill factor" which is the effective air temperature, taking into account the actual air temperature (in the absence of wind) and the wind speed. Assuming the air temperature remains constant at 20 degrees Fahrenheit, how does the wind chill factor depend on the wind speed?

Let w represent the wind speed and $r = f(w)$ represent the wind chill factor. Certainly, if there is no wind, then the wind chill factor is the same as the air temperature. Hence, $f(0) = 20$. Furthermore, as the wind speed increases, the wind chill factor goes down. The table below gives the wind chill factors for several different wind speeds at an air temperature of 20.

Wind speed	5	10	15	20	25	30	35
Wind chill factor	15	5	−5	−10	−15	−20	−20

These values are graphed in Figure 1.6.

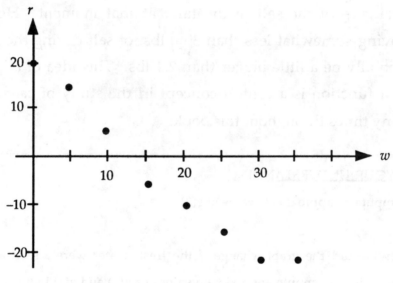

Fig. 1.6

Note that we've drawn the graph as a discrete set of points. Presumably, however, the wind chill can be determined for wind speeds in between those given in the table and, hence, the dots in the graph can be connected to form a continuous curve. ◆

TEST YOUR UNDERSTANDING

9. How would the graph change if the air temperature were 30 degrees?

EXAMPLE 1.4:

An open-topped box is created by cutting small squares from the corners of a 8" x 15" rectangular piece of cardboard and folding up the sides, as shown in Figure 1.7.

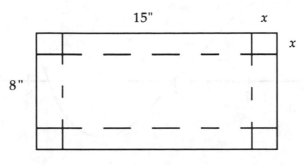

15" x

x

8"

Fig. 1.7

Determine the volume of the box as a function of size of the cutout squares.

Let x = side of the cutout squares and $V = g(x)$ be the corresponding volume.

Once the cardboard is folded, then x is the height of the box. If $x = 1$, then the dimensions of the base of the box are 6 and 13, so the volume is $g(1)$ = 1 x 6 x 13 = 78. If $x = 2$, the dimensions of the base are 4 and 11, so the volume is $g(2) = 2 \times 4 \times 11 = 88$. In general, the length and width of the box are $8 - 2x$ and $15 - 2x$ so that the volume is

$$g(x) := x(8 - 2x)(15 - 2x) = 120x - 46x^2 + 4x^3.$$

The graph of g is given in Figure 1.8. Note that although values of $g(x)$ can be computed for any real value of x, this function only makes sense physically for x-values between 0 and 4 since we cannot cut out squares bigger than 4 inches if the cardboard is only 8 inches wide. This is evident in the graph: If $0 \leq x \leq 4$, then $g(x) \geq 0$ while if $x > 4$, $g(x)$ becomes negative, a physical impossibility. Hence, the domain is $\{x \mid 0 \leq x \leq 4\}$.

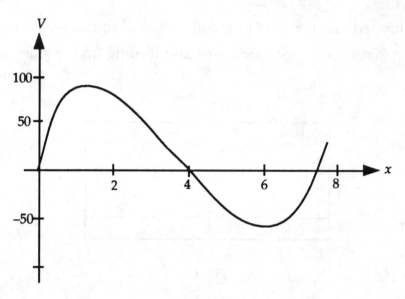

Fig. 1.8

It appears that the largest box that can be made in this fashion has a volume of approximately 90 cubic inches, obtained by cutting squares of approximately 1.7 inches from each corner. Determining the largest value of a function is one of the most important applications of calculus, one which we'll investigate in Chapter 5. ◆

- -

TEST YOUR UNDERSTANDING

10. Determine the volume of the box if 3 inch squares are cut out.

11. Approximately what size squares should be cut out to make the volume of the box 50 cubic inches?

- -

EXERCISES FOR SECTION 1.1:

1. Let $f(x) := \sqrt{x-2}$.

    (a) What is the domain of f?

    (b) What is $f(11)$?

    (c) For what value(s) of x is $f(x) = 4$?

2. Determine the domain of $f(x) := \dfrac{1}{x^2 + 4x + 3}$.

3. Let $g(x) := 4x - 8$.

    (a) For what values of x is $g(x) = 12$?

    (b) For what values of x is $g(x) > 0$?

4. Let $g(x) := x^2 + 2x$.

    (a) Determine $g(3) - g(2)$.

    (b) Determine $g(x + 1)$.

    (c) Determine $g(x) + g(1)$. Is your answer the same as in (b)?

5. Determine $h(2x + 1)$ if $h(x) := \dfrac{x}{x-5}$.

6. Let $f(x) := x^2 - x$. For what values of x is $f(x) + f(x + 2) = 6$?

7. Draw a graph of any function f defined for x-values between 0 and 5.

    (a) Draw a line segment whose length is $|f(4)|$.

    (b) Draw a segment whose length is $|f(4) - f(2)|$.

8. The graph below shows a function g.

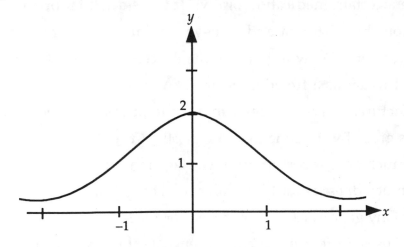

    (a) What are the domain and the range of g?

    (b) For what values of x is $g(x) = 1$?

    (c) For what values of x is $g(x) > 1$?

9. The graph below shows a function h.

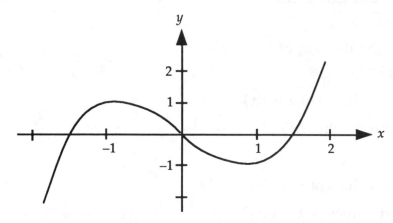

   (a) For what values of x is $h(x) \geq 0$?

   (b) For what values of x is $-2 \leq h(x) \leq 2$?

   (c) For what values of x is $h(x) > h(-1)$?

10. You cook a turkey until its internal temperature is 180 degrees Fahrenheit, remove it from the oven and place it in a room whose temperature is 70 degrees. Draw a graph of the temperature of the turkey as a function of the time elapsed since you removed it from the oven.

11. Draw a reasonable graph of the wind chill factor as a function of the air temperature if the wind speed remains constant at 20 mph.

12. You take a certain medication orally. It takes a while for the medication to enter your bloodstream and achieve maximum concentration. Then it starts to wear off. Draw a graph of the concentration of the medication in your bloodstream as a function of time.

13. A manufacturer has determined that the total cost of producing x gallons of gloop is given by the function $c(x) := 50 + 6x + x^2$.

   (a) How much does it cost to produce 10 gallons of gloop?

   (b) How much does it cost to produce the 11th gallon?

   (c) How many gallons can be produced for $482?

14. A farmer uses 80 feet of fencing to enclose three sides of a rectangular garden. The fourth side of the garden is his barn. Express the area of the garden as a function of the length of the side opposite the barn. Be sure to include the domain.

15. A woman 5 feet tall is standing on level ground near a 10 foot lamppost.

    (a) Express the length of her shadow as a function of her distance from the lamppost.

    (b) How far from the lamppost must she be in order for her shadow to be 12 feet long?

16. A baseball player runs at a constant speed of 30 feet per second. If he leaves first base at time $t = 0$ (heading towards second base, where he stops), express his distance from home plate as a function of t. (Note: A baseball diamond is a 90 foot square. "Distance" means shortest distance, not the distance along the basepaths.)

17. A car passes by a certain point at 4:00 heading east at 40 mph. At 5:00, another car passes by the same point heading north at 50 mph. Express the distance between the two cars as a function of t, where t is the number of hours that have elapsed since 5:00.

18. A right triangle has a hypotenuse of 12 feet.

    (a) Express the length of one leg as a function of the length of the other leg.

    (b) Express the area of the triangle as a function of the length of one leg.

PROBLEMS FOR SECTION 1.1:

1. A bowl is filled with water up to initial height h. The water drains through a hole in the bottom in such a way that the height at time t is given by $g(t) := \sqrt{h^2 - 2kt}$, for some constant k.

    (a) Express, in terms of h and k, the amount of time it takes for the bowl to empty completely.

    (b) How long does it take for the height of water in the bowl to reach one-half its initial value?

    (c) If the height of water decreases from 10 to 8 inches in the first 5 minutes, determine the value of k.

2. Let $f(x) := px^7 + qx^3 + rx - 4$, where p, q and r are constants and $f(-5) = 3$. What is the value of $f(5)$?

3. Let $f(x) := x^2 + 4x - 5$.

    (a) Express $\dfrac{f(2+h)-f(2)}{h}$ in terms of h.

    (b) Interpret the expression in part (a) in terms of the graph of f.

4. Let $f(x) := x^2 + 1$ and $g(x) := bx$. For what value(s) of b will the graphs of f and g have:

    (a) two points in common   (b) one point in common   (c) no points in common

5. Let $f(x) := 2x + 5$.

    (a) Show that $f(a + b) \neq f(a) + f(b)$.

    (b) Can you think of a function for which $f(a + b) = f(a) + f(b)$?

TYU Answers for Section 1.1

1. $s = g(t)$ 2. $v = f(p)$; $f(20)$ 3. $f(0) = 2$; $x = 5$ (approx.)

4. (a) $g(2) = 6, g(-2) = -6$ (b) $x = 1, -1, 0$ 5. (a) At $t = .4$ and 2.2 (approx.)

   (b) At $t = 2.5$ (approx.)   6. The vertex (turning point) would move up among other things.

7. $g(3) = 1.536$ 8. The new graph would be below the old but still above the t-axis;

   $g(1) = 1.8, g(2) = 1.08$ 9. The graph would be higher up on the vertical axis.

10. $g(3) = 54$ 11. At $x = 0.5$ and $x = 3.1$ (approx.)

1.2 ANALYZING AND DESCRIBING THE BEHAVIOR OF FUNCTIONS

Throughout the remainder of this book, we will be analyzing many functions. A first step in that analysis is to be able to recognize how the function behaves and to draw its graph (or at least a rough sketch).

Initially, we'll just look at polynomials, rational functions (quotients of polynomials) and algebraic functions (involving radicals). Later, we will learn about exponential, logarithmic and trigonometric functions (some of the so-called transcendental functions).

You may argue that there really is no need to do any of this since there are calculators and computers that will easily draw reasonably accurate graphs of any function. That argument is correct but only up to a certain point. First of all, there is the question of convenience. For very simple functions, it is faster to draw them by hand than to turn on the computer. (This is akin to using a calculator to add 3 + 5 or a food processor to chop one carrot.) Also, the technology is not perfect and sometimes computer-generated graphs exhibit features which shouldn't be there or do not exhibit features which should be. Determining what is real and what isn't requires some analysis. Most importantly, however, in the real world, functions often depend on quantities (or **parameters**) which cannot be measured accurately, or which may change over time. (For instance, consider Example 1.1, where we threw a ball from initial height of 8 feet. The graph depends on this initial height and on the initial velocity.) Rather than re-draw the graph each time one of these parameters changes, it is more expedient to express the behavior of the function in terms of these parameters. This is where calculus is useful.

<u>DIRECTION</u>

Consider the graph of the function $y = f(x)$ in Figure 1.9.

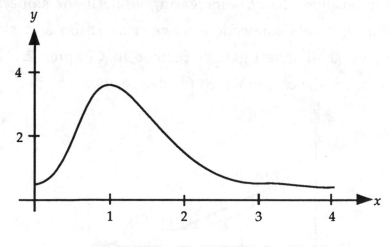

Fig. 1.9

As we move from left to right along the x-axis, the y-values increase until we get to $x = 1$, after which they start to decrease until we get to $x = 4$. We shall say that the function f is "increasing on the interval [0, 1] and decreasing on the interval [1, 4]". What this means is that if we pick any two x-values, p and q where $p < q$ and both are between 0 and 1, then $f(p) < f(q)$. Conversely if we pick p and q between 1 and 4, with $p < q$, then $f(p) > f(q)$. More formally, we have:

DEFINITION: A function f is said to be **increasing** on the interval I if, for *every* choice of p and q on I with $p < q$, then $f(p) < f(q)$. Similarly, f is **decreasing** on I if, for every choice of p and q with $p < q$, then $f(p) > f(q)$.

Notes: (1) The requirement that $p < q$ ensures that we move from left to right.

(2) Intervals are denoted by enclosing the endpoints either in parentheses or in square brackets, depending on whether or not the endpoint is included. For example, the open interval $\{x \mid a < x < b\}$ is denoted (a, b), while the closed interval $\{x \mid a \le x \le b\}$ is denoted $[a, b]$. Intervals may also be half-open, such as $[a, b)$ or $(a, b]$.

Geometrically, this definition implies that if we pick *any two points* $P(p, f(p))$ and $Q(q, f(q))$ on the graph of f, with $p < q$, and if the slope of the line PQ is positive, then f is increasing while if the slope is negative, then f is decreasing. This connection between direction and slope is very important and we shall investigate it further in Chapter 2. Figure 1.10 illustrates this idea for the case in which f is decreasing.

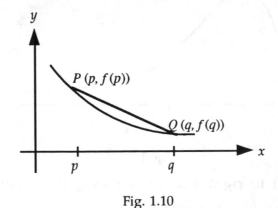

Fig. 1.10

We shall use the term **direction** to describe whether a function is increasing or decreasing; that is, the phrase "discuss the direction of a function" means "determine the intervals on which the function is increasing and those on which it is decreasing".

EXAMPLE 1.5:

Discuss the direction of the function pictured in Figure 1.11 below.

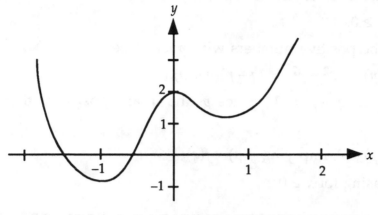

Fig. 1.11

This function is decreasing on (–∞, –1] and [0, .75] and increasing on [–1, 0] and [.75, ∞). Note that these values are approximate; you may get slightly different results, depending on how you read the graph. ◆

EXAMPLE 1.6:

Draw a function that is increasing on the intervals (–∞, –2] and [3, 5] and decreasing on the intervals [–2, 3] and [5, ∞).

Since we are not given any function values, there is not a unique answer to this question. One possibility is shown in Figure 1.12 below. There are infinitely many others.

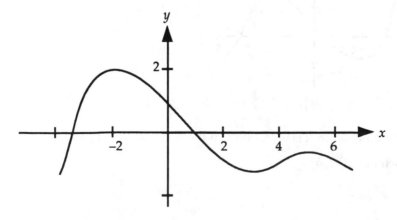

Fig. 1.12

◆

EXAMPLE 1.7:

Use the definition of an increasing function to show that $f(x) := x^2$ is increasing for $x \geq 0$.

Let p and q be positive numbers with $p < q$. Then
$$f(q) - f(p) = q^2 - p^2 = (q - p)(q + p).$$
Since $p < q$, then $q - p > 0$. Since p and q are positive, then $q + p > 0$. Therefore,
$$f(q) - f(p) > 0, \text{ implying } f(p) < f(q).$$
Thus, f is increasing for $x \geq 0$. ◆

- -

TEST YOUR UNDERSTANDING

1. Show by definition that $f(x) := x^2$ is decreasing for $x < 0$.

2. Show by definition that $f(x) := \frac{1}{x}$ is decreasing for $x > 0$.

3. Describe the direction of the function pictured below.

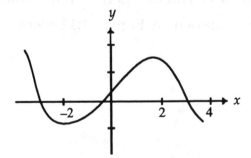

4. Draw a function that is increasing on the intervals $(-\infty, 1]$ and $[4, \infty)$ and decreasing on the interval $[1, 4]$.

- -

CONCAVITY

While determining the direction of a function tells us a lot about its behavior, there is more we can say. Consider the two functions graphed in Figure 1.13. Both are increasing on the interval [0, 3]. However, the one on the left is "bent upward", while the one on the right is "bent downward". The mathematical term for "bent" is **concave**. Thus, the graph on the left is **concave up**, and the one on the right is **concave down**. When we "discuss the concavity of a function", we mean determine the intervals on which it is concave up and those on which it is concave down.

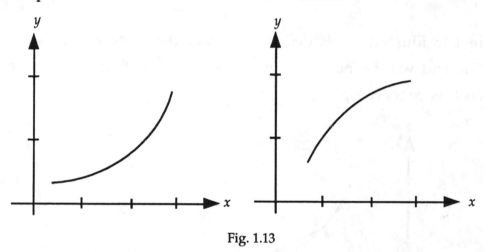

Fig. 1.13

Concavity also applies to decreasing functions. The function on the left in Figure 1.14 is decreasing and concave up; the one on the right is decreasing and concave down.

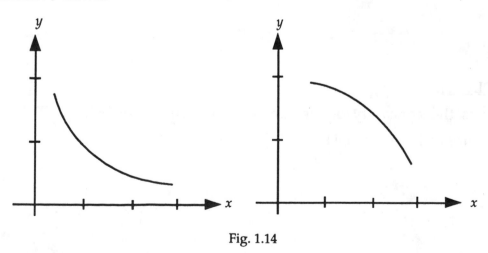

Fig. 1.14

Concavity is a property that can be determined from the graph but is a little hard to define precisely. Here's one possible definition.

DEFINITION: On an interval $[a, b]$, choose any three numbers p, q and r, where $a \leq p < q < r \leq b$. Let $P(p, f(p))$, $Q(q, f(q))$ and $R(r, f(r))$ be the corresponding points on the graph of f. If, *for every choice* of p, q and r, the slope of PQ is less than the slope of QR, then f is **concave up** on $[a, b]$. Similarly, if the slope of PQ is greater than the slope of QR for every p, q and r, then f is **concave down**.

Figure 1.15 illustrates this definition. Since the slope of PQ is less than that of QR and will be no matter we pick P, Q and R in that order, then this function is concave up.

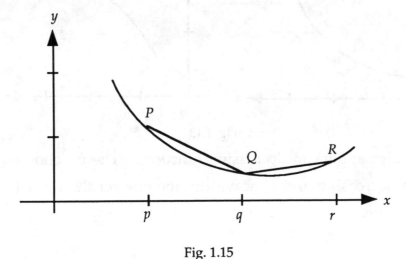

Fig. 1.15

EXAMPLE 1.8:

Discuss the concavity of the function in Figure 1.16 below. This is the same picture as in Figure 1.11.

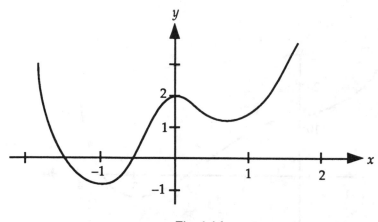

Fig. 1.16

It is very difficult to visually locate the points at which concavity changes. However, it appears that this function is concave up on $(-\infty, -.5]$ and $[0.5, \infty)$ and concave down on $[-.5, 0.5]$. (Again, your answers may be slightly different since we are approximating the values from the graph.) ◆

EXAMPLE 1.9:

Use the definition to show that $f(x) := x^2$ is concave up for all x.

Let $P(p, p^2)$, $Q(q, q^2)$ and $R(r, r^2)$ be any three points on the graph of f, where $p < q < r$. The slope of PQ is $\dfrac{q^2 - p^2}{q - p} = q + p$, while the slope of QR is $\dfrac{q^2 - r^2}{q - r} = q + r$. Since $p < r$, then $q + p < q + r$ and, hence, the slope of $PQ <$ slope QR, for every choice of p, q and r. Thus, f is concave up everywhere. ◆

EXAMPLE 1.10:

Draw a function that is decreasing on $(-\infty, 3]$, increasing on $[3, \infty)$, concave up on $(-\infty, 0]$ and $[2, \infty)$ and concave down on $[0, 2]$ and such that $f(0) = 12$, $f(2) = 0$ and $f(3) = -5$.

One possibility is shown in Figure 1.17.

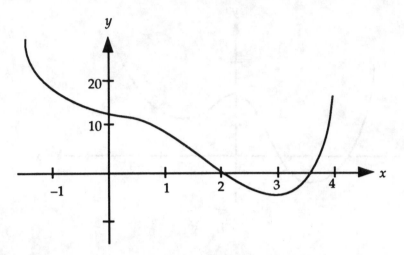

Fig. 1.17

◆

5. Discuss the concavity of the function graphed below.

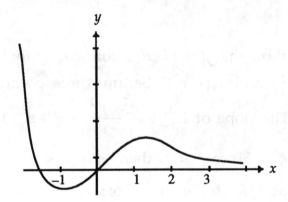

6. Draw a function that is decreasing for all x, concave up on the interval $(-\infty, 2]$ and concave down on $[2, \infty)$.

LOCAL EXTREMA

Look at the function f in Figure 1.18 below. The point on the graph at $x = 2$ has the largest y-value of any point "nearby". In other words, if we move a little to the left of $x = 2$ or a little to the right of $x = 2$, the values of $f(x)$ decrease. Similarly, the point on the graph at $x = 5$ has the smallest y-value of any point nearby, meaning that the function values a little bit on either side of $x = 5$ are bigger than $f(5)$.

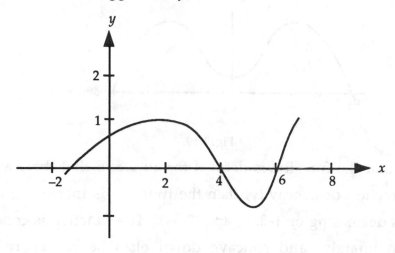

Fig. 1.18

This leads to the following:

DEFINITION: We say that f has a **local maximum** at $x = c$ if, for values of x very close to c, $f(x) < f(c)$. Similarly, f has a **local minimum** at $x = c$ if, for values of x very close to c, $f(x) > f(c)$.

Collectively, the local maxima and minima of a function are called the **local extrema**. Note that f has a local maximum at $x = c$ if f is increasing for x less than, but close to, c and decreasing for x greater than, but close to, c. In other words, as we move from *left to right* through $x = c$, the direction of f changes from increasing to decreasing. Similarly, f has a local minimum at $x = c$ if f the direction of f changes from decreasing to increasing as we move from left to right through $x = c$.

EXAMPLE 1.11:

Describe the function in Figure 1.19. That is, state where it is increasing, decreasing, concave up, and concave down. What are the local extrema?

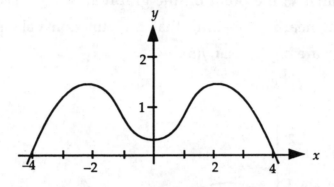

Fig. 1.19

Assuming that the function is defined for all x and that there are no other changes of direction or concavity, then the function is increasing on $(-\infty, -2]$ and $[0, 2]$; it is decreasing on $[-2, 0]$ and $[2, \infty)$. The function is concave up on $[-1, 1]$ (approximately) and concave down elsewhere. There is a local minimum at $x = 0$ and local maxima at $x = -2$ and $x = 2$. ◆

- -

TEST YOUR UNDERSTANDING

7. Below are the graphs of $f(x) := x^2$ on the left and $g(x) := x^3$ on the right Describe them in terms of direction and concavity. Are there any local extrema?

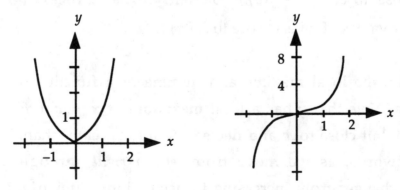

- -

◻ There is one more property of functions we should mention here-- continuity. Informally, a function is **continuous** on an interval [*a*, *b*] if its graph can be drawn in one piece--that is, without lifting your pencil. This definition will suffice for now; we'll give a more precise one in Chapter 3.

Most of the functions we've seen so far have been continuous on any interval on which they are defined. For an example of a discontinuous function, consider $f(x) := \frac{1}{x}$ whose graph is given in Figure 1.20.

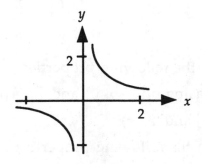

Fig. 1.20

This function is discontinuous at *x* = 0 (or on any interval containing *x* = 0).

We have to be a bit careful when describing the direction and concavity of a discontinuous function. In this case, *f* is decreasing and concave down for *x* on the open interval (–∞, 0) and decreasing and concave up on the open interval (0, ∞). There are no local extrema.

EXERCISES FOR SECTION 1.2:

1. Describe the direction, concavity, and local extrema of each of the following functions.

(a)

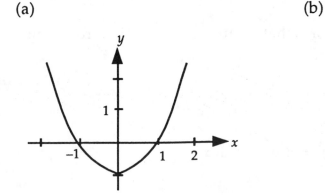

(b)

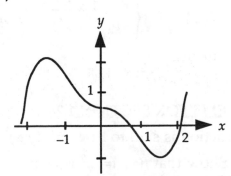

(c)

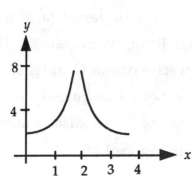

(d)

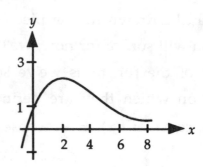

2. Sketch a function f with the following properties:

   $f(0) = 5$, $f(2) = 1$, increasing on $(-\infty, 0]$ and $[2, 4]$, decreasing elsewhere, concave down on $(-\infty, 1]$ and $[3, \infty)$.

3. Sketch a function h with the following properties:

   $0 \leq h(x) < 1$ for all x, decreasing on $(-\infty, 0)$, increasing on $(0, \infty)$, concave up on $(-2, 2)$, concave down elsewhere

4. Sketch a function g that is increasing and concave up on $(-\infty, 1]$, decreasing and concave down on $[1, \infty)$ and such that $g(1) = 3$.

5. A function f has a local maximum at $(1, -1)$, a local minimum at $(-1, 1)$ and no other local extrema. Is it possible for the function to be continuous? Explain.

6. Show algebraically that $f(x) := 2x$ is increasing for all x.

7. A continuous function f has roots at $x = -1$, $x = 2$ and $x = 5$. What is the minimum number of local extrema f can have?

8. Let $f(x) := \begin{cases} x^2 - 1 & x \geq 2 \\ kx & x < 2 \end{cases}$. For what value of k is this function continuous?

PROBLEMS FOR SECTION 1.2:

1. A function is said to be **even** if $f(x) = f(-x)$ for all x.
   (a) Show that $f(x) := x^2$ is even.
   (b) Is $f(x) := 2x^4 + 3x - 1$ even?

(c) Argue that the graph of an even function must be symmetric about the y-axis.

(d) Let $h(x) := f(x) + g(x)$, where f and g are even. Show that h is even.

2. A function is said to be **odd** if $f(x) = -f(-x)$ for all x.

(a) Show that $f(x) := x^3$ is odd.

(b) What kind of symmetry does the graph of an odd function possess?

(c) Let $h(x) := f(x) + g(x)$, where f and g are odd. Show that h is odd.

(d) Show that the graph of every odd function must pass through the origin.

(e) Let $p(x) := f(x)g(x)$, where f and g are odd. Is p odd or even or neither?

3. Use the definition of concavity given in this section to show that $f(x) := x^3$ is concave up on $[0, \infty)$. [Hint: $a^3 - b^3 = (a - b)(a^2 + ab + b^2)$.]

TYU Answers for Section 1.2

1. Suppose $p < q < 0$. Then $q + p < 0$ but $q - p > 0$. Thus, $f(q) - f(p) = q^2 - p^2 = (q - p)(q + p) < 0$ so f is decreasing.

2. Suppose $q > p > 0$. Then $f(q) - f(p) = 1/q - 1/p = (p - q)/pq < 0$ since $p - q < 0$ and $pq > 0$.   3. Increasing on $[-2, 2]$, decreasing elsewhere.

4. One possibility is below   6. One possibility is below

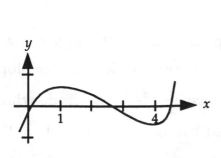

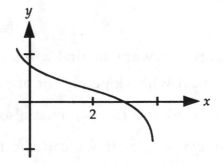

5. Concave up on $(-\infty, 0]$ and $[2, \infty)$, down on $[0, 2)$ 7. f is incr. on $[0, \infty)$ and decr. on $(-\infty, 0]$ while g is incr. for all x. f is conc. up for all x, while g is conc. up on $[0, \infty)$ and conc. down on $(-\infty, 0]$. f has a local min. at $x = 0$, g has no local extrema

1.3 SOME COMMON FUNCTIONS

There are some functions that occur so frequently as examples and in mathematical applications that they deserve to be studied in detail.

1. LINEAR FUNCTIONS

A **linear function** is of the form $f(x) := ax + b$, for some constants a and b. The domain is **R** and the range is **R**.

Consider any two points $P(x_1, f(x_1))$ and $Q(x_2, f(x_2))$ on the graph. The slope of the line PQ is

$$\frac{f(x_2) - f(x_1)}{x_2 - x_1} = \frac{(ax_2 + b) - (ax_1 + b)}{x_2 - x_1} = \frac{a(x_2 - x_1)}{x_2 - x_1} = a,$$

which is independent of the points chosen. Hence, the slope between any two points is the same, implying that the graph of f is a straight line. Figure 1.21 shows a linear function with $a > 0$. The function is increasing for all x and is neither concave up nor concave down.

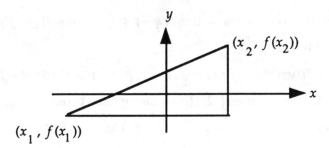

Fig. 1.21

Suppose we want to find a linear function that passes through a given point (x_0, y_0) with slope a. For any other point (x, y) on the line, the slope between (x, y) and (x_0, y_0) must also be a. Hence, $\frac{y - y_0}{x - x_0} = a$, from which $y - y_0 = a(x - x_0)$. If we call the function f (that is, $y = f(x)$), then the equation of the line is

(1) $f(x) := f(x_0) + a(x - x_0).$

EXAMPLE 1.12:

Write an equation of the line passing through the point (–8, 2), parallel to the line $2y + x = 7$.

Rewriting the given line as $y = -\frac{1}{2}x + \frac{7}{2}$, we see that it has a slope of $-\frac{1}{2}$. Since our line is to be parallel to this, it must also have a slope of $-\frac{1}{2}$. Therefore its equation is:

$$y - 2 = -\frac{1}{2}(x + 8) \text{ or, equivalently, } y = -\frac{1}{2}x - 2. \qquad \blacklozenge$$

EXAMPLE 1.13:

A candle is 10" long when it is lit. Twenty minutes later, it is 6" long. Assuming the candle burns at a constant rate, determine a function that gives the length of the candle in terms of the time elapsed since it was lit. How long does it take for the candle to burn completely?

Let $f(t) :=$ length of the candle at time t where $t = 0$ corresponds to the time the candle was lit. Then $f(0) = 10$ and $f(20) = 6$. The fact that the candle burns at a constant rate implies that f is a linear function. The slope of f is $\frac{6-10}{20-0} = -\frac{1}{5}$. Hence, $f(t) - 10 := -\frac{1}{5}(t - 0)$ or $f(t) := -\frac{1}{5}t + 10$.

The candle is completely burned when $f(t) = 0$ which occurs when $t = 50$ min. $\qquad \blacklozenge$

- -

TEST YOUR UNDERSTANDING

1. What can you say about the graph of a line with negative slope? zero slope?

2. Compare the graphs of $y = 2x$ and $y = 4x$.

3. Write an equation of the line passing through (4, –1) with a slope of 3.

4. Write an equation of the line passing through (1, 3) and (4, 2).

EXAMPLE 1.14:

A car travels at 60 mph for 2 hours, then slows down to 40 mph for the next 3 hours, then returns to 60 mph for another 2 hours. Determine a function $f(t)$ that gives the distance travelled by the car after t hours.

If $0 \leq t \leq 2$, then the distance travelled is just $60t$. If $2 \leq t \leq 5$, then the distance travelled is the total distance travelled in the first 2 hours plus 40 mph times the number of hours beyond 2; that is, $2(60) + 40(t - 2)$. Finally, for $5 \leq t \leq 7$, the distance travelled is the total distance from the first 5 hours plus 60 mph times the number of hours beyond 5; that is, $2(60) + 3(40) + 60(t - 5) = 240 + 60(t - 5)$. Putting this together, we have:

$$f(t) := \begin{cases} 60\,t, & 0 \leq t \leq 2 \\ 120 + 40(t - 2), & 2 \leq t \leq 5 \\ 240 + 60(t - 5), & 5 \leq t < 7 \end{cases}$$

A graph of this function is given in Figure 1.22.

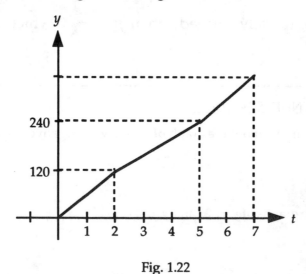

Fig. 1.22

Note that this graph consists of three linear segments glued together. Functions of this type are said to be **piecewise linear**.   ♦

---

5. After how many hours has the car travelled 180 miles?

---

2. QUADRATIC FUNCTIONS

A **quadratic function** is of the form $f(x) := ax^2 + bx + c$, where $a \neq 0$. Its graph is called a **parabola**. The domain clearly is **R**. First, let's look at a specific example. Let $f(x) := 2x^2 - 12x + 11$. After some algebra, we can write $f(x)$ in the form $f(x) := 2(x - 3)^2 - 7$, which we will call **completed-square form**. (It's okay if you didn't think of this manipulation. You should, however, verify that it is true.) The first term is a positive multiple of a perfect square and, therefore, can never be negative. Its minimum value is 0 when $x = 3$. Thus, the smallest value of $f(x)$ is –7. In other words, $f(x) \geq -7$ for all x. Since $f(x)$ can be made arbitrarily large by taking x large, then we conclude that the range of f is $\{y \mid y \geq -7\}$. See Figure 1.23. The point $(3, -7)$ is called the **vertex** of the parabola.

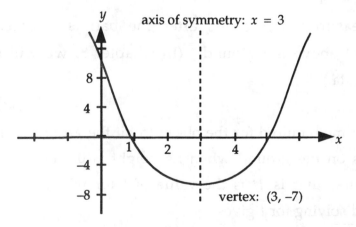

Fig. 1.23

More generally, the graph of $f(x) := ax^2 + bx + c$ has an **axis of symmetry** at $x = \dfrac{-b}{2a}$. If $a > 0$, the graph is decreasing for $x < \dfrac{-b}{2a}$ and increasing for $x > \dfrac{-b}{2a}$. Thus, there is a local minimum at $x = \dfrac{-b}{2a}$. The graph is concave up for all x. If $a < 0$, the graph is increasing for $x < \dfrac{-b}{2a}$ and decreasing for $x > \dfrac{-b}{2a}$ so there is a local maximum at $x = \dfrac{-b}{2a}$. The graph is concave down for all x.

EXAMPLE 1.15:

Determine the direction, concavity and local extrema (if any) of $f(x) := -x^2 + 4x - 3$.

The axis of symmetry is at $x = \dfrac{-4}{2(-1)} = 2$. Since $a = -1 < 0$, f is increasing for $x < 2$ and decreasing for $x > 2$. There is a local maximum at $x = 2$ and the graph is concave down for all x.   ♦

EXAMPLE 1.16:

A ball is dropped from a window h feet above the ground. Ignoring air resistance and assuming that the acceleration due to gravity is constant (32 ft./sec.^{2}), then it can be shown that the height of the ball off the ground at time t is given by the function

$$f(t) := h - 16t^2$$

where t is measured in seconds after the ball is released and $f(t)$ is measured in feet above the ground. (In Chapter 3, we will show how to derive this formula.)

(a) Express the time required for the object to hit the ground in terms of h.

The object is on the ground when its height is 0. Let t^* be the time at which this occurs; that is, t^* is the value of t for which $f(t) = 0$. Setting $h - 16t^2 = 0$ and solving for t gives

$$t^* = \sqrt{\frac{h}{16}} \text{ sec.}$$

Note that we can now find the domain of f. Since the object stops moving when it hits the ground, then the domain of the function is restricted to the values of t for which $f(t) \geq 0$; that is, to $\{t \mid 0 \leq t \leq \sqrt{\frac{h}{16}}\}$.

(b) How long does it take to reach the ground if $h = 100$?

Setting $h = 100$ in the answer to (a) gives $t^* = \sqrt{\frac{100}{16}} = 2.5$ seconds.

(c) What happens to the time required to hit the ground if the initial height is doubled?

"Doubling the initial height" means that instead of starting at height h, we now start at height $2h$. Replacing h by $2h$ in the answer to (a) gives t^* = $\sqrt{\frac{2h}{16}} = \sqrt{2}\sqrt{\frac{h}{16}}$, which is $\sqrt{2}$ times the time required for the ball to hit the ground when dropped from height h.

Figure 1.24 shows the graph of f for $h = 100$ and $h = 200$. The time to hit the ground is the value of t at which the graph intersects the t-axis.

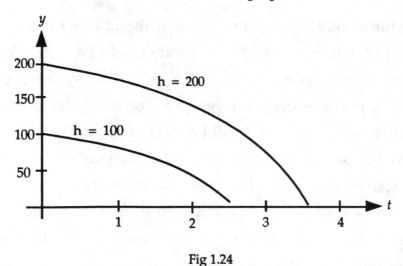

Fig 1.24

◆

TEST YOUR UNDERSTANDING

6. Express in terms of h the time at which the ball is half-way to the ground.

----

3. POWER FUNCTIONS

A **power function** is of the form $f(x) := x^n$, where n is an integer. The graphs of some power functions, when n is positive, are given in Figures 1.25(a) and (b).

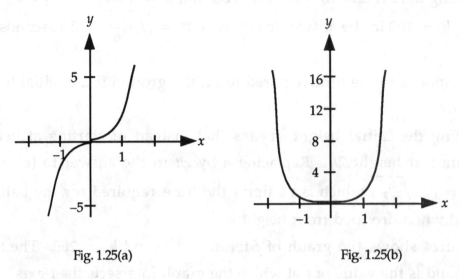

Fig. 1.25(a)   Fig. 1.25(b)

If n is a positive odd integer, the graph of the power function resembles Figure 1.25(a). That is, if n is odd, the function will be increasing for all x, concave up on $[0, \infty)$, concave down on $(-\infty, 0]$ and symmetric about the origin. If n is a positive even integer, the graph of the power function resembles Figure 1.25(b); that is, f will be increasing on $[0, \infty)$, decreasing on $(-\infty, 0]$, concave up for all x and symmetric about the y-axis.

If n is a negative integer, we get somewhat different behavior. First note that the functions are discontinuous at $x = 0$ since 0^n is not defined if $n < 0$. Figures 1.26(a) and (b) show the cases $n = -1$ and $n = -2$. In general, if n is a negative odd integer, then $f(x) > 0$ if and only if $x > 0$, so the graph resembles Figure 1.26(a). If n is a negative even integer, then $f(x) > 0$ for all x, so the graph resembles Figure 1.26(b).

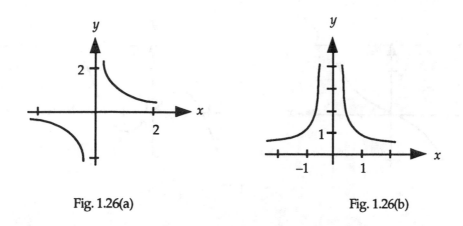

Fig. 1.26(a)   Fig. 1.26(b)

4. POLYNOMIAL FUNCTIONS

A **polynomial** is of the form

$$f(x) := a_n x^n + a_{n-1} x^{n-1} + \ldots + a_1 x + a_0,$$

where n is a positive integer (called the **degree** of the polynomial) and a_0, $a_1, \ldots, a_n$ are real numbers with $a_n \neq 0$ (so that the coefficient of the highest power of x is not 0). Linear functions are first-degree polynomials; quadratic functions are second-degree polynomials. Power functions with positive integer exponents are polynomials with just one term and leading coefficient $a_n = 1$. The function $f(x) := x^5 - 4x^3 + 2x^2 - 1$ is a fifth-degree polynomial.

In general, the behavior of polynomials is difficult to determine since it depends heavily on the nature of the coefficients. Consider, for example, a cubic polynomial of the form $f(x) := x^3 + bx$, where b is a constant. (This is not the most general type of cubic polynomial, since there are no x^2 or constant terms present.) Upon graphing this for several different values of b, we find that when $b \geq 0$, the graph is increasing for all x, while if $b < 0$, the graph increases, then decreases, then increases again. See Figure 1.27.

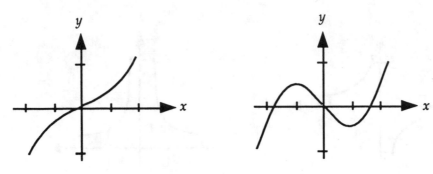

Fig. 1.27

One way to help us gain some insight into the behavior of polynomials is to look at what happens for large values of x. For example, let $f(x) := x^5 - 4x^3 + 2x^2 - 1$ whose graph is given in Figure 1.28. When x is large, the values of the polynomial are dominated by the highest-power term (x^5). This means that the value of this term is so much larger than the other terms combined that they can be ignored. For example $f(100) = 9,996,019,999 \approx 10,000,000,000 = 100^5$. Since the leading coefficient is positive, then $f(x) \to +\infty$ as $x \to +\infty$ and $f(x) \to -\infty$ as $x \to -\infty$. (The $\to$ means "approaches". To say that $x \to +\infty$ means that x is positive and becomes very large. To say that $x \to -\infty$ means that x is negative and becomes very large in absolute value.)

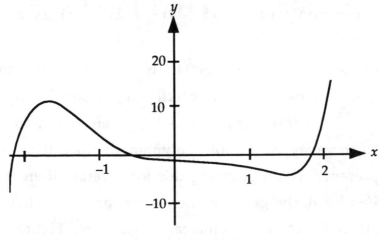

Fig. 1.28

In general, polynomials of odd-degree with positive leading coefficients come up from the lower left and go out to the upper right, with possibly some wiggles in the middle.

Now let $f(x) := x^4 + 3x^3 - x + 1$, whose graph is in Figure 1.29. Since the polynomial is of even degree and the leading coefficient is positive, then $f(x) \to +\infty$ as $x \to \pm\infty$.

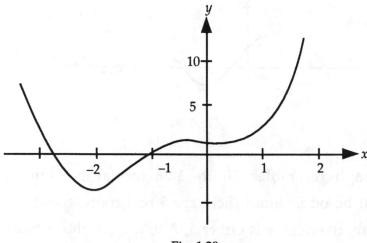

Fig. 1.29

In general, even degree polynomials with positive leading coefficient come down from the upper left, turn around, and go up to the upper right, again with some wiggles possible.

_____

TEST YOUR UNDERSTANDING

7. What would the graph of a fourth degree polynomial look like if the leading coefficient were negative?

_____

Determining what happens in the middle (for x near 0) is tricky without calculus. One possibility is to try to find the roots, which may be difficult if the polynomial does not factor. Every polynomial of degree n has n roots, some of which are real and some complex. Since the real roots correspond to places where the graph of the polynomial crosses the x-axis, then the graph of an nth degree polynomial can cross the x-axis in at most n places. This puts some restrictions on how many "wiggles" the graph can have.

EXAMPLE 1.17:

What are the possible degrees of the polynomial pictured in Figure 1.30?

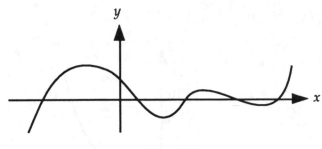

Fig. 1.30

Since the graph resembles Figure 1.28 for large x, the degree of the polynomial must be odd. Since there are 5 real roots, the degree must be at least 5. Therefore, the degree is either 5, 7, 9, ... (Without more information, we can't be more specific.) ♦

EXAMPLE 1.18:

Consider the salt-water problem of Example 1.2 of Section 1.1. Is it reasonable to expect that the function $p(t)$ would be a polynomial?

We argued that $p(t)$ approaches 0 as t increases. In other words, the graph of p "levels off at 0" after a long time. Since polynomials never "level off"--they either go to positive or negative infinity as the independent variable increases without bound--then $p(t)$ cannot be a polynomial. ♦

5. RATIONAL FUNCTIONS

Let $f(x) := \dfrac{g(x)}{h(x)}$, where g and h are polynomials. Functions of this type are called rational functions. In all the functions studied so far, the domain has been **R**. Here, because of the potential of dividing by 0, the domain may be restricted. Specifically, the domain is $\{x \mid h(x) \neq 0\}$.

Suppose $h(c) = 0$ and $g(c) \neq 0$. Then as x approaches c, $h(x)$ is close to 0 but $g(x)$ is not; thus, $f(x)$ becomes infinitely large, either positively or negatively. This means that the graph has a **vertical asymptote** at $x = c$.

For example, let $f(x) := \dfrac{x}{x^2-1}$. Thus, $g(x) := x$ and $h(x) := x^2 - 1$. Since $h(1) = 0$ and $g(1) \neq 0$, then there is a vertical asymptote at $x = 1$. Likewise, there is a vertical asymptote at $x = -1$. The graph of this function is shown in Figure 1.31.

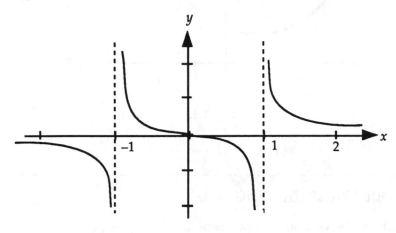

Fig. 1.31

EXAMPLE 1.19:

Determine the vertical asymptotes of:

$$\text{(a)} \quad g(x) := \frac{x^2+9}{x-4} \qquad \text{(b)} \quad h(x) := \frac{x^3-1}{x-1}.$$

(a) Since $x - 4 = 0$ when $x = 4$ (and the numerator $\neq 0$ there), then g has vertical asymptote at $x = 4$.

(b) It is tempting to say that h has a vertical asymptote at $x = 1$ since the denominator will be 0; however, since the numerator is also 0 when $x = 1$, then we can't say that there is a vertical asymptote there. Moreover, since $x^3 - 1 = (x - 1)(x^2 + x + 1)$, then $\dfrac{x^3-1}{x-1} = x^2 + x + 1$, if $x \neq 1$. The reduced function has no vertical asymptotes so neither does h.

The graph of h (Figure 1.32) is the same as that of $y = x^2 + x + 1$, except that there is a "hole punched" at $x = 1$ since h is not defined there.

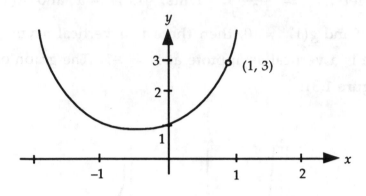

Fig. 1.32

♦

---

8. Determine the vertical asymptotes of $f(x) := \dfrac{x^2-1}{x\,(x+1)}$.

Look again at the function in Figure 1.31. Notice that as x becomes infinitely large positively or negatively, $f(x)$ approaches 0. More generally, we'll say that f has a **horizontal asymptote** at $y = b$ if $f(x)$ approaches b as x becomes infinitely large, either positively or negatively.

EXAMPLE 1.20:

Determine the horizontal asymptotes of $f(x) := \dfrac{x^3+1}{2x^3+x+4}$.

Let's evaluate f for increasingly large x: $f(10) = .4970209$, $f(100) = .4999745$, $f(1000) = .49999975$. It appears that $f(x) \to \frac{1}{2}$ as $x \to \infty$. Hence, there is a horizontal asymptote at $y = \frac{1}{2}$.

Notice that you would reach the same conclusion by ignoring all but the highest power terms in the numerator and denominator. This is justifiable since, for large x (either positive or negative), the x^3 in the numerator and the $2x^3$ in the denominator become much bigger than the other terms.

Hence, the values of $f(x)$ approach $\dfrac{x^3}{2x^3} = \dfrac{1}{2}$. So, $y = \dfrac{1}{2}$ is a horizontal asymptote for this function. See Figure 1.33.

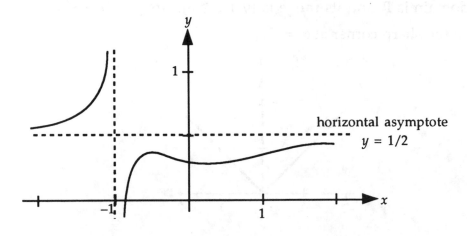

Fig. 1.33

EXAMPLE 1.21:

Determine the horizontal asymptote, if any, of $f(x) := \dfrac{x+1}{x^2-2x+4}$.

For large x, the numerator is approximately x, while the denominator is approximately x^2. Therefore, $f(x)$ behaves like $\dfrac{x}{x^2} = \dfrac{1}{x}$. This clearly approaches 0 as x approaches either positive or negative infinity. Hence, $y = 0$ is a horizontal asymptote.

TEST YOUR UNDERSTANDING

9. Find the horizontal asymptotes of (a) $g(t) := \dfrac{3t^2-1}{t-4t^2}$ (b) $h(x) := \dfrac{x^3+7x-5}{x^2+4}$.

----

6. THE ABSOLUTE VALUE FUNCTION

The function $f(x) := |x|$ is called the **absolute value function**. We can write this as $f(x) := \begin{cases} x & x \geq 0 \\ -x & x < 0 \end{cases}$. For example, $f(4) = 4$ and $f(-7) = -(-7) = 7$. Its domain is **R** and its range is $\{y \mid y \geq 0\}$. Its graph is shown in Figure 1.34. Note the sharp corner at $x = 0$.

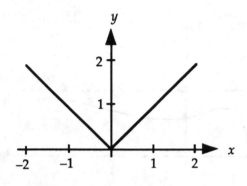

Fig. 1.34

7. EXPONENTIAL FUNCTIONS

An **exponential function** is of the form $f(x) := b^x$, where b is a positive constant. Note the difference between exponential functions and power functions. For power functions, the base is a variable and the exponent is a constant. For exponential functions, the base is constant and the exponent is a variable. For example, consider $f(x) := 2^x$ whose graph is shown in Figure 1.35. Note that the graph is strictly increasing and concave up and that there is a horizontal asymptote at $y = 0$. The function in the salt water problem (Example 1.2) could be exponential. We will study exponential functions, along with the related logarithmic functions, in detail in Chapter 4.

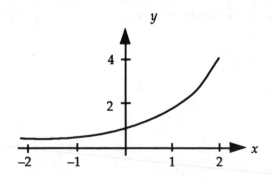

Fig. 1.35

8. TRIGONOMETRIC FUNCTIONS

There are six basic **trigonometric functions**--the sine, cosine, tangent, cotangent, secant and cosecant. You have probably studied them at some length in one of your previous mathematics courses. Figure 1.36 shows the graph of $f(x) := \sin(x)$. Note that the graph is **periodic**, meaning that a portion of the graph (for example, the piece between $x = 0$ and $x = 2\pi$) is repeated infinitely often. All trigonometric functions are periodic and thus are useful for describing situations in which some behavior repeats indefinitely. For example, the motion of a frictionless pendulum could be described by a trigonometric function. We'll study the calculus of trigonometric functions in detail in Chapter 7.

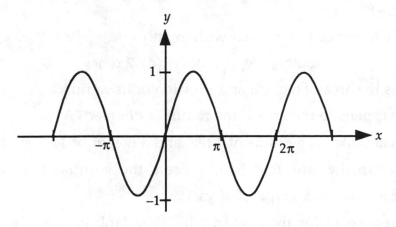

Fig. 1.36

EXERCISES FOR SECTION 1.3:

1. P dollars invested at r percent simple interest for t years grows to an amount $A = P + Prt$. At what interest rate will an investment of $2000 grow to $2500 in two years?

2. Write an equation for the line with slope -3 which passes through the point $(1, 2)$.

3. For what value of k will the line $2x + ky = 5$ be parallel to $4x - 8y = 3$?

4. Write an equation of the line that intersects the x-axis at $(3, 0)$ and the y-axis at $(0, -6)$.

5. Write an equation for the line passing through (3, –1) perpendicular to $y = 2x - 1$. (Remember that two lines are perpendicular if the product of their slopes is –1.)

6. An empty glass weighs 100 grams. It is filled with a liquid that weighs 6 grams per cubic centimeter. Express the total weight of the glass and liquid as a function of x, where x is the number of cubic centimeters of liquid in the glass.

7. Determine the points of intersection of the graphs of $y = 2x - 1$ and $y = x^2 - 2$.

8. Let P and Q be the points on the graph of $f(x) := x^2 - 4x$ corresponding to $x = 1$ and $x = 5$. Write an equation of the line PQ.

9. Determine a quadratic function that passes through the origin and has a vertex at (2, –8).

10. Sketch a fifth degree polynomial with exactly:

   (a) 5 roots   (b) 3 roots   (c) 1 root   (d) 2 roots

11. (a) Express the area of a circle as a function of its radius.

   (b) What happens to the area if the radius is doubled?

12. A cylindrical tank has a radius of 4 feet and a height of 12 feet. If the depth of the water in the tank is h feet, express the volume V of water as a function of h. Sketch a graph of V vs. h.

13. Repeat Exercise 12 for the case in which the tank is cone-shaped (point down) with a radius 10 feet and height 20 feet. (Hint: The volume of a cone is given by $V = \frac{1}{3}\pi r^2 h$.)

14. Repeat Exercise 12 for the case in which the tank is shaped as shown below.

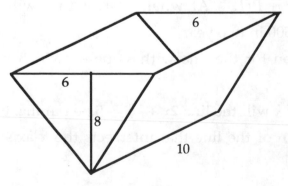

15. Sketch a function g with the following properties:

vertical asymptote at $x = 2$, $g(x) \to +\infty$ as $x \to 2$ from either direction, horizontal asymptote at $y = 1$, concave up on $(-\infty, 2)$ and $(2, \infty)$.

16. Determine all horizontal and vertical asymptotes of the function
$$f(x) := \frac{x(x-1)(x-3)}{x(2x-5)(3x+9)}.$$

17. Let $g(x) := x^2 - x$. Write the equation of the function obtained when the graph of g is reflected about the:

(a) x-axis

(b) y-axis

18. Express in terms of k the area of the triangle bounded by the lines $y = kx$, $y = -kx$ and $y = k$, where $k > 0$.

PROBLEMS FOR SECTION 1.3:

1. Let $(x_1, f(x_1))$ and $(x_2, f(x_2))$ be any two points on the graph of $f(x) := ax^2 + bx + c$. Compute the slope of the line segment joining these two points and show that, unlike for linear functions, the result depends on x_1 and x_2.

2. (a) Show that the general quadratic polynomial $f(x) := ax^2 + bx + c$ can be written as
$$f(x) := a\left(x + \frac{b}{2a}\right)^2 + \left(c - \frac{b^2}{4a}\right),$$
which we call the completed-square form.

(b) Use this to express the roots of $f(x) = 0$ in terms of the coefficients a, b and c.

3. Consider the quadratic function $f(x) := ax^2 + bx + c$, where $a > 0$. Under what conditions on a, b and c will the inequality $f(x) < 0$ have no solutions? Sketch the graph of f in this case.

4. Let f be a function such that $f(x) > 0$ for all x and $f(a + b) = f(a)f(b)$ for all a and b.

(a) Show that $f(2a) = [f(a)]^2$.

(b) What conclusion can you draw about $f(na)$, where n is a positive integer?

(c) Show that $f(0) = 1$.

(d) Can you think of a function with this property?

5. The **greatest integer function**, denoted $[x]$, is defined as the largest integer less than or equal to x.

(a) What is $[3.4]$? What is $[-3.4]$?

(b) What are all the values of x such that $[x] = 7$? $[x] = -6$?

(c) Sketch the graph of the greatest integer function.

(d) Is $[x + y] = [x] + [y]$ for all x and y? If not, for what x and y is it true?

(e) Suppose a shipping company charges \$3.00 for packages weighing less than one pound and \$2.00 for each additional pound or fraction thereof. Express the total cost of shipping a package weighing x pounds.

6. Is it possible for an odd degree polynomial to have no real roots? What about an even degree polynomial?

7. Let $f(x) := \dfrac{g(x)}{h(x)}$, where g and h are polynomials. Depending on the nature of g and h, f may or may not approach a finite value as $x \to \infty$. What must be true about g and h in order for f to approach a finite value (that is, have a horizontal asymptote)?

8. Determine the horizontal asymptotes of $f(x) := \dfrac{2x}{\sqrt{x^2 + 1}}$.

TYU Answers for Section 1.3

1. Lines with negative slope go from the upper left to the lower right; those with zero slope are horizontal   2. Both lines go through the origin with positive slope; $y = 4x$ is steeper

3. $y + 1 = 3(x - 4)$ or $y = 3x - 13$ 4. $y - 3 = -\frac{1}{3}(x - 1)$ or $y = -\frac{1}{3}x + \frac{10}{3}$ or

  $y - 2 = -\frac{1}{3}(x - 4)$ 5. 3.5 hours   6. $t = \sqrt{\dfrac{h}{32}}$

7. The graph comes up from the lower left, wiggles around and goes out to the lower right.

8. $x = 0$ only   9. (a) $y = -3/4$ only   (b) none

1.4 ALGEBRA OF FUNCTIONS

SKETCHING SIMPLE FUNCTIONS

We can use what we know about simple functions to draw graphs of more complicated functions. The next three examples illustrate this.

EXAMPLE 1.22:

Sketch the graph of $g(x) := x^3 - 2$.

We know what the graph of $f(x) := x^3$ looks like. The y-values for g are obtained by subtracting 2 from the y-values for f. This has the effect of moving the graph down by 2 units.

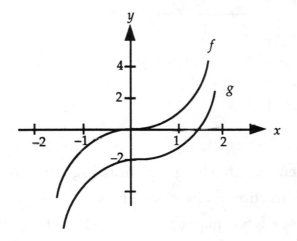

Fig. 1.37

♦

In general, let f be a function and define a new function g by $g(x) := f(x) + c$. The graph of g can be obtained by moving the graph of f upward (or downward if $c < 0$) by $|c|$ units. See Figure 1.38.

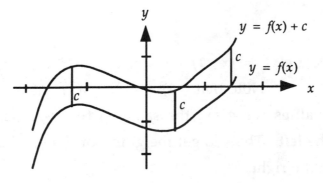

Fig. 1.38

page 1 - 47

EXAMPLE 1.23:

Sketch the graph of $g(x) := 2x^2$.

Start with $f(x) := x^2$. Each of the y-values of g is twice as big as the corresponding y-values of f. Thus the graph of g can be obtained from the graph of f by stretching it in the y-direction by a factor of 2.

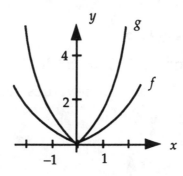

Fig. 1.39

♦

In general, if $h(x) := cf(x)$, where c is a positive constant, then the graph of h is obtained by stretching (or shrinking) the graph of f by a factor of c in the vertical direction. The case where c is negative is a little more complicated. Let's see what happens if $c = -1$, so that $h(x) = -f(x)$. Then each ordinate has its sign changed; that is, positive y-values become negative and negative y-values become positive. This means that the graph of h is a reflection of the graph of f across the x-axis. More generally, if $h(x) = cf(x)$ where $c < 0$, then the graph of h is obtained by flipping the graph of f over the x-axis and stretching by a factor of $|c|$.

EXAMPLE 1.24:

Sketch the graph of $g(x) := (x - 1)^4$.

Start with $f(x) := x^4$. Note that $g(2) = 1^4 = f(1)$, $g(3) = 2^4 = f(2)$, etc. In general, the y-values for g are the same as the y-values for f at an x-value one unit to the left. Thus, to get the graph of g, take the graph of f and move it one unit to the right.

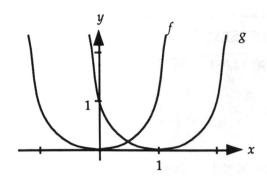

Fig. 1.40

It is important not to confuse $f(x + c)$ with $f(x) + c$. In the first case, the graph of $f(x)$ is moved c units to the left; in the latter case, the graph is moved c units up.

EXAMPLE 1.25:

Sketch the graph of $f(x) := (x - 2)^2 + 1$.

If we start with the graph of $y = x^2$ and shift it 2 units to the right, we get $y = (x - 2)^2$. Shifting 1 unit up gives the desired graph.

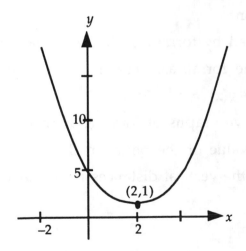

Fig. 1.41

----

1. Sketch the graph of $f(x) := -(x + 1)^3$.

2. Sketch the graph of $g(x) := |x + 4|$.

3. Sketch the graph of $g(x) := \dfrac{1}{(x - 2)^2}$.

ARITHMETIC OF FUNCTIONS

Given two functions f and g, it is possible to create a new function h that is the sum of f and g. This new function is defined by $h(x) = f(x) + g(x)$, for all x. In a similar manner, we can define the difference, product and quotient of functions.

If f and g are defined by formulas, then it is easy to find a formula for their sum--just add the formulas. For instance, if $f(x) := x^2$ and $g(x) := 2x + 5$, then $h(x) := f(x) + g(x) = x^2 + 2x + 5$.

Suppose we just have graphs of f and g, as in Figure 1.42. Since $h(c) = f(c) + g(c)$, then the y-value of the point on the graph of h corresponding to $x = c$ is the sum of the vertical distances from the x-axis to the graphs of f and g at $x = c$.

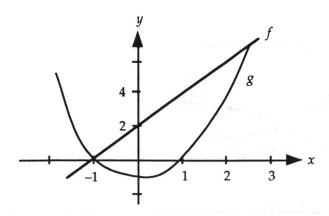

Fig. 1.42

So, for example, $h(0) = 2 + (-1) = 1$, $h(1) = 4 + 0 = 4$, $h(2) = 6 + 4 = 10$, $h(-1) = 0 + 0 = 0$, etc. Plotting these points (and some others) and connecting the dots gives us a graph of h, as in Figure 1.43.

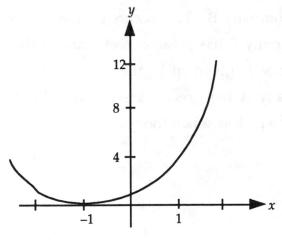

Fig. 1.43

EXAMPLE 1.26:

The graphs in Figure 1.44 show the net assets (in millions of dollars) for two different companies as a function of time. During which time intervals does company A have greater assests than company B? During which intervals does it have less? Graph the difference between their assests (company A minus company B) as a function of time.

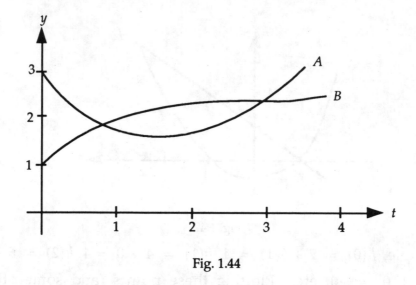

Fig. 1.44

Company A will have greater assets whenever the graph for company A is above the graph of company B. This occurs on the intervals [0, .9] and [3, 4], approximately. Company B has greater assets during the interval [.9, 3]. The graph of the difference is given in Figure 1.45. Note that the difference is positive when company A has greater assets. The difference is 0 when they have the same assets which is when the graphs intersect.

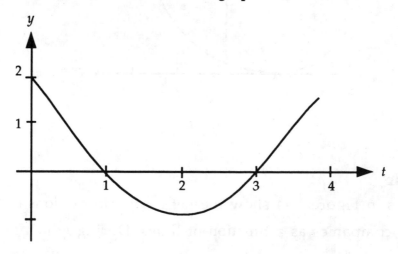

Fig. 1.45

COMPOSITE FUNCTIONS AND INVERSES

In the salt water problem of Example 1.2, we claimed that the amount of salt in the water is a function of time--that is, $p = g(t)$. (The fact that we had no formula for this function is irrelevant. The function still exists and its graph is in the accompanying diagram.) It is a scientific fact that the freezing point of a solution goes down as the concentration of solution increases. In other words, the more salt there is in the water, the lower the freezing point. Hence the freezing point z is a function of p and we write $z = f(p)$. Since p is a function of t and z is a function of p, it follows that z is a function of t--that is, $z = f(g(t)) = h(t)$. This new function h takes a value of t, runs it through the function g, takes the output $g(t)$ and runs it through f. We call h the **composite** of f and g, which is usually written as $h = f \circ g$. This is illustrated in Figure 1.46.

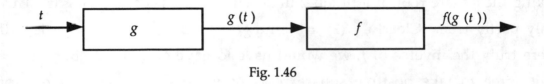

Fig. 1.46

Suppose $f(x) := \frac{1}{x}$ and $g(x) := 2x + 1$. Then $h(x) := f(g(x)) = f(2x + 1) = \frac{1}{2x + 1}$. Note the restriction on the domain: Even though the domain of g is **R**, the domain of h is $\{x \mid x \neq -1/2\}$. Also note that the order in which we compose the functions is important. If $k = g \circ f$, then $k(x) := g(f(x)) = 2(\frac{1}{x}) + 1$, which is not the same as h. (How do we know that h and k are different?)

Given an arbitrary function, it may be possible to express it as the composite of simpler functions. The function $h(x) := \frac{1}{\sqrt{x^2 - 1}}$ can be expressed as $f \circ g$, where $f(x) := \frac{1}{x}$ and $g(x) := \sqrt{x^2 - 1}$. This answer is not unique; there are many other choices for f and g.

TEST YOUR UNDERSTANDING

4. Find two other "decompositions" (choices of f and g) for the function h above.

It is possible that f and g will be defined in such a way that $f(g(x)) = x$ and $g(f(x)) = x$ for all x for which the composite functions are defined. In this case, whatever g does to x, f undoes and gives us back the original x and vice-versa. For example, if $f(x) := 2x$ and $g(x) := \frac{x}{2}$, then $f(g(x)) := x$ and $g(f(x)) := x$. If this happens, we say that f and g are **inverse functions** and we write $g = f^{-1}$ or $f = g^{-1}$. (The " $^{-1}$ " is a symbol that is often used in mathematics to represent inverses. It is not an exponent.)

Not all functions have an inverse; in fact, most do not. Suppose $f(x) := x^2$ and $g(x) := \sqrt{x}$. It is tempting to say that f and g are inverses since taking the square root of a number undoes the process of squaring it. This is only partly true. Clearly, $f(2) = 4$ and $g(4) = 2$. But, $f(-2) = 4$ also. If g were truly the inverse of f, we would have to have $g(4) = -2$. But $g(4) = 2$ (we agree to take positive square roots only) so g is not the inverse of f. Actually, if we redefine f by restricting its domain to $\{x \mid x \geq 0\}$, then g is the inverse of f. We will see this idea in Section 7.4 where we discuss inverse trigonometric functions.

The logical question to ask is: Which functions have inverses? The reason $f(x) := x^2$ does not have an inverse is that there are two different x-values having the same y-value. Thus, the inverse would have two different y-values for the same x-value and, hence, would not be a function. A function having the property that no two distinct x-values have the same $f(x)$ is said to be **one-to-one**. So, only one-to-one functions have inverses. Geometrically, the graph of a one-to-one function has the property that no *horizontal* line crosses it in more than one place.

If f has an inverse, then it is easy to get the graph of f^{-1} from the graph of f. Any point (a, b) on the graph of f has a corresponding point (b, a) on the graph of f^{-1} since $f^{-1}(b) = f^{-1}(f(a)) = a$. Since the points (a, b) and

(b, a) are placed symmetrically about the line $y = x$, the graph of f^{-1} can be obtained by reflecting the graph of f across the line $y = x$. See Figure 1.47.

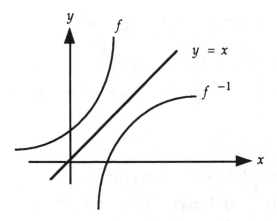

Fig. 1.47

Here's an algebraic method for finding the inverse of a function $y = f(x)$, if it exists. First, solve for x in terms of y, if possible. Then, switch x and y. The expression in x is $f^{-1}(x)$.

EXAMPLE 1.27:

Find the inverse of $f(x) := x^3 + 1$.

Solving $y = x^3 + 1$ for x gives

$x = (y - 1)^{1/3}$.

Now switch x and y, obtaining $f^{-1}(x) := y = (x - 1)^{1/3}$.   ◆

Although this is an interesting exercise, it is seldom possible to solve for x in terms of y. Consider, for example, $f(x) := y = x^5 + x$. This is a one-to-one function, but it is not possible to solve for x, so we won't be able to express f^{-1} in a closed form.

TEST YOUR UNDERSTANDING

5. Find the inverse of $f(x) := \dfrac{x}{x+1}$.

EXERCISES FOR SECTION 1.4:

1. Sketch the graphs of the following functions:

   (a) $y = -\frac{1}{2}x + 2$ (b) $y = 1 - x^2$ (c) $y = x^3 - 1$ (d) $y = \dfrac{1}{(x+3)^2}$

   (e) $y = (x-1)^2 - 3$ (f) $y = (x+2)^2$ (g) $y = |x| - 2$ (h) $y = \sqrt{9 - x^2}$

2. Given $f(2) = 4, f(4) = 7, f(7) = 2, g(2) = 7, g(4) = 4$, and $g(7) = 2$, what is:

   (a) $f \circ g(7)$ (b) $g \circ f(7)$

3. Let $f(x) := 1 + x$, and $g(x) := x^2$. Determine:

   (a) $f^{-1}(x)$, if it exists   (b) $f \circ g(x)$ (c) $g \circ f(x)$

4. Given $h(x) := 1 + \sqrt{x^2 + 1}$, and that $f \circ g = h$, find three possible choices for f and g.

5. Determine the inverse of :

   (a) $f(x) := \sqrt[3]{x + 4}$ (b) $f(x) := 1 + \sqrt{x}$

6. Let $c(x)$ be the total cost of producing x items.

   (a) What does $c(x + 1) - c(x)$ represent?

   (b) What does $c(x)/x$ represent?

PROBLEMS FOR SECTION 1.4:

1. Let f be the function whose graph is shown below and let $g(x) := xf(x)$. Sketch the graph of g.

   Hint: For what x values is $g(x) = 0$? For what x values is $g(x) > 0$? For what x values is $g(x) < 0$? If $f(x) > 0$, then for what x is $g(x) > f(x)$? What if $f(x) < 0$?

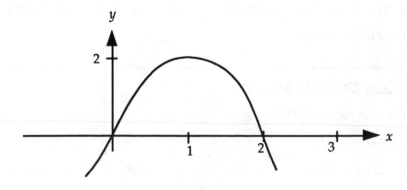

2. For the function in Problem 1, sketch $h(x) := x^2 f(x)$.

3. Economists define profit as the difference between total revenue and total costs; that is, $P = R - C$. The graphs of R and C, as a function of x, the number of items produced, are given below.

   (a) For what value of x is $P = 0$?

   (b) For what values of x is $P > 0$?

   (c) Sketch a graph of P as a function of x.

   (d) How much should this manufacturer produce to maximize profits?

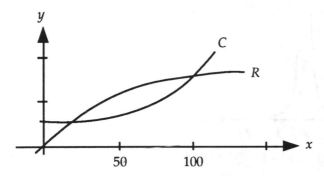

4. Suppose $f(x) := x$. Then clearly, $f(f(x)) := x$, implying that $f = f^{-1}$. Find two other functions with the property that they are their own inverses.

5. Let f be the function whose graph is given below.

   (a) Sketch a graph of $g(x) := |f(x)|$. Describe, in general, how to get the graph of $g(x) := |f(x)|$ from the graph of f.

   (b) Repeat part (a) for the function $h(x) := f(|x|)$.

   (c) Repeat part (a) for the functions $p(x) := f(-x)$, $q(x) := -f(x)$ and $r(x) := [f(x)]^2$.

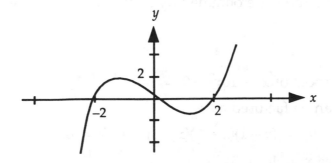

TYU Answers for Section 1.4

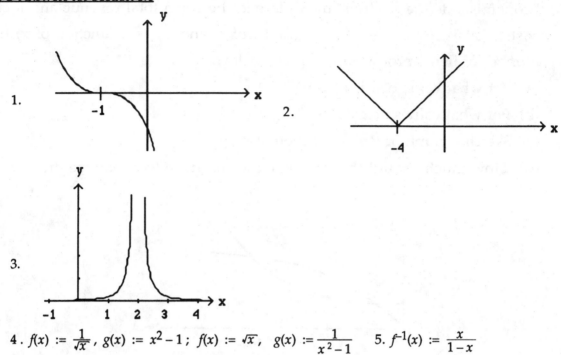

1.

2.

3.

4. $f(x) := \frac{1}{\sqrt{x}}$, $g(x) := x^2 - 1$; $f(x) := \sqrt{x}$, $g(x) := \frac{1}{x^2 - 1}$ 5. $f^{-1}(x) := \frac{x}{1-x}$

APPENDIX

SOLVING EQUATIONS AND INEQUALITIES

Throughout this course, we will have to solve many equations and inequalities. To help you, let's review some techniques.

All equations can be written in the form $f(x) = 0$ for some suitable function f. If f is a polynomial, then we can try to factor it into the product of linear factors. The roots are obtained by setting each factor equal to 0.

EXAMPLE A1.1:

Determine the roots of $x^4 - 10x^2 + 9 = 0$.

The equation can be factored as

$$(x^2 - 1)(x^2 - 9) = (x - 1)(x + 1)(x - 3)(x + 3) = 0.$$

Hence, the roots are $x = 1, -1, 3, -3$.   ♦

TEST YOUR UNDERSTANDING

1. Show that $x = -3$ is one root of $x^3 + 3x^2 - x - 3 = 0$. Find the other roots.

2. Solve $x^4 + x^3 - 4x^2 - 4x = 0$.

If f is not factorable, then other techniques must be employed. For quadratic equations, we can use the well-known quadratic formula. For higher degree polynomial equations, it is best to try to approximate the roots numerically. (There are formulas for third and fourth degree polynomial equations but they are complicated and not worth remembering. There is no formula, and it has been shown that there never will be, that will solve the general equation of 5th degree or higher.)

There are many numerical procedures available for solving equations. This is a topic for further investigation.

Once the roots of $f(x) = 0$ have been found, it is easy to solve the inequalities $f(x) > 0$ and $f(x) < 0$ if f is continuous. Suppose x_1 and x_2 are successive roots of $f(x) = 0$ (meaning that there are no roots between x_1 and x_2). Then, for all x between x_1 and x_2, $f(x)$ is either greater than or less than 0. To find out which, simply select a value of x between x_1 and x_2 and evaluate f.

EXAMPLE A1.2:

Solve $x^3 - 5x^2 + 6x > 0$.

Since $f(x) = x^3 - 5x^2 + 6x = x(x - 2)(x - 3)$, then the roots of the equation $f(x) = 0$ are 0, 2 and 3. Pick any number less than 0, say –1, and substitute. $f(-1) = -12 < 0$ so $f(x) < 0$ for $x < 0$. Now pick a number between 0 and 2, say 1. $f(1) = 2 > 0$ so $f(x) > 0$ for $0 < x < 2$. Next, pick a number between 2 and 3, say 2.5. $f(2.5) = -.625 < 0$, so $f(x) < 0$ for $2 < x < 3$. Finally, pick a number greater than 3, say 4. $f(4) = 8 > 0$, so $f(x) > 0$ for $x > 3$. Therefore, the solution is $\{x \mid 0 < x < 2 \text{ or } x > 3\}$. ♦

In the case where f is can be expressed as the product or quotient of functions, we can use a number line to help us solve the inequality. Consider the inequality in the example above. Draw a number line and indicate the roots 0, 2 and 3 of the corresponding equation. This partitions the number line into 4 disjoint segments: $(-\infty, 0)$, $(0, 2)$, $(2, 3)$ and $(3, \infty)$. The sign of each factor in each segment can be easily determined. In order for the product of the three factors to be positive, we need either three positive factors (occurring on the interval $(3, \infty)$) or two negative and one positive factors (occurring on the interval $(0, 2)$).

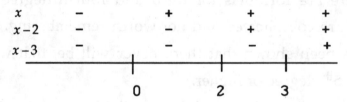

EXAMPLE A1.3:

Solve $\dfrac{x}{x^2-9} \le 0$.

Since $\dfrac{x}{x^2-9} = \dfrac{x}{(x-3)(x+3)}$, we will use the number line technique described above.

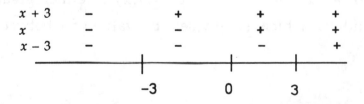

The expression is negative when all three factors are negative or when one is negative and two are positive. Thus, the solution is $(-\infty, -3)$ or $[0, 3)$. Note that $x = 0$ is included since it satisfies the equation $\frac{x}{x^2 - 9} = 0$. Neither -3 nor 3 is included since the expression is undefined there.   ♦

EXERCISES FOR APPENDIX:

1. Find the real roots of each of the following equations:

   (a) $x^4 - 13x^2 + 36 = 0$ (b) $x^3 - x - 6 = 0$

2. Solve the following inequalities:

   (a) $2x - 3 < 5x - 12$ (b) $x^2 + x - 2 \geq 0$ (c) $x^3 - x \leq 0$ (d) $x^4 - 4x^2 \geq 0$

   (e) $x^2 \geq 9$ (f) $x + \frac{1}{x} \geq \frac{5}{2}$

TYU Answers for Appendix

   1. Other roots are 1 and -1.   2. $x = 0, -1, 2, -2$

ANALYZING A CLASS OF RATIONAL FUNCTIONS

OBJECTIVE: Let $f(x) := \dfrac{x}{x^2 + b^2}$, where b is a constant. The purpose of this project is to describe the behavior of this function and to determine how that behavior is affected by changing the constant b.

PROCEDURE:

Part 1: Some preliminary analysis
   a. What is the domain of f?
   b. For what values of x is $f(x) > 0$? $f(x) < 0$?
   c. What happens to the values of $f(x)$ as $x \to \infty$? As $x \to -\infty$?

Part 2: Graphs of f
   a. Use a graphing calculator or computer graphing package to draw the graph of f for the cases $b = 1$, $b = 2$ and $b = 3$.
   b. Discuss the direction and concavity of the functions.
   c. Determine the (approximate) coordinates of all local maximum and minimum points.
   d. What happens to the range of f as b increases?
   e. What happens to the coordinates of the local extrema as b increases?
   f. What happens to the coordinates of the inflection points as b increases?

Part 3: Determining the range of f
   a. Let $b = 1$; that is, set $f(x) := \dfrac{x}{x^2 + 1} = y$.
   b. Show that the equation above can be rewritten as $yx^2 - x + y = 0$.
   c. Use the quadratic formula to solve for x in terms of y.
   d. Determine the values of y for which the roots of the quadratic equation are real. These y-values constitute the range of f.
   e. Repeat this calculation for the more general case $f(x) := \dfrac{x}{x^2 + b^2}$ and express the range in terms of b. Does this confirm your observation in Part 2d?

Part 4: Determining the local maxima and minima for the general case
   a. What are the y-values (in terms of b) of the local maxima and minima of f?
   b. Solve for the corresponding x-values and confirm the answer to 2e.

PROJECT 1.2

TRIGONOMETRIC FUNCTIONS

OBJECTIVE: In Section 1.3, we mentioned the existence of six trigonometric functions, the sine, cosine, tangent, cotangent, secant, and cosecant. Although we will postpone a formal discussion of these until Chapter 7, we can do some preliminary analysis. That is the objective of this project.

PROCEDURE:
Part 1: Radian measure
   The arguments of all trigonometric functions are real numbers, or angles expressed in radians, not degrees. Note: $180° = \pi$ radians.
   a. Convert each of the following degree-measures into radians
        (i) 60°   (ii) 225°   (iii) 810°   (iv) 31°
   b. In which quadrant would you find each of the following angles?
        (i) $3\pi/4$ (ii) $17\pi/6$ (iii) 4   (iv) 7.3   (v) –5.3
   c. Use your calculator (set in radian mode) to evaluate
        (i) $\sin(2)$ (ii) $\cos(3.91)$ (iii) $\tan(-1.4)$ (iv) $\sin(\cos(.5))$

Part 2: The sine and cosine functions
   a. Graph $y = \sin(x)$, for $-2\pi \le x \le 2\pi$. Note that the function is
      periodic, meaning that it repeats itself after a fixed distance along the
      x-axis. In this case, the period is 2π, since $\sin(x + 2\pi) = \sin(x)$ for all
      x. In general, a function f is periodic with period p if $f(x + p) =$
      $f(x)$ for all x, and p is the smallest number with this property.
   b. What is the range of $\sin(x)$?
   c. The **amplitude** of a periodic function is defined as one-half the
      difference between the maximum and minimum values of the
      function. What is the amplitude of $\sin(x)$?
   d. For what values of x between -2π and 2π is $\sin(x) > 0$? Indicate these
      on your graph.
   e. Repeat 2a, b, c and d for $y = \cos(x)$.
   f. Now consider the more general function $y = a\sin(bx)$. Graph this
      for the following cases: $a = 2, b = 1$; $a = 3, b = 1$;
         $a = 1, b = 2$; $a = 1, b = 3$.
      What effect does changing a and b have on the amplitude and
      period of the graph?

Part 3: Some identities

   a. Graph the function $f(x) := \sin^2(x) + \cos^2(x)$. What do you notice?

   b. Show that $\sin(\pi/6 + \pi/4) \neq \sin(\pi/6) + \sin(\pi/4)$.

   c. It can be shown that $\sin(x + y) = \sin(x)\cos(y) + \cos(x)\sin(y)$. Use this to get the correct value for $\sin(\pi/6 + \pi/4)$.

   d. Show that $\sin(x + \pi/2) = \cos(x)$ for all x. Illustrate this by graphing $f(x) := \sin(x + \pi/2)$ and comparing to your graph in 2e.

Part 4: A combination

Let $f(x) := a \sin(x) + b \cos(x)$.

   a. Graph this function for each of the following cases:

     (i) $a = 1, b = 1$ (ii) $a = 2, b = 1$ (iii) $a = 1, b = 2$
     (iv) $a = 3, b = 1$

   b. How does each graph compare to $y = \sin(x)$?

   c. For each of the cases above, determine the maximum value of f and the smallest positive value of x at which it occurs.

   d. Using the identity from 3c, show that f can be rewritten as

$$f(x) := r \sin(x + \alpha), \text{ where } r = \sqrt{a^2 + b^2} \text{ and } \cos(\alpha) = \frac{a}{\sqrt{a^2 + b^2}}.$$

     The angle α is called the **phase shift**.

   e. Use 3d to describe how you could easily graph
$$f(x) := a \sin(x) + b \cos(x).$$

   f. Compute r and (the smallest) α for each case in 4a.

Part 5: Some other trigonometric functions

The **tangent** function is defined by $\tan(x) := \dfrac{\sin(x)}{\cos(x)}$, and the **secant** function by $\sec(x) := \dfrac{1}{\cos(x)}$.

   a. What are the domains of $\tan(x)$ and $\sec(x)$?

   b. Graph $y = \tan(x)$ and $y = \sec(x)$. What are the ranges? What are the periods?

   c. Graph the function $f(x) := \dfrac{\sin(2x)}{1 + \cos(2x)}$. What do you notice?

   d. Prove your observation in 5c.

     Hint: $\sin(2x) = 2\sin(x)\cos(x)$ and $\cos(2x) = 2\cos^2(x) - 1$.

PROJECT 1.3

FUNCTION ITERATION

OBJECTIVE: Recall that h is the composite of f and g if $h(x) := f(g(x))$, for all x. In this project, we will look at a special case of function composition. In particular, let f be a function and define $f^{(2)}(x) := f(f(x))$; that is, $f^{(2)}$ is the composite of f with itself. Similarly, let $f^{(3)}(x) := f(f^{(2)})(x)$, $f^{(4)}(x) := f(f^{(3)})(x)$, etc. Put differently, let's define a sequence by $u_0 = x$, $u_1 = f(u_0) = f(x)$, $u_2 = f(u_1) = f^{(2)}(x)$, etc. In general, $u_n = f(u_{n-1}) = f^{(n)}(x)$. It turns out that, upon continuing this process indefinitely, something interesting happens to the sequence for certain functions and x-values.

PROCEDURE:
Part 1: Some calculations
 a. Let $f(x) := \sqrt{x}$ and $u_0 = 2$. Compute u_1 through u_{15}.
 b. Repeat 1a with $f(x) := \sqrt{x}$ and $u_0 = .1$.
 c. Repeat 1a with $f(x) := \sqrt{x}$ and any (positive) u_0 of your own choice.
 d. What can you say about $\lim_{n \to \infty} u_n$ in 1a, b and c?
 e. Let $f(x) := x^2 - 2$ and $u_0 = 2$. Compute u_1 through u_5. What do you notice?
 f. Repeat 1e with $f(x) := x^2 - 2$ and $u_0 = -1$.
 g. Repeat 1e with $f(x) := x^2 - 2$ and $u_0 = 3$.

Part 2: Fixed points and convergence
 A **fixed point** of a function f is a number c such that $f(c) = c$. For example, -1, 0 and 1 are fixed points of $f(x) := x^3$, since $f(-1) = -1, f(0) = 0$ and $f(1) = 1$.
 a. Explain graphically how to locate fixed points. Hint: Compare the graphs of $y = f(x)$ and $y = x$.
 b. Determine the fixed points of the function $f(x) := \sqrt{x}$.
 c. Determine the fixed points of the function $f(x) := x^2 - 2$.
 d. Does the function $f(x) := \dfrac{-1}{x}$ have any fixed points? Explain and illustrate graphically.
 e. For what values of b does the function $f(x) := x^2 + b$ have exactly one fixed point? For what values of b does it have more than one? Express the fixed points in terms of b. Illustrate graphically.

f. Let $u_n := f(u_{n-1})$ as we did in Part 1. Show that if $\lim\limits_{n \to \infty} u_n = L$, then L is a fixed point of f. In other words, if this sequence converges, then it converges to a fixed point. Note: At some point, you will need to use the fact that $f\left(\lim\limits_{n \to \infty} u_n\right) = \lim\limits_{n \to \infty} f(u_n)$, a fact which is intuitively pleasing and correct, if f is continuous.

Part 3: Cobweb diagrams

There is an interesting geometric interpretation to the sequence $\{u_1, u_2,...\}$ one which will illustrate whether or not it converges. (You should have seen in 1c that the sequence does not always converge.)

a. On the same set of axes, draw the graphs of $y = \sqrt{x}$ and $y = x$. (It is important to use the same scale on both the x- and y-axes.) Note the fixed points at $x = 0$ and $x = 1$.

b. Pick a value on the x-axis between 0 and 1. Call it u_0. Draw a vertical line up to the graph of $y = \sqrt{x}$. What are the coordinates of the point of intersection?

c. Now draw a horizontal line from this point to the graph of $y = x$. What are the coordinates of that point? In particular, show that the x-coordinate of that point is $u_1 = \sqrt{u_0}$.

d. Starting at the point obtained in 3c, draw a vertical line to the graph of $y = \sqrt{x}$ followed by a horizontal line to $y = x$ to obtain a point whose x-coordinate is u_2. Continue in this fashion to obtain u_3, u_4, etc. The resulting picture should look like a cobweb spiraling in towards the fixed point $x = 1$.

e. Is it possible to pick a starting point so that the sequence converges to the fixed point $x = 0$?

Part 4: Another example

a. Let $f(x) := bx(1 - x)$, where b is a constant. Show that the fixed points are $x = 0$ and $x = \dfrac{b-1}{b}$.

b. Compute the first 10 terms of the sequence if $b = 2$ and $u_0 = .6$. Does the sequence converge? If so, to which fixed point? Illustrate with a cobweb diagram.

c. Repeat 4b with $b = 2.5$ and $u_0 = .5$.

d. Repeat 4b with $b = 4$ and $u_0 = .8$.

e. Repeat 4b with $b = 4$ and $u_0 = .3$.

Part 5: An application

One reason for studying fixed points is that it gives us a method for solving certain equations that we would not otherwise be able to solve.

a. Consider the equation $\cos(x) = x$, which has a root between 0 and $\pi/2$. Draw a graph of $y = \cos(x)$ and $y = x$ and estimate the root.

b. Starting with some u_0 near the root, construct a sequence defined by $u_n = \cos(u_{n-1})$. Does the sequence converge? Compute the root of $\cos(x) = x$ to 4 decimal places.

c. Now consider the equation $x^3 - x - 7 = 0$. This can be written in the form $f(x) := x$, where $f(x) := x^3 - 7$. Sketch graphs of $y = f(x)$ and $y = x$ and estimate the root of $f(x) := x$.

d. Starting with some u_0 near the root, construct a sequence defined by $u_n = f(u_{n-1})$. Does the sequence converge?

e. The equation in 1c can also be written as $f(x) := x$, where $f(x) := \sqrt[3]{x+7}$. Repeat 5d with this function. Compute the root of $x^3 - x - 7 = 0$ to 4 decimal places.

CHAPTER 2

BASIC PROBLEMS OF CALCULUS

2.1 THE PROBLEM OF THE BROKEN SPEEDOMETER

Imagine that you are driving your car along a highway. The speedometer of your car is broken so that, at any given moment, you do not know how fast you are going. Can you use the odometer readings to determine your instantaneous velocity (actual speedometer reading) at any given time?

¤ Let $s(t)$ denote the odometer reading and let $v(t)$ represent your velocity at time t. One of the most important problems that calculus can solve is determining the relationship between $s(t)$ and $v(t)$. In this section, we will concentrate on determining $v(t)$, given $s(t)$. In Section 2.3 and again in Chapter 6, we'll consider the converse problem--namely, determining the odometer reading (or distance travelled) from the velocity function $v(t)$.

Figure 2.1 shows a typical graph of the function $s(t)$, where s is measured in miles and t is measured in minutes. If you are always driving forward, then s should be an increasing function of t.

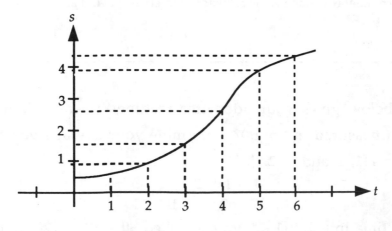

Fig. 2.1

Let's see what we can say about the velocity. During the first minute (i.e. the time interval [0, 1]), $s(t)$ changes from 0.5 to approximately 0.6, a change of 0.1 miles. This means that your **average velocity** during the first minute is 0.1 miles per minute (6 miles per hour). During the time interval [1, 2], $s(t)$ changes from 0.6 to 0.9, a change of 0.3 miles. Thus, your average velocity is 0.3 miles per minute. During the time interval [2, 3], $s(t)$ changes from 0.9 to 1.5, a change of 0.6 miles. Thus, your average velocity during this time interval is 0.6 miles per minute. During the interval [3, 4], there is even a bigger change in $s(t)$, from 1.5 to 2.6, so you really must have sped up (average velocity of 1.1 miles per minute). During the interval [4, 5], the change in $s(t)$ is a little bigger, from 2.6 to 3.8, so you are travelling at an average velocity of 1.2 miles per minute. During the interval [5, 6], however, the change is not as great, from 3.8 to 4.3, so you have slowed down to an average of 0.5 miles per minute.

We could subdivide the time intervals by reading the odometer every half minute. For example, during the interval [3, 3.5], the position changes from 1.5 to 2.0, a change of 0.5 miles. Since this occurs during an interval of 0.5 minutes, the average velocity is approximately $\frac{0.5}{0.5}$ = 1.0 miles per minute.

TEST YOUR UNDERSTANDING

1. Determine the average velocity over the intervals [4, 4.5] and [3.5, 4].

EXAMPLE 2.1:

The chart below gives your odometer readings (measured in miles) at various times (measured in hours)? Determine your average velocity during the time intervals [1, 2] and [2, 2.5].

t	0	1	2	2.5	3
$s(t)$	37	62	90	102	119

During the time interval [1, 2], you travelled $90 - 62$ = 28 miles, so your average velocity is 28 miles per hour.

During the time interval [2, 2.5], you travelled $102 - 90 = 12$ miles, so your average velocity is $\frac{12}{0.5} = 24$ miles per hour. ♦

TEST YOUR UNDERSTANDING

2. Compute the average velocity during the intervals [2.5, 3] and [1, 2.5] for the data in Example 2.1.

3. Compute your average velocity over the time interval [2, 5] if $s(5) = 8753$ km. and $s(2) = 8480$ km., where time is measured in hours.

Let's generalize these calculations. Consider the time interval $[t_1, t_2]$. Then, $s(t_1)$ is the odometer reading at the beginning of the interval and $s(t_2)$ is the reading at the end of the interval. The difference $\Delta s = s(t_2) - s(t_1)$ is the distance travelled during the time interval, and $\Delta t = t_2 - t_1$ is the length of the time interval. Thus, the quantity

(1) $$\bar{v} = \frac{s(t_2) - s(t_1)}{t_2 - t_1} = \frac{\Delta s}{\Delta t}.$$

is the **average velocity** during the time interval $[t_1, t_2]$.

Note: The symbol Δ (the capital Greek letter "delta") is often used in mathematics to indicate a change or difference in a quantity. Thus, Δs is the change in s.

EXAMPLE 2.2:

Suppose the odometer readings are given by $s(t) := t^2 + 53t + 8800$. Find the average velocity over the intervals: (a) [2, 4] and (b) [2, 2 + Δt]. (From now on, we'll omit the units of measurement, unless they are relevant.)

(a) The average velocity over the interval [2, 4] is

$$\bar{v} = \frac{s(4) - s(2)}{4 - 2} = \frac{9028 - 8910}{2} = 59.$$

(b) The average velocity over the interval $[2, 2 + \Delta t]$ is

$$\bar{v} = \frac{s(2 + \Delta t) - s(2)}{2 + \Delta t - 2} = \frac{(2 + \Delta t)^2 + 53(2 + \Delta t) + 8800 - 8910}{\Delta t}$$

$$= \frac{4 + 4\Delta t + (\Delta t)^2 + 106 + 53\Delta t - 110}{\Delta t} = \frac{57\Delta t + (\Delta t)^2}{\Delta t}. \qquad \blacklozenge$$

TEST YOUR UNDERSTANDING

4. Use the result of Example 2.2(b) to find the average velocity over the interval [2, 2.5].

5. Suppose odometer readings on a bicycle are given by the function $s(t) := t^3 + 3t$. Determine the average velocity over the interval [1, 3].

6. If $s(t) := 2t^2 + 12$, find the average velocity over the intervals:

    (a) [1, 3]   (b) [1, 2]   (c) $[1, 1 + \Delta t]$

Let's rewrite Eq.(1) in a slightly different form. Suppose the time interval begins at time $t_1 = c$ and is Δt time units long. Then it ends at time $t_2 = c + \Delta t$ and Eq.(1) becomes:

(2) $\bar{v} = \dfrac{s(c + \Delta t) - s(c)}{\Delta t}$.

□ The average velocity has an interpretation in terms of the graph of $s(t)$. Let $P(c, s(c))$ and $Q(c + \Delta t, s(c + \Delta t))$ be points on the graph of $s(t)$. Then $\bar{v}$ is the slope of the line PQ. We call a line joining two points on a curve a **secant line**, so the average velocity over an interval is the slope of the secant line joining the endpoints of the interval. See Figure 2.2.

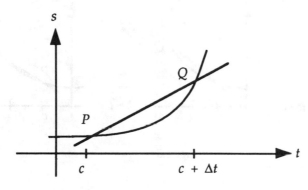

Fig. 2.2

Remember that what we've computed is the average velocity over an interval. This is *not the same* as $v(t)$, which represents the **instantaneous velocity** *at* time t. However, we can use the average velocity to determine the instantaneous velocity. One way to do it is to let Δt become small; that is, to consider the average velocity over shorter and shorter time intervals. In Example 2.2, if we evaluate the expression $\bar{v} = \dfrac{57\Delta t + (\Delta t)^2}{\Delta t}$ for small Δt, we get:

Δt	1	.1	.01	.001
$\bar{v}$	58	57.1	57.01	57.001

As Δt approaches 0, the average velocity near time $t = 2$ gets closer and closer to 57 and, in fact, we will say that the velocity at time $t = 2$ *equals 57*.

Geometrically, as Δt approaches 0, the point Q in Figure 2.2 approaches P. See Figure 2.3. As it does so, the secant line essentially just lies along the graph at P. We call a line that lies along a graph at a point a **tangent line**.

Hence, <u>the instantaneous velocity at time $t = c$ is the slope of the line tangent to the graph of the position function $s(t)$ at $t = c$</u>. This is a very important observation because it connects the physical notion of velocity with the geometric one of the tangent line. We will often exploit this and other similar connections throughout the rest of the book.

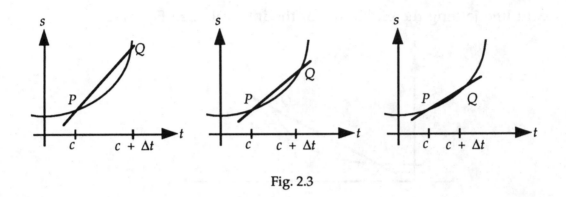

Fig. 2.3

Look again at the expression for $\bar{v}$ in Example 2.2. Note that we could divide the numerator and denominator by Δt, obtaining $\bar{v} = 57 + \Delta t$, *provided* $\Delta t \neq 0$. (This certainly agrees with the values in the table; e.g. when $\Delta t = .01$, $\bar{v} = 57 + .01 = 57.01$.) Then it is clear that $\bar{v}$ approaches 57 as Δt approaches 0.

¤ All of this may appear to be self-contradictory. Aren't we really letting Δt become 0 in Example 2.2 in order to get a velocity of exactly 57? But if we let $\Delta t = 0$ in the original expression for $\bar{v}$, we would get $\frac{0}{0}$, an expression with no meaning. (Remember the "reduced" form $\bar{v} = 57 + \Delta t$ is only valid if $\Delta t \neq 0$.) The problem lies with the word "equals". When we say that the instantaneous velocity at time $t = 2$ "equals" 57, what we really mean is that the average velocity over the time interval $[2, 2 + \Delta t]$ must be extremely close to 57 if Δt is sufficiently small and, moreover, we can make it as close as we like to 57 by making Δt *very* small.

While this may seem strange, it really is a concept you have seen before. Consider the rational number $\frac{1}{3}$, which we can express as the infinite repeating decimal .333... . Since we cannot actually write an infinite number of 3's, we have to interpret what we mean when we say that $\frac{1}{3}$ = .333.... . One way to think of it is that by taking enough 3's, we can make the difference between $\frac{1}{3}$ and the finite decimal .333...3 arbitrarily small. We are doing the same thing here: <u>To say the instantaneous velocity equals 57, we mean that we can make the average velocity arbitrarily close to 57 by making Δt sufficiently small</u>. This does not imply that the instantanteous velocity is an imprecise quantity. Indeed, the instantaneous velocity is as precise as the number $\frac{1}{3}$; we just obtain it through a sequence of ever-improving approximations.

In some sense, learning to deal with very small, non-zero quantities is at the heart of calculus. In fact, one of the discoverers of calculus, Gottfried Wilhelm von Leibniz, expressed his findings in terms of these very small quantities, which he called **infinitesimals**. Also, the first calculus textbook ever written was called *Analyse des infiniment petits pour l'intelligence des lignes courbes*, which can be translated as the "Analysis of infinitely small things for the study of curved lines". It was written in 1696 by Guillaume-François-Antoine de l'Hôpital, Marquis de Sainte-Mesme, Comte d'Entremont, whose name (suitably shortened) we shall come across later.

Needless to say, Leibniz and Isaac Newton, who invented calculus independently and more-or-less concurrently, were attacked for their radical (and fuzzy) thinking. Bishop George Berkeley referred to these infinitesimals as "ghosts of departed quantities". These attacks prompted later mathematicians to develop a more formal structure in which to study calculus. This task was not completed until late in the 19th century, roughly 200 years after calculus was invented. We shall examine some of this structure in the next chapter when we discuss limits. However, limits just provide a language in which to express these ideas; they won't help you if you don't understand the basic concept we have outlined here.

¤ Now let's generalize this a bit. Rather than you driving your car down a highway, imagine that a particle is moving along an axis. Let $s(t)$ be the position, relative to some fixed origin, of the particle on the axis. We'll allow the particle to move in either direction, so $s(t)$ may be increasing on some time intervals and decreasing on others. For convenience, assume that the axis is horizontal and that the "positive" direction is to the right.

One way to illustrate the motion of this particle is by a series of "snapshots", taken at equally spaced time intervals. Figure 2.4 shows such snapshots, taken at one second intervals. The particle starts at position $s(0) = 2$, moves to position $s(1) = 4$, then to $s(2) = 2$ and $s(3) = -2$.

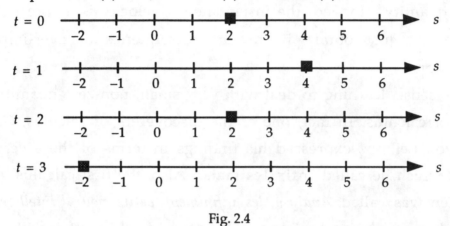

Fig. 2.4

Another way to represent this is by a graph with time on the horizontal axis and position on the vertical axis, as we did with the odometer readings in Figure 2.1. Figure 2.5 shows a typical graph of $s(t)$. The particle moves to the right whenever $s(t)$ is increasing which occurs on the time interval $[0, 1]$. It moves to the left when $s(t)$ is decreasing--that is, on the interval $[1, \infty)$. The particle passes the origin when the graph of $s(t)$ crosses the t-axis, at approximately $t = 2.5$. It is important to see that Figures 2.4 and 2.5 are just different graphical representations of the same path. The advantage to the graph in Figure 2.5 is that it gives us the position at every time between 0 and 3, not just at discrete points.

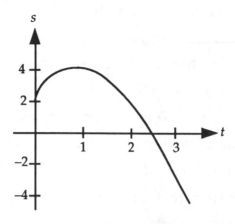

Fig. 2.5

If we have a formula for $s(t)$, we can derive a formula for $v(t)$, in much the same way as we did Example 2.2. We need to generalize the calculation to an arbitrary value of t, rather than just the specific value $t = 2$. In Example 2.2, we determined that the average velocity over the interval $[2, 2 + \Delta t]$ is

$$\bar{v} = \frac{s(2 + \Delta t) - s(2)}{2 + \Delta t - 2} = \frac{(2 + \Delta t)^2 + 53(2 + \Delta t) + 8800 - 8910}{\Delta t}.$$

Similarly the average velocity over the interval $[t, t + \Delta t]$ is

$$\bar{v} = \frac{s(t + \Delta t) - s(t)}{\Delta t} = \frac{(t + \Delta t)^2 + 53(t + \Delta t) + 8800 - (t^2 + 53t + 8800)}{\Delta t}$$

$$= \frac{2t\,\Delta t + (\Delta t)^2 + 53\Delta t}{\Delta t} = 2t + \Delta t + 53, \text{ if } \Delta t \neq 0.$$

Upon letting Δt approach 0, we find $v(t) := 2t + 53$.

EXAMPLE 2.3: Suppose $s(t) := t^2 - t$. Determine $v(t)$.

The average velocity over the time interval $[t, t + \Delta t]$ is

$$\bar{v} = \frac{(t + \Delta t)^2 - (t + \Delta t) - (t^2 - t)}{\Delta t} = \frac{2t\,\Delta t + (\Delta t)^2 - \Delta t}{\Delta t}$$

$$= 2t + \Delta t - 1, \text{ if } \Delta t \neq 0$$

Upon letting Δt approach 0, we find $v(t) := 2t - 1$. ◆

◻ This type of calculation is very important as it really underscores the meaning and geometric interpretation of instantaneous velocity. However, we shall postpone doing any more of these until the next chapter. What we will concentrate on here is using $v(t)$ to give us information about $s(t)$.

Suppose the particle moves to the right. Then $s(t)$ is increasing and the velocity $v(t)$ is positive. Similarly, $v(t)$ is negative when $s(t)$ is decreasing. If the particle changes direction, then $v(t)$ changes sign (either from positive to negative or from negative to positive). It follows that if $v(t)$ is continuous, then $v(t) = 0$ at any point where the direction changes. Physically, this means the particle must come to a complete stop (at least for an instant) before it can turn around.

In Example 2.3, we find that $v(t)$ is positive when $t > \frac{1}{2}$ and $v(t)$ is negative when $t < \frac{1}{2}$. Hence, the particle moves to the left for one-half second (on the interval $[0, \frac{1}{2}]$) and thereafter moves to the right.

TEST YOUR UNDERSTANDING

7. Describe the direction of motion for a particle whose velocity is:

(a) $v(t) := 12 - 4t$ (b) $v(t) := 4t - t^2$

EXAMPLE 2.4:

You start walking from home at 12:00 noon. You walk eastward at constant velocity of 3 mph for thirty minutes. Then you meet a friend and stop to chat for 10 minutes. You promised to be home in one hour, so you start walking home at constant velocity. Realizing that you will be late if you keep walking, you start accelerating to a jog, and arrive home exactly at 1:00. Draw a graph of $s(t)$ for $0 \le t \le 60$, where t is measured in minutes and $s(t)$ is measured in miles.

If your velocity is constant during a time interval, then the slope of the position function must be constant, implying that $s(t)$ is linear. While you are chatting with your friend, your position does not change. During the trip home, the velocity is negative and becomes more negative as you start to jog. This means the graph of $s(t)$ is decreasing evermore rapidly during this interval. See Figure 2.6.

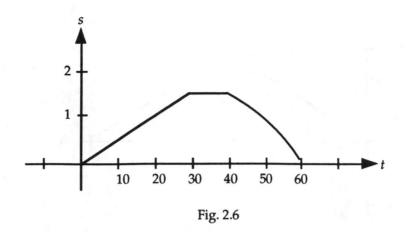

Fig. 2.6

EXERCISES FOR SECTION 2.1 :

1. The position of a particle is given by $s(t) := t^2 - 4$.

   (a) What is the average velocity over the interval [1, 3]?

   (b) What is the average velocity over the interval [1, 1 + Δt]?

2. The table below gives the position of a particle at various times.

t	0	1	3	6	8	10
$s(t)$	5	9	4	2	7	12

   (a) What is the average velocity during the interval [3, 6]?

   (b) What is the average velocity during the interval [3, 10]?

3. Sketch a position function for a particle whose velocity is positive on [0, 3] and negative on [3, ∞). (The answer is not unique.)

4. Repeat Exercise 3 for a particle whose velocity is positive on [0, 2] and [3, 6] and negative elsewhere, if the initial position of the particle is $s = 4$.

5. If the average velocity of a particle over the interval [2, 5] is $\bar{v} = 8$ and $s(2) = -3$, what is $s(5)$?

6. The graph below is the position function of a particle.

   (a) Estimate the average velocity over the interval [0, 1].

   (b) During what intervals is the instantaneous velocity positive?

   (c) Sketch the position function of another particle with the same velocity function.

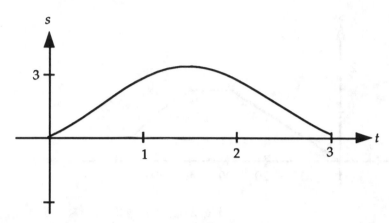

7. A train travels so that its position at time t is $s(t) := 5t^2 + 10t + 100$.

    (a) What is the average velocity of the train over the interval [2, 5]?

    (b) What is its instantaneous velocity when $t = 2$?

    (c) Determine $v(t)$, the instantaneous velocity at time t.

    (d) What is the initial velocity of the train?

    (e) At what time is the velocity of the train equal to 40?

8. The position of a particle is given by $s(t) := t^3 - 4t$.

    (a) During which time intervals is the particle to the right of the origin? (Assume the positive direction is to the right.)

    (b) The velocity of this particle is $v(t) := 3t^2 - 4$. During which time intervals is the particle moving to the right?

9. Two trucks leave from the same point and head in opposite directions along a straight highway. Each is travelling at a constant speed of 60 mph.

    (a) Draw the velocity function for each truck.

    (b) Draw the position function for each truck.

    (c) Draw a graph of the function b, where $b(t) = $ distance between the trucks at time t.

10. You drive down a straight country road at a constant rate of 50 mph. After 10 miles, you enter a town in which the speed limit is reduced to 30 mph. It takes 5 minutes to pass through the town, after which you resume travelling at 50 mph. Sketch your velocity and position functions.

PROBLEMS FOR SECTION 2.1 :

1. Two horses, Gorgeous George and Al's Pal, run a 1 mile race. Their position functions are graphed below. Write a description of the race, as if you were the track announcer. Who is leading at the quarter mile mark? the half-mile mark? the three-quarter mile mark? Who wins and by how much time?

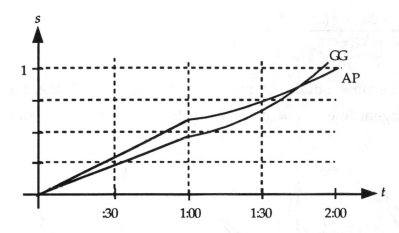

2. Argue that the repeating decimal .9999... is really the same as the number 1.

TYU Answers for Section 2.1

1. Using $s(4.5) = 3.4$ and $s(3.5) = 2.0$, we get 1.6 miles per minute over the interval [4, 4.5] and 1.2 miles per minute over the interval [3.5, 4]   2. 34 mph, 80/3 mph

3. 91 kmph   4. 57.5 mph   5. 16   6. (a) 8   (b) 6   (c) $\dfrac{4\Delta t + 2(\Delta t)^2}{\Delta t}$

7. (a) moves to right when $t < 3$, to left when $t > 3$ (b) moves to the right when $0 < t < 4$, to the left when $t > 4$

2.2 SLOPE FUNCTIONS

In the last section, we looked at the relationship between the position function $s(t)$ and the velocity function $v(t)$ of a particle. We argued that the velocity at time $t = c$ is the slope of the line tangent to the graph of $s(t)$ at $t = c$. In particular, we saw how the direction of $s(t)$ and the sign of $v(t)$ are related.

◻ In this section, we'll consider an arbitrary function $y = f(x)$. We'll define a **slope function**, $m(x)$, in much the same way we defined the velocity. The slope function will give us the same type of information about the behavior of $f(x)$ that $v(t)$ gave us about $s(t)$.

Let $P(c, f(c))$ and $Q(c + \Delta x, f(c + \Delta x))$ be two points on the graph of f, as shown in Figure 2.7 (which is the same as Figure 2.3, except for the names of the variables). The secant line PQ has slope given by:

$$\overline{m} = \frac{f(c + \Delta x) - f(c)}{c + \Delta x - c} = \frac{f(c + \Delta x) - f(c)}{\Delta x} = \frac{\Delta y}{\Delta x}$$

By letting Δx become small, Q moves closer to P and the secant lines approach the tangent line at $x = c$. As a result, their slopes approach $m(c)$.

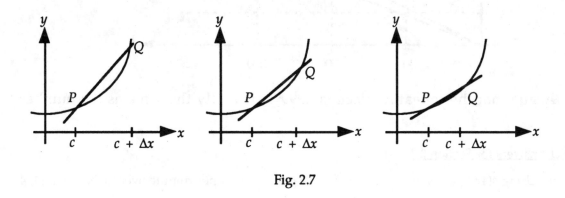

Fig. 2.7

Figure 2.8 illustrates a function with its tangent line at $x = c$. Note that the slope of the tangent line will change if we draw it at a different x-value.

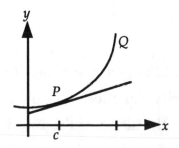

Fig. 2.8

We sometimes may speak of the "slope of a curve" at $x = c$. What we mean is the slope of the line tangent to the graph at that point.

To derive the slope of the tangent line at $x = c$ analytically, first find the slope of the secant line over the interval $[c, c + \Delta x]$, simplify (if possible) so that there is no Δx in the denominator and then let Δx become 0.

EXAMPLE 2.5:

Let $f(x) := x^2 + 2x - 3$.

(a) Determine the slope of the secant line joining the points $P(2, f(2))$ and $Q(4, f(4))$.

Since $f(2) = 5$ and $f(4) = 21$, the slope of PQ is $\dfrac{21 - 5}{4 - 2} = 8$.

(b) Determine the slope joining $P(2, f(2))$ and $R(2 + \Delta x, f(2 + \Delta x))$.

$f(2 + \Delta x) = (2 + \Delta x)^2 + 2(2 + \Delta x) - 3 = 5 + 6\Delta x + (\Delta x)^2$ so the slope of

PR is $\overline{m} = \dfrac{f(2 + \Delta x) - f(2)}{\Delta x} = \dfrac{5 + 6\Delta x + (\Delta x)^2 - 5}{\Delta x} = \dfrac{6\Delta x + (\Delta x)^2}{\Delta x}$.

(c) Determine the slope of the line tangent to the graph of f at $x = 2$.

If $\Delta x \neq 0$, then the expression above for the slope of the secant can be reduced to $\overline{m} = 6 + \Delta x$. By letting Δx approach 0, we conclude that the slope of the tangent to the curve at $x = 2$ is 6.   ◆

EXAMPLE 2.6:

Let $f(x) := 2x^3$. Determine the slope of the tangent to the curve at an arbitrary $x = c$.

The secant line joining the points $(c, f(c))$ and $(c + \Delta x, f(c + \Delta x))$ has

slope given by $\overline{m} = \dfrac{f(c + \Delta x) - f(c)}{\Delta x} = \dfrac{2(c + \Delta x)^3 - 2c^3}{\Delta x}$

$$= \dfrac{2c^3 + 6c^2\Delta x + 6c(\Delta x)^2 + 2(\Delta x)^3 - 2c^3}{\Delta x} = \dfrac{6c^2\Delta x + 6c(\Delta x)^2 + 2(\Delta x)^3}{\Delta x}$$

$$= 6c^2 + 6c(\Delta x) + 2(\Delta x)^2 \text{, if } \Delta x \neq 0$$

By letting Δx approach 0, we find that the slope of the tangent at $x = c$ is $m(c) = 6c^2$.

Hence, the slope of the tangent at $x = 1$ is $m(1) = 6(1)^2 = 6$; the slope of the tangent at $x = 2$ is $m(2) = 6(2)^2 = 24$; the slope of the tangent at $x = 0$ is $m(0) = 6(0)^2 = 0$; etc. ◆

TEST YOUR UNDERSTANDING

1. The slope of the secant line joining $(4, f(4))$ and $(4 + \Delta x, f(4 + \Delta x))$ for some function f is given by $\overline{m} = 51 + 12\Delta x + (\Delta x)^2$. What is the slope of the tangent line at $x = 4$?

2. Let $f(x) := 2x - x^2$. Determine the slope of the tangent to the curve at:

    (a) $x = -1$ (b) an arbitrary $x = c$

EXAMPLE 2.7:

The slope function for f is $m(x) := 8 + 2x$. For what values of x is f increasing?

f is increasing on an interval if the tangent line drawn at any point on the interval has positive slope--that is, if $m(x) > 0$. In this example, $m(x) > 0$ when $x > -4$. Similarly, f is decreasing if $m(x) < 0$. Here, $m(x) < 0$ for $x < -4$. ◆

¤ Given the graph of $f(x)$, we can draw the graph of $m(x)$.

EXAMPLE 2.8:

Figure 2.9 shows the graph of a function f. On what intervals will its slope function be positive? negative? Draw a graph of the slope function.

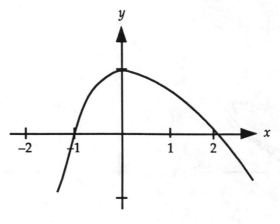

Fig. 2.9

Since f is increasing on $(-\infty, 0]$ and decreasing on $[0, \infty)$, then $m(x)$ will be positive on $(-\infty, 0]$ and negative on $[0, \infty)$. A plausible graph of m is given in Figure 2.10.

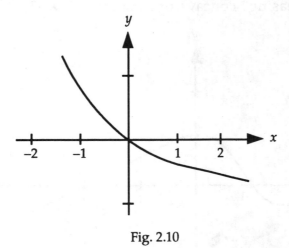

Fig. 2.10

♦

¤ The slope function can also be used to determine the concavity of f. Suppose $m(x)$ is increasing on some interval. Then the slopes of the lines tangent to the graph of $f(x)$ are increasing which, in turn, means that the graph of $f(x)$ is concave up. (Think about it!!). Similarly, if $m(x)$ is decreasing, then $f(x)$ is concave down. This is illustrated in the diagrams below. In Figure 2.11(a), the slopes of the tangent lines increase from negative to positive as we move from left to right; hence, the graph of $f(x)$ is concave up. In Figure 2.11(b), the slopes decrease from positive to negative and $f(x)$ is concave down.

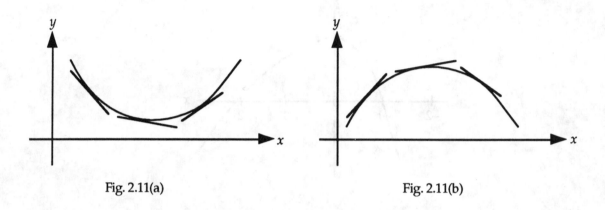

Fig. 2.11(a)   Fig. 2.11(b)

EXAMPLE 2.9:

Figure 2.12 shows the graph of the slope function for f. On what intervals is f increasing? decreasing? concave up? concave down?

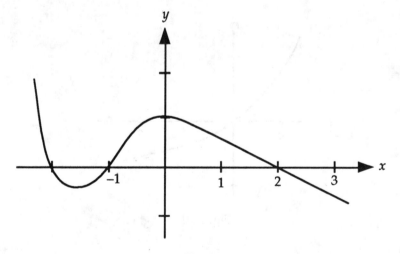

Fig. 2.12

Since $m(x) > 0$ on $(-\infty, -2]$ and $[-1, 2]$, then f is increasing on those intervals. Likewise, f is decreasing on $[-2, -1]$ and $[2, \infty)$. Since $m(x)$ is increasing on $[-1.5, 0]$, f is concave up there and concave down elsewhere. ♦

Recall that f has a local minimum at $x = c$ if the direction of f changes from decreasing to increasing as we move from left to right through $x = c$. This means that $m(x)$ changes from negative to positive at $x = c$. Likewise, f has a local maximum at $x = c$ if $m(x)$ changes from positive to negative at $x = c$. Consequently, the function whose slope function is given in Figure 2.12 will have local maxima at $x = -2$ and $x = 2$ and a local minimum at $x = -1$.

TEST YOUR UNDERSTANDING

3. Sketch the slope function for the function pictured below.

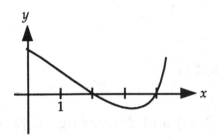

❑ The next two examples reinforce the idea that the velocity function is the slope function for the position function. Consequently, $s(t)$ is increasing whenever $v(t)$ is positive and $s(t)$ is decreasing whenever $v(t)$ is negative. Furthermore, $s(t)$ is concave up when $v(t)$ is increasing and $s(t)$ is concave down when $v(t)$ is decreasing. The rate at which the velocity changes is called the **acceleration**, denoted $a(t)$. Hence, $s(t)$ is concave up when $a(t)$ is positive and $s(t)$ is concave down when $a(t)$ is negative. Since the acceleration is, in essence, the "velocity of the velocity", we could find a formula for $a(t)$ from $v(t)$ by repeating the process we used to find $v(t)$ from $s(t)$. We won't do so here.

In Example 2.3, $v(t) := 2t - 1$ which is increasing for all t. Hence the acceleration of the particle is positive for all t, meaning that the graph of the position function is concave up for all t.

EXAMPLE 2.10:

The graph of a position function is given in Figure 2.13. Draw a graph of the velocity function.

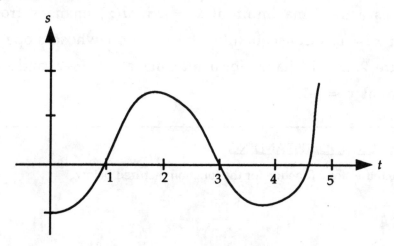

Fig. 2.13

Since $s(t)$ is increasing on $[0, 2]$ and $[4, \infty)$ and decreasing on $[2, 4]$, then $v(t)$ is positive on $[0, 2]$ and $[4, \infty)$ and negative on $[2, 4]$. Changes of direction occur at $t = 2$ and $t = 4$, so $v(2) = v(4) = 0$. Since $s(t)$ is concave up on $[0, 1]$ and $[3, \infty)$, then $v(t)$ is increasing on those intervals. It is decreasing on $[1, 3]$. See Figure 2.14.

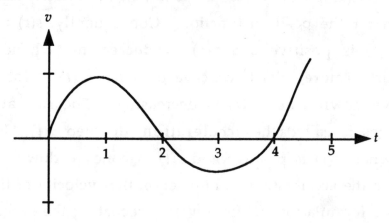

Fig. 2.14

◆

EXAMPLE 2.11:

Figure 2.15 is the graph of the velocity function. When is the particle moving to the right? to the left? When does it change direction? When is the acceleration positive? negative?

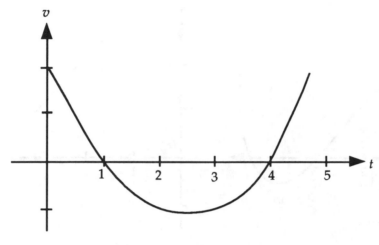

Fig. 2.15

The particle moves to the right on the time intervals [0, 1] and [4, ∞), when $v(t) > 0$. It moves to the left on [1, 4]. Direction changes occur at $t = 1$ and $t = 4$, since $v(1) = 0$ and $v(4) = 0$. The velocity is decreasing on [0, 2.5], so the acceleration is negative there. The velocity is increasing on [2.5 ∞), so the acceleration is positive on that interval.   ◆

▯ At this point, we might ask whether we can determine $f(x)$ from $m(x)$ or, equivalently, determine $s(t)$ from $v(t)$. The answer is, "not quite". The information given by $m(x)$ tells us the "shape" of $f(x)$--that is, the direction and concavity of $f(x)$. However, there are infinitely many graphs with the same shape. Imagine taking a graph and sliding it vertically--its shape doesn't change, but you get a different function. So, unless we have some additional information such as a point on the graph, the best we can do is determine the shape of $f(x)$, but not $f(x)$ itself. In the context of velocity, we would need to know the position at some specific time in order to draw the graph of the position function. For example, consider the velocity function in Example

2.11. If the initial position is $s(0) = 0$, we get a graph like the one in Figure 2.16(a). On the other hand, if $s(0) = 3$, we get a graph like the one in Figure 2.16(b). Note that the graphs are, in some sense, "parallel"; one is a vertical translation of the other.

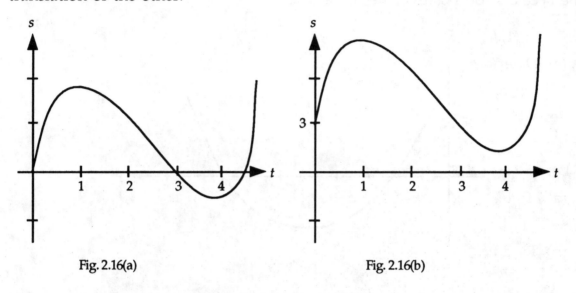

Fig. 2.16(a)   Fig. 2.16(b)

_____

TEST YOUR UNDERSTANDING

4. The velocity function of a particle is pictured below. Sketch a position function for which $s(0) = -1$.

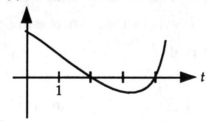

_____

EXERCISES FOR SECTION 2.2 :

1. Let $f(x) := x^2 + x$.

   (a) Determine the slope of the secant line between the points $P(1, f(1))$ and $R(3, f(3))$.

   (b) Determine (in terms of Δx) the slope of the secant line between $P(1, f(1))$ and $Q(1 + \Delta x, f(1 + \Delta x))$.

   (c) Determine the slope of the tangent line at $x = 1$.

   (d) Write an equation of the tangent line at $x = 1$.

   $y' = 2x + 1 \qquad m = 3$

   $y = 3m - 1$

2. Repeat Exercise 1 for the function $f(x) := 2x^3 - x + 3$.

3. Repeat Exercise 1 for the function $g(x) := 7x - 3$.

4. Let $f(x) := 1 - x^2$.

   (a) Determine the slope of the secant line between the points $P(c, f(c))$ and $Q(c + \Delta x, f(c + \Delta x))$.

   (b) Find the slope function of f.

5. Repeat Exercise 4 for the function $g(x) := 5x^2 - x$.

6. The slope of the secant joining $(c, f(c))$ and $(c + \Delta x, f(c + \Delta x))$ for some function f is $\overline{m} = 2c + 4 + \Delta x$.

   (a) What is the slope of the secant joining $(3, f(3))$ and $(5, f(5))$?

   (b) What is the slope of the tangent line at $x = 3$?

   (c) What is the slope function $m(x)$?

   (d) If $f(3) = 7$, write an equation of the tangent line at $x = 3$.

7. The slope function for a function f is $m(x) := 3x^2 + 6x$.

   (a) If $f(2) = 7$, write an equation of the line tangent to the graph of f at $x = 2$.

   (b) Write an equation of the line *perpendicular* to the tangent at $x = 2$.

   (c) At what values of x is the tangent line horizontal?

   (d) For what values of x is the tangent line parallel to $y = 3x - 10$?

8. The slope function for a function f is pictured below.

   (a) On what intervals is f increasing?

   (b) On what intervals is f concave up?

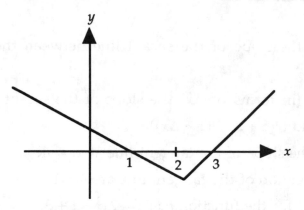

9. Sketch the velocity function for a particle whose position function is given below.

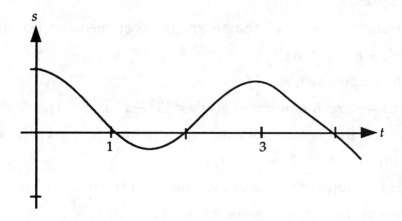

10. Functions f and g are shown in the graph below.

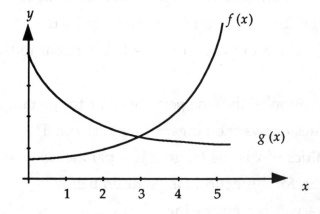

(a) For what values of x is $f(x) > g(x)$?

(b) For what values of x is the slope function of f greater than the slope function of g?

PROBLEMS FOR SECTION 2.2:

1. Let $f(x) := x^2 - x$. For what value of c does the tangent to the graph at $x = c$ pass through $(0, -1)$?

2. Let $f(x) := x^2$.

   (a) Compute, in terms of c, the slope of the secant line over the interval $[c, c + 1]$.

   (b) For what value of c is this secant line horizontal?

   (c) For what values of c is the slope of the secant positive?

   (d) Show that the tangent line at $x = c + 1/2$ is parallel to the secant line in (a).

   (e) Repeat (a) for the function $g(x) := x^3$.

   (f) Show that there is no value of h such that the line tangent to the graph of g at $x = c + h$ is parallel to the secant line in (e) for *every* value of c.

3. Suppose f is a function with slope function m such that $f(0) = 0$ and $0 \le m(x) \le 1$ for all x. What is the largest possible value for $f(2)$? Explain.

4. Let $f(x) := tx^2$ and $g(x) := tx^3$, where t is a constant. Their slope functions are $m_1(x) := 2tx$ and $m_2(x) := 3tx^2$, respectively.

   (a) Determine a value of t such that the lines tangent to the graph of f at $x = 1$ and $x = -1$ are perpendicular.

   (b) Show that for every c there exists a value of t such that the lines tangent to the graph of f at $x = c$ and $x = -c$ are perpendicular.

   (c) Show that for every t and c the lines tangent to the graph of g at $x = c$ and $x = -c$ are parallel.

   (d) At what value(s) of c are the lines tangent to the graphs of f and g at $x = c$ parallel? Show that the answer is independent of t.

TYU Answers for Section 2.2

   1. 51   2. (a) 4   (b) $2 - 2c$

3.

4.

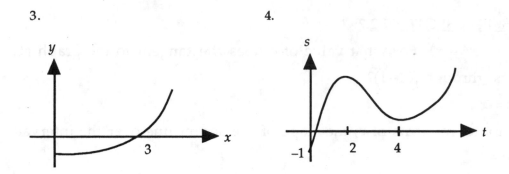

2.3 THE PROBLEM OF THE BROKEN ODOMETER

In Section 2.1, we considered the problem of determining the instantaneous velocity (speedometer reading) of an object, given that the speedometer was broken. Our approach was to take odometer readings at discrete time intervals, compute the average velocity over that interval, and then let the length of the interval get smaller.

In this section, we will consider the converse problem: Can you tell how far you've travelled if the odometer is broken but the speedometer works?

One way to approach this problem is to read the speedometer at regularly-spaced points in time $t_0, t_1, t_2, ..., t_n$ where $t_0 = a =$ time at which the journey starts and $t_n = b =$ time at which the journey ends. Since the readings are at equally-spaced times, then $t_2 - t_1 = t_3 - t_2 = t_4 - t_3 = ... = t_n - t_{n-1} = \Delta t$. ($\Delta t$ may be 1 minute or 5 minutes or 10 seconds or any other length of time.) What we've really done is subdivide (or **partition**, as it is usually described) the time interval $[a, b]$ into n equal subintervals. Each subinterval is of length $\Delta t = \dfrac{b - a}{n}$. See Figure 2.17.

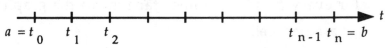

Fig. 2.17

Certainly, the total distance travelled during the time interval $[a, b]$ is the sum of the distances travelled during each subinterval $[t_{j-1}, t_j]$. Unfortunately, these "subdistances" are no easier to compute than the total distance.

To get out of this predicament, we make a bold assumption: The velocity during the entire subinterval $[t_{j-1}, t_j]$ is equal to $v(t_j)$ the velocity at time t_j. In effect, we are replacing the actual velocity function $v(t)$ by a "staircase approximation", as shown in Figure 2.18.

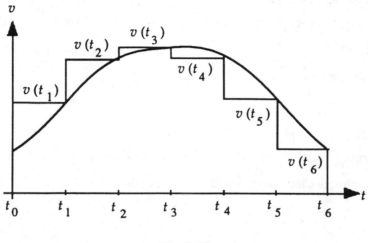

Fig. 2.18

If an object moves at a constant velocity v during an interval of length Δt, then the distance travelled during that interval is $v\Delta t$. Thus, the distance travelled during the interval $[t_{j-1}, t_j]$ is *approximately* $v(t_j)\Delta t$, and the total distance travelled during the interval $[a, b]$ is approximately:

$$(3) \qquad L \approx v(t_1)\Delta t + v(t_2)\Delta t + v(t_3)\Delta t + \ldots + v(t_n)\Delta t = \sum_{j=1}^{n} v(t_j)\Delta t \ .$$

Note: If you are unfamiliar with the notation $\sum_{j=1}^{n} v(t_j)\Delta t$, which is a shorthand for the summation of a bunch of similar terms, see the Appendix of this chapter.

For example, suppose you look at the speedometer every 15 minutes (1/4 hour) and the velocities in miles per hour are {57, 48, 55, 62, 51, 60, 53, 56, ... }. Then, assuming constant velocity during each interval, you travelled approximately 57(1/4) = 14.25 miles during the first 1/4 hour, 48(1/4) = 12 miles during the second 1/4 hour, 55(1/4) = 13.75 miles during the third 1/4 hour and so on. The total distance travelled during the first 1.5 hours (6 quarter hours) is approximately

$$L \approx 57(1/4) + 48(1/4) + 55(1/4) + 62(1/4) + 51(1/4) + 60(1/4) = 83.25$$

miles.

- -

TEST YOUR UNDERSTANDING

1. Suppose the speedometer readings were taken every 10 minutes and the result was {57, 55, 53, 52, 51, 50, 48, 50, 52, 53,...}. Approximate the distance travelled during the first 90 minutes.

2. Assuming the data in TYU#1 were recorded every 12 minutes, determine the approximate distance travelled during the first hour.

- -

At this point, all we have is an approximation to the total distance travelled. The reason it is an approximation is that we assumed the velocity in each subinterval is constant when, in fact, it may not be. However, the approximation will improve if we make Δt smaller. If we want to make Δt smaller, we will have to take more readings of the speedometer. In other words, making Δt smaller is equivalent to making n larger. We claim that we can get the exact distance travelled by making Δt "equal to" 0. This is similar to what we did in Section 2.1, where we obtained the instantaneous velocity at time t from the average velocity over the interval $[t, t + \Delta t]$ by letting Δt become "equal to" 0.

¤ This has a nice graphical interpretation. Suppose we modify Figure 2.18 by constructing rectangles as shown in Figure 2.19. The first rectangle has a height of $v(t_1)$ and a width of Δt, so its area is $v(t_1)\Delta t$. Similarly, the area of the second rectangle is $v(t_2)\Delta t$, the area of the third rectangle is $v(t_3)\Delta t$, etc. Thus, the approximate distance travelled is the sum of the areas of the rectangles.

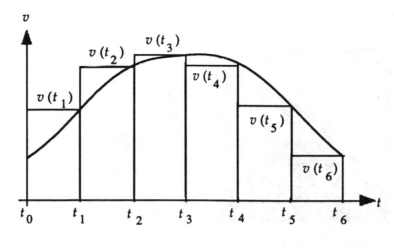

Fig. 2.19

TEST YOUR UNDERSTANDING

3. Using the data from TYU #1, draw a graph similar to Fig.2.19 such that the area under the bars is the approximate distance travelled during the first hour, assuming the data were recorded every 10 minutes.

As Δt gets smaller, the rectangles become thinner and they "fit the curve" better. Thus it seems plausible that the total distance travelled during the time interval $[a, b]$ is the area of the region R bounded by the graph of $v(t)$, the t-axis and the lines $t = a$ and $t = b$, as shown in Figure 2.20.

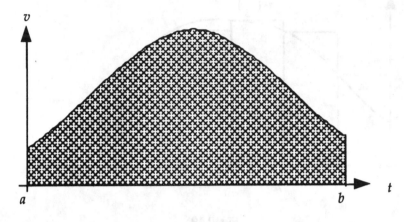

Fig. 2.20

EXAMPLE 2.12 :

The velocity of a particle is given by $v(t) := 2t + 4$. Determine the distance travelled by the particle during the time interval [1, 5].

The distance travelled is the area of the trapezoidal region shown in Figure 2.21.

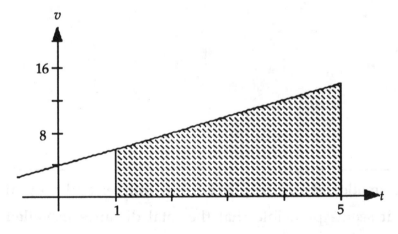

Fig. 2.21

The area of a trapezoid is given by $A = \dfrac{h(b_1 + b_2)}{2}$, where b_1 and b_2 are the bases and h is the altitude. Here, $h = 4$, $b_1 = 6$ and $b_2 = 14$. Thus, the distance is 40.   ♦

----

4. For the particle whose velocity is given in Example 2.12 , determine the distance travelled during the interval [2, 4].

▫ Now we come to a most crucial observation: If the velocity of a particle is positive during the time interval $[a, b]$, then the distance travelled by the particle is equal to the change in position (odometer reading). In other words, if $v(t)$ is the velocity and $s(t)$ is any corresponding position function, then the distance travelled during the interval $[a, b]$ is $s(b) - s(a)$.

To illustrate this point, recall Example 2.3 in which we showed that if $s(t)$:= $t^2 - t$, then $v(t)$:= $2t - 1$. During the time interval [2, 4], $v(t) > 0$. Hence the distance travelled during this interval is $s(4) - s(2)$ = $12 - 2$ = 10. This means that the area bounded by $v(t)$:= $2t - 1$, the t-axis and the lines $t = 2$ and $t = 4$ is 10, a fact that can be checked by geometry (cf. Example 2.12.)

While this may not seem terribly earthshattering at this point, it is actually a special case of the Fundamental Theorem of Calculus, the major result that ties the entire subject of calculus together.

EXERCISES FOR SECTION 2.3:

1. A bicyclist reads her speedometer every 12 minutes. The readings (in m.p.h.) are 10, 12, 15, 11, 16, 9, 13, 12,..., respectively. Assuming constant velocity during each time interval, approximately how far did she travel in the first hour?

2. Suppose the velocity of a particle is given by $v(t)$:= $3t + 1$. How far does the particle travel during the time interval [1, 4]? Sketch the region whose area represents the distance travelled.

3. The velocity of a particle is $v(t)$:= $\sqrt{1 + t^2}$. Approximate the distance travelled during the interval [0, 2] by using 4 subintervals of equal length.

PROBLEMS FOR SECTION 2.3:

1. Two horses, Cool Jule and Bonny Beth, run a race. Their velocity functions are pictured below.

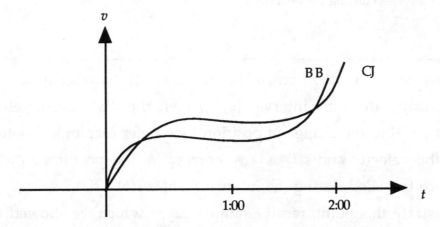

(a) At (approximately) what time(s) are the horses moving at the same speed? Who is leading at those times? Explain.

(b) If the race lasts approximately 2 minutes, who wins?

2. The argument that the distance travelled by a particle is equal to the area under the graph of the velocity function is valid only if the velocity is always positive during the given time interval. Suppose the velocity becomes negative at some point. Then part of the region is below the t-axis. How could we interpret the area under the curve in this case? Apply your interpretation to the velocity function pictured below.

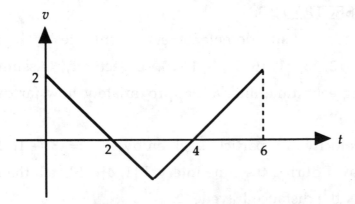

3. The velocity of a particle is given by $v(t) := 4t$. Another particle starts at the same point and moves at constant velocity k. Determine k so that the two particles have travelled the same distance at $t = 4$.

1. 78 miles   2. 53.6 miles   3.   4. 20

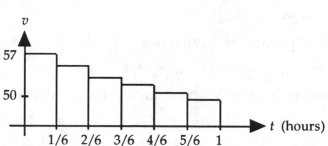

2.4 AREA AND RIEMANN SUMS

In Section 2.2, we showed that the physical problem of determining the instantaneous velocity of a particle is equivalent to the geometric problem of determining the slope of the line tangent to the graph of the position function. We then concentrated on the more general geometric problem of determining the slope of the line tangent to the graph of an arbitrary function f. In Section 2.3, we argued that the physical problem of determining the distance travelled during the time interval $[a, b]$ by a particle whose instantaneous velocity is $v(t)$ is equivalent to the geometric problem of finding the area bounded the graph of $v(t)$, the t-axis and the lines $t = a$ and $t = b$. Again, we'll concentrate just on the geometric problem.

Let R be the region bounded by the (non-negative) function $f(x)$, the x-axis and the vertical lines $x = a$ and $x = b$. We seek the area of R. See Figure 2.20.

In geometry, we define the area of a rectangle as the length times the width and the area of a circle to be π times the radius squared. We use these definitions to find the areas of other figures such as triangles, parallelograms, trapezoids, etc. The problem we face here is that the areas of the regions we consider, such as those in Figure 2.22, cannot be computed by any well-known formula (except in special cases such as when f is a linear function, in which case R is a trapezoid). We'll approach this problem as we did in the previous section.

◻ Partition the interval $[a, b]$ on the x-axis into n equal subintervals, each of length

$$\Delta x = \frac{b-a}{n}.$$

Label the points of division $x_0, x_1, \ldots, x_n$ where $x_0 = a, x_1 = a + \Delta x, x_2 = a + 2\Delta x, \ldots, x_j = a + j\Delta x, \ldots, x_n = b = a + n\Delta x$.

Construct rectangles by drawing horizontal lines between the points $(x_{j-1}, f(x_j))$ and $(x_j, f(x_j))$, for $j = 1, 2, 3, \ldots, n$. This means that the height of each rectangle will be the function value at the *right* side of the corresponding subinterval. Some of the rectangles will "fit inside" the region, while others will "stick out", but that doesn't matter. If Δx is very small, the rectangles will fill up the region quite nicely. See Figure 2.22.

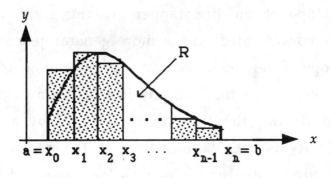

Fig 2.22

The first rectangle has a height of $f(x_1)$ and a width of Δx, so its area is $f(x_1)\Delta x$. Similarly, the area of the second rectangle is $f(x_2)\Delta x$, etc. Therefore, the total area of all the rectangles is given by:

$$S(n) := f(x_1)\Delta x + f(x_2)\Delta x + \ldots + f(x_n)\Delta x = \sum_{j=1}^{n} f(x_j)\Delta x.$$

The expression above is called a **Riemann sum** for the function f, named after the 19th century German mathematician George Friedrich Bernhard Riemann (pronounced Ree'-mahn).

EXAMPLE 2.13:

Let R be the region bounded by $f(x) := x^2 + 1$, the x-axis, the lines $x = 0$ and $x = 3$, as shown in Figure 2.23. Partition the interval $[0, 3]$ into 6 subintervals and compute the corresponding approximation to the area of R (i.e., Riemann sum).

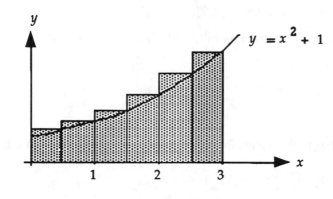

Fig. 2.23

Since $\Delta x = \dfrac{3-0}{6} = .5$, the partition points are:

$x_0 = 0, x_1 = .5, x_2 = 1, x_3 = 1.5, x_4 = 2, x_5 = 2.5$ and $x_6 = 3$.

Furthermore, $f(.5)\Delta x = (1.25)(.5) = .625$

$f(1)\Delta x = (2)(.5) = 1$

$f(1.5)\Delta x = (3.25)(.5) = 1.625$

$f(2)\Delta x = (5)(.5) = 2.5$

$f(2.5)\Delta x = (7.25)(.5) = 3.625$ and

$f(3)\Delta x = (10)(.5) = 5.$

So, the approximate area is $S(6) = 14.375$. ♦

- -

TEST YOUR UNDERSTANDING

1. Suppose, in Example 2.12, there were 5, rather than 6, subintervals. Find:

   (a) Δx (b) the subdivision points (c) $S(5)$

2. Let R be the region bounded by $y = 3x$, the x-axis, $x = 3$ and $x = 5$. Approximate the area of R using 4 rectangles.

3. Let $f(x) := x$ on the interval $[0, 2]$.

    (a) Show that if the interval is subdivided into 4 pieces, the resulting Riemann sum is 2.5.

    (b) What is the Riemann sum if the interval is divided into 8 pieces?

◻ We can now restate our observation at the end of Section 2.3 in more geometric terms: If $m(x)$ is the slope function of a continuous function $f(x)$ and $m(x)$ is non-negative over the interval $[a, b]$, then the area bounded by the graph of $y = m(x)$, the x-axis, the lines $x = a$ and $x = b$ is $f(b) - f(a)$. Again, this is a special case of the Fundamental Theorem of Calculus.

EXERCISES FOR SECTION 2.4:

1. For each of the following, approximate the area bounded by the graph of $f(x)$, the x-axis and the lines $x = a$ and $x = b$ by computing a Riemann sum with n terms:

    (a) $f(x) = x$, $a = 0$, $b = 4$, $n = 8$

    (b) $f(x) = 2x + 5$, $a = 1$, $b = 3$, $n = 4$

    (c) $f(x) = 2x^2 + 3$, $a = 0$, $b = 4$, $n = 4$

    (d) $f(x) = x^3 + x + 1$, $a = 0$, $b = 6$, $n = 3$

2. Some values of a function f are given in the chart below. Estimate the area under the graph of f between $x = 0$ and $x = 4$.

x	0	1	2	3	4
$f(x)$	7	9	3	5	10

TYU Answers for Section 2.4

1. 14.88   2. 25.5   3. (a) 2.5   (b) 2.25

QUESTIONS TO THINK ABOUT

1.   What is the geometrical interpretation of the average velocity and instantaneous velocity of a particle?

2. Given the graph of the velocity, what can you tell about the graph of the position function?

3. Describe how to get the approximate distance travelled by a particle, given its velocity. What is the geometric counterpart to this problem?

APPENDIX

SIGMA NOTATION

It is often the case that we are required to add up many terms which have some common characteristic. Rather than write out each term and connect them with plus signs, mathematicians have developed a shorthand notation.

Suppose we want to add up the cubes of the first 10 positive integers. We could write this as $1^3 + 2^3 + ... + 10^3$, where the ... represents the missing terms. Instead, we abbreviate this as $\sum_{j=1}^{10} j^3$ which is read "the sum of j^3 for j going from 1 to 10". The Σ is the upper case Greek letter "sigma". The letter j is called the **index of summation** and the numbers 1 and 10 are the **limits of the summation**. The choice of index is arbitrary; we could have used any other letter, although we typically use i, j, k, l, m or n. That is, $\sum_{j=1}^{10} j^3$, $\sum_{k=1}^{10} k^3$ and $\sum_{n=1}^{10} n^3$ all represent the sum of the cubes of the first 10 positive integers (which is equal to 3025).

More generally, we may write $\sum_{j=1}^{n} f(j)$, where $f(j)$ is any expression that can be evaluated when j takes on integer values. To interpret this symbol, first substitute the lower limit (in this case, 1) in the expression after the Σ. Write a plus sign. Then substitute the next higher integer value (2) of the index. Write a plus sign. Continue until the index reaches the upper limit (n).

EXAMPLE A2.1:

Evaluate $\sum_{j=3}^{6} j^2$.

Substituting $j = 3, 4, 5$ and 6 into j^2 and adding gives:

$$\sum_{j=3}^{6} j^2 = 3^2 + 4^2 + 5^2 + 6^2 = 86. \qquad \blacklozenge$$

EXAMPLE A2.2:

Evaluate $\displaystyle\sum_{k=2}^{4} \frac{1}{2k-1}$.

Substituting $k = 2, 3$ and 4 into $\dfrac{1}{2k-1}$ gives:

$$\sum_{k=2}^{4} \frac{1}{2k-1} = \frac{1}{3} + \frac{1}{5} + \frac{1}{7} = \frac{71}{105}. \qquad\qquad \blacklozenge$$

TEST YOUR UNDERSTANDING

1. Evaluate $\displaystyle\sum_{i=2}^{5} \frac{i}{i+1}$.

2. Evaluate $\displaystyle\sum_{k=1}^{6} 2^{k}$

In Section 2.3, we wrote $L \approx \displaystyle\sum_{j=1}^{n} v(t_j)\,\Delta t$. Now we can interpret this: First substitute $j = 1$, obtaining $v(t_1)\,\Delta t$. Then add the term $v(t_2)\,\Delta t$ obtained by substituting $j = 2$. Continue in this fashion until the last term, $v(t_n)\,\Delta t$ corresponding to $j = n$.

TYU Answers for Appendix

1. $183/60$ 2. 126

CHAPTER 3

THE DERIVATIVE

3.1 LIMITS AND THE DERIVATIVE

In Section 2.1, we studied the physical problem of the broken speedometer in which we learned to determine the instantaneous velocity of a particle, given its position. We did so by computing the average velocity of the particle over an interval of length Δt and then letting Δt "become small". In Section 2.2, we looked at the geometric equivalent of this problem, namely that of finding the slope of the line tangent to the graph of a function. There, we computed the slope of the secant line over an interval of length Δx and then let Δx "become small". Now, we will take another look at these problems from a more formal point of view. In particular, we will give a more precise meaning to the phrase "become small".

□ In order to do so, we need to define the concept of **limit**.

DEFINITION: We say that the **limit of $f(x)$ as x approaches a is L**, written $\lim_{x \to a} f(x) = L$, if the values of $f(x)$ can be made arbitrarily close to L by taking x sufficiently close, but not equal, to a.

When we say that one number is "close" to another, we mean that the absolute value of their difference is close to zero, since $|a - b|$ is simply the distance between a and b. Thus, our definition can be restated as: $\lim_{x \to a} f(x) = L$ if $|f(x) - L|$ can be made arbitrarily close to 0 by making $|x - a|$ sufficiently close to, but not equal to, 0.

In other words, if you tell me how close you want $f(x)$ to be to L (but without insisting that it be equal to L), I have to be able to find an interval of x's centered at a so that any x in the interval (except, possibly, $x = a$) will do the trick. Most importantly, *f need not be defined at a* in order for the limit to exist.

Figure 3.1 shows a function defined for all $x \neq a$. However, any x-value in the shaded portion of the x-axis (except $x = a$) produces a y-value in the shaded portion of the y-axis. Moreover, no matter how small a segment of the y-axis centered at L you pick, there is a segment of the x-axis, centered at a, with this property. This is exactly what the definition means. (We could actually have picked a slightly larger interval on the x-axis, as long as it is symmetric about $x = a$ and does not extend beyond the dotted lines.)

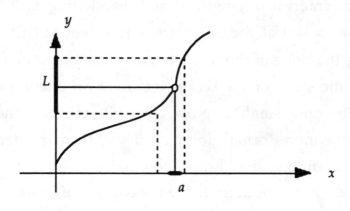

Fig. 3.1

Let $f(x) := x^2$. The table below shows values of $f(x)$ for x near 3. Observe that the values of $f(x)$ approach 9 as x approaches 3 from either direction. Hence, we'd be led to believe that $\lim\limits_{x \to 3} f(x) = 9$.

x	4	3.1	3.01	3.001	3	2.999	2.99	2.9	2
$f(x)$	16	9.61	9.06	9.006	?	8.994	8.94	8.41	4

To see how this fits the definition, suppose we want to get the function values within 1 unit of the proposed limit $L = 9$--that is, make $f(x)$ between 8 and 10. Any x within 0.1 units of $x = 3$--that is, x between 2.9 and 3.1--will do the trick since $f(2.9) = 8.41$ and $f(3.1) = 9.61$. On the other hand, if we want $f(x)$ within 0.1 units of 9 (between 8.9 and 9.1), we can take x-values within 0.01 units of 3 (between 2.99 and 3.01).

TEST YOUR UNDERSTANDING

1. It is not hard to believe that $\lim_{x \to 2} x^2 = 4$. How close to 2 must we make x in order to make $f(x)$ within 0.5 units of 4?

2. (a) Let $L = \lim_{x \to 2} x^3$. Determine L.

   (b) How close to 2 must we make x in order to make $f(x)$ within 1 unit of L?

In evaluating limits, we can make use of the following common-sense theorem:

THEOREM 3.1: Let f and g be functions such that $\lim_{x \to a} f(x)$ and $\lim_{x \to a} g(x)$ exist. Then:

(a) $\lim_{x \to a} (f(x) \pm g(x)) = \lim_{x \to a} f(x) \pm \lim_{x \to a} g(x)$.

(b) $\lim_{x \to a} (f(x) g(x)) = [\lim_{x \to a} f(x)][\lim_{x \to a} g(x)]$.

(c) $\lim_{x \to a} \left(\dfrac{f(x)}{g(x)} \right) = \dfrac{\lim_{x \to a} f(x)}{\lim_{x \to a} g(x)}$, if $\lim_{x \to a} g(x) \neq 0$.

In other words, suppose $f(x)$ approaches L and $g(x)$ approaches M as x approaches a. Then part (a) says that $f(x) + g(x)$ approaches $L + M$ as x approaches a. For example, consider $\lim_{x \to 4} (x^3 + 2x)$. Since $\lim_{x \to 4} x^3 = 64$ and $\lim_{x \to 4} 2x = 8$, then $\lim_{x \to 4} (x^3 + 2x) = 64 + 8 = 72$.

page 3 - 3

Since we do not have a formal definition of limit, we cannot prove this theorem. However, it is a rather intuitive result, so we shall accept it and use it without proof.

---

3. Evaluate each limit:

(a) $\lim_{x \to 1} (x^3 + 3x - 5)$ (b) $\lim_{x \to -2} \dfrac{x}{x + 5}$ (c) $\lim_{x \to 0} \sqrt{4 - x^2}$

◻ We might approach all limit problems by first asking whether $\lim_{x \to a} f(x) = f(a)$, as it is in the examples above. Unfortunately, the answer to this question is "no", as the next example illustrates.

Consider the function $f(x) = \dfrac{x^3 - 1}{x - 1}$. By examining the table of values below, we see that as $x \to 1$ from either direction, the values of $f(x)$ appear to approach 3 and, in fact, can be made arbitarily close to 3 by taking x sufficiently close to 1. Hence, we conclude that $\lim_{x \to 1} f(x) = 3$. However, f is not defined at $x = 1$ and so, $\lim_{x \to 1} f(x) \neq f(1)$.

x	0	.9	.99	.999	1	1.001	1.01	1.1	2
$f(x)$	1	2.71	2.97	2.997	?	3.003	3.03	3.31	7

We can show that this limit is correct by noting that $\dfrac{x^3 - 1}{x - 1} = \dfrac{(x - 1)(x^2 + x + 1)}{x - 1}$. As long as $x \neq 1$, we can reduce this fraction. Hence, $\lim_{x \to 1} \dfrac{x^3 - 1}{x - 1} = \lim_{x \to 1} x^2 + x + 1$. But $x^2 + x + 1$ is well-defined at $x = 1$ and, clearly, its values approach 3 as x approaches 1. The graph of $f(x) := \dfrac{x^3 - 1}{x - 1}$ is exactly the same as the graph of $f(x) := x^2 + x + 1$ except that there is a "hole punched" at the point $(1, 3)$. See Figure 3.2.

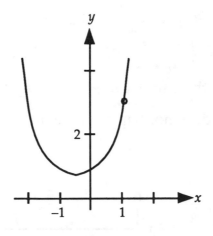

Fig. 3.2

◻ In Chapter 1, we informally defined what we meant by a function being continuous. A continuous function is one whose graph can be drawn without lifting your pencil. The function in Fig.3.2 is not continuous at $x = 1$ because there is a hole in the graph. The reason that $\lim_{x \to 1} f(x) \neq f(1)$ is a direct result of this discontinuity. In fact, we can now give a more formal definition of what it means for a function to be continuous.

DEFINITION: A function f is **continuous at** $x = a$ if $\lim_{x \to a} f(x) = f(a)$.

We will say that a function is **continuous** if it is continuous at each point in its domain.

A function fails to be continuous at $x = a$ for one of three reasons: Either $f(a)$ does not exist, or $\lim_{x \to a} f(x)$ does not exist, or both exist but $\lim_{x \to a} f(x) \neq f(a)$. We have already learned to recognize circumstances under which $f(a)$ fails to exist. Now let's investigate how $\lim_{x \to a} f(x)$ may not exist. Essentially, there are two possibilities for algebraic functions.

Consider the function $f(x) := \dfrac{|x|}{x}$. Since $|x| = x$ for $x > 0$ and $|x| = -x$ for $x < 0$, then $f(x) = \begin{cases} 1, & x > 0 \\ -1, & x < 0 \end{cases}$. Implicit in our definition of limit is that $f(x)$ must approach the same value L as x approaches a from the left and the right. Since that does not happen here, then $\lim\limits_{x \to 0} \dfrac{|x|}{x}$ does not exist. See Figure 3.3.

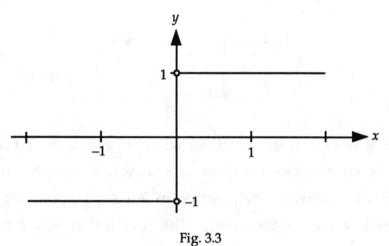

Fig. 3.3

The other situation in which $\lim\limits_{x \to a} f(x)$ fails to exist occurs when the values of the function grow very large as x approaches a. For example, consider $\lim\limits_{x \to 0} \dfrac{1}{x^2}$. By choosing x sufficiently close to 0, we can make $\dfrac{1}{x^2}$ as large as we like. See Figure 3.4. Although we will often write $\lim\limits_{x \to 0} \dfrac{1}{x^2} = \infty$ in this case, the limit does not exist.

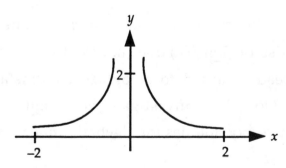

Fig. 3.4

Finally, it is possible for $\lim\limits_{x \to a} f(x)$ to exist and $f(a)$ to exist, but $\lim\limits_{x \to a} f(x) \neq f(a)$. For example, let

$$f(x) := \begin{cases} \dfrac{x^3 - 1}{x - 1} & \text{if } x \neq 1 \\[2ex] 4 & \text{if } x = 1 \end{cases}.$$

We have already seen that $\lim\limits_{x \to 1} \dfrac{x^3 - 1}{x - 1} = 3$. But $f(1) = 4$. Hence, f is not continuous at $x = 1$. The graph of this function resembles Figure 3.2, except that there is a dot at $(1, 4)$ which does *not* "fill in the hole".

Evaluating limits for continuous functions is not very challenging. The interesting case occurs when substituting $x = a$ in the formula for $f(x)$ leads to an **indeterminate form**, an expression with no fixed meaning. There are several indeterminate forms: $\dfrac{0}{0}, \dfrac{\infty}{\infty}, \infty - \infty, 0^0, 0(\infty), \infty^0$, and 1^∞. If $f(a)$ is one of these indeterminate forms, then $\lim\limits_{x \to a} f(x)$ sometimes exists and sometimes does not. We have already seen an example in which it does. Let $f(x) := \dfrac{x^3 - 1}{x - 1}$. We showed that $\lim\limits_{x \to 1} f(x) = 3$ even though $f(1)$ is an indeterminate form $\dfrac{0}{0}$. On the other hand, let $g(x) = \dfrac{x}{x^2}$. Here, $g(0)$ is an indeterminate form $\dfrac{0}{0}$. However, $\lim\limits_{x \to 0} \dfrac{x}{x^2} = \lim\limits_{x \to 0} \dfrac{1}{x}$ does not exist.

Note: Do NOT confuse the indeterminate form $\dfrac{0}{0}$ with expressions of the form $\dfrac{0}{a}$ or $\dfrac{a}{0}$, where $a \neq 0$. The first of these is always equal to 0; the second is undefined in the sense that it is infinitely large and any limit which results in an expression of this form does not exist.

Often, the indeterminate forms that arise can be handled by algebraic tricks such as reducing fractions or rationalizing numerators or denominators that replace the troublesome expression for $f(x)$ with one that may be evaluated. That's exactly what happened when we replaced $\dfrac{x^3 - 1}{x - 1}$ by $x^2 + x + 1$. Here are three more examples that illustrate these techniques.

EXAMPLE 3.1:

Evaluate $\lim\limits_{y \to -3} \dfrac{y^2 + 5y + 6}{y^2 - 9}$.

Upon substituting -3 for y, we get the indeterminate form $\dfrac{0}{0}$. However, we can factor both the numerator and denominator, obtaining $\dfrac{(y+3)(y+2)}{(y+3)(y-3)}$ which can be reduced if $y \neq -3$ (which it won't be since y is only near -3, but never is equal to -3). Therefore, $\lim\limits_{y \to -3} \dfrac{y^2 + 5y + 6}{y^2 - 9} = \lim\limits_{y \to -3} \dfrac{y+2}{y-3} = \dfrac{1}{6}$. ◆

EXAMPLE 3.2:

Determine $\lim\limits_{x \to 4} \dfrac{\sqrt{x} - 2}{x - 4}$.

Upon substituting 4 for x, we get the indeterminate form $\dfrac{0}{0}$. Let's rationalize the numerator by multiplying both the numerator and denominator by $\sqrt{x} + 2$.

$$\left(\dfrac{\sqrt{x} - 2}{x - 4}\right)\left(\dfrac{\sqrt{x} + 2}{\sqrt{x} + 2}\right) = \dfrac{x - 4}{(x - 4)(\sqrt{x} + 2)} = \dfrac{1}{\sqrt{x} + 2} \text{ , if } x \neq 4$$

Therefore, $\lim\limits_{x \to 4} \dfrac{\sqrt{x} - 2}{x - 4} = \lim\limits_{x \to 4} \dfrac{1}{\sqrt{x} + 2}$ which can now be evaluated by substitution, obtaining a limit of $\dfrac{1}{4}$. ◆

Note: Rationalizing the numerator is an algebraic trick that works in examples in which the denominator contains a square root or other irrational quantity. We'll use this trick again in later examples.

EXAMPLE 3.3:

Determine $\lim\limits_{x \to 0} \left(\dfrac{1}{x} - \dfrac{1}{x^2}\right)$.

If we try to substitute $x = 0$, we get the indeterminate form $\infty - \infty$ (which is not necessarily 0). Upon combining fractions, we have $\lim\limits_{x \to 0} \left(\dfrac{1}{x} - \dfrac{1}{x^2}\right) = \lim\limits_{x \to 0} \dfrac{x - 1}{x^2}$ which does not exist since substitution gives $\dfrac{-1}{0}$, an undefined expression (as opposed to indeterminate). ◆

---

4. Determine each of the following limits:

(a) $\lim_{x \to 2} \frac{1}{x}$ 　　　　(b) $\lim_{x \to 0} \frac{1}{x}$ 　　　　(c) $\lim_{x \to 0} \frac{x}{x+1}$

(d) $\lim_{x \to 1} \frac{x^2-1}{x^2+1}$ 　　(e) $\lim_{x \to 1} \frac{x^2-1}{x^2-3x+2}$ 　　(f) $\lim_{x \to 1} \frac{x^2-1}{x^2-2x+1}$

As a last example, consider the function $h(x) := \dfrac{2^x - 1}{x}$. Notice that $h(0)$ is an indeterminate form $\frac{0}{0}$. On the other hand, the chart below suggests that $\lim_{x \to 0} \dfrac{2^x - 1}{x}$ exists and is approximately .693. Unlike our other examples, an algebraic trick that would allow us to evaluate this limit without the table is not readily apparent.

x	1	.1	.01	.001	0	–.001	–.01	–.1	–1
$f(x)$	1	.717	.695	.693	?	.693	.690	.669	.5

We will investigate this limit in greater detail in Chapter 4.

¤ So far, we have talked about limits as x approaches a *finite* number a. It is also possible to define the limit of $f(x)$ as x approaches ∞.

DEFINITION: We say that the **limit of $f(x)$ as x approaches ∞ is L**, written $\lim_{x \to \infty} f(x) = L$, if the values of $f(x)$ can be made arbitrarily close to L by taking x sufficiently large.

If $\lim_{x \to \infty} f(x) = L$, then the graph of f has a horizontal asymptote at $y = L$. We saw some examples of this in Section 1.3. It follows that if f is a polynomial (which never has a horizontal asymptote), then $\lim_{x \to \infty} f(x)$ does not exist.

Let $f(x) := \dfrac{2x^3 + 1}{x^3 + 3x^2 + 2}$. The table below gives values of f for increasingly large values of x.

x	1	10	100	1000	10000
$f(x)$	.5	1.537	1.942	1.994	1.999

It is clear from the table that $\lim\limits_{x \to \infty} \dfrac{2x^3 + 1}{x^3 + 3x^2 + 2} = 2$. This is correct since for large values of x, the numerator is approximately equal to $2x^3$ while the denominator is approximately x^3.

TEST YOUR UNDERSTANDING

5. Evaluate each of the following limits:

(a) $\lim\limits_{x \to \infty} \dfrac{4x^2 + 1}{x^3 + 5x + 9}$

(b) $\lim\limits_{x \to \infty} \dfrac{x^4}{x^2 - 3}$

◻ We are now prepared to give a more formal approach to the slope function concept from Section 2.2. As we stated earlier, the slope of the secant joining $(c, f(c))$ and $(c + \Delta x, f(c + \Delta x))$ is $\dfrac{\Delta f}{\Delta x} = \dfrac{f(c + \Delta x) - f(c)}{\Delta x}$. For a fixed value of c, this is a function of Δx. The slope function is obtained by letting $\Delta x \to 0$ or, as we can now say more precisely, it is the limit of $\dfrac{\Delta f}{\Delta x}$ as $\Delta x \to 0$. To go along with this more formal approach, we'll give the slope function a more formal name, the derivative.

DEFINITION: The **derivative** of a function f is defined by
$$D_x f(x) := \lim_{\Delta x \to 0} \frac{\Delta f}{\Delta x} = \lim_{\Delta x \to 0} \frac{f(x + \Delta x) - f(x)}{\Delta x}.$$

If $D_x f(c)$ exists, then we say that f is **differentiable** at $x = c$.

Keep in mind that although we started out thinking of the derivative as a quantity which was approximated by taking the slope of a secant over shorter and shorter intervals, it actually is a precise quantity obtained by the limit process described above. Note that $\Delta f = 0$ when $\Delta x = 0$, so $\frac{\Delta f}{\Delta x}$ is always an indeterminate form. However, as we saw in the previous examples, this indeterminate form may approach a finite value as $\Delta x \rightarrow 0$. If it does, this value is the derivative; if it doesn't, then the derivative does not exist at that point.

It is *very important* to understand that the slope of the tangent line in general depends on the point at which it is drawn; that is, *the slope is a function of x.* Note that we generally express the derivative as a function of x, or whatever the dependent variable of the given function is. However, in order to get the slope of the tangent line, we must *evaluate the derivative* at the given point.

There are several different notations for derivatives. If $y = f(x)$, then the derivative is denoted by either $D_x f(x), f'(x), y'$, or $\frac{dy}{dx}$. The $D_x f(x)$ notation, although not commonly used in calculus texts, is sometimes used in more advanced courses. The $f'(x)$ notation is due to Lagrange, a French mathematician who worked on the foundations of the calculus at the end of the 18th century, about 100 years after calculus' invention. In the $\frac{dy}{dx}$ notation, the dy and dx are called **differentials** and represent the infinitesimally small changes in x and y, the ratio of which gives us the slope of the tangent line (i.e., the derivative). This notation is due to Leibniz; its advantage is that it is suggestive. The disadvantage to the y' and $\frac{dy}{dx}$ notations is that there is no place to indicate the x-value at which the derivative is being evaluated. Nonetheless, we shall use all of these notations where appropriate.

EXAMPLE 3.4:

Use the definition above to find the derivative of $g(x) := \sqrt{x}$.

$$g'(x) := \lim_{\Delta x \to 0} \frac{g(x + \Delta x) - g(x)}{\Delta x}$$

$$= \lim_{\Delta x \to 0} \frac{\sqrt{x + \Delta x} - \sqrt{x}}{\Delta x} = \lim_{\Delta x \to 0} \left(\frac{\sqrt{x + \Delta x} - \sqrt{x}}{\Delta x} \right) \left(\frac{\sqrt{x + \Delta x} + \sqrt{x}}{\sqrt{x + \Delta x} + \sqrt{x}} \right)$$

$$= \lim_{\Delta x \to 0} \left(\frac{x + \Delta x - x}{\Delta x (\sqrt{x + \Delta x} + \sqrt{x})} \right) = \lim_{\Delta x \to 0} \left(\frac{1}{\sqrt{x + \Delta x} + \sqrt{x}} \right)$$

$$= \frac{1}{2\sqrt{x}} .$$

Note that we have used the "rationalizing numerators" trick mentioned earlier. ♦

TEST YOUR UNDERSTANDING

6. Use the definition of the derivative to find dy/dx if $y = x^2 - x$.

EXAMPLE 3.5:

Write equations of the lines tangent to the graph of $g(x) := \frac{1}{x}$ at $x = -2$ and at $x = 1$.

First we find the derivative.

$$\frac{g(x + \Delta x) - g(x)}{\Delta x} = \frac{\frac{1}{x + \Delta x} - \frac{1}{x}}{\Delta x} = \frac{\frac{x - (x + \Delta x)}{x(x + \Delta x)}}{\Delta x} = \frac{\frac{-\Delta x}{x(x + \Delta x)}}{\Delta x}$$

$$= \frac{-1}{x(x + \Delta x)} \text{, if } \Delta x \neq 0.$$

By letting Δx approach 0, we find $D_x\, g(x) := \frac{-1}{x^2}$.

Therefore, the slope of the tangent line at $x = -2$ is $D_x\, g(-2) = -\frac{1}{4}$. The y-coordinate of the point of tangency is $g(-2) = -\frac{1}{2}$. So, an equation of the tangent line is:

$$y + \frac{1}{2} = -\frac{1}{4}(x + 2) \text{ or, equivalently, } y = -\frac{1}{4}x - 1.$$

At $x = 1$, the slope is $D_x\, g(1) = -1$ and the y-coordinate is $g(1) = 1$. Hence, an equation of the tangent line is:

$y - 1 = -1(x - 1)$ or, equivalently, $y = -x + 2$.

See Figure 3.5.

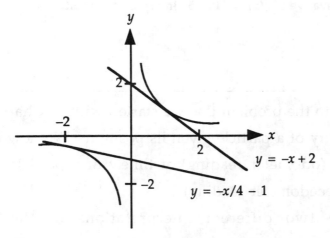

Fig. 3.5

TEST YOUR UNDERSTANDING

7. Describe the geometric interpretation of the derivative. Be specific.

8. Write an equation of the line tangent to the graph of g in Example 3.5 at $x = 3$.

9. Let $f(x) := 3x^2 - 4x$.

   (a) Find the slope of the secant line joining $(-1, f(-1))$ and $(2, f(2))$.

   b) Find $D_x\, f(x)$.

   (c) What is the slope of line tangent to the graph of f at $x = 1$? at $x = 4$?

   (d) Write an equation of the line tangent to f at $x = 1$.

(e) For what x-values is the tangent line horizontal?

10. Find the derivative of $g(x) := 4x - 5$. Interpret the result.

Now let's go back to the problem that we started with in Chapter 2--that of determining the velocity of a particle given its position. We now can say that if $s(t)$ is the position (odometer reading) at time t of a particle, then $s'(t) = v(t)$ is the velocity (speedometer reading).

Hence, we have two different interpretations of the derivative. Geometrically, it represents the slope of the line tangent to the graph of a function. Physically, it represents the instantaneous rate of change of the dependent variable (y or s, for example) with respect to the independent variable (x or t). We shall explore both of these interpretations, and the applications they generate, in the remainder of this chapter and in Chapters 4 and 5.

EXAMPLE 3.6:

A particle's position at time t is given by $s(t) := 3t^2 - 6t + 2$. At what time is its instantaneous velocity equal to 12?

$$\frac{\Delta s}{\Delta t} = \frac{s(t + \Delta t) - s(t)}{\Delta t} = \frac{3(t + \Delta t)^2 - 6(t + \Delta t) + 2 - \left(3t^2 - 6t + 2\right)}{\Delta t}$$

$$= \frac{3t^2 + 6t\,\Delta t + 3(\Delta t)^2 - 6t - 6\Delta t + 2 - (3t^2 - 6t + 2)}{\Delta t}$$

$$= \frac{6t\,\Delta t + 3(\Delta t)^2 - 6\Delta t}{\Delta t}$$

Dividing by Δt and letting Δt approach 0 gives $v(t) := s'(t) = 6t - 6$.

To find the time at which the velocity is 12, set $v(t) = 12$ and solve for t, obtaining $t = 3$. ◆

DERIVATIVES OF SIMPLE FUNCTIONS

Let's use this definition to find the derivatives of some of the common functions listed in Section 1.3.

1. <u>LINEAR FUNCTIONS</u>: $f(x) := ax + b$, where a and b are constants

Since the graph of a linear function is a straight line, then the line tangent to the graph at any point is just the function itself. Hence, the slope of the tangent line is the same as the slope of the function at any point. Then we should expect that $f'(x) := a$, for all x.

A special case of the linear function is the constant function which occurs where $a = 0$. Its graph is a horizontal line which has a slope (and, hence, derivative) of 0.

2. <u>QUADRATIC FUNCTIONS</u>: $f(x) := ax^2 + bx + c$, where a, b and c are constants

By definition, $f'(x) := \lim_{\Delta x \to 0} \dfrac{\Delta f}{\Delta x} = \lim_{\Delta x \to 0} \dfrac{f(x + \Delta x) - f(x)}{\Delta x}$

$$= \lim_{\Delta x \to 0} \frac{a(x + \Delta x)^2 + b(x + \Delta x) + c - (ax^2 + bx + c)}{\Delta x}$$

$$= \lim_{\Delta x \to 0} \frac{ax^2 + 2ax\,\Delta x + a(\Delta x)^2 + bx + b\,\Delta x + c - (ax^2 + bx + c)}{\Delta x}$$

$$= \lim_{\Delta x \to 0} 2ax + a\,\Delta x + b$$

$$= 2ax + b$$

Note that the derivative depends on x. This is not unexpected since the graph of a quadratic function is a parabola, not a straight line and, hence, the slope of the curve is not constant. Furthermore, $f'(x) = 0$ when $x = \dfrac{-b}{2a}$. Recall that the vertex occurs at $x = \dfrac{-b}{2a}$. This means that the tangent line at the vertex of the parabola (i.e., at the local maximum or minimum) is horizontal.

3. <u>POWER FUNCTIONS</u>: $f(x) := x^n$, where n is a positive integer

For a power function, $\dfrac{\Delta f}{\Delta x} = \dfrac{(x + \Delta x)^n - x^n}{\Delta x}$

At this point, we could either expand the first term in the numerator using the binomial theorem, or we could factor the numerator using the fact that $a^n - b^n = (a - b)(a^{n-1} + a^{n-2}b + a^{n-3}b^2 + \ldots + b^{n-1})$. We'll take the second approach.

$$\frac{\Delta f}{\Delta x} = \frac{(x + \Delta x - x)\left((x + \Delta x)^{n-1} + (x + \Delta x)^{n-2}x + (x + \Delta x)^{n-3}x^2 + \ldots + x^{n-1}\right)}{\Delta x}$$

$$= (x + \Delta x)^{n-1} + (x + \Delta x)^{n-2}x + (x + \Delta x)^{n-3}x^2 + \ldots + x^{n-1}, \quad \text{if } \Delta x \neq 0.$$

There are n terms, each of which approaches x^{n-1} as $\Delta x \to 0$. Hence,

$$f'(x) := \lim_{\Delta x \to 0}\left[(x + \Delta x)^{n-1} + (x + \Delta x)^{n-2}x + (x + \Delta x)^{n-3}x^2 + \ldots + x^{n-1}\right]$$
$$= nx^{n-1}.$$

Although technically we have only proved this result for positive integer exponents, it does in fact hold for all rational exponents, positive or negative. (Actually it holds for any real exponent, although an expression such as $3^{\sqrt{2}}$, in which the exponent is irrational, causes conceptual difficulties.)

This result is so important that we will state it as:

THEOREM 3.2 (POWER RULE FOR DERIVATIVES): If $f(x) := x^b$, where b is any real number, then $f'(x) := bx^{b-1}$.

In words, this says that the derivative of a power function is obtained by multiplying by the exponent and decreasing the exponent by 1.

EXAMPLE 3.7:

Find the derivative of (a) $f(x) := x^4$ (b) $g(x) := \frac{1}{x}$ (c) $h(x) := \sqrt[3]{x}$ (d) $y = x^\pi$.

Each of these is a power function to which Theorem 3.2 applies.

In (a), $b = 4$, so $f'(x) := 4x^3$. In (b), $b = -1$, so $g'(x) := -1x^{-2} = -\frac{1}{x^2}$.

In (c), $b = \frac{1}{3}$, so $h'(x) := \frac{1}{3}x^{-2/3}$. In (d), $b = \pi$, so $\frac{dy}{dx} = \pi x^{\pi - 1}$. ◆

---

11. Find the derivative of (a) $f(x) := \sqrt{x}$ (b) $g(x) := \frac{1}{\sqrt{x}}$ (c) $h(x) := x\sqrt{x}$

---

4. ABSOLUTE VALUE FUNCTION

Let $f(x) := |x| = \begin{cases} x, & \text{if } x \geq 0 \\ -x, & \text{if } x < 0 \end{cases}$. We know that, if a and b are both

positive, then $|a| - |b| = a - b$ while if a and b are both negative, then $|a| - |b| = b - a$.

By definition, $f'(x) := \lim_{\Delta x \to 0} \dfrac{|x + \Delta x| - |x|}{\Delta x}$. Remember that in order for

the derivative to exist, we must get the same limit whether Δx approaches 0 from the right or from the left. Let's consider the case where $x > 0$. If $\Delta x > 0$, then $x + \Delta x > 0$ and $\Delta f = \Delta x$. If, on the other hand, $\Delta x < 0$, then eventually it will become close enough to zero so that $x + \Delta x > 0$ and, once again, $\Delta f = \Delta x$. So, it follows that if $x > 0$, $\dfrac{\Delta f}{\Delta x} = 1$ and so $f'(x) := 1$. (This is perfectly reasonable if you look at the graph--the slope is 1 for all $x > 0$.)

A similar argument can be used to show that if $x < 0$, then $f'(x) := -1$.

As we said earlier, the problem occurs when $x = 0$. Then $f'(0) = \lim_{\Delta x \to 0} \dfrac{|\Delta x|}{\Delta x}$. If $\Delta x > 0$, this expression reduces to 1, while if $\Delta x < 0$, it reduces to -1. Therefore, the limit and, hence, $f'(0)$ does not exist. Geometrically, this corresponds to the fact that there is a sharp point at $x = 0$. Note that f is continuous at $x = 0$ although it is not differentiable there.

Using the definition of the derivative is not all that difficult for many algebraic functions. Usually there is some algebraic manipulation that can be done to simplify the indeterminate form and permit evaluation of the limit.

Transcendental functions are a different story. Let $f(x) := \sin(x)$. Then

$$f'(x) := \lim_{\Delta x \to 0} \frac{\sin(x + \Delta x) - \sin(x)}{\Delta x} .$$

Although there are some algebraic steps that can be taken (perhaps you remember a formula for expanding $\sin(x + y)$), there will remain some limits that are not easy to evaluate except by making a table of values. We will not pursue this here.

¤ Suppose f is not continuous at $x = c$. Is it possible that it is differentiable at $x = c$? The answer to this question is "no". To see why, imagine that f has a hole punched in it at $x = c$. Then it is impossible to draw a line tangent to the graph at that point because there is no point at which to draw it. On the other hand, if f takes a jump at $x = c$, then the slope of the tangent line cannot be obtained by taking the limit of the slope of the secant as Δx approaches 0. In both cases, f is not differentiable. We usually state this result as:

THEOREM 3.3: If f is differentiable at $x = c$, then f is continuous at $x = c$.

For instance, the function $f(x) := 1/x$ is not continuous at $x = 0$; therefore, it is not differentiable. Also, if $f(x) := x^2$, then $f'(x) := 2x$ which is defined for all x. Since f is differentiable everywhere, then it is continuous everywhere.

Caution: Do not make the mistake of thinking that every continuous function is differentiable. What we've said is the converse. For example, the absolute value function $f(x) := |x|$ is continuous at $x = 0$ but, as we shall see a bit later, is not differentiable there.

¤ The next two theorems tell us how to differentiate the sum of two functions and a constant multiple of a function.

THEOREM 3.4: Let f and g be differentiable functions and let $h(x) := f(x) + g(x)$. Then, $h'(x) := f'(x) + g'(x)$.

Proof: First note that $\Delta h = h(x + \Delta x) - h(x)$

$$= f(x + \Delta x) + g(x + \Delta x) - (f(x) + g(x))$$
$$= f(x + \Delta x) - f(x) + g(x + \Delta x) - g(x)$$
$$= \Delta f + \Delta g$$

Therefore, $\dfrac{\Delta h}{\Delta x} = \dfrac{\Delta f}{\Delta x} + \dfrac{\Delta g}{\Delta x}$. Now let $\Delta x \to 0$.

$$\lim_{\Delta x \to 0}\frac{\Delta h}{\Delta x} = \lim_{\Delta x \to 0}\left(\frac{\Delta f}{\Delta x} + \frac{\Delta g}{\Delta x}\right) = \lim_{\Delta x \to 0}\frac{\Delta f}{\Delta x} + \lim_{\Delta x \to 0}\frac{\Delta g}{\Delta x} \quad \text{by Theorem 3.1(a)}.$$

The conclusion follows from the definition of the derivative.

THEOREM 3.5: Let f be a differentiable function and let $h(x) := kf(x)$,

where k is a constant. Then, $h'(x) := kf'(x)$.

You are asked to prove Theorem 3.5 in the problems at the end of the section. Figure 3.6 shows the graphs of $y = f(x)$ and $y = h(x) := 2f(x)$ and their tangent lines at $x = c$. Theorem 3.5 says that the slope of the line tangent to the graph of h is twice as big as the slope of the line tangent to the graph of f.

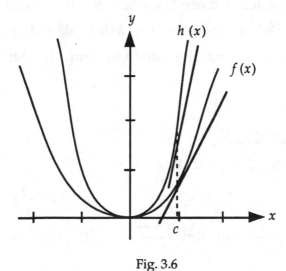

Fig. 3.6

We are now in a position to differentiate every polynomial function. A polynomial consists of the sum of constant multiples of power functions. Theorem 3.2 tells us how to differentiate power functions. Theorem 3.5 tells us that when we multiply a function by a constant, we multiply its derivative by the same constant. Theorem 3.4 tells us that when we add up two functions (or more than two, as well), we add up their derivatives.

EXAMPLE 3.8:

Find the derivative of $y = 4x^5 + 7x^2 - 5x + 2$.

Applying both Theorems 3.2 and 3.4 gives:

$$D_x y = 4D_x[x^5] + 7D_x[x^2] - 5D_x[x] + D_x[2]$$
$$= 4(5x^4) + 7(2x) - 5(1) + 0$$
$$= 20x^4 + 14x - 5. \qquad \blacklozenge$$

TEST YOUR UNDERSTANDING

12. Find the derivative of: (a) $y = 9x^3 - 7x^2 + 12$ (b) $g(x) := \dfrac{4}{x^5} - \dfrac{3}{x^2}$.

In Section 3, we will learn more theorems for finding derivatives without using the definition. Before doing so, we will look at the information about the behavior of functions that can be obtained from the derivative.

EXERCISES FOR SECTION 3.1:

1. Evaluate the following limits, if they exist:

(a) $\lim\limits_{x \to 4} x^3 - x^2$

(b) $\lim\limits_{x \to -2} \dfrac{x^2 - 4}{x + 2}$

(c) $\lim\limits_{x \to 0} \dfrac{1}{x^2}$

(d) $\lim\limits_{x \to \infty} \dfrac{5x^3 - 17x}{10x^3 + 3x^2 - 7}$

(e) $\lim\limits_{x \to 0} \dfrac{x^2 - 4}{x + 2}$

(f) $\lim\limits_{x \to \infty} \dfrac{x^5 - x^3 + 2}{x^4 + 16}$

2. The graph of the function f is given below. Does $\lim\limits_{x \to 1} f(x)$ exist? Explain.

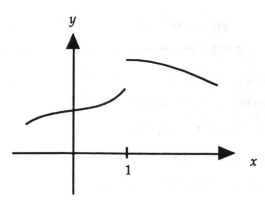

3. Let $f(x) := \begin{cases} x^2, & \text{for } x \leq 2 \\ 2x + k, & \text{for } x > 2 \end{cases}$.

   (a) What is $\lim_{x \to 1} f(x)$?

   (b) For what value of k does $\lim_{x \to 2} f(x)$ exist?

4. Use the definition of the derivative to find $\dfrac{dy}{dx}$ if:

   (a) $y = 4x^2 + 3x - 2$ (b) $y = \dfrac{1}{x + 2}$ (c) $y = x^3 + 2x$

5. Find the derivatives of each of the following functions:

   (a) $y = 3x - 7$ (b) $g(x) := 9$ (c) $q(x) := x^2 + 4x - 3$

   (d) $y = x^{1/3}$ (e) $f(x) := \dfrac{1}{x^2 \sqrt{x}}$ (f) $y = ax^3 + bx + c$

   (g) $z = 3t^2 - \dfrac{1}{t}$ (h) $p(t) := \dfrac{t}{2} + \dfrac{t^2}{4}$ (i) $g(x) := \dfrac{1}{\sqrt[3]{x^4}}$

6. (a) Write an equation of the line tangent to the graph of the function in Exercise 5(c) at the point $(4, 29)$.

   (b) Write an equation of the line tangent to the graph of the function in Exercise 5(d) at the point $(8, 2)$.

   (c) Write an equation of the line perpendicular to the graph of the function in Exercise 5(d) at the point $(8, 2)$.

7. Let $f(x) := 2x^2 - 12x + 3$.

   (a) For what x-values is the tangent line horizontal?

   (b) For what x-values is the tangent line parallel to $y = -6x + 7$?

8. Let $g(x) := x^2 + bx$. Determine the value of b such that the tangent line at $x = -1$ is horizontal.

9. Let $f(x) := x^3 + ax + b$. Determine the values of a and b so that the line $y = x + 3$ is tangent to the graph of f at $x = 1$.

10. Let $f(x) := x^2 + x + 3$. Determine the coordinates of the point of intersection of the lines tangent to the graph of f at $x = -1$ and $x = 0$.

11. The position of a particle is given by $s(t) := t^4 - 3t^3$.

    (a) At what time is the particle at the origin (position $= 0$)?

    (b) What is the initial velocity of the particle?

    (c) At what times is the particle at rest?

12. A train travels so that its position at time t is $s(t) := 3t^2 + 8t + 40$.

    (a) What is the average velocity of the train over the interval $[2, 5]$?

    (b) Determine $v(t)$, the instantaneous velocity at time t.

    (c) What is its instantaneous velocity at $t = 1$?

    (d) What is the initial velocity of the train?

    (e) At what time is the velocity of the train equal to 38?

PROBLEMS FOR SECTION 3.1:

1. Let f be a differentiable function and let
$$g(x) := \lim_{\Delta x \to 0} \frac{f(x + \Delta x) - f(x - \Delta x)}{\Delta x} .$$

    (a) Determine $g(x)$ if $f(x) := x^2 + x$.

    (b) How is $g(x)$ is related to the derivative of f?

2. Find the area of the triangle bounded by the x-axis and the tangents drawn to the curve $y = 8 - x^2$ at the points $(2, 4)$ and $(-2, 4)$.

3. In the text we showed that $\lim_{x \to 1} \frac{x^3 - 1}{x - 1} = 3$.

    (a) Generalize this result to find $\lim_{x \to 1} \frac{x^n - 1}{x - 1}$, where n is a positive integer.

    (b) Generalize even further to find $\lim_{x \to a} \frac{x^n - a^n}{x - a}$, where a is a real number.

4. Tangents are drawn to the graphs of $f(x) := \frac{x^3}{24}$ and $g(x) := \frac{x^2}{2}$ at $x = c$. For what value of c will those tangent lines be perpendicular to each other?

5. There are two tangent lines to the graph of $y = 4x - x^2$ that pass through the point $(2, 5)$. Find equations of these two lines.

6. Prove Theorem 3.5.

7. In the text, we showed that $\lim_{x \to 0} \dfrac{2^x - 1}{x} \approx .693$.

   (a) In a similar fashion, evaluate $\lim_{x \to 0} \dfrac{3^x - 1}{x}$ and $\lim_{x \to 0} \dfrac{6^x - 1}{x}$.

   (b) How are these three numbers related?

8. The graph of the function f is given below. Which of the following statements are true? (There may be more than one.) Explain.

   A. $\lim_{x \to 0} f(x)$ exists   B. $\lim_{x \to 0} |f(x)|$ exists   C. $|f(x)|$ is continuous at $x = 0$

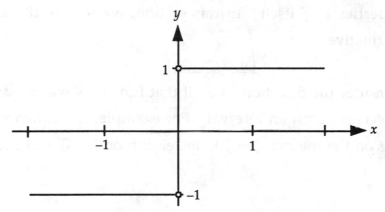

9. Let $f(x) := \dfrac{g(x)}{h(x)}$, where g and h are polynomials. Determine $\lim_{x \to \infty} f(x)$ if:

   (a) the degree of g is greater than the degree of h

   (b) the degree of g is less than the degree of h

   (c) the degree of g is the same as the degree of h

7. The derivative of f when evaluated at $x = c$ gives the slope of the line tangent to the graph of f at $(c, f(c))$.   8. $y = -\frac{1}{9}x + \frac{2}{3}$ 9. (a) -1 (b) $D_x f(x) = 6x - 4$

    (c) $D_x f(1) = 2; D_x f(4) = 20$ (d) $y = 2x - 3$ (e) $x = 2/3$

10. $D_x g(x) = 4$ for all x which is the slope of the line $y = 4x - 5$.

11. (a) $f'(x) := \frac{1}{2}x^{-1/2} = \frac{1}{2\sqrt{x}}$ (b) $g'(x) := -\frac{1}{2}x^{-3/2} = -\frac{1}{2x^{3/2}}$ (c) $h'(x) :=$

    $\frac{3}{2}x^{1/2} = \frac{3}{2}\sqrt{x}$ 12. (a) $y' = 27x^2 - 14x$ (b) $g'(x) := \frac{-20}{x^6} + \frac{6}{x^3}$

3.2 USING THE DERIVATIVE TO ANALYZE FUNCTIONS

In Chapter 2, we showed how the slope function for f could be used to determine properties of f itself. In this section, we restate those results in terms of the derivative.

DIRECTION

First let's consider the direction. Recall that functions will be described as increasing or decreasing on an interval. For example, the function in Figure 3.7 is increasing on the interval $(-\infty, 2)$, decreasing on $(2, 4)$ and increasing on $(4, \infty)$.

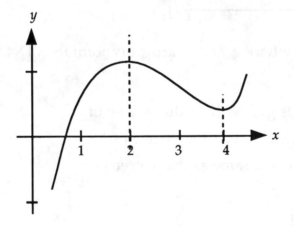

Fig. 3.7

Pick a point in one of the intervals on which f is increasing and draw the tangent line. Clearly, the slope of that tangent line will be positive (or at least non-negative). Similarly, at any point in the interval on which f is decreasing, the slope of the tangent will be negative (non-positive).

What we are claiming is the following:

1. If f is increasing on $[a, b]$ and c is any number between a and b, then $f'(c) \geq 0$.

2. If f is decreasing on $[a, b]$ and c is any number between a and b, then $f'(c) \leq 0$.

While these results are intuitively clear, they aren't what we want. We want to be able to find the intervals on which f is increasing and decreasing. In other words, we would like to state conditions that are *sufficient* to claim f is increasing (or decreasing). The next theorem gives us these conditions which, again, are intuitive. A proof of this theorem requires the **Mean Value Theorem** which we won't discuss here.

THEOREM 3.6: Suppose f is continuous on $[a, b]$.
  (a) If $f'(x) > 0$ for all x on (a, b), then f is increasing on $[a, b]$.
  (b) If $f'(x) < 0$ for all x on (a, b), then f is decreasing on $[a, b]$.
  (c) If $f'(x) = 0$ for all x on (a, b), then f is constant on $[a, b]$.

EXAMPLE 3.9:

Determine the direction of $f(x) := x^3 - 3x + 4$.

First, we find $f'(x) := 3x^2 - 3 = 3(x^2 - 1)$.

$f'(x) > 0$ whenever $x^2 > 1$ which occurs when $x > 1$ or $x < -1$.

Therefore, f is increasing on $(-\infty, -1]$ and $[1, \infty)$. It is decreasing on $[-1, 1]$. ♦

EXAMPLE 3.10:

Determine the direction of $g(x) := x^4 - 2x^2$.

$g'(x) := 4x^3 - 4x = 4x(x - 1)(x + 1)$

We can use the techniques of Chapter 1 to find the sign of $g'(x)$.

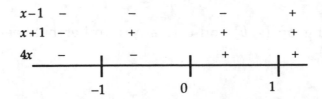

$g'(x) > 0$ for $-1 < x < 0$ or for $x > 1$ and $g'(x) < 0$ elsewhere. Therefore, g is increasing on the intervals $[-1, 0]$ and $[1, \infty)$ and decreasing on $(-\infty, -1]$ and $[0, 1]$. ◆

TEST YOUR UNDERSTANDING

1. What must be true about the derivative of a function (assuming it exists) in order for the function to be increasing on an interval?

2. Determine the direction of each of the following:

(a) $f(x) := 4x^2 + 16x - 2$

(b) $g(x) := x^3 + 9x^2$

(c) $y = x^4 - 4x + 2$

(d) $y = x^5 + x$

We would also like to be able to use the first derivative to determine the local maxima and minima of a function. If f has a local maximum at $x = c$, then $f'(x)$ must be positive for x less than (but near) c and negative for x greater than (but near) c. Conversely, if f has a local minimum at $x = c$, then $f'(x)$ must be negative for x less than c and positive for x greater than c. In other words, $f'(x)$ changes sign as we pass from left to right through any local extremum--from positive to negative at a local maximum and from negative to positive at a local minimum.

What can we say about $f'(x)$ at $x = c$, where f has a local extremum at $x = c$? In Figure 3.7, the tangents to the curve at $x = 2$ (the local maximum) and $x = 4$ (the local minimum) are both horizontal, so $f'(2) = f'(4) = 0$. See also Figure 3.8(a). While this is one possible condition that f' could satisfy at a local maximum or minimum, it is not the only one. We could also have a maximum or minimum at points for which f' does not exist.

There are two reasons why $f'(c)$ may not exist even though $f(c)$ is defined. One is that the tangent line is vertical (has infinite slope), as in Figure 3.8(b). The other reason is that the graph of f may have a sharp point. If this happens, then the derivative simply does not exist at $x = c$. To see why, recall that in order for a limit to exist as $\Delta x \rightarrow 0$ (and, hence, for the derivative to exist), it must be the same whether $\Delta x \rightarrow 0$ from the right or from the left. This is not the case if there is a sharp point.

As an example, consider the function $f(x) := |x|$. In Section 3.1, we showed that the derivative does not exist at $x = 0$ because the slope as we approach 0 from the left is different from the slope as we approach from the right. However, it does have a local minimum at $x = 0$, as Figure 3.8(c) illustrates.

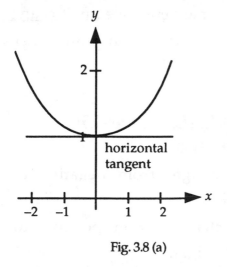

Fig. 3.8 (a)

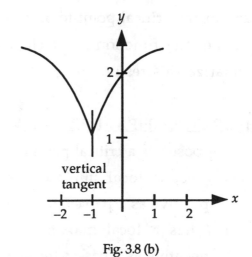

Fig. 3.8 (b)

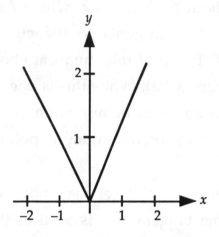

Fig. 3.8 (c)

Therefore, if there is a local maximum or minimum at $x = c$, then either $f'(c)$ equals 0 or $f'(c)$ does not exist.

This leads us to the following definition.

DEFINITION: The number c in the domain of f is said to be a **critical point** of f if either $f'(c) = 0$ or $f'(c)$ does not exist.

Every local maximum or minimum occurs at a critical point. However, not every critical point is a local extremum. It is entirely possible that the first derivative will be positive for $x < c$, zero at $x = c$ and positive for $x > c$. In order for the critical point to be a local extremum, the derivative must change sign (i.e. the function must change direction) at the critical point. Let's summarize this result:

THEOREM 3.7 (FIRST DERIVATIVE TEST FOR CRITICAL POINTS):
Suppose c is a critical point of the function f. Then:
(a) f has a local minimum at c if $f'(x)$ changes from negative to positive as x passes through c from left to right
(b) f has a local maximum at c if $f'(x)$ changes from positive to negative as x passes through c from left to right.

In other words, if the function changes from decreasing to increasing as we pass through $x = c$ (from left to right), then f has a local minimum at $x = c$. If the function changes from increasing to decreasing, then f has a local maximum at $x = c$. If the direction does not change, then there is neither a minimum nor a maximum at $x = c$.

In Example 3.10, we had $g(x) := x^4 - 2x^2$ and $g'(x) := 4x^3 - 4x$. If we set $g'(x) = 0$, we see that there are critical points at $x = 0$ and $x = \pm 1$. Since $g'(x) < 0$ for $x < -1$ and $g'(x) > 0$ for $-1 < x < 0$, then g has a local minimum at $x = -1$. Since $g'(x) < 0$ for $0 < x < 1$, then g has a local maximum at $x = 0$. Finally, since $g'(x) > 0$ for $x > 1$, then g has a local minimum at $x = 1$.

Keep in mind that these are *local* extrema. This means that the function value at, say, a local maximum is bigger than the function values nearby; it is not necessarily the biggest value the function can attain. In the example above, there is a local maximum at $x = 0$. Hence, the function values near $x = 0$ must be smaller than $g(0) = 0$. There are, however, values of x for which $g(x) > 0$. (Can you find one?) In Chapter 5, we'll talk about finding the largest and smallest values a function can attain anywhere in its domain-- the so-called "global" extrema.

EXAMPLE 3.11:

Determine all local extrema of the function $f(x) := x^3$.

The derivative is $f'(x) := 3x^2$.

Clearly, $f'(x) = 0$ if $x = 0$, so there is a critical point at $x = 0$. However, $f'(x)$ is positive both for $x < 0$ and $x > 0$, so f has neither a local maximum nor minimum at $x = 0$.

Interestingly, the line tangent to this function at $x = 0$ is horizontal (it actually is the x-axis) and therefore crosses the graph of f at the origin. See Figure 3.9 .

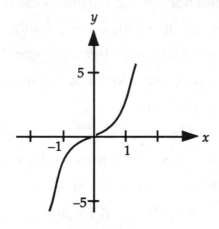

Fig. 3.9

EXAMPLE 3.12:

Determine the critical points of $g(x) := \frac{1}{x}$.

We have seen that $g'(x) = -\frac{1}{x^2}$.

There are no x-values for which $g'(x) = 0$, but $g'(0)$ does not exist. So, we may be tempted to think that $x = 0$ is a critical point. However, this is not correct since $x = 0$ is not in the domain of g. ◆

EXAMPLE 3.13:

Determine and classify the critical points of $f(x) := x^{2/3}$.

$$f'(x) := \frac{2}{3}x^{-1/3} = \frac{2}{3\sqrt[3]{x}}$$

Again, $f'(x)$ is never 0 but fails to exist when $x = 0$. This time, however, $x = 0$ is in the domain and therefore is a critical point of f.

Since $f'(x) < 0$ for $x < 0$ and $f'(x) > 0$ for $x > 0$, then f has a local minimum at $x = 0$. ◆

TEST YOUR UNDERSTANDING

3. How can we use the derivative to tell if a function has a local maximum at a critical point? a local minimum?

4. Determine and classify the critical points for each of the following functions:

   (a) $y = x^2 - 10x + 7$ (b) $y = -3x^2 + 24x$

   (c) $y = x^3 + 6x$ (d) $y = \sqrt[3]{x}$

5. Draw a graph of a function f which has a horizontal tangent at $x = 3$ but such that there is neither a local minimum nor maximum at $x = 3$. (The answer is not unique.)

6. Sketch a graph of a function for which $f'(2) = f'(-1) = 0$ and such that $f'(x) > 0$ on the interval $(-1, 2)$ and $f'(x) < 0$ elsewhere. (Again, the answer is not unique.)

- -

CONCAVITY

In Chapter 1, we had the following definition: If, for any points P, Q and R on the graph (in order from left to right, with x-coordinates on the interval $[a, b]$), the slope of PQ is less than the slope of QR, then f is concave up on $[a, b]$. It is clear from Figure 3.10 that if f is concave up on $[a, b]$, then the slope of the tangent line increases as we move from left to right. In other words, if f is concave up, then f' is increasing.

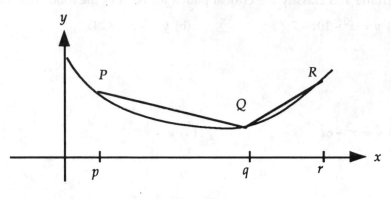

Fig. 3.10

Using an argument similar to the one needed to prove Theorem 3.6, we claim that the converse of this statement is also true. That is, _f is concave up on [a, b]_ if its derivative f' is increasing. But f' is just another function and we can tell if it is increasing by determining where _its_ derivative is positive.

Thus, concavity is characterized by the derivative of the derivative, which we call (obviously) the **second derivative**. The second derivative is denoted

either $D_x^2 f(x), f''(x), y''$ or $\dfrac{d^2 y}{dx^2}$.

THEOREM 3.8: Suppose $f''(x)$ exists on (a, b).

(a) If $f''(x) > 0$ for all x on the interval (a, b), then f is concave up on $[a, b]$.

(b) If $f''(x) < 0$ for all x on the interval (a, b), then f is concave down on $[a, b]$.

(Again we have a theorem whose proof depends on the Mean Value Theorem.)

EXAMPLE 3.14:

Determine the concavity of the function $f(x) := x^3 - 3x + 4$ from Example 3.9.

Since $f'(x) := 3x^2 - 3$, then $f''(x) := 6x$. Since $6x > 0$ if and only if $x > 0$, then f is concave up on $[0, \infty)$ and concave down on $(-\infty, 0]$.   ◆

EXAMPLE 3.15:

Determine the concavity of the function $g(x) := x^4 - 2x^2$ from Example 3.10.

Since $g'(x) := 4x^3 - 4x$, then $g''(x) := 12x^2 - 4$.

$g''(x) < 0$ when $x^2 < \frac{1}{3}$; that is, when $-\sqrt{\frac{1}{3}} < x < \sqrt{\frac{1}{3}}$. Therefore, g is concave down on $[-\sqrt{\frac{1}{3}}, \sqrt{\frac{1}{3}}]$ and concave up on $(-\infty, -\sqrt{\frac{1}{3}}]$ and $[\sqrt{\frac{1}{3}}, \infty)$. ♦

EXAMPLE 3.16:

For the function g pictured in Figure 3.11 , sketch the first and second derivatives.

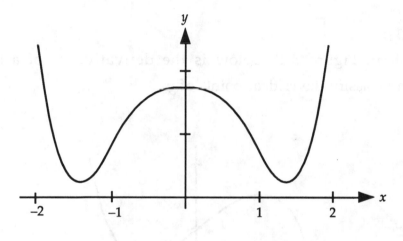

Fig. 3.11

First observe that g has a local maximum and $x = 0$ and local minima at $x = \pm 1.5$, approximately. Since the tangents are horizontal at these points, it must be that $g'(x) = 0$ when $x = 0$ and $x = \pm 1.5$.

Since g is increasing on $[-1.5, 0]$ and $[1.5, \infty)$ and decreasing elsewhere, it must be that $g'(x) > 0$ on $(-1.5, 0)$ and $(1.5, \infty)$ and $g'(x) < 0$ elsewhere.

The graph indicates that g is concave up approximately on $(-\infty, -1]$ and $[1, \infty)$, then g' is increasing and g'' is positive on those intervals. (It is a little hard to tell exactly where the concavity changes just by looking at the graph.) Similarly, g' is decreasing and g'' is negative on the interval $(-1, 1)$. See Figures 3.12 (a) and (b).

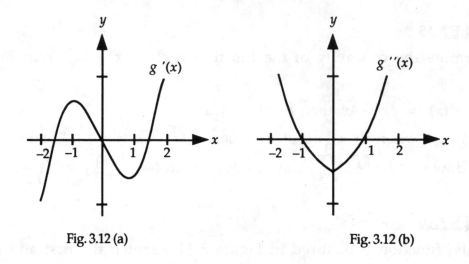

Fig. 3.12 (a)   Fig. 3.12 (b)

♦

EXAMPLE 3.17:

The graph in Figure 3.13 below is the derivative g' of a function g. Determine and classify the critical points of g.

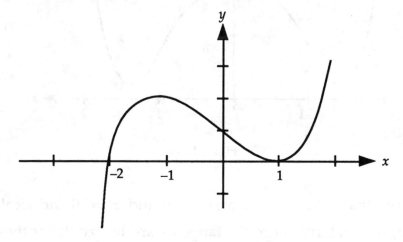

Fig. 3.13

Since $g'(x) = 0$ when $x = -2$ and when $x = 1$, then these are the critical points. (We assume g' is defined everywhere so there are no critical points at which g' is undefined.) Now $g'(x) < 0$ for $x < -2$ and $g'(x) > 0$ for $x > -2$ which means g has a local minimum at $x = -2$. On the other hand, g' does not change sign in the vicinity of $x = 1$, so g has neither a maximum nor a minimum at $x = 1$. ♦

◻ A point on the graph of f at which f changes from concave up to concave down or vice-versa is called an **inflection point**. In order for the concavity to change, the second derivative must either be 0 or fail to exist. So, the inflection points occur at those values of x for which $f''(x) = 0$ or $f''(x)$ does not exist. However, as we saw with critical points and local extrema, not every value of x for which $f''(x) = 0$ or $f''(x)$ does not exist is an inflection point. We must check that the second derivative does indeed change sign there.

The second derivative also gives us another way of characterizing certain critical points as local maxima or minima. Suppose c is a critical point for which $f'(c) = 0$. If f is concave up on some interval containing $x = c$, then there must be a local minimum at $x = c$, while if f is concave down at $x = c$, then there must be a local maximum at $x = c$. In Figure 3.13, there is a local maximum at $x = -1$ and the function is concave down in the vicinity of $x = -1$. Likewise, there is a local minimum at $x = 1$ and the function is concave up in the vicinity of $x = 1$.

THEOREM 3.9 (SECOND DERIVATIVE TEST FOR CRITICAL POINTS):

Let c be a critical point of f for which $f'(c) = 0$ and suppose $f''(x)$ is continuous for x near c.

(a) If $f''(c) > 0$, then f has a local minimum at $x = c$.

(b) If $f''(c) < 0$, then f has a local maximum at $x = c$.

(c) If $f''(c) = 0$, then no conclusion can be drawn.

Note: When we say no conclusion can be drawn, we mean that f could have a local maximum, a local minimum, or neither at $x = c$. To tell which is the case, we must resort to Theorem 3.7 or some other argument.

In Example 3.9, $f(x) := x^3 - 3x + 4$, $f'(x) := 3x^2 - 3$ (so $x = 1, -1$ are critical points), and $f''(x) := 6x$. Since $f''(1) = 6 > 0$, then f has a local minimum at $x = 1$, while $f''(-1) = -6 < 0$ implies f has a local maximum at $x = -1$. This agrees with our earlier conclusions.

In Example 3.11, $f''(x) := 6x$ as well. The critical point $x = 0$ cannot be classified using Theorem 3.9 since $f''(0) = 0$. (In this case it is neither a maximum nor a minimum as we argued from Theorem 3.7.)

TEST YOUR UNDERSTANDING

7. State two equivalent conditions that guarantee that a function f is concave up on an interval.

8. Determine the concavity of each of the following functions:

   (a) $y = -2x^2 + 9x - 2$ (b) $y = 2x^3 + 12x^2 + 4x - 3$

   (c) $y = \sqrt{x}$ (d) $y = \frac{1}{x}$

9. Suppose f is a function for which $f'(4) = 0$ and $f''(x) = 6 - 2x$. What conclusion can you draw about f at $x = 4$?

10. Suppose g is a function for which $g'(-1) = 0$ and $g''(x) = x^2 - 1$. What conclusion can you draw about g at $x = -1$?

Now let's look at an example of how we put this all together to get the graph of a function.

EXAMPLE 3.18:

Let $y = 2x^3 - 6x^2 - 18x + 20$. Determine the direction, local maxima and minima, and concavity of y. Sketch the graph.

$$\frac{dy}{dx} = 6x^2 - 12x - 18 = 6(x-3)(x+1)$$

There are critical points when $x = 3$ and $x = -1$.

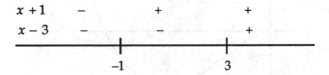

As we can see, $\frac{dy}{dx} > 0$ when $x < -1$ or $x > 3$ and $\frac{dy}{dx} < 0$ when $-1 < x < 3$. Hence, y is increasing on $(-\infty, -1]$ and $[3, \infty)$ and decreasing on $[-1, 3]$. Furthermore, there is a local maximum at $x = -1$ and a local minimum at $x = 3$. The corresponding y-values are 30 and -34, respectively.

$\frac{d^2y}{dx^2} = 12x - 12$ which is positive when $x > 1$. Therefore, y is concave up on $[1, \infty)$ and concave down on $(-\infty, 1]$. There is an inflection point at $x = 1$ where $y = -2$.

The graph is shown in Figure 3.14.

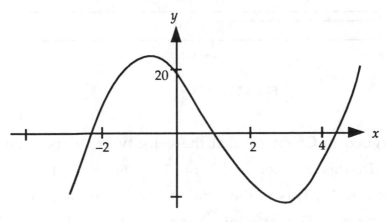

Fig. 3.14

VELOCITY AND ACCELERATION

Suppose a particle moves back and forth along a straight line; its position at time t is given by the function $s(t)$. For example, let $s(t) := t^3 - 3t^2$, for $t \geq 0$. A graph of this function is given in Figure 3.15.

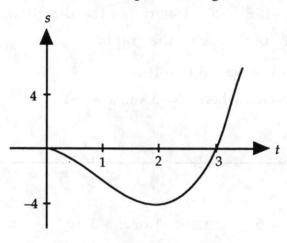

Fig. 3.15

The particle starts at position $s = 0$ when $t = 0$. It then moves *backwards* to position $s = -4$ when $t = 2$. At this point, it turns around and begins moving forward. It passes its initial position at $t = 3$ and continues forward forever. Figure 3.16 shows the actual path followed by the particle.

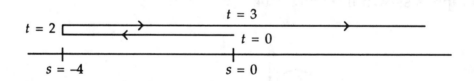

Fig. 3.16

We have argued in Chapter 2 that the velocity of the particle is given by $v(t) = s'(t)$. In this example, $v(t) := 3t^2 - 6t = 3t(t - 2)$. Note that $v(t) < 0$ for $0 < t < 2$. This is the time interval over which the particle is moving backwards. The rate of change of the velocity is called the **acceleration**; that is, $a(t) = v'(t)$. Since the velocity is the derivative of the position, then the acceleration is the second derivative of the position; $a(t)$

$= s''(t)$. If both the velocity and acceleration are positive, then the particle is speeding up; positive velocity and negative acceleration means the particle is slowing down. Conversely, if the velocity and acceleration are both negative, then the particle is moving backwards and its velocity is decreasing--that is, becoming more negative. This means that the particle is moving backwards at an ever-increasing speed. Finally, if the velocity is negative and the acceleration is positive, then the particle is moving backwards at an ever-decreasing speed.

In our example, $a(t) := 6t - 6$ which is positive for $t > 1$ and negative for $t < 1$. Thus, for $0 < t < 1$, the particle moves backwards but its speed increases; for $1 < t < 2$, the speed decreases until the particle stops and turns around at $t = 2$. For $t > 2$, both the velocity and acceleration are positive, meaning that the particle moves forward and speeds up.

EXERCISES FOR SECTION 3.2:

1. Determine the direction and concavity of each function below. Determine and classify the critical points. Sketch the graph.

    (a) $f(x) := 2x^2 + 4x$ (b) $f(x) := x^3 - x$ (c) $g(x) := x + \dfrac{1}{x}$

    (d) $y = x^3 - 6x^2 - 15x$ (e) $y = \sqrt[5]{x}$ (f) $y = x^{1/2} - 3$

    (g) $f(x) := x^4 - 8x^3$ (h) $h(x) := x^5 - 20x$ (i) $f(x) := \dfrac{x^2}{2} + \dfrac{1}{x}$

    (j) $y = x^{-1/2}$

2. Sketch a continuous function g for which $g'(-2) = 0$, $g'(x) < 0$ on $(-\infty, -2)$, $g'(x) > 0$ on $(-2, \infty)$, $g''(x) < 0$ on $(-1, 1)$ and $g''(x) > 0$ on $(1, \infty)$ and $(-\infty, -1)$.

3. Sketch a continuous function f for which $f'(x) > 0$ on $(-\infty, 0)$ and $(3, \infty)$, $f''(x) > 0$ for all x, $f(0) = 5$ and $f(3) = 2$.

4. A function f is continuous on the interval $[-3, 3]$ with $f(-3) = 4$ and $f(3) = 1$. Also,

x	$-3 < x < -1$	$x = -1$	$-1 < x < 1$	$x = 1$	$1 < x < 3$
$f'(x)$	pos.	d.n.e.	neg.	0	neg.
$f''(x)$	pos.	d.n.e.	pos.	0	neg.

(a) Determine all local maxima and minima of f on the interval $[-3, 3]$.

(b) Determine all inflection points of f.

(c) Sketch a graph of f.

5. A function f is graphed below. Graph its derivative and second derivative.

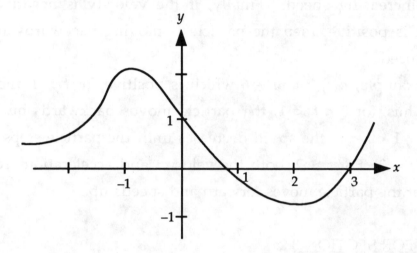

6. Each graph below is the *derivative f'* of a function. For each one, determine the direction, concavity, critical points, inflection points of f and sketch a graph of f consistent with the information obtained. (The graph is not unique.)

(a)   (b)

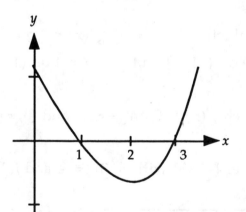 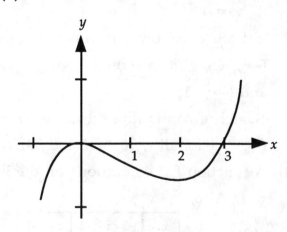

(c)

(d)

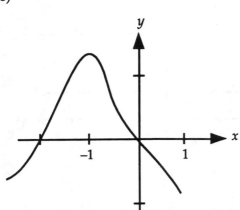

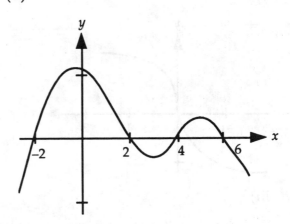

7. Sketch the graph of f in the vicinity of $x = 1$ if:

   (a) $f(1) = 2,\ f'(1) = 0,\ f''(1) = 4$

   (b) $f(1) = -3,\ f'(1) = 0,\ f''(1) = -2$

   (c) $f(1) = 0,\ f'(1) = 0,\ f''(1) = 0,\ f''(x) < 0$ for $x < 1,\ f''(x) > 0$ for
   $x > 1$

   (d) $f(1) = -1,\ f'(1) = 3,\ f''(1) = -2$

   (e) $f(1) = 4,\ f'(1) = \infty$ (undefined), $f''(x) > 0$ for x near 1

8. Suppose $g'(x) := (x - 1)(x - 5)(x + 2)$.

   (a) Determine and classify the critical points of g.

   (b) Write an equation of the line tangent to the graph of g at $x = 2$ if
   $g(2) = 7$.

9. Match each function with its derivative.

<u>$f(x)$</u>   <u>$f'(x)$</u>

i)   (a)

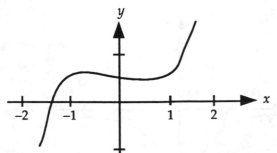

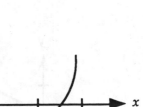

ii)

(b)

iii)

(c)

iv)

(d)

v)

(e)

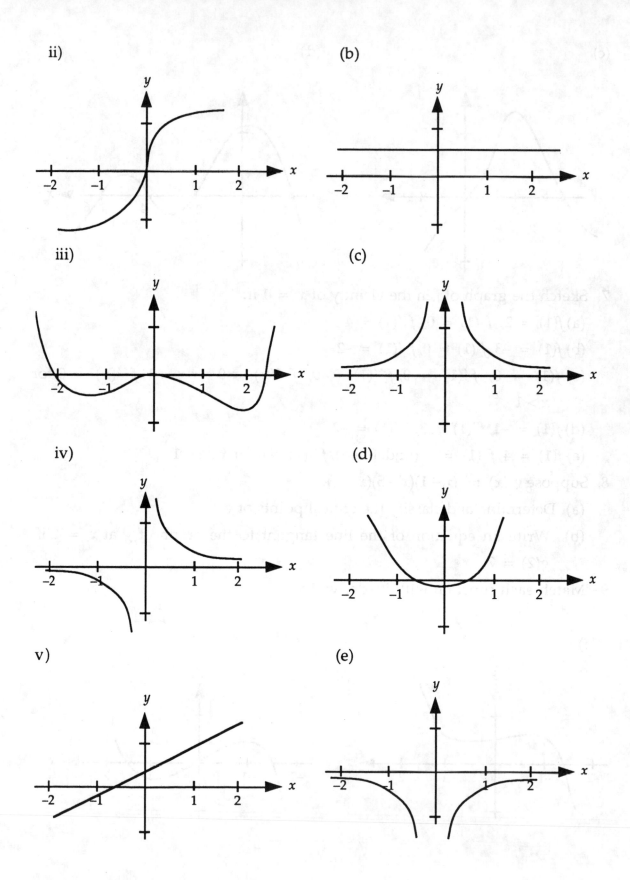

10. Write an equation of the line tangent to the graph of $f(x) := x^3 - 6x^2 + 12x$ at $x = 1$.

11. The derivative of a function is $g'(x) := x(x - 2)(x - 4)$. If g is defined for all x, determine and classify the critical points of g.

12. Repeat Exercise 11 if $g'(x) := (x + 1)(x - 5)^3$.

13. Repeat Exercise 11 if $h'(x) := (x - 3)^2(x + 1)$.

14. Repeat Exercise 11 if $h'(x) := \dfrac{x^2 - 1}{x^2 + 1}$.

15. Sketch a function f for which $f'(x) := x(x - 4)$ for all x, $f(0) = 2$ and $f(4) = -5$.

16. Sketch a function f with all of the following properties:

$f'(x) > 0$ for x on the intervals $(-\infty, -2)$ and $(2, \infty)$, $f'(x) < 0$ for x on the interval $(-2, 2)$

$f'(x)$ is increasing for x on the intervals $(-\infty, -4)$ and $(0, 4)$

$f'(x)$ is decreasing for x on the intervals $(-4, 0)$ and $(4, \infty)$

$f(-2) = 7$, $f(2) = -1$, $f(-4) = 3$, $f(0) = 3$, $f(4) = 5$

17. Find the minimum value of the slope of the tangent to the graph of $y = x^5 + x^3 - 2x$.

18. Determine the concavity of a function h if $h'(x) := x^3 - 12x$.

19. Let $f(x) := 2x^2 + 9x + 4$.

(a) Determine an equation of the line perpendicular to f at $(-2, -6)$.

(b) At what other point does the perpendicular intersect the graph of f?

20. For what value of k will the function $g(x) := x^3 - kx^2$ be decreasing on $[0, 3]$ and increasing elsewhere?

21. The position of a particle at time t is given by $s(t) := t^3 - 6t^2$.

(a) Determine the velocity function $v(t)$.

(b) At what times is the particle moving forward?

(c) At what times is the particle at rest?

(d) What is the minimum velocity of the particle?

(e) What is the acceleration of the particle?

22. The velocity of a particle is given by $v(t) := (t-1)(t-4)^2$. Its acceleration is $a(t) := 3(t-2)(t-4)$.

    (a) During what time intervals is the particle moving backwards?

    (b) During what time intervals is the acceleration positive?

    (c) If the initial position is $s(0) = 3$, sketch a graph of the position function.

PROBLEMS FOR SECTION 3.2:

1. Determine constants p and q such that $f(x) := x^3 + px + q$ has a local minimum at $(2, -9)$.

2. (a) Show that a quadratic function has no inflection points.

   (b) Show that every cubic function has exactly one inflection point.

3. Let $f(x) := x(x-k)^2$, for some $k > 0$.

   (a) Determine and classify the critical points of f.

   (b) Show that the x-value at the point of inflection lies midway between the x-values at the local minimum and maximum of f.

4. Consider a cubic polynomial of the form $f(x) := x^3 + bx$, for some constant b. Describe the direction and concavity of the polynomial for the cases where b is positive and those where b is negative.

5. Let $f(x) := x^4 + x^3 + kx^2$. For what values of k does f have exactly one local extremum?

6. Let $p(x) := x^4 + ax^3 + bx^2 + cx + d$. The graph of $p(x)$ is symmetric about the y-axis, has a local maximum at $x = 0$ and a local minimum at $x = q$.

   (a) Determine a, b and c in terms of q.

   (b) If $p(0) = 1$ and $p(q) = -15$, determine q and d.

TYU Answers for Section 3.2

   1. Its derivative must be positive on that interval.   2. (a) incr. on $[-2, \infty)$, decr. on $(-\infty, -2]$

     (b) incr. on $[0, \infty)$ and $(-\infty, -6]$, decr. on $[-6, 0]$ (c) incr. on $[1, \infty)$, decr. on $(-\infty, 1]$

     (d) incr. for all x 3. Local max if f' changes from positive to negative; local min if f' changes from negative to positive.

4. (a) There is a min at $x = 5$. 　　　(b) There is a max at $x = 4$.

　　(c) No critical points 　　　　　　(d) There is neither a min nor a max at $x = 0$.

5. 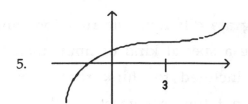 　　　6.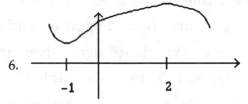

7. f' is increasing or f'' is positive 　8. (a) conc. dn. for all x 　(b) conc. up on $[-2, \infty)$, dn. on

$(-\infty, -2]$ 　(c) conc. dn on $[0, \infty)$, (not defined for $x < 0$) (d) conc. dn. on $(-\infty, 0)$, conc. up on

$(0, \infty)$ 　9. There is a local max at $x = 4$ 　　10. no conclusion

3.3 SHORTCUTS FOR FINDING DERIVATIVES

So far, we have used a definition to find the derivatives of some simple functions. While this definition is extremely important (arguably the most important concept in this course) and you *must never forget it*, it is, admittedly, very difficult to use, especially for more complicated functions. Since we do want to be able to use these derivatives, it will be useful to know shortcuts for finding them that disguise the use of the definition. This is *not an excuse* for forgetting the definition; indeed, later, we will encounter functions for which our shortcuts won't work so we will have to come back to the definition once again.

Our ultimate goal is to be able to differentiate all algebraic functions without recourse to the definition. An algebraic function is one whose rule involves a finite number of additions, subtractions, multiplications, divisions and root-taking (radicals). One approach for handling complex functions is to "break them down into pieces", differentiate the pieces, and "glue the pieces back together" in some suitable fashion (not necessarily the same way you broke them down). As all amateur repairmen know, taking things apart is easy; putting them back together is hard. We'll need some theorems to help us in this regard.

We have already seen how to differentiate power functions and polynomials easily. Once we get past these, things get a little more complicated. We need to deal with products, quotients and composites of functions. Although we will work just with algebraic functions in this chapter, these rules apply to all functions.

Let's do products first. Suppose f and g are differentiable functions and that $h(x) = f(x)g(x)$. Since derivatives are a special kind of limit, then in view of Theorem 3.1(b), we might be inclined to think that $h'(x) = (f'(x))(g'(x))$. To determine whether or not this is correct, we'll try an example. Suppose $f(x) := x^2$ and $g(x) := x^3$. Then $f'(x) := 2x, g'(x) := 3x^2$, so $(f'(x))(g'(x)) = 6x^3$. But, $h(x) := (x^2)(x^3) = x^5$, so $h'(x) := 5x^4 \neq 6x^3$. So much for that theory!

What should we do next? The "obvious" result is wrong and it is not at all clear what the right result is. (Knowing that Leibniz did not get the correct rule the first time he tried it should make you feel better.) To give us a clue as to what the right result might be, let's try a special case. Suppose $f(x) := x$, so that $h(x) := xg(x)$.

$$h'(x) := \lim_{\Delta x \to 0} \frac{(x + \Delta x)g(x + \Delta x) - xg(x)}{\Delta x}$$

$$= \lim_{\Delta x \to 0} \frac{xg(x + \Delta x) + (\Delta x)g(x + \Delta x) - xg(x)}{\Delta x}$$

$$= \lim_{\Delta x \to 0} \frac{x[g(x + \Delta x) - g(x)] + (\Delta x)g(x + \Delta x)}{\Delta x}$$

$$= \lim_{\Delta x \to 0} \frac{x \Delta g + (\Delta x)g(x + \Delta x)}{\Delta x}$$

$$= x \lim_{\Delta x \to 0} \frac{\Delta g}{\Delta x} + \lim_{\Delta x \to 0} g(x + \Delta x).$$

Therefore, $h'(x) := xg'(x) + g(x)$.

So, we see that there are two terms in the answer, one involving $g(x)$, the other involving $g'(x)$.

Note: We have used the fact that $g(x + \Delta x) \to g(x)$ as $\Delta x \to 0$. This is only true if g is continuous. We have assumed that g is differentiable which, as we stated in Theorem 3.3, implies that g is continuous.

Let's look at a slightly more complicated special case and see if a pattern emerges. Maybe then we can generalize. Suppose $h(x) := x^2g(x)$. Then:

$$h'(x) := \lim_{\Delta x \to 0} \frac{(x + \Delta x)^2 g(x + \Delta x) - x^2 g(x)}{\Delta x}$$

$$= \lim_{\Delta x \to 0} \frac{x^2[g(x + \Delta x) - g(x)] + 2x \Delta x\, g(x + \Delta x) + (\Delta x)^2 g(x + \Delta x)}{\Delta x}$$

$$= x^2 \lim_{\Delta x \to 0} \frac{\Delta g}{\Delta x} + \lim_{\Delta x \to 0}(2x + \Delta x)g(x + \Delta x).$$

Therefore, $h'(x) := x^2 g'(x) + 2xg(x)$.

Let's keep going. Suppose $h(x) := x^3g(x)$. A similar calculation will show $h'(x) := x^3g'(x) + 3x^2g(x)$. In each case, there are two terms, one with $g(x)$ and one with $g'(x)$.

Careful inspection reveals that, at least in these cases, if $h(x) := f(x)g(x)$, then $h'(x) := f(x)g'(x) + f'(x)g(x)$. The question that remains is: Is this true in general? Let's try a proof.

$$h(x + \Delta x) - h(x) = f(x + \Delta x)g(x + \Delta x) - f(x)g(x)$$

Now it appears we are stuck. There seems to be no algebraic manipulation that we can do at this point that will enable us to divide by Δx. However, not all is lost. Let's subtract and add $f(x + \Delta x)g(x)$ from the expression above. (Admittedly this is somewhat unmotivated but surely, subtracting and adding the same expression does not change the value.) Thus,

$$h(x + \Delta x) - h(x) = f(x + \Delta x)g(x + \Delta x) - f(x + \Delta x)g(x)$$
$$+ f(x + \Delta x)\, g(x) - f(x)g(x)$$
$$= f(x + \Delta x)[g(x + \Delta x) - g(x)] + g(x)[f(x + \Delta x) - f(x)]$$

Now divide by Δx and rearrange:

$$\frac{\Delta h}{\Delta x} = f(x + \Delta x)\left(\frac{g(x + \Delta x) - g(x)}{\Delta x}\right) + g(x)\left(\frac{f(x + \Delta x) - f(x)}{\Delta x}\right)$$

As $\Delta x \to 0$, $f(x + \Delta x) \to f(x)$, $\dfrac{g(x + \Delta x) - g(x)}{\Delta x} \to g'(x)$ and $\dfrac{f(x + \Delta x) - f(x)}{\Delta x}$

$\to f'(x)$. Hence, we get:

$h'(x) := f(x)g'(x) + f'(x)g(x)$, as we surmised.

THEOREM 3.10   (PRODUCT RULE FOR DERIVATIVES): If f and g are differentiable functions and $h(x) := f(x)g(x)$, then h is differentiable and $h'(x) := f(x)g'(x) + f'(x)g(x)$.

In words, this says "the derivative of the product of two functions is equal to the first function times the derivative of the second function plus the second function times the derivative of the first function".

If the proof above seems contrived, here's another, less "magical" (but unfashionable) one.   Let $y = h(x)$, $u = f(x)$ and $v = g(x)$. As x is increased by Δx, u is increased by Δu and v is increased by Δv. In other words, $f(x + \Delta x) = u + \Delta u$, $g(x + \Delta x) = v + \Delta v$ and $h(x + \Delta x) = y + \Delta y$. Therefore,

$$\Delta y = (u + \Delta u)(v + \Delta v) - uv = u\Delta v + v\Delta u + (\Delta u)(\Delta v).$$

Dividing by Δx, we get:

$$\frac{\Delta y}{\Delta x} = u\frac{\Delta v}{\Delta x} + v\frac{\Delta u}{\Delta x} + (\Delta u)\frac{\Delta v}{\Delta x} .$$

Since u and v are differentiable, then they are continuous. Hence, as $\Delta x \to 0$, so do $\Delta u \to 0$ and $\Delta v \to 0$. Furthermore, $\frac{\Delta u}{\Delta x} \to \frac{du}{dx}$, $\frac{\Delta v}{\Delta x} \to \frac{dv}{dx}$ and $(\Delta u)\frac{\Delta v}{\Delta x} \to 0(\frac{dv}{dx}) = 0$. Therefore

$$\frac{dy}{dx} = \frac{d(uv)}{dx} = u\frac{dv}{dx} + v\frac{du}{dx}.$$

Let's see if our theorem works for the example considered earlier. If $f(x) := x^2$ and $g(x) := x^3$, then $f(x)g'(x) + f'(x)g(x) = (x^2)(3x^2) + (2x)(x^3) = 3x^4 + 2x^4 = 5x^4$ which is the derivative of x^5.

EXAMPLE 3.19:

Find y' if $y = (x^3 - 3x^2 + 2)(2x^2 + 5x - 23)$

Since y is the product of two functions, we invoke Theorem 3.10 with $f(x) := x^3 - 3x^2 + 2$ and $g(x) := 2x^2 + 5x - 23$. So, $f'(x) := 3x^2 - 6x$ and $g'(x) := 4x + 5$. Therefore,

$$\frac{dy}{dx} = (x^3 - 3x^2 + 2)(4x + 5) + (3x^2 - 6x)(2x^2 + 5x - 23)$$

$$= 10x^4 - 4x^3 - 114x^2 + 146x + 10. \qquad \blacklozenge$$

TEST YOUR UNDERSTANDING

1. Verify the result of Example 3.19 by multiplying the factors first and then differentiating.

2. Find the derivatives of each of the following:

   (a) $y = \sqrt{x}\,(x^2 + 1)$ (b) $f(x) := (ax^2 + bx)(cx + d)$

3. Suppose $f(3) = 2, f'(3) = -4, g(3) = 5$ and $g'(3) = 3$. If $h(x) := f(x)g(x)$:

   (a) Determine $h'(3)$.

   (b) Write an equation of the line tangent to the graph of h at $x = 3$.

❑ Next we consider the quotient of two functions. One way to handle this is to think of the quotient $\frac{f(x)}{g(x)}$ as the product $(f(x))\left(\frac{1}{g(x)}\right)$ and use the product rule. In order to do so, we need to know how to find the derivative of $\frac{1}{g(x)}$. (It is *not* simply $\frac{1}{g'(x)}$. Think about $y = \frac{1}{x^2}$. Is $\frac{dy}{dx} = \frac{1}{2x}$?)

Let $u = g(x)$ and $y = h(x) = \frac{1}{g(x)} = \frac{1}{u}$. Then

$$h(x + \Delta x) = \frac{1}{g(x + \Delta x)} = \frac{1}{u + \Delta u} \qquad \text{and}$$

$$\Delta y = h(x + \Delta x) - h(x) = \frac{1}{u + \Delta u} - \frac{1}{u} = \frac{-\Delta u}{(u + \Delta u)(u)} .$$

Thus, $\frac{\Delta y}{\Delta x} = \frac{-\Delta u /\Delta x}{(u + \Delta u)(u)}$. Letting $\Delta x \to 0$ (implying $\Delta u \to 0$), we get $\frac{dy}{dx}$

$= \frac{-1}{u^2} \frac{du}{dx}$. We state this result as:

THEOREM 3.11: If g is a differentiable function and $h(x) := \frac{1}{g(x)}$, then h is differentiable and $h'(x) := \frac{-g'(x)}{[g(x)]^2}$, provided $g(x) \neq 0$.

EXAMPLE 3.20:

Determine the derivative of $h(x) := \frac{1}{x^2 + 2x + 4}$.

Applying Theorem 3.11 with $g(x) := x^2 + 2x + 4$ (and, consequently, $g'(x) := 2x + 2$), we have $h'(x) := -\frac{2x + 2}{\left(x^2 + 2x + 4\right)^2}$. ◆

We are now prepared to state a rule for finding the derivative of the quotient of two functions.

THEOREM 3.12 (QUOTIENT RULE FOR DERIVATIVES): If f and g are differentiable functions and $h(x) := \frac{f(x)}{g(x)}$, then h is differentiable and $h'(x) := \frac{g(x)f'(x) - f(x)g'(x)}{[g(x)]^2}$, if $g(x) \neq 0$.

EXAMPLE 3.21:

Find $\dfrac{dy}{dx}$ if $y = \dfrac{x^3 + 4x}{x^2 + 2}$.

Applying Theorem 3.12 with $f(x) := x^3 + 4x$ and $g(x) := x^2 + 2$ gives

$$\frac{dy}{dx} = \frac{(x^2 + 2)(3x^2 + 4) - 2x(x^3 + 4x)}{(x^2 + 2)^2}$$

$$= \frac{x^4 + 2x^2 + 8}{(x^2 + 2)^2}. \qquad \blacklozenge$$

TEST YOUR UNDERSTANDING

4. Find the derivatives of each of the following:

   (a) $y = \dfrac{x + 1}{x + 2}$ (b) $g(t) := \dfrac{t^2}{2t^2 + 1}$ (c) $f(x) := \dfrac{2x}{x^3 + 6}$

5. Suppose $f(2) = 3$, $f'(2) = 1$, $g(2) = -2$ and $g'(2) = 4$. If $h(x) := f(x)/g(x)$, find $h'(2)$.

◻ Our last task is to find the derivative of the composite of two functions. Let's consider a special case. Suppose $h(x) := [g(x)]^n$, for some positive integer n. We might be tempted to invoke the power rule and claim $h'(x) = n[g(x)]^{n-1}$.

Let's try an example to see if this is correct. Suppose $g(x) := x^3 + 1$ and $h(x) := [g(x)]^2 = x^6 + 2x^3 + 1$. If our claim is correct, then $h'(x)$ should be $2(x^3 + 1) = 2x^3 + 2$. However, $h'(x)$ is, in fact, $6x^5 + 6x^2$. This disproves the claim. Note that $6x^5 + 6x^2 = 3x^2(2x^3 + 2)$ and that $3x^2 = g'(x)$. So, perhaps the correct rule is $h'(x) := n[g(x)]^{n-1}g'(x)$.

Before trying to prove this in general, let's try another example. Let $h(x) := [g(x)]^3 = x^9 + 3x^6 + 3x^3 + 1$. Then $h'(x) := 9x^8 + 18x^5 + 9x^2 = 9x^2(x^6 + 2x^3 + 1) = 3(x^3 + 1)^2(3x^2) = n[g(x)]^{n-1}g'(x)$ with $n = 3$.

We're now ready to try a general proof. To do so, we go back to the definition of the derivative. Let $u = g(x)$. As x increases by Δx, then u increases by Δu, so $\Delta h = h(x + \Delta x) - h(x) = (u + \Delta u)^n - u^n$. Factoring, we get

$$\Delta h = [u + \Delta u - u][(u + \Delta u)^{n-1} + (u + \Delta u)^{n-2}u + (u + \Delta u)^{n-3}u^2 + \ldots + u^{n-1}]$$

$$= \Delta u[(u + \Delta u)^{n-1} + (u + \Delta u)^{n-2}u + (u + \Delta u)^{n-3}u^2 + \ldots + u^{n-1}]$$

$$\frac{\Delta h}{\Delta x} = \frac{\Delta u}{\Delta x}\left[(u + \Delta u)^{n-1} + (u + \Delta u)^{n-2}u + \cdots + u^{n-1}\right]$$

As $\Delta x \to 0$, $\Delta u \to 0$ and $\dfrac{\Delta u}{\Delta x} \to \dfrac{du}{dx}$. Each term in the brackets approaches u^{n-1}. Therefore, $h'(x) := nu^{n-1}\dfrac{du}{dx} = n[g(x)]^{n-1}g'(x)$, as we surmised.

So the power rule has to be modified when it is applied to a function raised to a power.

THEOREM 3.13: Let g be a differentiable function and let $h(x) := [g(x)]^n$, for some positive integer n. Then $h'(x) := n[g(x)]^{n-1}g'(x)$.

Notes:

1. If $g(x) := x$, then $g'(x) := 1$ and this theorem reduces to the original power rule.

2. As with Theorem 3.2, this result holds for all exponents.

3. If $n = -1$, we get Theorem 3.11.

EXAMPLE 3.22:

Find y' if $y = \sqrt[3]{x^2+4} = (x^2+4)^{1/3}$

This is the composite of two functions so we use Theorem 3.13 with $g(x) := x^2+4$ and $f(x) = x^{1/3}$. Thus,

$$y' = \frac{1}{3}(x^2+4)^{-2/3}(2x) = \frac{2x}{3}(x^2+4)^{-2/3}. \qquad \blacklozenge$$

TEST YOUR UNDERSTANDING

6. Find the derivatives of each of the following:

   (a) $f(x) := (4x+1)^{3/2}$ (b) $h(t) := \left(t+\frac{1}{t}\right)^5$ (c) $z = \dfrac{1}{(x^3+6x+7)^3}$

7. Find y'' for the function in Example 3.22.

8. Find the instantaneous velocity and acceleration of a particle whose position is given by $s(t) := \sqrt{2t+1}$.

Now let's apply these rules to analyze functions and draw graphs.

EXAMPLE 3.23:

Sketch the graph of $f(x) := \dfrac{1}{x^2+1}$, making use of the direction, concavity, critical points, asymptotes and symmetry.

$$f'(x) := \frac{-2x}{(x^2+1)^2}$$

Since the denominator of f' is positive for all x, then $f'(x) > 0$ when the numerator is positive--i.e., when $x < 0$. Thus, f is increasing on $(-\infty, 0]$ and decreasing on $[0, \infty)$. There is a local maximum at $x = 0$.

Applying the quotient rule, we get:

$$f''(x) := \frac{(x^2 + 1)^2(-2) - (-2x)(2)(x^2 + 1)(2x)}{(x^2 + 1)^4} = \frac{6x^2 - 2}{(x^2 + 1)^3}$$

Again, the denominator is always positive, so $f''(x) < 0$ when the numerator is negative; that is, when $x^2 < \frac{1}{3}$. Therefore, f is concave down on $[-\sqrt{\frac{1}{3}}, \sqrt{\frac{1}{3}}]$ and concave up elsewhere.

We also note that f is an even function and that $\lim_{x \to \pm\infty} f(x) = 0$, implying that $y = 0$ is a horizontal asymptote.

The graph is in Figure 3.17.

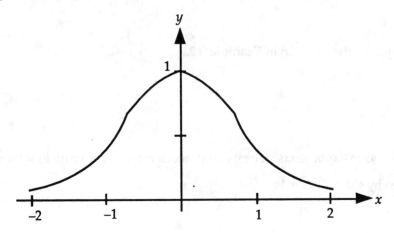

Fig. 3.17

$\blacklozenge$

EXAMPLE 3.24:

Write an equation of the line tangent to the graph of $f(x) := x^2\sqrt{x + 1}$ at $x = 3$.

$$f'(x) := \frac{1}{2}\frac{x^2}{\sqrt{x + 1}} + 2x\sqrt{x + 1}$$

Since $f'(3) = \frac{57}{4}$ and $f(3) = 18$, the desired equation is:

$y - 18 = \frac{57}{4}(x - 3).$

$\blacklozenge$

Now let's consider the general composite function $h(x) := f(g(x))$. In Theorem 3.13, $f(x) := x^n$ and we showed that $h'(x) := n[g(x)]^{n-1}g'(x)$ $= f'(g(x))g'(x)$. We now show that this is true for any differentiable functions f and g.

THEOREM 3.14 (CHAIN RULE): Let f and g be differentiable functions and
let $h(x) := f(g(x))$. Then h is also differentiable and
$$h'(x) := f'(g(x))g'(x).$$

"Proof": Let $y = h(x) = f(u)$, where $u = g(x)$.

Certainly, $\dfrac{\Delta y}{\Delta x} = \dfrac{\Delta y}{\Delta u}\dfrac{\Delta u}{\Delta x}$ if $\Delta u \neq 0$. Now let $\Delta x \to 0$.

$\dfrac{\Delta y}{\Delta x} \to h'(x)$, $\dfrac{\Delta y}{\Delta u} \to f'(u) = f'(g(x))$ and $\dfrac{\Delta u}{\Delta x} \to g'(x)$ which gives us our result.

Caution: This proof is not strictly correct. Can you find the problem?

Sometimes it is convenient to remember the chain rule in "differential form"; that is, if $y = f(u)$ where $u = g(x)$, then
$$\frac{dy}{dx} = \frac{dy}{du}\frac{du}{dx}.$$
If we treat the differentials as individual quantities and the derivatives as ratios (which they really are not), then this statement is algebraically correct since the du "cancels out". Furthermore, if y is the composite of 3 or more functions, we can extend the chain rule. For example, if $y = f(u)$, $u = g(v)$ and $v = h(x)$, then $\dfrac{dy}{dx} = \dfrac{dy}{du}\dfrac{du}{dv}\dfrac{dv}{dx}$, etc.

For now, we will not have to use the generality of Theorem 3.14 very often since most of the functions we consider are power functions or rational functions and can be handled by Theorem 3.13. In Chapters 4 and 7, we will learn about other functions and then we will really need all the power of the chain rule.

EXAMPLE 3.25:

Suppose $g(x) := f\left(\frac{1}{x}\right)$. Find $g'(2)$ if $f'\left(\frac{1}{2}\right) = 3$.

By Theorem 3.13, $g'(x) := f'\left(\frac{1}{x}\right)\left(\frac{-1}{x^2}\right)$. Therefore, $g'(2) = f'\left(\frac{1}{2}\right)\left(\frac{-1}{4}\right) = \frac{-3}{4}$.

♦

----

9. Suppose $h(x) := f(\sqrt{x})$. Find $h'(9)$ if $f'(3) = -3$.

EXERCISES FOR SECTION 3.3:

1. Find the derivative of the following functions:

   (a) $f(x) := 3x^2 - x$

   (b) $y = x^{1/3}(1 + \sqrt{x})$

   (c) $f(x) := 1 - \dfrac{1}{x^2}$

   (d) $p(t) := \dfrac{t+2}{t+3}$

   (e) $y = (x^2 + x)^{-2}$

   (f) $v = \dfrac{9z^2 + 12z - 2}{3}$

   (g) $y = \dfrac{ax}{x+b}$

   (h) $y = \dfrac{1}{5x+9}$

   (i) $h(x) := x^5 + 3x^3 - x + \dfrac{1}{x^2}$

   (j) $y = \dfrac{1}{(z^2 + 9)^3}$

   (k) $f(x) := (2x^2 - 5)^{4/3}$

   (l) $g(x) := \dfrac{\sqrt{1+x^2}}{x^2}$

   (m) $h(x) := \sqrt{\dfrac{x+1}{x-3}}$

   (n) $g(x) := \left(\dfrac{1+x^2}{1-x^2}\right)^{10}$

   (o) $g(x) := \sqrt[3]{x(x+5)}$

   (p) $s(t) := \left(t + \dfrac{1}{t}\right)^{2/3}$

2. Determine and classify the critical points of each of the following:

   (a) $y = x^4 - 16x^2$ (b) $y = \dfrac{x}{x+1}$ (c) $g(x) := \dfrac{x}{x^2+9}$

   (d) $f(x) := x + \dfrac{1}{x}$ (e) $f(x) := x^2 + \dfrac{1}{x^2}$

3. Write an equation of the line tangent to the graph of the function in Exercise 2(b) at $x = 0$.

4. Write an equation of the line joining the two local extrema of the function in Exercise 2(d).

5. Suppose $f(3) = 5, g(3) = 2, f'(3) = -4$ and $g'(3) = 1$.

   (a) If $h(x) := f(x)/g(x)$, find $h'(3)$.

   (b) Write an equation of the line tangent to the graph of h at $x = 3$.

6. Let $g(x) := \dfrac{f(x)}{x^2}$. If $y = 3x - 5$ is an equation of the line tangent to the graph of f at $x = 1$, write an equation of the line tangent to the graph of g at $x = 1$.

7. Let $g(x) := xf(x)$, for all x. Suppose f has a local maximum at $(1, 3)$.

   (a) Determine $g'(1)$.

   (b) Show that $g''(1) < 0$.

8. The table below contains information about functions f and g at $x = 1, 2$ and 3.

	f	f'	g	g'
$x = 1$	5	4	2	-2
$x = 2$	3	6	1	0
$x = 3$	-1	7	-2	3

   (a) If $h(x) := x^3 f(x)$, determine $h'(3)$.

   (b) If $h(x) := g(x) - f(x)$, write an equation of the line tangent to the graph of h at $x = 1$.

   (c) If $h(x) := f[g(x)]$, determine $h'(2)$.

9. Determine the direction and concavity of $f(x) := \dfrac{x^2}{x^2 - 4}$. Sketch the graph.

10. Repeat Exercise 9 for $f(x) := x - \dfrac{1}{x}$.

11. Repeat Exercise 9 for $f(x) := \dfrac{x}{x + 3}$.

12. A population of 100 bacteria is introduced into a culture. The number of bacteria at time t is given by the function $N(t) := 100\left(1 + \dfrac{3t}{50 + t^2}\right)$. Find the rate at which the population is growing when $t = 2$.

13. The concentration C of a certain chemical in the bloodstream t hours after injection into muscle tissue is given by $C = \dfrac{3t}{27 + t^3}$. When is the concentration greatest?

14. Suppose $g(x) := \sqrt{f(x)}$. If $f(9) = 16$ and $f'(9) = 2$, what is $g'(9)$?

PROBLEMS FOR SECTION 3.3:

1. (a) If $p(x) := f(x)g(x)$, determine $p''(x)$ and $p'''(x)$.

    (b) If $p(x) := f(x)g(x)h(x)$, where f, g and h are differentiable, determine $p'(x)$.

2. Prove the quotient rule.

3. Let f be the function pictured below and let $g(x) := [f(x)]^2$. Determine the direction and critical points of g and sketch its graph.

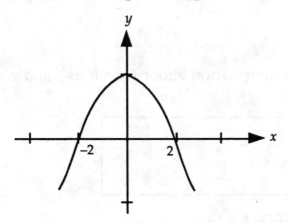

4. Repeat Problem 3 for the function pictured below.

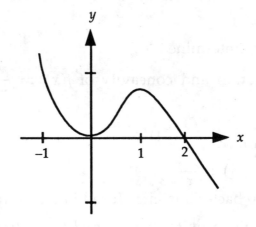

5. Let f and g be functions such that $f(2) = 2, f(5) = 5, g(2) = 5, g(5) = 2,$ $f'(2) = 4, f'(5) = -3, g'(2) = -4$ and $g'(5) = 6$.

    (a) If $p(x) := f(g(x))$, determine $p'(2)$.

    (b) If $q(x) := g(f(x))$, determine $q'(5)$.

    (c) If $r(x) := [f(x)]^2$, determine $r'(5)$.

    (d) If $s(x) := g(x)\sqrt{f(x)}$, determine $s'(5)$.

6. Suppose f is a differentiable function for which $f(x) > 0$ for all x and that $g(x) := [f(x)]^2$.

   (a) Show that any local minimum of f is also a local minimum of g and conversely. Is this statement also true for local maxima?

   (b) Show that part (a) holds if $g(x) := [f(x)]^n$, where n is a positive integer.

7. Find the minimum value of $f(x) := \sqrt{x^2 + 4x + 7}$. (Hint: You may want to use the result of problem 6.)

8. Let f be a function with the following properties:

   $f(0) = 2$, $f'(x) > 0$ for all x, $f''(x) > 0$ for $x > 0$ and $f''(x) < 0$ for $x < 0$

   Let $g(x) := f(x^2)$.

   (a) Find $g(0)$.

   (b) Find the x-coordinates of all local minimum points of g.

   (c) Where is g concave up?

   (d) Sketch a graph of g.

1. $y = 2x^5 - x^4 - 38x^3 + 73x^2 + 10x - 46$ from which y' is correct.

2. (a) $y' = \sqrt{x}\,(2x) + \frac{1}{2}x^{-1/2}(x^2 + 1)$ (b) $f'(x) := (2ax + b)(cx + d) + c(ax^2 + bx)$

3. (a) $h'(3) = -14$ (b) $y - 10 = -14(x - 3)$ or $y = -14x + 52$

4. (a) $y' = \dfrac{(x + 2)(1) - (x + 1)(1)}{(x + 2)^2} = \dfrac{1}{(x + 2)^2}$ (b) $g'(t) := \dfrac{(2t^2 + 1)(2t) - (t^2)(4t)}{(2t^2 + 1)^2}$

   $= \dfrac{2t}{(2t^2 + 1)^2}$ (c) $f'(x) := \dfrac{(x^3 + 6)(2) - (3x^2)(2x)}{(x^3 + 6)^2} = \dfrac{12 - 4x^3}{(x^3 + 6)^2}$ 5. $h'(2) = -7/2$

6. (a) $f'(x) := 6\sqrt{4x + 1}$ (b) $h'(t) := 5\left(t + \frac{1}{t}\right)^4\left(1 - \frac{1}{t^2}\right)$

   (c) $\dfrac{dz}{dx} = -3(x^3 + 6x + 7)^{-4}(3x^2 + 6) = \dfrac{-3(3x^2 + 6)}{(x^3 + 6x + 7)^4}$

7. $y'' = \frac{2x}{3}\left(-\frac{2}{3}\right)(x^2 + 4)^{-5/3}(2x) + \frac{2}{3}(x^2 + 4)^{-2/3} = \frac{-8x^2}{9}(x^2 + 4)^{-5/3} + \frac{2}{3}(x^2 + 4)^{-2/3}$

8. $v(t) := (2t + 1)^{-1/2}$; $a(t) := -(2t + 1)^{-3/2}$ 9. $-1/2$

3.4 ANTIDERIVATIVES

Let's ask the following question: Given the derivative $f'(x)$, is it possible to find $f(x)$? The answer, as we said in Chapter 2, is "yes, if we are given additional information", such as the value of f at some point.

Finding f given its derivative is still a hard problem, much harder than finding the derivative given f. For now, we'll stick to very simple problems; in Chapters 6 and 8, we'll develop techniques for tackling somewhat more complicated ones. Even then, we won't be able to do anything very difficult.

As we hinted earlier, there are infinitely many functions with the same derivative but all those functions differ by a constant. More formally:

THEOREM 3.15: If $f'(x) = g'(x)$ for all x, then $f(x) = g(x) + c$ for all x, where c is a constant.

Before proving Theorem 3.15, here's something you'll believe: If $h'(x) = 0$ for all x, then $h(x) := c$; that is, any function whose derivative is 0 for all x is a constant function. (Again, a proof involves the Mean Value Theorem.)

Now let $h(x) := f(x) - g(x)$. This implies $h'(x) := f'(x) - g'(x) = 0$ for all x. Therefore, $h(x) := c$ implying $f(x) - g(x) = c$ for all x, from which the result follows.

Geometrically, this says that the graphs of f and g are "parallel". See Figure 3.18.

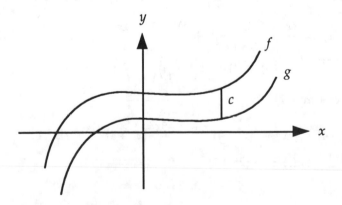

Fig. 3.18

Suppose we are given $f'(x) := 3x^2$. From the power rule, we recognize that this is the derivative of x^3, so f must be of the form $f(x) := x^3 + c$. To find c, we must be given more information. For instance, if we are told that $f(2) = 4$, then $4 = 2^3 + c$ from which $c = -4$. If, instead, $f(3) = 6$, then $6 = 3^3 + c$, from which $c = -21$, etc.

TEST YOUR UNDERSTANDING

1. Suppose $f'(x) := 4x^3$ and $f(2) = 10$. Determine $f(x)$.

DEFINITION: Suppose F and f are functions such that $F'(x) = f(x)$, for all x. Then, we will say that F is an **antiderivative** of f.

Theorem 3.15 implies that if f has any antiderivative, then it has infinitely many antiderivatives, all of which differ from each other by constants. It is also true (and we shall prove this in Chapter 6) that every continuous function has an antiderivative and, hence, infinitely many antiderivatives, although it generally is not possible to express any of them in a nice form.

We need a symbol to represent antiderivatives. Since finding an antiderivative is the inverse of the process of finding derivatives, and since we use $D_x f(x)$ to represent derivatives, then we should use $D_x^{-1} f(x)$ to represent antiderivatives. (The subscript $_x$ is there to remind you that x is the variable in the problem.) For example, since $D_x(x^3) = 3x^2$, then $D_x^{-1}(3x^2) = x^3$. But, as we noted earlier, there are infinitely many other antiderivatives of $3x^2$. If we want to represent all of them, we may write

$$D_x^{-1}(3x^2) = x^3 + c$$

where c is an arbitrary constant.

This is not the only symbol used to represent antiderivatives and, despite the logic behind it, it is not often used. The more common notation makes use of a symbol which will appear a bit odd at this point. If F is an antiderivative of f, then we write $F(x) = \int f(x)\,dx$. The $\int$ is called an **integral sign** and the process of finding antiderivatives is sometimes called **integration**. Again, the "dx" is there to remind you that x is the variable in the problem. We will see why the integral sign is used in Chapter 6, although we hinted at the reason in Chapter 2--the $\int$ is an elongated "S" which stands for "sum", as in Riemann sum. We'll use the two notations interchangeably.

To help us find antiderivatives, we need some rules. First, let's develop a "power rule". The power rule for derivatives says to multiply by the exponent and decrease the exponent by 1. To undo this, we should add 1 to the exponent and divide by the new exponent. Thus, we have:

THEOREM 3.16 (POWER RULE FOR ANTIDERIVATIVES):

$$D_x^{-1}[x^n] = \frac{x^{n+1}}{n+1} + c \ , \ n \neq -1.$$

Why doesn't this hold if $n = -1$? We will consider the case $n = -1$ in Chapter 4.

EXAMPLE 3.26:

Evaluate (a) $D_x^{-1}[x^4]$ (b) $D_x^{-1}[\sqrt{x}]$ (c) $D_x^{-1}\left[\frac{1}{x^3}\right]$

In (a), we invoke Theorem 3.16 with $n = 4$, obtaining $D_x^{-1}[x^4] = \frac{x^5}{5} + c$.

In (b), we use $n = 1/2$, so $D_x^{-1}[\sqrt{x}] = \frac{x^{3/2}}{3/2} + c = \frac{2}{3}x^{3/2} + c$

In (c), we use $n = -3$, so $D_x^{-1}\left[\dfrac{1}{x^3}\right] = \dfrac{x^{-2}}{-2} + c = -\dfrac{1}{2x^2} + c$. ◆

<u>TEST YOUR UNDERSTANDING</u>

2. Evaluate (a) $D_x^{-1}[x^6]$ (b) $D_x^{-1}\left[\dfrac{1}{\sqrt{x}}\right]$ (c) $\displaystyle\int \sqrt[3]{x}\, dx$ (d) $D_x^{-1}[5]$

There are analogs to Theorems 3.4 and 3.5 which we state without proof.

THEOREM 3.17: $D_x^{-1}[f(x) + g(x)] = D_x^{-1}[f(x)] + D_x^{-1}[g(x)]$.

THEOREM 3.18: $D_x^{-1}[kf(x)] = k\,D_x^{-1}[f(x)]$, where k is a constant.

We can now find antiderivatives of all polynomials and certain other rational and algebraic functions.

EXAMPLE 3.27:

Find an antiderivative of $f(x) := 2x^5 - 9x^2 + 4x + 3$.

Using Theorems 3.17 and 3.18, we have:

$$\int \left(2x^5 - 9x^2 + 4x + 3\right) dx = 2\int x^5\, dx - 9\int x^2\, dx + 4\int x\, dx + \int 3\, dx$$

$$= \frac{2x^6}{6} - \frac{9x^3}{3} + \frac{4x^2}{2} + 3x + c$$

$$= \frac{x^6}{3} - 3x^3 + 2x^2 + 3x + c.$$ ◆

EXAMPLE 3.28:

Determine a function f whose derivative is $f'(x) := 4x^3 - 2x + 1$ and whose graph passes through the point (1, 4).

$$f(x) := D_x^{-1}\left[4x^3 - 2x + 1\right] = x^4 - x^2 + x + c$$

To find c, we use the fact that $f(1) = 4$. Substituting $x = 1$ and $f(1) = 4$ gives $4 = 1 - 1 + 1 + c$, from which $c = 3$. Thus, $f(x) := x^4 - x^2 + x + 3$.

$\blacklozenge$

EXAMPLE 3.29:

Evaluate $\int \sqrt{x^3 + 1}\, dx$.

This does not fit the basic power rule since the dx tells us that x is the variable, but it is $x^3 + 1$, not just plain x, that is being raised to the 1/2 power. Therefore, we cannot complete this example with the information we have so far. There are other techniques for finding antiderivatives that we will learn in later chapters, although none of them would help for this particular example.

$\blacklozenge$

This idea of not being able to complete a problem may seem strange since you have always done mathematics in which every problem had an answer or, perhaps, several answers. In fact, many mathematics problems simply don't have answers that can be written down in a "nice" form. One approach to handling such problems is to approximate the answer; we'll learn some techniques for that in later chapters. For now, it is important to recognize when a problem can't be done and leave it at that.

TEST YOUR UNDERSTANDING

3. Complete this statement: If $g'(x) = f(x)$ for all x, then $g(x)$ is called

    _____ and we write $g(x) = $ _____.

4. Evaluate each antiderivative:

    (a) $D_x^{-1}[5x^4 - 6x^2 + 4x - 5]$ (b) $\int (x + 4)(x - 3)\, dx$

(c) $\int \dfrac{x^2+x}{x+1}\,dx$　　　　　　(d) $D_t^{-1}\left[3pt^2+qt+r\right]$

5. Determine a function g such that $g'(x) := \dfrac{1}{x^2}$ and $g(2) = 1$.

❑ There are no "product and quotient rules" for antiderivatives, as there were for derivatives. There is, however, what we might call a "reverse chain rule". Let f and g be differentiable functions and let F be any antiderivative of f. Consider the composite function $h(x) := F(g(x))$. By Theorem 3.14, $h'(x) := F'(g(x))g'(x) = f(g(x))g'(x)$, since f is the derivative of F. Upon antidifferentiating this equation, we have:

THEOREM 3.19: If F is an antiderivative of f, then
$$\int f(g(x))g'(x)\,dx = F(g(x))+c.$$

Or, using the other notation, $D_x^{-1}\left[f(y)\dfrac{dy}{dx}\right] = F(y)+c$, where $y = g(x)$.

As with the chain rule, we will not need Theorem 3.19 in all its generality here. Rather we will primarily need the special case in which f is a power function. In other words, we have:

COROLLARY: $\int [g(x)]^n\, g'(x)\,dx = \dfrac{[g(x)]^{n+1}}{n+1}+c,\ n \neq -1.$

EXAMPLE 3.30:

Evaluate $\int \left(\sqrt{x^2+1} \right)(2x)\,dx$.

If we let $f(x) := \sqrt{x}$ and $g(x) := x^2 + 1$, then $f(g(x)) := \sqrt{x^2+1}$ and $g'(x) := 2x$. This example is exactly of the form in the corollary to Theorem 3.19 with $n = 1/2$. Hence,

$$\int \left(\sqrt{x^2+1} \right)(2x)\,dx = \frac{2(x^2+1)^{3/2}}{3} + c. \text{ You can check this by finding}$$

$D_x\left[\dfrac{2(x^2+1)^{3/2}}{3} \right]$. ◆

EXAMPLE 3.31:

Can Theorem 3.19 be used to evaluate $\int x(x^3+4)^{5/2}\,dx$?

If we let $g(x) := x^3 + 4$, then $g'(x) := 3x^2$. The integrand contains only a factor of x, not $3x^2$. Hence, the integrand is not of the form $[g(x)]^n\,g'(x)$ and Theorem 3.19 does not apply. ◆

Theorem 3.19 will be very useful in Chapter 4 when we solve differential equations and, more importantly, is the basis for the so-called substitution technique for finding antiderivatives that we will study in Chapter 8.

TEST YOUR UNDERSTANDING

6. Evaluate (a) $\int 2(2x+5)^{5/2}\,dx$ (b) $D_x^{-1}\left[(\sqrt{x}+3)^2\left(\frac{1}{2\sqrt{x}}\right) \right]$.

◻ There are many, many applications of antiderivatives. For example, we may be given the velocity of an object $v(t)$. The position $s(t)$ is then obtained--up to a constant-- by finding an antiderivative of v. If we are given some additional information, such as the initial position, then we can find $s(t)$ exactly.

In Chapter 2, we claimed that if an object is dropped from an initial height h, then its height at time t is given by the function $s(t) := h - 16t^2$. We can now prove and generalize this claim.

Assume that the only force acting on the object is gravity (no air resistance) and that the acceleration due to gravity is a constant g. (In English units, $g = 32$ ft./sec.^{2}; in metric units, $g = 9.8$ m./sec.^{2} .) If the ground corresponds to $s = 0$ and the positive direction is upward, then

$$a(t) = s''(t) = -g.$$

(The negative sign is needed because gravity is pulling the object down in the negative direction.)

Taking the antiderivative of both sides, we get

$$v(t) = D_t^{-1}[a(t)] = D_t^{-1}[-g] = -gt + c.$$

Substituting $t = 0$, we get $c = v(0) = v_0$, where v_0 is the initial velocity of the object. Hence,

$$v(t) := -gt + v_0.$$

To get the position function, we take the antiderivative of the velocity function, obtaining

$$s(t) = D_t^{-1}[-gt + v_0] = -\frac{1}{2}gt^2 + v_0t + c.$$

Again substituting $t = 0$, we get $c = s(0) = s_0$, where s_0 is the initial position. Putting it all together, we have:

The distance to the ground of an object subjected only to gravitational acceleration is given by the function $s(t) := -\frac{1}{2}gt^2 + v_0t + s_0$, where v_0 is the initial velocity and s_0 is the initial height.

For example, if the object is just dropped from height h, then $v_0 = 0$ and $s_0 = h$, so $s(t) := -\frac{1}{2}gt^2 + h = h - 16t^2$ if g is measured in ft./sec.^{2} and h is measured in ft.

EXAMPLE 3.32:

Suppose the ball is thrown upward with initial velocity 24 ft./sec. from inital height 40 ft. At what time does the ball begin to fall and when does it hit the ground?

Since $v_0 = 24$ and $s_0 = 40$, we have $s(t) := -16t^2 + 24t + 40$.

The ball begins to fall when its velocity is 0. $v(t) := -32t + 24 = 0$ when $t = 3/4$.

The ball hits the ground when $s(t) = 0$.

$$-16t^2 + 24t + 40 = 0$$

$$-8(2t - 5)(t + 1) = 0$$

Therefore, $t = 5/2$. (The root $t = -1$ makes no sense physically.) ◆

TEST YOUR UNDERSTANDING

7. An object, dropped from a tower, hits the ground after 3 seconds. How tall is the tower?

EXERCISES FOR SECTION 3.4:

1. Evaluate the following antiderivatives, if possible:

(a) $D_x^{-1}[2x^2 + 1]$

(b) $D_x^{-1}\left[\dfrac{1}{x^4}\right]$

(c) $\displaystyle\int 4\,dt$

(d) $D_y^{-1}[ay + b]$

(e) $\displaystyle\int \dfrac{1}{x}\,dx$

(f) $\displaystyle\int (1 - 5x)\,dx$

(g) $D_x^{-1}\left[\dfrac{1}{5}x^4 + \dfrac{1}{2}x^3 - \dfrac{1}{x^2}\right]$

(h) $D_t^{-1}\left[(t^2 + 1)^2\right]$

(i) $\displaystyle\int \dfrac{v^2 + 4}{v^2}\,dv$

(j) $\displaystyle\int x^2(x - 5)\,dx$

(k) $\displaystyle\int \dfrac{1}{(x^3 + 1)^2}\,dx$

(l) $\displaystyle\int \left(3p\,t^2 + qt\right)dt$

2. Determine a function g such that $g'(x) := 4x + 6$ and $g(1) = 2$.

3. Determine a function h such that $h'(x) := 3x^2 + 2x - 3$ and $h(2) = 6$.

4. Determine a function f such that $f'(x) := \dfrac{1}{x^2}$ and $f(1) = 1$.

5. Determine $f(x)$ if $f(1) = 2$, $f'(1) = -3$, and $f''(x) := 2$ for all x.

6. Determine $g(x)$ if $g''(x) := 4x$, $g(-1) = 4$ and $g(-1) = 5$.

7. Sketch 3 different functions whose derivatives are $f'(x) = 2x + 1$.

8. Evaluate each of the following antiderivatives, if possible:

   (a) $\int 5(5x - 8)^{2/3}\, dx$ (b) $D_x^{-1}\left[\dfrac{1}{(2x + 5)^3}\right]$ (c) $\int 3x^2(x^3 + 1)^5\, dx$

   (d) $\int x^2\sqrt{x^4 + 2x + 1}\, dx$ (e) $\int \dfrac{1}{y^2}\left(1 - \dfrac{1}{y}\right)^3 dy$

9. An object is dropped from a balloon at 1600 ft. Express its height above the ground as a function of t. How long does it take the object to reach the ground?

10. An object is dropped from initial height h. Three seconds later it is 126 ft off the ground. What is h?

11. A ball is thrown upward from the ground with initial velocity v. Two seconds later it is 104 ft. off the ground. What is v?

12. A stone is thrown vertically upward with an initial velocity of 64 ft/sec. from an initial height of 80 ft.

    (a) How long will it take the stone to stop rising?

    (b) How high will the stone go?

    (c) When will the stone strike the ground?

13. A car travels in a straight line with constant acceleration $a = 6$ ft/sec². If its initial velocity is $v = 40$ ft/sec.,

    (a) how long does it take for the car to travel 147 ft?

    (b) what is its velocity at that time?

14. Verify by differentiating that $D_x^{-1}\left[x^3\sqrt{x^2 - 1}\right] = \dfrac{(x^2 - 1)^{5/2}}{5} + \dfrac{(x^2 - 1)^{3/2}}{3} + c$

PROBLEMS FOR SECTION 3.4:

1. Let f be a function whose second derivative is $f''(x) = 4x + 6$. An equation of the line tangent to the graph at $x = 3$ is $y = 8x - 9$. Determine f.

2. (a) Determine all functions with the property that the slope of the tangent to the curve at any point is equal to the square of the x-coordinate at the point of tangency.

(b) Determine the specific function with the property above that passes through the point (1, 2).

3. An object is dropped from a height of 64 ft. Another object is thrown downward from a height of 112 ft. What should its initial velocity be so that the two objects hit the ground at the same time?

4. A ball is thrown upward with initial velocity of 48 ft./sec. from a hotel balcony 160 feet above the ground. After 2 seconds, a guest in her room saw the ball pass her.

   (a) How fast was the ball going when she saw it?

   (b) Was it going up or down when she saw it?

   (c) Was her room above or below the balcony?

   (d) A guest whose room was 96 feet above the ground also saw the ball pass his window. How many seconds after it was thrown did he see it?

   (e) How fast was it going when he saw it?

5. Find a cubic polynomial that has a local maximum at (2, 4), a local minimum at (4, 2) and an inflection point at (3, 3).

6. An object is thrown upward with initial velocity v_0 from height h. Let $t^* =$ time the object hits the ground. Express t^* in terms of v_0 and h. If h is constant, how does t^* depend on v_0?

7. A 1970 429CJ Mustang could run the standing quarter mile in 13.20 seconds. Determine the acceleration assuming that it is a constant.

TYU Answers for Section 3.4

1. $f(x) := x^4 - 6$ 2. (a) $\frac{x^7}{7} + c$ (b) $2\sqrt{x} + c$ (c) $\frac{3}{4}x^{4/3} + c$ (d) $5x + c$

3. an antiderivative of f; $\int f(x)\,dx$ or $D_x^{-1}[f(x)]$ 4. (a) $x^5 - 2x^3 + 2x^2 - 5x + c$

   (b) $\frac{x^3}{3} + \frac{x^2}{2} - 12x + c$ (c) $\frac{x^2}{2} + c$ (d) $pt^3 + \frac{qt^2}{2} + rt + c$ 5. $g(x) := \frac{-1}{x} + \frac{3}{2}$

6. (a) $\frac{2}{7}(2x+5)^{7/2} + c$ (b) $\frac{1}{3}(\sqrt{x}+3)^3 + c$ 7. 144 feet or 44.1 meters

QUESTIONS TO THINK ABOUT

1. Explain what is meant by the statement $\lim_{x \to a} f(x) = L$.

2. State the definition (involving limits) of the derivative of a function and explain it in geometric terms.

3. Explain the relationships among the graphs of f and its derivatives. That is, relate the geometric and algebraic information available from one graph to the same kind of information about the other graphs.

4. Discuss the following statement: If you know the position of a falling body at some time and its velocity at some time, you know everything about its motion.

PROJECT 3.1

DERIVATIVES OF TRIGONOMETRIC FUNCTIONS

OBJECTIVE: In Chapter 2, we briefly mentioned the existence of transcendental functions, such as trigonometric, exponential and logarithmic functions. When we attempted to find the derivatives of these functions in this chapter, we ran into difficulties evaluating certain limits. In this project, we will investigate the trigonometric functions $f(x) := \sin(x)$ and $g(x) := \cos(x)$ in more detail and actually determine their derivatives.

PROCEDURE:

Part 1: Graphical analysis

    a. Use a computer or calculator to draw graphs of $f(x) := \sin(x)$ and $g(x) := \cos(x)$ on separate axes, for $-2\pi \le x \le 2\pi$.

    b. For what values of x is $f(x)$ positive? increasing? concave up? Where are the local extrema? the inflection points?

    c. Repeat 1b for $g(x)$.

    d. Do you see a connection between the direction of f and the sign of g? between the direction of g and the sign of f?

Part 2: Using the definition of the derivative

    a. By definition, $f'(x) := \lim\limits_{\Delta x \to 0} \dfrac{\sin(x + \Delta x) - \sin(x)}{\Delta x}$. Using the fact that $\sin(a + b) = \sin(a)\cos(b) + \cos(a)\sin(b)$, show that

$$f'(x) := \sin(x)\lim_{\Delta x \to 0} \frac{\cos(\Delta x) - 1}{\Delta x} + \cos(x)\lim_{\Delta x \to 0} \frac{\sin(\Delta x)}{\Delta x}$$

    b. Both of the limits in the expression above are indeterminate forms $(0/0)$. Use a calculator to evaluate $\dfrac{\sin(\Delta x)}{\Delta x}$ and $\dfrac{\cos(\Delta x) - 1}{\Delta x}$ for $\Delta x = 1, .1, .01$ and $.001$. What conclusion might you draw about $\lim\limits_{\Delta x \to 0} \dfrac{\sin(\Delta x)}{\Delta x}$ and $\lim\limits_{\Delta x \to 0} \dfrac{\cos(\Delta x) - 1}{\Delta x}$?

    c. Assuming your conclusion in Part 2b is correct, what is $f'(x)$?

    d. Repeat these steps to find $g'(x)$. This time you will need the fact that $\cos(a + b) = \cos(a)\cos(b) - \sin(a)\sin(b)$.

    e. Do your answers to 2c and 2d agree with 1d? Explain.

    f. Determine $f''(x)$ and $g''(x)$. What are the implications of these results for the concavity of f and g?

Part 3: Some practice

   a. Suppose $y = \sin(u)$ where u is a function of x. Use the chain rule to determine $\dfrac{dy}{dx}$.

   b. Find the derivative of each of the following:

      (i) $y = 3\cos(x)$ (ii) $y = \sin(4x)$ (iii) $y = [\sin(x)]^3$

      (iv) $y = x^2\cos(x)$ (v) $y = \sin(x)\cos(x)$ (vi) $y = \dfrac{\sin(x)}{x}$

Part 4: A trigonometric identity

   a. Let $h(x) := [f(x)]^2 + [g(x)]^2 = \sin^2(x) + \cos^2(x)$. Express $h'(x)$ in terms of $f(x), f'(x), g(x)$ and $g'(x)$.

   b. Show that $h(x)$ is a constant function; that is, $h(x) := c$, for all x.

   c. If $f(0) = 0$ and $g(0) = 1$, determine c.

Part 5: Other trigonometric functions

   a. The **tangent** function is defined by $\tan(x) := \dfrac{\sin(x)}{\cos(x)}$. Determine the derivative of $\tan(x)$.

   b. The **secant** function is defined by $\sec(x) := \dfrac{1}{\cos(x)}$. Determine the derivative of $\sec(x)$.

ANALYZING CUBIC POLYNOMIALS

OBJECTIVE: In this project, we will analyze cubic polynomials of the form $p(x) := x^3 + ax^2 + bx + c$, where a, b and c are constants. Unlike quadratic polynomials, whose graphs are always parabolas, cubic polynomials may take several different shapes depending on the coefficients a, b and c.

PROCEDURE:

Part 1: Preliminary observations

  a. Let $p(x)$ be a cubic polynomial of the form described above. Determine $\lim_{x \to \infty} p(x)$ and $\lim_{x \to -\infty} p(x)$. What does this mean about the graph of p?

  b. Can the equation $p(x) = 0$ have no real roots? one real root? two real roots? three real roots? more than three real roots? Draw a rough sketch of a cubic polynomial for each of these cases, if possible.

  c. What effect does the constant term c have on the graph?

Part 2: A special case

  a. Let $p(x) := x^3 + bx$ (that is, with $a = c = 0$). Graph $p(x)$ for the cases $b = -4, b = -1, b = 0, b = 1$ and $b = 4$.

  b. For each case above, describe the direction, concavity and local extrema of p. What are the roots of $p(x) = 0$?

  c. What general statements can you make about the behavior of $p(x) := x^3 + bx$? You might consider two cases: $b < 0$ and $b \geq 0$.

  d. Use calculus to verify your statements in 2c.

Part 3: The more general case

  a. Now let $p(x) := x^3 + ax^2 + bx + c$. Determine $p'(x)$.

  b. Determine the roots of the equation $p'(x) = 0$. Under what conditions are the roots real?

  c. Sketch a graph of $p'(x)$ if the roots of $p'(x) = 0$ are not real numbers. What can we say about the direction of p in this case?

  d. Repeat 3c for the case when the roots of $p'(x) = 0$ are real numbers.

  e. Summarize your conclusions about the general shape of $p(x)$ in terms of its coefficients. Choose some representative values of a, b and c illustrating the different cases. Draw a graph of $p(x)$ in each case.

PROJECT 3.3

THE MEAN VALUE THEOREM

OBJECTIVE: One of the most important theoretical results in calculus is the Mean Value Theorem. It is used to prove many of the results in this chapter such as the theorem that says that a function is increasing wherever its derivative is positive. In this project, we'll ask you to derive the Mean Value Theorem, then use it to prove some results.

PROCEDURE:

Part 1: The intuitive basis

Claim: If you average v miles per hour on a trip, then at some point during the trip, your instantaneous velocity must have been v.

a. Do you believe this claim? Support your answer with an argument using your intuitions about instantaneous and average velocity.

b. What information do you need about a trip to find the average velocity over a given time interval $[a, b]$? How would you find the average velocity if you knew this information?

Suppose the position of a particle at any time t in the time interval $[0, 3]$ is given by $s(t) := 2t^3 - 9t^2 + 12t$.

c. What is the average velocity of the particle over this time interval?

d. At what time during the interval $[0, 3]$ is the instantaneous velocity of the particle equal to its average velocity? How many such times are there?

Part 2: The Mean Value Theorem

Let f be a function that is continuous and differentiable on a closed interval $[a, b]$. Then there is a number c, between a and b, such that

$$f'(c) = \frac{f(b) - f(a)}{b - a}.$$

a. Explain this theorem in terms of tangent lines and secant lines.

b. Explain this theorem in terms of instantaneous and average velocity.

c. Let $f(x) := x^3 + x$. Find the value of c guaranteed by the Mean Value Theorem on the interval $[0, 4]$. Draw a graph of f and interpret the result using this graph.

d. Repeat 2c for the function $f(x) := x^4 - 2x^2$ on the interval $[-2, 2]$.

e. Show for $f(x) := \dfrac{1}{x^2}$ that there is no value of c on the interval $[-3, 3]$ such that $f'(c) = \dfrac{f(3)-f(-3)}{3-(-3)}$. Why doesn't this invalidate the Mean Value Theorem?

f. Show for $f(x) := x^{2/3}$ that there is no value of c on the interval $[-1, 1]$ such that $f'(c) = \dfrac{f(1)-f(-1)}{1-(-1)}$. Why doesn't this invalidate the Mean Value Theorem?

Part 3: Some consequences

a. Let $f(x) := x^2 + px + q$, where p and q are constants. Show that for any interval $[a, b]$, the value of c guaranteed by the Mean Value Theorem is the midpoint of the interval $[a, b]$.

b. Let $f(x) := \sqrt{1+x}$. Show that $f'(x) < \dfrac{1}{2}$ for all $x > 0$. Then use this and the Mean Value Theorem to show that $f(x) < 1 + \dfrac{1}{2}x$, for all $x > 0$.   Hint: Consider the interval $[0, t]$, for some $t > 0$.

c. Show that $(1 + x)^p < 1 + px$, for $x > 0$ and $0 < p \le 1$.

d. A **fixed point** of a function f is a number c such that $f(c) = c$. Show that if $f'(x) < 1$ for all x, then f has no more than one fixed point. Hint: Assume there are two fixed points, a and b. Use the Mean Value Theorem on the interval $[a, b]$ to show a contradiction.

Part 4: More consequences

We have said throughout the text that the Mean Value Theorem can be used to prove many results that we intuitively believe are correct. Here, we ask you to prove some of them.

a. Show that if $f'(x) = 0$ for all x on some interval $[a, b]$, then f is a constant function on that interval.

b. Use 4a to show that if $f'(x) = g'(x)$ for all x on $[a, b]$, then f and g differ by a constant. Hint: Let $h(x) := f(x) - g(x)$.

c. Show that if $f'(x) > 0$ for all x on some interval $[a, b]$, then f is increasing on that interval.

PROJECT 3.4

APPROXIMATING FUNCTIONS BY POLYNOMIALS

OBJECTIVE: There are many practical instances in which it is difficult to evaluate functions exactly. For example, suppose we wanted to find $\sqrt{4.1}$. Unless you have a calculator handy, this is not so easy to do. The purpose of this project is to develop a method for approximating the value of a function. Our approach is to derive a sequence $p_1(x)$, $p_2(x)$,..., where $p_n(x)$ is a polynomial of degree n. The polynomials are chosen so that their values approach $f(x)$, at least for x near some number c. The reason for using polynomials is that they can be evaluated easily, requiring only addition and multiplication. The polynomials we obtain are called **Taylor polynomials**, named after the 17th century mathematician Brook Taylor.

PROCEDURE:
Part 1: Tangent line approximation--the first degree polynomial
  Let f be a function that is differentiable in an interval containing $x = c$.
  a. Show that the line tangent to f at $x = c$ is represented by the function
     $$p_1(x) := f(c) + f'(c)(x - c)$$
  b. What is the y-value on the tangent line where $x = c + \Delta x$?
  c. Why should the y-value in 1b--that is, $p_1(c + \Delta x)$-- be a good
     approximation to $f(c + \Delta x)$ if Δx is small? Draw a picture to
     illustrate.
  d. To compute $\sqrt{4.1}$, let $f(x) := \sqrt{x}$, $c = 4$ and $\Delta x = .1$. Write an
     equation of the tangent line at $x = 4$ and compute the value of y on
     the tangent line corresponding to $x = 4.1$. This is the approximation
     to $\sqrt{4.1}$. Note: We chose $c = 4$ because it is close to 4.1 and because
     $f(4)$ and $f'(4)$ are easy to compute.

Part 2: Some more examples
  a. Use this technique to approximate $\sqrt{3.8}$ and $\sqrt{9.08}$. In each case, what is
     the best choice for c and Δx?
  b. Let $f(x) := x^3 - 4x$. Use this technique to approximate $f(2.05)$ and
     $f(0.1)$. Use your calculator to compute $f(2.05)$ and $f(0.1)$ exactly and
     compare to your approximations.
  c. Use tangent line approximation to estimate $\sqrt[3]{8.1}$ and $\dfrac{1}{4.05}$. What
     should you use for $f(x)$?

    d. The radius of a circle increases from 5 to 5.2 inches. Use tangent line approximation to estimate the increase in the area of the circle.

    e. A rope is wrapped around the earth on the surface along the equator. If the length of the rope is increased by 1 mile and formed into a circle along the equator, approximately how far above the surface will it lie? (Assume the earth is a perfect sphere of radius 4000 miles.)

    f. Approximate the volume of water needed to cover the surface of the earth to a depth of one foot. (Hint: One foot = .00019 miles. Find the change in the volume of the sphere.)

Part 3: Better approximations

The tangent line only gives good approximations when Δx is small. To get better approximations, we might try using a curve that is bent the same way as f in the vicinity of $x = c$; that is, a function whose second derivative (concavity) agrees with f at $x = c$.

    a. Show that the function p_1 in 1a satisfies $p_1(c) = f(c)$ and $p_1'(c) = f(c)$.

    b. Let $p_2(x) = f(c) + f'(c)(x - c) + \dfrac{f''(c)}{2}(x - c)^2$. Show that $p_2(c) = f(c)$, $p_2'(c) = f'(c)$ and $p_2''(c) = f''(c)$.

    c. Notice that $p_2(x) = p_1(x)$ + another term. If x is very near c, would you expect this additional term to be large or small in value? Explain.

    d. For the function $f(x) = \sqrt{x}$ and $c = 4$, determine the function p_2.

    e. Graph f and p_2 on the same axes for $0 \le x \le 9$.

    f. Use p_2 to estimate $\sqrt{4.1}$. Is this is closer to the "real answer" than the estimate obtained by p_1? Use your graph to explain.

Part 4: Even better approximations

In Part 3, we used a quadratic function to approximate f. We claimed that the resulting estimates are closer to the real answers than the estimates obtained in Parts 1 and 2. It seems logical that we could get even better approximations by using a cubic or higher degree polynomial.

    a. What additional property should the third degree polynomial have?

    b. Let $p_3(x) = f(c) + f'(c)(x - c) + \dfrac{f''(c)}{2}(x - c)^2 + B(x - c)^3$. For what value of B (in terms of some derivative of f) will r have the desired properties? Use p_3 to estimate $\sqrt{4.1}$.

    c. What would the fourth degree approximating polynomial look like?

    d. What would the nth degree polynomial look like?

PROJECT 3.5

NEWTON'S METHOD

OBJECTIVE: There are many situations in mathematics that require solving equations for which an explicit algebraic solution is difficult, or impossible, to obtain. Some examples are polynomials of degree 3 or higher that don't factor and equations involving trigonometric or other transcendental functions.

One approach to solving equations of this type is to write them in the form $f(x) = 0$ for some function f, graph f and estimate where the graph crosses the x-axis. This approach is limited by the resolution and accuracy of the graph. In this project, we develop a numerical method, called **Newton's method**, for solving equations that, under most circumstances, produces results to a high degree of accuracy in a relatively short time.

PROCEDURE:

Part 1: A motivational example

In Chapter 1, we considered the following problem: An open-topped box is formed by cutting squares from the corners of an 8" x 15" piece of cardboard and folding up the sides. We showed that if x is the length of the side of the cut-out square, then the volume of the box is given by the function $V(x) := x(8 - 2x)(15 - 2x)$, where x is restricted to the domain $\{x \mid 0 \le x \le 4\}$ so that we don't cut more cardboard than is there. The question is: For what value of x will the box have a volume of 50 cu. in.?

a. Determine a function f such that the question above is equivalent to solving the equation $f(x) = 0$.

b. Make a table of values of the function f for $x = 0, 1, 2, 3$ and 4.

c. Why can we claim that the equation $f(x) = 0$ has two roots on the interval [0, 4]--one between 0 and 1, the other between 3 and 4?

d. Draw a graph of the function f and indicate the two roots.

e. Is the root between 0 and 1 closer to 0 or 1? To what integer is the root between 3 and 4 closest?

Part 2: An example of Newton's method

Let x^* be the positive root of the equation $x^2 - 2 = 0$. Our goal is to find x^*.

a. Draw a graph of $f(x) := x^2 - 2$ and indicate x^*.

b. Clearly, x^* is between 1 and 2. Let $x_0 = 1$. Write an equation of the line tangent to the graph at $x = 1$.

c. At what point does the tangent line in 2b intersect the x-axis? Call this value x_1. Is x^* closer to x_1 than it is to 1?

d. Write an equation of the line tangent to the graph at x_1. Determine its intersection with the x-axis. Call that value x_2.

e. Repeat the procedure in 2d once more to determine a new value x_3. Each of the successive values obtained in 2c, 2d and 2e should be closer to x^*. This is the basis of Newton's method.

Part 3: A generalization

Let f be a continuous function and let x^* be a root of $f(x) = 0$. Let x_0 be a number near x^*.

a. Write an equation of the line tangent to the graph of f at x_0.

b. Show that the line in 3a intersects the x-axis at $x_1 = x_0 - \dfrac{f(x_0)}{f'(x_0)}$.

More generally, it follows that the nth estimate of x^* is given by

$x_n = x_{n-1} - \dfrac{f(x_{n-1})}{f'(x_{n-1})}$, $n \geq 1$. This procedure of generating successive estimates to the root of an equation is Newton's method. If the function is nicely behaved, the values generated by Newton's method should get closer to x^* rapidly. It can be shown that it is rarely necessary to use more than 4 or 5 steps (or iterations) of Newton's method to get as much accuracy as any calculator can handle.

c. Use 3 iterations of Newton's method to estimate the root of the equation in 1a that is between 3 and 4.

d. Repeat 3c to estimate the root between 0 and 1.

Part 4: More problems

a. Use Newton's method to estimate $\sqrt[3]{4}$ to 3 decimal places. Hint: $\sqrt[3]{4}$ is a root of the equation $x^3 - 4 = 0$.

b. Draw a graph of $y = 2\sin(x)$ and $y = x$ on the same axes and estimate the positive root of $2\sin(x) = x$ to the nearest integer. Then use Newton's method to calculate this root to 3 decimal places.

c. Suppose we use Newton's method to find $\sqrt{k}$. Show that the formula in 3b can be written as $x_n = \dfrac{1}{2}\left[x_{n-1} + \dfrac{k}{x_{n-1}}\right]$. Apply this formula to find $\sqrt{20}$.

d. Derive a formula similar to the one in 4c for finding cube roots.

Generally, Newton's method converges to the desired root quickly.
However, there are cases where "bad" things happen.

e. Suppose we wanted to find the root of $x^3 - 3x + 1 = 0$ between 1 and 2.
Can we start Newton's method with $x_0 = 1$?

f. Repeat 4b starting with $x_0 = 1$. What happens to successive estimates?
Illustrate with a graph showing the tangent lines.

g. Repeat 4b with $x_0 = .9$. To which root do the estimates converge?

CHAPTER 4

DIFFERENTIAL EQUATIONS AND EXPONENTIAL FUNCTIONS

4.1 DIFFERENTIAL EQUATIONS

In Section 1.1, we studied the following problem: A 10 gallon tank of water has 3 pounds of salt dissolved in it. Fresh water is poured into the tank at a rate of 2 gallons per day. We argued that the amount of salt in the tank would decrease toward zero as t increases.

Now let's consider a variation of that problem. Rather than pouring in fresh water, we'll pour in salt water, whose concentration is 0.5 lbs./gal. Let $p(t)$:= number of pounds of salt in the tank at time t (measured in days). During a short time interval $[t, t + \Delta t]$, some of the salt water in the tank is removed and replaced by other salt water. Since $\frac{1}{5}$ of the contents of the tank (and, hence, $\frac{1}{5}$ of the salt) is removed per day, then the amount of salt removed in Δt days is approximately $\frac{p(t)}{5} \Delta t$. (We say "approximately" because $p(t)$ is not constant during the time interval $[t, t + \Delta t]$. However, we'll assume that if Δt is small, the error introduced by assuming that $p(t)$ is constant is negligible.) The amount of salt added per day is (2 gal)(0.5 lb/gal) = 1 lbs.; hence, the amount of salt added in Δt days is $(1)\Delta t = \Delta t$.

Since the amount of salt at time $t + \Delta t$ is the amount of salt at time t minus the amount removed plus the amount added, we have:

(1) $\qquad p(t + \Delta t) \approx p(t) - \frac{p(t)}{5} \Delta t + 1 \Delta t.$

The approximation improves as Δt approaches 0.

Upon subtracting $p(t)$ and dividing by Δt, Eq. (1) becomes:

(2) $$\frac{p(t+\Delta t)-p(t)}{\Delta t} \approx 1-\frac{p(t)}{5}.$$

By taking the limit as $\Delta t \to 0$ and recalling the definition of the derivative, we get:

(3) $$\frac{dp}{dt} = 1-\frac{p}{5}.$$

Let's see what information we can derive about $p(t)$ from Eq.(3). First note that $\frac{dp}{dt} > 0$ whenever $p < 5$. Since $p(0) = 3$ (we started with 3 lbs. of salt in the tank), then p is increasing initially. If p ever equals 5, then $\frac{dp}{dt} = 0$ and p will stop increasing. If $p > 5$, then $\frac{dp}{dt} < 0$, so p would decrease.

By differentiating Eq.(3) with respect to t (invoking the chain rule) we get:

(4) $$\frac{d^2 p}{dt^2} = \frac{-1}{5}\frac{dp}{dt} = \frac{-1}{5}\left(1-\frac{p}{5}\right) = \frac{p-5}{25}$$

Thus, p is concave down if $p < 5$ and concave up if $p > 5$. Putting this all together, we get a function like the one pictured in Figure 4.1. (Admittedly, we've waved our hands a bit here. You might try to make the argument more precise.) Notice how much information we can get about p, even though we don't yet have a formula for p in terms of t.

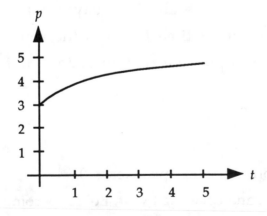

Fig. 4.1

Note: This result is rather intuitive. Eventually, all the water originally in the tank is drained away to be replaced by the water whose salt concentration is 0.5 lbs./gal. So, in a 10 gallon tank, there should eventually be (10)(0.5) = 5 lbs. of salt. Furthermore, the rate at which the solutions are exchanged, in our case 2 gal./day, has no effect on the limiting value of p.

◻ Eq.(3) is an example of a **differential equation**. Quite simply, a differential equation is an equation involving a function and one or more of its derivatives. Many important applications of calculus involve differential equations. Some examples of differential equations are:

(5) $$\frac{dy}{dx} - 5y = 0$$

(6) $$\frac{d^2 y}{dx^2} + x\frac{dy}{dx} - 7y = x^2 + 1$$

(7) $$\left(\frac{dy}{dt}\right)^2 - \frac{4}{y} = \sin(t)$$

The highest derivative that appears in the equation is called the **order** of the differential equation. Eqs. (5) and (7) above are **first-order** equations; Eq.(6) is **second-order**. (Note: The first term in Eq.(7) is the square of the first derivative, not the second derivative; hence, it is a first-order equation.) We've chosen to use the $\frac{dy}{dx}$ notation for derivatives; we could have used y', in which case Eq.(5) becomes $y' - 5y = 0$. The disadvantage to doing so is that it is not clear what the independent variable is.

We have already solved some differential equations. Whenever we find an antiderivative, we are actually solving a first-order differential equation. If we write $\int 3x^2\,dx = x^3 + c$, we are really describing all functions whose derivative with respect to x is $3x^2$. In other words, we are finding all the solutions of the first-order differential equation

$$\frac{dy}{dx} = 3x^2 .$$

Note that there are infinitely many solutions, one for each value of c. Solutions corresponding to $c = -3$, 0 and 3 are shown in Figure 4.2.

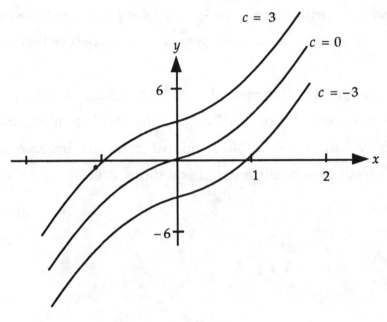

Fig. 4.2

If we are given additional information such as the value of y for some x (i.e., a point on the solution curve), then we can solve for c. For instance, if $y = 1$ when $x = 0$, then c must equal 1.

We need to be a bit more specific about what we mean by "solving" a differential equation. Unlike algebraic equations (such as $x^2 - 4x + 3 = 0$), for which the solutions are numbers, <u>the solutions of a differential equation are functions</u>. Typically, there are infinitely many functions that satisfy a given differential equation. The **general solution** is a function (or functions) expressed in terms of one or more constants that represents *every possible* solution of the equation. In other words, by changing the values of the constants, we get different functions, all of which satisfy the differential equation. Sometimes, we may be given enough information to determine the constants, in which case we have a **specific solution** (possibly unique) satisfying some initial conditions.

Thus, the general solution of the equation $\frac{dy}{dx} = 3x^2$ is $y = x^3 + c$. The specific solution satisfying the condition $y(0) = 1$ is $y = x^3 + 1$.

- -

TEST YOUR UNDERSTANDING

1. (a) Find the general solution of the differential equation $\frac{dy}{dx} = 4x$.

(b) Sketch several solutions of this equation.

(c) Find the specific solution of $\frac{dy}{dx} = 4x$ satisfying $y(2) = 3$.

- -

EXAMPLE 4.1:

(a) Show that every function of the form $y = ax^2 + bx$, where a and b are constants, satisfies the differential equation

$$x^2 \frac{d^2 y}{dx^2} - 2x \frac{dy}{dx} + 2y = 0.$$

(b) Find the specific solution to the differential equation above that satisfies $y(1) = 3$ and $y(2) = 10$.

If $y = ax^2 + bx$, then $\frac{dy}{dx} = 2ax + b$ and $\frac{d^2 y}{dx^2} = 2a$. Substituting into the differential equation, we get:

$$x^2(2a) - 2x(2ax + b) + 2(ax^2 + bx) = 2ax^2 - 4ax^2 - 2bx + 2ax^2 + 2bx$$

$= 0$, for all x. Thus, $y = ax^2 + bx$ is a solution for every value of a and b.

In (b), we are looking for is values of a and b so that $y = 3$ when $x = 1$ and $y = 10$ when $x = 2$.

Substituting $x = 1$ and $y = 3$ gives $3 = a + b$.

Substituting $x = 2$ and $y = 10$ gives $10 = 4a + 2b$.

The solution to this system of equations is $a = 2$ and $b = 1$; hence, the specific solution of the differential equation is $y = 2x^2 + x$. ♦

<u>TEST YOUR UNDERSTANDING</u>

2. Show that every function of the form $y = \sqrt{a^2 + x^2}$ satisfies the differential equation $y \dfrac{dy}{dx} = x$.

Note that we have not claimed that *every* solution of the differential equation in Example 4.1 is of the form $y = ax^2 + bx$, for some a and b. There may be solutions that don't look anything like $y = ax^2 + bx$ (although, in this particular case, that happens not to be true).

It is not hard to believe that the general solution of a first-order equation contains one constant and that it is sufficient to specify a point on the solution curve--that is, the value of y corresponding to some value of x--in order to determine that constant. An interesting question is what happens for second-order equations? There should be two constants, but what kind of information guarantees a unique specific solution?   In Example 4.1, we specified two points on the curve but this is not the only possibility. We won't answer this question here since we will only deal with first-order differential equations in this chapter. However, we will look at it in Chapter 7 when we deal with second-order equations.

¤ In general, solving differential equations is difficult and there is no universal method that can be applied to every equation. However, there are techniques that can be applied to certain simple equations. We will consider one of those techniques here. In Chapters 7 and 11, we will look at a few others. If you want to learn more about solving differential equations, you should take an entire course in the subject.

Let's look more carefully at the equation $\frac{dy}{dx} = 3x^2$. Both the left and right sides of this equation are functions of x so we can antidifferentiate both sides with respect to x:

$$D_x^{-1}\left[\frac{dy}{dx}\right] = D_x^{-1}\left[3x^2\right]$$

Since an antiderivative of $\frac{dy}{dx}$ is y, we have

$$y = x^3 + c.$$

(Technically, there should be a constant of integration on each side of the equation--that is, $y + c_1 = x^3 + c_2$. This, however, is the same as $y = x^3 + c_2 - c_1$. Since c_2 and c_1 are constants, then so is $c_2 - c_1$, which we will simply call c. From now on, we will only put the constant of integration on one side of the equation when we find the antiderivatives.)

Here's another way of thinking about this. If we consider $\frac{dy}{dx}$ as the ratio of the infinitesimal quantities dy and dx, then we can multiply both sides of this equation by dx, obtaining:

$$dy = 3x^2\,dx$$

Now find the antiderivative of both sides.

$$\int dy = \int 3x^2\,dx$$

or, in other words, $y = x^3 + c$.

Note: This is really a bit of sleight-of-hand. Technically, dy and dx are not separate quantities and the derivative is not their quotient. So it really makes no sense to "multiply by dx". However, one of the benefits of using this notation is that we can do mechanical things that produce the right answers, even though they are technically suspect.

- -

TEST YOUR UNDERSTANDING

3. (a) Find the general solution of the differential equation $\frac{dy}{dx} = x^{-2}$.

   (b) Find the specific solution of $\frac{dy}{dx} = x^{-2}$ satisfying $y(1) = 3$.

- -

It is clear that any differential equation of the form $\frac{dy}{dx} = g(x)$ can be solved in the same manner, provided we can find an antiderivative of g in closed form. Let's go one step further. Suppose we had an equation which could be written in the form

(8) $\quad h(y)\dfrac{dy}{dx} = g(x)$.

Again, if y is a function of x, then both sides of this equation are functions of x, so we can antidifferentiate with respect to x.

(9) $\quad D_x^{-1}\left[h(y)\dfrac{dy}{dx}\right] = D_x^{-1}[g(x)]$

Let H be an antiderivative of h. Then by Theorem 3.19, the left side of Eq.(9) is $H(y)$. If G is an antiderivative of g, then the right side of Eq.(9) is $G(x)$. Hence, the solution of Eq.(8) can be expressed as:

(10) $\quad H(y) = G(x) + c$

where c is an arbitrary constant.

Again, it is easier to think of this by treating dy and dx as separate quantities. Upon multiplying both sides of Eq.(8) by dx, we get:

(11) $\quad h(y)\,dy = g(x)\,dx$.

Written in this form, it suggests we antidifferentiate both sides (in principle, if not in practice).

$$\int h(y)\,dy = \int g(x)\,dx$$

which is the same as Eq.(10).

Newton thought of this problem--given a relationship between the derivatives, find the relationship between the functions--in a form like Eq.(11). He viewed x and y as functions of some third variable, usually time. In his intepretation, the dy stood for $\frac{dy}{dt}$, the dx stood for $\frac{dx}{dt}$. (His notation was different from ours; he would have written $\dot{y}$ for dy or $\frac{dy}{dt}$.)

Not every first-order differential equation can be expressed in the form of Eq. (11); indeed, most cannot. An equation which can be so expressed is said to be **separable** and this technique for solving equations is called **separation of variables**.

EXAMPLE 4.2:

(a) Determine the general solution of the equation $\frac{dy}{dx} = 4xy^2$.

(b) Find the specific solution satisfying $y(1) = -\frac{1}{3}$.

After separating variables, we see this is equivalent to:

$$\frac{1}{y^2}\, dy = 4x\, dx$$

which is of the required form. Antidifferentiating both sides, we get:

$$\int \frac{1}{y^2}\, dy = \int 4x\, dx \quad \text{or, equivalently,}$$

$$-\frac{1}{y} = 2x^2 + c$$

Therefore, $y = \dfrac{-1}{2x^2 + c}$ is the general solution.

Several specific solutions (for various values of c) are depicted in Figure 4.3.

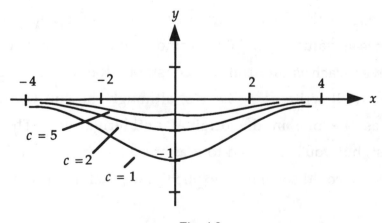

Fig. 4.3

For (b), we substitute $x = 1$ and $y = -\frac{1}{3}$.

$$-\frac{1}{3} = \frac{-1}{2+c}$$

from which $c = 1$. Therefore, the specific solution is

$$y = \frac{-1}{2x^2+1} .$$

Note that we can check that the general solution to the equation in Example 4.2 is correct by differentiation:

If $y = \dfrac{-1}{2x^2+c}$, then

$$\frac{dy}{dx} = \frac{4x}{(2x^2+c)^2} = 4x\left(\frac{-1}{2x^2+c}\right)^2 = 4xy^2,$$

which is the original equation.

EXAMPLE 4.3:

Solve the equation $\dfrac{dy}{dx} = \dfrac{3x^2}{y^3}$.

"Cross multiplying" allows us to write the equation in "separated form"

$$y^3\, dy = 3x^2\, dx.$$

Antidifferentiating gives:

$$\frac{y^4}{4} = x^3 + c \quad \text{or, equivalently,}$$

$$y^4 = 4x^3 + 4c = 4x^3 + c_1, \text{ where } c_1 = 4c.$$

Notice that each value of c determines a value of c_1, and conversely, each c_1 produces a value of c. Furthermore, c and c_1 may take on any values whatsoever--each is an arbitrary constant. Rather than get involved with subscripts, we'll write $y^4 = 4x^3 + c$, although the c in this equation is not the same as the one in the original antiderivative. This might be confusing at first, but you'll get used to it after several more examples.

At this point, we could solve for y explicitly; we shall not do so here. ◆

EXAMPLE 4.4:

Solve $\dfrac{dy}{dx} = x + y$.

We can write this as $dy = (x + y)dx = x\,dx + y\,dx$. After some thought, we see that there is no way to isolate terms containing only y and dy on one side and terms containing only x and dx on the other. Hence, this equation is not separable. Other techniques, beyond the scope of this book, must be used to solve this equation. ♦

Let's try to solve the equation $\dfrac{dp}{dt} = 1 - \dfrac{p}{5}$ for the salt water problem. This equation can be separated as $\dfrac{1}{5-p}\,dp = \dfrac{1}{5}\,dt$. We cannot proceed at this point since we can't find an antiderivative of the left side. We'll learn to do so later in the chapter.

TEST YOUR UNDERSTANDING

4. Determine the general solution of each of the following differential equations, if possible:

(a) $\dfrac{dy}{dx} = -\dfrac{x}{y}$ (b) $\dfrac{dy}{dx} = \sqrt{y}$ (c) $y^2 - x^3\dfrac{dy}{dx} = 0$ (d) $\dfrac{dy}{dx} = \dfrac{1}{x^2 + y^2}$

5. Sketch solutions to the equation in 4(a) above for several values of c.

6. Determine the specific solution to TYU 4(a) satisfying $y(1) = 2$.

¤ There are many interesting applications of differential equations in addition to the salt water problem that motivated this section. (Arguably, the main reason for studying calculus is to learn how to solve them.) Recall that one of the interpretations of the derivative is the instantaneous rate of change of one quantity with respect to another. In many cases, the independent variable is time, so the derivative is the instantaneous velocity or growth rate.

Suppose we are told that the velocity of a particle is equal to the square root of its position. Since the velocity is the derivative of the position, then this statement is equivalent to the differential equation:

$$\frac{ds}{dt} = \sqrt{s}.$$

This is a separable equation that can be rewritten as:

$$\frac{1}{\sqrt{s}} ds = dt \qquad \text{or, upon antidifferentiating,}$$

$$2\sqrt{s} = t + c .$$

If we were given additional information, we could solve for c. Suppose the particle starts at the origin; that is, $s(0) = 0$. Then, $c = 0$ and we have (after solving for s) that the position of the particle at time t is given by:

$$s(t) := \frac{t^2}{4}.$$

Now consider a slight modification of the problem above: The velocity of a particle is **proportional** to the square root of its position. The words "proportional to" can be translated as "is equal to a constant times". Hence, the differential equation is:

$$\frac{ds}{dt} = k\sqrt{s}$$

where k is a constant. How does this change the solution?

EXAMPLE 4.5:

An investment increases in value at a rate inversely proportional to the size of the investment.

(a) Determine the size of the investment as a function of time, given that the initial investment is $100.

(b) If the value of the investment after 1 year is $110, determine how long it takes to reach $200.

Let $P(t)$:= size of the investment at time t. The words "inversely proportional to" are equivalent to "equals a constant divided by". Thus, the first sentence implies:

$$\frac{dP}{dt} = \frac{k}{P}$$

Separating variables (by cross-multiplying) gives:

$$P \, dP = k \, dt$$

or, upon antidifferentiating

$$\frac{P^2}{2} = kt + c.$$

At this point, we can plug in the initial conditions to solve for c. Substituting $P = 100$ and $t = 0$ gives $c = 5000$. Therefore, $\frac{P^2}{2} = kt + 5000$ or, upon solving for P, we have:

$$P = \sqrt{2kt + 10000}$$

For (b), we are told that $P = 110$ when $t = 1$. This allows us to find k.

$$110 = \sqrt{2k + 10000}$$

$$12100 = 2k + 10000 \text{ so } k = 1050.$$

Therefore,

$$P = \sqrt{2100t + 10000}$$

whose graph is given in Figure 4.4. Note that the graph is concave down, implying that the rate of increase is decreasing. This agrees with the hypothesis: As t increases, P increases, but $\frac{dP}{dt}$ $(= \frac{k}{P})$ decreases.

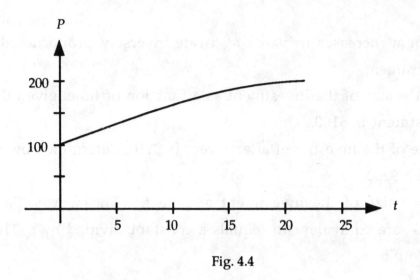

Fig. 4.4

Now set $P = 200$ and solve for t.

$200 = \sqrt{2100t + 10000}$

$40000 = 2100t + 10000$ so $t \approx 14.28$ years.   ♦

TEST YOUR UNDERSTANDING

7. (a) Write a differential equation that says that the rate of change of y with respect to x is proportional to y^2.

    (b) Find the specific solution of the equation in (a) such that $\dfrac{dy}{dx} = 3$ at the point (2, 1).

EXAMPLE 4.6:

A spherical snowball evaporates at a rate proportional to its surface area. Determine the volume of the snowball as a function of t, given that the initial volume is 27 cu. in.

The rate of evaporation is the instantaneous rate of change of the volume of the snowball. The statement of the problem expresses this rate in terms of the surface area. In order for this to be useful, we need to express the volume in terms of the surface area.

The volume and surface area of a sphere are given by $V = \frac{4}{3}\pi r^3$ and $S = 4\pi r^2$, respectively. Therefore, $V^{2/3} = kr^2 = k_1 S$, for some k and k_1, from which we claim that S is proportional to $V^{2/3}$. (The actual values of k and k_1, although computable, are not particularly important.)

Hence, if $V(t) :=$ volume of snowball at time t, then:

$$\frac{dV}{dt} = -b V^{2/3}, \text{ where } b > 0 \text{ is a constant.}$$

The minus sign is needed because the volume is decreasing. So, $\frac{dV}{dt}$ must be negative, even though V is positive.

Upon separating variables, we have:

$$V^{-2/3}\, dV = -b\, dt$$

Upon antidifferentiating, we get:

$$3V^{1/3} = -bt + c.$$

Substituting the initial condition $V(0) = 27$ gives $c = 9$. Hence,

$$V(t) := \left(\frac{9 - bt}{3}\right)^3 . \qquad\qquad \blacklozenge$$

TEST YOUR UNDERSTANDING

8. How would the problem change if the "snowball" were a cube instead of a sphere?

AN APPLICATION

A cylindrical can of radius R has a circular hole of radius r punched in the bottom. The can is filled with water up to height h_0 which then drains through the hole. How long will it take for the water to drain out?

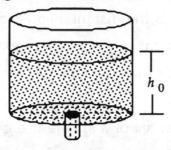

Fig. 4.5

We'll solve this problem by first finding a function that tells us the height of the water at any time t. Then we'll find the time at which the height of the water is zero.

Let $h(t)$ represent the height of the water in the can as a function of time. In a small time interval Δt, the height changes by an amount Δh and therefore, the volume of water changes by an amount

(12) $\Delta V_1 = A\Delta h,$

where $A = \pi R^2 = $ cross-sectional area of the can. (Note that ΔV_1 is negative since Δh is negative. This agrees with the fact that the volume is decreasing.)

In the same time interval, the amount of water draining through the hole is

(13) $\Delta V_2 = B\Delta s,$

where $B = \pi r^2 = $ area of the hole and $\Delta s = $ distance travelled by the water. But

(14) $\Delta s = v \Delta t,$

where v is the velocity of the water as it flows through the hole.

Now we invoke a principle from physics called Torricelli's Law which says that, under ideal conditions (ignoring surface tension and other factors), the velocity of the water coming through the hole is given by

(15) $v = \sqrt{2gh}\,,$

where g is the acceleration due to gravity and h is the height of the water in the can. Although we won't prove Torricelli's law (the proof is derived from the principle of conservation of energy), it is, at least qualitatively, plausible. Our intuition tells us that the more water there is in the can, the more downward pressure it exerts, so the water should flow more rapidly through the hole. Eq.(15) certainly implies this.

Substituting Eqs.(14) and (15) into Eq.(13), we get:

(16) $\Delta V_2 = B\sqrt{2gh}\,\Delta t.$

(Note that ΔV_2 is positive.)

Finally, we realize that the amount of water draining through the hole is exactly equal to the amount by which the volume decreased in the can; that is, $\Delta V_2 = -\Delta V_1$.   (The minus sign is needed because ΔV_1 and ΔV_2 have opposite signs.) Therefore,

(17) $-A\Delta h = B\sqrt{2gh}\,\Delta t$

Divide both sides of Eq.(17) by $-A$ and Δt and let $\Delta t \to 0$. Recalling that $\frac{\Delta h}{\Delta t} \to \frac{dh}{dt}$ as $\Delta t \to 0$, we find that $h(t)$ must satisfy the differential equation

(18) $\qquad \dfrac{dh}{dt} = -k\sqrt{h}$,

where $k = \dfrac{B}{A}\sqrt{2g}$ is a constant.

This is a first-order separable equation which fortunately we can solve.

$$\dfrac{dh}{\sqrt{h}} = -k\ dt$$

$$\int \dfrac{dh}{\sqrt{h}} = \int -k\ dt$$

$2h^{1/2} = -kt + c$, for some constant c.

Now we use the fact that the height at time $t = 0$ is $h(0) = h_0$. This implies $c = 2\sqrt{h_0}$.

Putting this all together, we get:

$$h^{1/2} = -\dfrac{k}{2}t + \sqrt{h_0} \qquad \text{or, equivalently,}$$

(19) $\qquad h(t) := \left(-\dfrac{k}{2}t + \sqrt{h_0}\right)^2$

where $k = \dfrac{B}{A}\sqrt{2g}$.

Note that h is a quadratic function whose graph is a concave-up parabola. Furthermore, since $h(t)$ is the square of some quantity, then $h(t) \geq 0$ for all t. Thus, the graph of h should start at h_0, decrease to 0, then increase again. However, the physical reality of the situation tells us that h cannot increase once it reaches 0. Thus, the domain of h is restricted to the interval $[0, t^*]$, where t^* is the value of t for which $h(t) = 0$; i.e., the time at which the can is empty.

Suppose the can has radius $R = 5$ cm and the hole has radius $r = 0.6$ cm. Then, using $g = 980$ cm/sec^2, we get $k = 0.638$. If $h_0 = 10$ cm, then $h(t) := (3.16 - 0.319t)^2$. Therefore, $t^* = \dfrac{3.16}{0.319} = 9.91$ sec. If $h_0 = 20$, then $h(t) := (4.47 - 0.319t)^2$, from which $t^* = \dfrac{4.47}{0.319} = 14.02$ sec. If $h_0 = 30$, then

$h(t) := (5.47 - 0.319t)^2$ from which $t^* = \dfrac{5.47}{0.319} = 17.17$ sec.

Figure 4.6 shows the graph of $h(t)$ vs. t for the three values of h_0 above.

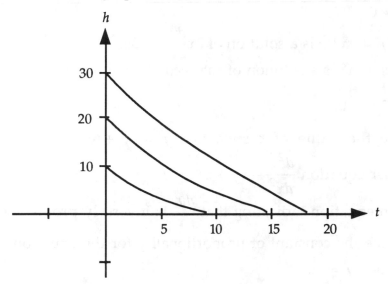

Fig. 4.6

More generally, if we set $h(t) = 0$ in Eq.(19) and solve for t, we get:

$$t^* = \frac{2}{k}\sqrt{h_0} = \frac{A}{B}\sqrt{\frac{2h_0}{g}} = \frac{R^2}{r^2}\sqrt{\frac{2h_0}{g}}\,.$$

From this, it is apparent that doubling the initial height multiplies the time required for the can to empty by a factor of $\sqrt{2}$, tripling the initial height multiplies the time by $\sqrt{3}$, and so on.

EXERCISES FOR SECTION 4.1:

1. Find the general solution of each of the following, if possible:

(a) $\dfrac{dy}{dx} = \dfrac{x}{y}$ (b) $\dfrac{dy}{dx} = x^2y^2$ (c) $\dfrac{dy}{dx} = 5 - xy$

(d) $(1 + y)dy = 2x\,dx$ (e) $\dfrac{dy}{dx} = xy^2 - x^4y^2$ (f) $\dfrac{dy}{dx} = x + y$

(g) $\dfrac{dy}{dx} = \dfrac{4 - y^2}{x}$ (h) $\sqrt{y} - \sqrt{x}\,\dfrac{dy}{dx} = 0$

2. Find the specific solution to the equation in Exer. 1(a) that passes through the point (1, 1).

3. Find the specific solution to the equation in Exer. 1(h) such that $y(4) = 9$.

4. Find the specific solution of $\dfrac{dy}{dx} = \dfrac{\sqrt{x}}{2y}$, if $y(0) = 2$.

5. Show that $y = (c^2 - x^2)^{1/2}$ is a solution of the differential equation
$y\dfrac{dy}{dx} + x = 0$.

6. Show that $y = cx^{3/2}$ is a solution of $2x\dfrac{dy}{dx} = 3y$.

7. Show that $y = x^4$ is a solution of the second-order equation
$x^2\dfrac{d^2y}{dx^2} - 12y = 0.$

8. Determine the value of k such that $y = x^3 + 6x$ is a solution of the second-order equation $\dfrac{d^2y}{dx^2} - ky + x^3 = 0$

9. (a) Write an equation indicating that $\dfrac{dy}{dx}$ is inversely proportional to y^3.

(b) Determine the constant of proportionality for the equation in (a) if $\dfrac{dy}{dx}$ = 1 when $y = 2$.

(c) Find the specific solution to the equation in (b) if $y = 2$ when $x = 0$.

10. Write, but do not solve, an equation indicating that the velocity of a particle at time t is inversely proportional to the position and directly proportional to the time.

PROBLEMS FOR SECTION 4.1:

1. A psychologist theorizes that the amount of knowledge acquired by a chimpanzee increases at a rate inversely proportional to the square root of the knowledge already acquired. Express this as a differential equation and solve if the chimpanzee knows nothing at time $t = 0$.

2. Water flows into a tank in such a way that the rate of change in the height of water at time t is equal to 4 times the cube root of the height.

(a) Express as a differential equation and solve if the tank is empty at time $t = 0$.

(b) If the tank is 10 feet deep, how long will it take to fill?

3. (a) Determine all functions with the property that the slope of the tangent to the graph of the function at any point (x, y) is given by x^2y^2.

(b) Find the specific function with the property in (a) that passes through (2, 1).

4. Let v and y be functions of x. The product rule for derivatives says that
$$\frac{d}{dx}(vy) = v\frac{dy}{dx} + y\frac{dv}{dx}.$$
Consider the differential equation $\quad x^2\frac{dy}{dx} + 2xy = 4x + 1.$

(a) Determine a function v such that the left side of the differential equation is $\frac{d}{dx}(vy)$.

(b) Antidifferentiate both sides with respect to x and solve for y to obtain the general solution of this equation.

5. Referring to the can problem at the end of this section, what happens to the time required for the can to drain completely if

(a) the radius of the can (R) is tripled?

(b) the radius of the hole (r) is doubled?

6. The model for the hole-in-the-can problem assumes that there is no friction between the water and the can as the water drains. Clearly friction slows the water down. One way to account for this is to modify Torricelli's law as $v = \alpha\sqrt{2gh}$, where α is a constant. Experimental evidence shows that $\alpha = 0.6$ for water. Modify Eq.(19) to account for this and then recompute t^* for the values of R, r and h_0 used in the text.

7. Suppose the can has square cross-sections of side length q. Modify the derivation of Eq.(19) and then recompute t^* for the values of R, r and h_0 used in the text.

TYU Answers for Section 4.1

1. (a) $y = 2x^2 + c$ (b) The graphs are parabolas with vertex at $(0, c)$. (c) $y = 2x^2 - 5$

2. $y' = \frac{x}{\sqrt{a^2+x^2}}$; $yy' = \sqrt{a^2+x^2}\,\frac{x}{\sqrt{a^2+x^2}} = x$ 3. (a) $y = -\frac{1}{x} + c$ (b) $y = -\frac{1}{x} + 4$

4. (a) $y^2 + x^2 = c$ (b) $2\sqrt{y} = x + c$ (c) $\frac{1}{2x^2} = \frac{1}{y} + c$ (d) can't be solved by sep. of var.

5. Graphs are circles, centered at origin with radius $\sqrt{c}$ 6. $y^2 + x^2 = 5$

7. (a) $\frac{dy}{dx} = ky^2$ (b) $y = \frac{1}{7-3x}$.   8. The form would be the same but with a different constant b.

4.2 EXPONENTIAL FUNCTIONS

Let's return once again to the salt water problem that motivated this chapter. Suppose that, instead of adding salt water to replace the water that is removed, we add fresh water. Now, since no salt is being added, Eq.(1) becomes:

$$p(t + \Delta t) \approx p(t) - \frac{p(t)}{5} \Delta t + 0\, \Delta t = p(t) - \frac{p(t)}{5} \Delta t .$$

From this, we get

$$\frac{p(t + \Delta t) - p(t)}{\Delta t} \approx -\frac{p(t)}{5}$$

or, upon taking the limit as $\Delta t \to 0$,

$$(20) \qquad \frac{dp}{dt} = \frac{-1}{5} p .$$

If we try to solve this by separation of variables, we get:

$$\frac{1}{p}\, dp = \frac{-1}{5}\, dt .$$

The expression on the left side is of the form $p^{-1}\, dp$, which we cannot antidifferentiate at this time. (The power rule for antiderivatives does not apply when the exponent is -1.)

The differential equation (20) is a special case of the more general equation

$$(21) \qquad \frac{dy}{dt} = ry$$

where r is a constant. This equation arises in many applications in biology, chemistry, economics and other disciplines.

Important note: Pay particular attention to the form of Eq. (21). It says that the derivative of a function equals a constant times the function. The discussion that follows applies only to equations which precisely match this form; e.g., $dy/dt = 3y$, $dz/dx = -7z$, $dp/dq = 9.3p$. It does not apply to equations such as $dy/dt = 3y^2$, which we already can solve by separation of variables. The resulting antiderivative $\int y^{-2}\, dy$ can be handled by the power rule. It also does not apply to $dy/dt = 4t$ which also is easily solved by separation of variables. (Do so.)

Let's see what we can say about the solution to Eq. (21). Assume that $y > 0$. If $r > 0$, then $\dfrac{dy}{dt} > 0$, implying that y is an increasing function of t. Conversely, if $r < 0$, then $\dfrac{dy}{dt} < 0$, implying that y is decreasing. Furthermore, we can differentiate Eq.(21) with respect to t (invoking the chain rule), obtaining:

$$(22) \qquad \frac{d^2y}{dt^2} = r\frac{dy}{dt} = r^2y \, .$$

Since $r^2 > 0$ for all r, then $\dfrac{d^2y}{dt^2} > 0$, implying that y is concave up. These behaviors are depicted in Figures 4.7(a) and (b).

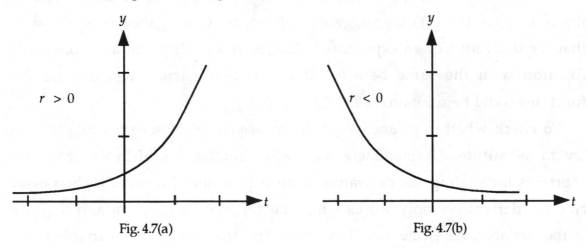

Fig. 4.7(a)   Fig. 4.7(b)

While having a graph of the solution is useful, it would be nice to have a formula for the solution as well. As we said before, Eq.(21) is separable, but the antiderivative $\int \frac{1}{y}\,dy$ that results is one which we cannot find yet.

No polynomial function f could possibly satisfy Eq. (21) since if f were of degree n, then its derivative would be of degree $n - 1$ and it is impossible for a polynomial of degree n to be equal to (or be a constant multiple of) a polynomial of degree $n - 1$, for all t.

◻ In Chapter 1, we briefly mentioned **exponential functions**. An exponential function is of the form

(23) $f(x) := b^x,$

for some constant b. In order to avoid raising negative numbers to fractional exponents such as $1/2$, we ought to have $b > 0$ and to keep the function interesting, we will require $b \neq 1$. (Otherwise, $f(x) = 1$ for all x.) Given these restrictions on b, the domain of any exponential function is **R** and the range is $\{y \mid y > 0\}$.

For example, $y(t) := 3^t$ is an exponential function. Note that $y(0) = 1$, $y(1) = 3, y(2) = 9, y(3) = 27$, etc. Thus, $y(1) - y(0) = 2, y(2) - y(1) = 6$, $y(3) - y(2) = 18$, etc. In general, it can be shown that for this particular exponential function, $y(t + 1) - y(t) = 2(3^t) = 2y(t)$. Since differences of the form $y(t + 1) - y(t)$ are suggestive of the derivative, then it is plausible that the derivative of an exponential function is a multiple of an exponential function with the same base b. If this is really true, then exponential functions could be solutions of Eq. (21). Let's try it!

To check whether a function of the form $y(t) := b^t$ satisfies Eq.(21), we try to substitute. Immediately we realize another problem--we have no shortcuts for finding the derivative of an exponential function. (The power rule for derivatives only works when the *exponent* is constant and the *base* is the variable; here, the *base* is constant and the *exponent* is variable.) So, we are forced to resort to the definition of the derivative to find $\dfrac{dy}{dt}$.

$$\Delta y = y(t + \Delta t) - y(t) = b^{t+\Delta t} - b^t = b^t b^{\Delta t} - b^t$$
$$= b^t(b^{\Delta t} - 1)$$

Therefore, $\dfrac{\Delta y}{\Delta t} = b^t \left(\dfrac{b^{\Delta t} - 1}{\Delta t} \right)$ and so

(24) $\dfrac{dy}{dt} = \lim\limits_{\Delta t \to 0} \dfrac{\Delta y}{\Delta t} = b^t \lim\limits_{\Delta t \to 0} \left(\dfrac{b^{\Delta t} - 1}{\Delta t} \right).$

We have a slight problem, because we can't evaluate the limit in Eq. (24) (note that it is an indeterminate form $\frac{0}{0}$). For now, let's assume that the limit exists and is a constant which depends on b; that is, let

$$k_b = \lim_{\Delta t \to 0}\left(\frac{b^{\Delta t} - 1}{\Delta t}\right).$$

Thus, $\dfrac{dy}{dt} = k_b\, b^t = k_b\, y(t)$.

Note: Although we are writing b as a subscript, we need not restrict b to be an integer so we may write expressions such as $k_{1.5}$ or $k_{0.2}$.

So, we've done it--we've found a function whose derivative is just a constant times the function itself. If we can find the value of b such that $k_b = r$, then we will have solved Eq.(21).

THE NUMBER e

For any exponential function $f(x) := b^x$, we've shown that $f'(x) := k_b f(x)$ for every x. Thus $\dfrac{f'(x)}{f(x)} = k_b$ for every x. In particular, this is true for $x = 0$. Since $f(0) = 1$, then for every $b, f'(0) = k_b$.

Let's take advantage of this property to do a little exploring. Since $f'(x) \approx \dfrac{f(x + \Delta x) - f(x)}{\Delta x}$ for values of Δx near 0, we can use our calculators to approximate $f'(0) = k_b$:

$$k_b = f'(0) \approx \frac{f(0 + \Delta x) - f(0)}{\Delta x} = \frac{f(\Delta x) - 1}{\Delta x} = \frac{b^{\Delta x} - 1}{\Delta x}.$$

Here's a table of values of $\dfrac{b^{\Delta x} - 1}{\Delta x}$ for $b = 2, 2.5$ and 3 and $\Delta x = 0.01, 0.001,$ and 0.0001.

b \ Δx	0.01	0.001	0.0001
2	0.695555	0.6933875	0.693171
2.5	0.9205015	0.9167107	0.916333
3	1.1046692	1.0992160	1.098673

We might reasonably surmise from the table that k_2 is approximately 0.693, that $k_{2.5}$ is approximately 0.916 and that k_3 is approximately 1.099. This might lead us to ask whether there is a number b such that $k_b = 1$.

TEST YOUR UNDERSTANDING

1. Suppose there is a b such that $k_b = 1$. Using the data we collected above, guess an approximate value for b.

2. Test your guess using the technique we tried. Can you find a value for b that is accurate in the first decimal place?

Indeed, there is such a number b; it is approximately 2.718. That is, $k_{2.718} \approx 1$. This number is so important that we give it a special name, e. (The letter e was chosen to commemorate Leonhard Euler (pronounced Oiler), an 18th century Swiss mathematician who first discovered it.) It is a transcendental number, as is π. To 10 digits, $e = 2.718281828$.

Remember that if $f(x) := b^x$, then $f'(x) := k_b b^x$. For the special case $b = e$, we have $k_b = 1$. Thus, the special exponential function $f(x) := e^x$ has the property that $f'(x) := e^x$. This special function occurs in many applications. It is generally referred to as **the** **exponential function** (as opposed to other exponential functions).

Figure 4.8 shows the graph of $f(x) := e^x$. Note that $f(x) = f'(x) = f''(x) := e^x > 0$, for all x, so f is positive, increasing and concave up for all x.

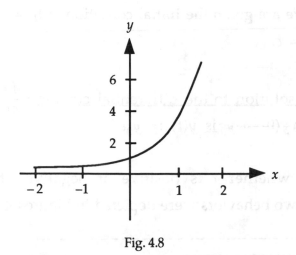

Fig. 4.8

¤   Now let's go back to the problem that motivated this discussion. Recall that we were trying to solve the differential equation $\dfrac{dy}{dt} = ry$. We have shown that exponential functions have the desired property that their derivatives are proportional to the function values. So we could claim that the solution to this equation is $y(t) := ab^t$, where b is chosen so that $k_b = r$. However, rather that messing around with different bases, we will express everything in terms of e. Observe that if $y(t) := e^{rt}$, then, by the chain rule,

$$\frac{dy}{dt} = e^{rt}(r) = ry(t).$$

So, $y(t) := e^{rt}$ is a solution to the differential equation $\dfrac{dy}{dt} = ry$.

   While this is one solution, we would like to have the general solution. Let $z(t) := cy(t) = ce^{rt}$. Then $\dfrac{dz}{dt} = cre^{rt} = rz(t)$. Hence $z(t)$ also satisfies Eq.(21); that is, every constant multiple of $y(t)$ is a solution of Eq.(21). In Problem 8 at the end of this section, you are asked to show that every solution of Eq.(21) must be a constant multiple of y. For now, we will accept it as fact and claim:

The general solution of the differential equation $\dfrac{dy}{dt} = ry$ is $y = ce^{rt}$.

Now suppose we are given the initial condition $y(0) = y_0$. Then

$$y_0 = ce^{r(0)} = c.$$

Thus, <u>the specific solution to the differential equation</u> $\dfrac{dy}{dt} = ry$, <u>subject to</u> <u>the initial condition</u> $y(0) = y_0$ <u>is</u> $y(t) := y_0 e^{rt}$.

Depending on whether r is positive or negative, the graph behaves differently. These two behaviors were depicted in Figures 4.7(a) and 4.7(b).

TEST YOUR UNDERSTANDING

3. (a) Find the general solution of the differential equation $\dfrac{dy}{dt} = 8y$.

   (b) Find the general solution of the differential equation $\dfrac{dy}{dt} = 8y^2$.

   (c) Explain why different techniques were used for parts (a) and (b).

Let's return to the salt water problem that motivated this section. The differential equation for this problem is $\dfrac{dp}{dt} = \dfrac{-1}{5}p$. We now know that, since this equation is of the form of Eq.(21) with $r = \dfrac{-1}{5}$, the solution to this equation is $p = p_0 e^{-t/5}$, where p_0 is the number of pounds of salt initially in the tank. Since $r = \dfrac{-1}{5} < 0$, then the graph is decreasing, concave up and approaches 0 as t increases, as in Figure 4.7(b).

THE EXPONENTIAL FUNCTION

Let's review what we know about the exponential function $f(x) := e^x$.

1. The domain of f is **R**, the range is $\{y \mid y > 0\}$.

2. f is increasing and concave up for all x.

3. $f'(x) = e^x = f(x)$.

4. $e^0 = 1$

5. $\lim_{x \to \infty} e^x = \infty$; $\lim_{x \to -\infty} e^x = 0$.

6. By laws of exponents, $e^{a+b} = e^a e^b$, $e^{a-b} = e^a / e^b$, $e^{ab} = (e^a)^b$ $= (e^b)^a$.

It follows from property 3 that $f''(x) := e^x$, $f'''(x) := e^x$, etc., and that

7. $\int e^x \, dx = e^x + c$.

All the other rules for derivatives can be used with exponential functions. In particular, the chain rule (Theorem 3.14) is needed to differentiate functions of the form $y = e^{g(x)}$. Thinking of this as a composite $f(g(x))$, where $f(x) = e^x$, then the derivative will be $\frac{dy}{dx} = f'(g(x))g'(x) = e^{g(x)}g'(x)$.

EXAMPLE 4.7:

Find the derivatives of:

(a) $f(x) := e^{2x^3}$ (b) $y = x^2 e^x$ (c) $g(x) := (e^x + 1)^3$ (d) $y = \frac{e^x}{x}$

(a) Using the chain rule with $g(x) := 2x^3$ and, consequently, $g'(x) := 6x^2$, we have $f'(x) := e^{2x^3}(6x^2) = 6x^2 e^{2x^3}$.

(b) The product rule gives $\frac{dy}{dx} = x^2 \frac{d}{dx}(e^x) + 2x e^x = x^2 e^x + 2x e^x$.

(c) Again, the chain rule gives $g'(x) := 3(e^x + 1)^2 \frac{d}{dx}(e^x + 1) = 3(e^x + 1)^2 e^x$.

(d) The quotient rule gives $\frac{dy}{dx} = \frac{x e^x - e^x (1)}{x^2} = \frac{e^x(x-1)}{x^2}$. ◆

In Example 4.7(a), we saw that $D_x[e^{2x}] := 2e^{2x}$. This implies $D_x^{-1}[2e^{2x}] := e^{2x} + c$, or upon dividing both sides by 2,

$$D_x^{-1}[e^{2x}] := \frac{1}{2}e^{2x} + c.$$

This can easily be generalized, enabling us to find antiderivatives of functions of the form $f(x) := e^{bx}$, for any constant b. In Chapter 8, we will learn how to find antiderivatives of more complicated exponential functions.

_____

TEST YOUR UNDERSTANDING

4. Simplify each of the following:

   (a) $e^2 e^5$ (b) $\dfrac{e^x}{e^3}$ (c) $(e^{4x})^3$ (d) $\sqrt{e^{64x^2}}$

5. Is there a value of x such that $e^x = -1$? Explain.

6. Find the derivative of:

   (a) $y = e^{3t^2}$ (b) $v = t e^{-t}$ (c) $g(x) := \sqrt{1 + e^x}$ (d) $q(x) := \dfrac{e^x}{x^2}$

7. Find the general solution of the differential equation $\dfrac{dy}{dx} = e^x y^2$.

_____

EXAMPLE 4.8:

Determine the direction and concavity of $y = xe^x$ and sketch.

By the product rule, $\dfrac{dy}{dx} = xe^x + e^x = e^x(x + 1)$.

Since $e^x > 0$ for all x, then $\dfrac{dy}{dx} > 0$ if and only if $x + 1 > 0$. Therefore, y is increasing on the interval $[-1, \infty)$ and decreasing on $(-\infty, -1]$.

There is a critical number at $x = -1$ which is easily seen to be a local minimum.

Again by the product rule, $\dfrac{d^2 y}{dx^2} = e^x(x + 1) + e^x = e^x(x + 2)$. By a similar argument, we see that y is concave up on $[-2, \infty)$ and concave down on $(-\infty, -2]$.

To aid with the sketching, note that $y > 0$ if and only if $x > 0$, so the graph lies in the first and third quadrants only.

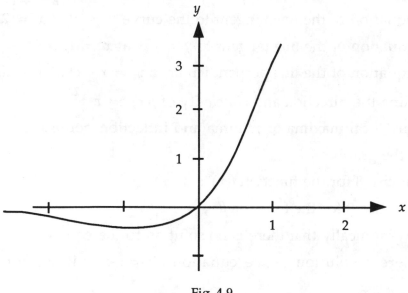

Fig. 4.9

Note that y appears to go to 0 as $x \to -\infty$; in other words, $\lim\limits_{x \to -\infty} xe^x = 0$. This is interesting because direct substitution gives the indeterminate form $(-\infty)(0)$, which need not equal 0 (although in this case it does). We'll prove this limit is correct in Section 4.4. In the meantime, you might use your calculator to compute values of xe^x for large negative values of x.   ♦

EXERCISES FOR SECTION 4.2:

1. (a) Determine the general solution to the differential equation $\dfrac{dy}{dt} = 3y$.

   (b) Determine the specific solution of the equation $\dfrac{dy}{dt} = 3y$ satisfying $y(0) = 6$.

   (c) Sketch the graph of the solution in part (b).

2. (a) Determine the general solution to the differential equation $\dfrac{dy}{dx} = -4x$.

   (b) Determine the specific solution of this equation satisfying $y(0) = 10$.

   (c) Sketch the graph of the solution in part (b).

3. Sketch the graphs of $f(x) := e^x$ and $g(x) := e^{-x}$ on the same axes.

4. Find the derivative of the following:

   (a) $f(x) := e^{1-3x}$ (b) $f(x) := e^{\sqrt{x}}$ (c) $f(x) := x^3 e^x$

   (d) $y = \dfrac{e^{4x}}{x}$ (e) $y = (e^x + x^2)^3$ (f) $g(x) := \dfrac{e^{2x}}{e^{2x}+1}$

5. Write an equation of the line tangent to the curve $y = e^x$ at $x = 2$.

6. Write an equation of the line tangent to $y = e^{2x}$ at $x = 1$.

7. Write an equation of the line perpendicular to $y = x + e^x$ at $x = 0$.

8. (a) Determine the direction and concavity of $f(x) := e^{-x^2}$.

   (b) Find any local maxima or minima and inflection points.

   (c) Sketch the graph.

9. Repeat Exercise 8 for the function $f(x) := x^2 e^x$.

10. Repeat Exercise 8 for the function $f(x) := xe^{-x}$.

11. (a) Show graphically that there is no solution to the equation $x = e^x$.

    (b) Is there a solution to the equation $e^x = -x$? If so, approximate it.

12. Write the general solution of the differential equation $\dfrac{dy}{dx} = \dfrac{e^x}{y}$.

PROBLEMS FOR SECTION 4.2:

1. A population of amœbas (amœbae?) increases at a rate equal to 10% of the current population per day. Write and solve a differential equation for the size of the population given that there are initially 5000 amœbas.

2. Let $y(t)$ be the gross national product (GNP) of a certain country and let $x(t)$ be its total capital. The **Domar model** says that the rate of growth of the capital is a fixed percentage k of the GNP and that the GNP is a fixed percentage m of the capital. Write and solve a differential equation for x.

3. At the beginning of Section 4.1, we derived a differential equation $\frac{dp}{dt} = 1 - \frac{p}{5}$ for the salt water problem. We said that the differential equation is separable but we could not solve it because the resulting antiderivative was beyond our means at this time. However, it can be shown that the solution is of the form $p(t) := a + be^{-t/5}$, for some constants a and b.

    (a) Determine a and b if $p(0) = 3$.

    (b) What happens to $p(t)$ as t increases?

4. Let $u(n) := \left(1 + \frac{1}{n}\right)^n$.

    (a) Use a calculator to evaluate $u(1)$, $u(10)$, $u(100)$, $u(1000)$, $u(10000)$.

    (b) Does it appear that $u(n)$ is approaching a limit as $n \to \infty$? If so, what?

5. Let $A(r)$ be the area of the rectangle inscribed under the curve $y = e^{-x^2}$ as shown below.

    (a) Determine $A(1)$.

    (b) What value of r maximizes $A(r)$?

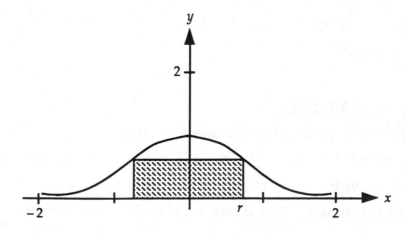

6. Let $f(x) := e^x - x - 1$.

    (a) Show that f is increasing for $x \geq 0$.

(b) Use this to show that $e^x > x + 1$ for all $x > 0$. Hint: What is $f(0)$?

7. Consider the function $f(x) := xe^{-kx}$, for some positive constant k.

   (a) Determine the local maximum of f.

   (b) Write an equation for the set of local maximum points of f as k varies through positive values.

8. In the text, we claimed that any function of the form $y = ce^{rt}$ satisfies the equation $\dfrac{dy}{dt} = ry$. Now we'll show that the *only* solutions of $\dfrac{dy}{dt} = ry$ are of the form $y = ce^{rt}$.

   (a) Let z be any other solution of this differential equation and set $h(t) := \dfrac{z(t)}{y(t)}$. Show that $h'(t) := \dfrac{y(t)z'(t) - y'(t)z(t)}{(y(t))^2}$. (Note that h is defined for all t since $y > 0$ for all t.)

   (b) Show that $h'(t) := 0$ for all t.

   (c) What must be true about $h(t)$?

   (d) Conclude that z must be a constant multiple of y.

TYU Answers for Section 4.2

1. Between 2.5 and 3.   2. 2.7; $k_{2.7} = .993$ 3. (a) $y = ce^{8t}$ (b) $1/y = -8t + c$

   (c) The power rule for antiderivatives does not work for (a), but it does for (b).

4. (a) e^7 (b) e^{x-3} (c) e^{12x} (d) e^{32x^2} 5. No, $e^x > 0$ for all x.   6. (a) $y' = 6te^{3t^2}$

   (b) $v' = -te^{-t} + e^{-t}$ (c) $g'(x) = \dfrac{e^x}{2\sqrt{1+e^x}}$ (d) $q'(x) = \dfrac{x^2e^x - 2xe^x}{x^4} = \dfrac{e^x(x-2)}{x^3}$

7. $-\dfrac{1}{y} = e^x + c$ *or* $y = \dfrac{-1}{e^x + c}$

4.3 THE NATURAL LOGARITHM

In the last section, we argued that the number of pounds of salt in the tank at time t is given by $p(t) := p_0 e^{-t/5}$, where p_0 is the initial amount of salt. Suppose we start with 3 pounds and would like to know at what time there are 1.5 pounds remaining. That is, we want to find the value of t such that $1.5 = 3e^{-t/5}$ or, upon dividing by 3, $0.5 = e^{-t/5}$. What algebraic step should we do next to allow us to solve for t? The answer is not clear.

One way to do this is graphically: look at $y = 0.5$ on the graph of $y = e^{-t/5}$ and find the corresponding t. (It appears from the graph in Figure 4.10 that $t \approx 3.5$ or so.) This is not entirely satisfactory. There should be some functional way of solving the equation $e^{-t/5} = 0.5$ or, more generally, $e^x = z$, for any $z > 0$. What we need is some way of "undoing" the exponential function, just like squaring a number undoes taking its square root.

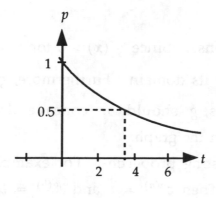

Fig. 4.10

You may have guessed that what we are looking for is the inverse function of $f(x) := e^x$. Certainly, f is one-to-one; hence, it has an inverse. Let $g = f^{-1}$; that is, g is the function defined by $e^{g(x)} = x$ and $g(e^x) = x$. The domain of g will be $\{x \mid x > 0\}$, the same as the range of f. The range of g will be $\mathbf{R}$, the same as the domain of f. We can get the graph of g by reflecting the graph of f across the line $y = x$. See Figure 4.11.

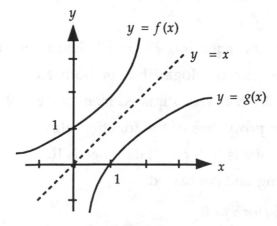

Fig. 4.11

Although we don't have a formula for g, we can tell a lot about it. For instance, if we differentiate both sides of the equation $e^{g(x)} = x$ with respect to x (making sure to use the chain rule), we get:

$$e^{g(x)} g'(x) = 1 \qquad \text{from which}$$

$$g'(x) = \frac{1}{e^{g(x)}} .$$

But $e^{g(x)} = x$, so

$$g'(x) := \frac{1}{x} .$$

Let's see if this makes sense. Since $g'(x) > 0$ for $x > 0$, then g should be increasing everywhere on its domain. Furthermore, $g''(x) := \frac{-1}{x^2}$ which is negative for all x. Thus, g should be concave down. Both of these properties are evident from the graph.

There are other interesting properties. For example, let a and b be any two positive numbers. Then $e^{g(a)} = a$ and $e^{g(b)} = b$. Multiplying these two equations and using laws of exponents, we get $e^{g(a) + g(b)} = ab$. But $e^{g(ab)} = ab$, also. Therefore, since $f(x) := e^x$ is one-to-one, $g(a) + g(b) = g(ab)$. Similarly, $g(a) - g(b) = g(a/b)$ and $g(a^b) = b g(a)$.

◻ You may have encountered other functions with these properties--they are called **logarithmic functions**. Hence, g is just a special type of logarithmic function which we will call the **natural logarithm**, abbreviated ln; that is, $g(x) := \ln(x)$. Your calculator probably has a key that evaluates $\ln(x)$ for any $x > 0$.

So, the solution to the equation $e^x = 5$ is just $x = \ln(5) = 1.609$. To solve $e^{-t/5} = .5$, we take the logarithm of both sides, obtaining $-t/5 = -.693$, from which $t = 3.465$ as we estimated from our graph.

Let's summarize the properties of the function $g(x) := \ln(x)$:

1. The domain of g is $\{x \mid x > 0\}$; its range is **R**.

2. g is increasing and concave down.

3. $\dfrac{d \ln(x)}{dx} = \dfrac{1}{x}$, for $x > 0$

4. $\ln(1) = 0$

5. $\ln(e^x) = x$, for all x; $e^{\ln(x)} = x$, for all $x > 0$.

6. $\ln(ab) = \ln(a) + \ln(b)$; $\ln(a/b) = \ln(a) - \ln(b)$; $\ln(a^b) = b\ln(a)$

Once again the rules for derivatives apply. In particular, if $y = \ln(h(x))$, the chain rule gives $\dfrac{dy}{dx} = \dfrac{1}{h(x)}h'(x) = \dfrac{h'(x)}{h(x)}$.

EXAMPLE 4.9:

Find the derivative of:

(a) $y = \ln(2x)$ (b) $f(x) := x^2 \ln(x)$ (c) $g(t) := \ln(t^3)$

(d) $z = (\ln(x) + x)^4$

(a) From the chain rule, $\dfrac{dy}{dx} = \dfrac{1}{2x}(2) = \dfrac{1}{x}$. Note that $y = \ln(2x) = \ln(2) + \ln(x)$ from which $\dfrac{dy}{dx} = \dfrac{1}{x}$ directly. (Remember: $\ln(2)$ is a constant.)

(b) By the product rule, $f'(x) := x^2\dfrac{d}{dx}(\ln(x)) + 2x\ln(x) = x^2\left(\dfrac{1}{x}\right) + 2x\ln(x)$
$\qquad\qquad = x + 2x\ln(x)$.

(c) As in (a), $g'(t) := \dfrac{1}{t^3}(3t^2) = \dfrac{3}{t}$. Or, note that $g(t) = 3\ln(t)$ from which $g'(t) := \dfrac{3}{t}$.

(d) $\dfrac{dz}{dx} = 4(\ln(x) + x)^3\dfrac{d}{dx}(\ln(x) + x) = 4(\ln(x) + x)^3\left(\dfrac{1}{x} + 1\right)$.   ◆

TEST YOUR UNDERSTANDING

1. Given that $\ln(3) = 1.098$ and $\ln(2) = .693$, determine (without using the ln button on your calculator):

(a) $\ln\left(\dfrac{1}{2}\right)$ (b) $\ln(1.5)$ (c) $\ln(12)$ (d) $\ln(\sqrt{3})$ (e) $\ln\left(\dfrac{e}{2}\right)$

2. Simplify:

   (a) $\ln(e^3)$ (b) $e^{\ln(2x)}$ (c) $e^{2\ln(x)}$ (d) $e^{-3\ln(2)}$

3. Solve for x:

   (a) $\ln(x) = 2$ (b) $e^x = 4$ (c) $\ln(x) + \ln(x+1) = \ln(12)$

4. Find the derivative of:

   (a) $y = \dfrac{\ln(x)}{x}$ (b) $y = \ln(x^2 + 1)$ (c) $y = \dfrac{1}{1 + \ln(x)}$

5. Write an equation of the line tangent to the graph of $y = \ln(1+x)$ at $x = 0$.

EXAMPLE 4.10:

Determine the direction and concavity of $g(x) := x \ln(x)$ and sketch the graph.

First note that the domain of g is $\{x \mid x > 0\}$ since $\ln(x)$ is not defined for negative values of x and that $g(x) > 0$ when $\ln(x) > 0$; that is, when $x > 1$.

By the product rule, $g'(x) := x(1/x) + \ln(x) = 1 + \ln(x)$. Thus, g is increasing when

$$1 + \ln(x) > 0; \text{ that is, when}$$

$$\ln(x) > -1.$$

This occurs when $x > e^{-1} \approx .37$.

There is a critical number at $x = e^{-1}$ which we can see is a local minimum.

The second derivative is $g''(x) := 1/x$ which is positive when $x > 0$. Therefore, g is concave up everywhere on its domain.

The graph is in Figure 4.12.

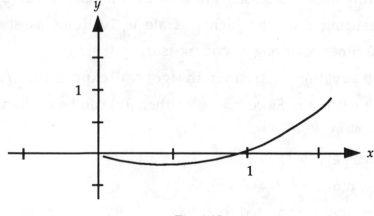

Fig. 4.12

Note that even though g is not defined at $x = 0$, it appears that $g(x) \to 0$ as $x \to 0$; in other words, $\lim_{x \to 0} x \ln(x) = 0$. Indeed this is the case, although as before we shall have to wait until Section 4.4 to prove it. You might verify this with your calculator by computing values of $x \ln(x)$ for values of x very near to 0.

♦

EXAMPLE 4.11:

Find y' if $y = \ln\left(\dfrac{x(x+1)^3}{\sqrt{x^2+1}}\right)$.

Although this looks like quite a formidable problem, it actually can be greatly simplified if we first rewrite y using the properties of logarithms.

$$y = \ln(x) + 3\ln(x+1) - \tfrac{1}{2}\ln(x^2+1)$$

It now follows that

$$\frac{dy}{dx} = \frac{1}{x} + \frac{3}{x+1} - \frac{1}{2}\left(\frac{1}{x^2+1}\right)(2x) = \frac{1}{x} + \frac{3}{x+1} - \frac{x}{x^2+1}. \qquad \blacklozenge$$

◻ The natural logarithm is sometimes described as a logarithm to the base e. There are logarithms to other bases. The most notable is the base 10 logarithm, called the **common logarithm** and abbreviated log. Many physical quantities such as the pH scale for measuring the strengths of acids and bases in chemistry, the Richter scale for measuring earthquakes and the decibel scale for measuring sound intensity are based on logarithms in base 10. (An earthquake measuring 6 on the Richter scale is 10 times as strong as one measuring 5, 100 times as strong as one measuring 4, etc.)

One more observation: Consider the general exponential function $f(x) := b^x$, for some $b > 0, b \neq 1$. Since $b = e^{\ln(b)}$, then $f(x)$ can be written as

$$f(x) := e^{(\ln(b))x}.$$

Differentiating, we get

$$f'(x) := (\ln(b))\, e^{(\ln(b))x} = (\ln(b))f(x).$$

But, in the last section, we showed that $f'(x) = k_b\, f(x)$. Therefore,

$$\ln(b) = k_b = \lim_{\Delta t \to 0}\left(\frac{b^{\Delta t} - 1}{\Delta t}\right).$$

You should use the natural logarithm button on your calculator to confirm the values of k_b that we deduced near the beginning of the section on the number e.

◻ Finally, since $\frac{d}{dx}(\ln x) = \frac{1}{x}$, it follows that:

$$\int \frac{1}{x}\, dx = \ln(x) + c \ , x > 0$$

and we have partially filled in the gap in the power rule for antiderivatives (when $n = -1$). Applying this to the differential equation $\frac{1}{y} dy = r\, dt$, we get

$$\ln(y) = rt + c.$$

Thus, $e^{\ln(y)} = e^{rt + c} = e^{rt}\, e^{c}$.

Since c is an arbitrary constant, then e^c is also a constant which we will just call C. Therefore, the solution to the differential equation $\frac{dy}{dt} = ry$ is

$$y = Ce^{rt},$$

as we discovered before.

To fill in the other half of the gap in the power rule (i.e., for $x < 0$), note that if $x < 0$, then $|x| = -x > 0$ and $\frac{d}{dx}(\ln|x|) = \frac{d}{dx}(\ln(-x)) = \frac{1}{-x}(-1) = \frac{1}{x}$. Thus, for any $x \neq 0$, $\frac{d}{dx}(\ln|x|) = \frac{1}{x}$. So we have:

THEOREM 4.1: $\displaystyle\int \frac{1}{x}\, dx = \ln|x| + c,\ x \neq 0.$

It follows from this theorem that $\frac{d\,[\ln|x|]}{dx} = \frac{1}{x}$, which extends Property 3 on page 4-36 to all $x \neq 0$.

- -

TEST YOUR UNDERSTANDING

6. Evaluate: (a) $\displaystyle\int \frac{5}{x}\, dx$ (b) $\displaystyle\int \frac{x^3 + 4x}{x^2}\, dx$

7. Write the general solution the differential equation $\frac{dy}{dx} = x^2 y$.

- -

EXAMPLE 4.12:

Let $f(x) := \ln(a - bx)$.

(a) Determine $f'(x)$.

(b) Determine $\displaystyle\int \frac{b}{a-bx}\, dx$.

(c) Determine $\displaystyle\int \frac{1}{a-bx}\, dx$.

By the chain rule, $f'(x) := \left(\dfrac{1}{a-bx}\right)(-b) = \dfrac{-b}{a-bx}$.

Now it follows that

$$\int \frac{-b}{a-bx}\, dx = \ln|a-bx| + c. \text{ Upon multiplying by } -1, \text{ we have:}$$

$$\int \frac{b}{a-bx}\, dx = -\ln|a-bx| + c.$$

Since b is a constant, we can divide both sides of the equation above by b obtaining:

$$\int \frac{1}{a-bx}\, dx = -\frac{1}{b}\ln|a-bx| + c. \qquad \blacklozenge$$

EXERCISES FOR SECTION 4.3:

1. Find the derivative of the following:

   (a) $f(t) := \ln(2t^3)$

   (b) $y = \ln(e^{5x})$

   (c) $f(x) := \ln(x^5 e^{3x})$

   (d) $h(x) := 2x\ln(x)$

   (e) $z = (1 + \ln(t))^4$

   (f) $v = \ln(x^2 + 2x)$

   (g) $s(t) := e^t \ln(t)$

   (h) $y = e^{x\ln(x)}$

2. Use the laws of logarithms to simplify each of the following into a single expression:

   (a) $\ln(x-2) + \ln(x+2)$

   (b) $3\ln(x) + \ln(x+1) - 2\ln(x^2+9)$

3. Solve for x:

   (a) $e^{x+1} = 3$

   (b) $\ln(x) = 1.5$

   (c) $\ln(x+1) - \ln(2x-1) = \ln(3)$

4. Write an equation of the line tangent to the function in Exer. 1(d) at $x = 1$.

5. What is the domain of $f(x) := \ln(4 - x^2)$?

6. Find $f(x)$ if $f'(x) := \dfrac{3}{x}$ and $f(e) = 2$.

7. Find $f(x)$ if $f''(x) := \dfrac{2}{x^2}$, $f'(1) = -1$, and $f(1) = 3$.

8. Determine the direction and concavity of the function $g(x) := \ln(1 + x^2)$.

9. Repeat Exercise 8 for $f(x) := x^2 \ln(x)$.

10. Repeat Exercise 8 for $h(x) := \dfrac{1}{x^2} + \ln(x^2)$.

11. For what value of k does the graph of $f(x) := \ln(x) - kx$ have a horizontal tangent at $x = 1$?

12. Determine the area of the triangle formed by the y-axis, the line tangent to $y = \ln(x)$ at $x = 1$ and the line perpendicular to $y = \ln(x)$ at $x = 1$.

13. Determine the general solution for each of the following differential equations:

   (a) $\dfrac{dy}{dx} = 2xy$ (b) $\dfrac{dy}{dx} = \dfrac{y}{x}$

14. Show that $y = x \ln(x)$ satisfies the differential equation $x\dfrac{dy}{dx} - y = x$.

15. The value of an investment at time t is given by $y(t) := 500e^{.08t}$.

   (a) What is the initial value of the investment?

   (b) At what time is the investment worth $600?

   (c) How long does it take for the investment to double in value?

16. Evaluate each of the following:

   (a) $\displaystyle\int \dfrac{1}{6x}\,dx$ (b) $\displaystyle\int \dfrac{x^2-1}{x}\,dx$ (c) $\displaystyle\int \dfrac{4}{4x+1}\,dx$

PROBLEMS FOR SECTION 4.3:

1. An investment is compounded continuously at interest rate r so that its value at time t is given by $y(t) := y_0 e^{rt}$, where y_0 is the initial investment.

   (a) Show that the time required for the investment to double in value is independent of its current value; that is, there is some t^* such that $y(t + t^*) = 2y(t)$ for all t.

   (b) Express t^* in terms of r.

2. Consider the function $g(x) := \ln\!\left(x + \sqrt{x^2+1}\right)$.

   (a) Show that g is odd; that is, show that $g(-x) = -g(x)$, for all x.

   (b) Show that $g'(x) := \dfrac{1}{\sqrt{x^2+1}}$.

(c) Determine the direction and concavity of g.

(d) Determine the general solution of the differential equation $\frac{dy}{dx} = \frac{y}{\sqrt{x^2+1}}$.

3. (a) Mimic the discussion following Example 4.7 to find $D_x^{-1}[e^{5x}]$ and $D_x^{-1}[e^{12x}]$.

(b) Generalize to find $D_x^{-1}[e^{ax}]$ in terms of a.

(c) Determine $D_x^{-1}[b^x]$. [Hint: $b = e^{\ln b}$ and use the result above.]

4. Use an argument similar to the one in the text to show that $\ln(a/b) = \ln(a) - \ln(b)$ and $\ln(a^b) = b\ln(a)$.

5. (a) Determine the derivative of $f(x) := [\ln(x)]^2$.

(b) Find the general solution of the differential equation $\frac{dy}{dx} = \frac{-xy}{\ln(y)}$.

(c) Find the specific solution to the equation in (b) for which $y = e^2$ when $x = 0$.

6. (a) Show that, for x near 0, $\ln(1 + x) \approx x$. (Hint: Think about the line tangent to the graph of $f(x) := \ln(1 + x)$ at $x = 0$.)

(b) Let $f(x) := (1+x)^{1/x}$ and let $g(x) := \ln f(x)$. Use (a) to evaluate $\lim_{x \to 0} g(x)$. What does this tell you about $\lim_{x \to 0} f(x)$?

TYU Answers for Section 4.3

1. (a) $-.693$ (b) $.405$ (c) 2.484 (d) $.549$ (e) $.307$

2. (a) 3 (b) $2x$ (c) x^2 (d) $1/8$ 3. (a) $x = e^2$ (b) $x = \ln(4)$ (c) $x = 3$

4. (a) $y' = \frac{1-\ln(x)}{x^2}$ (b) $y' = \frac{2x}{x^2+1}$ (c) $y' = \frac{-1/x}{(1+\ln(x))^2}$ 5. $y = x$

6. (a) $5\ln|x| + c$ (b) $\frac{x^2}{2} + 4\ln|x| + c$ 7. $\ln|y| = \frac{x^3}{3} + c$

4.4 L'HÔPITAL'S RULE

In Example 4.8, we claimed that $\lim\limits_{x \to -\infty} x e^x = 0$. In Example 4.10, we claimed that $\lim\limits_{x \to 0} x \ln(x) = 0$. Since direct substitution leads to the indeterminate form $(0)(-\infty)$ in both cases, we justified these conclusions by evaluating the first expression for large negative values of x and the second expression for values of x very near 0. In this section, we will learn a theorem, called l'Hôpital's Rule, to help us evaluate limits of indeterminate expressions. Recall in Chapter 3, we mentioned l'Hôpital as the author of the first calculus textbook, in 1696. The rule first appears in this book.

THEOREM 4.2 (L'HÔPITAL'S RULE): Suppose $h(x) := \dfrac{f(x)}{g(x)}$, where either $\lim\limits_{x \to a} f(x) = 0$ and $\lim\limits_{x \to a} g(x) = 0$, or $\lim\limits_{x \to a} f(x) = \pm\infty$ and $\lim\limits_{x \to a} g(x) = \pm\infty$. Then, $\lim\limits_{x \to a} h(x) = \lim\limits_{x \to a} \dfrac{f'(x)}{g'(x)}$, if the limit exists.

This says is that if you need to evaluate the limit of the quotient of two functions and that limit turns out to be an indeterminate expression of the form $\dfrac{0}{0}$ or $\dfrac{\infty}{\infty}$, you can evaluate the limit of the quotient of the derivatives of the two functions. (This is NOT the same as the derivative of the quotient of the two functions, for which you would need the quotient rule.)

There is an interesting story connected with l'Hôpital's rule. Apparently, it was not discovered by l'Hôpital but rather by Johann Bernoulli, whom l'Hôpital paid to do mathematics for him and to keep quiet about it. L'Hôpital subsequently published Bernoulli's work as his own. Although Bernoulli claimed the rule as his own after l'Hôpital's death, nobody believed him since Bernoulli was guilty of sleazy shenanigans, such as stealing results from his brother Jacques. It wasn't until 250 years later that correspondence between l'Hôpital and Bernoulli was unearthed which proved that, at least this once, Bernoulli was telling the truth. It is, however, too late to start calling Theorem 4.2 "Bernoulli's Rule".

We shall not prove l'Hôpital's Rule here, although we include the original proof, somewhat as it appeared in l'Hôpital's book, in the Appendix.

EXAMPLE 4.13:

Evaluate $\lim\limits_{x \to 3}\dfrac{x^2-5x+6}{x^2-9}$.

Direct substitution leads to the indeterminate form $\dfrac{0}{0}$. We could simplify this expression by factoring and canceling $(x - 3)$ from the numerator and denominator, or we could invoke Theorem 4.2.

$$\lim\limits_{x \to 3}\dfrac{x^2-5x+6}{x^2-9} = \lim\limits_{x \to 3}\dfrac{2x-5}{2x} = \dfrac{1}{6} .$$ ♦

EXAMPLE 4.14:

Evaluate $\lim\limits_{x \to 0}\dfrac{e^x-1}{x^2}$.

This is another example of the indetermine form $\dfrac{0}{0}$. Applying Theorem 4.2, we have $\lim\limits_{x \to 0}\dfrac{e^x-1}{x^2} = \lim\limits_{x \to 0}\dfrac{e^x}{2x}$. Since the numerator approaches 1 and the denominator approaches 0 as x approaches 0, then $\lim\limits_{x \to 0}\dfrac{e^x}{2x}$ does not exist. Therefore, $\lim\limits_{x \to 0}\dfrac{e^x-1}{x^2}$ does not exist. ♦

Sometimes we have to use l'Hôpital's Rule more than once, as the next example illustrates.

EXAMPLE 4.15:

Evaluate $\lim\limits_{x \to \infty}\dfrac{x^2+4x-7}{3x^2+7}$.

This results in an indeterminate form $\dfrac{\infty}{\infty}$. Thus $\lim\limits_{x \to \infty}\dfrac{x^2+4x-7}{3x^2+7} = \lim\limits_{x \to \infty}\dfrac{2x+4}{6x}$. This is still indeterminate so we use l'Hôpital's Rule once more. Thus, $\lim\limits_{x \to \infty}\dfrac{2x+4}{6x} = \lim\limits_{x \to \infty}\dfrac{2}{6} = \dfrac{1}{3}$. Note that we could have obtained this results by other methods such as those discussed in Chapter 1. ♦

EXAMPLE 4.16:

Evaluate $\lim_{x \to 0} x \ln |x|$.

As we said earlier, direct substitution results in the indeterminate form $(0)(\infty)$, which at first glance, does not appear to be of the types covered by Theorem 4.2. However, we can rewrite $x \ln |x|$ as $\frac{\ln |x|}{1/x}$ which does result in the indeterminate form $\frac{\infty}{\infty}$ upon substitution.

Thus, $\lim_{x \to 0} x \ln |x| = \lim_{x \to 0} \frac{\ln |x|}{1/x} = \lim_{x \to 0} \frac{1/x}{-1/x^2} = \lim_{x \to 0} (-x) = 0.$ ◆

EXERCISES FOR SECTION 4.4:

1. Evaluate each limit below:

   (a) $\lim_{x \to \infty} \frac{\ln(x)}{x}$ (b) $\lim_{x \to \infty} x e^{-x}$ (c) $\lim_{x \to 1} \frac{x^3 - 8x^2 + 4x + 3}{x^2 - 1}$

   (d) $\lim_{x \to \infty} x^2 e^{-x}$ (e) $\lim_{x \to 0} x^2 \ln |x|$ (f) $\lim_{x \to 0} \frac{e^x}{x}$

2. Evaluate $\lim_{x \to 1} \left(\frac{1}{\ln(x)} - \frac{1}{x-1} \right).$

QUESTIONS TO THINK ABOUT

1. Explain what it means to say that $y = f(x)$ is a solution of a differential equation. Discuss the difference between general and specific solutions.

2. What problems were we trying to solve when we were "forced" to introduce exponential and logarithmic functions? You should consider both physical and mathematical problems in your answer.

3. Discuss the technique for solving separable differential equations and explain why it works.

4. Discuss the relative rates of growth of $y = e^x$, $y = \ln(x)$ and $y = x^n$ for large positive values of n.

5. Discuss the origin, value and importance of the number e.

APPENDIX

PROOF OF L'HÔPITAL'S RULE

We now provide a proof of l'Hôpital's Rule, in somewhat the way l'Hôpital (or was it Bernoulli?) did it. We have modernized the proof to include words such as "limit" and "derivative", which were not known to l'Hôpital. (They came along a bit later.) The proof is not completely correct; a more rigorous proof requires something called the Extended Mean Value Theorem, which we will not discuss.

The diagram below shows the graphs of f, g and their quotient f/g. Let A have coordinates $(a, 0)$. Then $f(a) = g(a) = 0$. What we want is the value of $f(a)/g(a)$ or, more precisely, $\lim_{x \to a} \dfrac{f(x)}{g(x)}$. In the graph, this value is the length of the segment AB.

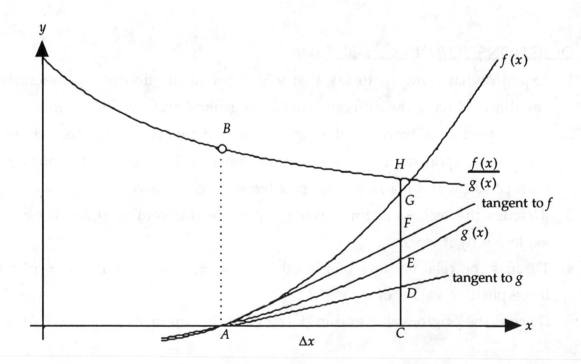

Let C have coordinates $(a + \Delta x, 0)$. The corresponding change in f is Δf $= f(a + \Delta x) - f(a) = f(a + \Delta x) = CG$ while the change in g is $\Delta g =$ $g(a + \Delta x) - g(a) = g(a + \Delta x) = CE$.

For small Δx, $AB \approx CH = CG/CE$. Also, $CG \approx CF = f'(a) \Delta x$ and $CE \approx CD = g'(a) \Delta x$. Therefore, $AB \approx \dfrac{f'(a) \Delta x}{g'(a) \Delta x} = \dfrac{f'(a)}{g'(a)}$. The approximation becomes exact as $\Delta x \to 0$. Hence, we have shown that if $f(a)$ $= g(a) = 0$, then $\lim\limits_{x \to a} \dfrac{f(x)}{g(x)} = \dfrac{f'(a)}{g'(a)}$, provided $f'(a)$ and $g'(a)$ exist and $g'(a) \neq 0$. This is (half of) l'Hôpital's Rule.

By the way, the first example in l'Hôpital's book (*Analyse des Infiniment Petits*) involving l'Hôpital's Rule is the following:

Find the value of y when $x = a$ if $y = \dfrac{\sqrt{2a^3x - x^4} - a\sqrt[3]{aax}}{a - \sqrt[4]{ax^3}}$.

Note that he does not use an exponent of 2; he writes aa for a^2. We leave this as an exercise for the adventuresome reader.

PROJECT 4.1

THE HYPERBOLIC SINE AND COSINE FUNCTIONS

OBJECTIVE: In this project, we will define two new functions, called the **hyperbolic sine** (abbreviated sinh) and **hyperbolic cosine** (cosh), and study their properties. Let:

$$\sinh(x) := \frac{e^x - e^{-x}}{2} \quad \text{and} \quad \cosh(x) := \frac{e^x + e^{-x}}{2}.$$

PROCEDURE:

Part 1: Some preliminary analysis
  a. What are the domains of $\sinh(x)$ and $\cosh(x)$?
  b. Evaluate $\sinh(x)$ and $\cosh(x)$ for $x = -2, -1, 0, 1$ and 2.
  c. What is $\sinh(x) + \cosh(x)$?
  d. Show that $\sinh(-x) = -\sinh(x)$ and $\cosh(-x) = \cosh(x)$ for all x. What does this imply about the graphs of sinh and cosh?
  e. Graph $y = \sinh(x)$ and $y = \cosh(x)$. What are their ranges?
  f. For each x-value in Part 1b, compute $(\cosh(x))^2 - (\sinh(x))^2$. What do you notice? Is there a general result? If so, prove it.
  g. Show that $\sinh(2x) = 2\cosh(x)\sinh(x)$.

Part 2: Calculus of hyperbolic functions
  a. Show that $\frac{d}{dx}[\sinh(x)] = \cosh(x)$ and $\frac{d}{dx}[\cosh(x)] = \sinh(x)$.
  b. Discuss the direction of $\sinh(x)$ and $\cosh(x)$.
  c. Determine $\frac{d^2}{dx^2}[\cosh(x)]$ and $\frac{d^2}{dx^2}[\sinh(x)]$. What does this imply about concavity?
  d. Conjecture a general result about higher-order derivatives of $\sinh(x)$ and $\cosh(x)$.
  e. Evaluate $\int \sinh(x)\,dx$ and $\int \cosh(x)\,dx$.

Part 3: Differential equations and hyperbolic functions
  a. Show that $y = \sinh(x)$ and $y = \cosh(x)$ both satisfy the second-order equation $y'' - y = 0$.
  b. Show that $y = a\sinh(x) + b\cosh(x)$ also satisfies $y'' - y = 0$ for any constants a and b. (We shall show in Chapter 7 that this actually is the general solution to the differential equation.)

c. Determine the specific solution of $y'' - y = 0$ satisfying the initial conditions $y(0) = 3$ and $y'(0) = 2$.

Part 4: The inverse hyperbolic sine function

a. Since $\sinh(x)$ is a one-to-one function, it has an inverse, denoted $\sinh^{-1}(x)$. Sketch a graph of $y = \sinh^{-1}(x)$.

b. Let $y = \sinh^{-1}(x)$, implying $\sinh(y) = x$. Use Part 1f to show that $\cosh(y) = \sqrt{x^2 + 1}$. Add these equations for $\sinh(y)$ and $\cosh(y)$, making use of 1c to simplify. Now solve for y, obtaining an equivalent expression for $\sinh^{-1}(x)$.

c. Show that the derivative of $y = \sinh^{-1}(x)$ is $y' = \dfrac{1}{\sqrt{x^2 + 1}}$.

PROJECT 4.2

COMPARING EXPONENTIAL AND POWER FUNCTIONS

OBJECTIVE: A problem which intrigued mathematicians for many years is: Which is bigger, e^π or π^e ? In the days before calculators, this was a non-trivial question since the values are quite close. In this project, we will show that $e^x \geq x^e$ for all x (with equality only when $x = e$) and, hence, e^π is bigger than π^e. We will then consider the more general question of comparing the exponential function b^x with the power function x^b.

PROCEDURE:

Part 1: An unusual beginning

    a. Let $f(x) := \dfrac{\ln(x)}{x}$. (You'll see why we chose this function later.) Use a computer or graphing calculator to draw a graph of f, for $0 < x < 5$.

    b. Determine $f'(x)$ and show that the direction of f agrees with your graph.

    c. What is the maximum value of $f(x)$?

Part 2: Comparing e^x and x^e

    a. Use Part 1c to argue that $\dfrac{\ln(x)}{x} \leq \dfrac{1}{e}$ for all $x > 0$.

    b. This implies $e \ln(x) \leq x$, for all $x > 0$. Show that $x^e \leq e^x$ for all $x > 0$.

    c. Graph the functions $y = e^x$ and $y = x^e$ (for $0 \leq x \leq 4, 0 \leq y \leq 50$) on the same axes and verify the inequality in 2b.

    d. Clearly the graphs meet at $x = e$. Show that they have the same slope at that point.

Part 3: Comparing $f(x) := x^b$ and $g(x) := b^x$

    a. On the same axes, graph f and g for the case $b = 2$. Where do they intersect?

    b. Repeat Part 3a for the case $b = 4$ and $b = 5$. Make sure to include enough of the graph to show all points of intersection.

    c. In all cases, there are 2 points of intersection. One is obvious: $x = b$. Is the other intersection point at an x-value greater than b or less than b?

    d. Call the other intersection point x^*. For what values of x is $f(x) \leq g(x)$?

e. Let $h(x) = f(x) - g(x) = x^b - b^x$. How many roots does the
   equation $h(x) = 0$ have?

f. Use a root-finding procedure (available on many calculators) to find the
   roots of $h(x) = 0$ for the cases $b = 2, b = 3, b = 5$ and $b = 6$.

PROJECT 4.3

LOGARITHMIC DIFFERENTIATION

OBJECTIVE: So far, we have learned to differentiate power functions ($f(x) :=$ x^n, for some constant n) and exponential functions ($f(x) := b^x$, for some constant $b > 0$, $b \neq 1$). In this project, we will study a function which is a hybrid of these two types; namely, let $f(x) := x^x$. Since both the base and exponent are variables, none of the rules we learned for derivatives apply to this function. We will develop a new technique, called logarithmic differentiation, specifically designed to handle functions of this type.

PROCEDURE:

Part 1: Some graphical and numerical analysis

a. Use a computer or graphing calculator to draw a graph of $f(x) := x^x$ for $0 < x < 3$.

b. Note that $f(0) = 0^0$ is an indeterminate quantity. By computing values of $f(x)$ for x very near 0, guess the value of $\lim_{x \to 0} x^x$. Does it agree with what your graph shows?

c. Describe the direction of f. Does f have any local extrema? If so, where (approximately)?

d. Write a formula, in terms of Δx, for the slope of the secant joining the points $(1, f(1))$ and $(1 + \Delta x, f(1 + \Delta x))$. Evaluate the slope for $\Delta x = 1, .1, .01$ and $.001$. What do you notice?

e. Use 1d to estimate $f'(1)$.

Part 2: Determining $f'(x)$

a. Let $g(x) := \ln[f(x)] = \ln(x^x)$. Use some laws of logarithms to express $g(x)$ in a simpler form.

b. Differentiate your answer to 2a to find $g'(x)$.

c. Since $g(x) = \ln[f(x)]$, then by the chain rule, $g'(x) := \frac{1}{f(x)} f'(x)$. Use this and your answer to 2b to show that $f'(x) := x^x[1 + \ln(x)]$.

d. What is $f'(1)$? Compare to your answer to Part 1e.

e. What are the critical numbers of f? Do they agree with your graph?

Part 3: Some more examples
This technique in which we take the logarithm of a complicated expression and then differentiate is called, quite naturally, **logarithmic differentiation**. Try it on the following examples.

a. $f(x) := x^{1/x}$ b. $f(x) := x^{\ln(x)}$ c. $f(x) := \dfrac{x(x+1)^2}{\sqrt[3]{x+2}}$

Note that we could do 3c by other methods, but logarithmic differentiation is much easier.

Part 4: A surprising result
a. Let $f(x) := x^{1/\ln(x)}$. What is $f(e)$?
b. Use logarithmic differentiation to find $f'(x)$.
c. What does your answer to 4a imply about f?
d. Draw a graph of f.

PROJECT 4.4

SECOND-ORDER DIFFERENTIAL EQUATIONS

OBJECTIVE: In this chapter, we learned to solve some first-order differential equations by separation of variables. In this project, we will learn how to solve second-order differential equations of the form $\dfrac{d^2y}{dx^2} + a\dfrac{dy}{dx} + by = 0$, where a and b are constants.

PROCEDURE:

Part 1: Some observations

   a. Why can't the solution of this differential equation be a polynomial?

      [Hint: Consider the degrees of $\dfrac{dy}{dx}$ and $\dfrac{d^2y}{dx^2}$.]

   b. Why is it reasonable to think that the solutions might be exponential functions? [Hint: If y is an exponential function, then what are $\dfrac{dy}{dx}$ and $\dfrac{d^2y}{dx^2}$?]

   c. The general solution of a first-order differential equation has one constant in it. It is not hard to believe that the general solution of a second-order equation has two constants in it. Show that if $y_1(x)$ and $y_2(x)$ are solutions to the differential equation, then $c_1y_1(x) + c_2y_2(x)$ is also a solution for every choice of constants c_1 and c_2. Moreover, it can be shown (you don't have to show it) that if y_1 is not a multiple of y_2, then every solution of a second-order equation of this type is of the form $y(x) := c_1y_1(x) + c_2y_2(x)$.

   d. Show that $y = e^{2x}$ and $y = e^{3x}$ both satisfy the equation $\dfrac{d^2y}{dx^2} - 5\dfrac{dy}{dx} + 6y = 0$.

   e. In view of 1c, write another solution of the equation in 1d.

Part 2: The characteristic equation

   a. Let $y = e^{rx}$, where r is a constant. Determine $\dfrac{dy}{dx}$ and $\dfrac{d^2y}{dx^2}$.

   b. Show that the values of r for which $y = e^{rx}$ is a solution of the equation $\dfrac{d^2y}{dx^2} + a\dfrac{dy}{dx} + by = 0$ are precisely the roots of the polynomial equation $r^2 + ar + b = 0$.

c. The polynomial in 2b is called the **characteristic polynomial** for the differential equation. Write and solve the characteristic polynomial for the equation $\dfrac{d^2y}{dx^2} - 5\dfrac{dy}{dx} + 6y = 0$ from 1d. Does this confirm 1d?

d. Let r_1 and r_2 be the roots of the characteristic polynomial. If r_1 and r_2 are real and distinct, then the general solution of the differential equation is $y = c_1 e^{r_1 x} + c_2 e^{r_2 x}$. Write the general solution for the equation in 2c.

e. Write the general solution for each of the following equations:

   (i) $\dfrac{d^2y}{dx^2} - 4\dfrac{dy}{dx} - 5y = 0$ (ii) $\dfrac{d^2y}{dx^2} - 8\dfrac{dy}{dx} + 12y = 0$

Part 3: Initial conditions

The general solution to the equations above contains two arbitrary constants, c_1 and c_2. Specifying the values of y and $\dfrac{dy}{dx}$ at the same x-value is sufficient to uniquely determine c_1 and c_2.

a. For the equation in 2e(i), show that $y(0) = c_1 + c_2$ and $y'(0) = -c_1 + 5c_2$.

b. Determine c_1 and c_2 if $y(0) = 2$ and $y'(0) = 4$. Graph the corresponding solution to the differential equation and indicate the value of $y(0)$. What is the significance of $y'(0)$?

c. Repeat 3b if $y(0) = 0$ and $y'(0) = -6$.

d. Determine the specific solution of the equation in 2e(ii) if $y(0) = 3$ and $y'(0) = 14$.

e. Determine the specific solution of $\dfrac{d^2y}{dx^2} - 9y = 0$ satisfying $y(0) = 4$ and $y'(0) = -4$.

Part 4: Imaginary roots or equal roots

So far, we have only solved equations for which the characteristic polynomial has real, distinct roots. Here, we briefly consider what happens if the roots are either not real or not distinct.

a. Consider the equation $\dfrac{d^2y}{dx^2} - 6\dfrac{dy}{dx} + 9y = 0$. Show that the roots of the corresponding characteristic polynomial are equal.

b. Show that $y = e^{3x}$ and $y = xe^{3x}$ both satisfy the differential equation.

c. The general solution to this equation is $y = c_1 e^{3x} + c_2 x e^{3x}$. Graph this solution for the case $c_1 = c_2 = 1$.

d. If the roots of the characteristic polynomial are not real, then they must be conjugate pairs; that is, $r_1 = p + qi, r_2 = p - qi$. It can be shown that the corresponding general solution is

$$y = e^{px}(c_1 \cos(qx) + c_2 \sin(qx)).$$

Consider the equation $\dfrac{d^2y}{dx^2} - 2\dfrac{dy}{dx} + 2y = 0$. Show that the roots of the characteristic polynomial are $r = 1 \pm i$. Write the general solution of the differential equation.

e. Graph the specific solution for the case $c_1 = c_2 = 1$.

f. Repeat 4e for the equation $\dfrac{d^2y}{dx^2} + 2\dfrac{dy}{dx} + 2y = 0$.

CHAPTER 5

APPLICATIONS OF DERIVATIVES

5.1 OPTIMIZATION

One of the most frequently encountered problems in mathematics involves finding the best way (most efficient, cheapest, etc.) of doing something. Consider the following three examples:

EXAMPLE A: An open-top box is formed by cutting small squares from the corners of an 8" x 15" piece of cardboard and folding up the sides. (We considered a similar problem in Chapter 1.) What size squares should be cut out to maximize the volume of the box?

Let x = side of the cut-out square. Then the length of the box will be $15 - 2x$, the width will be $8 - 2x$ and the height will be x. Note that $0 \leq x \leq 4$, lest we cut out more cardboard than is there. (See Figure 5.1.) Thus, the objective is to maximize the volume:

(1) $$V(x) := x(8 - 2x)(15 - 2x) = 120x - 46x^2 + 4x^3$$

for x in the closed interval $[0, 4]$.

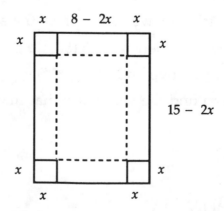

Fig. 5.1

---

1. How would the formulation of Example A change if the cardboard were 6" x 12"?

EXAMPLE B: A farmer has 100 feet of fence with which to enclose a rectangular garden. What are the dimensions of the garden of largest area that can be so enclosed?

The problem asks us to find the rectangular garden with the largest area. Thus, if x = width of rectangle and y = length of rectangle, then the goal is to maximize the enclosed area $A = xy$.

Note that A is a function of two variables, unlike the previous example in which V is a function of x only. Since we have dealt only with functions of one variable, we seek a relationship between x and y that will allow us to express A in terms of x or y alone. We are told that the farmer must fence the garden with 100 feet of fencing. This means that

$$2x + 2y = 100, \text{ or}$$

$$x + y = 50.$$

Once we have this restriction, we can express the area in terms of a single variable: Since $y = 50 - x$, then $A = x(50 - x) = 50x - x^2$. Note that both x and y must be non-negative; thus, $0 \leq x \leq 50$.

Therefore, the goal is to find the value of x that maximizes the function

(2) $\qquad A(x) = 50x - x^2,$

for x in the closed interval $[0, 50]$.

- -

TEST YOUR UNDERSTANDING

2. How would the formulation of Example B change if the farmer had 200 feet of fencing with which to enclose the garden?

3. Suppose the garden is to be built against a barn so that the farmer need only construct 3 sides of the garden with his 100 feet of fence. (The fourth side is the barn.) How does this change the formulation of Example B?

- -

EXAMPLE C: A cylindrical can is designed to hold 100 cc of liquid. What dimensions will use the least amount of material?

The "dimensions" of a cylinder are its height h and radius r. Using "the least amount of material" is equivalent to minimizing the surface area of the cylinder. Think of the cylinder as being made of 3 pieces--the top, the bottom (each circles of radius r) and the sides (which can be "unrolled" to form a rectangle whose height is h and whose length is the circumference of a circle of radius r). See Figure 5.2. Thus, the total surface area is given by:

(3) $S = 2\pi r^2 + 2\pi rh$

The goal is to minimize S.

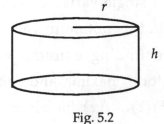

Fig. 5.2

The variables r and h are related because the can is to have a fixed volume of 100cc. Hence,

$$V = \pi r^2 h = 100$$

If we rewrite this as $h = \dfrac{100}{\pi r^2}$ and substitute in Eq.(3), we see that the objective is to minimize

$$(4) \qquad S(r) := 2\pi r^2 + \frac{200}{r}$$

where $r > 0$.

TEST YOUR UNDERSTANDING

4. Suppose the material used to construct the top and bottom of the can in Example C cost \$4 per sq. cm. while the material used to construct the sides cost \$3 per sq. cm. The objective is to minimize the total cost. Express this cost as a function of r.

▫ Problems in which the goal is to maximize or minimize a quantity subject to certain conditions are called **optimization** problems. The quantity being optimized is called the **objective function**. The conditions to which the objective function is subjected are called **constraints**. They limit how big or small the objective function can get.

In each of the examples above, either the objective function is inherently a function of one variable, or we were able to use the constraints to express the objective function in terms of a single variable. Having done so, we can use the techniques of calculus to find its optimum value.

We have some experience finding extreme values of a function. In Chapter 3, we learned about local maxima and minima. Recall that f has a local maximum at $x = c$ if $f(c) > f(x)$ for all x near c. We recognize a local maximum on the graph of f if f is increasing to the left of $x = c$ and decreasing to the right. Here we are interested in the **global** extreme values of a function--that is, the largest or smallest value the function can attain anywhere in its domain. More formally, we have:

DEFINITION: $f(c)$ is the **global maximum value** of f if $f(c) \geq f(x)$ *for all* x in the domain of f. Similarly, $f(c)$ is the **global minimum value** of f if $f(c) \leq f(x)$ for all x in the domain of f.

Note the change in semantics. For local extrema, we say, for instance, that "f has a local minimum at $x = 3$", often without regard to the function value there. Here, we would say "the global minimum value of f is 8, occurring at $x = 2$". In many cases, the global extrema occur at the same x-values as one or more of the local extrema, but not necessarily. Furthermore, a function need not have a global maximum or minimum.

Consider the function $f(x) := x^2 + 1$. Clearly, this has a local minimum at $x = 0$. Since for all $x, f(x) \geq 1 = f(0)$, then 1 is the global minimum value of f, occurring at $x = 0$. There is no global maximum since $f(x)$ can be made arbitrarily large by taking x large (either positive or negative).

EXAMPLE 5.1:

Find the global maximum and minimum values of $f(x) := x^4 - 8x^3 + 10x^2 + 40$.

Since $f'(x) := 4x^3 - 24x^2 + 20x = 4x(x - 1)(x - 5)$, then f has critical numbers at $x = 0, x = 1$ and $x = 5$. Furthermore, $f''(x) := 12x^2 - 48x + 20$. Since $f''(0)$ and $f''(5)$ are positive and $f''(1)$ is negative, then there are local minima at $x = 0$ and $x = 5$ and a local maximum at $x = 1$.

Observe that $\lim_{x \to -\infty} f(x) = \lim_{x \to +\infty} f(x) = +\infty$ so, with no other restriction on the values of x, f has no global maximum. On the other hand, since $f(0) = 40$ and $f(5) = -85$, the global minimum value of f is -85, occurring when $x = 5$. See Figure 5.3.

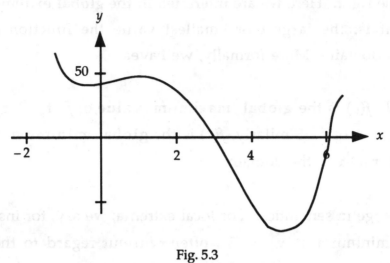

Fig. 5.3

♦

It would be nice if things were really this simple. Unfortunately, there is a complication that may arise. In each of the 3 problems considered earlier, the domain of the variable is restricted to a subinterval of the real numbers. Whenever this happens, we need to do additional analysis to determine the global extreme values.

For instance, consider the function $f(x) := x^2 + 1$ with domain restricted to the closed interval [–3, 1]. Since $x = 0$ is in this interval and it is the only critical number, then $f(0)$ must still be the global minimum. But what about the global maximum? There are no local maxima; however, it is clear from the graph in Figure 5.4 that the largest function value is $f(–3) = 10$.

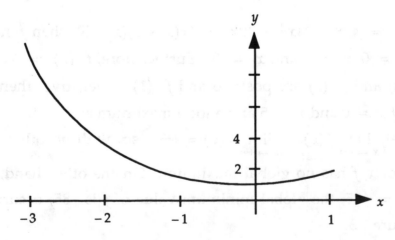

Fig. 5.4

This suggests that, in order to find the global extrema of a function defined on a closed interval, we must expand our set of candidates to include not only the critical numbers of f but also the endpoints of the interval on which f is defined.

EXAMPLE 5.2:

Consider the function $f(x) := x^4 - 8x^3 + 10x^2 + 40$ from Example 5.1. Determine the global maximum and minimum of f if its domain is restricted to the closed interval $[-1, 4]$.

Since $x = 5$ is not in this domain, the only critical numbers are $x = 0$ (a local minimum) and $x = 1$ (a local maximum). Let's evaluate f at each critical number and at the endpoints of the domain:

$$f(0) = 40, \quad f(1) = 43, \quad f(-1) = 59, \quad f(4) = -56$$

Thus, the global maximum is 59, occurring when $x = -1$, and the global minimum is -56, occurring when $x = 4$. See Figure 5.5.

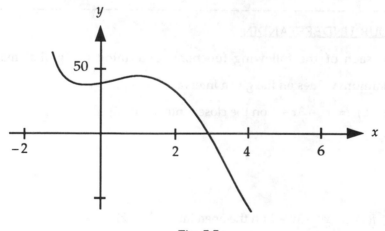

Fig. 5.5

◆

The moral of this is that we must remember to check the endpoints of the domain when looking for the global extrema of a function.

This assumes that f is defined on a closed interval; open intervals have no endpoints. If $f(x) := x^2 + 1$ were defined on the open interval $(-3, 1)$, there would be no global maximum. If there were, it would have to be smaller than 10, but for any value less than 10 you might choose, there is an x on the interval $(-3, 1)$ for which $f(x)$ is bigger than your choice but still less than 10.

Note: It is true that 10 is the smallest number greater than or equal to all the function values on the interval $(-3, 1)$. However, since -3 is not in the restricted domain, $f(x)$ is never equal to 10, so 10 cannot be the global maximum. In more advanced mathematics courses, you will say that 10 is the **least upper bound** on the values of f on the interval $(-3, 1)$.

It appears (and it is true) that <u>if f is continuous and defined on a closed interval, then it always has a global maximum and minimum</u>. The only places these can occur are at the critical numbers or at the endpoints of the interval. (This is a well-known result called the **Extreme Value Theorem**, which you might prove in a more advanced course.)

If f is defined on an open interval (or any other non-closed interval) or if f is discontinuous, then anything can happen--it may have both a maximum and minimum, one or the other, or neither.

- -

TEST YOUR UNDERSTANDING

5. For each of the following functions, determine the global maximum and minimum values on the given interval.

    (a) $f(x) := x^3 - 3x + 1$ on the closed interval $[0, 2]$.

    (b) $f(x) := x^3 - 3x + 1$ on the open interval $(0, 2)$.

    (c) $f(x) := 1/x$ on the closed interval $[1, 6]$.

(d) $g(x) := 9 - x^2$ on the half-open interval $(-1, 3]$.

¤ Now let's solve the three problems posed earlier.

Solution to Example A: Differentiating Eq.(1) gives:

$$V'(x) := 120 - 92x + 12x^2 = 4(3x - 5)(x - 6)$$

and we see that there are critical numbers at $x = 5/3$ (a local maximum) and $x = 6$ (which is not in the domain). Since $V(0) = V(4) = 0$, then the global maximum of V must occur when $x = 5/3$.

Thus, it is optimal to construct the box with dimensions 35/3" x 14/3" x 5/3".

Solution to Example B: From Eq.(2), we want to maximize
$$A(x) := 50x - x^2$$
for x in the closed interval $[0, 50]$.

Since $A'(x) := 50 - 2x$, there is a critical number at $x = 25$. Convince yourself that it is a local maximum. Thus, the only candidates for the global maximum are at $x = 25$ and the endpoints $x = 0$ and $x = 50$. Since $A(0) = A(50) = 0$ and $A(25) = 625$, then the global maximum occurs when $x = 25$. The maximum area is 625. Note that $x = 25$ implies $y = 25$ also, so the maximum area occurs when the garden is square.

In fact, it is always true that the area of a rectangle of fixed perimeter P is maximized by making the rectangle into a square whose side is $P/4$. (See Problem 1 at the end of this section.)

----

6. Solve the variation of this problem in TYU #3 in which one side of the garden is a barn.

Solution to Example C: From Eq. (4), the objective is to minimize $S(r) :=$ $\frac{200}{r} + 2\pi r^2$, where $r > 0$. (Note that S is not defined for $r = 0$. This means that S is defined on an open interval so there might not be a global minimum.) Differentiating gives

$$S'(r) := 4\pi r - \frac{200}{r^2} = \frac{4\pi}{r^2}\left(r^3 - \frac{50}{\pi}\right).$$

Setting $S'(r) = 0$ gives $r = \sqrt[3]{\frac{50}{\pi}} \approx 2.5$ cm as the only critical number.

To convince ourselves that this critical number is indeed a global minimum, note that $S'(r) < 0$ for all $r < \sqrt[3]{\frac{50}{\pi}}$ and $S'(r) > 0$ for all $r >$ $\sqrt[3]{\frac{50}{\pi}}$. Therefore, the global minimum must occur at the critical number. See Figure 5.6 for a graph of S.

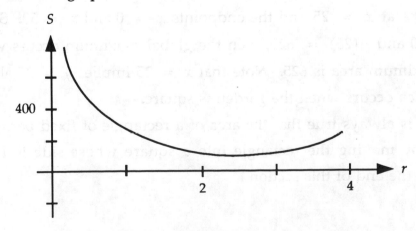

Fig. 5.6

Upon substitution, we find the optimal $h = \dfrac{100}{\pi r^2} = \dfrac{100}{\pi}\left(\dfrac{50}{\pi}\right)^{-2/3} = 2\left(\dfrac{50}{\pi}\right)^{1/3}$ $= 2r$. Thus, it is optimal to build the can so that its height is equal to its diameter.

Look through your cupboards to see how many cans are constructed this way. Can you think of some reasons for not constructing a can in this manner?

¤ We conclude this section by presenting several more examples.

EXAMPLE 5.3: A beam of rectangular cross-section is to be cut from a circular log of diameter 16 inches. What is the stiffest such beam that can be cut?

In order to solve this problem, we need to define what we mean by "stiffness". Engineers define the stiffness of a beam as being equal to the product of the width and the cube of the height of the rectangular cross-section.

Let x = width and y = height of the beam. The stiffness is given by $S = xy^3$. This is the objective function; we would like to maximize S. As the diagram indicates, x and y are the legs of a right triangle whose hypotenuse is the diameter of the log. Therefore, the constraint is $x^2 + y^2 = 16^2 = 256$. See Figure 5.7.

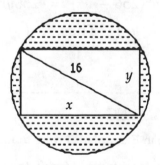

Fig. 5.7

Solving for x in terms of y gives $x = \sqrt{256 - y^2}$.

Hence, the objective is to find the value of y that maximizes

(5) $S = y^3 \sqrt{256 - y^2}$

where $0 \le y \le 16$. From Eq.(5), the objective is to maximize $S(y) :=$ $y^3 \sqrt{256 - y^2}$ for y on the closed interval $[0, 16]$. Differentiating gives:

$$S'(y) := 3y^2 \sqrt{256 - y^2} + y^3 \left(\frac{1}{2}\right)(256 - y^2)^{-1/2}(-2y)$$

$$= 3y^2 \sqrt{256 - y^2} - y^4(256 - y^2)^{-1/2} = y^2(256 - y^2)^{-1/2}[3(256 - y^2) - y^2]$$

$$= y^2(256 - y^2)^{-1/2}[768 - 4y^2]$$

Setting $S'(y) = 0$ yields $y = 0$ and $y = \sqrt{192} = 8\sqrt{3}$. There is also a critical number at $y = 16$ since $S'(16)$ is undefined. (Note that both endpoints are also critical numbers.)

Since $S(0) = S(16) = 0$ and $S(8\sqrt{3}) = 12288\sqrt{3} \approx 21283$, then the stiffest beam has height $y = 8\sqrt{3}$. The corresponding value of x is 8. Thus, the stiffest beam is 8 inches wide and $8\sqrt{3}$ inches high.

Here's another, somewhat easier, approach. Since $S(y) \ge 0$ for all possible y, then $[S(y)]^2$ is a maximum when $S(y)$ is. (See Problem 4 in Section 3.3.) Letting $T(y) := [S(y)]^2 = y^6(256 - y^2) = 256y^6 - y^8$, we see that $T'(y) :=$ $256(6y^5) - 8y^7 = 8y^5(192 - y^2)$. Thus, $T'(y) = 0$ when $y = 0$ or $y = \sqrt{192} = 8\sqrt{3}$, as before.   ◆

- -

TEST YOUR UNDERSTANDING

7. Suppose the objective in Example 5.3 were to maximize the cross-sectional area of the beam, rather than its stiffness. Modify the formulation for this case and solve.

- -

EXAMPLE 5.4:

The amount of light perceived at a point r yards away from its source is directly proportional to the intensity of the light and inversely proportional to r^2. Suppose 2 light bulbs, one of 60 watts and one of 120 watts, are 100 yards apart. Find the point on the line joining the bulbs where the light intensity is minimal.

Let x = distance from the 60 watt bulb. Then $100 - x$ = distance from the 120 watt bulb. The perceived brightness of the 60 watt bulb = $k\left(\dfrac{60}{x^2}\right)$ for some k, and the perceived brightness of the 120 watt bulb = $k\left(\dfrac{120}{(100-x)^2}\right)$.

The total perceived light is $k\left(\dfrac{60}{x^2}\right) + k\left(\dfrac{120}{(100-x)^2}\right)$.

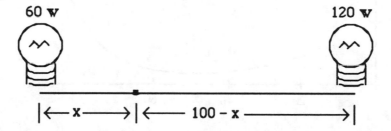

Since the value of k does not affect the location of the critical numbers, we can arbitrarily set $k = 1$. Therefore, the objective is to find x that minimizes

$$I(x) := \frac{120}{(100-x)^2} + \frac{60}{x^2}.$$

Differentiating with respect to x, we get

$$\frac{dI}{dx} = \frac{240}{(100-x)^3} - \frac{120}{x^3}.$$

Setting $\dfrac{dI}{dx} = 0$ gives

$$\frac{x^3}{(100-x)^3} = \frac{120}{240} = .5 \qquad \text{from which}$$

$$\frac{x}{(100-x)} = \sqrt[3]{.5} = .79.$$

Solving, we get $x = 44.25$ as a critical number which you can verify to be a local minimum. See Figure 5.8.

Technically, I is defined for x on the open interval (0, 100) so there are no endpoints to check. Since there is only one critical number and it is a local minimum, it must be the global minimum and, hence, the point of least brightness is 44.3 yards from the 60 watt bulb.

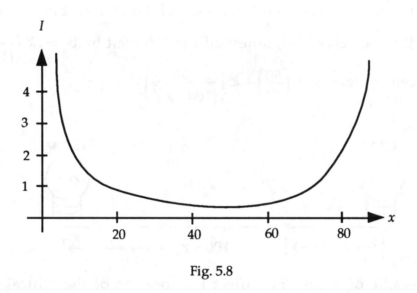

Fig. 5.8

Observe that the graph of I is nearly flat for most of the domain so if we were to just rely on graphical techniques, it would be difficult to determine the optimal solution. ♦

◻ After solving a problem such as this, it is important and interesting to do some "what if" analysis to see if the optimal solution behaves as we think it should. Also, the optimal solution will depend on some data in the problem which may be subject to change. It may be important to estimate the magnitude of the effect a change in data will have on the optimal solution.

For example, what if the 60 watt bulb is replaced by one of greater intensity? What happens to the optimal location? Clearly, the point of minimum total intensity will be further from that light source, but the question is how much?

To answer these questions, consider the intensity of the replacement bulb to be a variable s. Then

$$I = \frac{120}{(100-x)^2} + \frac{s}{x^2} \quad \text{from which}$$

$$\frac{dI}{dx} = \frac{240}{(100-x)^3} - \frac{2s}{x^3}.$$

Setting $\frac{dI}{dx} = 0$, we get

$$\frac{x^3}{(100-x)^3} = \frac{s}{120}.$$

Let $c = \sqrt[3]{\frac{s}{120}}$. Then $\frac{x}{100-x} = c$, from which $x = \frac{100c}{1+c}$. In other words, the optimal location is given in terms of the wattage of the replacement bulb by the function $x(s) := \frac{100c}{1+c}$, where $c = \sqrt[3]{\frac{s}{120}}$.

Suppose s is increased from 60 to 75. Then $c = \sqrt[3]{\frac{75}{120}} = .855$ so the new optimal position is $x(75) = \frac{(.855)(100)}{1.855} = 46.1$.

EXAMPLE 5.5:

A cable television company has its master antenna located at point A on the bank of a straight river 1 mile wide. It is going to run a cable from point A to a point P on the opposite side and then straight along the river to a town T, 3 miles downstream from A. See Figure 5.9. If it costs 5 dollars per foot to run the cable under water and 3 dollars per foot to run it along the bank, what location of P minimizes the total cost?

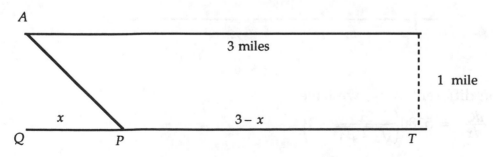

Fig. 5.9

Let's look at some extreme cases first. Suppose they lay the cable straight across the river to point Q, then along the bank of the river to T. The cost of laying the cable under water is 5280 ft./mi. $\times$ 5 dollars/ft. $\times$ 1 mi. = 5280(5). The cost of laying the cable along the bank is 5280 ft./mi. $\times$ 3 dollars/ft. $\times$ 3 mi. = 5280(9). Thus, the total cost is 5280(14).

Now suppose they laid the cable directly under water to T. The total distance is $\sqrt{3^2 + 1^2} = \sqrt{10}$ and, hence, the total cost is 5280($5\sqrt{10}$). Note that this is more expensive than laying it straight across the river.

Now let's see what happens if P is located strictly between Q and T. Let x = number of miles downstream that P is from Q. Then the distance from P to T is $3 - x$ and the distance from A to P is $\sqrt{x^2 + 1}$. So the total cost of laying the cable is

$$C = 5280[5\sqrt{x^2 + 1} + 3(3 - x)].$$

Since P will not be downstream from T nor upstream from Q, then x is restricted to the closed interval [0, 3]. A graph of this function, with the y-values divided by 5280 for simplicity, is given in Figure 5.10.

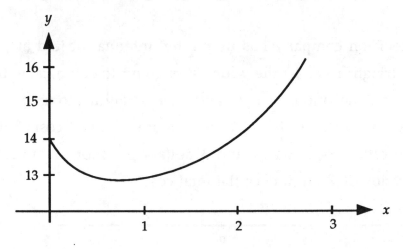

Fig. 5.10

Upon differentiating, we have:

$$\frac{dC}{dx} = 5280\left(\frac{5x}{\sqrt{x^2 + 1}} - 3\right).$$

Setting $\frac{dC}{dx} = 0$, we have:

$$5x = 3\sqrt{x^2 + 1}.$$

Squaring both sides and simplifying yields $16x^2 = 9$ from which

$$x = \sqrt{\frac{9}{16}} = .75 \text{ miles.}$$

Since $C(.75) = 68640$, $C(0) = 73920$ and $C(3) = 83424$, then the minimum cost is \$68640, obtained by locating P .75 miles from Q.

Clearly, the optimal solution depends on the costs of laying the cable under water and along the bank. In particular, if the cost of laying it under water goes up, then x should decrease, while if the cost of laying it along the bank increases, x should increase. Let w and b represent the cost per foot of laying the cable under water and along the bank, respectively. Then the total cost is

$$C = 5280[w\sqrt{x^2 + 1} + b(3 - x)] \text{ from which}$$

$$\frac{dC}{dx} = 5280\left(\frac{wx}{\sqrt{x^2 + 1}} - b\right).$$

Setting $\frac{dC}{dx} = 0$ yields $wx = b\sqrt{x^2 + 1}$, from which

$$x = \frac{b}{\sqrt{w^2 - b^2}} \text{ if } w > b.$$

Upon dividing the numerator and denominator by b, we see that the optimal value of

$$x = \frac{1}{\sqrt{r^2 - 1}}$$

where $r = w/b > 1$.

Since $\frac{dx}{dr} = \frac{-r}{(r^2 - 1)^{3/2}} < 0$ when $r > 0$, then x decreases if r increases. Thus, if it becomes more expensive to lay the cable under water, P should move closer to Q.

(See Problem 5 at the end of this section for some additional questions about this example.) ◆

The last example is a variation of Example B considered earlier in this section.

EXAMPLE 5.6: A farmer has a barn that is 50 ft. long. He has 200 ft. of fence with which to enclose a rectangular garden one of whose sides is to be along the barn. What are the dimensions of the largest garden that can be so enclosed?

Let x and y be the dimensions of the garden, as shown in Figure 5.11. As before, the objective is to maximize the area $A = xy$. Since there is only 200 ft. of fence available, then $2x + y = 200$. Furthermore, since one side of the garden is the barn, the width of the garden cannot exceed 50 ft.; that is, $y \leq 50$.

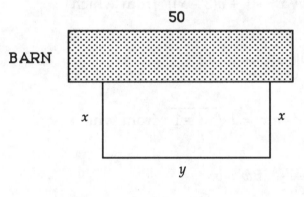

Fig. 5.11

Solving the constraint for x, we get $x = 100 - \frac{y}{2}$. Hence our problem is to maximize $A(y) := y\left(100 - \frac{y}{2}\right)$, where $0 \leq y \leq 50$.

$A'(y) := 100 - y = 0$ when $y = 100$. However, this is not in the domain so we must look at the endpoints. Clearly, A is an increasing function of y for $y < 100$ so the maximum value of A should occur when $y = 50$. Thus, the farmer should build a garden 50 ft. wide and 75 ft. long. ♦

EXERCISES FOR SECTION 5.1:

1. Determine the global maxima and minima for the following functions on the given interval:

   (a) $f(x) := 2x^3 - 24x$, $[0, 1]$ (b) $f(x) := \dfrac{x^2}{2x^2 + 2}$, $[-2, 2]$

   (c) $f(x) := 9 - x^2$, $(-2, 4)$

2. The deflection D of a particular beam of length L is given by $D = 2x^4 - 5Lx^3 + 3L^2x^2$, where x is the distance from one end of the beam. At what point is the deflection maximum?

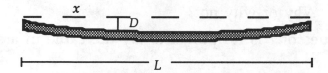

3. Find the dimensions of the right triangle whose area is 2 sq. cm. if the length of the hypotenuse is to be as small as possible.

4. What positive number x minimizes the sum of x and its reciprocal?

5. The sum of one positive number and three times a second positive number is 120. Find the two numbers so that their product is maximum.

6. What are the dimensions of the largest rectangle that can be inscribed in the region bounded by the graph of $y = 24 - x^2$ and the x-axis?

7. Find the maximum vertical distance between the graphs of $y = x^2 - 1$ and $y = 1 - x$ on the interval $-2 \leq x \leq 1$.

8. What is the minimum velocity of a particle whose position is given by the function $s(t) := t^3 - 12t + 15$?

9. Suppose for aesthetic reasons the box in Example A had to be at least 2" deep. How does this change the answer?

PROBLEMS FOR SECTION 5.1:

1. Determine the maximum area of a rectangle whose perimeter is P.

2. Determine the minimum perimeter of a rectangle whose area is A.

3. Find the point on the line $y = x - 2$ which is nearest to the point $(5, 2)$.

4. An office manager observes that one person will work approximately 30 hours per week. However, if additional people are hired, the resulting conversations reduce the effective number of work hours per week per person by $\dfrac{30(x-1)^2}{33}$ hours per week, where x is the total number of people hired. How many people should be hired to maximize the amount of work done?

5. Consider the cable TV problem of Example 5.5.

   (a) Does the optimal solution depend on the distance from A to T downstream? Why or why not?

   (b) For what values of r is it optimal to lay the cable in a straight line towards T?

   (c) For what values of r is it optimal to lay the cable straight across the river?

6. Suppose you wish to construct a cylindrical can as described in Example C but, now, the material used for the top and bottom of the can is twice as expensive as that used for the sides. Determine the dimensions of the can that minimizes the cost of the materials.

7. Circle O has radius 1 and is centered at the origin. Tangents to the circle from the point $R(r, 0)$ outside the circle meet the circle at P and Q. What is the maximum area of triangle OPQ and what is the corresponding value of r?

8. We have shown in Example C that it is optimal to have the height of the can equal to the diameter for the case when the volume is 100. Show that this is true if the volume is an arbitrary number V.

TYU Answers for Section 5.1

    1. Maximize $V(x) := x(6-2x)(12-2x), 0 \le x \le 3$

    2. Constraint becomes $2x + 2y = 200$, or $x + y = 100$. Maximize $A(x) := x(100 - x)$, $0 \le x \le 100$ 3. Constraint becomes $y + 2x = 100$. Max $A(x) := x(100 - 2x), 0 \le x \le 50$

    4. Cost $= 4(2\pi r^2) + 3(2\pi rh) = 8\pi r^2 + \dfrac{600}{r}$

    5. (a) Max is 3 (when $x = 2$), min is -1 (when $x = 1$) (b) No max, min is -1 (when $x = 1$)

(c) Max is 1 (when $x = 1$), min is 1/6 (when $x = 6$) (d) Max is 9 ($x = 0$), min is 0 ($x = 3$)

6. Dimensions are 25 by 50   7. Dimensions are $8\sqrt{2}$ by $8\sqrt{2}$.

5.2 ECONOMIC APPLICATIONS

One area where calculus is frequently used is economics. Before looking at some examples, we need to define some terms. Suppose you manufacture an item, say widgets, which you sell to the general public. Let

x = number of widgets demanded   and

$p(x)$:= price *per unit* given that you sell x widgets.

We will call the function p the **price function**. Typically, p is a decreasing function of x.

Note: It may be easier to think of x as a function of p, in which case it is clearly true that the demand usually goes down as the price goes up. Thus, x is a decreasing function of p which implies p is a decreasing function of x. A graph of this function, with p on the vertical axis and x on the horizontal axis, is what economists call the **demand curve**.

The total **revenue** is the amount of money the manufacturer takes in by selling x widgets. If each widget sells for $p(x)$ dollars, then the revenue is:

$R(x) := xp(x)$.

An interesting question is whether the revenue increases or decreases as a function of x. If you lower the price, you will sell more widgets but it is not clear whether the extra sales volume will compensate for the lower price.

Let $\Delta R = R(x + 1) - R(x)$ be the additional revenue received by selling the $(x + 1)^{\text{st}}$ widget. Since the slope of the secant, $\dfrac{\Delta R}{\Delta x}$, is approximately the same as the slope of the tangent, $R'(x)$, we have, by setting $\Delta x = 1$,

$\Delta R \approx R'(x)(1) = R'(x)$.

Thus, we can use the derivative to approximate the change in revenue incurred by selling one more widget. (Derivatives are called **marginals** in economics. Hence, $R'(x)$ is **marginal revenue**.)

Since $R(x) := xp(x)$, then by the product rule,

$R'(x) := xp'(x) + p(x)$.

Thus, the revenue is increasing whenever $xp' + p > 0$; that is, whenever $\frac{p}{xp'} < -1$. The quantity

$$\eta = \frac{p}{xp'}$$

is called the **elasticity** of the demand. (η is the Greek letter "eta" as in "I η bit too much for dinner".)

Generally speaking, the elasticity is a function of the demand, although for some demand functions, it is a constant (see Problem 4 at the end of this section). Furthermore, since $p' < 0$, then $\eta < 0$. So, if $|\eta| > 1$, the revenue is increasing, while if $|\eta| < 1$, the revenue is decreasing. In the former case, the demand is said to be **elastic**, meaning that a decrease in price will be accompanied by an increase in demand large enough to drive the revenue up. Otherwise, the demand is **inelastic**.

Note: In some economics books, the elasticity is expressed as $\eta = \frac{dx/x}{dp/p}$. The ratio dx/x can be interpreted as the percentage (or fraction) change in x. Thus, the elasticity is the ratio of the percentage change in demand to the percentage change in price.

There is a nice geometric representation of this. Consider the demand curve in Figure 5.12. Let $S(x_0, p_0)$ and $S'(x_0 + \Delta x, p_0 + \Delta p)$ be two points on the curve and draw rectangles $OUST$ and $OU'S'T'$ as shown. The revenue when the demand is x_0 is:

$$R(x_0) = x_0 p_0 = \text{area of rectangle } OUST.$$

Similarly, the revenue when the demand is $x_0 + \Delta x$ is

$$R(x_0 + \Delta x) = (x_0 + \Delta x)(p_0 + \Delta p) = \text{area of rectangle } OU'S'T'.$$

The increased demand will result in increased revenue only if the area of rectangle $OU'S'T'$ is greater than the area of rectangle $OUST$. This will happen only if the area of rectangle $UU'S'V$ is greater than the area of rectangle $STT'V$. But the area of rectangle $UU'S'V$ is $\Delta x(p_0 + \Delta p)$ while the area of rectangle $STT'V$ is $-x_0 \Delta p$ (note that $\Delta p < 0$, so we need a minus sign to make the area positive). Therefore, the revenue will increase only if

$$\Delta x(p_0 + \Delta p) > -x_0 \Delta p \text{ or, equivalently,}$$

$$p_0 + \Delta p > -x_0 \frac{\Delta p}{\Delta x}.$$

Upon letting $\Delta x \to 0$ (and, consequently, $\Delta p \to 0$), we see that the revenue will increase if and only if $-x_0 p' < p_0$ or, equivalently, $\dfrac{p_0}{x_0 p'} < -1$. (Remember $p' < 0$). But $\dfrac{p_0}{x_0 p'} = \eta$ and we have our previous result.

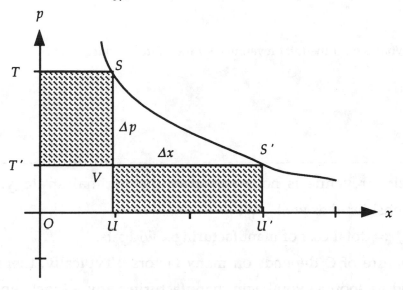

Fig. 5.12

EXAMPLE 5.7:

An express railroad train between two large cities carries 10000 passengers per year at a one-way fare of $50. If the fare goes up, ridership will decrease since more people will drive or take other more economical transportation. It is estimated that each $10 increase in fare will result in 1000 fewer passengers per year. What fare will maximize revenue?

Let p = fare and x = number of passengers. We know $x = 10000$ when $p = 50$. Since x goes down by 1000 whenever p goes up by 10, we'll assume that p is a linear function of x with slope $-10/1000 = -.01$. Therefore $p = -.01x + b$. Substituting the given data, we find $b = 150$, so

$$p(x) := 150 - .01x.$$

This means $R(x) := 150x - .01x^2$, so that $R'(x) := 150 - .02x$.

Setting $R' = 0$ gives $x = 7500$, implying $p = 150 - .01(7500) = \$75$. So, to maximize revenue, the railroad should charge $75. The maximum revenue is R(7500) = $562,500.   ◆

---

1. In the example above, what price should be charged to get 5000 passengers?

2. What would the total revenue be if the railroad charged $80?

◻ Maximizing revenue is not necessarily the optimal strategy. There are costs to be considered as well. Let

   $C(x) :=$ total cost of manufacturing x widgets.

The exact nature of C depends on many factors. Typically, there is a set-up cost incurred as soon as you begin manufacturing any widgets and a variable cost (which may or may not be constant) per widget made. At any rate, it is safe to assume C is positive and increasing. It also is usually concave up, at least for large x.

The **profit** you make is just the difference between the revenue and the costs; that is,

   $P(x) := R(x) - C(x)$.

In many cases, $P(x)$ is negative for small x, then $P(x)$ becomes positive as the revenue exceeds costs. A value of x for which $P(x) = 0$ is called a **break-even point**.

Ultimately, your goal is to maximize profit. In order to do so, set $P'(x) = 0$ which, in turn, implies $R'(x) = C'(x)$. In other words, if the profit is maximized, then the marginal revenue equals the marginal cost. Of course, just because $P'(x) = 0$ does not mean that the profit is maximized. We need other conditions to insure that the critical number is indeed a maximum. One possibility is to have $P''(x) < 0$; that is, $R''(x) < C''(x)$.

Let's look at a special case: Suppose the total cost consists of a constant set-up cost c and a constant cost per widget b. Then

$$C(x) := c + bx$$

is a linear function, $C'(x) := b > 0$ and $C''(x) = 0$. Furthermore, let's assume that the price is a linear function of the demand; that is,

$p(x) := r - sx$, where r and s are positive constants. Then

$R(x) := rx - sx^2$,

$R'(x) := r - 2sx$,

$R''(x) := -2s < 0$.

Hence, $R''(x) < C''(x)$ for all x and, hence, any critical number will be a global maximum. Moreover, the profit is maximized when $r - 2sx = b$ or, equivalently,

$$x = \frac{r-b}{2s}.$$

In order for this to make sense, we need $r > b$. See Figure 5.13.

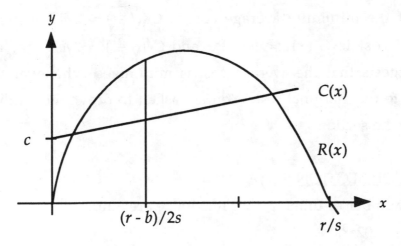

Fig. 5.13

Note that since $x = \frac{r-p}{s}$, then $x < 0$ if the price, p, exceeds r. Since the demand cannot realistically be negative, we will just say that it is 0. In other words, people stop buying if the price is too high.

▫ Another quantity of interest is the **average cost per unit** manufactured $\bar{C}(x) := \frac{C(x)}{x}$. If $C(x) := a + bx$, then $\bar{C}(x) := \frac{a}{x} + b$ which is a strictly decreasing function for $x > 0$. A more realistic model might have C concave up; for example, $C(x) := a + bx + cx^2$, where $c > 0$. In this case $\bar{C}(x) := \frac{a}{x} + b + cx$. A graph of this function is in Figure 5.14.

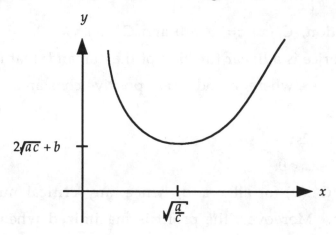

Fig. 5.14

Note that the minimum average cost is $\bar{C}(\sqrt{\frac{a}{c}}) = 2\sqrt{ac} + b$. However, the marginal cost is $C'(x) := b + 2cx$ and $C'(\sqrt{\frac{a}{c}}) = 2\sqrt{ac} + b$, also. This example suggests that the average cost is minimized whenever the average cost is equal to the marginal cost. You are asked to prove this in the problems at the end of the section.

EXERCISES FOR SECTION 5.2:

1. Find the number of units, x, that maximizes revenue, R, if
   $R = 600x^2 - 0.02x^3$.

2. Find the number of units, x, that minimizes average cost per unit, $\bar{C}$, if the total cost is $C = 0.001x^3 - 5x + 250$.

3. A certain company's profit is given by $P = 230 + 20s - \frac{1}{2}s^2$, where s is the amount (in hundreds of dollars) spent on advertising. What amount of advertising gives the maximum profit?

4. A manufacturer of radios charges $90 per unit when the average production cost per unit is $60. However to encourage large orders from distributors, the manufacturer will reduce the charge $0.10 per unit for

each unit ordered in excess of 100. Find the largest order the manufacturer should allow so as to realize a maximum profit.

5. Suppose the price equation is $p(x) := 20 - \sqrt{x}$.

   (a) Find η when $x = 4$.

   (b) Find the values of x and p that maximize the total revenue.

   (c) Show that $|\eta| = 1$ for the value of x found in (b).

6. Given the revenue function $R(x) := -x^2 + 80x$,

   (a) Find the marginal revenue at $x = 10$.

   (b) Compare your answer from (a) to $R(11) - R(10)$.

7. A company finds that its cost for producing x units of a commodity is $C(x) := 3x^2 + 5x + 10$. Find the approximate cost for making the 21st unit.

8. If the marginal cost is $C'(x) := 2 + 8x + 12x^2$ and the fixed costs are $20, determine the total cost function.

9. If the marginal revenue is $R'(x) := 100 - 5x$, find the revenue and demand functions.

PROBLEMS FOR SECTION 5.2:

1. A critical piece of data in Example 5.7 is the estimate of 1000 fewer passengers for each $10 increase in fare. Suppose we treat that number as an unknown parameter w. Determine the optimal price in terms of w.

2. The graphs of the total cost and revenue functions are given below. Sketch the profit function. Determine graphically the value of x which maximizes profits. Sketch the marginal cost and marginal revenue functions.

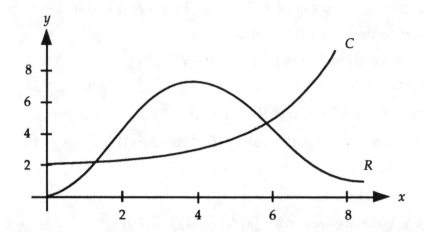

3. Show that average cost is minimized when the average cost equals the marginal cost.

4. Show that if $p(x) := \frac{k}{x}$, then the elasticity is constant for all x.

5. A monopolist is an industrial manager who can manipulate the price of his commodity, and usually does so in order to maximize profits. When the government taxes output, the tax, in effect, becomes an additional cost, and the monopolist is forced to decide how much of the cost to absorb and how much to pass on to the consumer.

    Suppose a particular monopolist assumes that when he produces x units, the total cost will be $C(x) := \frac{7}{8}x^2 + 5x + 100$ dollars and that the market price will be $p(x) := 15 - \frac{3}{8}x$ dollars per unit. Furthermore, assume that the government impose a tax of t dollars on each unit produced.

    (a) Show that profit is maximized when $x = \frac{2}{5}(10 - t)$.

    (b) Suppose the government assumes that the monopolist will always act so as to maximize total profit. What value of value of t should be chosen to maximize total tax revenue $T = tx$?

TYU Answers for Section 5.2

   1. $100   2. $560000

5.3 RELATED RATES

In the first two sections of this chapter, we have looked at applications of the derivative based on its interpretation as the slope of the tangent line. In this section and the next, we investigate applications based on the interpretation of the derivative as a rate of change.

Imagine that you are flying a kite at a constant altitude of 100 ft. The wind moves the kite downwind at 5 ft./sec. Let $x(t)$ be the kite's distance downwind at time t. Assume that at time $t = 0$, the kite is 20 ft. downwind; that is, $x(0) = 20$. Then $x(1) = 25$, $x(2) = 30$, $x(3) = 35$, etc. In general, $x(t) := 20 + 5t$.

The question that we are interested in is: What happens to the length of the string as the kite moves downwind? Certainly it gets longer but does it lengthen at a constant rate? If not, how fast is it lengthening as a function of time?

Let $s(t) :=$ length of string at time t. By the Pythagorean theorem,

(6) $\qquad (x(t))^2 + 100^2 = (s(t))^2.$

Substituting for $x(t)$ and solving for $s(t)$ gives:

$$s(t) := \sqrt{10000 + (20 + 5t)^2} = \sqrt{10400 + 200t + 25t^2}.$$

In particular, $s(0) = \sqrt{10400} = 101.98$, $s(10) = \sqrt{14900} = 122.06$, $s(20) = \sqrt{24400} = 156.20$, $s(30) = \sqrt{38900} = 197.23$.

Now compute the differences between these values of s: $s(30) - s(20) = 41.03$, $s(20) - s(10) = 34.14$, $s(10) - s(0) = 20.08$. Since the differences of the lengths are not constant but the time intervals are, then s is not increasing at a constant rate.

---

1. How much string is let out during the time interval from $t = 0$ to $t = 5$?

2. Suppose the kite flew at an altitude of 50 feet. (All other data remain unchanged.) Derive a formula for $s(t)$ and use it to compute the amount of string let out during the first 10 seconds.

To find the rate at which s is increasing, let's compute the derivative $s'(t)$.

$$s'(t) := \frac{1}{2}(10400 + 200t + 25t^2)^{-1/2}(200 + 50t) = \frac{100 + 25t}{\sqrt{10400 + 200t + 25t^2}}$$

So, for instance, $s'(10) = 2.87$, $s'(20) = 3.84$, $s'(30) = 4.31$.

Suppose we wanted to know how fast the string is lengthening when the kite is 400 ft. downwind. One way to do this is to find the time at which the kite is 400 ft. away; that is, find t such that $x(t) = 400$. It is easy to see that $t = 76$ is the answer. Therefore, the string is lengthening at a rate of $s'(76) = 4.85$ ft./sec.

Let's look at this problem from a slightly different point of view. Suppose we didn't know that the kite was moving at a constant rate but we did know that at time $t = 0$ it was 20 feet downwind. We can still define $x(t)$ to be the distance downwind at time t, although we won't be able to write an explicit formula for it. Furthermore, assuming the kite is always 100 ft. above the ground, Eq.(6) is still true.

To find the rate at which the string is lengthening, differentiate both sides of Eq.(6) *with respect to t*. This necessitates invoking the chain rule. We get:

(7) $2x(t)x'(t) = 2s(t)s'(t)$

Now suppose that, at some (unspecified) time t, the kite is 400 ft. downwind and moving at a rate of 5 ft./sec. This means that $x(t) = 400$ and $x'(t) = 5$. Substituting in Eq.(6) gives $s(t) = 412.3$. Now substitute in Eq.(7):

$2(400)(5) = 2(412.3)s'(t)$ from which

$s'(t) = 4.85$ ft./sec.

as we had before. Note that the specific value of t at which this occurs is irrelevant.

TEST YOUR UNDERSTANDING

3. How fast would the length of the string be changing if the kite were 100 ft. off the ground, 300 ft. downwind and moving at 8 ft./sec.?

4. Suppose the kite flew at an altitude of 50 feet as in TYU #2. How fast would the length of the string be changing when the kite is 200 ft. downwind and moving at 4 ft./sec.?

¤ The identifying feature of a problem of this type is that there are two quantities (in this case x and s) which are changing over time. The quantities do not behave independently, but rather are related in some way such as Eq.(6). The objective is to find a relationship between the rates of change of these two quantities, such as given by Eq.(7). Then, if we are given the rate at which one of the quantities is changing (and any other information that might be necessary), we can find the rate of change of the other. Problems of this type are often called **related rates problems**.

Newton conceived this problem as one of the two basic problems of calculus: Given the relationship between two quantities, find the relationship between their rates of change. The other problem is the inverse: Given the relationship between the rates of change, find the relationship between the quantities. Clearly (we hope), one is the derivative problem, the other is the antiderivative problem.

EXAMPLE 5.8:

A spherical balloon is inflated at a rate of 100 cc./min. How fast is the radius changing when the radius is 4 cm.?

The two quantities that are changing over time are the volume $V(t)$ and the radius $r(t)$. They are related by the formula

$$V(t) := \frac{4}{3}\pi[r(t)]^3.$$

Differentiating with respect to t (remember the chain rule) gives

$$V'(t) := 4\pi[r(t)]^2 r'(t)$$

We are given $V'(t) = 100, r(t) = 4$. Substituting and solving for $r'(t)$ gives

$$r'(t) = \frac{100}{64\pi} \approx .5 \text{ cm/min.}$$

Thus, the radius is increasing at an approximate rate of .5 cm./min. at the instant that the radius is 4 cm. ◆

TEST YOUR UNDERSTANDING

5. How fast is the radius changing when the volume of the balloon is 36π cc. and the balloon is being deflated at a rate of 30cc./min.?

EXAMPLE 5.9:

A 15 foot ladder is leaning against a wall as shown in Figure 5.15. The base of the ladder is sliding away from the wall at a rate of 1 ft./min. How fast is the top sliding down the wall when the base of the ladder is 12 feet from the wall?

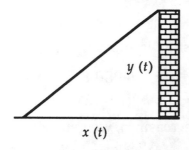

Fig. 5.15

Let $x(t)$ be the distance from the wall to the base of the ladder and let $y(t)$ be the distance from the ground to the top of the ladder. At any t, $x(t)$ and $y(t)$ are the legs of a right triangle whose hypotenuse is 15, the length of the ladder. Thus,

$$[x(t)]^2 + [y(t)]^2 = 225.$$

Differentiating with respect to t gives

$$2x(t)x'(t) + 2y(t)y'(t) = 0.$$

We are given $x(t) = 12$, which implies $y(t) = 9$. Substituting these, along with the fact that $x'(t) = 1$ gives $24 + 18y'(t) = 0$, from which $y'(t) = \dfrac{-3}{4}$.

Thus, the top of the ladder is sliding down at a rate of $\dfrac{3}{4}$ ft./min.   ♦

EXAMPLE 5.10:

According to Boyle's Law, the pressure and volume of a gas (at constant temperature) are inversely proportional. A cylinder of radius 2 inches has a movable piston at one end. When the cylinder is 6 inches high, the pressure inside is 20 psi (pounds per square inch). If the piston is moving in at 0.5 in./min, how fast is the pressure changing when the cylinder is 3 inches high?

Let $P(t)$ and $V(t)$ be the pressure and volume, respectively, at time t. Boyle's Law implies that, at any time t,

$P(t)V(t) = k$,   where k is a constant.

Differentiating with respect to t (invoking the product rule) gives

$P'(t)V(t) + P(t)V'(t) = 0$.

We are given that the piston is moving at 1 in./min. This means that the height $h(t)$ of the cylinder is changing at that rate. Since $V(t) = \pi r^2 h(t) = 4\pi h(t)$, then $V'(t) = 4\pi h'(t)$. When $h(t) = 3$ and $h'(t) = -0.5$ (negative because $h(t)$ is decreasing), we get $V(t) = 12\pi$ and $V'(t) = -2\pi$.

We still don't have enough information to find $P'(t)$; we need to find $P(t)$. We know that at some time t_0, $V(t_0) = \pi(2^2)(6) = 24\pi$ and $P(t_0) = 20$. This means that $k = 480\pi$. Hence, when $V(t) = 12\pi$, $P(t)$ must equal 40. Substituting this data above gives

$P'(t) = \dfrac{20}{3}$ psi/min.

So the pressure is increasing (as it should since the volume is decreasing) at $\dfrac{20}{3}$ psi/min when the height of the cylinder is 3 inches.   ♦

EXERCISES FOR SECTION 5.3:

1. Suppose $y = x^2$. If $\dfrac{dx}{dt} = 4$ when $x = 5$, what is $\dfrac{dy}{dt}$?
2. Suppose $y = \dfrac{1}{x}$. If $\dfrac{dy}{dt} = 3$ when $y = 2$, what is $\dfrac{dx}{dt}$?
3. The radius of a circle is increasing at a rate of 2 cm./min. How fast is the area changing?

PROBLEMS FOR SECTION 5.3:

1. A tank is shaped like an inverted cone whose radius is 3 ft. and height is 6 ft. Water is poured into the tank at a rate of 5 cu.ft./min. How fast is the water level rising when the water is 4 ft. deep?

2. The intensity of light perceived by a woman standing at a distance x from a light source is given by the formula $I = \dfrac{36}{x^2}$. If the woman is moving away from the source at 2 ft./sec., how fast is the light intensity changing when she is 10 feet away?

3. A man 6 feet tall is moving away from a 10 foot lamppost at a rate of 2 ft./sec. How fast is the length of his shadow changing when he is 15 feet away?

4. A baseball player is running from first base to second base at a rate of 30 ft./sec. How fast is his distance from home plate changing when he is 20 feet from second base? (A baseball diamond is a square 90 feet on each side. The distance to home plate means the shortest distance, not along the basepaths.)

5. Is the ladder in Example 5.9 sliding down at an increasing or decreasing rate? Explain.

6. A particle starts at the origin O and moves along the curve $y = x^3$. At time t, the particle is at point P, whose coordinates are $x(t)$ and $y(t)$.

   (a) Determine $y'(t)$ if $x'(t) = 3$ when $x = 2$.

   (b) How fast is the slope of the line OP changing at that time?

   (c) How fast is the length of the segment OP changing at that time?

7. A car starts from point B and travels west at 60 m.p.h. Another car starts from B at the same time and travels south at 50 m.p.h. How fast is the distance between them changing after 3 hours?

8. The perceived temperature (in $^\circ$C) felt by a woman standing x meters from a fire is given by the function $T(x) := \dfrac{200}{1 + x^2}$.

   (a) If the woman moves away from the fire at 2 meters per second, how fast is the temperature changing when she is 5 meters away?

   (b) At what distance from the fire is the perceived temperature changing the fastest?

1. 7.68 ft.   2. $s(t) = \sqrt{2900 + 200t + 25t^2}$, 32.17 ft.   3. $s'(t) = 7.59$ ft./sec.

4. $s'(t) = 3.88$ ft./sec.   5. $r'(t) = \dfrac{-5}{6\pi}$ cm./min. (negative since r is decreasing)

5.4 MORE APPLICATIONS OF DIFFERENTIAL EQUATIONS

In Chapter 4, we looked at several applications of first-order differential equations. In this section, we will explore several other important applications.

POPULATION GROWTH

One important application of exponential functions is the study of the growth of populations of organisms such as bacteria. Experimental evidence has shown that it is reasonable to assume that the rate at which such populations grow is proportional to the current population size. (This is true as long as there is abundant food to eat and space for the organisms to grow in. Determining what happens if this is not true is a topic for further investigation.)

Under the assumption above, the population size $y(t)$ satisfies the differential equation

$$\frac{dy}{dt} = ry.$$

(Note this is the same as Eq. (21) of Chapter 4.) Here, r can be interpreted as the net per capita growth rate--that is, the difference between the per capita birth rate and the per capita death rate. For instance, if $r = .5$, then the instantaneous rate of change in the population is equal to 50% of whatever the population is at that time.

We showed in Chapter 4 that solutions to this equation are exponential functions. In particular, the population size is given by:

$$y(t) = y_0 e^{rt},$$

where y_0 is the initial population.

EXAMPLE 5.11:

A population of organisms grows according to the differential equation $\frac{dy}{dt} = ry$. At time $t = 0$, there are 200 organisms. At time $t = 2$, there are 300. How many are there at time $t = 3$?

Since $y_0 = 200$, then $y(t) := 200e^{rt}$, where r is a constant to be determined. To find r, we use the fact that $y(2) = 300$; that is,

$$300 = 200e^{2r}.$$

Upon dividing by 200 and taking the logarithm of both sides, we have:

$$\ln(1.5) = 2r$$

from which $r = \frac{\ln(1.5)}{2} \approx .203$. Then, $y(3) = 200e^{(.203)(3)} \approx 367$. ♦

TEST YOUR UNDERSTANDING

1. At a certain time, there are 1000 bacteria in a culture. Four hours later, there are 2000. Assuming that the population size grows at a rate proportional to the present population, find the time at which the population is 6000.

RADIOACTIVE DECAY

Suppose we had a substance such as uranium or radium which decays radioactively. One theory about the behavior of such substances is that they decay at a rate proportional to the amount of the substance present. Note the similarity to the salt water example in Sections 1.1 and 4.1 in which the amount of salt decreases at a rate proportional to the current amount of salt.

Let $y(t)$ be the amount of substance present at time t. Our basic assumption implies that $y(t)$ satisfies the differential equation

$$\frac{dy}{dt} = -ky.$$

where k is a positive constant. (The minus sign indicates that y is decreasing over time.) The solution of this equation is obtained similarly to the exponential growth case, the only difference being the minus sign. Hence,

(8) $\qquad y = y_0 e^{-kt},$

where y_0 is the amount of substance at time $t = 0$.

Often, the rate of decay for radioactive substances is expressed in terms of the **half-life**-- that is, the time until half the original amount of substance decays. Some substances such as uranium-238 have half-lives on the order of 4 billion years (which is why we have to worry about nuclear wastes--they don't decay very quickly), while others such as radon-217 have half-lives on the order of a thousandth of a second.

Let t^* be the half-life. Then by definition, $y(t^*) = \frac{1}{2}y_0$. Substituting in Eq.(8), we get

$$\frac{1}{2}y_0 = y_0 e^{-kt^*}.$$

Dividing by y_0 and taking the natural logarithm of both sides gives
$$-kt^* = \ln(\tfrac{1}{2}) = -\ln(2).$$
Therefore,
$$k = \frac{\ln(2)}{t^*} \quad \text{and, hence,}$$

(9) $\qquad y = y_0 e^{-(\ln 2)t / t^*}.$

Since $e^{-\ln 2} = \frac{1}{2}$, Eq.(9) can be rewritten as:

(10) $\qquad y = y_0\left(\frac{1}{2}\right)^{t / t^*}.$

In this form it is easier to see that the amount of substance decreases by a factor of $1/2$ every t^* time units. See Figure 5.16.

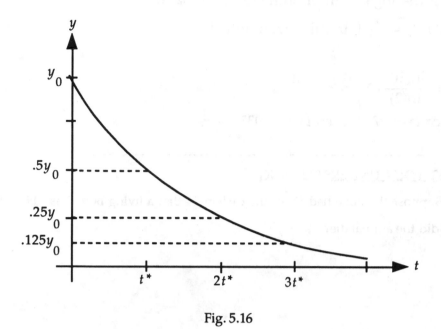

Fig. 5.16

A very important application of this is carbon-14 dating which is used to determine how old organic fossils are. Carbon-14 is a radioactive isotope of carbon with a half-life of 5730 years. Living organisms breathe in small amounts of carbon-14. When they die, the carbon-14 decays in the organism. It is possible to measure the concentration of carbon-14 remaining in the fossil and thus determine the age.

EXAMPLE 5.12:

Suppose a bone is found which contains 10% of the carbon-14 that a living bone has. Determine the approximate length of time since the animal died.

Let y_0 = the amount of carbon-14 present when the animal died. Then
$$y(\bar{t}) = \frac{1}{10} y_0,$$
where $\bar{t}$ is the number of years since the animal died. Since $y(t) = y_0 \left(\frac{1}{2}\right)^{t/t^*}$, then
$$\frac{1}{10} y_0 = y_0 \left(\frac{1}{2}\right)^{\bar{t}/t^*} \text{ or, } \frac{1}{10} = \left(\frac{1}{2}\right)^{\bar{t}/t^*}.$$

Upon taking the logarithm of both sides, we have:

$$-\ln(10) = \frac{\bar{t}}{t*} [-\ln(2)], \quad \text{from which}$$

$$\bar{t} = \frac{\ln(10)}{\ln(2)} t*.$$

Finally, since $t* = 5730$, then $\bar{t} \approx 19035$ years. ◆

- -

TEST YOUR UNDERSTANDING

2. Suppose the bone had 5% of the carbon-14 that a living bone has. How long ago did the animal die?

- -

NEWTON'S LAW OF COOLING

Suppose you cook a turkey until its internal temperature is 85° C and remove it from the oven. You leave it at room temperature (20° C) to cool down. How long will it take for the temperature of the turkey to reach 40° C?

In order to answer this question, we need to characterize the temperature $z(t)$ of the turkey as a function of time. At time $t = 0$, $z(0) = 85$. Furthermore, $z(t)$ steadily decreases towards 20 and never drops below 20; that is, $z(t) \to 20$ as $t \to \infty$. This behavior is depicted in Figure 5.17.

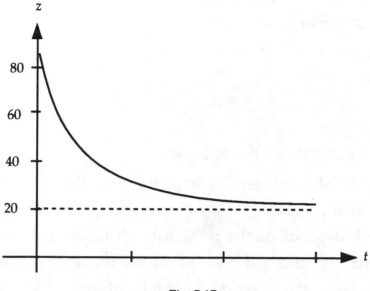

Fig. 5.17

What about the rate of cooling? Initially, the turkey cools rapidly but after a while, the rate of cooling decreases as the temperature gets closer to 20. One way to express this mathematically is that the rate of cooling is proportional to the difference between the current temperature and 20. But the rate of cooling is just $\frac{dz}{dt}$, so z must satisfy the differential equation

(11) $\qquad \frac{dz}{dt} = -k(z - 20)$

for some positive constant k. The minus sign insures $\frac{dz}{dt} < 0$ when z > 20. Eq.(11) is known as **Newton's Law of Cooling**.

Separating variables, we get

$$\frac{1}{z - 20}\, dz = -k\; dt\; .$$

Although technically we don't know how to evaluate $\int \frac{1}{z - 20}\, dz$, it is not too hard to believe that it is ln(z − 20). (See Example 4.12 for comparison or check by differentiating.) Thus,

$$\ln(z - 20) = -kt + c \qquad \text{from which}$$
$$z - 20 = e^{-kt+c} = Ce^{-kt}, \qquad \text{for some constant } C.$$

Substituting $z = 85$ and $t = 0$ gives us $C = 85 - 20 = 65$.

So, the temperature at time t is given by the function

(12) $z(t) = 20 + 65e^{-kt}$.

Notes:

1. Since $e^{-kt} > 0$ for all t, then $z(t) > 20$ for all t.

2. As $t \to \infty$, $e^{-kt} \to 0$, so $z(t) \to 20$, implying that the temperature does indeed level off at $z = 20$.

3. The constant k depends on the particular substance being heated. It is related to what physicists and chemists call the **thermal conductivity** of the object. If k is large, the object does not retain heat well and cools down quickly.

4. We are assuming that the surrounding temperature is not affected by placing the hot object in it.

Now let's see if we can answer our original question: When does the temperature of the turkey reach $40°$? That is, for what t is $40 = 20 + 65e^{-kt}$?

After simplifying, we get $e^{-kt} = \dfrac{40 - 20}{65} = .3077$. Upon taking the logarithm of both sides, we get $-kt = -1.179$ or $t = \dfrac{1.179}{k}$. In order to determine t, we need to find k. This can be accomplished with more information, such as the temperature of the turkey at some specific time. For instance, suppose the turkey had cooled to $60°$ C after 30 minutes. Then,

$$z(30) = 20 + 65e^{-k(30)} = 60, \text{ or equivalently,}$$

$$e^{-30k} = \dfrac{60 - 20}{65} = .6154.$$

Upon taking the logarithm of both sides, we get $-30k = -.4855$ so that $k = .0162$.

Substituting this value of k in the expression above, we get $t = \dfrac{1.179}{.0162} = 72.8$ minutes.

----

3. When was the turkey at 50° C?

We can generalize this problem: Suppose an object is heated to initial temperature z_0 and placed in a surrounding medium whose temperature is b. By modifying the calculations above, we can show that the temperature of the object at time t is given by:

(13) $z(t) := b + (z_0 - b)e^{-kt}$

for some constant k. If $z_0 > b$ (meaning that the object is heated to a temperature greater than its surroundings), the graph of Eq.(13) resembles Figure 5.17.

EXAMPLE 5.13:

A cup of black coffee is poured from a pot, whose contents are at 95°C, into a noninsulated cup at room temperature (20°C). After 2 minutes, the coffee has cooled to 85°C. How long will it take to cool to 60°C?

We are given $z_0 = 95$ and $b = 20$. Therefore,

$z(t) := 20 + 75e^{-kt}$, for some k.

To find k, we use the additional information that $z(2) = 85$. Substituting, we get

$85 = 20 + 75e^{-2k}$,   from which

$e^{-2k} = 65/75 = .87$.

Now take the natural logarithm of both sides:

$$-2k = \ln(.87) \approx -.143.$$

Thus $k \approx .072$.

Using this value of k and setting $z = 60$, we solve for t.

$$60 = 20 + 75e^{-.072t}$$

$$e^{-.072t} = 40/75 = .53$$

$$-.072t = \ln(.53) = -.629$$

Therefore, it takes $t = 8.7$ minutes for the coffee to cool down. ♦

TEST YOUR UNDERSTANDING

4. Suppose the coffee in the pot is at 90° C, the room is still at 20° C and it takes two minutes to cool to 80° C. How long does it take for the coffee to cool to 60°?

We have explored just one possible model. It may be more reasonable to assume $\frac{dz}{dt} = -k(z-b)^2$ or $\frac{dz}{dt} = -k(z-b)^{1/2}$ or any other exponent. Each choice will lead to a different solution. One way to determine whether any particular model is correct is to compare the predictions given by the model to actual data. (See Problem 4 at the end of this section.)

PROBLEMS FOR SECTION 5.4:

1. A hospitalized criminal has been running a fever of 40°C. At 11:00 PM, a nurse finds him shot to death. At that time his body temperature is 37°C. An hour later, his temperature is down to 35°C. If the room is maintained at 20°C, when did he die?

2. Ten grams of a radioactive substance has decayed to 8 grams in 2 hours.
   (a) Determine the half-life of the substance.
   (b) How long will it take for the substance to decay to 6 grams?

3. Sketch Eq.(13) for the case when the object is cooled to initial temperature z_0 and placed in surroundings of temperature $b > z_0$.

4. Another possible model for describing the temperature of a cooling object is $\frac{dz}{dt} = -k(z - b)^2$. Determine the specific solution of this equation satisfying $z(0) = z_0 > b$. Compare the graph of the solution to Figure 5.17.

TYU Answers for Section 5.4

   1. 10.3 hours   2. 24765 years 3. 47.7 minutes   4. 7.26 minutes

QUESTIONS TO THINK ABOUT

1. For each of the following economic terms, define the term and describe its relationship to the other terms on the list.
   (a) price function (demand curve)   (b) marginal
   (c) elasticity of demand   (d) break even point

2. Describe in general terms how a differential equation might arise in a problem. What physical or geometric quantities involve the derivative? Give examples to show how they enter problems.

3. Discuss the relationship between radioactive decay and population growth as mathematical problems. What factors might limit the usefulness of the models we used to discuss these problems?

4. What is Newton's Law of Cooling? How could you test this model? What are some of its limitations? How might you improve the model, assuming you did not have to solve it (at least right away)?

PROJECT 5.1

AN OPTIMIZATION PROBLEM

OBJECTIVE: A man in a rowboat on a river is 1 mile from the nearest shore point A. He hears a fire alarm and must report to the fire station, which is 5 miles down shore from A. He decides to row to a point P along the shore, then run the rest of the way. He rows at 4 miles/hr. and runs at 5 miles/hr. The objective is to find the location of P that minimizes the total time for the trip.

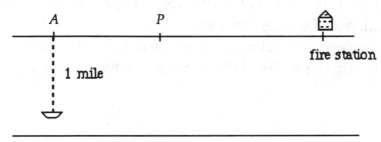

PROCEDURE:

Part 1: Some preliminary calculations

   a. Suppose P were 1 mile from A. How far would the man have to row? How far would he have to run? How long would the entire journey take?

   b. Repeat Part 1a if P were 2 miles from A.

   c. Let x = distance from P to A. Express the total rowing distance in terms of x. Express the total running distance in terms of x.

   d. Let $T(x)$:= total time for the journey. Express $T(x)$ in terms of x. What restrictions do the physical reality of the problem put on the domain of T?

   e. Graph $T(x)$ for $0 < x < 5$. Approximate the value of x that minimizes $T(x)$?

Part 2: Analytical solution

   a. Determine $T'(x)$.

   b. Use your answer to 2a to find the critical numbers of T. Classify those critical numbers.

   c. What is the (global) minimum value of T?

   d. Suppose the man does not know calculus and could not derive the exact solution. He decides arbitrarily to row to a point 2 miles from A. How much time will he have wasted by doing so?

e. Repeat 2d if he rows directly to the fire station. What if he rows directly to A and runs the 5 miles down the shore?

Part 3: Some further analysis
   a. Suppose he could row faster than 4 miles/hr. Would this move the optimal location of P closer to A or further from A?
   b. In general, let r = rowing rate. Express $T(x)$ in terms of x and r.
   c. Graph $T(x)$ for $r = 2$, $r = 3$ and $r = 5$. Do the graphs support your conclusion in 3a?
   d. Let $x^*(r)$:= value of x that minimizes T, expressed in terms of r. Determine and expression for $x^*(r)$.
   e. What is the smallest value of r for which it is optimal for the man to row directly to the fire station; that is, for what r is $x^*(r) = 5$?

PROJECT 5.2

REFLECTION IN A PARABOLA

OBJECTIVE: A **parabola** is defined as the set of points equidistant from a fixed point F, called the **focus**, and a straight line L, called the **directrix**. Let Q be any point inside the parabola. The objective of the project is to determine a point P on the parabola such that the total distance from F to P to Q is a minimum. We'll show that it is optimal to pick P such that PQ is parallel to the axis of symmetry of the parabola. Then, we'll show that the angle between FP and the tangent to the parabola at P is the same as the angle between the tangent and PQ.

PROCEDURE:

Part 1: Deriving an equation of the parabola

    For simplicity, assume that the parabola is symmetric about the y-axis and that its vertex is at the origin. Then the focus is at the point $F(0, r)$ and the directrix is the line $L\colon y = -r$, for some constant $r \neq 0$.

    a. Let $P(x, y)$ be any point on the parabola. Determine the length of FP.

    b. Determine the distance from P to L.

    c. Equate your answers to 1a and 1b and simplify. Show that the equation of the parabola is $y = \dfrac{x^2}{4r}$.

    d. Sketch the parabolas for $r = 1$ and $r = 2$. Indicate the focus and directrix for each. How does increasing r change the graph?

Part 2: The shortest distance

    Let $Q(a, b)$ be any point inside the parabola $y = \dfrac{x^2}{4}$. (Note that we are working with the special case $r = 1$ for simplicity; the result is true for every r.) As in Part 1, let $P(x, y)$ be a point on the parabola.

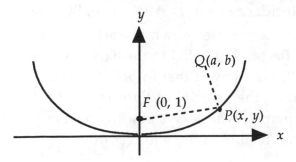

a. Show that $FP + PQ = \frac{1}{4}x^2 + 1 + \sqrt{(x-a)^2 + (\frac{1}{4}x^2 - b)^2}$.

b. The quantity in 2a, which we'll denote by z, represents the total distance from F to P to Q and is what we want to minimize. Determine $\frac{dz}{dx}$.

c. Show that $\frac{dz}{dx} = \frac{1}{2}a + \dfrac{(\frac{1}{4}a^2 - b)(\frac{1}{2}a)}{\sqrt{(\frac{1}{4}a^2 - b)^2}}$ when $x = a$.

d. Argue that $\sqrt{(\frac{1}{4}a^2 - b)^2} = -(\frac{1}{4}a^2 - b)$ and, hence, $\frac{dz}{dx} = 0$ when $x = a$.

The fact that $\frac{dz}{dx} = 0$ when $x = a$ would not normally imply that z is minimized when $x = a$. In this case, however, that happens to be true. Think about how you might convince yourself of this. We'll accept it.

Part 3: Equal angles

Let T be the tangent to the graph of the parabola at P. Let α be the angle between T and FP and β be the angle between T and PQ.

a. Determine the slope of T.

b. Determine the slope of FP.

c. It can be shown that if lines L_1 and L_2 have (finite) slopes m_1 and m_2, respectively, where $m_1 > m_2$, then the acute angle θ between the lines satisfies $\tan(\theta) = \dfrac{m_1 - m_2}{1 + m_1 m_2}$. Use this to find $\tan(\alpha)$.

d. We can't use the formula in 3c to find $\tan(\beta)$ because the slope of PQ is not finite. Show geometrically that $\tan(\beta) = \dfrac{1}{\text{slope } T}$.

e. Use 3c and d to conclude that $\alpha = \beta$.

Application: Imagine that the parabola is a reflecting surface and there is a light bulb at the focus F. It is well-known that when light reflects off a surface, the angle of incidence (α in Part 3) is equal to the angle of reflection (β). If we believe this, then we've shown in Part 3 that every light ray striking the surface reflects off parallel to the axis of the parabola. Furthermore, in Part 2, we showed that in doing so, the light ray travels the shortest path. Assuming the velocity of light is constant, then we have justified **Fermat's principle**, which says that to go from point A to point B, light travels a path that results in the shortest time.

PROJECT 5.3

LOGISTIC GROWTH

OBJECTIVE: In the text, we studied a model of population growth. Under the assumption that the rate of change in the population is proportional to the size of the population, we get the differential equation $\frac{dy}{dt} = ry$, where r is a constant representing the fractional increase in population per unit time. In practice, it may be unreasonable to assume that r is a constant. The purpose of this project is to explore what happens if we assume that r is not constant, but rather depends on the population size.

PROCEDURE:

Part 1: What's wrong with the old model?

    a. Solve the equation $\frac{dy}{dt} = ry$, subject to $y(0) = y_0$.

    b. Graph the solution to 1a, assuming $r > 0$. What happens to y as
        $t \to \infty$?

    c. Why is the behavior you observe in 1b unreasonable in the real world, particularly for large organisms such as fish or deer or humans?

Part 2: A new model

    Recall that the net growth rate r = birth rate – death rate. Let's assume the birth rate is constant but the death rate depends on the size of the population.

    a. Is the death rate an increasing or decreasing function of the population size? In other words, as the population goes up, would we expect a larger or smaller fraction of the population to die? Why?

    b. Does your answer to 2a imply that r is an increasing or decreasing function of the population size y?

    c. One model assumes $r = a - by$, where a and b are *positive* constants. Does this agree with your answer to 2b?

    d. Substituting in the differential equation gives $\frac{dy}{dt} = (a - by)y$. Show that this equation is separable but that you cannot completely solve it yet. Why?

Part 3: What can we do without solving the equation?

    We would like to sketch possible graphs of y as a function of t.

Remember that y is the dependent variable and t is the independent variable. Normally, we would say that "y is an increasing function of t for some values of t". Here, we will say "y is an increasing function of t for some values of y".

Notice that $y(t) > 0$ for all t and thus, $\dfrac{dy}{dt} = 0$ if and only if $y = \dfrac{a}{b}$.

a. Suppose $y > \dfrac{a}{b}$. What is the direction of y? What is the direction of y if $y < \dfrac{a}{b}$? Sketch an approximation to the curve in the cases $y(0) = y_0 > \dfrac{a}{b}$ and $y(0) = y_0 < \dfrac{a}{b}$.

b. Did your curves in part 3a reach the line $y = \dfrac{a}{b}$? Think about what must happen if the curve ever touches that line. Explain why, if it touches the line, it can neither rise above nor fall below the line after that.

   [Hint: If $y(t_0) = \dfrac{a}{b}$ for some t_0, what must be true about $y(t)$ for all $t > t_0$?]

c. Suppose the curve in 3a never reaches the line $y = \dfrac{a}{b}$. What can you say about $\lim\limits_{t \to \infty} y(t)$?

d. Differentiate the differential equation with respect to t and show that
$$\frac{d^2 y}{dt^2} = (a - 2by)\frac{dy}{dt} = (a - 2by)(a - by)y.$$
   Remember that y is a function of t so that when differentiating the right side, you must invoke the chain rule.

e. For what values of y is the solution concave up? Use the new information to modify your sketches in 3a.

Part 4: The actual solution

a. Let $f(y) := \ln\left(\dfrac{y}{a - by}\right)$. Show that $f'(y) = \dfrac{a}{y\,(a - by)}$.

b. Use 4a to help get past the roadblock you encountered in 2d. Show that
$$\frac{y}{a - by} = C\,e^{at}, \text{ for some constant } C.$$

c. Use the initial condition $y(0) = y_0$ to show that $C = \dfrac{y_0}{a - b\,y_0}$.

d. Substitute and simplify to show $y(t) := \dfrac{y_0 a\,e^{at}}{a + b\,y_0(e^{at} - 1)}$.

e. Graph the solution for the case $a = 3, b = 1, y_0 = 2$. Does the graph agree with your sketch in 3e? Repeat with $y_0 = 5$.

f. Show that if $a \neq 0$ and if $y(t) = \dfrac{a}{b}$ for any t, then $y_0 = \dfrac{a}{b}$ and $y(t) = \dfrac{a}{b}$ for all t.

PROJECT 5.4

A FAMILY OF EXPONENTIAL FUNCTIONS

OBJECTIVE: Consider the set of functions $f_k(x) := (x^2 - k^2)e^{-x^2}$, where k is a positive constant. The graph of f_k crosses the x-axis at two distinct points P and Q. The triangle formed by the x-axis and the tangents drawn to f_k at P and Q has area $A(k)$. The objective of this project is to explore properties of f_k and to determine the value of k that maximizes $A(k)$.

PROCEDURE:

Part 1: Graphical observations

a. Use your computer or graphing calculator to draw the graphs of f_1, f_2 and $f_{1/2}$ on separate axes for x between -3 and 3.

b. For each graph in 1a, describe the direction, concavity and intercepts.

c. Judging from your graphs, what do you think $\lim_{x \to \infty} f_k(x)$ is?

d. For each graph in 1a, draw the triangle described in the objective and estimate its area.

Part 2: Some analysis

a. Express the x- and y-intercepts of f_k in terms of k.

b. Compute $f_k{'}(x)$ and use it to find the local extrema of f_k.

c. What happens to the x-coordinate of the local maxima as k increases? Does this agree with your graphs in 1a?

d. What happens to the y-coordinate of the local maxima and minima as k increases? Does this agree with your graphs in 1a?

e. Let P and Q be the x-intercepts that you found in 2a. Write equations of the lines tangent to f_k at P and Q.

f. Determine the coordinates of R, the point of intersection of the tangent lines in 2e.

Part 3: Some results about a triangle

Consider triangle PQR, where P and Q are the x-intercepts of f_k and R is the intersection point of the tangent lines found in 2f.

a. Let $A(k)$ be the area of triangle PQR. Show that $A(k) := 2k^3 e^{-k^2}$.

b. Determine $A'(k)$.

c. For what value(s) of k is $A(k)$ maximized?

d. Show that $QR = PR = k\sqrt{1 + 4k^2e^{-2k^2}}$.

e. Let $g(k) := k^2e^{-2k^2}$. Show that the maximum value of $g(k)$ is $\dfrac{1}{2e}$ and, hence, $g(k) < \dfrac{1}{4}$ for all k.

f. Use 3e to show that $QR < k\sqrt{2}$ and, thus, there is no value of k for which triangle PQR is equilateral. (Hint: How long is the third side of the triangle?)

PROJECT 5.5

A FAMILY OF LOGARITHMIC FUNCTIONS

OBJECTIVE: The goal of this project is to investigate some interesting properties of the set of functions $f_k(x) := x \ln\left(\frac{x^2}{k}\right)$, where k is a positive constant and $x \neq 0$.

PROCEDURE:

Part 1: Limits and symmetry
  a. Show that $f_k(x) = 0$ when $x = \pm\sqrt{k}$.
  b. Argue that $f_k(x)$ is an odd function--that is, $f_k(-x) = -f_k(x)$, for all
     $x \neq 0$.
  c. Show that $f_k(x) = 2x \ln(x) - x \ln(k)$, if $x > 0$.
  d. Show that if we try to evaluate $\lim_{x \to 0} f_k(x)$ by substitution, we get the
     indeterminate form $0(-\infty)$.
  e. Use 1c to argue that $\lim_{x \to 0} f_k(x)$ is independent of k.
  f. By evaluating $f_k(x)$ for small values of x, conclude that $\lim_{x \to 0} f_k(x) = 0$.

Part 2: Critical points and graphs
  a. Determine $f_k'(x)$.
  b. Show that $f_k(x)$ has a local minimum when $x = \frac{\sqrt{k}}{e}$.
  c. Use 1b to argue that $f_k(x)$ has a local maximum when $x = -\frac{\sqrt{k}}{e}$.
  d. Discuss the concavity of $f_k(x)$.
  e. Use the information gathered so far to sketch graphs of $f_k(x)$ for $k = 1, 4$ and 9 for $0 < x \leq 3$.

Part 3: Maximizing the area of a triangle
  Let $P(u, v)$ be a point on the graph of f_k, where $0 < u < \sqrt{k}$. Draw a line tangent to the graph of f_k at P; let Q be the point where the tangent line crosses the y-axis. Let $R(u, 0)$ be the point on the x-axis directly above P.

  a. Show that the area of triangle PQR is given by $A = \frac{-1}{2} uv$
     $= \frac{-1}{2} u^2 \ln\left(\frac{u^2}{k}\right)$. Why do we need the minus sign?
  b. Compute $\frac{dA}{du}$. Show that the area of triangle PQR is maximized when

$$u = \sqrt{\tfrac{k}{e}}.$$

From here on, assume that triangle PQR is drawn so that its area is maximum--that is with $u = \sqrt{\tfrac{k}{e}}$.

c. Show that the slope of $PQ = 1$.

d. Show that $v = -\sqrt{\tfrac{k}{e}}$.

e. Write an equation for PQ and determine the coordinates of Q.

f. Show that the ratio $PR:PQ:QR = 1:\sqrt{2}:\sqrt{5}$.

g. Let Δ_k represent triangle PQR when $u = \sqrt{\tfrac{k}{e}}$. Part 3f shows that all triangles Δ_k are similar since the ratio of their sides is independent of k. On the graph in 2e, draw Δ_1, Δ_4 and Δ_9 and verify this result visually.

CHAPTER 6

INTEGRATION

6.1 THE PROBLEM OF THE BROKEN ODOMETER REVISITED

In Section 2.3, we considered the following problem: Can you tell how far you've travelled given your velocity $v(t)$ at time t?

We argued that if your velocity is positive on the interval $[a, b]$, then the distance travelled is $s(b) - s(a)$, where $s(t)$ is any position function corresponding to the velocity function $v(t)$. We can now state this more formally using the language of Chapter 3:

OBSERVATION: If $v(t) \geq 0$ on the time interval $[a, b]$, and $s(t)$ is any antiderivative of $v(t)$, then the distance travelled during the interval $[a, b]$ is given by $L = s(b) - s(a)$.

EXAMPLE 6.1:

The velocity of a particle is given by $v(t) := 3t^2$. How far does the particle travel during the time interval $[1, 4]$?

Since $v(t) \geq 0$ on the given interval (and, indeed, for all t), then the conditions of our observation are met. An antiderivative of $v(t)$ is $s(t) := t^3$. Hence, the distance travelled is $L = s(4) - s(1) = 64 - 1 = 63$ units. ♦

TEST YOUR UNDERSTANDING

1. Use another antiderivative of $v(t)$ in Example 6.1 and show that you get the same distance.

2. Find the distance travelled during the interval [0, 2] by a particle whose instantaneous velocity is $v(t) := 2t + 1$.

❑ In order to use our observation, we need to have a formula for $v(t)$ and to be able to find an antiderivative of $v(t)$. There are certainly situations in which one of these requirements would not be met. Suppose you were driving down the highway. Even if you had some way of recording your velocity at every instant, it would be virtually impossible to find any formula that precisely fit the data. Or, we might have a formula such as $v(t) := \sqrt[3]{1 + t^2}$ for which no simple antiderivative exists. The question then becomes: Can we find the distance travelled if we don't have a formula for $v(t)$ or if we can't find an antiderivative of $v(t)$? In other words, what happens if our observation can't be applied?

As we showed in Section 2.3, one way to approach this problem is to read the speedometer at regularly-spaced points in time $t_0, t_1, t_2, ..., t_n$ where $t_0 = a =$ time at which the journey starts and $t_n = b =$ time at which the journey ends. Since the readings are at equally-spaced times, then $t_2 - t_1 = t_3 - t_2 = t_4 - t_3 = ... = t_n - t_{n-1} = \Delta t$. ($\Delta t$ may be 1 minute or 5 minutes or 10 seconds or any other length of time.) What we've really done is partition the time interval $[a, b]$ into n equal subintervals. Each subinterval is of length $\Delta t = \dfrac{b - a}{n}$. See Figure 6.1.

Fig. 6.1

By assuming that the velocity is a constant $v(t_j)$ during the entire subinterval $[t_{j-1}, t_j]$, we argued that the distance travelled during the interval $[t_{j-1}, t_j]$ is *approximately* $v(t_j)\Delta t$, and the total distance travelled during the interval $[a, b]$ is approximately:

(1) $\qquad L \approx v(t_1)\Delta t + v(t_2)\Delta t + v(t_3)\Delta t + \ldots + v(t_n)\Delta t = \sum_{j=1}^{n} v(t_j)\Delta t$.

At this point, all we have is an approximation to the total distance travelled. The reason it is an approximation is that we assumed the velocity in each subinterval is constant when, in fact, it may not be. However, the approximation will improve if we make Δt smaller. To make Δt smaller, we'll have to take more speedometer readings. That is, making Δt smaller is equivalent to making n larger. We claim that we can get the exact distance travelled by taking the limit of the expression in Eq.(1) as $n \to \infty$; that is,

(2) $\qquad L = \lim_{n \to \infty} \sum_{j=1}^{n} v(t_j)\Delta t$.

Now let's go back to the observation on page 6-1 which says that the total distance travelled during the interval $[a, b]$ is $s(b) - s(a)$, where $s(t)$ is any antiderivative of $v(t)$. We can now claim that

(3) $\qquad \lim_{n \to \infty} \sum_{j=1}^{n} v(t_j)\Delta t = s(b) - s(a)$.

This is a result that we will see again in a more general context in Section 6.3.
¤ Eq.(2) has a nice graphical interpretation. Suppose we construct rectangles under the graph of $v(t)$ as shown in Figure 6.2. The first rectangle has a height of v_1 and a width of Δt, so its area is $v_1\Delta t$. Similarly, the area of the second rectangle is $v_2\Delta t$, the area of the third rectangle is $v_3\Delta t$, etc. Thus,

the approximate distance travelled is the sum of the areas of the rectangles.

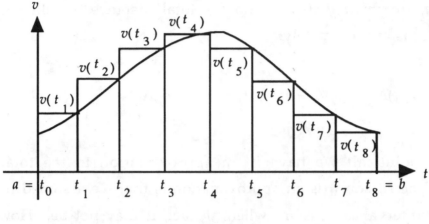

Fig. 6.2

As Δt gets smaller, the rectangles become thinner and they "fit the curve" better. Thus it seems plausible that the total distance travelled during the time interval $[a, b]$ is the area of the region R bounded by the graph of $v(t)$, the t-axis and the lines $t = a$ and $t = b$, as shown in Figure 6.3. Furthermore, in view of Eq.(5), it follows that the area of $R = s(b) - s(a)$, where $s(t)$ is an antiderivative of $v(t)$.

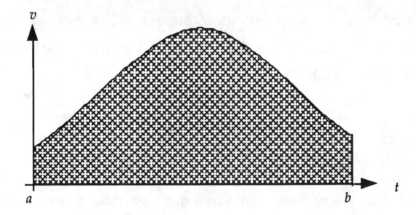

Fig. 6.3

EXERCISES FOR SECTION 6.1:

1. The velocity of a particle is given by $v(t) := 4t^3 - 6t^2$. How far does the particle travel during the interval $[2, 3]$?

2. The velocity of a particle is given by $v(t) := 3t^2$. During the time interval $[1, b]$, the particle travels 26 units. Determine b.

3. Determine the distance travelled by a particle whose velocity is $v(t) := \sqrt{9-t^2}$ during the interval $[0, 3]$. [Hint: Draw a picture and use a geometric formula.]

4. A particle moves with velocity $v(t) := t + 2$ for 3 seconds, then moves at constant velocity 5 for 3 seconds. How far has it travelled?

5. A particle moves with velocity $v(t) := \sqrt{1+t^3}$ during the time interval $[0, 2]$. Approximate the distance travelled by the particle by partitioning the interval into 4 equal subintervals and computing the corresponding Riemann sum (as in Eq. (1)).

6. Repeat Exercise 5 if $v(t) := \dfrac{1}{t+1}$ on the interval $[0, 3]$. Use 3 subintervals.

PROBLEMS FOR SECTION 6.1:

1. A particle starts at rest and undergoes a constant acceleration of r m/sec^2.
    (a) Determine the velocity $v(t)$ and sketch.
    (b) Show that the distance travelled during the interval $[a, b]$ is $L = \dfrac{r(b^2 - a^2)}{2}$.

2. A particle starts at rest, accelerates at 3 m/sec^2 for 4 seconds, remains at that velocity for 6 seconds and then decelerates to 0 in 2 seconds.
    (a) Sketch the velocity $v(t)$.
    (b) Determine the total distance travelled by the particle.
    (c) At what time did the particle complete exactly half its journey?

3. Two particles start at the same time from the origin. One moves with velocity $v_1(t) := 4t + 2$, the other with velocity $v_2(t) := 6t$.
    (a) At what time are they moving at the same velocity?

(b) At what time will the particles be at the same location? Interpret this in terms of the graphs of v_1 and v_2.

(c) At what time would they be at the same location if particle 2 started 1 second later than particle 1?

4. What is the interpretation of $s(b) - s(a)$ if the velocity is not always positive; that is, if the object can move forward and backward during the interval $[a, b]$?

<u>TYU Answers for Section 6.1</u>

    1. If $s(t) := t^3 + c, s(4) - s(1) = (64 + c) - (1 + c) = 63$ 2. 6 miles

6.2 AREA AND RIEMANN SUMS

In the last section, we argued that the physical problem of determining the distance travelled during the time interval $[a, b]$ by a particle whose instantaneous velocity is $v(t)$ is equivalent to the geometric problem of finding the area bounded the graph of $v(t)$, the t-axis and the lines $t = a$ and $t = b$. Now, we'll concentrate just on the geometric problem. Let R be the region bounded by the (non-negative) function $f(x)$, the x-axis and the vertical lines $x = a$ and $x = b$. We seek the area of R.

In view of our observations about distance and velocity, we might conclude that the area of this region is $F(b) - F(a)$, where F is any antiderivative of f. We will prove this truly remarkable fact called the Fundamental Theorem of Calculus later in this chapter. For now, let's try to use what we know (e.g. areas of rectangles) to approximate the area of R.

¤ As we did earlier, partition the interval $[a,b]$ on the x-axis into n equal subintervals, each of length

$$\Delta x = \frac{b - a}{n}.$$

Construct rectangles by drawing horizontal lines between the points $(x_{j-1}, f(x_j))$ and $(x_j, f(x_j))$, for $j = 1, 2, 3, \ldots, n$, as shown in Figure 6.4.

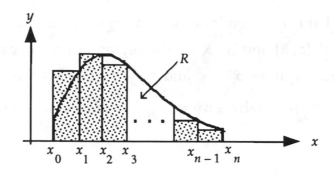

Fig. 6.4

The total area of all the rectangles is given by the **Riemann sum**:

$$(6) \qquad S(n) := f(x_1)\Delta x + f(x_2)\Delta x + \ldots + f(x_n)\Delta x = \sum_{j=1}^{n} f(x_j)\,\Delta x.$$

where $x_0 = a$, $x_1 = a + \Delta x$, $x_2 = a + 2\Delta x$, ..., $x_j = a + j\Delta x$,..., $x_n = b = a + n\Delta x$.

Note that we have chosen to draw the rectangles so that their heights are the y-values at the right side of each subinterval. This is not necessary; we could have used the y-values at the left side, anywhere within the subinterval, or any combination thereof. Many calculus books refer to **inscribed rectangles** and **circumscribed rectangles**. In the former, the height is chosen to be the smallest y-value in each interval (so that all rectangles fit inside the region); in the latter, the height is the largest y-value (so all rectangles stick out). It really doesn't matter how you draw them, as long as the height is the function value at some point in each subinterval.

As $n \to \infty$, the rectangles get thinner ($\Delta x \to 0$), but they also "fit better" in R. The "missing pieces" and parts that "stick out" get smaller. Eventually, we should get a "perfect fit". This leads to the following definition:

DEFINITION: Let f be a continuous, non-negative function defined on the closed interval $[a, b]$ and let R be the region bounded by the graph of f, the x-axis and the lines $x = a$ and $x = b$. The **area** of R is defined by

$$A = \lim_{n \to \infty} \sum_{j=1}^{n} f(x_j) \Delta x \text{, where } \Delta x = \frac{b-a}{n} \text{ and } x_j = a + j\Delta x.$$

EXAMPLE 6.2:

Let R be the region bounded by a non-negative function $y = f(x)$, the x-axis and the lines $x = -1$ and $x = 2$. Suppose a Riemann sum for this function is $S(n) := 3 + \dfrac{9}{2n^2} + \dfrac{9}{2n}$.

(a) What is the approximation to the area of R using 4 rectangles?

The desired approximation is $S(4) = 3 + 9/32 + 9/8 \approx 4.406$.

(b) What is the exact area of R?

The exact area is $A = \lim_{n \to \infty}\left(3 + \dfrac{9}{2n^2} + \dfrac{9}{2n}\right) = 3.$ ♦

TEST YOUR UNDERSTANDING

1. The Riemann sum for a non-negative continuous function f over the interval $[2, 4]$ is $S(n) := \dfrac{12 + 56n + 60n^2}{n^2}$. What is the area of the region bounded by $y = f(x)$ and the x-axis, the lines $x = 2$ and $x = 4$?

In Example 6.2, we were given a formula for $S(n)$ in terms of n. Deriving such a formula for a given function f is difficult, except for very simple functions as in the following example. What this means is that it is usually not possible to compute areas from the definition.

This does not, however, make the definition any less valid. There are many examples of definitions in mathematics that are impractical or impossible to use on all but the simplest of cases. In order to circumvent the use of the definition, we develop theorems that allow us to do more complicated examples. We have seen this in Chapter 3 (rules for derivatives). We'll see it in this chapter and in Chapters 11, 13 and 14, as well.

EXAMPLE 6.3:

Use the definition to find the area of the region bounded by $f(x) = 2x$, the x-axis and the lines $x = 1$ and $x = 3$.

Partition the interval $[1, 3]$ into n subintervals of length $\Delta x = \dfrac{3-1}{n} = \dfrac{2}{n}$. Then $x_0 = 1, x_1 = 1 + \Delta x, x_2 = 1 + 2\Delta x, ..., x_j = 1 + j\Delta x, ..., x_n = 3$.

$$S(n) := \sum_{j=1}^{n} f(x_j)\,\Delta x \;=\; \sum_{j=1}^{n} 2x_j\,\Delta x \;=\; \sum_{j=1}^{n} 2(1 + j\,\Delta x)\,\Delta x \;=\; \sum_{j=1}^{n} 2\!\left(1 + \frac{2j}{n}\right)\frac{2}{n}$$

$$= \sum_{j=1}^{n} \frac{4}{n} + \sum_{j=1}^{n} \frac{8j}{n^2} = \frac{4}{n} \sum_{j=1}^{n} 1 + \frac{8}{n^2} \sum_{j=1}^{n} j \;.$$

Certainly, $\displaystyle\sum_{j=1}^{n} 1 = 1 + 1 + 1 + ... + 1$ (n times) $= n$ and, it can be shown that (see the problems at the end of the section) $\displaystyle\sum_{j=1}^{n} j = \frac{n(n+1)}{2}$.

Therefore, $S(n) := 4 + \dfrac{8n(n+1)}{2n^2} = 4 + 4\!\left(1 + \dfrac{1}{n}\right)$.

Upon taking the limit as $n \to \infty$, we find that the area is 8.

We can check that this is correct by noting that the region is a trapezoid with bases $b_1 = 2$ and $b_2 = 6$ and altitude $h = 2$, so that the area is $A = \dfrac{h}{2}(b_1 + b_2) = 8$. See Figure 6.5.

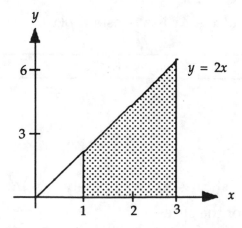

Fig. 6.5

◻ It is important to realize that the problem of finding the area under a curve is not particularly interesting in its own right. We use it as a prototype for other applications because it has nice geometric qualities--it's easy to draw pictures. This is not unlike our discussion of the derivative in terms of the slope of the tangent line; by itself, it is not earth-shattering, but it provides a foundation upon which to base other more important applications-- optimization, differential equations, etc. We've already seen one of these applications of the "area prototype", that of finding distance travelled. We'll look at one more now; in Section 4, we will look at some others.

A cylindrical rod is constructed in such a way that its density (measured in units of mass per unit length, such as grams/m) at a point x meters from one end is given by the function $\rho(x)$. What is the total mass of the rod?

If the density were constant, then the total mass would just be the product of the density and the length of the rod. (This is analogous to the fact that the distance travelled during a time interval when the velocity is constant is the product of the velocity and the length of the interval or to the fact that the area of a rectangle is the product of its width and its height.) If the density is not constant, then we can slice the rod into small slices of width Δx. See Figure 6.6. As we did with velocity, we'll assume that the density of the slice of the rod between x_j and $x_j + \Delta x$ is a constant $\rho(x_j)$.

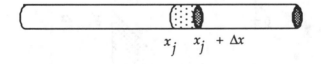

$$x_j \quad x_j + \Delta x$$

Fig. 6.6

Thus, the mass of this slice is approximately $\rho(x_j)\Delta x$ and the total mass is the sum of the masses of the slices; i.e.

$$M \approx \rho(x_1)\Delta x + \rho(x_2)\Delta x + ... + \rho(x_n)\Delta x = \sum_{j=1}^{n} \rho(x_j)\Delta x$$

This is nothing more than a Riemann sum for the density function $\rho(x)$.

To get the exact mass, just take the limit as $n \to \infty$; that is,

$$M = \lim_{n \to \infty} \sum_{j=1}^{n} \rho(x_j)\Delta x.$$

Equivalently, if we drew a graph of the density function, the total mass would be the area under the graph and above the x-axis.

Note: Here we are evaluating the density at the *left* side of each subinterval. As we said earlier, it doesn't matter where you evaluate the function within each subinterval.

TEST YOUR UNDERSTANDING

2. A rod, 3 meters long, is divided into 6 equal segments. The density of the rod (in kg./m)at the endpoints of each segment are given by the sequence {12, 18, 10, 15, 16, 20}. Use this data to estimate the total mass of the rod.

3. A rod is divided into n equal segments. Suppose the approximate total mass is given by $S(n) = \dfrac{12 + 4n + 2n^2 + 6n^3}{n^3}$ grams. What is the exact total mass of the rod?

EXERCISES FOR SECTION 6.2:

1. Find the area bounded by $f(x) = x$, $x = 3$, $x = -3$, and the x-axis.

2. A Riemann sum for approximating the area of a region R using n rectangles is $S(n) := 10 + \dfrac{8}{n}$. What is the area of R?

3. A rod is 2 meters long. The density at a point x meters from one end is given by $\rho(x) := \sqrt{x + 1}$ grams/meter. Approximate the total mass of the object by dividing it into 4 equal slices.

PROBLEMS FOR SECTION 6.2:

1. Use the definition to find the area of the region bounded by $y = 4x + 2$, the x-axis and the lines $x = 0$ and $x = 2$. (See Example 6.3.) Verify geometrically.

2. Use the definition to find the area of the region bounded by $y = x^2$, the x-axis and the lines $x = 0$ and $x = 1$. (Hint: You'll need to know that $\sum\limits_{j=1}^{n} j^2 = \dfrac{n(n+1)(2n+1)}{6}$.)

3. In Example 6.3, we claimed that $\sum\limits_{j=1}^{n} j = \dfrac{n(n+1)}{2}$. In this problem, we'll prove this claim.

    (a) Let $S = \sum\limits_{j=1}^{n} j$; that is, $S = 1 + 2 + 3 + \ldots + (n-1) + n$. We can also write $S = n + (n-1) + \ldots + 2 + 1$. Add these two expressions for S and show that you get $2S = n(n+1)$ from which the result follows.

    (b) Verify that this formula is correct for $n = 3$ and $n = 5$.

    (c) When the mathematician Karl Gauss was about 8 years old, his teacher tried to punish him by making him add the first 1000 integers. Young Karl, much to his teacher's chagrin, returned the answer very quickly. What is the answer?

    (d) Use a similar proof to find the sum of the first n odd integers; that is, the sum $S = 1 + 3 + \ldots + (2n - 1)$.

TYU Answers for Section 6.2

   1. 60   2. 91/2 kg.   3. 6 g.

6.3 DEFINITE INTEGRALS AND THE FUNDAMENTAL THEOREM OF CALCULUS

We have now seen three different applications--distance, area and mass-- that give rise to Riemann sums. We've also seen that, at least in the case of distance, the Riemann sum is equivalent to an expression involving an antiderivative of the function involved in the sum. In this section, we'll formalize and generalize this connection. First, a definition:

DEFINITION: Let f be continuous on the closed interval $[a, b]$. The **definite integral of** $f(x)\, dx$ **from** $x = a$ **to** $x = b$ is

$$\int_a^b f(x)\, dx = \lim_{n \to \infty} \sum_{j=1}^{n} f(x_j)\, \Delta x,$$

where $x_0 = a, x_1 = a + \Delta x, x_2 = a + 2\Delta x, ..., x_j = a + j\Delta x, ..., x_n = b$ and $\Delta x = \dfrac{b-a}{n}$.

The function f is called the **integrand**; the numbers a and b are called the **limits of integration**.

The symbol is valid for any function f; however, if f is non-negative, then $\int_a^b f(x)\, dx$ represents the area of the region R defined earlier. Note the similarity of this notation to the notation used for antiderivatives. This is not a coincidence but a reflection of the aforementioned relationship between antiderivatives and the distance problem.

EXAMPLE 6.4:

Write a definite integral that is equivalent to $\displaystyle\lim_{n \to \infty} \sum_{j=1}^{n} \left(1 + \frac{2j}{n}\right)^3 \frac{2}{n}$.

The expression after the summation sign must be of the form $f(x_j)\, \Delta x$, for some function f and some a and b such that $x_j = a + j\Delta x$ and $\Delta x = \dfrac{b-a}{n}$.

One possibility is to let $f(x) := x^3$, $a = 1$ and $\Delta x = \frac{2}{n}$. Then $b - a = 2$ so that $b = 3$. Hence, the summation is equivalent to $\int_1^3 x^3 \, dx$. ◆

▢ As Examples 6.3 and 6.4 illustrate, this definition is very difficult to use on a regular basis, much worse than the definition of the derivative that we encountered in Chapter 3. So, let's see if we can find a better way to evaluate definite integrals. (This does not mean you should forget the definition since we will have to refer to it when we do other applications.)

Let f be a continuous function on $[a, b]$ and let F be any antiderivative of f. The quantity $\dfrac{F(x_j) - F(x_{j-1})}{\Delta x}$ represents the slope of the secant line joining $(x_j, F(x_j))$ and $(x_{j-1}, F(x_{j-1}))$. For small Δx, the slope of the secant is approximately the same as the slope of the tangent at $(x_j, F(x_j))$.

Since the slope of the tangent is just $F'(x_j)$, then:

$$F(x_j) - F(x_{j-1}) \approx F'(x_j)\Delta x.$$

But, $F'(x) = f(x)$, so

$$F(x_j) - F(x_{j-1}) \approx f(x_j)\Delta x.$$

Moreover, the approximation improves as Δx gets smaller.

Now we have $S(n) := \displaystyle\sum_{j=1}^{n} f(x_j)\Delta x \approx F(x_n) - F(x_0) = F(b) - F(a)$.

Therefore, by letting $n \to \infty$, (equivalently, $\Delta x \to 0$)

$$(8) \qquad \int_a^b f(x)\,dx = \lim_{n \to \infty} S(n) = \lim_{n \to \infty} [F(b) - F(a)] = F(b) - F(a).$$

Hence, we have the following remarkable result:

THEOREM 6.1 (THE FUNDAMENTAL THEOREM OF CALCULUS):

Let f be a continuous function defined on the interval $[a, b]$ and let F be *any* antiderivative of f. Then, $\int_a^b f(x)\,dx = F(b) - F(a)$.

What this theorem says is: If you want to evaluate a definite integral, just find an antiderivative of the given function (a possibly non-trivial or even impossible task), evaluate the antiderivative at the upper and lower limits of integration and subtract. This is precisely the observation we made on page 6-1 about distance travelled.

EXAMPLE 6.5:

Find the exact area of the region bounded by $f(x) := x^2 + 1$, the x-axis, $x = 0$ and $x = 3$.

Since $f(x) := x^2 + 1$, then an antiderivative of f is $F(x) := \frac{1}{3}x^3 + x$. So, the area is $F(3) - F(0) = 12 - 0 = 12$. We will usually abbreviate this calculation as follows:

$$A = \int_0^3 (x^2 + 1)\, dx = \left(\frac{1}{3}x^3 + x\right)\Big|_{x=0}^{x=3} = 12 - 0 = 12$$

where the vertical bar means to evaluate at the upper limit, then at the lower limit, and subtract.

Observe that, if we had used any other antiderivative of f, say $F(x) := \frac{1}{3}x^3 + x + 7$, we would get $A = \left(\frac{1}{3}x^3 + x + 7\right)\Big|_{x=0}^{x=3} = 19 - 7 = 12$, the same answer. ◆

EXAMPLE 6.6:

Evaluate $\int_1^3 2x\, dx$ and verify the result of Example 6.3.

Since $F(x) := x^2$ is an antiderivative of $f(x) := 2x$, then

$$\int_1^3 2x\, dx = x^2\Big|_{x=1}^{x=3} = 9 - 1 = 8$$

as we found earlier (with a lot more effort). ◆

EXAMPLE 6.7:

Evaluate $\int_1^e \left(y + \frac{1}{y}\right) dy$.

$$\int_1^e \left(y + \frac{1}{y}\right) dy \;=\; \left(\frac{y^2}{2} + \ln(y)\right)\Bigg|_{y=1}^{y=e} \;=\; \frac{e^2}{2} + \ln(e) - \left(\frac{1}{2} + \ln(1)\right) \;=\; \frac{e^2+1}{2}\,.$$

◆

TEST YOUR UNDERSTANDING

1. State the Fundamental Theorem of Calculus and explain its significance.

2. Evaluate each of the following integrals:

(a) $\displaystyle\int_{-1}^2 (3x^2 + 4x)\, dx$ (b) $\displaystyle\int_0^2 (x^3 + x - 4)\, dx$ (c) $\displaystyle\int_1^3 \frac{1}{x^2}\, dx$ (d) $\displaystyle\int_{-1}^1 e^x\, dx$

3. Find the area bounded by $y = 12 - x^2$, the x-axis, the lines $x = -1$ and $x = 3$.

4. The velocity of a particle is given by $v(t) := 3t^2 + 2t$. Determine the distance travelled by the particle during the time interval $[1, 4]$.

5. The density of a bar at a point x units from one end is $\rho(x) := 3x^2 + 2x$. If the bar is 4 units long, find its mass.

▢ Although the Fundamental Theorem of Calculus is an extremely important and useful result, there is some bad news. The theorem requires us to be able to find an antiderivative for the given function. As of now, we can only do this in very special cases. In Chapters 7 and 8, we will learn to solve some more of these problems. Even then, we won't be able to find very many antiderivatives and this theorem won't do us any good. (In fact, there are many functions that don't have antiderivatives that can be expressed in terms of "nice" functions.) If we can't find an antiderivative, then we will have to resort to other methods for finding the value of the definite integral.

EXAMPLE 6.8:

Evaluate $\int_0^2 \sqrt{4-x^2}\, dx$.

After some thought, we realize that we can't yet find an antiderivative for the function $f(x) := \sqrt{4-x^2}$. (We'll learn to do this problem in Chapter 8.) Hence, we cannot invoke the Fundamental Theorem of Calculus.

However, the graph of $y = \sqrt{4-x^2}$ is the top half of a circle of radius 2 centered at the origin. Thus, the integral represents the area of a quarter circle of radius 2 as shown in Figure 6.7 below. From geometry, we know that the area of a circle is πr^2, so $\int_0^2 \sqrt{4-x^2}\, dx = \frac{1}{4}\pi(2^2) = \pi.$

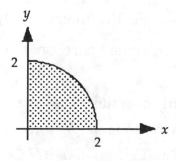

Fig. 6.7

◻ We must be careful that f is continuous on the interval $[a, b]$; otherwise, ridiculous answers might result, as the next example illustrates.

EXAMPLE 6.9:

Evaluate $\int_{-1}^{1} \frac{1}{x^2} \, dx$.

Proceeding blindly, we have $\int_{-1}^{1} \frac{1}{x^2} \, dx = \frac{-1}{x} \Big|_{-1}^{1} = -1 -1 = -2.$

This an absurd answer since the function is non-negative on the interval $[-1, 1]$ and, hence, the integral represents the area of a region which must be positive. See Figure 6.8.

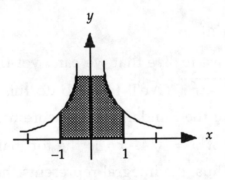

Fig. 6.8

◆

The reason that the Fundamental Theorem fails us is that the function $f(x) := \frac{1}{x^2}$ is not bounded on the interval $[-1, 1]$. In other words, the function gets infinitely large somewhere on the interval (at $x = 0$ in this case).

This raises an interesting question. Can we evaluate this integral? Or, more precisely: Is there a reasonable way to extend our definition of the integral to include this one and others like it? Our first reaction may be that since such functions "blow up", then the area "underneath" them should be infinite. However, it is possible to extend the definition in a logical way which sometimes gives a finite area under these unbounded functions.

Although that seems counter-intuitive, you should think of it as an extension of your concept of area. Integrals involving discontinuous or unbounded functions are said to be **improper** and are a topic for further investigation. We'll also see another type of improper integral, in which the function is continuous but the interval of integration is infinitely long, in Chapter 11.

EXAMPLE 6.10:

Determine the area bounded by $y = x - 1$, the x-axis, the lines $x = 0$ and $x = 4$.

Proceeding blindly, we might think that the area is given by the definite integral $\int_0^4 (x - 1)\,dx = \left(\dfrac{x^2}{2} - x\right)\Big|_{x=0}^{x=4} = 4$. However, this is incorrect. The integrand is *not* non-negative on the interval [0, 4], so the region consists of two triangles, one below the x-axis and one above as in Figure 6.9.

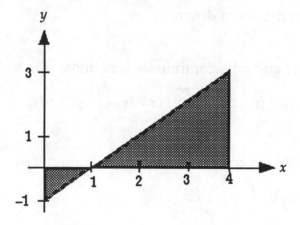

Fig. 6.9

The small triangle has a base of 1 and height of 1, so its area is $\dfrac{1}{2}$. The larger triangle has a base of 3 and height of 3, so its area is $\dfrac{9}{2}$. Therefore, the *area* of the entire shaded region is $\dfrac{9}{2} + \dfrac{1}{2} = 5$. ◆

EXAMPLE 6.11:

The velocity of a particle is given by $v(t) := \begin{cases} 4t + 2, & 0 \le t \le 3 \\ 20 - 2t, & 3 \le t \le 6 \end{cases}$. What is the distance travelled during the time interval [0, 6]?

Since v is defined by one formula on the interval [0, 3] and another formula on the interval [3, 6], we need to use 2 separate integrals to determine the distance. Hence,

$$L = \int_0^6 v(t)\, dt = \int_0^3 (4t + 2)\, dt + \int_3^6 (20 - 2t)\, dt$$
$$= 24 + 33 = 57. \qquad \blacklozenge$$

In the previous example, we made implicit use of the following theorems. Theorems 6.2 and 6.3 resemble Theorems 3.17 and 3.18 of Chapter 3. Theorem 6.4 has a nice geometric interpretation. The proofs of these theorems follow directly from the definition of the definite integral and we shall not bother to write them down.

THEOREM 6.2: Let f and g be continuous functions. Then:
$$\int_a^b (f(x) + g(x))\, dx = \int_a^b f(x)\, dx + \int_a^b g(x)\, dx \quad .$$

THEOREM 6.3: Let f be a continuous function and let k be a constant. Then:
$$\int_a^b kf(x)\, dx = k \int_a^b f(x)\, dx \quad .$$

THEOREM 6.4: $\int_a^b f(x)\, dx + \int_b^c f(x)\, dx = \int_a^c f(x)\, dx \quad .$

Usually, when we write $\int_a^b f(x)\, dx$, it is assumed that $a < b$. However, we can define the symbol if $a \ge b$, as well. If $a = b$, then we are finding the area of a region over an interval of length 0. Intuitively, this area should be 0; that is,

$$\int_a^a f(x)\,dx \ = \ 0.$$

We define the integral for the case when $a > b$ in order to make Theorem 6.4 true for all choices of a, b and c (not necessarily with $a < b < c$). Suppose $a = c$. Then the theorem becomes

$$\int_a^b f(x)\,dx \ + \ \int_b^a f(x)\,dx \ = \ \int_a^a f(x)\,dx \ .$$

But $\int_a^a f(x)\,dx \ = \ 0$. Therefore,

$$\int_a^b f(x)\,dx \ = \ -\int_b^a f(x)\,dx \ .$$

Thus, switching the limits of integration changes the sign of the integral. (See Exercise 13.)

EXERCISES FOR SECTION 6.3:

1. Evaluate the following definite integrals:

   (a) $\displaystyle\int_0^1 2x\,dx$

   (b) $\displaystyle\int_1^2 (5x^4 + 5)\,dx$

   (c) $\displaystyle\int_1^4 \frac{1}{y}\,dy$

   (d) $\displaystyle\int_4^9 \frac{1}{\sqrt{u}}\,du$

   (e) $\displaystyle\int_{-1}^1 \sqrt[3]{t}\,dt$

   (f) $\displaystyle\int_{-2}^0 (x+4)^2\,dx$

   (g) $\displaystyle\int_{-2}^2 (z^3 + z)\,dz$

   (h) $\displaystyle\int_0^6 (ax + b)\,dx$

2. Find the area bounded by the graph of $f(x) := 4x - x^2$ and the x-axis.

3. Evaluate $\displaystyle\int_0^3 e^x\,dx$ and sketch the region whose area is given by this integral.

4. Write, but do not evaluate, a definite integral which can be used to determine the area bounded by $f(x) := 8x - x^4$ and the x-axis.

5. Evaluate $\displaystyle\int_{-1}^1 |x^3|\,dx$.

6. The velocity of a particle is given by $v(t) := t^3 + 3t$. Find the distance travelled over the time interval $[1, 4]$.

7. Sketch the region whose area is given by $\int_0^5 \sqrt{9-x}\, dx$.

8. If the Riemann sum for a function f over the interval [3, 5] is $S(n) :=$
$\dfrac{24 + 18n + 6n^2 + 30n^3}{2n^3}$, what is $\int_3^5 f(x)\, dx$?

9. Evaluate each of the following integrals by sketching the region and using an appropriate geometry formula.

 (a) $\int_0^2 (4-2x)\, dx$ 　　　(b) $\int_1^5 |x-4|\, dx$ 　　　(c) $\int_{-4}^4 \sqrt{16-x^2}\, dx$

10. If $\int_0^4 f(x)\, dx = A$ and $\int_4^9 f(x)\, dx = B$, express each of the following in terms of A and B:

 (a) $\int_0^9 f(x)\, dx$ 　　　(b) $\int_9^4 f(x)\, dx$

11. The density of a bar at a point x meters from one end is given by $\rho(x) :=$ $2x^3 + 4x$ grams/meter. If the bar is 2 meters long, find the total mass.

12. A cylindrical rod is 1 meter long. The density of the rod at a point x meters from one end is given by the function $\rho(x) := 1 + x - x^2$ kg/m. What is the total mass of the rod?

13. Draw a picture illustrating Theorem 6.4 for the case in which f is non-negative.

PROBLEMS FOR SECTION 6.3:

1. (a) Argue geometrically that if f is an odd function, then $\int_{-c}^c f(x)\, dx = 0$.

 (b) Argue geometrically that if f is an even function, then $\int_{-c}^c f(x)\, dx =$ $2\int_0^c f(x)\, dx$.

 (c) Evaluate $\int_{-3}^3 (x^5 + 3x^3 - 4x)\, dx$.

2. Prove that if $f(x) \le g(x)$ for $a \le x \le b$, then $\int_a^b f(x)\, dx \le \int_a^b g(x)\, dx$.

3. Express, in terms of n, the area in the first quadrant bounded by $y = x^n$, the x-axis and the line $x = 1$. What happens to the area as n increases?

4. At time $t = 0$, a jogger is running at a velocity of 300 meters per minute. The jogger is slowing down with a negative acceleration that is directly proportional to time t. This brings the jogger to a stop in 10 minutes.

   (a) Determine the velocity of the jogger at time t.

   (b) What is the total distance traveled by the jogger in that 10-minute interval?

5. Suppose f and g are functions such that $f(x) = g'(x)$ for all x. If $g(1) = 3$ and $g(4) = 9$, evaluate $\int_1^4 f(x)\,dx$.

6. Consider the region R bounded by $y = 3x^2 + 1$, the x-axis, the lines $x = b$ and $x = b + 4$, for some constant b.

   (a) Express the area of R in terms of b.

   (b) For what value of b is the area of R minimized?

7. A region is bounded by the curve $y = x^2$ and the line $y = h$.

   (a) Express the area of the region in terms of h.

   (b) If h is increasing at 3 units/min., how fast is the area changing when $h = 4$?

<u>TYU Answers for Section 6.3</u>

   1. The FTC allows us to use antiderivatives, rather than the definition, to evaluate definite integrals.

   2. (a) 15 (b) –2 (c) 2/3 (d) $e - 1/e$ 3. 116/3   4. 78   5. 80

6.4 APPLICATIONS OF DEFINITE INTEGRALS

As we said earlier in this chapter, the problem of finding the area of a region is merely a prototype for many other applications of Riemann sums and definite integrals. It is used because it has a nice geometric flavor and we can draw pictures to illustrate the concepts. In this section, we will consider several other applications of integrals. First let's do a few more area problems to review and extend the basic technique of creating and evaluating Riemann sums.

Before we started this chapter, the only regions for which we could find areas were rectangles. Rectangles are special because they have a constant height and constant width. The regions we encountered in this chapter had variable height. We chopped those regions into n very small pieces, each of which is approximately rectangular. Then we computed the area of each piece and added them up, obtaining a Riemann sum. To get the exact area, we let $n \to \infty$. This turned the Riemann sum into a definite integral which, if we were lucky, could be evaluated by finding an antiderivative and using the Fundamental Theorem of Calculus.

EXAMPLE 6.12:

Find the area in the first quadrant bounded by the curves $f(x) := x$ and $g(x) := x^2$, as pictured in Figure 6.10 below.

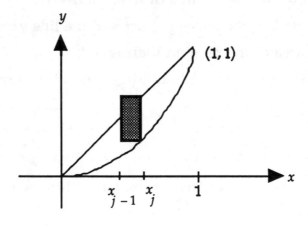

Fig. 6.10

This region differs from the ones we've considered so far since the lower boundary is a curve, not the x-axis. Notice that the curves intersect at $(0, 0)$ and $(1, 1)$.

Partition the interval $[0, 1]$ into n subintervals. Let $x_j = 0 + j\Delta x = j\Delta x$ be the jth partition point. Draw a vertical line between the points $(x_j, f(x_j))$ and $(x_j, g(x_j))$ and construct rectangles using this line as the height and Δx as the width, as shown. The height of the jth rectangle is $f(x_j) - g(x_j) = x_j - x_j^2$. The sum of the areas of the n rectangles is:

$$S(n) := \sum_{j=1}^{n} \left(x_j - x_j^2 \right) \Delta x.$$

To get the exact area, take the limit as $n \to \infty$, obtaining:

$$A = \lim_{n \to \infty} \sum_{j=1}^{n} \left(x_j - x_j^2 \right) \Delta x = \int_0^1 \left(x - x^2 \right) dx = \left. \frac{x^2}{2} - \frac{x^3}{3} \right|_0^1 = \frac{1}{6}. \quad \blacklozenge$$

- -

TEST YOUR UNDERSTANDING

1. Let $f(x) := x^2 - 1$ and $g(x) := x + 1$. (a) Show that the graphs of f and g intersect at two points. (b) Determine the area of the region bounded by f and g between those points.

- -

EXAMPLE 6.13:

Find the area in the first quadrant bounded by $y = \ln(x)$, the x-axis and the line $x = e$ as shown in Figure 6.11.

At first glance, this appears to be a problem just like the ones we solved earlier in the chapter, in which case,

$$A = \int_1^e \ln(x)\, dx.$$

While this is correct, it is not very useful since we cannot yet find an antiderivative of $f(x) := \ln(x)$. (We'll learn how in Chapter 8.) Thus, we cannot invoke the Fundamental Theorem of Calculus.

To get around this, let's turn the problem on its side. If x is between 1 and e, then $y = \ln(x)$ is between 0 and 1. Try partitioning the interval $[0, 1]$ on the y-axis into n subintervals of length $\Delta y = 1/n$ and drawing in the rectangles horizontally. The height of any rectangle is the difference between the x-values at its right and left boundaries. Note that we will have to express the height in terms of y since we will eventually be integrating with respect to y.

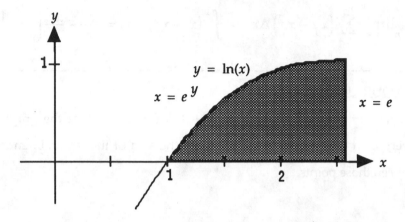

Fig. 6.11

The right boundary of each rectangle is the vertical line $x = e$; the left boundary is the curve $y = \ln(x)$ or, upon solving for x, $x = e^y$. Therefore, the sum of the areas of the rectangles is $S(n) := \sum_{j=1}^{n} (e - e^{y_j}) \Delta y$.

The exact area, obtained by taking the limit as $n \to \infty$, is:

$$A = \int_0^1 (e - e^y)\, dy = ey - e^y \Big|_0^1 = e - e - 0 + 1 = 1.$$ ♦

¤   Other problems that make use of definite integrals are finding the distance travelled by an object or the mass of an object. If the velocity is constant, there is nothing to it--just multiply the velocity by the time. Similarly, if the density of the object is constant, just multiply the density by the length. It's when the velocity or density is not constant that we need to invoke calculus.

The common theme is that the quantity we are looking for (area, distance, mass) is the "product" of two other quantities. If those quantities are constant, then all we need do is multiply. Calculus is needed when those quantities are not constant. In the remainder of this chapter, we will look at several other applications of this same idea.

VOLUMES OF SOLIDS

Suppose S is a 3-dimensional solid with the property that all cross-sections perpendicular to some axis are geometrically similar. For example, if we slice a cone perpendicular to its axis, all the cross-sections are circles which decrease in radius as we get near the point. Our objective is to find the volume of such a solid.

If all the cross-sections were exactly the same shape and size, then the volume of the solid would be given by $V = Ah$, where A is the area of the cross-section and h is the height of the solid. For instance, if the solid were a circular cylinder of radius r, then $A = \pi r^2$, so $V = \pi r^2 h$.

A more interesting case is when the cross-sections are the same shape but not necessarily the same size. Then A is not constant. In order to find the volume, we slice the solid into slices, much as you would a loaf of bread. If the slices are sufficiently thin, then we may assume each slice has constant cross-sectional area. We can then find its approximate volume. The total volume is approximately the sum of the volumes of the slices. The exact volume is obtained by making the slices thinner (i.e. taking more slices).

Suppose we want to find the volume of a pyramid with square base of side $s = 4$ and height $h = 8$. While the cross-sections are all squares, they get smaller as we go up the pyramid.

When solving problems of this type, it is convenient to introduce a coordinate system. Here, let's invert the pyramid so that its point is at the origin and the y-axis runs through the middle. Then, slice the pyramid horizontally into small slices. (Each slice resembles a slice of square bread with beveled edges.) Let $y_j = y$-coordinate of the bottom edge of the jth slice (or any other point in the jth slice, for that matter) and let $\Delta y = $ thickness of each slice. See Figure 6.12.

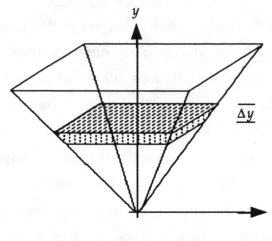

Fig. 6.12

Let l_j be the length of the side of the slice. Using similar triangles (see Figure 6.13), l_j can be obtained from the proportion $\dfrac{l_j}{4} = \dfrac{y_j}{8}$ from which $l_j = \dfrac{y_j}{2}$.

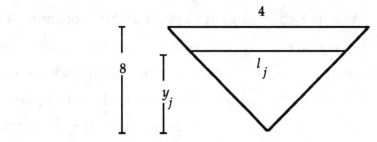

Fig. 6.13

Thus, the area of the square is $A = \left(\dfrac{y_j}{2}\right)^2$ and the volume of the jth slice is approximately $V_j = \left(\dfrac{y_j}{2}\right)^2 \Delta y$. To get the approximate volume, let's add up the volumes of all the slices:

$$V \approx \sum_{j=1}^{n} \left(\dfrac{y_j}{2}\right)^2 \Delta y \ .$$

This is a Riemann sum for the function $A(y) := \left(\dfrac{y}{2}\right)^2$ and is very similar to the ones we obtained when computing areas.

Notice also that the approximation improves as $n \to \infty$ (or, $\Delta y \to 0$). The exact volume is obtained by taking the limit as $n \to \infty$: $V = \lim\limits_{n \to \infty} \sum\limits_{j=1}^{n} \left(\dfrac{y_j}{2}\right)^2 \Delta y$. Rather than evaluate the sum directly, we convert it to an integral to which we then apply the Fundamental Theorem of Calculus.

$$V = \int_0^8 \frac{y^2}{4}\, dy = \left.\frac{y^3}{12}\right|_0^8 = \frac{128}{3}.$$

This is the correct answer since there is a well-known result in solid geometry that gives the volume of any pyramid as $V = \dfrac{1}{3} Ah$, where A is the area of the base. Here $A = 16$ and $h = 8$; hence, $V = \dfrac{128}{3}$.

Pay particular attention to the limits of integration. The reason we integrate from $y = 0$ to $y = 8$ in this example is that there is a slice of the pyramid for each y-value in that interval.

TEST YOUR UNDERSTANDING

2. Suppose we cut a small pyramid off the bottom of the whole inverted pyramid by slicing it parallel to the base at a point 2 inches from the vertex. Use integration to find the volume of the remaining part.

3. Suppose the base of the pyramid is a square of side $s = 10$ and the height is 5. Use integration to find the volume of the pyramid.

Let's try another example. Suppose we want to find the volume of a sphere of radius R. Place the sphere so that the x- and y-axes run through the center and slice the sphere as you would a tomato. (Each slice looks like a disk or hockey puck. See Figure 6.14.) We'll slice it vertically although, in this case, it doesn't matter. Let x_j be the x-coordinate of the jth slice and let Δx = thickness of the slices.

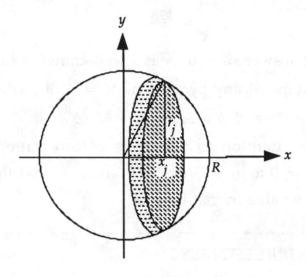

Fig. 6.14

Since each slice has circular cross-section, we need to find the radius r_j of the jth slice. By the Pythagorean Theorem, $r_j^2 + x_j^2 = R^2$, so $r_j^2 = R^2 - x_j^2$. Therefore, the cross-sectional area of the jth slice is

$$A_j = \pi r_j^2 = \pi(R^2 - x_j^2)$$

and the volume of the slice is approximately

$$V_j = \pi(R^2 - x_j^2)\Delta x.$$

The total volume is approximately

$$V \approx \sum_{j=1}^{n} \pi(R^2 - x_j^2)\,\Delta x,$$

a Riemann sum for the function $A(x) := \pi(R^2 - x^2)$. After taking the limit and converting to an integral, we get

$$V = \int_{-R}^{R} \pi(R^2 - x^2)\,dx = \pi\left(R^2 x - \frac{x^3}{3}\right)\Bigg|_{-R}^{R} = \frac{4}{3}\pi R^3 ,$$

another well-known result. Again note the limits of integration. There is a slice for each x between $-R$ and R; hence, we integrate from $-R$ to R.

TEST YOUR UNDERSTANDING

4. Use integration to show that the volume of a circular cone that has a base of radius 3 and a height of 4 is 12π.

WORK

In physics, you may have learned that, by definition, if a force of magnitude F moves an object a distance x, then the work done is $W = Fx$. This assumes that the force is constant. For example, suppose an object of mass m kg. is lifted x meters. Assuming no air resistance and that the acceleration due to gravity is a constant g, then the only force required is to overcome gravity. By Newton's law, force = (mass)(acceleration) = mg. Therefore, the work done in lifting the object is $W = mgx$ Joules.

Note: A Joule is a Newton-meter, or kg-m^2/sec^2 and is one of the units in which work is measured in the metric system. Another metric unit for work is the erg, defined as a dyne-cm. or g-cm^2/sec^2. In the English system, the unit of force (or weight) is the pound which is the mass times the acceleration of gravity. (The English unit of mass, the slug, is not commonly used.) Hence, work is measured in foot-pounds.

In many applications, however, the force exerted is not constant in which case this simple formula does not apply. A classic example is the spring.

Experience tells us that the more you stretch a spring, the more force required to keep it from contracting (or the more force the spring exerts on you). In fact, the force required is proportional to the amount the spring is stretched. This is known as **Hooke's Law** and can be stated as:

The amount of force exerted by a spring when it is stretched x units beyond its natural length is given by $F(x) := kx$, where k is a constant that depends on the spring.

The question we'd like to answer is how much work is done by stretching the spring from $x = a$ to $x = b$ meters beyond its natural length?

As with areas, we partition the interval $[a, b]$ into n subintervals of length Δx. Assume that the force required while stretching the spring from x_{j-1} to $x_j = x_{j-1} + \Delta x$ is (approximately) constant $F(x_j)$. The work done by doing so is

$$W_j = F(x_j)\Delta x = kx_j\Delta x.$$

The total work done is approximately

$$W \approx \sum_{j=1}^{n} k x_j \, \Delta x \,,$$

a Riemann sum for the function $F(x) := kx$. By taking the limit as $n \to \infty$, we get

$$W = \int_a^b kx \, dx = \frac{k}{2}\left(b^2 - a^2\right).$$

EXAMPLE 6.14:

A spring exerts a force of 20 Newtons (1 Newton $= 1$ kg-m/sec^2) when stretched 2 meters beyond its natural length. How much work is done in stretching the spring from 2 meters to 4 meters beyond its natural length?

Since $F = 20$ when $x = 2$, then Hooke's law tells us that the proportionality constant for this spring is $k = 10$. Thus, the work done is

$$W = \int_2^4 10x \, dx = 60 \text{ Joules.} \qquad \blacklozenge$$

In general, if $F(x)$ is the force exerted on an object at point x, then the work done in moving the object from $x = a$ to $x = b$ is $W = \int_a^b F(x)\,dx$.

---

5. Suppose a spring exerts a force of 50 Newtons when stretched 10 meters beyond its natural length. How much work is done by stretching the spring from 5 meters to 15 meters beyond its natural length?

6. Suppose the force required to move a body is *inversely* proportional to its distance from some point O. How much work is done by moving the object from 2 meters to 4 meters from O?

Let's consider a slightly different problem. Suppose we have a cylindrical tank of radius R and height h which is full of water. We want to determine how much work is required to pump the water out over the top of the tank.

In this problem, the force is constant but different "parts" of the water are moved different distances. (The water at the bottom must travel further than the water at the top.) So once again we need to create a Riemann sum. Introduce a coordinate system with the y-axis down the center of the tank and the origin at the center of the bottom and slice the water into thin disks of thickness Δy. The volume of water in the slice is $\pi R^2 \Delta y$ and so the mass is $\rho \pi R^2 \Delta y$, where ρ is the density of water (approx. 1 gram/cc). Let y_j be the y-coordinate of any point in the jth slice. Then the water in the jth slice must be moved a distance $h - y_j$. See Figure 6.15.

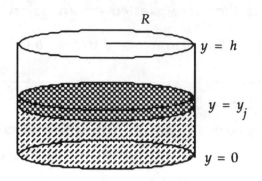

Fig. 6.15

Therefore, the work required to pump the water in the jth slice out of the tank is

$$W_j = \text{mass} \times \text{acceleration} \times \text{distance moved} = \rho g \pi R^2 (h - y_j) \Delta y.$$

The total work to pump out all the water is approximately

$$W \approx \sum_{j=1}^{n} \rho g \pi R^2 (h - y_j) \Delta y,$$

a Riemann sum for the function $p(y) := \rho g \pi R^2 (h - y)$. Taking the limit as $n \to \infty$, we get

$$W = \int_0^h \rho g \pi R^2 (h - y)\, dy = \frac{\rho g \pi R^2 h^2}{2}.$$

- -

TEST YOUR UNDERSTANDING

7. Suppose, instead of cylindrical, the tank was a rectangular solid with a square base 10 feet on a side and 40 feet high. How much work is required to pump the water out the top? (For your information, water weighs 62.4 pounds per cubic foot. Recall from an earlier note about units that, in the English system, this number already includes the acceleration of gravity; that is, $62.4 = \rho g$.)

PROBLEMS FOR SECTION 6.4:

1. What is the area of the closed region bounded by the curve $y = e^{2x}$ and the lines

    (a) $x = 1$ and $y = 1$?

    (b) $x = 1$ and $y = e$?

2. Find the area bounded by the graph of $y = 8 - x^2$ and the secant line joining the points $(-2, 4)$ and $(1, 7)$.

3. (a) Find the area of the region bounded above by the graph of $f(x) := x^2$, below by the line tangent to that graph at $x = 1/4$, on the left by the y-axis, and on the right by the line $x = 1$.

    (b) Repeat (a) using the tangent line at an arbitrary point, $x = c$. Your answer should be a function of c.

    (c) Call the function you found in (b) $A(c)$. What value of c minimizes $A(c)$?

    (d) For $n > 0$, let $A_n(c)$ be the area of the region bounded above by the graph of $f(x) := x^n$, below by the line tangent to that graph at $x = c$, on the left by the y-axis, and on the right by the line $x = 1$. Prove that for all n, the same value of c minimizes $A_n(c)$.

4. A tower is constructed in such a way that all its cross-sections are squares. The side of the square at the base is 50 ft. and the tower tapers in such way that at height y above the ground, the side of the cross-sectional square is $s(y) := 50e^{-ky}$ for some k.

    (a) If the tower is 200 feet tall and the length of the side of the cross-section at the top is 10 ft., determine k.

    (b) Determine the volume of the tower.

5. The gravitational force between an object and the earth is given by the formula $F = \dfrac{GMm}{r^2}$, where M is the mass of the earth, m is the mass of the object, G is a universal constant and r is the distance between the object and the center of the earth. How much work is required to lift a 1000 kg. satellite from the earth's surface to an altitude of 400 km.? (The radius of the earth is approximately 6400 km.)

6. A bowl is shaped in such a way that its cross-sections perpendicular to the axis of the bowl are circles of radius $r(y) := \sqrt{y}$, where y is the distance from the bottom of the bowl. Determine the volume of the bowl if it is h inches deep.

7. The base of a right circular cone has radius r and the height of the cone is h. Show that the volume of the cone is $V = \frac{1}{3}\pi r^2 h$.

8. A conical tank has radius = 4 ft. and height = 6 ft. as shown below. If the tank is full of water, how much work is required to pump all the water out over the top of the tank?

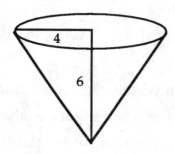

TYU Answers for Section 6.4

1. (a) $x = -1, x = 2$ (b) $\displaystyle\int_{-1}^{2} (x+1) - (x^2-1)\,dx = 9/2$ 2. $\displaystyle\int_{2}^{8} \frac{y^2}{4}\,dy = 42$

3. $\displaystyle\int_{0}^{5} (2y)^2\,dy = \frac{500}{3}$ 4. $\displaystyle\int_{0}^{4} \pi\left(\frac{3}{4}y\right)^2\,dy = 12\pi$ 5. 500 Joules

6. $W = \displaystyle\int_{2}^{4} \frac{k}{x}\,dx = k\,\ln(2)$ 7. $6240\displaystyle\int_{0}^{40} (40-y)\,dy = 800(6240) = 4992000$ ft.-lbs.

6.5 FUNCTIONS DEFINED BY INTEGRALS

Up to this point, all the functions we have considered have been defined by explicit formulas that can be evaluated in a finite number of arithmetical operations or, in the case of e^x and $\ln(x)$, in a few strokes on your calculator. For example, consider $f(x) := x^2 + 1$; for any given x, this can be evaluated with one multiplication (x by x) and one addition. In reality, there are other ways of defining functions which aren't necessarily so "tidy". We will consider one such method here. (We'll look at another one in Chapter 11 when we study power series.)

Consider the region bounded above by the graph of the non-negative function $y = f(t)$, below by the t-axis, on the left by the line $t = a$ and on the right by the "movable" line $t = x$. (You should think of x as a variable.) See Figure 6.16. The area of this region is a function of x and is given by:

$$g(x) := \int_a^x f(t)\, dt\,.$$

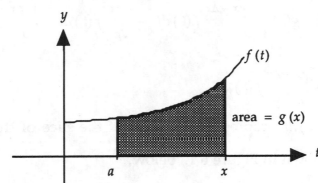

Fig 6.16

If f were antidifferentiable, then we could invoke the Fundamental Theorem of Calculus and express g in closed form. For example, let

$$g(x) := \int_1^x 3t^2\, dt\,.$$

Then $\quad g(x) := t^3\big|_{t=1}^{t=x} = x^3 - 1$.

Now consider the function

$$g(x) := \int_0^x \sqrt{t^3 + 1}\, dt\,.$$

The function $f(t) := \sqrt{t^3 + 1}$ has no closed form antiderivative; nevertheless, g is still a well-defined function of x, although difficult to compute. One way to evaluate g (at least approximately) is by computing an appropriate Riemann sum with sufficiently many terms.

As long as we agree that functions defined by integrals are bona-fide functions, then we can ask many of the same questions about them that we did about functions defined in a more traditional manner. The main question we'd like to answer is how fast is $g(x)$ changing as a function of x. In other words, what is $g'(x)$? (Once we know this, then the standard questions about direction, concavity, etc., are easily answered.)

If we could express g in closed form, we could then just differentiate to find g'. For example, with $g(x) := \int_1^x 3t^2\,dt = x^3 - 1$, we have $g'(x) := 3x^2$. However, even if we can't express g in closed form, we can still find g' by resorting to the definition of the derivative from Chapter 3.

$$\Delta g = g(x + \Delta x) - g(x) = \int_a^{x+\Delta x} f(t)\,dt - \int_a^x f(t)\,dt = \int_x^{x+\Delta x} f(t)\,dt .$$

So,

$$\frac{\Delta g}{\Delta x} = \frac{1}{\Delta x} \int_x^{x+\Delta x} f(t)\,dt .$$

Now, $\int_x^{x+\Delta x} f(t)\,dt$ represents the area of the slice of the region between x and $x + \Delta x$, as shown in Figure 6.17 below.

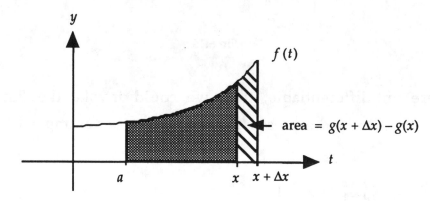

Fig 6.17

If Δx is very small, then this slice is approximately a very thin rectangle with height $f(x)$ and width Δx. Therefore,

$$\int_x^{x+\Delta x} f(t)\,dt \approx f(x)\,\Delta x,$$

from which $\frac{\Delta g}{\Delta x} \approx f(x)$. Letting $\Delta x \to 0$ establishes the following theorem:

THEOREM 6.5: Let f be a continuous function and let $g(x) := \displaystyle\int_a^x f(t)\,dt$.

Then $g'(x) := f(x)$, for all x.

This theorem is very important because it tells us that *every* continuous function has an antiderivative, even if we can't express the antiderivative in a nice form.

EXAMPLE 6.15:

Let $g(x) := \displaystyle\int_1^x \frac{1}{t^2+1}\,dt$

(a) Determine $g'(x)$.

According to Theorem 6.5, $g'(x) := \dfrac{1}{x^2+1}$.

(b) Write an equation of the line tangent to the graph of g at $x = 1$.

Since $g(1) = \displaystyle\int_1^1 \frac{1}{t^2+1}\,dt = 0$ and $g'(1) = \frac{1}{2}$, the equation is

$$y - 0 = \tfrac{1}{2}(x-1), \text{ or}$$
$$y = \tfrac{1}{2}x - \tfrac{1}{2}.$$

               ◆

Note that if $h(x) := \displaystyle\int_2^x \frac{1}{t^2+1}\,dt$, then $h'(x) := \dfrac{1}{x^2+1}$, as well. The lower limit of integration has no effect on the derivative. In fact, by Theorem 6.4, $g(x) - h(x) = \displaystyle\int_1^x \frac{1}{t^2+1}\,dt - \int_2^x \frac{1}{t^2+1}\,dt = \int_1^2 \frac{1}{t^2+1}\,dt$, which is a constant. By taking the derivative of both sides, we have $g'(x) - h'(x) = 0$, or $g'(x) = h'(x)$.

EXAMPLE 6.16:

Determine the direction and concavity of $f(x) := \displaystyle\int_1^x \left(1 - e^{-t}\right) dt$.

From Theorem 6.5, $f'(x) := 1 - e^{-x}$ which is positive whenever $e^{-x} < 1$.

This happens when $x > 0$. Hence, f is increasing for $x > 0$ and decreasing for $x < 0$.

$f''(x) := e^{-x}$ which is always positive. Thus, f is concave up for all x.

$\blacklozenge$

TEST YOUR UNDERSTANDING

1. Determine $g'(x)$ if: (a) $g(x) := \displaystyle\int_0^x \ln(t^2 + 4)\,dt$ (b) $g(x) := \displaystyle\int_2^x \ln(t^2 + 4)\,dt$

2. Let $g(x) := \displaystyle\int_0^x t(e^t - 2)\,dt$. Determine the critical points of g and classify them as local maximum, minimum or neither.

◻ Some texts refer to Theorem 6.5 as the "Fundamental Theorem of Calculus" and use it to prove Theorem 6.1 (which we called the Fundamental Theorem of Calculus). We include the following proof of Theorem 6.1 for completeness.

Let f be a continuous function and let $G(x) := \displaystyle\int_a^x f(t)\,dt$. Theorem 6.5 tells us that G is an antiderivative of f. Let F be any antiderivative of f. Then, by Theorem 3.15, F and G must differ by a constant; that is,

$$F(x) = G(x) + c.$$

Therefore,

$$F(b) - F(a) = [G(b) + c] - [G(a) + c] = G(b) - G(a)$$
$$= \int_a^b f(t)\,dt - \int_a^a f(t)\,dt$$
$$= \int_a^b f(t)\,dt$$

which is the result of Theorem 6.1.

THE NATURAL LOGARITHM AS A DEFINITE INTEGRAL

One consequence of Theorem 6.5 is that it allows us to give another definition to the natural logarithm function. We showed that the derivative of $\ln(x)$ is $\frac{1}{x}$ so, $\ln(x)$ is an antiderivative of $\frac{1}{x}$. Although there are infinitely many such antiderivatives, all of them can be expressed in the form

$$f(x) := \int_a^x \frac{1}{t}\, dt \quad \text{for some } a > 0.$$ In order to determine a, we use the fact that $\ln(1) = 0$. Since $f(1) = \int_a^1 \frac{1}{t}\, dt$, then $a = 1$ implies $f(1) = 0$.

DEFINITION: $\ln(x) = \int_1^x \frac{1}{t}\, dt \quad$ for $x > 0$.

Thus, if $x > 1$, $\ln(x)$ is the area under the graph of $f(t) := \frac{1}{t}$ between $t = 1$ and $t = x$. If $0 < x < 1$, then we use the fact that $\int_1^x \frac{1}{t}\, dt = -\int_x^1 \frac{1}{t}\, dt$ and so $\ln(x)$ is the negative of the area under the graph of f between $t = x$ and $t = 1$. See Figure 6.18.

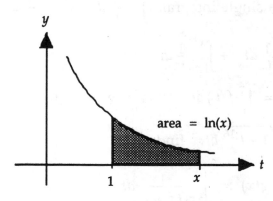

Fig. 6.18

It can be shown that this definition implies all the properties that the natural logarithm should have such as $\ln(a) + \ln(b) = \ln(ab)$. This is a topic for further investigation.

EXERCISES FOR SECTION 6.5:

1. Use the Fundamental Theorem of Calculus to evaluate the following integrals, then differentiate the resulting function of x and verify Theorem 6.5:

   (a) $g(x) := \int_{-2}^{x} \left(t^2 + 2t \right) dt$

   (b) $g(x) := \int_{1}^{x} \frac{1}{t^2} dt$

2. Determine the derivative of each of the following:

   (a) $g(x) := \int_{4}^{x} t \ln(t) dt$

   (b) $y = \int_{-3}^{x} \sqrt{1 + e^t} \, dt$

3. Determine the direction and concavity of $g(x) := \int_{0}^{x} \sqrt{t^2 + 1} \, dt$.

4. Let $g(x) := x \int_{3}^{x} e^{-t^2} dt$. Determine $g'(3)$.

5. Suppose $5x^3 + 40 = \int_{c}^{x} f(t) \, dt$ for some constant c.

   (a) Determine $f(x)$.   (b) Determine the value of c.

PROBLEMS FOR SECTION 6.5:

1. (a) Simplify into a single integral: $\int_{1}^{x^2} \frac{1}{t} \, dt + \int_{1}^{x^3} \frac{1}{t} \, dt$

   (b) Simplify: $\int_{1}^{x^a} \frac{1}{t} \, dt + \int_{1}^{x^b} \frac{1}{t} \, dt$

2. (a) Suppose $g(x) := \int_{x}^{a} f(t) \, dt$. What is $g'(x)$? Justify your claim.

   (b) If $g(x) := \int_{x}^{3} \sqrt{1 + t^{16}} \, dt$, find $g'(x)$.

3. Determine $g'(x)$ if $g(x) := \int_{2}^{x^2} \frac{1}{t^3 + 1} \, dt$.

4. (a) Let $g(x) := \int_{x}^{x^2} f(t) \, dt$. Determine $g'(x)$.

   (b) Let $g(x) := \int_{u(x)}^{v(x)} f(t) \, dt$. Determine $g'(x)$.

   (c) Suppose that g is defined as in (b), and that $u(2) = 3$, $u'(2) = -1$, $v(2) = 6$, $v'(2) = 3$, $f(3) = 1$ and $f(6) = -4$. Determine $g'(2)$.

5. Let f be a continuous function and let $g(x) := \int_1^x f(t)\,dt$. Suppose that g has the property that $g(ab) = g(a) + g(b)$ for all $a > 0$ and $b > 0$ and $g'(1) = 3$.

(a) Find $f(1)$.

(b) Show that $ag'(ax) = g'(x)$ for every $a > 0$.

(c) Use the results of (a) and (b) to find $f(x)$.

6. (a) Prove that if $f'(x) = g'(x)$ for all x and $f(a) = g(a)$ for some a, then $f(x) = g(x)$ for all x.

(b) Let $f(x) := \int_0^x \dfrac{1}{\sqrt{1+t^2}}\,dt$ and $g(x) := \ln\!\left(x + \sqrt{x^2+1}\right)$. Use (a) to show that $f(x) = g(x)$ for all x.

(c) Determine the area bounded by the graph of $y = \dfrac{1}{\sqrt{1+x^2}}$, the x-axis and the lines $x = 0$ and $x = 3$.

TYU Answers for Section 6.5

1. (a) $\ln(x^2 + 4)$ (b) same as (a)

2. There is a local max at $x = 0$ and a local min at $x = \ln(2)$

QUESTIONS TO THINK ABOUT

1. Define the definite integral in terms of Riemann sums. Your definition should include the definition of a Riemann sum.

2. How are the problems of the broken speedometer, area under a curve, and work related? Your answer should include some information about approximation by sums.

3. Interpret $\int_a^b f(x)\,dx$ as an area problem, as a distance traveled problem, as a mass problem, as a volume problem and as a work problem.

4. State the Fundamental Theorem of Calculus and explain its importance.

PROJECT 6.1

CYLINDRICAL SHELLS

OBJECTIVE: In Section 6.5, we learned how to find the volume of a certain type of solid--those for which all cross-sections perpendicular to some axis are geometrically similar.   In this project, we will look at a different method for finding volume. It is called the method of **cylindrical shells**.

PROCEDURE:
Part 1: Some geometry
   A cylindrical shell consists of a cylinder of radius R from which a smaller cylinder of radius r has been removed, leaving a ring or shell of thickness $\Delta r = R - r$.

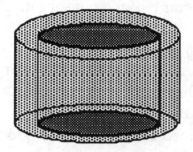

a. Compute the exact volume of a cylindrical shell of height $h = 4$ if $R = 6$ and $r = 5$.
b. Repeat 1a if $h = 4, R = 5.1$ and $r = 5$.
c. Argue that if Δr is small, then the volume of the cylindrical shell is given approximately by $\Delta V \approx 2\pi rh\Delta r$. Hint: "Unroll" the cylindrical shell, obtaining a rectangular solid.

Part 2: An example of finding volume by the method of cylindrical shells
   Consider the cone formed by rotating the triangle bounded by $y = 0, x = 0$ and $y = 4 - 2x$ around the y-axis, as shown.

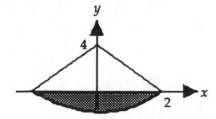

a. Find the volume of this cone by using the formula $V = \frac{1}{3}\pi r^2h$.

Partition the interval [0, 2] of the x-axis into n equal subintervals of length Δx. Choose an arbitrary subinterval $[x_j, x_{j+1}]$ and construct a rectangle whose height is $4 - 2x_j$. Rotate this rectangle around the y-axis obtaining a cylindrical shell.

b. What is the inner radius r of this shell?

c. What is the height h of the shell?

d. Show that the volume of the shell is approximately

$$\Delta V \;=\; 2\pi x_j(4 - 2x_j)\Delta x.$$

e. Create a Riemann sum equal to the sum of the volumes of the shells that approximates the volume of the cone.

f. Use 2e to obtain an integral whose value is the volume of the cone. Evaluate this integral and show that the answer is the same as 2a.

Part 3: Generalizations

Let R be the region bounded by the graph of the non-negative function $y = f(x)$, the x-axis, and the lines $x = a$ and $x = b$, where $0 \le a \le b$. Let S be the solid obtained by rotating R around the y-axis. Partition the interval $[a, b]$ into equal subintervals and construct shells as in Part 2.

a. Show that the volume of the jth shell is $\Delta V = 2\pi x_j f(x_j)\, \Delta x$.

b. Write an integral whose value is the volume of S.

c. Find the volume of the solid obtained by rotating the region bounded by $y = 4x - x^2$ and the x-axis around the y-axis.

d. Find the volume of the solid obtained by rotating the region bounded by $y = x^2 + 1$, the x-axis, the y-axis and $x = 1$ around the y-axis.

e. Find the volume of the solid obtained when the region in 3d is rotated around the line $x = 2$.

f. Find the volume of the solid obtained when the region bounded above by $y = 4x - x^2$ and below by $y = x$ is rotated around the y-axis.

g. Set up an integral that gives the volume of the doughnut obtained when the region bounded by $(x - 1)^2 + y^2 = 1$ is rotated around the y-axis.

PROJECT 6.2

A FAMILY OF PARABOLAS

OBJECTIVE: Let $f_k(x) := kx^2 + (1 - 4k)x + 3k$, where k is a non-zero constant. In this project, we'll first show that there are two points, P and Q, which lie on the graph of f_k for every k. Then, we'll consider the triangle whose vertices are P, Q and the point of intersection of the lines tangent to the graph of $y = f_k(x)$ at P and Q. We'll show that the graph of f_k divides this triangle into two pieces whose areas are in the same ratio for all k.

PROCEDURE:

Part 1: Intersection points
  a. Graph f_1 and f_2 on the same axes.
  b. At what two points, P and Q, do the graphs of f_1 and f_2 intersect?
  c. Show that the two points you found in 1b lie on the graph of f_k for every k.
  d. Write an equation of PQ.

Part 2: Tangent lines and a triangle
  a. Determine, in terms of k, the slopes of the lines drawn tangent to the graph of f_k at P and Q.
  b. Write equations of the tangent lines in 2a.
  c. Show that the tangent lines intersect at the point R whose coordinates are $(2, 2 - 2k)$.
  d. Write an equation of the line through R perpendicular to PQ.
  e. Show that the line in 2d intersects PQ at $S(2 - k, 2 - k)$.
  f. Determine the length of RS and use it to show that the area of triangle PQR is $2k$.

Part 3: The ratio
  The graph of f_k divides triangle PQR into two pieces--an "interior" piece bounded by the curve and PQ, and an "exterior" piece bounded by the curve PR and QR. Let A_1 and A_2 be the areas of the interior and exterior pieces, respectively.
  a. Write and evaluate an integral to find A_1.
  b. Use 3a and 2f to find A_2.
  c. Determine the ratio $A_1 : A_2$ and show that it is independent of k.

PROJECT 6.3

CENTER OF MASS

OBJECTIVE: Suppose two people sit on a see-saw. If they are of equal weight and sit equally distant from the fulcrum (pivot point), then they will balance each other and the see-saw will remain horizontal. On the other hand, if they are not of equal weight, then the heavier one will have to sit closer to the fulcrum in order for the see-saw to balance. Or, if they each sit at one end of the see-saw, then the fulcrum will have to be moved closer to the heavier person to balance the see-saw.

   In this project, we consider the more general problem: Let R be the region in the xy-plane bounded by $y = f(x)$, the x-axis and the lines $x = a$ and $x = b$. Imagine that we cut the region out of a uniformly thick piece of cardboard and would like to balance the region on the edge of a ruler. Along what vertical line (i.e. at what x-value) should we place the ruler so that the region balances?

PROCEDURE:
Part 1: Some physics and a few simple examples
   Suppose an object exerts a downward force of magnitude F at a distance R from the fulcrum of a lever. We say that the object exerts a **torque** whose magnitude is given by $T = FR$.

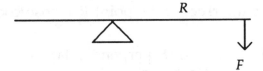

The lever will be in balance if the total torques on each side of the fulcrum are equal.
a. A 10 lb. object is placed 6 ft. to the right of the fulcrum and a 25 lb. object is placed 3 ft. to the left. Will the lever balance? If so, why? If not, which way will it tilt?
b. Jason, who weighs 60 lbs, and his sister Amanda, who weighs 40 lbs, get on a see-saw. If Amanda sits 8 ft. from the fulcrum, where should Jason sit so they balance?
c. Jason sits 6 ft. from the fulcrum and his friend Julian, who weighs 80 lbs, sits on the same side as Jason, 4 ft. from the fulcrum. Amanda sits 8 ft. from the fulcrum and her friend Ashley, who weighs 45 lbs, sits on the same side as Amanda. Where should Ashley sit to balance

the see-saw?

d. A lever is 20 ft. long. A 3 lb weight is placed on one end and a 2 lb weight is placed on the other end. Where should the fulcrum be placed so that the weights balance?

Part 2: A more general example

Suppose the lever is of length L. Introduce a coordinate system so that one end of the lever corresponds to $x = 0$ and the other corresponds to $x = L$. Place n objects of weights $m_1, m_2, \ldots m_n$ at coordinates $x_1, x_2, \ldots, x_n$, respectively. Let $\bar{x}$ be the coordinate of the fulcrum.

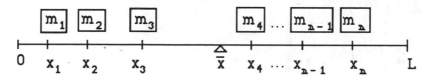

a. How much torque is exerted by object 1? by object 2? by object 4?

b. More generally, if object j is to the left of the fulcrum, how much torque does it exert? How much does it exert if it is to the right?

c. If k of the n objects are to the left of the fulcrum, argue that the total torque they exert is $\sum\limits_{j=1}^{k} m_j(\bar{x} - x_j)$ and that the total torque exerted by the remaining $n - k$ objects to the right of the fulcrum is

$$\sum_{j=k+1}^{n} m_j(x_j - \bar{x}).$$

d. The underlying physical principle says that these two quantities should be equal in order for the lever to balance; that is, $\sum\limits_{j=1}^{k} m_j(\bar{x} - x_j) = \sum\limits_{j=k+1}^{n} m_j(x_j - \bar{x})$. Rearrange terms to show that this is equivalent to $\sum\limits_{j=1}^{n} m_j x_j = \sum\limits_{j=1}^{n} m_j \bar{x}$ and, hence, the fulcrum should be placed at

$$\bar{x} = \frac{\sum\limits_{j=1}^{n} m_j x_j}{\sum\limits_{j=1}^{n} m_j} \quad \text{in order for the lever to balance.}$$

The quantity $\bar{x}$ is called the **center of mass** of the system.

e. Objects of mass 3, 5, 9, 4 and 12 are placed at coordinates 2, 4, 6, 8 and 10. Where should the fulcrum be placed to balance the lever?

Part 3: The continuous case

Now suppose we have a rod of length L. One end of the rod is at $x = a$, the other at $x = b$. The rod need not be uniform; let $\rho(x)$ be the density (in units of mass/unit length) at the point whose coordinate is x. Partition the rod into n equal segments of length Δx.

a. If Δx is small, then we can assume the density in the jth segment is approximately constant $\rho(x_j)$. What is the approximate mass of the jth segment?

b. Use 2d to argue that the fulcrum should be placed approximately at

$$\bar{x} = \frac{\displaystyle\sum_{j=1}^{n} x_j \, \rho(x_j) \, \Delta x}{\displaystyle\sum_{j=1}^{n} \rho(x_j) \, \Delta x} .$$

c. By taking the limit as $n \to \infty$, show that the fulcrum should be placed exactly at

$$\bar{x} = \frac{\displaystyle\int_a^b x \, \rho(x) \, dx}{\displaystyle\int_a^b \rho(x) \, dx} .$$

d. A baseball bat is in the shape of a tapered cylinder, 36" long. The diameter at one end is 1", the diameter at the other end is 2". Assuming the bat tapers uniformly, argue that the diameter at a point x" from the narrow end is $d = 1 + \frac{x}{36}$.

e. If the wood used to make the bat is uniform, then the density of the bat x" from the narrow end should be proportional to the cross-sectional area or, equivalently, to the square of the diameter. In other words, $\rho(x) := k\left(1 + \frac{x}{36}\right)^2$, for some constant k. Use this and the result of 3c to find the point at which the bat balances (i.e. the center of mass).

f. Let R be the region in the xy-plane bounded by $y = f(x)$, the x-axis, and the lines $x = a$ and $x = b$. If we cut the region out of a uniformly thick piece of cardboard, then the density at the point whose coordinate is x is the same as the height of the region there.

Thus, $\bar{x} = \dfrac{\displaystyle\int_a^b x \, f(x) \, dx}{\displaystyle\int_a^b f(x) \, dx}$. Use this to find the center of mass of the region bounded by $y = x^2$, the x-axis, $x = 0$ and $x = 2$.

g. Modify the result of 3f to find the center of mass of the region in the first quadrant bounded by $y = x^2$ and $y = x$.

PROJECT 6.4

NUMERICAL INTEGRATION

OBJECTIVE: In this chapter, we learned how to evaluate definite integrals by using the Fundamental Theorem of Calculus. However, using this theorem requires us to find an antiderivative, a task which may be difficult or impossible. Another possibility is that we will only be given the value of the function at a discrete set of points (such as the velocity readings at discrete times), rather than a formula for the function. Without a formula, finding an antiderivative is impossible.

If we can't invoke the Fundamental Theorem, then we must use numerical techniques to approximate the value of the integral. One possibility is to compute the value of the corresponding Riemann sum $S(n)$ for some large value of n (where n is the number of subintervals). While this will work, it may require a very large value of n to get an accurate answer. In this project, we look at two related methods--the trapezoidal rule and Simpson's rule--for evaluating definite integrals when the Fundamental Theorem can't be applied.

PROCEDURE:

Part 1: An example

A function that appears in many applications, particularly in probability and statistics is $f(x) := e^{-x^2}$. Of particular importance is finding the area under a portion of the graph of this function.

a. Draw a graph of $f(x) := e^{-x^2}$ for $-2 \le x \le 2$ and indicate a region

whose area is given by $A = \int_0^1 e^{-x^2}\,dx$.

b. Explain why it is not possible to evaluate this integral with the Fundamental Theorem of Calculus.

c. Approximate the value of A by using a Riemann sum with $n = 4$ subintervals and evaluating the heights of the rectangles at the right endpoint of each subinterval (as we do in the text). Would you expect the actual value of A to be less than or greater than the Riemann sum approximation?

d. An improved approximation may be obtained by evaluating the heights of the rectangles at the midpoint of each subinterval. Do so and compare your answer to the value obtained in 1c.

Part 2: The trapezoidal rule

Consider the region R bounded by the non-negative function f, the x-axis and the lines $x = a$ and $x = b$. Partition the interval $[a, b]$ into n equal subintervals; let $x_j = a + j \Delta x$, where $\Delta x = \dfrac{b-a}{n}$, be the jth partition point, $j = 0, 1, 2, ..., n$. Construct trapezoids by drawing line segments between the points $(x_j, f(x_j))$ and $(x_{j+1}, f(x_{j+1}))$, $j = 0, 1, 2, ..., n - 1$. (The trapezoids are "standing on end".)

a. Argue that the area of the first trapezoid is $A_1 = \dfrac{f(x_0) + f(x_1)}{2} \Delta x$ and, more generally, the area of the jth trapezoid is $A_j = \dfrac{f(x_{j-1}) + f(x_j)}{2} \Delta x$.

b. Show that the total area of the n trapezoids is given by
$$T(n) := \frac{f(x_0) + 2f(x_1) + 2f(x_2) + ... + 2f(x_{j-1}) + f(x_j)}{2} \Delta x .$$
Note that the first and last terms in the numerator do not have coefficient 2. This formula is known as the **Trapezoidal Rule**.

c. Use the trapezoidal rule with $n = 4$ to approximate the area of the region in Part 1a. How does your answer compare to the approximations obtained in 1c and 1d?

d. Use the trapezoidal rule with $n = 6$ to approximate $\displaystyle\int_0^3 \sqrt{x^3 + 1}\; dx$.

Part 3: Simpson's Rule

One potential source of error incurred by using either rectangles or trapezoids to approximate a definite integral comes from the fact that we are, in essence, replacing the function by straight line segments (horizontal in one case, diagonal in the other). We might be able to get more accurate approximations by replacing the function by a curve. Simpson's Rule uses parabolic arcs to approximate the function.

a. Redraw the picture from Part 2 without the trapezoids. Let P_i be the point on the graph with coordinates $(x_i, f(x_i))$.

It is a fact that there is a unique parabola that can be drawn through any three non-collinear points. Let $p(x)$ be the parabola passing through $P_{i-1}, P_i,$ and P_{i+1} as shown. It turns out that the area bounded by $y = p(x)$ over the interval $[x_{i-1}, x_{i+1}]$ is given by
$$A_i = \int_{x_{i-1}}^{x_{i+1}} p(x)\, dx = \frac{\Delta x}{3} \left[f(x_{i-1}) + 4f(x_i) + f(x_{i+1}) \right].$$

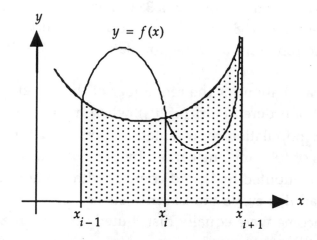

b. Since each parabola covers two subintervals, we need to have an even number of subintervals in order to have an integral (no pun intended) number of parabolas. Show that the total area of the $n/2$ parabolic regions is given by

$$B(n) \; := \; \frac{\Delta x}{3} \left[f(x_0) + 4f(x_1) + 2f(x_2) + 4f(x_3) + 2f(x_4) + \ldots \right.$$
$$\left. + 2f(x_{n-2}) + 4f(x_{n-1}) + f(x_n) \right].$$

Note that each "even" term except the 0th and n^{th} has a coefficient of 2, while each "odd" term has a coefficient of 4. This formula is known as **Simpson's Rule**.

c. Use Simpson's Rule to approximate the value of the integrals in 1a (with $n = 4$) and 2d (with $n = 6$). How do your answers compare with the trapezoidal rule?

Part 4: An application

A question of interest in economics concerns the distribution of income throughout a given society. In a perfectly equitable distribution in which everyone earns the same amount of money, $p\%$ of the total income will be earned by $p\%$ of the population. In reality, there will be a small percentage of rich people who earn a relatively high percentage of the total income.

Imagine a society with 10 people whose incomes are given in the table below. Note that we've listed them in increasing numerical order.

Person	1	2	3	4	5	6	7	8	9	10
Income (thousands)	12	15	21	24	30	40	45	47	50	100

The total income for the entire society is 384. Person 1, who represents .1 of the population, earns 12/384 = .031 = 3.1% of the income. Persons 1 and 2 together, who represent .2 of the population, earn 27/384 = .07 = 7% of the income.

a. Complete this calculation for the remainder of the society; that is, compute a set of ordered pairs (x_n, y_n), where x_n = cumulative fraction of the population represented by persons 1 through n, and y_n = fraction of total income earned by persons 1 through n.

b. Plot the points computed in 4a and connect with a smooth curve. Economists call this curve the **Lorentz curve**.

c. Argue that if income were equally distributed, the Lorentz curve would be the straight line $y = x$.

d. Show that since by listing the incomes in increasing order, then $L(x) \le x$ for all x.

e. One way to measure the income distribution is by the **Gini coefficient**
$$g = \frac{\text{Area between the Lorentz curve and the line } y = x}{\text{Area between the line } y = x \text{ and the } x\text{-axis}}$$ over the interval [0, 1].

   Show that if $L(x)$ is the Lorentz curve, then $g = 2 \int_0^1 (x - L(x))\, dx$.

e. The case $g = 0$ corresponds to equal distribution of income. Describe a scenario in which g is close to 1. (Certainly, g cannot exceed 1.)

f. Since it is highly unlikely that we will have a formula for $L(x)$, g will have to be approximated numerically. Use the given data and Simpson's rule to approximate g for this society.

CHAPTER 7

TRIGONOMETRIC FUNCTIONS

7.1 UP AND DOWN, BACK AND FORTH

There are many examples in the real world of phenomena which behave in a **periodic** fashion; that is, the behavior pattern repeats itself after a fixed amount of time. For example, suppose we examined the average daily high temperature in a given city. Typically, the warmest time of year (in the northern hemisphere) occurs in late July or early August. After that, the temperature cools down (slowly at first, then a bit more rapidly) until February when a warming trend begins. This pattern repeats itself on a yearly cycle. (Note that we are talking about *average temperatures*; the actual temperatures may deviate considerably.) If we were to plot the average temperature versus time of year, we might get something like the graph in Figure 7.1.

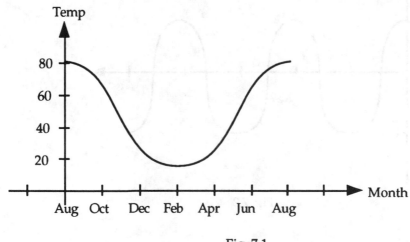

Fig. 7.1

Another example of periodic behavior is a pendulum. A bob of mass m pivots on an arm of length L. Let θ be the angle between the arm of the pendulum and the vertical, as shown in Figure 7.2.

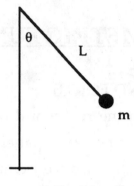

Fig. 7.2

Suppose at time $t = 0$, we move the pendulum bob so that $\theta = \theta_0$. Then, in the absence of friction, θ oscillates between θ_0 and $-\theta_0$. This is illustrated in Figure 7.3. The time required for the pendulum to return to its initial position is called its **period**.

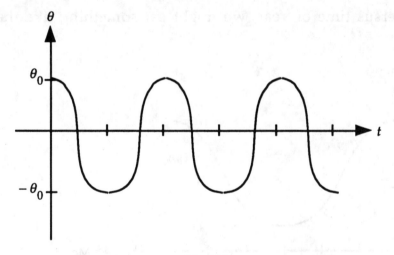

Fig. 7.3

¤ The periodic phenomenon we would like to analyze in some detail is the **spring-mass system**. An object of mass m lies on a table. It is attached to a vertical wall by a spring. The spring is stretched out a bit and the object is released. Assuming that the table is frictionless and that there is no air resistance, then the object should oscillate back and forth, alternately stretching and compressing the spring.

Let's introduce a coordinate system. Let $y(t)$ = position of the object at time t. The rest position (in which the spring is neither stretched nor compressed) corresponds to $y = 0$. Positive values of y are to the right (spring stretched), negative values to the left (spring compressed). See Figure 7.4.

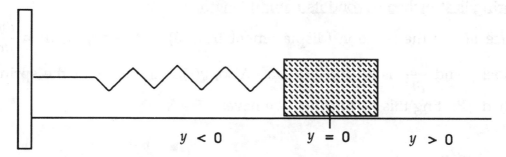

Fig. 7.4.

A graph of the position of the object as a function of time is given in Figure 7.5.

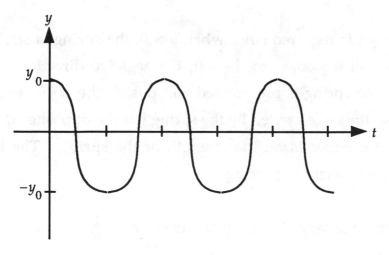

Fig. 7.5.

In order to analyze this system, we need to review a bit of physics. The first fact we need is Newton's Second Law of Motion (which we've seen before in Chapter 6), which says:

<u>The sum of the forces acting on an object is equal to the product of the mass of the object and its acceleration</u>; in short, $F = ma$.

Since the object is resting on a table and we are ignoring friction and air resistance, then the only force acting on the object comes from the spring. Hooke's Law (which we also saw in Chapter 6 when we studied work) says:

The force exerted by a spring is proportional to the amount by which the spring is stretched beyond its natural length.

Since $y(t)$ is the position (displacement from 0) of the object, then $\dfrac{dy}{dt}$ is its velocity and $\dfrac{d^2y}{dt^2}$ is its acceleration. Also, $y(t)$ is the amount the spring is stretched. Putting this all together, we have:

(1) $m\,\dfrac{d^2y}{dt^2} = -ky(t)$

where k is a positive constant.

Notes:

1. The minus sign is required since when $y > 0$, the spring is stretched and will tend to pull the object to the left, the negative direction. Similarly, when $y < 0$, the spring is compressed and pushes the object to the right. In either case, the force exerted by the spring has the opposite sign of y.

2. The constant k depends on the strength of the spring. The larger the value of k, the stronger the spring.

Let's divide both sides of Eq.(1) by m and set $b = \dfrac{k}{m}$. Then the equation can be written as:

(2) $\dfrac{d^2y}{dt^2} + by = 0,$

where b is a positive constant.

This is a second-order differential equation for which we as yet have no method of solving. (The only technique we know for solving differential equations is separation of variables, which does not generally work on second-order equations.) Consider the special case when $b = 1$; that is, the equation

$$\frac{d^2y}{dt^2} + y = 0 \quad \text{or, equivalently,}$$

$$\frac{d^2y}{dt^2} = -y.$$

This calls for a function whose second derivative is the negative of the function. Convince yourself that none of the functions we have studied so far has this property.

Since $\frac{d^2y}{dt^2}$ and y have opposite signs, then the graph of y will be concave up whenever $y < 0$, and concave down whenever $y > 0$.

PROBLEMS FOR SECTION 7.1:

1. What factors do you think influence the period of the pendulum?

2. Sketch a graph similar to Figure 7.5 for the case in which the table is not frictionless or air resistance is accounted for .

3. Consider the equation $\frac{d^2y}{dt^2} - y = 0$. Do you know any functions that satisfy this equation? Can you find more than one? How about $\frac{d^2y}{dt^2} - by = 0$ where $b > 0$?

7.2   SECOND-ORDER DIFFERENTIAL EQUATIONS

In this section, we will solve the equation $\frac{d^2y}{dt^2} + by = 0$, where b is a positive constant. This is a special case of the more general equation $\frac{d^2y}{dt^2} + a\frac{dy}{dt} + by = 0$ which we will consider in Section 7.5.

We will need to develop some of the theory of second-order differential equations. To help motivate these results, let's review what we know about first-order equations. Consider the equation

(3) $\dfrac{dy}{dt} + ay = 0$

that we studied in Chapter 5. We can separate the variables, obtaining:

$\dfrac{1}{y}\,dy \ = -a\,dt$

Integrating both sides gives:

$\ln(y) \ = -at + c$

where c is an arbitrary constant. Solving for y , we get:

$y \ = e^{-at+c} \ = e^{-at}e^{c} \ = Ce^{-at}$

for some C. We could determine C if we were given additional information such as the value of y for some specific value of t.

So, although the first-order equation $\dfrac{dy}{dt} + ay \ = \ 0$ has infinitely many solutions (one for each value of C), we can think of it as having just one "basic" or "fundamental" solution $y(t) \ = \ e^{-at}$ with all other solutions being constant multiples of that one basic solution.

Furthermore, if we specify that the solution must satisfy the condition $y(t_0) \ = \ u_0$, then the equation $\dfrac{dy}{dt} + ay \ = \ 0$, has a *unique* solution of the form $y(t) \ = \ Ce^{-at}$. In Chapter 5, we called $y(t) \ = \ Ce^{-at}$ the **general solution** of the differential equation; the solution satisfying a given condition is called the **specific** or **particular solution**.

□ Before considering what happens for second-order equations, we need the following:

DEFINITION: Two functions $y_1(t)$ and $y_2(t)$ are said to be **independent** if neither is a constant multiple of the other, for all t.

For example, the functions $y_1(t) := t^2$ and $y_2(t) := 2t + 3$ are independent. To see why, consider the equation $y_1(t) = ky_2(t)$--that is, $t^2 = k(2t + 3)$. There is no constant k which makes this equation true simultaneously for all t. (Suppose $t = 1$. Then k would have to be 1/5.

But if $t = 2$, then k would be 4/7. The same k must work for every t.) Similarly, there is no k such that $kt^2 = 2t + 3$, for all t. On the other hand, $y_1(t) := e^{2t}$ and $y_2(t) := 4e^{2t}$ are not independent since $y_2(t) = 4y_1(t)$, or $y_1(t) = \frac{1}{4}y_2(t)$, for all t.

TEST YOUR UNDERSTANDING

1. Show that the functions $y_1(t) := e^{2t}$ and $y_2(t) := e^{3t}$ are independent.

2. Are $y_1(t) := e^t$ and $y_2(t) := te^t$ independent? Explain.

◻ Now for the results about second-order equations:

1. Every equation of the form $\dfrac{d^2y}{dt^2} + a\dfrac{dy}{dt} + by = 0$ has two independent solutions $y_1(t)$ and $y_2(t)$.

2. If $y_1(t)$ and $y_2(t)$ are independent solutions of the equation, then the general solution (i.e. every solution) of the equation is of the form $y(t) := c_1y_1(t) + c_2y_2(t)$, where c_1 and c_2 are constants.

The interesting question is, what kind of information (initial conditions) do we need to uniquely determine the constants c_1 and c_2? Simply specifying the value of y at some value of t (e.g. $y(t_0) = u_0$ as we did for first-order equations) is insufficient since, upon substituting that value of t, we would get one equation in c_1 and c_2 which could not possibly have a unique solution.

What other information is available to us? In practice, not only do we know the position but we might also know the velocity at some time t_0. For example, in Chapter 3, we derived an equation for the position $s(t)$ of a falling object. This is equivalent to solving the second-order equation $s''(t) = -g$. In order to get a unique answer, we had to specify the initial position $s_0 = s(0)$ and the initial velocity $v_0 = s'(0)$.

It turns out that specifying the values of y and $\dfrac{dy}{dt}$ *at the same value of t* always leads to a unique solution for c_1 and c_2.

We summarize this result in the following:

THEOREM 7.1: Every second-order differential equation of the form $\dfrac{d^2y}{dt^2} + a\dfrac{dy}{dt} + by = 0$ with initial conditions $y(t_0) = u_0$ and $y'(t_0) = u_1$, where t_0, u_0 and u_1 are given real numbers has a unique solution. Moreover, if y_1 and y_2 are any pair of independent solutions, then the general solution of the differential equation is $y(t) := c_1y_1(t) + c_2y_2(t)$, where the values of c_1 and c_2 (i.e. the specific solution) are uniquely determined from the initial conditions.

For example, it is easy to see that both $y_1(t) := e^t$ and $y_2(t) := e^{-t}$ satisfy the second-order differential equation $\dfrac{d^2y}{dt^2} - y = 0$ and that they are independent. Thus, the general solution is $y(t) := c_1e^t + c_2e^{-t}$.

Suppose we were given the initial condition $y(0) = 3$. Upon substituting $t = 0$, we get $c_1 + c_2 = 3$, an equation with infinitely many solutions. We have chosen 5 of these solutions (see table below) and graphed the corresponding function $y(t)$ in Figure 7.6.

Graph	$\underline{1}$	$\underline{2}$	$\underline{3}$	$\underline{4}$	$\underline{5}$
c_1	1	4	2	−1	3
c_2	2	−1	1	4	0

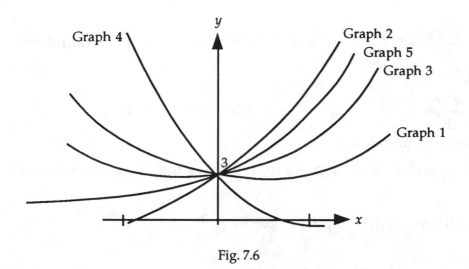

Fig. 7.6

Note that all the graphs pass through the point $(0, 3)$ (why?) but with different slopes. Since $y'(t) := c_1 e^t - c_2 e^{-t}$, then $y'(0) = c_1 - c_2$. Computing this quantity for each of the 5 cases, we see that graph 2 has the largest positive slope, 5, while graph 4 has the most negative slope, –5. Theorem 7.1 guarantees that there is only one curve that passes through $(0, 3)$ with a given slope. Hence, c_1 and c_2 can be uniquely determined by specifying a point through which the curve must pass and the slope with which it passes through that point.

For example, suppose we wanted $y(0) = 3$ and $y'(0) = -1$. Since $y(0) = c_1 + c_2$, then $c_1 + c_2 = 3$. Also, $y'(t) := c_1 e^t - c_2 e^{-t}$. Thus, $y'(0) = c_1 - c_2 = -1$. These two conditions imply $c_1 = 1$ and $c_2 = 2$, the solution depicted in Graph 1.

EXAMPLE 7.1:

Show that $y_1(t) = e^{2t}$ and $y_2(t) = e^{3t}$ both satisfy the equation $\dfrac{d^2 y}{dt^2} - 5\dfrac{dy}{dt} + 6y = 0$. What is the general solution of the equation? Determine the specific solution satisfying $y(0) = 3, y'(0) = 7$.

$$\frac{dy_1}{dt} = 2e^{2t}, \quad \frac{dy_2}{dt} = 3e^{3t}, \quad \frac{d^2 y_1}{dt^2} = 4e^{2t}, \frac{d^2 y_2}{dt^2} = 9e^{3t}.$$

Thus,

$$\frac{d^2y_1}{dt^2} - 5\frac{dy_1}{dt} + 6y_1 = 4e^{2t} - 10e^{2t} + 6e^{2t} = 0 \quad \text{for all } t \text{ and}$$

$$\frac{d^2y_2}{dt^2} - 5\frac{dy_2}{dt} + 6y_2 = 9e^{3t} - 15e^{3t} + 6e^{3t} = 0 \quad \text{for all } t.$$

Hence, both y_1 and y_2 are solutions.

Since y_1 and y_2 are independent, it follows that the general solution is:

$$y(t) := c_1y_1(t) + c_2y_2(t) = c_1e^{2t} + c_2e^{3t}.$$

We use the given initial conditions to find c_1 and c_2. First, we have:

$$y(0) = c_1 + c_2 = 3$$

Since $y'(t) := 2c_1e^{2t} + 3c_2e^{3t}$, we have:

$$y'(0) = 2c_1 + 3c_2 = 7.$$

Solving these two equations simultaneously gives $c_1 = 2$ and $c_2 = 1$. Hence, the (unique) specific solution is $y(t) := 2e^{2t} + e^{3t}$. ◆

- -

TEST YOUR UNDERSTANDING

3. For what value of b is $y = e^{4t}$ a solution of the second-order equation

$$\frac{d^2y}{dt^2} - 6\frac{dy}{dt} + by = 0?$$

4. The general solution of a differential equation is $y = c_1e^{4t} + c_2e^{-t}$. Find the specific solution satisfying:

   (a) $y(0) = 2, y'(0) = 13$ (b) $y(0) = 3, y'(0) = 12$

- -

SOLUTION OF THE SPRING–MASS SYSTEM

Theorem 7.1 is a classic example of what is called an "existence and uniqueness theorem". It tells us that a certain problem has a solution and, if we can find a solution, we are guaranteed that it is unique. What it doesn't tell us is how to find the solution. We'll deal with the general case $\frac{d^2y}{dt^2} + a\frac{dy}{dt} + by = 0$ later. Now let's just consider the special case motivated by our interest in the spring-mass system; i.e., the equation

$$(4) \qquad \frac{d^2y}{dt^2} + y = 0.$$

Theorem 7.1 guarantees that Eq.(4) has a unique solution for each set of initial conditions. Let's define the following two of these solutions, corresponding to different initial conditions:

1. $C(t)$ is the unique solution of Eq.(4) satisfying the initial conditions $C(0) = 1, C'(0) = 0$.

2. $S(t)$ is the unique solution of Eq.(4) satisfying the initial conditions $S(0) = 0, S'(0) = 1$.

In other words, C passes through the point $(0, 1)$ with a slope of 0, while S passes through $(0, 0)$ with a slope of 1.

We can establish several facts about the functions C and S just by using Eq.(4).

PROPERTY 1: The general solution of Eq.(4) is $y(t) := c_1C(t) + c_2S(t)$.

Proof: This will be true if S and C are independent. Suppose to the contrary that S and C are dependent; i.e. there is a constant k such that $C(t) = kS(t)$, for all t. In particular, for $t = 0$, we would have $C(0) =$

$kS(0)$. But $S(0) = 0$ and $C(0) = 1$. Since there is no k such that $1 = k(0) = 0$, then $C(t) \neq kS(t)$ for all t. Similarly, if $S(t) = kC(t)$, then $0 = k(1) = k$. This implies $S(t) = 0$ for all t. In that case, $S'(0)$ is 0, not 1. Thus, $S(t) \neq kC(t)$ either. Hence, S and C are independent.

Theorem 7.1 now guarantees that all solutions of Eq.(4) can be expressed as

$$(5) \qquad y(t) = c_1 C(t) + c_2 S(t).$$

PROPERTY 2: $S'(t) = C(t)$ and $C'(t) = -S(t)$ for all t.

Proof: Since $S'' + S = 0$, then by differentiating with respect to t, we have $S''' + S' = 0$.

Let $z(t) := S'(t)$. Then $z''(t) := S'''(t)$ and, hence, $z'' + z = 0$. This implies that S' is a solution of the Eq.(4).

Furthermore, by the definition of $S, z(0) = S'(0) = 1$. Also, $z'(0) = S''(0) = -S(0) = 0$. Therefore, z is a solution of Eq.(4) satisfying $z(0) = 1$, $z'(0) = 0$. But by definition, C is the solution of Eq.(4) satisfying $C(0) = 1$ and $C'(0) = 0$. Since Theorem 7.1 tells us there can't be two, it must be that $z = C$; i.e., $S'(t) = C(t)$, for all t.

The proof that $C'(t) = -S(t)$ is similar. (See Problem 7.)

PROPERTY 3: $S^2(t) + C^2(t) = 1$, for all t.

Proof: Let $f(t) := S^2(t) + C^2(t)$. Then,

$$(6) \qquad f'(t) = 2S(t)S'(t) + 2C(t)C'(t) = 2S(t)C(t) + 2C(t)(-S(t))$$
$$= 0$$

by Property 2. Thus, f is a function whose derivative is identically 0. It follows that f must be a constant function; that is,

(7) $S^2(t) + C^2(t) = K,$

for some constant K. Substituting $t = 0$ in Eq. (7) shows that $K = S^2(0) + C^2(0) = 0 + 1 = 1.$

This result implies that $|S(t)| \leq 1$ and $|C(t)| \leq 1$, for all t; that is:

$$-1 \leq S(t) \leq 1 \text{ and } -1 \leq C(t) \leq 1.$$

Assuming that S and C are continuous functions, we can now construct graphs of C and S. For instance, since $C(0) = 1$ and $C(t)$ cannot exceed 1, then C must decrease for $t > 0$ (at least for a while). It is also concave down, since $C'' = -C < 0$. Therefore, there is some $t_1 > 0$ such that $C(t_1) = 0$. Once C becomes negative, it changes to concave up.

Since $C(t) > 0$ on the interval $[0, t_1]$ and $S'(t) = C(t)$, then S must be increasing on that interval. Furthermore, since $S(0) = 0$, then $S(t) > 0$, and hence, concave down, on $[0, t_1]$. However, $S(t)$ cannot exceed 1. S has a horizontal tangent at t_1 since $S'(t_1) = C(t_1) = 0$. After this point, S must decrease (which agrees with the fact that C has become negative). Hence, there is some t_2 such that $S(t_2) = 0$ and after which S becomes negative. Once S becomes negative, C starts to increase since $C'(t) = -S(t) > 0$.

Although we've "waved our hands" a bit here, we could formalize this argument which shows, indeed, that S and C are periodic functions which oscillate between –1 and 1.

¤ At this point, you may be reminded of something you learned about in your trigonometry class. There, you learned about the functions $\sin(t)$ and $\cos(t)$. They are periodic and take on values between –1 and 1. Also, one of the fundamental identities relating these two function is that $\sin^2(t) + \cos^2(t) = 1$, for all t. Furthermore, $\cos(0) = 1$ and $\sin(0) = 0$. Perhaps, $C(t) := \cos(t)$ and $S(t) := \sin(t)$. (Talk about suggestive notation!!)

Admittedly, we haven't proved that S and C must be the sine and cosine--there may be other functions with these same properties--but at least we have some evidence. There are many other properties of S and C that we can prove, just based on Eq.(4), that are identical to properties of the sine and cosine functions. (See, for example, Problem 8.) We shall not do so here; rather, we will accept the fact that indeed, S and C are the well-known sine and cosine. We are therefore claiming:

> The general solution to the second-order differential equation
> $$\frac{d^2y}{dt^2} + y = 0$$
> is $y(t) := c_1 \cos(t) + c_2 \sin(t)$,   where c_1 and c_2 are constants.

◻ Recall that this differential equation arose as a special case of the spring-mass system $\frac{d^2y}{dt^2} + by = 0$, with $b = 1$, where $b = k/m$. There are initial conditions inherent in the problem which will allow us to solve for c_1 and c_2. Let's assume the object is moved y_0 units to the right at time $t = 0$ and released. Then $y(0) = y_0$ and $y'(0) = 0$ (initial velocity of 0).

Since $\cos(0) = 1$ and $\sin(0) = 0$, then $y(0) = c_1 \cdot 1 + c_2 \cdot 0 = c_1$. Thus $c_1 = y_0$. Moreover, since $\frac{d}{dt}(\cos(t)) = -\sin(t)$ and $\frac{d}{dt}(\sin(t)) = \cos(t)$, then
$$y'(t) := -c_1 \sin(t) + c_2 \cos(t).$$
Hence, $y'(0) = c_1 \cdot 0 + c_2 \cdot 1 = c_2$ and so $c_2 = 0$.

Thus, the specific solution of the spring-mass problem for the case $b = 1$ is

(8) $y(t) := y_0 \cos(t)$.

TEST YOUR UNDERSTANDING

5. (a) Solve the differential equation $\frac{d^2y}{dt^2} + y = 0$ subject to the initial conditions
   $y(0) = 0, y'(0) = v_0$.

    (b) How would you interpret the initial conditions in (a) in terms of the spring-mass system?

In the more general case (where b need not equal 1), we claim that the solutions of the equation $\dfrac{d^2 y}{dt^2} + by = 0$ can be expressed as

(9) $\quad y(t) := c_1 \cos(\sqrt{b}\ t) + c_2 \sin(\sqrt{b}\ t)$.

To see why, note that, by the chain rule,

$$\frac{dy}{dt} = -\sqrt{b}\ c_1 \sin(\sqrt{b}\ t) + \sqrt{b}\ c_2 \cos(\sqrt{b}\ t) \text{ and}$$

$$\frac{d^2 y}{dt^2} = -b\, c_1 \cos(\sqrt{b}\ t) - b\, c_2 \sin(\sqrt{b}\ t) = -by(t).$$

So, $\dfrac{d^2 y}{dt^2} + by = 0$.

TEST YOUR UNDERSTANDING

    6. Write the general solution of the differential equation $y'' + 16y = 0$.

The initial conditions $y(0) = y_0$ and $y'(0) = 0$ and their implications about c_1 and c_2 remain the same. (Convince yourself of this.) Thus, the specific solution to the spring-mass system with the original initial conditions is:

(10) $\quad\quad y(t) := y_0 \cos(\sqrt{b}\ t)$.

Note: It is common to let $\omega^2 = b$ (ω is the Greek letter "omega"). Then the differential equation is $\dfrac{d^2y}{dt^2} + \omega^2 y = 0$. The general solution is $y(t) := c_1 \cos(\omega t) + c_2 \sin(\omega t)$ and the specific solution satisfying the initial conditions is $y(t) := y_0 \cos(\omega t)$.

An interesting question is: What effect does changing ω have on the solution?   Let's see how long it takes for the object to return to its inital position y_0. The first time this happens is when $\cos(\omega t) = 1$, implying $\omega t = 2\pi$ or $t = \dfrac{2\pi}{\omega}$. So, as ω increases, the time required to complete one oscillation (which is called the **period** of the oscillation) decreases, meaning that the object oscillates more rapidly.   Since $\omega^2 = k/m$, then ω increases if k increases or if m decreases.   Therefore, strengthening the spring or using a less massive object causes the oscillations to occur more rapidly.   This is a very intuitive result.   Figure 7.7 shows the graph of the solution for the cases $\omega = 1$ and $\omega = 2$.

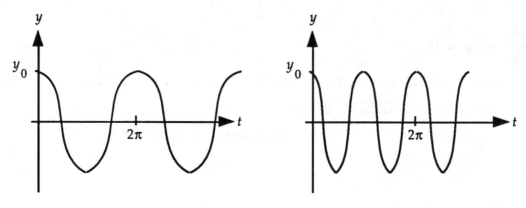

Fig. 7.7

EXERCISES FOR SECTION 7.2:

1. Write the general solution of the differential equation $\dfrac{d^2y}{dt^2} + 4y = 0$.

2. Find the specific solution to the equation in Exercise 1 satisfying the initial conditions $y(0) = 0$ and $y'(0) = 2$.

3. Determine the value of dy/dt at $t = 0$ for each of the following:

   (a) $y = S(2t)$ (b) $y = S(t^2)$ (c) $y = tC(t)$

   (d) $y = S(t) + C(t)$ (e) $y = S^2(t) + C^2(t)$ (f) $y = \dfrac{S(t)}{C(t)}$

4. Write an equation of the line tangent to the graph of $y = S(t)$ at $t = 0$.

5. A 5 kg book is attached to the wall by a spring. A force of 10 Newtons (1 Newton $= 1$ kg-m/sec.^{2}) moves the book 1 meter to the right at which time it is released. Write the differential equation governing the motion of the book and solve it. (Hint: What is $ky(0)$?)

6. If the spring constant k of a spring is doubled, what happens to the period of the oscillations?

7. Objects of mass 20g and 80g are attached to springs of equal strength. Which will oscillate faster? By how much?

8. Show that the coefficients in the general solution in Eq.(9) are given by $c_1 = y(0)$ and $c_2 = y'(0)$.

9. The general solution of the differential equation $\dfrac{dy}{dt} + ay = 0$ is $y(t) := Ce^{-at}$. Show that the initial condition $y(t_0) = u_0$ implies $C = u_0 e^{at_0}$ and, hence, $y(t) := u_0 e^{-a(t - t_0)}$.

10. Two solutions of $\dfrac{d^2y}{dt^2} + a\dfrac{dy}{dt} + by = 0$ are $y = e^{3t}$ and $y = e^{-t}$. Determine a and b.

PROBLEMS FOR SECTION 7.2:

1. Show that $y_1(t) = e^{at}$ and $y_2(t) = e^{bt}$ are independent if $a \neq b$.

2. Let $y_1(t)$ and $y_2(t)$ be solutions of the differential equation $y'' + ay' + by = 0$. Show that any function of the form $y(t) = c_1y_1(t) + c_2y_2(t)$ is also a solution.

3. Consider the equation $x^2\dfrac{d^2y}{dx^2} - 2x\dfrac{dy}{dx} + 2y = 0$.

   (a) Show that $y_1 = x$ and $y_2 = x^2$ are solutions to this equation.

   (b) Assuming the conclusion of Theorem 7.1 applies to this equation, find the general solution and the specific solution satisfying $y(1) = 0$ and $y'(1) = 3$.

4. Determine a and b (in terms of r and s) such that $y = c_1 e^{rx} + c_2 e^{sx}$ is the general solution of $\dfrac{d^2 y}{dx^2} + a\dfrac{dy}{dx} + by = 0$.

5. An object of mass m is attached to a spring suspended from the ceiling. Now an additional force, gravity, acts on the object. The corresponding differential equation is $\dfrac{d^2 y}{dt^2} + \omega^2 y = -g$, where g is the acceleration due to gravity.

   (Note $y(t)$ still represents the amount the spring is stretched beyond its natural length. Our coordinate system is chosen so that $y = 0$ is the point where the object would be when the spring is not stretched at all, as if being supported from below, and the positive direction is up; that is, $y > 0$ when the spring is compressed.)

   (a) Show that $y(t) := c_1 \cos(\omega t) + c_2 \sin(\omega t) - g/\omega^2$ satisfies this equation.

   (b) Assuming the object is moved to initial position y_0 and released, find c_1 and c_2 and sketch the solution.

6. Consider the equation $y'' - y = 0$ that we solved earlier. We showed that $y_1(t) := e^t$ and $y_2(t) := e^{-t}$ were solutions. In some cases, it is more convenient to express the solutions in a different form. Let $f(t) := \dfrac{e^t - e^{-t}}{2}$ and $g(t) := \dfrac{e^t + e^{-t}}{2}$. (These functions are called the **hyperbolic sine** and **cosine**, respectively, denoted sinh(t) and cosh(t).)

   (a) Show that $f'(t) = g(t)$ and $g'(t) = f(t)$. What can you say about higher order derivatives of f and g?

   (b) Show that f and g satisfy the differential equation $y'' - y = 0$.

   (c) Determine constants c_1 and c_2 such that the solution $y(t) := c_1 \sinh(t) + c_2 \cosh(t)$ satisfies the initial conditions $y(0) = u_0$ and $y'(0) = u_1$.

   (d) Express the solutions of $y'' - \omega^2 y = 0$ in terms of sinh(t) and cosh(t).

7. Adapt the proof of Property 2 to show that $C'(t) = -S(t)$.

8. Let $u(t) = S(t + a)$ and $v(t) = C(t + a)$, where a is a constant.

   (a) Use the chain rule to show that $\dfrac{d^2u}{dt^2} = -u(t)$ and $\dfrac{d^2v}{dt^2} = -v(t)$. Hence u and v satisfy the differential equation $y'' + y = 0$.

   (b) By Property 1, $u(t) := a_1 S(t) + a_2 C(t)$ and $v(t) := b_1 S(t) + b_2 C(t)$ for some constants a_1, a_2, b_1, and b_2. Substitute $t = 0$ to determine these constants and write expressions for $S(t + a)$ and $C(t + a)$. Do you recognize the results?

   (c) Use (b) to show that $S(2t) = 2S(t)C(t)$ and $C(2t) = [C(t)]^2 - [S(t)]^2$.

<u>TYU Answers for Section 7.2</u>

1. Suppose $e^{2t} = ke^{3t}$. Since e^{3t} is never 0, this implies $e^{-t} = k$, which is not true. Similarly, $e^{3t} \neq ke^{2t}$. 2. Yes, they are independent. Use similar argument as in TYU 1. 3. $b = 8$. 4. (a) $y = 3e^{4t} - e^{-t}$ (b) $y = 3e^{4t}$.

5. (a) $y = v_0 \sin(t)$ (b) Object pushed from initial position $y = 0$ (spring unstretched) with initial velocity v_0. 6. $y = c_1\cos(4t) + c_2\sin(4t)$

7.3 MORE ON TRIGONOMETRIC FUNCTIONS

In the last section, we introduced two "new" functions, each of which is the solution to a certain second-order differential equation. (This is similar to what we did in Chapter 4--the exponential function was introduced as a solution to a certain first-order differential equation.) In this section, we will investigate some more properties of these functions.

Let $f(x) := \sin(x)$ and $g(x) := \cos(x)$. Note that x is either a real number or an angle measured in **radians**; it is *not* an angle measured in degrees. (If you are not sure what this means, see the Appendix for a review of basic trigonometry.) Furthermore, f and g are defined for all real x.

Property 3 of the last section says that $-1 \leq \sin(x) \leq 1$ and $-1 \leq \cos(x) \leq 1$ for all x. This means that the range of f and g is $\{y \mid -1 \leq y \leq 1\}$.

Values of sin(*x*) and cos(*x*) for some commonly used *x*-values are given in the chart below. Other values can be obtained either by calculator or, in some cases, by using reference angles. (Again, see the Appendix if this idea is not familiar to you.)

x	0	$\pi/6$	$\pi/4$	$\pi/3$	$\pi/2$	π	$3\pi/2$
sin(x)	0	$\frac{1}{2}$	$\frac{\sqrt{2}}{2}$	$\frac{\sqrt{3}}{2}$	1	0	−1
cos(x)	1	$\frac{\sqrt{3}}{2}$	$\frac{\sqrt{2}}{2}$	$\frac{1}{2}$	0	−1	0

Both the sine and cosine are periodic functions; that is, their values repeat after a while. Furthermore, it can be shown that the period--i.e, the length of one cycle--is 2π. Thus, sin($x + 2\pi$) = sin(x) and cos($x + 2\pi$) = cos(x) for all *x* (and 2π is the smallest number with this property).

Based on this information, we are able to draw the graphs of y = sin(x) and y = cos(x). See Figure 7.8.

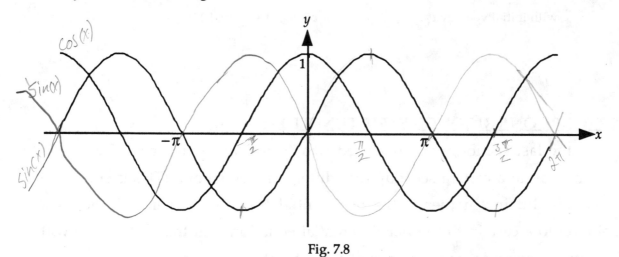

Fig. 7.8

DERIVATIVES OF SINE AND COSINE

We proved in property 2 of the last section that $S'(t)$ = $C(t)$ and $C'(t)$ = $-S(t)$. Let's state this formally as:

__THEOREM 7.2__: (a) $\frac{d}{dx}[\sin(x)]$ = cos(x);   (b) $\frac{d}{dx}[\cos(x)]$ = $-\sin(x)$

This is a rather remarkable fact: The derivative of the sine function is simply the cosine and the derivative of the cosine is the negative of the sine. Although we initially proved this directly from the differential equation $\frac{d^2y}{dx^2} + y = 0$, we can also prove it using the definition of the derivative that we studied in Chapter 3.

Before doing so, we need a couple of facts about sine and cosine which we state from trigonometry:

(11) $\quad \sin(x + y) = \sin(x)\cos(y) + \cos(x)\sin(y)$

(12) $\quad \cos(x + y) = \cos(x)\cos(y) - \sin(x)\sin(y)$

Now let's find the derivative of $f(x) := \sin(x)$.

$$\Delta f = f(x + \Delta x) - f(x) = \sin(x + \Delta x) - \sin(x)$$
$$= \sin(x)\cos(\Delta x) + \cos(x)\sin(\Delta x) - \sin(x) \quad \text{by Eq.(11)}$$
$$= \sin(x)[\cos(\Delta x) - 1] + \cos(x)\sin(\Delta x)$$

Therefore,

$$f'(x) := \lim_{\Delta x \to 0} \frac{\Delta f}{\Delta x} = \lim_{\Delta x \to 0} \frac{\sin(x)[\cos(\Delta x) - 1] + \cos(x)\sin(\Delta x)}{\Delta x}$$

$$= \sin(x)\lim_{\Delta x \to 0}\frac{[\cos(\Delta x) - 1]}{\Delta x} + \cos(x)\lim_{\Delta x \to 0}\frac{\sin(\Delta x)}{\Delta x}$$

if these limits exist.

Note that both of the limits are indeterminate expressions of the form $\frac{0}{0}$. In order to evaluate the two limits, let's make a table of values. As we can see, it appears that $\lim_{\Delta x \to 0}\frac{[\cos(\Delta x) - 1]}{\Delta x} = 0$ and $\lim_{\Delta x \to 0}\frac{\sin(\Delta x)}{\Delta x} = 1$.

Δx	$\sin(\Delta x)$	$\cos(\Delta x)$	$\dfrac{\sin(\Delta x)}{\Delta x}$	$\dfrac{\cos(\Delta x) - 1}{\Delta x}$
1	.8415	.5403	.8415	−.4597
.1	.0998	.9950	.9980	−.0499
.01	.0099	.9999	.9999	−.0049
.001	.0010	.9999	.9999	−.0005

TEST YOUR UNDERSTANDING

1. Make a chart similar to the one above showing values of $\sin(\Delta x)/\Delta x$ and $[\cos(\Delta x) - 1]/\Delta x$ as Δx approaches 0 from the left (through negative values).

There are more formal proofs of these results, one of which is outlined in the problems at the end of the section. Note that we could not have used L'Hôpital's Rule to evaluate these limits since that would require knowing the derivatives of $\sin(x)$ and $\cos(x)$. But that's what we're trying to show.

Let us emphasize once again that these results are only valid if x and Δx are measured in radians (real numbers). Try computing $\sin(\Delta x)/\Delta x$ for small values of Δx measured in degrees and see what you get. For example, $\dfrac{\sin(.1°)}{.1}$ = .0174, not terribly close to 1.

It now follows that:

$$f'(x) := (0) \sin(x) + (1) \cos(x) = \cos(x)$$

as we expect.

We can use the same technique to prove that $\frac{d}{dx}[\cos(x)] = -\sin(x)$. (See Problem 8 at the end of the section.)

Let's see if this makes sense in terms of the direction and concavity. Since $\cos(x) > 0$ on the intervals $(-\pi/2, \pi/2)$, $(3\pi/2, 5\pi/2)$, $(7\pi/2, 9\pi/2)$, etc., it follows that $\sin(x)$ should be increasing on these intervals. Inspection of the graph reveals that this is the case. Furthermore, $\sin(x) > 0$ on the intervals $(0, \pi)$, $(2\pi, 3\pi)$, $(4\pi, 5\pi)$, etc. Since $\dfrac{d^2}{dx^2}[\sin(x)] = -\sin(x)$, then the sine function should be concave down on these intervals. Again, this seems to be the case.

◻ All of the shortcuts for derivatives can now be adapted to these functions.

EXAMPLE 7.2:

Find the derivative of (a) $y = \sin(x^2)$ (b) $y = \sin^2(x)$.

(a) Using the chain rule, we get

$$\frac{dy}{dx} = \cos(x^2)\frac{d}{dx}[x^2] = 2x\cos(x^2).$$

(b) Noting that $\sin^2(x)$ means $(\sin(x))^2$, we again use the chain rule to get $\dfrac{dy}{dx} = 2\sin(x)\dfrac{d}{dx}[\sin(x)] = 2\sin(x)\cos(x).$ ◆

EXAMPLE 7.3:

Determine the direction of $f(x) := \cos(2x)$, for $x \geq 0$.

The derivative is $f'(x) := 2(-\sin(2x)) = -2\sin(2x)$. Therefore, f is increasing whenever $\sin(2x) < 0$. This happens when $\pi < 2x < 2\pi$, $3\pi < 2x < 4\pi$, $5\pi < 2x < 6\pi$, etc.; i.e, for x on the intervals, $[\pi/2, \pi]$, $[3\pi/2, 2\pi]$, $[5\pi/2, 3\pi]$, etc. Then f is decreasing everywhere else.   ◆

EXAMPLE 7.4:

Write an equation of the line tangent to the graph of $f(x) := e^x \sin(x)$ at $x = 0$.

Using the product rule, we get

$$f'(x) := e^x(\sin(x)) + e^x(\cos(x)) = e^x(\sin(x) + \cos(x)).$$

Therefore, the slope of the tangent line is $f'(0) = 1$. Since $f(0) = 0$, an equation of the tangent line is:

$$y - 0 = 1(x - 0) \quad \text{or, equivalently,} \quad y = x. \quad ◆$$

EXAMPLE 7.5:

Determine the critical numbers of $f(x) := x \cos(x)$ on the interval $-\pi \le x \le \pi$.

Using the product rule, we get

$$f'(x) := -x \sin(x) + \cos(x).$$

Since we cannot solve the equation $-x \sin(x) + \cos(x) = 0$ explicitly, we use the graph (or the "solve" button on a calculator) to show that there are roots at $x = \pm .86$ (approx.) Since $f'(-\pi/2) = -\pi/2$, $f'(0) = 1$ and $f'(\pi/2) = -\pi/2$, we conclude that f has a local minimum at $x = -.86$ and a local maximum at $x = .86$. See Figure 7.9.

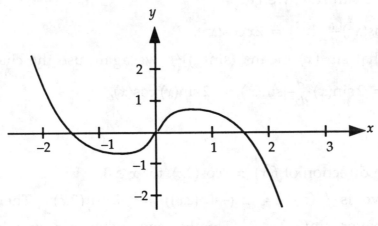

Fig. 7.9

♦

TEST YOUR UNDERSTANDING

2. Find the derivative of each of the following:

(a) $y = \sin^5(x)$ (b) $f(x) := \cos(2x + 1)$ (c) $g(x) := \dfrac{\cos(x)}{1 + \sin(x)}$

(d) $f(x) := \sin(\sqrt{x})$ (e) $y = \sin^2(t)\cos^2(t)$

3.   Write an equation of the line tangent to the graph of $y = \sin(x)$ at $x = \pi/6$.

4.   Find the maximum value of the function $f(x) := \sin(x) + \cos(x)$ for $0 \le x \le \pi$.

¤   Higher-order derivatives of the sine and cosine functions follow a nice pattern:

y	$\sin(x)$	$\cos(x)$
dy/dx	$\cos(x)$	$-\sin(x)$
d^2y/dx^2	$-\sin(x)$	$-\cos(x)$
d^3y/dx^3	$-\cos(x)$	$\sin(x)$
d^4y/dx^4	$\sin(x)$	$\cos(x)$
d^5y/dx^5	$\cos(x)$	$-\sin(x)$

Note that the derivatives repeat in cycles of 4; that is, the fifth derivative is the same as the first derivative, the sixth derivative is the same as the second derivative, etc.

EXAMPLE 7.6:

Find the 39th derivative of $g(x) := \sin(2x)$.

If we follow the cyclic pattern, we find that the 39th derivative will be "similar to" the third derivative, namely $-\cos(2x)$. However, each time we take the derivative, the chain rule introduces another factor of 2. Therefore, $g^{(39)}(x) := -2^{39}\cos(2x)$.

(Those with calculators can show that $2^{39} \approx 5.5 \times 10^{11}$, or about 550 billion.) ♦

ANTIDERIVATIVES INVOLVING SINE AND COSINE

From Theorem 7.2, we immediately see:

THEOREM 7.3: (a) $\int \sin(x)\,dx = -\cos(x) + c$ (b) $\int \cos(x)\,dx = \sin(x) + c$.

EXAMPLE 7.7:

Find the area under one "arch" of the curve $y = \sin(x)$ as shown in Figure 7.10.

Since $\sin(\pi) = \sin(0) = 0$ and $\sin(x) > 0$ for $0 < x < \pi$, then the desired area can be found by evaluating

$$\int_0^\pi \sin(x)\,dx = -\cos(x)\Big|_{x=0}^{x=\pi} = -\cos(\pi) + \cos(0) = 2.$$

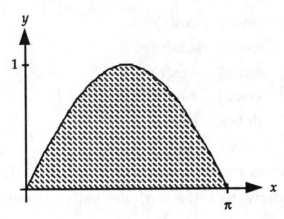

Fig. 7.10

$\blacklozenge$

EXAMPLE 7.8:

Find the derivative of $f(x) := \sin(3x)$ and use the result to evaluate $\int \cos(3x)\,dx$.

By the chain rule, $f'(x) := 3\cos(3x)$. Thus,

$$\int 3\cos(3x)\,dx = \sin(3x) + c, \text{ from which (upon dividing by 3)}$$
$$\int \cos(3x)\,dx = \tfrac{1}{3}\sin(3x) + c. \qquad \blacklozenge$$

For now, we are restricted to very simple antiderivatives involving trigonometric functions. We will learn to solve others in Chapter 8.

<u>TEST YOUR UNDERSTANDING</u>

5. Evaluate each of the following:

(a) $\displaystyle\int 5\sin(x)\,dx$

(b) $\displaystyle\int_0^\pi [\sin(x)+\cos(x)]\,dx$

6. Determine the area under one arch of the curve $y = \cos(x)$.

7. (a) A particle travels with velocity given by $v(t) := 3\cos(t)$. What is the change in position of the particle over the time interval $[0, \pi/2]$?

(b) The density of a rod x units from one end is $r(x) := 3\cos(x)$. If the rod is $\pi/2$ units long, what is its total mass?

OTHER TRIGONOMETRIC FUNCTIONS

So far, we have restricted ourselves to two trigonometric functions--sine and cosine. There are some others that we also want to consider.

1. **Tangent:** Let $\tan(x) := \dfrac{\sin(x)}{\cos(x)}$. The domain contains all values of x for which $\cos(x) \neq 0$; that is, $\{x \mid x \neq \pm\pi/2, \pm3\pi/2, \pm5\pi/2, \ldots\}$. The range is **R**.

2. **Secant:** Let $\sec(x) := \dfrac{1}{\cos(x)}$. Its domain is the same as the tangent. However, since $-1 \le \cos(x) \le 1$, it follows that $\sec(x) \ge 1$ or $\sec(x) \le -1$; that is, the range is $\{y \mid y \ge 1 \text{ or } y \le -1\}$.

The tangent and secant are related by the identity $\tan^2(x) + 1 = \sec^2(x)$. Graphs of the tangent and secant are given in Figures 7.11(a and b).

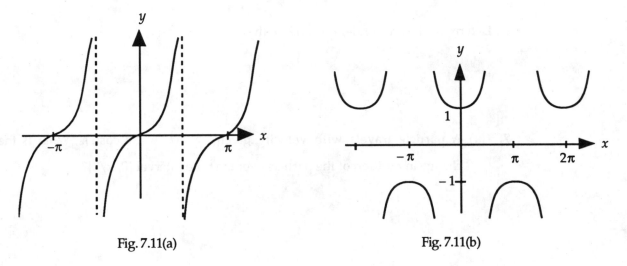

Fig. 7.11(a)   Fig. 7.11(b)

The derivatives of the tangent and secant functions are given in:

THEOREM 7.4: (a) $\dfrac{d\,[\tan(x)]}{dx} = \sec^2(x)$ (b) $\dfrac{d}{dx}[\sec(x)] = \sec(x)\tan(x)$

Proof: We prove part (a). Part (b) is a problem at the end of the section.
By invoking the quotient rule, we have

(13) $\quad \dfrac{d\,[\tan(x)]}{dx} = \dfrac{\cos(x)\cos(x) - \sin(x)(-\sin(x))}{\cos^2(x)} = \dfrac{\cos^2(x) + \sin^2(x)}{\cos^2(x)}$

$\qquad = \dfrac{1}{\cos^2(x)} = \sec^2(x).$

Observe that the derivative of the tangent function is always positive, implying that the tangent is strictly increasing on each interval in its domain, as the graph indicates.

There are two other common trigonometric functions, the **cotangent** (the reciprocal of the tangent) and **cosecant** (the reciprocal of the sine), which are occasionally useful. However, we shall not discuss them here.

EXERCISES FOR SECTION 7.3:

1. Find the derivative of each of the following:

    (a) $y = \sin(2x)$ (b) $y = \tan(x^2)$ (c) $f(x) := \cos(x)\sin(x)$

    (d) $g(x) := e^{\sin(x)}$ (e) $y = (\cos(t) + \sin(t))^2$ (f) $f(x) := \dfrac{\sin(x)}{1+\cos(x)}$

    (g) $y = x\sec(x)$ (h) $h(x) := \sqrt[3]{\tan(x)}$ (i) $g(x) := \tan^2(x)\cos^2(x)$

2. Write an equation of the line tangent to the function in Exercise 1(c) at $x = \pi$.

3. Write an equation of the line perpendicular to the function in Exercise 1(d) at $x = 0$.

4. Write an equation of the line tangent to the graph of $f(x) := \tan(3x)$ at $x = \pi/12$.

5. Determine the critical points of the function $f(x) := e^x \sin(x)$.

6. Discuss the direction and concavity of:

    (a) $y = x + \sin(x)$ (b) $y = x - 2\sin(x)$ (c) $y = \cos\left(\dfrac{x}{3}\right)$

7. What is largest value of b such that $f(x) := \cos(x^2)$ is decreasing on the interval $[0, b]$?

8. For what value of k does the function $f(x) := \sin(x) + k\cos(x)$ have a local maximum at $x = \pi/6$?

9. (a) Argue by drawing a graph that the only solution to the equation $\sin(x) = x$ is $x = 0$.

    (b) How many solutions are there to the equation $\sin(x) = x/2$? Give approximate values of these solutions.

10. The position of a particle is given by $s(t) := \sin(4t)$, $t \geq 0$.

    (a) Determine the velocity and acceleration of the particle.

    (b) What is the first time at which the velocity of the particle is equal to 2?

11. Evaluate each of the following definite integrals:

(a) $\displaystyle\int_0^{\pi/2} \sin(x)\,dx$ (b) $\displaystyle\int_0^{\pi/4} \sec^2(x)\,dx$

12. Determine the area bounded $y = \cos(3x), y = 0, x = 0$ and $x = \pi/6$.

PROBLEMS FOR SECTION 7.3:

1. Eq.(12) says that $\cos(x + y) = \cos(x)\cos(y) - \sin(x)\sin(y)$ for all x and y.

(a) Use this to show that $\cos(2x) = \cos^2(x) - \sin^2(x)$.

(b) Modify your answer to (a) to show that $\cos(2x) = 1 - 2\sin^2(x)$. Hence,
$$\sin^2(x) = \frac{1 - \cos(2x)}{2}.$$

(c) Use (b) to evaluate $\displaystyle\int \sin^2(x)\,dx$.

2. A projectile is launched from the ground with velocity v at an angle θ with the horizontal. It can be shown (and we will do so in Chapter 9) that, in the absence of air resistance, the projectile will travel $R = \dfrac{v^2}{g} \sin(2\theta)$ feet downrange, where $g = 32$ ft./sec^2 is the acceleration due to gravity.

(a) At what angle should the projectile be launched to maximize R?

(b) What is the maximum value of R?

(c) What effect will doubling the initial velocity v have on R?

3. The height of the projectile in problem 2 is given by
$$y = (\tan(\theta))x - \frac{g}{2v^2 \cos^2(\theta)}\,x^2,$$

where x is the distance downrange the projectile has travelled. Show that the maximum height is $h = \dfrac{v^2}{2g} \sin^2(\theta)$. (Note: The angle θ is constant. You are to maximize y as a function of x.)

4. (a) Evaluate $\displaystyle\lim_{x \to 0}\frac{\sin(mx)}{x}$ for $m = 2, 3$ and 4 by making a table of values similar to the one in the text.

(b) What do you think $\displaystyle\lim_{x \to 0}\frac{\sin(mx)}{x}$ is equal to in general? Prove your claim.

5. (a) Starting with the formulas $\sin(x + y) = \sin(x)\cos(y) + \cos(x)\sin(y)$ and $\cos(x + y) = \cos(x)\cos(y) - \sin(x)\sin(y)$, show that
$$\tan(x + y) = \frac{\tan(x) + \tan(y)}{1 - \tan(x)\tan(y)}.$$

   (b) Use the result of (a) to show that the function $f(x) := \tan(x)$ is periodic with period π.

6. A Christmas ornament is shaped in such a way that its cross-sections perpendicular to its axis are circles with radius $r(x) := \sin(x)$, where x is the distance from the top. If the total distance from top to bottom is 2 units, find the volume of the ornament. (Hint: Use the result of Problem 1(c).)

7. In this problem, we will prove geometrically that $\lim\limits_{\theta \to 0} \dfrac{\sin(\theta)}{\theta} = 1$. The diagram below has a circle of radius 1 with line segment $\overline{OC}$ drawn at angle θ with the x-axis.

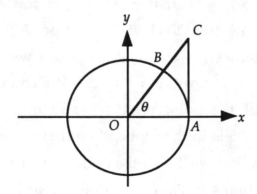

   (a) Show that the coordinates of B and C are $(\cos(\theta), \sin(\theta))$ and $(1, \tan(\theta))$, respectively.

   (b) Show that the area of $\triangle OAB = \frac{1}{2}\sin(\theta)$ and the area of $\triangle OAC = \frac{1}{2}\tan(\theta)$.

   (c) Show that the area of sector $OAB = \frac{1}{2}(\theta)$.

   (d) It is clear that area of $\triangle OAB \le$ area of sector $OAB \le$ area of $\triangle OAC$; that is, $\frac{1}{2}\sin(\theta) \le \frac{1}{2}(\theta) \le \frac{1}{2}\tan(\theta)$, for all θ. Multiply this inequality by $\dfrac{2}{\sin(\theta)}$.

   (e) What conclusion can you draw by letting $\theta \to 0$?

8. Use the definition of the derivative to prove $\frac{d}{dx}[\cos(x)] = -\sin(x)$.

9. Prove $\frac{d}{dx}[\sec(x)] = \sec(x)\tan(x)$.

10. Derive formulas for the derivative of $y = \cot(x)$ and $y = \csc(x)$.

TYU Answers for Section 7.3

1. $\sin(\Delta x)/\Delta x$ values are the same; $[\cos(\Delta x) - 1]/\Delta x$ values are of opposite sign as one

given   2. (a) $y' = 5\sin^4(x)\cos(x)$ (b) $f'(x) := -2\sin(2x+1)$

(c) $g'(x) := \dfrac{-(1+\sin(x))\sin(x) - \cos^2(x)}{(1+\sin(x))^2} = \dfrac{-1}{1+\sin(x)}$ (d) $f'(x) = \dfrac{1}{2\sqrt{x}}\cos(\sqrt{x})$

(e) $dy/dt = 2\sin(t)\cos(t)(\cos^2(t) - \sin^2(t))$ 3. $y - \dfrac{1}{2} = \dfrac{\sqrt{3}}{2}\left(x - \dfrac{\pi}{6}\right)$ 4. $\sqrt{2}$

5. (a) $-5\cos(x) + c$ (b) 2   6. 2   7. (a) 3   (b) 3

7.4 INVERSE TRIGONOMETRIC FUNCTIONS

Consider the mass-spring system with $b = 1$ subject to the initial conditions $y(0) = 0$, $y'(0) = 1$; that is, the object starts at position 0 with velocity 1. We can show (see TYU #5 in Section 7.2) that its motion is described by the function $y(t) := \sin(t)$. Suppose we wanted to find the time at which the object is at position $y = .25$. We could do it graphically-- find the t-coordinate of the point on the graph of $y = \sin(t)$ whose y-coordinate is .25. Since .25 is in the range, then there is such a point; in fact, there are infinitely many, but we'll take the one closest to 0 for now. (We saw a similar problem in Section 4.3: Find the value of t such that $e^{-t/5} = 0.5$.)

More generally, what we're looking for is the inverse of the sine function --that is, a function g such that $\sin(g(x)) = x$ and $g(\sin(x)) = x$, for all x. At this point, you might ask whether the sine function has an inverse function? Let's see: We know that $\sin(\pi) = 0$ which means that $g(0)$ would have to equal π. But $\sin(2\pi) = 0$ also so $g(0)$ would have to equal 2π. Since $g(0)$ cannot have two different values, we have a problem.

Recall that in order for a function to have an inverse, it must be one-to-one. Graphically, this means that no horizontal line can intersect the curve in more than one place. Clearly, this is not true about the sine function (or any other periodic function). In fact, we could say that the sine function is "infinitely-many-to-one".

In order to circumvent this problem, we can restrict the domain of the sine function to a portion of the *x*-axis on which the graph is one-to-one. The easiest (but by no means unique) way to do this is to restrict the domain to $\{x \mid -\pi/2 \le x \le \pi/2\}$. Then the inverse function will exist.

Let $f(x) := \sin(x)$, $-\pi/2 \le x \le \pi/2$. Then $f^{-1}(x)$ exists. Its domain is $\{x \mid -1 \le x \le 1\}$; its range is $\{y \mid -\pi/2 \le y \le \pi/2\}$. We will denote the inverse function by **arcsin(x)**. In other words,

$$y = \text{arcsin}(x) \text{ if and only if } x = \sin(y) \text{ and } -\pi/2 \le y \le \pi/2.$$

The graph of the arcsine function can be obtained by reflecting the graph of $y = \sin(x)$, on the restricted domain, across the line $y = x$. See Figure 7.12.

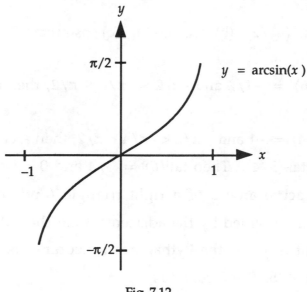

Fig. 7.12

In a similar manner, we can define the inverse of the cosine function. (See Problem 6 at the end of the section.)

Finally, we'll define the inverse of the tangent function, the **arctangent**. The tangent function is one-to-one on the domain $\{-\pi/2 < x < \pi/2\}$; its range is **R**. Therefore, the inverse function $g(x) := \text{arctan}(x)$ has domain **R** and range $\{y \mid -\pi/2 < y < \pi/2\}$. See Figure 7.13 for a graph.

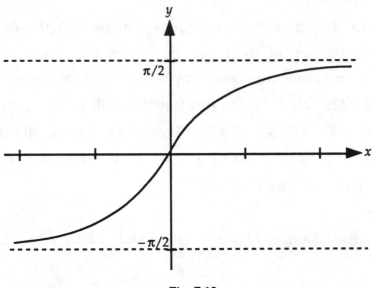

Fig. 7.13

EXAMPLE 7.9:

Evaluate (a) arcsin(−1/2) (b) arctan(−1) (c) cos(arctan(3/4))
(d) arcsin(sin(5π/6)).

(a) Since sin(−π/6) = −1/2 and −π/2 ≤ −π/6 ≤ π/2, then arcsin(−1/2) =
−π/6.

(b) Since tan(−π/4) = −1 and −π/2 < −π/4 < π/2, then arctan(−1) = −π/4.

(c) Let θ = arctan(3/4). Then tan(θ) = 3/4 and 0 < θ< π/2. Thinking
of θ as one of the acute angles of a right triangle (and recalling that the
tangent is the opposite divided by the adjacent), then the side opposite θ is 3
and the side adjacent is 4. By the Pythagorean theorem, the hypotenuse is 5
from which cos(θ) = 4/5. See Figure 7.14.

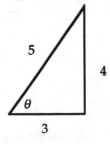

Fig. 7.14

(d) We're immediately tempted to say that, since arcsin(x) and sin(x) are inverse functions, then arcsin(sin(5π/6)) = 5π/6. But the range of arcsin(x) does not include 5π/6, so this must be wrong. Proceeding more carefully, we have sin(5π/6) = 1/2, so arcsin(sin(5π/6)) = arcsin(1/2) = π/6. ◆

- -

TEST YOUR UNDERSTANDING

1. Evaluate (a) arcsin$\left(\dfrac{\sqrt{2}}{2}\right)$ (b) arctan$\left(\sqrt{3}\right)$ (c) tan(arcsin(3/4)) (d) arctan(tan(3π/4))

- -

□ The next theorem gives the derivatives of these functions.

THEOREM 7.5: (a) $\dfrac{d}{dx}[\arcsin(x)] = \dfrac{1}{\sqrt{1-x^2}}$ (b) $\dfrac{d}{dx}[\arctan(x)] = \dfrac{1}{1+x^2}$

Proof: Again we prove part (a) only. Part (b) can be found in the Problems at the end of the section.

Let y = arcsin(x). Then, sin(y) = x. Differentiating both sides with respect to x gives $\cos(y)\dfrac{dy}{dx}$ = 1. Since $\sin^2(y) + \cos^2(y)$ = 1, then cos(y) = $\pm\sqrt{1-\sin^2(y)}$ = $\pm\sqrt{1-x^2}$. Since $-\pi/2 \le y \le \pi/2$, then cos(y) $\ge$ 0. Therefore, $\dfrac{d}{dx}[\arcsin(x)]$ = $\dfrac{1}{\sqrt{1-x^2}}$.

Observe that $\dfrac{dy}{dx}$ is undefined when x = ± 1. This implies that the lines tangent to the graph of y = arcsin(x) at x = ± 1 are vertical. Also, $\dfrac{dy}{dx} > 0$ for all x on the domain, so the arcsine function is strictly increasing. We've seen both of these properties in Figure 7.12.

The corresponding antiderivative formulas are given in:

THEOREM 7.6: (a) $\displaystyle\int \frac{1}{\sqrt{1-x^2}}\,dx = \arcsin(x) + c$

(b) $\displaystyle\int \frac{1}{1+x^2}\,dx = \arctan(x) + c$

Note that we have not been able to find either of these antiderivatives prior to this. Furthermore, it is rather interesting to see that the antiderivative of an algebraic function turns out to be transcendental.

EXAMPLE 7.10:

Determine dy/dx if: (a) $y = x\arcsin(x)$ (b) $y = \arctan(\frac{1}{x})$

(c) $y = \arctan(bx)$, where b is a constant.

(a) Using the product rule, we have:

$$\frac{dy}{dx} = x\,\frac{d}{dx}[\arcsin(x)] + (1)\,\arcsin(x) = \frac{x}{\sqrt{1-x^2}} + \arcsin(x)$$

(b) Using the chain rule, we have:

$$\frac{dy}{dx} = \frac{1}{1+\left(\frac{1}{x}\right)^2}\left(\frac{-1}{x^2}\right) = \frac{-1}{1+x^2}.$$

(c) Again using the chain rule, we have:

$$\frac{dy}{dx} = \frac{1}{1+(bx)^2}(b) = \frac{b}{1+b^2x^2}. \qquad \blacklozenge$$

EXAMPLE 7.11:

Determine $\displaystyle\int \frac{2}{1+4x^2}\,dx$.

The integrand matches the result of Example 7.10(c) with $b = 2$. Hence,

$$\int \frac{2}{1+4x^2}\,dx = \arctan(2x) + c. \qquad \blacklozenge$$

- -

TEST YOUR UNDERSTANDING

2. Determine $g'(x)$ if $g(x) := \arcsin(x^2)$.

3. Evaluate (a) $\int \dfrac{4}{1+16x^2}\,dx$ (b) $\int \dfrac{4}{\sqrt{1-16x^2}}\,dx$.

EXERCISES FOR SECTION 7.4:

1. Evaluate each of the following:

   (a) arcsin(.5)   (b) arctan(−1)   (c) cos(arcsin(1/3))

   (d) sin(arcsin(4/5))   (e) arctan(tan(7π/6))

2. Find the derivative of each of the following:

   (a) y = arcsin(2x)   (b) $g(t)$:= arctan(e^t)   (c) $f(x)$:= $(\text{arcsin}(x))^3$

   (d) y = cos(arcsin(x))   (e) $h(x)$:= tan(arctan(x))   (f) y = x^2 arctan(x)

3. Determine the concavity of $f(x)$ = arcsin(x).

4. Determine and classify the critical points of:

   (a) $f(x)$:= 2x − arcsin(x)   (b) $f(x)$:= $\dfrac{x}{2}$ − arcsin(x)

5. Discuss the direction of $f(x)$:= arcsin(x^2).

6. What is the domain of y = arcsin(2x)? Sketch the graph.

7. At what value(s) of x will the line tangent to y = arctan(x) be parallel to $5x - 4y = 3$?

8. Write an equation of the line tangent to $f(x)$:= arctan(x) at $x = 1$.

9. For what value of k does $g(x)$:= kx − arctan(x) have a horizontal tangent at $x = 3$?

10. Evaluate each integral:

   (a) $\displaystyle\int_0^{1/2} \dfrac{1}{\sqrt{1-x^2}}\,dx$ (b) $\displaystyle\int_0^1 \dfrac{1}{1+x^2}\,dx$

11. Argue by drawing a graph that $\displaystyle\int_0^1 \text{arcsin}(x)\,dx < \dfrac{\pi}{4}$. What similar statement could you make about $\displaystyle\int_0^{1/2} \text{arcsin}(x)\,dx$?

PROBLEMS FOR SECTION 7.4:

1. (a) Find the derivative of $f(x) := x \arcsin(x) + \sqrt{1-x^2}$

   (b) Use your answer to (a) to evaluate $\int_0^1 \arcsin(x)\, dx$.

2. A mass attached to a spring is released from initial position y_0. How long does it take for the mass to move from its rest position ($y = 0$) to one-half its maximum displacement? How does your answer depend on ω?

3. (a) Show that $\displaystyle\int \frac{1}{x^2 + 2bx + b^2 + a^2}\, dx = \frac{1}{a} \arctan\left(\frac{x+b}{a}\right) + c$.

   (b) Use (a) to evaluate $\displaystyle\int \frac{1}{x^2 + 6x + 25}\, dx$.

4. The bottom edge of a painting is 4 feet above eye-level. The painting is 6 feet tall. How far from the wall should an observer stand to maximize the angle θ subtended by the painting? (See diagram below.)

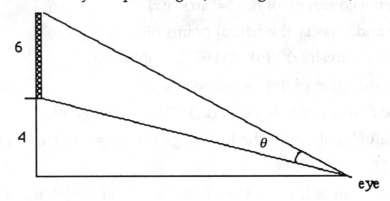

5. A boat is being towed by a rope attached to a pier 6 feet above water level. If the rope is being pulled in at 2 feet per second, how fast is the angle between the rope and the horizontal changing when the rope is 15 feet long?

6. One way to define the arccosine function is by $\arccos(x) = y$ if and only if $x = \cos(y)$ and $0 \le y \le \pi$; that is the arccosine is the inverse of the cosine function restricted to the range $[0, \pi]$.

   (a) Show that $\arcsin(x) + \arccos(x) = \pi/2$, for all x between -1 and 1.

   (b) Use (a) to find the derivative of the arccosine function.

   (c) Define the arcsecant function by $\operatorname{arcsec}(x) = \arccos(1/x)$, for $|x| \ge 1$. Use (b) to find the derivative of the arcsecant function.

7. Show that, for $x \neq 0$, $\arctan(\frac{1}{x}) = \frac{\pi}{2} - \arctan(x)$. [Hint: See Example 7.10(b).]

8. Prove that the derivative of $y = \arctan(x)$ is $\frac{dy}{dx} = \frac{1}{1+x^2}$.

TYU Answers for Section 7.4

1. (a) $\frac{\pi}{4}$ (b) $\frac{\pi}{3}$ (c) $\frac{3}{\sqrt{7}}$ (d) $-\frac{\pi}{4}$ 2. $g'(x) := \frac{2x}{\sqrt{1-x^4}}$

3. (a) $\arctan(4x) + c$ (b) $\arcsin(4x) + c$

7.5 THE DAMPED OSCILLATOR

Let's return to the problem which motivated this chapter--the spring-mass system. One of the assumptions we made was that there was no air resistance affecting the movement of the object. In this section, we'll see what happens if we relax this assumption, although we will still assume that the table on which the object rests is frictionless.

The differential equation that we derived was based on Newton's Second Law. Without air resistance, the only force acting on the object is from the spring. Now, however, there is another force-- air resistance--acting on the object. We need a way of quantifying this force (in much the same way that Hooke's Law quantified the force of the spring).

One theory is that the force exerted by air resistance is proportional to the velocity of the object. In other words, if the object is not moving, there is no resistance. As the object's velocity increases, the resistive force increases proportionally. This is not the only theory but it is simple and, as we shall see, gives (at least qualitatively) plausible results.

The differential equation in the no-resistance case was $m\frac{d^2y}{dt^2} = -ky$. The term on the right is the force from the spring. Now we have to add another term $h\frac{dy}{dt}$ to account for the resistance. So, the equation is

(14) $m\frac{d^2y}{dt^2} = -ky - h\frac{dy}{dt}$.

The minus sign in front of the $h\dfrac{dy}{dt}$ needs some explanation: If $\dfrac{dy}{dt} > 0$, then the object is moving to the right and the resistive force will tend to pull it back towards the left. The reverse is true if $\dfrac{dy}{dt} < 0$. Thus, the resistive force always opposes the direction of motion. (We will see later that if we had the wrong sign on the resistance term, we would get ridiculous results.)

Rearranging terms and letting $\omega^2 = k/m$ and $\rho = h/2m$, we have:

(15) $$\dfrac{d^2y}{dt^2} + 2\rho\dfrac{dy}{dt} + \omega^2 y = 0$$

This is a special case of the general second-order equation $\dfrac{d^2y}{dt^2} + a\dfrac{dy}{dt} + by = 0$ which we haven't learned to solve yet (unless $a = 0$). We might be tempted to try trigonometric functions as the solution to this equation. For example, suppose $y = \sin(kt)$ for some k. Then, $\dfrac{dy}{dt} = k\,\cos(kt)$ and $\dfrac{d^2y}{dt^2} = -k^2\,\sin(kt)$. Upon substituting, we get

$$-k^2\,\sin(kt) + ak\,\cos(kt) + b\,\sin(kt) = 0.$$

Convince yourself that there are no values of k that make this equation true for all t. So, trigonometric functions are not the answer. (You can try cosine or any other trig function but you'll come to the same conclusion.)

What other functions might we try? In Section 7.1, we showed that the general solution of the equation $\dfrac{d^2y}{dt^2} - y = 0$ (a special case of the equation we're considering) is $y = c_1 e^t + c_2 e^{-t}$. This suggests that the solutions of the more general equation might be exponential functions. Let's try it. Assume that there is a solution of the form $y = e^{rt}$, for some r. Then, $\dfrac{dy}{dt} = re^{rt}$ and $\dfrac{d^2y}{dt^2} = r^2 e^{rt}$. Substituting in the differential equation gives:

$$r^2 e^{rt} + ar e^{rt} + b e^{rt} = 0 \text{ or, equivalently,}$$

$$e^{rt}(r^2 + ar + b) = 0.$$

Since e^{rt} is never 0 (in fact, it's always positive), then

(16) $\quad r^2 + ar + b = 0.$

This is a quadratic equation whose roots can be found either by factoring or by using the quadratic formula. It is called the **characteristic equation** for the corresponding differential equation. There are three possibilities for the roots: Either the roots are real and distinct, or the roots are real and equal, or the roots are complex (imaginary). Let's concentrate for now on the first case.

CASE 1: Suppose the roots of $r^2 + ar + b = 0$ are r_1 and r_2, where $r_1 \neq r_2$. Then $y_1(t) := e^{r_1 t}$ and $y_2(t) := e^{r_2 t}$ are both solutions to the differential equation. Furthermore, since y_1 and y_2 are independent, we can conclude that the general solution of the differential equation $\dfrac{d^2 y}{dt^2} + a\dfrac{dy}{dt} + by = 0$ is $y(t) := c_1 e^{r_1 t} + c_2 e^{r_2 t}$, where c_1 and c_2 are constants.

EXAMPLE 7.12:

Determine all solutions of the equation $\dfrac{d^2 y}{dt^2} - 3\dfrac{dy}{dt} - 4y = 0$. Find the specific solution satisfying the conditions $y(0) = 3$ and $y'(0) = 2$.

The characteristic equation is $r^2 - 3r - 4 = 0$ whose roots are $r = -1$ and $r = 4$. Therefore, the general solution is $y(t) := c_1 e^{-t} + c_2 e^{4t}$.

To find the specific solution, first differentiate y with respect to t.

$$y'(t) := -c_1 e^{-t} + 4c_2 e^{4t}.$$

Substituting $t = 0$ in $y(t)$ and $y'(t)$ gives

$$y(0) = c_1 + c_2 \quad \text{and} \quad y'(0) = -c_1 + 4c_2.$$

The solution to the system

$$c_1 + c_2 = 3, \qquad -c_1 + 4c_2 = 2$$

is $c_1 = 2$, $c_2 = 1$. Thus, the specific solution to the differential equation is

$$y(t) := 2e^{-t} + e^{4t}.$$

The graph of this function, for $t > 0$, is in Figure 7.15.

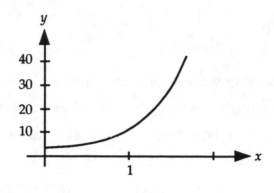

Fig. 7.15

EXAMPLE 7.13:

Solve the equation $\dfrac{d^2y}{dt^2} - y = 0$.

The characteristic equation is $r^2 - 1 = 0$ whose roots are $r = \pm 1$. Thus, the general solution is

$$y(t) := c_1 e^t + c_2 e^{-t}.$$

◆

CASE 2:   If the roots of the characteristic equation are not real (but assuming a and b are real), then the roots occur in conjugate pairs; that is, $r_1 = p + qi$ and $r_2 = p - qi$, for some real numbers p and q, where $i = \sqrt{-1}$. We claim (this takes some justification which we won't do here) that the solution is

(17) $y(t) := e^{pt}[c_1 \cos(qt) + c_2 \sin(qt)].$

If $p = 0$, then the solution is some combination of $\sin(qt)$ and $\cos(qt)$ which will oscillate with constant amplitude. This happens when $a = 0$ and the equation is one we've solved already: $\dfrac{d^2y}{dt^2} + by = 0$. However, if $p > 0$, then $e^{pt} > 1$ for $t > 0$ and increases as t increases. Therefore, the amplitude of the waves increases as t increases. On the other hand, if $p < 0$, then $e^{pt} < 1$ for $t > 0$ and decreases as t increases. This means the amplitude of the waves decreases as t increases.

---

1. Sketch each of the following:

   (a) $y = e^{t/10} \sin(t)$ (b) $y = e^{t/10} \cos(t)$ (c) $y = e^{-t/10} \sin(t)$

EXAMPLE 7.14:

Solve the equation $y'' - 2y' + 5y = 0$.

The characteristic equation is $r^2 - 2r + 5 = 0$ whose roots are $r_1 = 1 + 2i$ and $r_2 = 1 - 2i$. These are of the form $p \pm qi$ with $p = 1$ and $q = 2$. Therefore, the general solution of the differential equation is

$$y(t) := e^t \left[c_1 \cos(2t) + c_2 \sin(2t) \right].$$

A graph of this solution for the case $c_1 = 0, c_2 = 1$ is in Figure 7.16. Note that since $p > 0$, the amplitude of the oscillations increases as t increases.

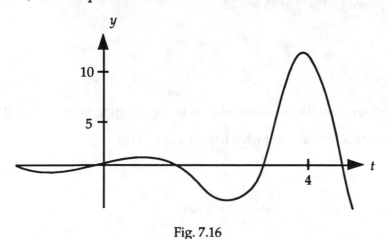

Fig. 7.16

♦

The only case we have not considered is the one in which the roots are real and equal. This is discussed in the problems at the end of the section.

TEST YOUR UNDERSTANDING

2. Find the general solution of each of the following differential equations:

(a) $y'' - 3y' - 18y = 0$ (b) $y'' - 4y' + 13y = 0$

(c) $y'' + 25y = 0$ (d) $y'' + 6y' = 0$

3. Determine the specific solution of the equation in 1(d) that satisfies the initial conditions $y(0) = 1$, $y'(0) = -12$.

4. Sketch any specific non-zero solution to the equation in 2(b) with $y(0) = 0$, making sure to take into account what happens as t increases.

5. How would the sketch in 4 change if the equation were $y'' + 4y' + 13y = 0$?

◻ Now let's go back to the spring-mass system with air resistance. The characteristic equation is $r^2 + 2\rho r + \omega^2 = 0$ whose roots, as given by the quadratic formula are $r_1 = -\rho + \sqrt{\rho^2 - \omega^2}$ and $r_2 = -\rho - \sqrt{\rho^2 - \omega^2}$.

We have several cases to consider:

1. If $\rho < \omega$, then the roots of the characteristic equation are complex and the general solution of the differential equation is

$$(18) \qquad y(t) := e^{-\rho t}[c_1 \cos(qt) + c_2 \sin(qt)],$$

where $q = \sqrt{\omega^2 - \rho^2}$. Upon substituting initial conditions $y(0) = y_0$ and $y'(0) = 0$, we find $c_1 = y_0$ and $c_2 = \rho y_0/q$. Thus, the specific solution is

$$(19) \qquad y(t) = y_0 e^{-\rho t}\left[\cos(qt) + \frac{\rho}{q}\sin(qt)\right].$$

A graph of this solution is given in Figure 7.17. Note that since ρ is presumed to be positive, then $-\rho$ is negative and the amplitude of the oscillations decreases as t increases. We say that the oscillations are **damped**.

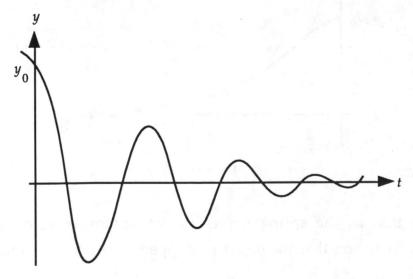

Fig. 7.17

2. If $\rho > \omega$, then the roots are real and the general solution is

(20) $$y(t) := c_1 e^{r_1 t} + c_2 e^{r_2 t}.$$

Furthermore, since $\rho^2 - \omega^2 < \rho^2$, then $\sqrt{\rho^2 - \omega^2} < \rho$; thus both r_1 and r_2 are negative. Imposing the initial conditions $y(0) = y_0$ and $y'(0) = 0$ yields (after some algebra which you are asked to verify in the problems) $c_1 = \dfrac{-r_2 y_0}{r_1 - r_2}$ and $c_2 = \dfrac{r_1 y_0}{r_1 - r_2}$. Therefore, the specific solution is:

$$y(t) := \frac{y_0}{r_1 - r_2} \left(r_1 e^{r_2 t} - r_2 e^{r_1 t} \right).$$

A graph of this solution is given in Figure 7.18. Note that the function is strictly decreasing and never crosses the t-axis. In this case, the oscillations are said to be **overdamped**.

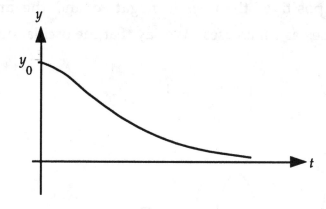

Fig. 7.18

This means that as the spring moves the object towards the origin, the resistance is so strong that the object is stopped "dead in its tracks" without getting there.

There is a third case to consider, when $\rho = \omega$. However, we shall not discuss this here, except to say that the solution resembles case 2.

EXERCISES FOR SECTION 7.5:

1. Find the general solution of each of the following differential equations:

    (a) $y'' - 4y' + 3y = 0$ (b) $y'' + 6y' - 7y = 0$

    (c) $y'' + 4y = 0$ (d) $y'' + 4y' + 8y = 0$

    (e) $y'' - 5y' + 9y = 0$ (f) $y'' - 2y' = 0$

2. For each equation in Exercise 1, state whether the solutions oscillate. If so, what happens to the magnitude of the oscillations as t increases?

3. Find the specific solution to the equation in Exercise 1(a) that satisfies the initial conditions $y(0) = 2, y'(0) = 6$.

4. Find the specific solution to the equation in Exercise 1(c) that satisfies the initial conditions $y(0) = -1, y'(0) = 6$.

5. For what values of k will the solutions of the equation $y'' - 4y' + ky = 0$ oscillate?

6. Suppose $y_1(t) := e^{3t} \cos(2t)$ is a solution of a differential equation of the form $y'' + ay' + by = 0$.

    (a) Write the general solution of the equation.

    (b) Determine a and b.

7. The graph below is a solution to the equation $y'' + ay' + 4y = 0$. What are all the possible values of a for which this could be true?

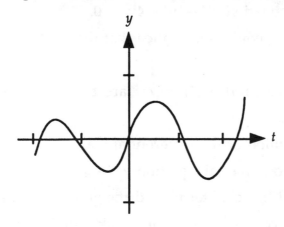

PROBLEMS FOR SECTION 7.5:

1. Verify the values of c_1 and c_2 obtained in both cases of the damped oscillator problem in section 7.5.

2. Suppose we had inadvertently gotten the wrong sign on the resistance term in the differential equation for the damped oscillator; that is, we had written the equation as $y'' - 2py' + \omega^2 y = 0$. Solve this equation (assuming $p < \omega$) and graph the solution for some values of p and ω. Why is the solution absurd?

3. Consider the differential equation $y'' - 2py' + (p^2 + q^2)y = 0$, where p and q are constants.

   (a) Show that $y'' - 6y' + 10y = 0$ is of this form, for some p and q.

   (b) Determine the roots of the characteristic equation of the differential equation in (a).

   (c) More generally, write the characteristic equation for the differential equation $y'' - 2py' + (p^2 + q^2)y = 0$ and show that its roots are $r_1 = p + qi$ and $r_2 = p - qi$.

   (d) Show that $y_1(t) := e^{pt} \cos(qt)$ and $y_2(t) = e^{pt} \sin(qt)$ satisfy the equation.

4. (a) Show that the solution of $y'' + \omega^2 y = 0$ can be expressed as
   $$y = A \sin(\omega t + \alpha), \text{ where } A = \sqrt{c_1^2 + c_2^2} \text{ and } \cos(\alpha) = c_1/A.$$

   (b) Sketch for the case $c_1 = 1, c_2 = 1, \omega = 2$.

   (Note: α is called the **phase angle** of the solution.)

5. Consider the differential equation $y'' - 4y' + 4y = 0$.

   (a) Write the characteristic equation. Notice that the roots are equal ($r_1 = r_2 = 2$).

   (b) Show that $y_1(t) = te^{2t}$ and $y_2(t) = e^{2t}$ are solutions. Are y_1 and y_2 independent?

   (c) Write the general solution of the differential equation.

6. Consider the third order differential equation $y''' - y' = 0$.

   (a) Adapt the methods of this chapter to find the general solution.

   (b) What kind of initial conditions do you think should be specified in order to guarantee a unique solution?

TYU Answers for Section 7.5

1. (a)

(b)

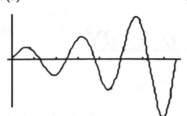

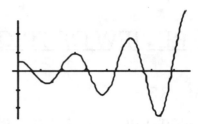

(c)

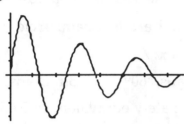

2. (a) $y = c_1 e^{6t} + c_2 e^{-3t}$

(b) $y = e^{2t}(c_1 \cos(3t) + c_2 \sin(3t))$

(c) $y = c_1 \cos(5t) + c_2 \sin(5t)$

(d) $y = c_1 + c_2 e^{-6t}$

3. $y = -1 + 2e^{-6t}$

4. Graph has increasing amplitude.

5. Graph will have decreasing amplitude.

QUESTIONS TO THINK ABOUT

1. Describe the physical spring-mass system and explain the corresponding differential equation:

   (a) in the case in which no friction or air resistance is considered

   (b) in the case in which air resistance is taken into account

2. Discuss the general theory of second-order linear differential equations. Include an explanation of "independent solutions", "general solutions" and "particular solutions".

3. Extend your discussion in question 2 to the specific case in which $y'' + ay' + by = 0$. Discuss the characteristic equation and its relationship to the solutions of the differential equation.

4. Define and discuss the inverse trigonometric functions. Include an explanation of the domain restrictions.

APPENDIX

REVIEW OF TRIGONOMETRY

RADIAN MEASURE

Let θ be a central angle in a circle of radius r. If the length of the arc (piece of the circle) subtended by θ is s, then the radian measure of θ is s/r. For example, if $\theta = 180^\circ$, then the subtended arc is a semicircle, whose length is πr. Therefore, the radian measure of θ is $\pi r/r = \pi$.

Similarly, $360^\circ = 2\pi$ radians, $90^\circ = \pi/2$ radians, $60^\circ = \pi/3$ radians, $45^\circ = \pi/4$ radians, etc. An angle of 1 radian is approximately equivalent to 57.3°.

Throughout this book, angles and arguments of trigonometric functions are measured in radians.

DEFINITIONS OF TRIGONOMETRIC FUNCTIONS

Let $P(x, y)$ be a point on a circle of radius r and let θ be the angle between the positive x-axis and the radius OP (measured counter-clockwise). See Figure 7.19. We define the following 6 trigonometric functions:

$$\sin(\theta) = \frac{y}{r} \qquad \cos(\theta) = \frac{x}{r} \qquad \tan(\theta) = \frac{y}{x}$$
$$\csc(\theta) = \frac{r}{y} \qquad \sec(\theta) = \frac{r}{x} \qquad \cot(\theta) = \frac{x}{y}$$

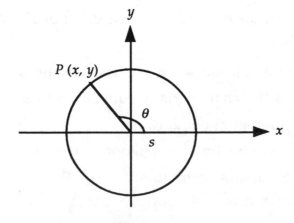

Fig. 7.19

If P is in the first quadrant, then x and y are both positive (r is always positive), so all 6 functions of θ are positive. If P is in the second quadrant, then $x < 0$. Thus, only $\sin(\theta)$ and $\csc(\theta)$ are positive. Similarly, if P is in the third quadrant, then x and y are both negative, so only $\tan(\theta)$ and $\cot(\theta)$ are positive. In the fourth quadrant, only $\cos(\theta)$ and $\sec(\theta)$ are positive.

Some often-used angles and their corresponding trigonometric function values are given in the table below:

θ	0	$\pi/6$	$\pi/4$	$\pi/3$	$\pi/2$	π	$3\pi/2$
$\sin(\theta)$	0	$\frac{1}{2}$	$\frac{\sqrt{2}}{2}$	$\frac{\sqrt{3}}{2}$	1	0	-1
$\cos(\theta)$	1	$\frac{\sqrt{3}}{2}$	$\frac{\sqrt{2}}{2}$	$\frac{1}{2}$	0	-1	0
$\tan(\theta)$	0	$\frac{\sqrt{3}}{3}$	1	$\sqrt{3}$	∞	0	∞

Values of trigonometric functions for angles in other quadrants can be expressed in terms of the reference angle, which is the angle between the radius and the "closest part" of the x-axis. For instance, if θ is in the second quadrant, its reference angle is $\pi - \theta$; if θ is in the third quadrant, its reference angle is $\theta - \pi$; if θ is in the fourth quadrant, its reference angle is $2\pi - \theta$. The trig function of any angle is equal to the same function of its reference angle with the sign adjusted according to the quadrant the angle is in.

EXAMPLE A7.1:

Find (a) $\tan(5\pi/6)$ (b) $\cos(7\pi/4)$

The reference angle for $5\pi/6$ is $\pi - 5\pi/6 = \pi/6$. Since the tangent is negative in the second quadrant, then $\tan(5\pi/6) = -\tan(\pi/6) = \frac{\sqrt{3}}{3}$.

The reference angle for $7\pi/4$ is $2\pi - 7\pi/4 = \pi/4$. Since the cosine is positive in the fourth quadrant, then $\cos(7\pi/4) = \cos(\pi/4) = \frac{\sqrt{2}}{2}$. ◆

TRIGONOMETRIC IDENTITIES

The following statements are true for all values of θ:

1. $\tan(\theta) = \dfrac{\sin(\theta)}{\cos(\theta)}$

2. $\sec(\theta) = \dfrac{1}{\cos(\theta)}$

3. $\csc(\theta) = \dfrac{1}{\sin(\theta)}$

4. $\cot(\theta) = \dfrac{1}{\tan(\theta)} = \dfrac{\cos(\theta)}{\sin(\theta)}$

5. $\sin^2(\theta) + \cos^2(\theta) = 1$

6. $1 + \tan^2(\theta) = \sec^2(\theta)$

7. $1 + \cot^2(\theta) = \csc^2(\theta)$

PROJECT 7.1

SOME TRIGONOMETRIC INTEGRALS

OBJECTIVE: In this project, we will investigate some more complicated integrals involving trigonometric functions. In particular, we will be concerned with integrals of functions of the form $\sin(ax)\sin(bx)$, $\sin(ax)\cos(bx)$ and $\cos(ax)\cos(bx)$.

PROCEDURE:

Part 1: Some simple cases

a. Let $f(x) := \sin(ax)$ and $g(x) := \cos(ax)$, where $a \neq 0$. Find $f'(x)$ and $g'(x)$.

b. Use your results above to determine $\int \sin(ax)\,dx$ and $\int \cos(ax)\,dx$.

c. Recall the addition formula:
$$\sin(x + y) = \sin(x)\cos(y) + \cos(x)\sin(y).$$
Use this to show $\sin(2x) = 2\sin(x)\cos(x)$.

d. Use 1b and 1c to evaluate $\int \sin(x)\cos(x)\,dx$.

e. Evaluate $\int \sin(5x)\cos(5x)\,dx$

f. Evaluate $\int \sin(ax)\cos(ax)\,dx$.

Part 2: The general case

a. Write a formula for $\sin(x - y)$.

b. Use 2a and the addition formula from 1c to show that $\sin(x)\cos(y) = \dfrac{\sin(x + y) + \sin(x - y)}{2}$.

c. Use 2b to find an expression for $\sin(3x)\cos(5x)$ in terms of $\sin(8x)$ and $\sin(2x)$.

d. Modify 2b to obtain a formula for $\sin(ax)\cos(bx)$ in terms of $\sin((a+b)x)$ and $\sin((a-b)x)$.

e. Use 2c or 2d to evaluate $\int \sin(3x)\cos(5x)\,dx$.

f. Use 2d to evaluate $\int \sin(ax)\cos(bx)\,dx$.

g. Starting with the formulas $\cos(x + y) = \cos(x)\cos(y) - \sin(x)\sin(y)$ and $\cos(x - y) = \cos(x)\cos(y) + \sin(x)\sin(y)$, derive formulas for $\cos(ax)\cos(bx)$ and $\sin(ax)\sin(bx)$.

h. Evaluate $\int \sin(3x)\sin(5x)\,dx$ and $\int \cos(3x)\cos(5x)\,dx$.

i. Evaluate $\int \sin(ax)\sin(bx)\,dx$ and $\int \cos(ax)\cos(bx)\,dx$.

Part 3: Some definite integrals

In more advanced mathematics courses, you will learn the following definition: Two functions f and g are said to be **orthogonal** on the interval $[a, b]$ if $\int_a^b f(x)g(x)\,dx = 0$.

a. Consider the set of functions $\{1, \sin(x), \cos(x), \sin(2x), \cos(2x),\ldots\}$.
   Show that any two distinct functions in this set are orthogonal on the interval $[-\pi, \pi]$.

b. Show that no function in this set is orthogonal to itself.

PROJECT 7.2

NON-HOMOGENEOUS DIFFERENTIAL EQUATIONS

OBJECTIVE: A second-order differential equation is said to be **homogeneous** if it can be expressed in the form $\dfrac{d^2y}{dx^2} + p(x)\dfrac{dy}{dx} + q(x)y = 0$. The equations we studied in this chapter are homogeneous. If the right hand side of the equation is a function of x alone--that is, $\dfrac{d^2y}{dx^2} + p(x)\dfrac{dy}{dx} + q(x)y = g(x)$--then the equation is said to be **non-homogeneous**. In this project, we will solve some non-homogenous equations.

PROCEDURE:

Part 1: A little bit of theory of differential equations

It can be shown that the general solution of a non-homogeneous differential equation can be expressed as $y = y_h + y_p$, where y_h is the general solution of the corresponding homogeneous equation--that is, the equation obtained by replacing the right side by 0--and y_p is *any* particular function satisfying the non-homogeneous equation. Let's try an example.

a. Consider the non-homogeneous equation $\dfrac{d^2y}{dx^2} - 5\dfrac{dy}{dx} + 4y = 8$. Write the general solution of the corresponding homogeneous equation-- that is, the equation obtained by replacing whatever is on the right-hand side (in this case, 8) by 0.

b. Show that $y_p = 2$ is a particular solution of the non-homogeneous equation.

c. Write the general solution of the non-homogeneous equation.

d. Determine the specific solution to this equation satisfying the initial conditions $y(0) = 6$ and $y'(0) = 7$.

e. Now consider the equation $\dfrac{d^2y}{dx^2} - 5\dfrac{dy}{dx} + 4y = 2x + 6$. Since the right side is a linear function of x, then the particular solution y_p might be a linear function of x; that is, $y_p = ax + b$, for some a and b. By substituting $y_p = ax + b$ in the differential equation, determine the values of a and b that make this particular solution work.

f. What is the general solution of $\dfrac{d^2y}{dx^2} - 5\dfrac{dy}{dx} + 4y = 2x + 6$?

g. Show that if y_1 and y_2 are solutions of $\dfrac{d^2 y}{dx^2} + p(x)\dfrac{dy}{dx} + q(x)y = g(x)$, then $y_1 - y_2$ is a solution of $\dfrac{d^2 y}{dx^2} + p(x)\dfrac{dy}{dx} + q(x)y = 0$.

Part 2: The forced oscillator equation

A car is equipped with springs that cause the car to oscillate back and forth at some frequency ω that depends on the strength of the spring and the mass of the car. Now suppose we drive the car over a bumpy road that causes the tires to bounce up and down with amplitude B at some frequency $\lambda \neq \omega$. This will cause a disruption in the natural oscillation of the car. In this case, we will say that the oscillations are **forced**. Assuming the car has no shock absorbers to damp the oscillations of the springs, it can be shown that this system can be represented approximately by the differential equation $\dfrac{d^2 y}{dt^2} + \omega^2 y = B \sin(\lambda t)$.

a. Write the general solution of the corresponding homogeneous equation.

b. A particular solution to this equation is $y_p = A \sin(\lambda t)$, where A is a constant. Why is this a plausible choice?

c. Determine $y_p{}'$ and $y_p{}''$ for the function in 2b.

d. Substitute the answers to 2c in the differential equation. By equating coefficients of $\sin(\lambda t)$, show that $A = \dfrac{B}{\omega^2 - \lambda^2}$.

e. Write the general solution of the non-homogeneous equation.

f. Assuming initial conditions $y(0) = y_0$ and $y'(0) = 0$, show that the specific solution of the non-homogenous equation is:

$$y = y_0 \cos(\omega t) - \frac{\lambda B}{\omega(\omega^2 - \lambda^2)} \sin(\omega t) + \frac{B}{\omega^2 - \lambda^2} \sin(\lambda t).$$

Part 3: Further analysis of the forced oscillator

a. Graph the solution if $y_0 = 1$, $\omega = 3$, $\lambda = 2$, $B = 2$. Describe the graph. Is the solution periodic? If so, with what period? What is the maximum amplitude?

b. Repeat 3a with $\lambda = 1$. (The other parameters remain the same.) Give a physical explanation of why this solution is different from the one in 3a. Hint: The fact that ω is a multiple of λ is significant.

c. Repeat 3a, this time with $B = 4$. How does the increase in B change the solution?

PROJECT 7.3

SNELL'S LAW

OBJECTIVE: It is well-known in physics that if a ray of light passes from one medium into another, it is refracted (bent). Try sticking your finger at an angle into a glass of water; if you look at it from the correct viewpoint, it appears that your finger is bending even though it is straight. **Snell's Law** allows us to determine how much the light ray will refract as it passes from one medium to the other. Specifically, it says that if v_1 and v_2 are the velocities of light in the two media, respectively, and if θ_1 and θ_2 are the angles shown in the diagram, then $\dfrac{\sin(\theta_1)}{v_1} = \dfrac{\sin(\theta_2)}{v_2}$. The objective of this project is to prove Snell's Law.

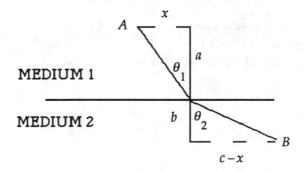

PROCEDURE:
Part 1: A specific example

Suppose $v_1 = 1, v_2 = 1.5, \theta_1 = 30^\circ, a = 4$ and $b = 2$.

a. Use Snell's Law to compute θ_2 to the nearest degree.

b. Compute x and c.

c. Compute the total distance travelled by the light ray as it goes from A to B.

d. Compute the total time required for the ray to travel from A to B.

Part 2: Further investigation

Proof of Snell's Law requires Fermat's principle which states that, when travelling between two points, light follows the path of shortest time.

a. Let $T(x)$ be the total time required for the light to travel from A to B. Referring to the diagram above, show in general (not just for the numbers in Part 1) that

$$T(x) := \frac{\sqrt{x^2 + a^2}}{v_1} + \frac{\sqrt{b^2 + (c - x)^2}}{v_2}.$$

b. Suppose $a = 5, b = 3, c = 7, v_1 = 2$ and $v_2 = 2.5$. Use a computer or graphing calculator to graph $T(x)$.

c. Estimate the value of x that minimizes $T(x)$.

d. Use your answer to 2c to compute θ_1 and θ_2.

e. Show that Snell's Law holds for this data.

Part 3: The proof

a. Compute $T'(x)$, where $T(x)$ is defined in 2a.

b. Show that T has a local minimum if and only if

$$\frac{x}{v_1 \sqrt{x^2 + a^2}} = \frac{c - x}{v_2 \sqrt{b^2 + (c - x)^2}}.$$

c. Show that 3b is equivalent to Snell's Law.

CHAPTER 8

MORE ABOUT INTEGRATION

8.1 INTEGRATION BY SUBSTITUTION

As of now, we can find the derivatives of all algebraic functions and many important transcendental functions. However, our prowess with antiderivatives is much more limited. The goal of this chapter is to expand the number of functions for which we can find antiderivatives.

Before doing so, let's review what we know at this point. We have learned 8 basic formulas:

1. $\displaystyle\int x^n \, dx \; = \; \frac{x^{n+1}}{n+1} \; + \; c, \text{ if } n \neq -1$

2. $\displaystyle\int \frac{1}{x} \, dx \; = \; \ln |x| \; + \; c$

3. $\displaystyle\int e^x \, dx \; = \; e^x + c$

4. $\displaystyle\int \sin(x) \, dx \; = \; -\cos(x) + c$

5. $\displaystyle\int \cos(x) \, dx \; = \; \sin(x) + c$

6. $\displaystyle\int \sec^2(x) \, dx \; = \; \tan(x) + c$

7. $\displaystyle\int \frac{1}{\sqrt{1-x^2}} \, dx \; = \; \arcsin(x) + c$

8. $\displaystyle\int \frac{1}{1+x^2} \, dx \; = \; \arctan(x) + c$

In this section, we will learn how to extend these formulas to allow us to solve many antiderivative problems. The technique we will use is based on Theorem 3.19, the so-called "reverse chain rule". Recall that if F is an antiderivative of f and $u = g(x)$, then

$$D_x^{-1}\left[f(u)\frac{du}{dx}\right] = F(u) + c \qquad \text{or, equivalently,}$$

$$\int f(u)\frac{du}{dx}\,dx = F(u) + c.$$

Each of the Formulas 1 through 8 can be generalized to make use of this theorem. For instance, Formula 1 can be written as:

1'. $\qquad \displaystyle\int u^n \frac{du}{dx}\,dx = \frac{u^{n+1}}{n+1} + c,\ n \neq -1$

while Formula 2 becomes:

2'. $\qquad \displaystyle\int \frac{1}{u}\frac{du}{dx}\,dx = \ln|u| + c,$

where, in each case, u is a function of x.

Similarly, the remaining formulas become:

3'. $\qquad \displaystyle\int e^u \frac{du}{dx}\,dx = e^u + c$

4'. $\qquad \displaystyle\int \sin(u)\frac{du}{dx}\,dx = -\cos(u) + c$

5'. $\qquad \displaystyle\int \cos(u)\frac{du}{dx}\,dx = \sin(u) + c$

6'. $\qquad \displaystyle\int \sec^2(u)\frac{du}{dx}\,dx = \tan(u) + c$

7'. $\qquad \displaystyle\int \frac{1}{\sqrt{1-u^2}}\frac{du}{dx}\,dx = \arcsin(u) + c$

8'. $\qquad \displaystyle\int \frac{1}{1+u^2}\frac{du}{dx}\,dx = \arctan(u) + c$

Depending on the specific function u, these modified formulas can take on different appearances. For example, suppose $u = g(x) := x^2 + 1$. Then $\frac{du}{dx} = 2x$. Substituting in Formula 1' with $n = 2$ gives:

$$\int (x^2 + 1)^2 (2x)\, dx = \frac{(x^2+1)^3}{3} + c .$$

On the other hand, if $u = g(x) := x^3 + 4x$, then $\frac{du}{dx} = 3x^2 + 4$, in which case we have:

$$\int (x^3 + 4x)^2 (3x^2 + 4)\, dx = \frac{(x^3+4x)^3}{3} + c .$$

Similarly, if we let $u = x^2$ and $\frac{du}{dx} = 2x$ in Formula 4', then we have

$$\int 2x\, \sin(x^2)\, dx = -\cos(x^2) + c.$$

Note that you can verify all of these antiderivatives by differentiation, making sure to invoke the chain rule each time.

TEST YOUR UNDERSTANDING

1. Substitute the given function u into the given formula to obtain a correct antiderivative:

(a) Formula 2', $u = 3x + 4$

(b) Formula 3', $u = 4x^2 + 2x$

(c) Formula 7', $u = e^x$

(d) Formula 5', $u = \ln(x)$

2. Does $\displaystyle\int \frac{4x^3}{x^4 + 9}\, dx$ match Formula 2'? If so, what is u?

3. Why doesn't $\int \sin(\sqrt{x})\,dx$ match Formula 4'?

Why, you may reasonably ask, are we doing this? The point is that dissimilar looking integrands may be structurally very much the same. For example, $\int 2x\sqrt{x^2+1}\,dx$ and $\int e^x\sqrt{e^x+4}\,dx$ are both of the form $\int u^{1/2}\frac{du}{dx}\,dx$. In the first case, $u = x^2 + 1$ so that $\frac{du}{dx} = 2x$. In the second case $u = e^x + 4$, so that $\frac{du}{dx} = e^x$.

Our task is to take a complicated integrand and, by a judicious choice of a function u, rewrite it in one of the forms given by Formulas 1' through 8', if possible. In other words, the entire integrand must be expressible in the form $f(u)\frac{du}{dx}\,dx$, where f is a function whose antiderivative we can find. It is *very important* that both $f(u)$ and $\frac{du}{dx}$ be present and that there be no extra terms or factors in the integrand. This method is known as **integration by substitution** and is a very important technique.

EXAMPLE 8.1:

Determine $\int (3x^2 + 1)\sqrt{x^3+x}\,dx$.

We note that $3x^2 + 1$ is the derivative of $x^3 + x$, so this suggests the substitution $u = x^3 + x, \frac{du}{dx} = (3x^2 + 1)$. The antiderivative, in terms of u, is:

$$\int \sqrt{u}\,\frac{du}{dx}\,dx = \int u^{1/2}\frac{du}{dx}\,dx .$$

Now invoking Formula 1' with $n = 1/2$, we have

$$\int u^{1/2}\frac{du}{dx}\,dx = \frac{u^{3/2}}{3/2} + c = \frac{2u^{3/2}}{3} + c$$

Upon substituting for u, we have:

$$\int (3x^2 + 1)\sqrt{x^3+x}\,dx = \frac{2(x^3+x)^{3/2}}{3} + c . \qquad \blacklozenge$$

EXAMPLE 8.2:

Determine $\int x\, e^{x^2/2}\, dx$.

The presence of the $\frac{x^2}{2}$ and a factor x suggests that $u = \frac{x^2}{2}$ is a wise substitution. Then $\frac{du}{dx} = x$ and the antiderivative is of the form

$$\int e^u \frac{du}{dx}\, dx = e^u + c.$$

Therefore, $\int x\, e^{x^2/2}\, dx = e^{x^2/2} + c.$ ◆

EXAMPLE 8.3:

Evaluate $\int 3x^2 \sec^2(x^3)\, dx$.

Here we let $u = x^3$, so that $\frac{du}{dx} = 3x^2$. Then

$$\int 3x^2 \sec^2(x^3)\, dx = \int \sec^2(u)\frac{du}{dx}\, dx$$

$$= \tan(u) + c = \tan(x^3) + c. \quad ◆$$

We can do a bit of notational chicanery to simplify this process somewhat. If we think of $\frac{du}{dx}$ as a fraction, then $\frac{du}{dx}\, dx$ "reduces to" just du. (We did a similar kind of manipulation in Chapter 4, when we "separated the variables" in a differential equation.) So, Formula 1' can be rewritten as $\int u^n\, du = \frac{u^{n+1}}{n+1} + c$, $n \neq -1$, which, of course, is correct. When evaluating an integral that requires a substitution, we will let $u = g(x)$ and $du = g'(x)\, dx$. Thus, in Example 8.3, we would let $u = x^3$, $du = 3x^2\, dx$. Then,

$$\int 3x^2 \sec^2(x^3)\, dx = \int \sec^2(u)\, du = \tan(u) + c = \tan(x^3) + c.$$

EXAMPLE 8.4:

Evaluate $\int \sin^3(x)\cos(x)\, dx$.

Let $u = \sin(x)$, $du = \cos(x)\, dx$. Then

$$\int \sin^3(x)\cos(x)\, dx = \int u^3\, du = \frac{u^4}{4} + c = \frac{\sin^4(x)}{4} + c. \quad ◆$$

TEST YOUR UNDERSTANDING

4. Evaluate (a) $\int 5x^4(x^5 - 9)^7 \, dx$ (b) $\int (1 + \ln(x))^2 \left(\frac{1}{x}\right) dx$.

(c) $\int 3x^2 \cos(x^3 + 1) \, dx$ (d) $\int \cos(x) \, e^{\sin(x)} \, dx$

◻ Suppose the problem in Example 8.3 had been $\int x^2 \sec^2(x^3) \, dx$. The substitution $u = x^3$ does not quite work since $\frac{du}{dx} = 3x^2$ but we only have a factor of x^2. However, by Theorem 3.19,

$$\int x^2 \sec^2(x^3) \, dx = \frac{1}{3} \int 3x^2 \sec^2(x^3) \, dx = \frac{1}{3} \tan(x^3) + c.$$

We see here that the substitution technique can be used even if the integrand cannot be written in one of the forms given by Formulas 1' through 8', provided that the only discrepancy is a constant factor. If any variables are missing, then the substitution will not work. For instance, the substitution $u = x^3$ is inappropriate for the integral $\int x \sec^2(x^3) \, dx$ since $\frac{du}{dx} = 3x^2$ but we only have a factor of x. There is no other substitution that will work for this problem, so this is an antiderivative we can't evaluate.

EXAMPLE 8.5:

Evaluate $\int x^2\sqrt{2x^3+7}\,dx$.

Let $u = 2x^3 + 7,\ du = 6x^2\,dx$. Then

$$\int x^2\sqrt{2x^3+7}\,dx = \frac{1}{6}\int 6x^2\sqrt{2x^3+7}\,dx = \frac{1}{6}\int u^{1/2}\,du$$

$$= \frac{1}{6}\frac{u^{3/2}}{3/2} = \frac{(2x^3+7)^{3/2}}{9} + c\,. \qquad \blacklozenge$$

EXAMPLE 8.6:

Evaluate $\int \frac{x}{x^2-4}\,dx$.

Let $u = x^2 - 4,\ du = 2x\,dx$. Then

$$\int \frac{x}{x^2-4}\,dx = \frac{1}{2}\int \frac{2x}{x^2-4}\,dx = \frac{1}{2}\int \frac{1}{u}\,du$$

$$= \frac{1}{2}\ln(u) + c = \frac{1}{2}\ln(x^2-4) + c\,. \qquad \blacklozenge$$

EXAMPLE 8.7:

Evaluate $\int e^{5x}\,dx$.

Let $u = 5x,\ du = 5\,dx$. Then

$$\int e^{5x}\,dx = \frac{1}{5}\int e^u\,du = \frac{1}{5}e^u = \frac{1}{5}e^{5x} + c\,.$$

This is a result that we had gotten in Chapter 4. $\qquad \blacklozenge$

TEST YOUR UNDERSTANDING

5. Evaluate each of the following integrals:

(a) $\int \sqrt{2x+3}\,dx$ 　　　　　　　　(b) $\int x^3 e^{x^4}\,dx$

(c) $\displaystyle\int \frac{x^2}{x^3+8}\, dx$

(d) $\displaystyle\int \cos^4(x)\sin(x)\, dx$

- -

It is very important to remember that we can only fix things up if a constant factor is missing; if any variables are missing, then our choice of u is incorrect. For instance, suppose the problem in Example 8.6 were to determine $\displaystyle\int \frac{1}{x^2-4}\, dx$. The substitution $u = x^2 - 4$, $du = 2x\, dx$ will not work since there is no x in the original integrand.

We can actually evaluate this integral using an algebraic trick which sometimes is useful for evaluating antiderivatives. See Problem 5 at the end of this section.

On the other hand, if there are extra variables, we *may* be able to transform them into equivalent expressions in u which we can antidifferentiate. The important thing to remember is to transform the *entire integrand* into expressions involving u--do not leave any x's in the integrand.

EXAMPLE 8.8:

Determine $\displaystyle\int x\sqrt{x-4}\, dx$.

Let $u = x - 4$, $du = dx$. You might think that this won't work because of the extra factor of x in the integrand. However, if $u = x - 4$, then $x = u + 4$. So,

$$\int x\sqrt{x-4}\, dx \;=\; \int (u+4)\sqrt{u}\, du \;=\; \int \left(u^{3/2} + 4u^{1/2}\right) du$$

$$= \frac{2}{5}u^{5/2} + \frac{8}{3}u^{3/2} + c$$

$$= \frac{2}{5}(x-4)^{5/2} + \frac{8}{3}(x-4)^{3/2} + c.$$

♦

TEST YOUR UNDERSTANDING

6. Evaluate $\int \dfrac{x}{\sqrt{x-4}}\,dx$.

◻ When using substitution on a definite integral, be careful about the limits of integration. Suppose you want to evaluate $I = \displaystyle\int_0^4 \sqrt{2x+1}\,dx$.

The 0 and 4 are x-values; if you substitute for x, you must transform the limits also.

Let $u = 2x + 1$, $du = 2\,dx$. Then, when $x = 0$, $u = 2(0) + 1 = 1$ and when $x = 4$, $u = 2(4) + 1 = 9$. So,

$$I = \frac{1}{2}\int_1^9 \sqrt{u}\,du = \frac{1}{2}\frac{u^{3/2}}{3/2}\Big|_{u=1}^{u=9} = \frac{1}{3}\left(9^{3/2} - 1^{3/2}\right) = \frac{26}{3} .$$

PLEASE DO NOT WRITE:

$$\int_0^4 \sqrt{2x+1}\,dx = \frac{1}{2}\int_0^4 \sqrt{u}\,du .$$ That's wrong!!

Another way to handle definite integrals by substitution is to take away the limits altogether and first find the antiderivative, expressing it in terms of the original variable. Then substitute the original limits and subtract.

$$\int \sqrt{2x+1}\,dx = \frac{1}{2}\int \sqrt{u}\,du = \frac{1}{3}u^{3/2} = \frac{1}{3}(2x+1)^{3/2}$$

Therefore, $I = \frac{1}{3}(2x+1)^{3/2}\Big|_{x=0}^{x=4} = \frac{26}{3}$.

EXAMPLE 8.9:

Evaluate $\int_1^3 \frac{x^2}{x^3+1}\, dx$.

Let $u = x^3 + 1$, $du = 3x^2\, dx$. When $x = 1$, $u = 2$; when $x = 3$, $u = 28$. Thus,

$$\int_1^3 \frac{x^2}{x^3+1}\, dx = \frac{1}{3}\int_2^{28} \frac{1}{u}\, du = \frac{1}{3}\ln(u)\Big|_{u=2}^{u=28} = \frac{1}{3}[\ln(28) - \ln(2)] = \frac{1}{3}\ln(14). \quad \blacklozenge$$

TEST YOUR UNDERSTANDING

7. Suppose the substitution $u = g(x)$ changes the integral $\int_1^3 f(x)\, dx$ into $\int_a^b h(u)\, du$. What are a and b if $g(x) :=$ (a) $x^2 + 1$ (b) $\sin(\pi x/2)$ (c) $\ln(x)$ (d) $\sqrt{x^2+3}$

AN APPLICATION

In Chapter 3, we studied the behavior of an object thrown with initial velocity v_0 from initial height h. We showed that, in the absence of air resistance, the height of the object at time t is given by the function $y(t) := -\frac{1}{2}gt^2 + v_0 t + h$. In this section, we will consider what happens if we take air resistance into account.

Remember that in the last chapter we hypothesized that air resistance is proportional to the velocity. So, Newton's law implies that:

$$m\frac{d^2y}{dt^2} = -mg - k\frac{dy}{dt},$$

where k is a positive constant of proportionality. (Remember, $\frac{dy}{dt}$ is the velocity.) Note the negative sign is required since the resistive force is opposite to the direction of motion; in other words, if the object is moving upward ($\frac{dy}{dt} > 0$), the air resistance pulls downward (the negative direction).

Upon dividing by m and setting $b = k/m$, we have:

$$\frac{d^2y}{dt^2} = -g - b\frac{dy}{dt}$$

which looks very much like the equations we considered in Chapter 7. Unfortunately, we have a term in this equation that does not contain y or its derivatives. While we've solved some first-order equations with this characteristic by separating variables, this technique won't work here.

To solve this equation, we resort to a trick. Notice that if we let $v = \frac{dy}{dt}$ = object's velocity, then $\frac{dv}{dt} = \frac{d^2y}{dt^2}$ and the equation becomes:

$$\frac{dv}{dt} = -g - bv = -(g + bv),$$

a separable first-order equation. This can be re-written as:

(1) $\dfrac{1}{g + bv}\, dv = -dt\,.$

To integrate the left side of Eq. (1), let $u = g + bv, du = b\, dv$. Upon substituting, we have:

$$\frac{1}{b}\int \frac{1}{u}\, du = -\int dt \qquad \text{whence}$$

(2) $\dfrac{1}{b}\ln(g + bv) = -t + c$

Assume that the object is dropped at time $t = 0$; that is, $v(0) = 0$. Substituting in Eq.(2) gives $c = \frac{1}{b}\ln(g)$. Therefore,

$$\frac{1}{b}\ln(g + bv) - \frac{1}{b}\ln(g) = -t \quad \text{or, equivalently,}$$

$$\frac{g + bv}{g} = e^{-bt}$$

Upon solving for v, we get:

(3) $v = \dfrac{g}{b}\left(e^{-bt} - 1\right).$

A plot of v vs. t for the case $g = 32, b = 2$ is shown in Figure 8.1.

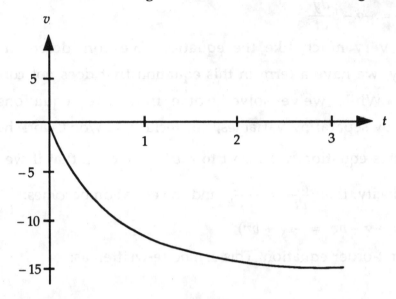

Fig. 8.1

Note that as $t \to \infty$, $e^{-bt} \to 0$, so $v \to -g/b$ which is -16, in this case. This means that after a while, the object virtually stops accelerating because the air resistance becomes strong enough to overcome the gravitational acceleration. The limiting value of v is called the **terminal velocity** of the object. (It is negative because the object is moving downward, the negative direction.)

Once we have an expression for the velocity $v(t) = y'(t)$, we can integrate once more to find the height $y(t)$ at any time t. We leave this for you to do in the problems at the end of the section.

EXERCISES FOR SECTION 8.1:

1. Evaluate the following integrals:

(a) $\int x^2 (x^3 - 1)^4 \, dx$

(b) $\int \frac{x^2}{(x^3 - 1)^2} \, dx$

(c) $\int \frac{4x}{\sqrt{1 + x^2}} \, dx$

(d) $\int 5x \sqrt[3]{1 + x^2} \, dx$

(e) $\int 3(x - 3)^{5/2} \, dx$

(f) $\int \frac{x + 1}{(x^2 + 2x - 3)^2} \, dx$

(g) $\int \left(1 + \frac{1}{t}\right)^3 \left(\frac{1}{t^2}\right) dt$

(h) $\int \frac{\sin(\sqrt{x})}{\sqrt{x}} \, dx$

(i) $\int x^2 \sqrt{x - 3} \, dx$

(j) $\displaystyle\int \frac{\ln(x)}{x}\,dx$ (k) $\displaystyle\int \frac{e^{\sqrt{x+1}}}{\sqrt{x+1}}\,dx$ (l) $\displaystyle\int \frac{x}{\sqrt{1-x^4}}\,dx$

2. Find the equation of the curve $f(x)$ which passes through the point $(0, \frac{4}{3})$, given that $f'(x) := x\sqrt{1-x^2}$.

3. Determine a function f such that $f''(x) := \sqrt{2x-1}$ for all x, $f'(1) = 3$ and $f(1) = 5$.

4. Evaluate:

   (a) $\displaystyle\int_0^{\ln(3)} e^{2x}\,dx$ (b) $\displaystyle\int_1^2 \frac{1}{2x+1}\,dx$ (c) $\displaystyle\int_0^6 \sqrt[3]{4x+3}\,dx$ (d) $\displaystyle\int_{-1}^1 (y+3)(y-4)\,dy$

5. Determine each of the following antiderivatives:

   (a) $\displaystyle\int x\,\cos(x^2)\,dx$ (b) $\displaystyle\int e^t\,\sin(e^t)\,dt$ (c) $\displaystyle\int e^{\tan(x)}\sec^2(x)\,dx$

   (d) $\displaystyle\int \tan^2(x)\,dx$ (e) $\displaystyle\int \frac{\sin(x)}{\sqrt{\cos(x)}}\,dx$ (f) $\displaystyle\int \tan^2(x)\sec^4(x)\,dx$

6. Find the area bounded by the curve $f(x) := x^2 e^{x^3}$ and the x-axis from $x = 0$ to $x = 2$.

7. Find the area bounded by $y = \cos(2x)$ and the x-axis from $x = 0$ to $x = \pi/4$.

8. Find the area bounded by $y = \dfrac{1}{x+2}$, $y = \dfrac{x}{8}$ and the y-axis.

9. Determine a value of k such that the area bounded by $y = x\,\sin(x^2)$ from $x = 0$ to $x = k$ is $1/4$.

10. For what value of n is $\displaystyle\int_0^1 x(1-x^2)^n\,dx = \frac{1}{10}$?

PROBLEMS FOR SECTION 8.1:

1. Show that if f is continuous on $[a, b]$, then
   $$\int_a^b f(a+b-x)\,dx = \int_a^b f(x)\,dx.$$

2. Show that $\displaystyle\int x\sqrt{ax+b}\,dx = \frac{2(3ax-2b)}{15a^2}(ax+b)^{3/2} + c.$

3. Let f be a function defined for all $x > -3$ and having the properties that $f''(x) = \dfrac{1}{\sqrt{x+3}}$ and the tangent to the graph of f at $(6, 1)$ has slope 1. Determine $f(x)$.

4. Integrate Eq. (3) to obtain $y(t)$, the height of the object thrown upward.

5. Determine $\displaystyle\int \frac{1}{x^2-4}\,dx$ using the fact that $\displaystyle\frac{1}{x^2-4} = \frac{1}{4}\left(\frac{1}{x-2} - \frac{1}{x+2}\right)$.

TYU Answers for Section 8.1

1. (a) $\displaystyle\int \frac{3}{3x+4}\,dx = \ln|3x+4| + c$ (b) $\displaystyle\int (8x+2)e^{4x^2+2x}\,dx = e^{4x^2+2x} + c$

   (c) $\displaystyle\int \frac{e^x}{\sqrt{1-e^{2x}}}\,dx = \arcsin(e^x) + c$ (d) $\displaystyle\int \frac{\cos(\ln(x))}{x}\,dx = \sin(\ln(x)) + c$

2. Yes, $u = x^4 + 9$.   3. If $u = \sqrt{x}$, then $\frac{du}{dx} = \frac{1}{2\sqrt{x}}$, which is missing.

4. (a) $\frac{(x^5-9)^8}{8} + c$ (b) $\frac{1}{3}(1+\ln(x))^3 + c$ (c) $\sin(x^3+1) + c$ (d) $e^{\sin(x)} + c$

5. (a) $\frac{1}{3}(2x+3)^{3/2} + c$ (b) $\frac{1}{4}e^{x^4} + c$ (c) $\frac{1}{3}\ln|x^3+8| + c$ (d) $\frac{-1}{5}\cos^5(x) + c$

6. $\frac{2}{3}(x-4)^{3/2} + 8(x-4)^{1/2} + c$ 7. (a) $a = 2, b = 10$ (b) $a = 1, b = -1$

   (c) $a = 0, b = \ln(3)$ (d) $a = 2, b = \sqrt{12}$

8.2 INTEGRATION BY PARTS

While the substitution technique of Section 8.1 greatly expands our capability of finding antiderivatives, there are still many antiderivatives we can't evaluate. For example, suppose we wanted to find the area of a circle of radius r. Let $f(x) := \sqrt{r^2-x^2}$. The region bounded by $y = f(x)$ and the x-axis is a semicircle whose area is given by the definite integral $A = \displaystyle\int_{-r}^{r} \sqrt{r^2-x^2}\,dx$. (To get the area of the circle, just multiply by two.) There is no substitution that will allow us to evaluate this integral. (Try it.)

There are many other techniques that we could develop to help us calculate more antiderivatives. Many calculus books will cover several such methods, each of which applies to a special class of problems. This does not seem like an efficient way of doing things. Furthermore, there are computer programs that can calculate many more antiderivatives than all these techniques put together. Nevertheless, it is still useful to learn some methods of integration. Specifically, we will learn one of the more powerful techniques--integration by parts. Then we will learn to use tables of integrals to help us with many other problems.

⌐ Recall the product rule for derivatives: If f and g are differentiable functions, then:

$$\frac{d}{dx}[f(x)g(x)] = f(x)g'(x) + f'(x)g(x).$$

This can be rewritten (if we don't ask too many questions) as:

$$f(x)g'(x)\,dx = d[f(x)g(x)] - f'(x)g(x)\,dx \quad.$$

Integrating both sides gives:

$$\int f(x)g'(x)\,dx = f(x)g(x) - \int f'(x)g(x)\,dx \quad.$$

Let $u = f(x)$, $v = g(x)$. Then $du = f'(x)\,dx$ and $dv = g'(x)\,dx$. The equation above can then be expressed as:

$$(4) \qquad \int u\,dv = uv - \int v\,du \quad.$$

Eq.(4) is called the **integration by parts** formula.

To make use of this formula, the integrand must be able to be expressed as the product $u\,dv$, where u and v are functions (dv is the derivative of v). There may be many ways in which u and dv can be chosen. However, in order to be useful, two criteria must be met.

1. dv must be easily antidifferentiated so that v can be obtained.

2. $\int v\,du$ must be, in some sense, "simpler" than $\int u\,dv$.

EXAMPLE 8.10:

Determine $\int x\,\sin(x)\,dx$.

The integrand does not match any of the basic forms given in the last section. Let's see if we can use integration by parts.

Let $u = x$, $dv = \sin(x)\,dx$. Then $du = dx$ and $v = -\cos(x)$.

Substituting in the formula gives:

$$\int x \sin(x)\,dx = -x \cos(x) + \int \cos(x)\,dx = -x \cos(x) + \sin(x) + c.$$

Suppose we had made a different choice of parts: $u = \sin(x)$ and $dv = x\,dx$. The first criterion is satisfied since we can integrate dv to get $v = \frac{x^2}{2}$. Then, since $du = \cos(x)\,dx$, we have

$$\int x \sin(x)\,dx = \frac{x^2}{2} \sin(x) - \int \frac{x^2}{2} \cos(x)\,dx.$$

The integral on the right is apparently worse than the original (or at least no easier) and, hence, this choice of parts does not help us.   ◆

EXAMPLE 8.11:

$$\int x e^{2x}\,dx$$

Again, let's try letting $u = x, dv = e^{2x}\,dx$. Then $du = dx$ and $v = \frac{1}{2}e^{2x}$. (We've actually skipped a step here in going from dv to v. There's an implicit substitution, say $z = 2x, dz = 2\,dx$ required. Write out the details, if necessary.)

Substituting in the integration by parts formula gives:

$$\int x e^{2x}\,dx = \frac{1}{2} x e^{2x} - \int \frac{1}{2} e^{2x}\,dx = \frac{1}{2} x e^{2x} - \frac{1}{4} e^{2x} + c.$$ ◆

TEST YOUR UNDERSTANDING

1. Use integration by parts to evaluate:

(a) $\int x \cos(x)\,dx$

(b) $\int x e^{-3x}\,dx$

Sometimes we need to use the integration by parts formula more than once, as the next example illustrates.

EXAMPLE 8.12:

Evaluate $\int x^2 e^x \, dx$

First let $u = x^2$ and $dv = e^x \, dx$. Then $du = 2x \, dx$ and $v = e^x$. Therefore,

$$\int x^2 e^x \, dx = x^2 e^x - 2 \int x e^x \, dx \ .$$

While we still can't evaluate the integral on the right, it is "simpler" than the original. We'll integrate by parts once more.

Let $u = x$, $dv = e^x \, dx$ so that $du = dx$ and $v = e^x$.

Then:

$$\int x^2 e^x \, dx = x^2 e^x - 2(xe^x - \int e^x \, dx\,)$$

$$= x^2 e^x - 2(xe^x - e^x) + c$$

$$= x^2 e^x - 2xe^x + 2e^x + c. \qquad \blacklozenge$$

EXAMPLE 8.13:

$\int x^{3/2} e^x \, dx$

This looks like Example 8.12 so let's try a similar approach. Let $u = x^{3/2}$, $dv = e^x dx$. Then $du = \frac{3}{2} x^{1/2} dx$ and $v = e^x$. Thus,

$$\int x^{3/2} e^x \, dx = x^{3/2} e^x - \int \frac{3}{2} x^{1/2} e^x \, dx \ .$$

We cannot evaluate this last antiderivative and another application of integration by parts (or a different initial choice of parts) doesn't help. (Try it!) So, we're stuck. This is an example of an antiderivative that cannot be evaluated in closed form by any technique. $\qquad \blacklozenge$

EXAMPLE 8.14:

Evaluate $\int x \ln(x)\, dx$.

In view of Examples 8.10 - 8.12, we might be tempted to let $u = x$, $dv = \ln(x)\, dx$. However, we quickly see that, if we do so, we won't be able to find v easily, since we don't know any antiderivatives of $\ln(x)$. So, we'll try $u = \ln(x)$, $dv = x\, dx$. Then $du = \frac{1}{x}\, dx$ and $v = \frac{x^2}{2}$. Hence,

$$\int x \ln(x)\, dx \;=\; \frac{x^2}{2} \ln(x) - \int \frac{x}{2}\, dx \;=\; \frac{x^2}{2} \ln(x) - \frac{x^2}{4} + c. \qquad \blacklozenge$$

EXAMPLE 8.15:

$$\int \ln(x)\, dx$$

At first glance, it might not appear that the integrand is the product of two functions. However, we can think of it as $(1)(\ln(x))\, dx$. For reasons similar to those stated in Example 8.14, we must choose $u = \ln(x)$ and $dv = 1\, dx$. Then $du = \frac{1}{x}\, dx$ and $v = x$. Therefore,

$$\int \ln(x)\, dx \;=\; x \ln(x) - \int x\left(\frac{1}{x}\right) dx \;=\; x \ln(x) - x + c. \qquad \blacklozenge$$

The last example in this section is one in which it appears that integration by parts will lead us in circles (as it sometimes will if we're not careful), but it really does work.

EXAMPLE 8.16:

$$\int e^x \sin(x)\, dx$$

Since we can find an antiderivative of both factors in the integrand, there seems to be no compelling reason to choose one of them over the other for u. So, let's try $u = \sin(x)$ and $dv = e^x\, dx$. Then $du = \cos(x)\, dx$ and $v = e^x$. Then,

$$\int e^x \sin(x)\,dx \;=\; e^x \sin(x) - \int e^x \cos(x)\,dx\,.$$

This doesn't seem to have helped since we have replaced one integral with another which is equally difficult. However, let's persevere.

Let $u = \cos(x)$ and $dv = e^x\,dx$. Then $du = -\sin(x)\,dx$ and $v = e^x$. So,

$$\int e^x \sin(x)\,dx \;=\; e^x \sin(x) - \int e^x \cos(x)\,dx$$

$$= \; e^x \sin(x) - e^x \cos(x) - \int e^x \sin(x)\,dx\,.$$

This is where it appears we are going in circles. But it isn't so. Collecting similar terms gives

$$2\int e^x \sin(x)\,dx \;=\; e^x \sin(x) - e^x \cos(x)$$

or, in other words,

$$\int e^x \sin(x)\,dx \;=\; \frac{e^x \sin(x) - e^x \cos(x)}{2} + c.$$

You can differentiate to show that, indeed, we have found the desired antiderivative. ♦

EXERCISES FOR SECTION 8.2:

1. Evaluate each of the following antiderivatives:

(a) $\displaystyle\int x\, e^{-x}\,dx$ (b) $\displaystyle\int x^2 \cos(x)\,dx$ (c) $\displaystyle\int x\, e^{x^2}\,dx$ (d) $\displaystyle\int x^3 \ln(x)\,dx$

(e) $\displaystyle\int \arcsin(x)\,dx$ (f) $\displaystyle\int x^3 \sin(x^2)\,dx$ (g) $\displaystyle\int x\, \sin(3x)\,dx$ (h) $\displaystyle\int \frac{\ln(x)}{x}\,dx$

(i) $\displaystyle\int \frac{\ln(x)}{x^2}\,dx$ (j) $\displaystyle\int x\, \tan^2(x)\,dx$ (k) $\displaystyle\int x\, \sqrt{x+4}\,dx$ (l) $\displaystyle\int x^3 \sqrt{x^2+4}\,dx$

2. Evaluate $\displaystyle\int_0^{\pi/4} x \cos(2x)\,dx$.

3. Find the area of the region bounded by the graph of $y = 1 + \ln(x)$ and the x-axis over the interval $[1/e, 3]$.

4. Find the area bounded the graph of $y = xe^{-x}$ and the x-axis over the interval $[0, 2]$.

5. In the Problems in Section 7.3, we determined $\int \sin^2(x)\,dx$ by writing $\sin^2(x)$ in terms of $\cos(2x)$. It can also be evaluated using integration by parts. Do so. [Hint: $\sin^2(x) = \sin(x)\sin(x)$.]

6. The velocity of a particle is given by $v(t) := te^{-2t}, t \geq 0$. Find the distance travelled during the time interval $[0, 3]$.

PROBLEMS FOR SECTION 8.2:

1. Use integration by parts and a trigonometric identity to evaluate $\int \sec^3(x)\,dx$.

2. (a) Prove that $\int x^n \sin(x)\,dx = -x^n \cos(x) + n \int x^{n-1} \cos(x)\,dx$.

    (b) Prove that $\int x^n \cos(x)\,dx = x^n \sin(x) - n \int x^{n-1} \sin(x)\,dx$.

    (c) Use (a) and (b) to evaluate $\int x^3 \sin(x)\,dx$.

3. A vase is 6 inches high. The cross-section at a distance x from the bottom is a circle whose radius is $r(x) := 1 + xe^{-x}$ inches. Determine the volume of the vase.

TYU Answers for Section 8.2

1. (a) $x\sin(x) + \cos(x) + c$ (b) $\dfrac{-1}{3} xe^{-3x} - \dfrac{1}{9} e^{-3x} + c$

8.3 INTEGRATION BY TABLES

As we said earlier, we will not bother learning many techniques for finding antiderivatives. Instead, we will concentrate on using a table of integrals. Most calculus books have such tables, some of which contain hundreds of formulas. We have provided an abbreviated table at the end of this chapter.

The key to using tables successfully is pattern recognition. You must take the problem that you are trying to solve and match it to one of the formulas on the table. In some cases, it will be necessary to substitute or integrate by parts first.

First note that the table is divided into sections according to the kind of function involved in the problem. For example, the first section is titled "Forms involving e^u ". So, if your integral has an expression containing e^u, for some function u, then this is where you should look first.

VERY IMPORTANT FACT: Throughout the table, _u always represents a variable,_ possibly a function of some other variable such as x, in which case du must match. Letters such as _a, b, etc. always represent constants_ (in some cases, positive constants). The letter n, often used as an exponent, is usually restricted to be a positive integer.

Some of the formulas in the table (such as #1, 7, 8, etc.) are familiar and are included as a reminder. Of the remaining formulas, some (such as #9, 15, 19, etc.) can be derived easily, either by substitution or integration by parts. Deriving the rest of the formulas is less trivial and, fortunately, we don't have to derive them; we accept them as true or, if we are skeptical, we can always check them by differentiation. We will also lead you through the derivation of some of the more difficult formulas in the Problems at the end of the section.

In addition, some of the formulas (such as #2, 11, 12, etc.) express the given integral in terms of another integral, much as you would get from integration by parts. However, the new integral is in some sense "simpler" than the original. Repeated use of the formula may eventually lead to an integral you can handle. We'll see an example a little later.

Finally, some formulas such as #27 and #28 contain ± signs. This means that if your integral has a + sign, use the + signs throughout, while if your integral has a − sign, use the − signs throughout.

Let's begin by solving a problem from Section 8.1 which we showed led to a function we could not antidifferentiate.

EXAMPLE 8.17:

Determine the area of a circle of radius r.

We showed earlier that the desired area is given by $A = 2\int_{-r}^{r} \sqrt{r^2 - x^2}\, dx$.

In order to do this, we need to evaluate the antiderivative $\int_{-r}^{r} \sqrt{r^2 - x^2}\, dx$.

This comes under the heading "Forms involving $\sqrt{a^2 - u^2}$ ". Formula #31, with $a = r$ and $u = x$ (and, consequently, $du = dx$) is a perfect match. Thus,

$$\int \sqrt{r^2 - x^2}\, dx = \tfrac{1}{2}\left(x\sqrt{r^2 - x^2} + r^2 \arcsin\!\left(\tfrac{x}{r}\right) \right) + c .$$

Then the area

$$A = x\sqrt{r^2 - x^2} + r^2 \arcsin\!\left(\tfrac{x}{r}\right)\Big|_{x\,=\,-r}^{x\,=\,r} = r^2 \arcsin(1) - r^2 \arcsin(-1)$$

$$= r^2\!\left(\tfrac{\pi}{2}\right) - r^2\!\left(\tfrac{-\pi}{2}\right) = \pi r^2 . \text{ (What a surprise!!!)} \qquad \blacklozenge$$

EXAMPLE 8.18:

Evaluate $\int \sin^4(x)\, dx$.

This matches formula #11 with $n = 4$. So,

$$\int \sin^4(x)\, dx = -\frac{\sin^3(x)\cos(x)}{4} + \frac{3}{4}\int \sin^2(x)\, dx .$$

The last term can be evaluated using formula #11 again with $n = 2$ or formula #9 directly. Therefore,

$$\int \sin^4(x)\, dx = -\frac{\sin^3(x)\cos(x)}{4} + \frac{3}{4}\int \sin^2(x)\, dx$$

$$= -\frac{\sin^3(x)\cos(x)}{4} + \frac{3}{8}\left(x - \sin(x)\cos(x)\right) + c . \qquad \blacklozenge$$

EXAMPLE 8.19:

Evaluate $\displaystyle\int \frac{1}{\sqrt{x^2-9}}\, dx$.

Since $x^2 - 9 \neq 9 - x^2$, we have to be careful to pick a formula with the terms in the correct order. Formula #28, with $u = x, du = dx, a = 3$ fits. Hence,

$$\int \frac{1}{\sqrt{x^2-9}}\, dx = \ln |x + \sqrt{x^2-9}| + c. \qquad \blacklozenge$$

EXAMPLE 8.20:

Evaluate $\displaystyle\int e^{2x}\cos(3x)\, dx$.

Although we could use integration by parts to evaluate this integral (it comes out something like Example 8.16), it is easier to use the table. Since the integrand contains an exponential function, we first look in the "forms involving e^u " section of the table, where we see that formula #4 is a perfect match. (Had we not found a match in this section, we might have tried the "Forms involving sin (u) or cos (u)" section.)

Letting $u = x, du = dx, a = 2$ and $b = 3$, we have:

$$\int e^{2x}\cos(3x)\, dx = \frac{e^{2x}}{13}[2\cos(3x) + 3\sin(3x)] + c. \qquad \blacklozenge$$

TEST YOUR UNDERSTANDING

1. Evaluate each of the following:

(a) $\displaystyle\int \tan^3(x)\, dx$ 　　　(b) $\displaystyle\int \frac{1}{\sqrt{x^2-25}}\, dx$ 　　　(c) $\displaystyle\int \frac{1}{\sqrt{25-x^2}}\, dx$

◻ Sometimes we have to make a substitution in order to use the table.

EXAMPLE 8.21:

Evaluate $L = \int_0^1 \sqrt{1 + 4x^2}\, dx$.

Since $1 + 4x^2 = 4x^2 + 1$, then this comes under the heading "Forms involving $\sqrt{u^2 \pm a^2}$ ". (Remember u is the function, a is the constant.) It almost matches formula #27 but we need a substitution.

Let $u = 2x$, $du = 2\, dx$ and $a = 1$. Then

$$\int \sqrt{1 + 4x^2}\, dx = \frac{1}{2} \int \sqrt{1 + u^2}\, du = \frac{1}{4}\left(2x\sqrt{4x^2 + 1} + \ln\left|2x + \sqrt{4x^2 + 1}\right|\right) + c .$$

Therefore, $L = \frac{1}{4}\left(2x\sqrt{4x^2 + 1} + \ln\left|2x + \sqrt{4x^2 + 1}\right|\right)\Big|_0^1$

$$= \frac{1}{4}\left[\left(2\sqrt{5} + \ln\left|2 + \sqrt{5}\right|\right) - \ln(1)\right] \approx 1.47894 \qquad \blacklozenge$$

EXAMPLE 8.22:

Evaluate $\int \dfrac{x^3}{1 + x^2}\, dx$.

Our first inclination is to look at the "Forms involving $a^2 \pm u^2$" section. However, there are no matches in that section. (Formula #25 would work if the numerator were constant, not x^3.) Since the integrand contains a binomial expression of the form $a + bu$, where $u = x^2$, then let's make that substitution and see if we can match a formula from the "Forms involving $a + bu$" section.

Let $u = x^2$, $du = 2x\, dx$, $a = b = 1$. Then $\dfrac{2x^3}{1 + x^2}\, dx =$

$\dfrac{x^2}{1 + x^2}(2x\, dx) = \dfrac{u}{a + bu}\, du$. Now look at formula #21. Except for the factor of 2, we're in business.

So, $\int \dfrac{x^3}{1 + x^2}\, dx = \dfrac{1}{2} \int \dfrac{u}{1 + u}\, du$

$$= \frac{1}{2}\left(u - \ln|1 + u|\right) = \frac{1}{2}\left(x^2 - \ln(1 + x^2)\right) + c . \qquad \blacklozenge$$

You might try Example 8.22 a different way. Let $u = 1 + x^2$ so that $x^2 = u - 1$. See what you get.

It is important to remember that <u>if you make a u-substitution to try to match a formula, then you must also substitute for the corresponding du</u>.

TEST YOUR UNDERSTANDING

    2. Evaluate each of the following:

        (a) $\displaystyle\int \frac{1}{4-9x^2}\, dx$
        (b) $\displaystyle\int \frac{x}{9+4x^4}\, dx$

EXERCISES FOR SECTION 8.3:

1. Evaluate each of the following antiderivatives:

    (a) $\displaystyle\int e^{2x} \sin(3x)\, dx$
    (b) $\displaystyle\int \sqrt{x^2+4}\, dx$
    (c) $\displaystyle\int \frac{x}{(1+4x)^2}\, dx$

    (d) $\displaystyle\int \frac{1}{x(4+x)}\, dx$
    (e) $\displaystyle\int \tan^4(x)\, dx$
    (f) $\displaystyle\int x\sqrt{9-x^4}\, dx$

    (g) $\displaystyle\int \frac{\cos(x)}{1-4\sin^2(x)}\, dx$
    (h) $\displaystyle\int \frac{1}{(x+2)(x+3)}\, dx$
    (i) $\displaystyle\int \frac{e^x}{\sqrt{e^{2x}-1}}\, dx$

    (j) $\displaystyle\int x^3 e^{2x}\, dx$
    (k) $\displaystyle\int \sin(x)\sqrt{\cos^2(x)+4}\, dx$
    (l) $\displaystyle\int \frac{dx}{x+2x^2}$

    (m) $\displaystyle\int \cos^3(x)\, dx$
    (n) $\displaystyle\int x \arcsin(x^2)\, dx$
    (o) $\displaystyle\int \frac{1}{x\sqrt{x^4+16}}\, dx$

2. Verify formula #22 by differentiation.

3. The velocity of a particle is given by $v(t) := e^{-t}\sin(t)$. Find the distance travelled by the particle during the time interval $[0, \pi]$.

4. Write the general solution of the differential equation $\dfrac{dy}{dx} = \sqrt{1+y^2}$.

5. Write the general solution of the differential equation $\dfrac{dy}{dx} = y(1-y)$.

6. Determine the area bounded by $y = \arcsin(x)$, the x-axis over the interval $[0, 1]$.

7. Derive formula #13 by writing $\tan(x) := \dfrac{\sin(x)}{\cos(x)}$.

8. Use a well-known trigonometric identity to derive formula #15.

PROBLEMS FOR SECTION 8.3:

1. Derive formula #11 as follows:

   (a)   Use integration by parts with $u = \sin^{n-1}(x)$ to show that
   $$\int \sin^n(x)\,dx = -\sin^{n-1}(x)\cos(x) + (n-1)\int \sin^{n-2}(x)\cos^2(x)\,dx$$

   (b) Substitute $1 - \sin^2(x)$ for $\cos^2(x)$ in the last integral, expand, collect like terms and simplify.

2. Verify the integration formula

   $$\int \frac{\sqrt{a^2-u^2}}{u}\,du = \sqrt{a^2-u^2} - a\,\ln\!\left(\frac{a+\sqrt{a^2-u^2}}{u}\right) + c$$

3. A boat is located at the point $(r, 0)$ and is attached to a rope r feet long being held by a child standing at the origin. (See diagram.) As the child walks along the y-axis, the boat follows a curved path called a **tractrix**.

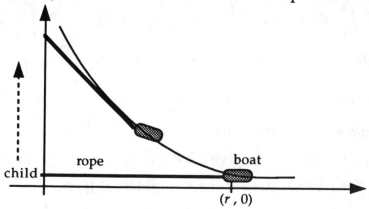

Let $P(x, y)$ be an arbitrary point on the tractrix and let $Q(0, b)$ be the corresponding position of the child on the y-axis.

   (a) Find the slope and length of PQ in terms of x, y and b.

(b) Use the fact that the length of PQ must be r and that its slope is y' to show that the tractrix is defined by the differential equation

$$y' = -\frac{\sqrt{r^2 - x^2}}{x}.$$

(c) Solve this differential equation, subject to the condition that $y = 0$ when $x = r$ thus giving the equation of the tractrix. Use problem 2.

4. (a) Evaluate $\displaystyle\int_0^{\pi/2} \cos(x)\, dx$.

(b) Evaluate $\displaystyle\int_0^{\pi/2} \cos^3(x)\, dx$.

(c) Use formula #12 repeatedly to show that

$$\int_0^{\pi/2} \cos^n(x)\, dx = \left(\frac{2}{3}\right)\left(\frac{4}{5}\right)\left(\frac{6}{7}\right)\cdots\left(\frac{n-1}{n}\right) \text{ if } n \text{ is odd and greater than 1.}$$

(d) $\displaystyle\int_0^{\pi/2} \cos^n(x)\, dx = \left(\frac{1}{2}\right)\left(\frac{3}{4}\right)\left(\frac{5}{6}\right)\cdots\left(\frac{n-1}{n}\right)\left(\frac{\pi}{2}\right)$ if n is even.

These results are known as **Wallis' formulas**.

5. Derive a "reduction" formula similar to #11 or #12 for $\displaystyle\int (\ln(x))^n\, dx$ and use it to evaluate $\displaystyle\int (\ln(x))^3\, dx$.

<u>TYU Answers for Section 8.3</u>

1. (a) $\dfrac{\tan^2(x)}{2} - \ln|\sec(x)| + c$ (b) $\ln\left|x + \sqrt{x^2 - 25}\right| + c$ (c) $\arcsin\left(\frac{x}{5}\right) + c$

2. (a) $\frac{1}{12}\ln\left|\dfrac{3x+2}{3x-2}\right| + c$ (b) $\frac{1}{12}\arctan\left(\dfrac{2x^2}{3}\right) + c$

8.4 ARC LENGTH AND THE HANGING CABLE PROBLEM

A flexible cable of uniform density is suspended between two poles and is allowed to hang under its own weight. (The cable has no other load on it.) We would like to find an equation of the curve formed by the cable.

Introduce a coordinate system with the origin at the lowest point of the cable. Consider the segment OP, where O is the origin and $P(x, y)$ is a point on the cable. (The choice of the origin as one endpoint of the segment makes the derivation of the equation simpler.) The two poles induce a tension in the cable. At O, the tension T_O is horizontal; at P, the tension T_P is in the direction of the tangent to the curve. See Figure 8.2.

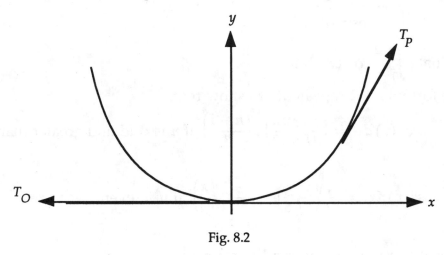

Fig. 8.2

Since the cable is not moving, then all the forces acting on it must cancel out (or, more formally, the forces are in equilibrium). Specifically, the weight of the cable--which pulls downward--must be counterbalanced by the "vertical part" of the tension at P and the tension at O must be counterbalanced by the "horizontal part" of the tension at P. (In physics, quantities such as force that have a direction associated with them are called **vectors**. The horizontal and vertical parts of a vector are called the **components** of the vector. We will discuss vectors in more detail in Chapter 9.)

Let θ be the angle between the tangent to the curve at P and the horizontal and let T_v and T_h be the vertical and horizontal components of T_P, as shown in Figure 8.3. It is easy to imagine that $T_h = T_P \cos(\theta)$ and $T_v = T_P \sin(\theta)$.

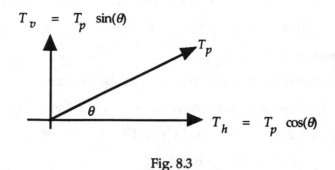

Fig. 8.3

Finally, let w = density of the cable (weight per unit length) and let s = length of the segment OP. Then, the weight of segment OP is ws.

Putting this all together, we have:

(5) $ws = T_p \sin(\theta)$ (vertical forces balance)

(6) $T_O = T_p \cos(\theta)$ (horizontal forces balance)

Divide Eq.(5) by Eq.(6), obtaining:

$\tan(\theta) = ks$

where $k = w/T_O$.

Note that $\tan(\theta) = dy/dx = f'(x)$ and so, at this point, we have:

(7) $\dfrac{dy}{dx} = ks.$

What we need to determine is s, the length of the segment OP.

ARC LENGTH

Recall that in Chapter 6, we wanted to find the area of a region. In some special cases (in particular, rectangles), computing the area was easy. We were able to make use of the idea of a Riemann sum to reduce the problem of finding the area of a region to one of calculating the areas of some rectangles,

page 8 - 29

adding them up and taking the limit. This led to the development of the definite integral which, in some cases, could be evaluated using the Fundamental Theorem of Calculus.

We will do something similar here. Again we rely on something we know how to do. In this case, we know how to find the length of the straight line segment joining any two points on the curve; specifically, the line segment joining (x_1, y_1) and (x_2, y_2) has length

$$s = \sqrt{(x_2 - x_1)^2 + (y_2 - y_1)^2} = \sqrt{(\Delta x)^2 + (\Delta y)^2} = \sqrt{1 + \left(\frac{\Delta y}{\Delta x}\right)^2} \, \Delta x \ .$$

For a straight line, $\dfrac{\Delta y}{\Delta x}$ is a constant, so the length is just the product of two constant quantities.

For an arbitrary curve, $\dfrac{\Delta y}{\Delta x}$ is not constant but depends on the value of x.. So, we need to use calculus. Suppose we want to find the length of the curve $y = f(x)$ from $x = a$ to $x = b$. Let's divide the interval $[a, b]$ into subintervals of length Δx as we did when finding area. This chops the curve up into small segments which, for small Δx, can be considered as straight line segments. (See Figure 8.4). The length of the jth segment is approximately

$$L_j \approx \sqrt{1 + \left(\frac{\Delta y_j}{\Delta x}\right)^2} \, \Delta x \ ,$$

where $\Delta y_j = f(x_{j+1}) - f(x_j)$ is the change in y-values over the jth subinterval.

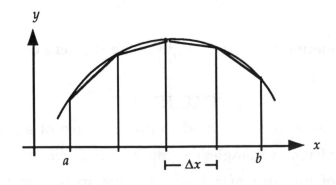

Fig. 8.4

The total length of the curve is approximated by adding up the lengths of the segments:

$$(8) \qquad L \approx \sum_{j=1}^{n} \sqrt{1 + \left(\frac{\Delta y_j}{\Delta x}\right)^2} \; \Delta x \; .$$

To illustrate, suppose we want to find the length of the parabola $y = x^2$ on the interval $[0, 1]$. Using $n = 2$ subintervals, we have $\Delta x = .5$, $x_0 = 0$, $x_1 = .5$, $x_2 = 1$, $y_0 = 0^2 = 0$, $y_1 = .5^2 = .25$ and $y_2 = 1^2 = 1$. Thus, $\Delta y_1 = .25 - 0 = .25$ and $\Delta y_2 = 1 - .25 = .75$. Hence,

$$L_1 \approx (.5)\sqrt{1 + \left(\frac{.25}{.5}\right)^2} = \frac{\sqrt{5}}{4} = .5590 \text{ and}$$

$$L_2 \approx (.5)\sqrt{1 + \left(\frac{.75}{.5}\right)^2} = \frac{\sqrt{13}}{4} = .9014$$

so $L \approx .5590 + .9014 = 1.4604$.

With $n = 5$, we get $L \approx 1.4760$, with $n = 10$, we get $L \approx 1.4782$ and with $n = 20$, we get $L \approx 1.4788$.

Strictly speaking, a Riemann sum is of the form $\sum_{j=1}^{n} f(x_j) \Delta x$ for some suitable function f. The expression in Eq.(8) is not quite of that form due to the presence of the $\frac{\Delta y_j}{\Delta x}$ term. However, we can still get the exact length L by letting $n \to \infty$ (or $\Delta x \to 0$). Note that as $\Delta x \to 0$, $\frac{\Delta y_j}{\Delta x} \to f'(x_j)$. Therefore,

THEOREM 8.1: The length of the curve given by $y = f(x)$ from $(a, f(a))$ to $(b, f(b))$ is given by $L = \int_{a}^{b} \sqrt{1 + (f'(x))^2} \; dx$.

Note: A formal proof of this Theorem requires (you guessed it!) the Mean Value Theorem.

EXAMPLE 8.23:

Find the length of the curve $y = \frac{2}{3} x^{3/2}$ from $x = 0$ to $x = 3$.

Since $\frac{dy}{dx} = x^{1/2}$, then

$$L = \int_0^3 \sqrt{1+x} \, dx = \frac{2(1+x)^{3/2}}{3} \Big|_0^3 = \frac{2(4^{3/2}) - 2(1^{3/2})}{3} = \frac{14}{3}.$$ ◆

EXAMPLE 8.24:

Find the length of the curve $y = x^2$ from $x = 0$ to $x = 1$.

Since $\frac{dy}{dx} = 2x$, then the length of the curve is given by $L = \int_0^1 \sqrt{1+4x^2} \, dx$. This is exactly the same integral we evaluated in Example 8.21, where we found its value to be approximately 1.47894. This is reasonable in view of our earlier calculations.   ◆

TEST YOUR UNDERSTANDING

1. Write an integral that can be used to find the length of the curve $y = \sqrt{x}$ between $x = 0$ and $x = 4$. Do not evaluate the integral.

◻ Now let's go back to the hanging cable problem. By Theorem 8.1, the length of the segment OP is given by

(9) $s = \int_0^x \sqrt{1 + (f'(t))^2} \, dt$.

Hence, Eq. (7) becomes:

(10) $f'(x) = k \int_0^x \sqrt{1 + (f'(t))^2} \, dt$

Differentiating both sides of Eq. (10) with respect to x (invoking Theorem 6.5 on the right) yields:

$$f''(x) = k \sqrt{1 + (f'(x))^2} \, .$$

In other words, the equation of the curve formed by the cable must satisfy the differential equation

$$(11) \qquad \frac{d^2 y}{d x^2} = k \sqrt{1 + \left(\frac{dy}{dx}\right)^2} \, .$$

Although this appears to be a second-order equation, it can easily be changed into a first-order equation, using the same trick as in Section 8.1. Let $v = \frac{dy}{dx}$, whence $\frac{dv}{dx} = \frac{d^2 y}{d x^2}$. The equation becomes

$$(12) \qquad \frac{dv}{dx} = k \sqrt{1 + v^2},$$

which is a first-order separable equation. (This trick works since Eq. (11) has no y in it, only $\frac{dy}{dx}$ and $\frac{d^2 y}{d x^2}$.)

Upon separating variables, we have:

$$\frac{dv}{\sqrt{1 + v^2}} = k \, dx$$

The left side can be integrated with the help of formula #28.

$$\ln(v + \sqrt{1 + v^2}) = kx + c$$

Since the tangent to the curve at O is horizontal, then $v(0) = 0$. This implies $c = \ln(1) = 0$. Therefore,

$$(13) \qquad \ln(v + \sqrt{1 + v^2}) = kx.$$

Solving this for v takes some work, but here we go:

$$v + \sqrt{1 + v^2} = e^{kx}$$

$$\sqrt{1 + v^2} = e^{kx} - v$$

$$1 + v^2 = (e^{kx} - v)^2 = e^{2kx} - 2ve^{kx} + v^2$$

$$2ve^{kx} = e^{2kx} - 1$$

Thus,

$$(14) \qquad v = \frac{e^{2kx} - 1}{2e^{kx}} = \frac{e^{kx} - e^{-kx}}{2}$$

In Problem 6 in Section 7.2 we defined a function called the hyperbolic sine by $\sinh(x) := \dfrac{e^x - e^{-x}}{2}$. Therefore, $v = \sinh(kx)$. Integrating both sides gives:

$$(15) \qquad y = \frac{e^{kx} + e^{-kx}}{2k} = \frac{1}{k}\cosh(kx) + c.$$

The initial condition $y(0) = 0$ implies that $c = -\dfrac{1}{k}$ and, hence, $y = \dfrac{1}{k}\cosh(kx) - \dfrac{1}{k}$.

So, a freely hanging flexible cable suspended from both ends takes the shape of the curve $y = \dfrac{1}{k}\cosh(kx)$, which is called a **catenary**, from the Latin "catena", meaning chain. (The additional $-\dfrac{1}{k}$ term merely translates the curve downward but does not affect the shape, so we omit it.) You might be interested to know that the Gateway Arch in St. Louis (that structure in the background when you watch Cardinals' games) is built in the shape of an inverted catenary.

Note that although the catenary resembles a parabola, they are not the same. Catenaries and parabolas have different geometric properties. However, it can be shown that if the cable is subjected to a uniformly distributed load (such as if it were holding up a bridge), then its shape would indeed be parabolic.

This problem was solved independently in 1691 by Leibniz, Johann Bernoulli (of L'Hopital's Rule fame) and Christiaan Huygens. Huygens, at age 17, showed that Galileo's contention that the shape assumed by a hanging cable is a parabola was incorrect, but it was 45 years before he and the others determined the correct answer. Johann Bernoulli, gloating over his brother James's failure to solve this problem wrote in 1718: "The efforts of my brother were without success. For my part, I was more fortunate, for I found the skill (I say it without boasting; why should I conceal the truth?) to solve it in full...It is true that it cost me study that robbed me of rest for an entire night. It was a great achievement for those days and for the slight age and experience I then had. The next morning, filled with joy, I ran to my brother, who was still struggling with the Gordian knot without getting anywhere, always thinking like Galileo that the catenary was a parabola. Stop! Stop! I say to him, don't torture yourself any more trying to prove the identity of the catenary with the parabola, since it is entirely false."

EXERCISES FOR SECTION 8.4:

1. Write, but do not evaluate, an integral that can be used to find the length of:

(a) $y = x^3$ from $x = -1$ to $x = 1$

(b) $y = \sin(x)$ from $x = 0$ to $x = \pi$

(c) $y = \ln(x)$ from $x = 1$ to $x = 4$

(d) $y = 1/x$ from $x = 2$ to $x = 5$

2. Determine a function f such that the length of $y = f(x)$ from $x = a$ to $x = b$ is given by $L = \int_a^b \sqrt{x^2 + 2x + 2}\, dx$.

3. Approximate the length of $y = \frac{1}{x}$ from $x = 1$ to $x = 3$ by partitioning the interval $[1, 3]$ into 4 subintervals of equal length and computing an appropriate Riemann sum.

PROBLEMS FOR SECTION 8.4:

1. Consider the hanging cable whose shape is given by the equation $y = \dfrac{e^{kx} + e^{-kx}}{2k} = \dfrac{1}{k}\cosh(kx)$. Suppose there are supports at $x = c$ and $x = -c$. Show that the length of the cable is

$$L = \frac{e^{kc} - e^{-kc}}{k} = \frac{2\sinh(kc)}{k}.$$

2. Determine the length of the curve $y = \dfrac{x^2}{4} - \dfrac{\ln(x)}{2}$ from $x = 1$ to $x = 3$.

3. Find the length of the curve defined by $y = \displaystyle\int_{1}^{x} \sqrt{t^2 - 1}\, dt$ from $x = 1$ to $x = 3$.

4. Use an integral to find the length of $y = \dfrac{a}{b}x$ from $x = 0$ to $x = b$. Do you recognize the result?

TYU Answers for Section 8.4

1. $L = \displaystyle\int_{0}^{4} \sqrt{1 + \dfrac{1}{4x}}\, dx$.

QUESTIONS TO THINK ABOUT

1. Explain how you choose an appropriate expression to use for u in a substitution.

2. Explain how you choose an appropriate expressions to use for u and dv in integration by parts.

3. Explain why the substitution process works by relating it to the chain rule.

4. Explain why integration by parts works by relating it to the product rule.

5. Derive the formula for finding the length of the curve $y = f(x)$ for $a \le x \le b$.

TABLE OF INTEGRALS

FORMS INVOLVING e^u:

1. $\int e^u \, du = e^u + c$

2. $\int u^n e^u \, du = u^n e^u - n \int u^{n-1} e^u \, du$

3. $\int e^{au} \sin(bu) \, du = \dfrac{e^{au}}{a^2 + b^2}[a \, \sin(bu) - b \, \cos(bu)] + c$

4. $\int e^{au} \cos(bu) \, du = \dfrac{e^{au}}{a^2 + b^2}[a \, \cos(bu) + b \, \sin(bu)] + c$

FORMS INVOLVING $\ln(u)$:

5. $\int \ln(u) \, du = u \, [\ln(u) - 1] + c$

6. $\int u^n \ln(u) \, du = \dfrac{u^{n+1}}{(n+1)^2}[(n+1) \ln(u) - 1] + c$

FORMS INVOLVING $\sin(u)$ or $\cos(u)$:

7. $\int \sin(u) \, du = -\cos(u) + c$

8. $\int \cos(u) \, du = \sin(u) + c$

9. $\int \sin^2(u) \, du = \frac{1}{2}(u - \sin(u) \cos(u)) + c$

10. $\int \cos^2(u) \, du = \frac{1}{2}(u + \sin(u) \cos(u)) + c$

11. $\int \sin^n(u) \, du = -\dfrac{\sin^{n-1}(u) \cos(u)}{n} + \dfrac{n-1}{n} \int \sin^{n-2}(u) \, du$

12. $\int \cos^n(u) \, du = \dfrac{\cos^{n-1}(u) \sin(u)}{n} + \dfrac{n-1}{n} \int \cos^{n-2}(u) \, du$

FORMS INVOLVING tan (u) or sec (u):

13. $\displaystyle\int \tan(u)\,du \;=\; \ln|\sec(u)| + c$

14. $\displaystyle\int \sec(u)\,du \;=\; \ln|\sec(u) + \tan(u)| + c$

15. $\displaystyle\int \tan^2(u)\,du \;=\; \tan(u) - u + c$

16. $\displaystyle\int \sec^2(u)\,du \;=\; \tan(u) + c$

17. $\displaystyle\int \tan^n(u)\,du \;=\; \frac{\tan^{n-1}(u)}{n-1} - \int \tan^{n-2}(u)\,du$

18. $\displaystyle\int \sec^n(u)\,du \;=\; \frac{\sec^{n-2}(u)\,\tan(u)}{n-1} + \frac{n-2}{n-1}\int \sec^{n-2}(u)\,du$

FORMS INVOLVING arcsin(u) or arctan(u):

19. $\displaystyle\int \arcsin(u)\,du \;=\; u\,\arcsin(u) + \sqrt{1 - u^2} + c$

20. $\displaystyle\int \arctan(u)\,du \;=\; u\,\arctan(u) - \ln\sqrt{1 + u^2} + c$

FORMS INVOLVING $a + bu$:

21. $\displaystyle\int \frac{u}{a+bu}\,du \;=\; \frac{1}{b^2}\left(bu - a\,\ln|a+bu|\right) + c$

22. $\displaystyle\int \frac{u}{(a+bu)^2}\,du \;=\; \frac{1}{b^2}\left(\frac{a}{a+bu} + \ln|a+bu|\right) + c$

23. $\displaystyle\int \frac{1}{u(a+bu)}\,du \;=\; \frac{1}{a}\left(\ln\left|\frac{u}{a+bu}\right|\right) + c$

24. $\displaystyle\int \frac{u^2}{(a+bu)^2}\,du \;=\; \frac{1}{b^3}\left(bu - \frac{a^2}{a+bu} - 2a\,\ln|a+bu|\right) + c$

FORMS INVOLVING $a^2 \pm u^2$, $a > 0$:

25. $\int \dfrac{1}{a^2 + u^2}\, du = \dfrac{1}{a}\left(\arctan\left(\dfrac{u}{a}\right)\right) + c$

26. $\int \dfrac{1}{a^2 - u^2}\, du = \dfrac{1}{2a}\left(\ln\left|\dfrac{u+a}{u-a}\right|\right) + c$

FORMS INVOLVING $\sqrt{u^2 \pm a^2}$:

27. $\int \sqrt{u^2 \pm a^2}\, du = \dfrac{1}{2}\left(u\sqrt{u^2 \pm a^2} \pm a^2 \ln\left|u + \sqrt{u^2 \pm a^2}\right|\right) + c$

28. $\int \dfrac{1}{\sqrt{u^2 \pm a^2}}\, du = \ln\left|u + \sqrt{u^2 \pm a^2}\right| + c$

29. $\int \dfrac{1}{u\sqrt{u^2 + a^2}}\, du = \dfrac{-1}{a}\ln\left|\dfrac{a + \sqrt{u^2 + a^2}}{u}\right| + c$

30. $\int \dfrac{\sqrt{u^2 + a^2}}{u}\, du = \sqrt{u^2 + a^2} - \ln\left|\dfrac{a + \sqrt{u^2 + a^2}}{u}\right| + c$

FORMS INVOLVING $\sqrt{a^2 - u^2}$, $a > 0$:

31. $\int \sqrt{a^2 - u^2}\, du = \dfrac{1}{2}\left(u\sqrt{a^2 - u^2} + a^2 \arcsin\left(\dfrac{u}{a}\right)\right) + c$

32. $\int \dfrac{1}{\sqrt{a^2 - u^2}}\, du = \arcsin\left(\dfrac{u}{a}\right) + c$

PROJECT 8.1

INTEGRATION BY TRIGONOMETRIC SUBSTITUTION

OBJECTIVE: At this point, the only way we can find an antiderivative such as $\int \sqrt{1-x^2}\, dx$ is to look it up on a table of integrals. The purpose of this project is to learn a new technique for finding antiderivatives that will enable us to solve problems in which the integrand contains expressions of the form $a^2 - x^2$, $a^2 + x^2$ or $x^2 - a^2$, where a is a constant.

PROCEDURE:

Part 1: Some warm-up calculations
  a. Suppose $y = 1 - x^2$, and $x = \sin(t)$. Express y in terms of t.
  b. Repeat 1a if $y = 1 + x^2$ and $x = \tan(t)$.
  c. Repeat 1a if $y = x^2 - 1$ and $x = \sec(t)$.
  d. Suppose $x = \sin(t)$, where $0 \le t \le \pi/2$. Express $\cos(t)$, $\tan(t)$ and $\sec(t)$ in terms of x.
  e. Suppose $y = 4 - x^2$. How should we substitute for x in terms of t so that y "simplifies" as in 1a?   What if $y = a^2 - x^2$?   What if $y = a^2 + x^2$?

Part 2: Using trigonometric substitution to evaluate $\int \sqrt{1-x^2}\, dx$
  a. Let $x = \sin(t)$. Express dx in terms of t.
  b. Substitute for x and dx in the integrand and show that
  $$\int \sqrt{1-x^2}\, dx = \int \cos^2(t)\, dt .$$
  c. Evaluate the integral on the right side in 2b. (You may use integration by parts, the tables, or remember a formula from trigonometry.)
  d. Use your answers to 1d to express your answer in terms of x.
  e. Use this same substitution to evaluate $\int \dfrac{1}{(1-x^2)^{3/2}}\, dx$.
  f. Use your answer to 1e and this technique to evaluate $\int \sqrt{4-x^2}\, dx$.

Part 3: More trigonometric substitutions
  a. What substitution might you try to evaluate $\int \sqrt{1+x^2}\, dx$? (Think about 1b.) Try it.
  b. What about $\int \sqrt{x^2-1}\, dx$?

c. In general, what substitution should you try if the integrand contains an expression of the form $a^2 - x^2$? $a^2 + x^2$? $x^2 - a^2$? (This assumes no simpler method works.)

Part 4: A mixed bag of problems

a. $\displaystyle \int \frac{1}{(x^2+1)^{3/2}}\, dx$ b. $\displaystyle \int \frac{x^2}{\sqrt{4-x^2}}\, dx$ c. $\displaystyle \int \frac{dx}{(x^2-16)^{3/2}}$

d. $\displaystyle \int \frac{x}{\sqrt{x^2+9}}\, dx$ e. $\displaystyle \int x^3\sqrt{1-x^2}\, dx$ f. $\displaystyle \int \frac{dx}{(x^2+4)^2}$

PROJECT 8.2

THE BETA FUNCTION

OBJECTIVE: In many applications of mathematics such as probability and statistics, we are required to evaluate an integral of the form $\int_0^1 x^m (1-x)^n \, dx$, where m and n are non-negative numbers. Since the value of the integral depends on m and n, we will denote it $B(m, n)$. The purpose of this project is to derive an explicit formula for $B(m, n)$ in the case where m and n are non-negative integers. $B(m, n)$ is called the **Beta function**.

PROCEDURE:

Part 1: A geometrical interpretation

Let $f(x) := x^m (1-x)^n$.

a. Sketch the graph of f and indicate the region whose area is given by $B(m, n)$ for the cases: (i) $m = 0, n = 1$ (ii) $m = 2, n = 0$ (iii) $m = n = 1$

b. Use a computer or graphing calculator to draw a graph of f for $0 < x < 1$ for each of the following cases: (i) $m = n = 2$ (ii) $m = 3, n = 2$ (iii) $m = 3, n = 4$
What do you observe about the shapes of the graphs? (Hint: You might consider three cases: $m = n, m < n$ and $m > n$.

c. Show that $f'(x) := x^{m-1}(1-x)^{n-1}(m - (m+n)x)$.

d. For what value of x does f attain its maximum value on the interval $[0, 1]$? What is that maximum value?

e. Use a geometric argument to show that $B(m, n) < 1$ for all m, n.

Part 2: A few special cases

a. Evaluate $B(m, n)$ for each of the 3 cases in 1a.

b. Express $B(m, 0)$ in terms of m.

c. Express $B(0, n)$ in terms of n.

d. Use the substitution $u = 1 - x$ to show that $B(m, n) = B(n, m)$.

Part 3: A harder example

a. Use integration by parts with $u = x^3$ to show that $B(3, 6) = \frac{3}{7} B(2, 7)$.
Note that m has decreased by 1 and n has increased by 1. The coefficient $\frac{3}{7}$ is $\frac{m}{n+1}$.

b. Continue in this fashion to show $B(2, 7) = \frac{2}{8}B(1, 8)$. Express $B(3, 6)$ as a multiple of $B(1, 8)$. Again note the pattern.

c. For what value of k is $B(1, 8) = kB(0, 9)$? Express $B(3, 6)$ as a multiple of $B(0, 9)$.

d. Use Part 2c and 3c to determine a numerical value of $B(3, 6)$.

Part 4: Generalization

a. Use integration by parts with $u = x^m$ to show that
$$B(m, n) = \frac{m}{n+1}B(m-1, n+1).$$

b. It follows that $B(m-1, n+1) = \frac{m-1}{n+2}B(m-2, n+2)$. Express $B(m, n)$ in terms of $B(m-2, n+2)$.

c. In a similar manner, express $B(m, n)$ in terms of $B(0, n+m)$.

d. Evaluate $B(0, n+m)$ from Part 2c and substitute in 4c to show that
$$B(m, n) := \frac{m(m-1)(m-2)\ldots(2)(1)}{(n+1)(n+2)(n+3)\ldots(n+m)(n+m+1)}.$$

e. Multiply the numerator and denominator of the expression above by $n!$ to show that $B(m, n) = \frac{n!\,m!}{(n+m+1)!}$.

f. Show that this formula agrees with your calculation in Part 3d.

g. Evaluate $B(5, 7)$ and $B(4, 9)$.

PROJECT 8.3

THE CIRCUMFERENCE OF AN ELLIPSE

OBJECTIVE: Consider the ellipse given by the equation $\frac{x^2}{9} + \frac{y^2}{4} = 1$. The goal of this project is to determine the circumference of this curve using the standard formula for arc length: $L = \int_a^b \sqrt{1 + [f'(x)]^2}\, dx$. We will show that this integral cannot be evaluated in closed form by standard techniques. Rather, we will approximate it numerically.

PROCEDURE:

Part 1: The integral

a. Sketch the ellipse $\frac{x^2}{9} + \frac{y^2}{4} = 1$.

b. Show that the upper half of the ellipse is given by the function
$$f(x) := \frac{2}{3}\sqrt{9 - x^2}.$$

c. Argue that the circumference of the ellipse is $L = 4\int_0^3 \sqrt{1 + [f'(x)]^2}\, dx$.

d. Show that, for this particular ellipse, $L = \frac{4}{3}\int_0^3 \sqrt{\frac{81 - 5x^2}{9 - x^2}}\, dx$.

Convince yourself that no technique we've learned so far will allow us to evaluate this integral.

Part 2: Elliptic integrals

a. Make the substitution $x = 3\sin(\theta)$, $dx = 3\cos(\theta)\, d\theta$ in the integral in 1d and show that $L = 12\int_0^{\pi/2} \sqrt{1 - \frac{5}{9}\sin^2(\theta)}\, d\theta$. Make sure to justify the limits of integration.

Integrals of the form $E(k) = \int_0^{\pi/2} \sqrt{1 - k^2\sin^2(\theta)}\, d\theta$, where $k > 0$ are called **elliptic integrals**. A table of values of $E(k)$ is given at the end of this project. Note that the table does not list points $(k, E(k))$, but rather lists points of the form $(\arcsin(k), E(k))$, with $\arcsin(k)$ measured in degrees. This is the traditional way of tabulating this function. In many applications, the value of k is obtained as the sine of some angle α --$k =$ $\sin(\alpha)$--with the angle often measured in degrees. The tables are set up to make it possible to go straight from the angle α to the value of the integral without needing to determine k.

b. Use the table to determine an approximate value for the integral in 2a. Note that we do not have the value of k given as the sine of a known angle, so you will have to determine $\alpha = \arcsin(k)$ in degrees. You will probably not find a value of α in the table exactly equal to the value you compute. Make the best estimate you can.

c. Use a similar technique to show that the circumference of the ellipse

$$\frac{x^2}{25} + \frac{y^2}{4} = 1 \text{ is given by } L = \frac{4}{5} \int_0^5 \sqrt{\frac{625 - 21x^2}{25 - x^2}}\, dx .$$

d. Use an appropriate substitution and the table to evaluate this integral.

Part 3: A variation

Consider the ellipse $x^2 + \dfrac{y^2}{4} = 1$.

a. Show that $L = 4 \displaystyle\int_0^1 \sqrt{\frac{1 + 3x^2}{1 - x^2}}\, dx .$

b. In view of past experience, we might attempt the substitution $x = \sin(\theta)$. Show that doing so gives $L = 4 \displaystyle\int_0^{\pi/2} \sqrt{1 + 3\sin^2(\theta)}\, d\theta$, which is not of the required form (there is a plus sign under the square root).

c. Instead, let $x = \cos(\theta)$ and show that $L = 4 \displaystyle\int_0^{\pi/2} \sqrt{1 + 3\cos^2(\theta)}\, d\theta .$

d. Replace $\cos^2(\theta)$ by $1 - \sin^2(\theta)$ and evaluate the integral.

VALUES OF ELLIPTIC INTEGRALS

arcsin(k)	E(k)	arcsin(k)	E(k)
0°	1.571	45	1.351
1	1.571	46	1.342
2	1.570	47	1.333
3	1.570	48	1.324
4	1.569	49	1.315
5	1.568	50	1.306
6	1.566	51	1.296

7	1.565	52	1.287
8	1.563	53	1.278
9	1.561	54	1.268
10	1.559	55	1.259
11	1.556	56	1.249
12	1.554	57	1.240
13	1.551	58	1.230
14	1.548	59	1.221
15	1.544	60	1.211
16	1.541	61	1.202
17	1.537	62	1.192
18	1.533	63	1.183
19	1.528	64	1.173
20	1.524	65	1.164
21	1.519	66	1.155
22	1.514	67	1.145
23	1.509	68	1.136
24	1.504	69	1.127
25	1.498	70	1.118
26	1.492	71	1.110
27	1.486	72	1.101
28	1.480	73	1.093
29	1.474	74	1.084
30	1.467	75	1.076
31	1.461	76	1.069
32	1.454	77	1.061
33	1.447	78	1.054
34	1.440	79	1.047
35	1.432	80	1.040
36	1.425	81	1.034
37	1.417	82	1.028
38	1.409	83	1.022
39	1.401	84	1.017
40	1.393	85	1.013
41	1.385	86	1.009
42	1.376	87	1.005
43	1.368	88	1.003
44	1.359	89	1.001
45	1.351	90	1.000

CHAPTER 9

VECTORS AND PARAMETRIC EQUATIONS

9.1 A MOTIVATIONAL EXAMPLE: VECTORS IN THE PLANE

In Chapters 3 and 6 we studied the problem of an object thrown straight up into the air. In particular, we showed that, in the absence of air resistance, the height of the object at time t is given by $s(t) := -\dfrac{gt^2}{2} + v_0 t + h$, where v_0 is the initial velocity, h is the initial height and g is the acceleration due to gravity (32 ft./sec.^{2} or 9.8 m/sec.^{2}). Furthermore, the velocity at time t is given by $v(t) = s'(t) := -gt + v_0$. This problem is simplified by the fact that the motion of the object is confined to one dimension; either it is moving up or it is moving down. Once we decide whether up is the positive or negative direction, then the velocity of the object at any time becomes a signed number. If "up" is the positive direction, then the object is travelling up whenever $v(t)$ is positive; when $v(t)$ is negative, the object is moving down. Furthermore, the speed of the object is just the magnitude (absolute value) of the velocity. It is important to distinguish between velocity and speed: When we talk about the velocity of an object, we must describe its magnitude and direction (e.g., 3 mph upward); when we talk about speed, we specify only the magnitude (3 mph). We can represent the velocity by an arrow pointing either upward or downward. The length of the arrow is the speed.

¤   In this chapter we consider a more complicated version of this problem in which the object can travel in directions other than straight up and down. For example, think about throwing a ball. The ball moves along a curved path through space until it hits the ground. Hence, at any given time, the ball could be moving in any one of infinitely many directions (as opposed to just two). For simplicity, assume that the object's motion is confined to a plane (no curve balls or hooks or slices) so that we now have a two-dimensional problem.

We can still describe the velocity of the object by giving its speed and direction; e.g. 5 mph at an angle of 30° with the horizontal. Geometrically, we can generalize our discussion of velocity in one dimension and represent the velocity by an arrow pointing in the correct direction with the speed as its length.

VECTORS

Quantities such as velocity that are characterized by both direction and magnitude are called **vectors**. As we have seen, we can represent vectors geometrically by arrows. The pointed end of the arrow is called the **head**; the other end is the **tail**. We'll denote vectors by bold-faced letters like *u* or *v* or *w*, although it is also common to use letters with an arrow over it like $\vec{u}$ or $\vec{v}$ or $\vec{w}$.

Note that changing either the direction or magnitude of the vector gives us another vector. For example, the vector *v* in Figure 9.1 has the same direction as the vector *u* but a different magnitude; the vector *w* has the same magnitude as *u* but a different direction. Hence, all 3 are different vectors. On the other hand, the vector *z* has both the same magnitude and direction as *u* and, thus, is the same vector. In other words, sliding a vector in the plane without rotating or stretching it does not change the vector.

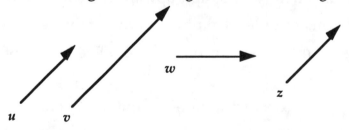

Fig. 9.1

In addition to velocity, there are many other physical quantities such as acceleration and force that may be represented by vectors.

¤ We'll now describe a way of doing calculations with these vectors. For now, we'll show how to multiply a vector by a real number, and how to add two vectors. Later, we'll talk about multiplying two vectors.

Scalar multiplication: Imagine an object travelling in the same direction as *u* but at twice the speed. It seems natural to say the velocity of this object is 2*u*; that is, 2*u* is a vector that has the same direction as *u* but is twice the length of *u*. In general, if *k* is any positive number, then *ku* is a vector that is *k* times as long as *u* but has the same direction as *u*. Similarly, if *k* is a negative number, then *ku* is a vector that is | *k* | times as long as *u* but has the opposite direction from *u*. The number *k* is called a **scalar** because it changes the size (scale) of *u* and the operation we just described is called **scalar multiplication**. See Figure 9.2.

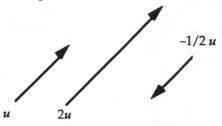

Fig. 9.2

In particular, the vector −*u* is a vector which is the same length as *u* but points in the opposite direction.

Vector addition: Imagine a small motor boat out on a very windy lake. The pilot of the boat keeps the boat pointed in a fixed direction and keeps the speed of the boat constant. Thus, the direction and speed given to the boat by the pilot is some vector *v*. On the other hand, the wind blows the boat in another direction at another speed, so its effect is represented by another vector *u*. What is the actual velocity (speed and direction) of the boat? The answer is the **sum** of the two vectors, *u* + *v*.

Here's how vector addition works. Slide the two vectors without turning them until their tails are together. Think of this configuration as two sides of a parallelogram. Complete the parallelogram. Now the vector *u* + *v* is the arrow that starts at the intersection of *u* and *v* and has its head at the opposite vertex of the parallelogram, as shown in Figure 9.3(a).

Here's another way to think about vectors and vector addition. Think of *v* as a journey in the plane. The journey begins at the tail of *v* and ends at its head. Two journeys are the same if they go in the same direction for the same distance, without respect to where they start. Now $u + v$ is the journey u followed by the journey v. We can represent this by placing the tail of the vector v at the head of the vector u. Then $u + v$ goes from the tail of u to the head of v. Notice, from Figure 9.3(b), that this vector is the same as the one we found in the last paragraph. Notice also that it is the same as $v + u$.

Fig. 9.3(a)   Fig. 9.3(b)

An interesting special case occurs when we add u and $-u$. In terms of the boating example, this means the wind is blowing at the same speed as the boat is travelling but in precisely the opposite direction. If this happens, the boat won't move at all. We can represent this motion by a vector of length 0. Such a vector is called a **zero vector**, denoted by **0**. Thus, we have $u + (-u)$ = **0**. Technically, the zero vector has no direction since it doesn't matter which way you're pointing if you aren't going to move.

At this point, we can also define vector subtraction by $u - v = u + (-v)$. In other words, to subtract v from u, first turn v in the opposite direction and add it to u. This is illustrated in Figure 9.4.

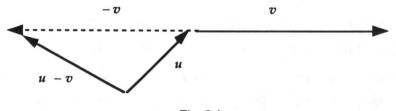

Fig. 9.4

Notice also that $u - v$ is the other diagonal of the parallelogram in Figure 9.3(a)--that is, the vector from the head of v to the head of u.

COMPONENTS OF A VECTOR

Now think again about a ball. As it moves along its trajectory, both its horizontal and vertical positions are changing; that is, part of its motion is in the x-direction and part is in the y-direction. Since, ultimately, we may want to know how far the ball travels before hitting the ground (a question about the horizontal motion) or how high it goes before starting to come down (a question about the vertical motion), then it will be useful to analyze the motion of the ball in terms of its horizontal and vertical components.

Let i be the vector that points in the direction of the positive x-axis and has length 1 and let j be the vector that points in the direction of the positive y-axis and has length 1. We claim that any vector v can be written in the form $v = ai + bj$, where a and b are **scalars**. To see why, construct a right triangle with v as the hypotenuse by drawing a horizontal vector from the tail of v and a vertical vector to the head of v. (See Figure 9.5). The horizontal vector is in the same direction as i (or in the opposite direction) and, hence, is a scalar multiple of i; that is, ai. The vertical vector is in the same direction as j (or in the opposite direction) and must be a scalar multiple of j; that is, bj. Using what we know about vector addition, it follows that $v = ai + bj$. The vectors ai and bj are called the **horizontal and vertical components** of **v**, respectively. The numbers a and b are called the **horizontal and vertical coordinates**.

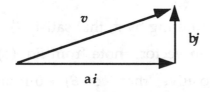

Fig. 9.5

It should be clear that the vector v is uniquely determined by specifying its coordinates. Hence, we will often denote a vector by writing its coordinates in angle brackets; that is, $v = \langle a, b \rangle$. Do not confuse this notation with the ordered pair (a, b), representing a point on the xy-plane. However, if we draw the vector $v = \langle a, b \rangle$ so that its tail is at the origin, then its head will be at the point (a, b). See Figure 9.6.

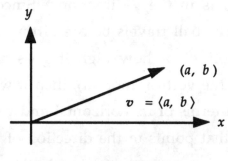

Fig. 9.6

Redraw Figure 9.5 with the arrowheads removed. Then you have a right triangle whose sides are a, b and r, where r is the length of the vector v. Let θ be the angle between v and its horizontal component. Using a bit of trigonometry, we have:

(1) $a = r \cos(\theta)$ and $b = r \sin(\theta)$.

Conversely, if we know a and b, then

(2) $r = \sqrt{a^2 + b^2}$ and $\dfrac{b}{a} = \tan(\theta)$.

There are two angles, differing by π, that satisfy $\dfrac{b}{a} = \tan(\theta)$. To determine which is correct for a given vector, note from Eq. (1) that $\dfrac{a}{r} = \cos(\theta)$. If we agree that r is always positive, then $\cos(\theta) > 0$ if and only if $a > 0$. If $a > 0$ and $b > 0$, then θ must be a first quadrant angle ($0 < \theta < \pi/2$) while if $a > 0$ and $b < 0$, then θ must be a fourth quadrant angle ($-\pi/2 < \theta < 0$). Similarly, if $a < 0$, then $\cos(\theta) < 0$. It follows that if $a < 0$ and $b > 0$, then θ must be a second quadrant angle ($\pi/2 < \theta < \pi$) while if $a < 0$ and $b < 0$, then θ must be a third quadrant angle ($\pi < \theta < 3\pi/2$).

We'll use the symbol $\|v\|$ to denote the **length** (or **magnitude**) of the vector v. Thus, if $v = \langle a, b \rangle$, then, $\|v\| = r = \sqrt{a^2 + b^2}$. Moreover, $\frac{b}{a}$ is the slope of any line parallel to v.

EXAMPLE 9.1:

A vector v has length 8 and makes an angle of $\frac{5\pi}{6}$ with the positive x-axis. Find the horizontal and vertical coordinates of v.

The horizontal coordinate is $a = 8\cos\left(\frac{5\pi}{6}\right) = 8\left(-\frac{\sqrt{3}}{2}\right) = -4\sqrt{3}$; the vertical coordinate is $b = 8\sin\left(\frac{5\pi}{6}\right) = 8\left(\frac{1}{2}\right) = 4$. Thus, we'll write $v = \langle -4\sqrt{3}, 4 \rangle$. ◆

EXAMPLE 9.2:

The vector u has horizontal component $2i$ and vertical component $-2j$; that is $u = \langle 2, -2 \rangle$. How long is u and what angle does u make with the positive x-axis?

The length of u is $\|u\| = \sqrt{2^2 + (-2)^2} = 2\sqrt{2}$ and the tangent of the angle θ that it makes with the positive x-axis is $\frac{-2}{2} = -1$. Therefore θ is either $3\pi/4$ or $-\pi/4$. Since the horizontal coordinate is $2 > 0$, then $\cos(\theta) > 0$ and the angle must be $-\pi/4$.

Note that if $u = \langle -2, 2 \rangle$, $\tan(\theta)$ would still be -1; however, since the horizontal coordinate is negative, then θ would be $3\pi/4$. ◆

TEST YOUR UNDERSTANDING

1. Determine the horizontal and vertical coordinates of a vector v whose length is 12 and which makes an angle of $\pi/3$ with the positive x-axis.

2. Let $w = \langle 5, -10 \rangle$. Determine the length of w. What angle does w make with the positive x-axis?

EXAMPLE 9.3:

A child pulls a wagon with a rope that makes an angle of 30° with the horizontal. If the child exerts a force of 10 Newtons, what is the magnitude of the force in the horizontal direction?

The magnitude of the horizontal component is $a = 10 \cos (30°) = 5\sqrt{3}$ Newtons. ◆

¤ Next, we'd like to see how the coordinates of ku and $u + v$ can be obtained from the coordinates of u and v. First, let's do scalar multiplication. Remember the definition of ku: It is a vector $|k|$ times as long as u and in the same or opposite direction, depending on whether k is positive or negative. We can use similar triangles to see that if a and b are the coordinates of u, then ka and kb are the coordinates of ku. See Figure 9.7.

Fig. 9.7

TEST YOUR UNDERSTANDING

3. What are the coordinates of w if w is twice as long as the vector v in Example 9.1 and w points in the same direction as v?

4. What are the coordinates of z if z is half as long as the vector v in Example 9.1 and z points in the opposite direction from u?

Seeing that the coordinates of $u + v$ are the sums of the coordinates of u and v is only slightly more difficult. The trick here is to use the "tail-to-head" definition of addition (Figure 9.3(b)) rather than our original "sides-of-a-parallelogram" definition. We'll ask you to work out the details in a problem at the end of the section. Here's a theorem summarizing our results:

THEOREM 9.1: Let $u = \langle a_1, b_1 \rangle$ and $v = \langle a_2, b_2 \rangle$. For any real number k,
$$ku = \langle k a_1, k b_1 \rangle \text{ and } u + v = \langle a_1 + a_2, b_1 + b_2 \rangle.$$

Note that the zero vector $0 = u + (-u) = \langle a_1, b_1 \rangle + \langle -a_1, -b_1 \rangle = \langle a_1 - a_1, b_1 - b_1 \rangle = \langle 0, 0 \rangle$. Furthermore, $u - v = \langle a_1 - a_2, b_1 - b_2 \rangle$.

EXAMPLE 9.4:

An airplane is traveling at 400 mph at an angle of 150° with the positive x-axis (i.e. N 60° W in navigator's parlance). The wind is blowing due north at 100 mph. What is resultant speed and direction of the plane?

Let u be the velocity vector of the airplane in still air and let v be the velocity vector of the wind. Then

$$u = \langle 400 \cos (150°), 400 \sin (150°) \rangle = \langle -200\sqrt{3}, 200 \rangle \text{ and}$$

$$v = \langle 100 \cos (90°), 100 \sin (90°) \rangle = \langle 0, 100 \rangle.$$

Therefore, $u + v = \langle -200\sqrt{3}, 300 \rangle$.

The speed of the airplane is $\|u + v\| = \sqrt{(-200\sqrt{3})^2 + (300)^2} = 458.3$ mph; its direction is given by $\tan (\theta) = -\dfrac{300}{200\sqrt{3}}$, from which $\theta = 139.1°$. ◆

❑ Sometimes it is convenient to work with vectors whose length is 1. Such vectors are called **unit vectors**. Given any non-zero vector v, it is possible to create a unit vector u in the same direction as v, simply by dividing v by its length; that is, $u = \dfrac{1}{\|v\|} v$. To see why, note that since u is a positive scalar multiple of v, then u and v are in the same direction. Moreover, $\|u\| = \left\| \dfrac{1}{\|v\|} v \right\| = \dfrac{1}{\|v\|} \|v\| = 1$. Hence, u is a unit vector.

So far, we have talked about adding two vectors and multiplying a vector by a scalar. Next, we'll discuss multiplication of two vectors.

DEFINITION: Let $u = \langle a_1, b_1 \rangle$ and $v = \langle a_2, b_2 \rangle$ be vectors. The **dot product of** u **and** v is defined by $u \cdot v = a_1 a_2 + b_1 b_2$.

NOTE: The dot product of two vectors is a scalar (real number), not another vector.

EXAMPLE 9.5:

Find the dot product of $u = \langle 4, 7 \rangle$ and $v = \langle 3, 2 \rangle$.

By definition, $u \cdot v = (4)(3) + (7)(2) = 26$. ◆

- -

TEST YOUR UNDERSTANDING

5. Find the dot product of $w = \langle 2, -3 \rangle$ and $v = \langle 1, 5 \rangle$.

6. Let $w = \langle 4, 6 \rangle$ and $v = \langle -2, b \rangle$. Find the value of b such that $w \cdot v = 10$.

7. Find a unit vector u in the same direction as $v = \langle 1, 5 \rangle$.

- -

The dot product has many interesting properties. We state a few of them in the following:

THEOREM 9.2:

(a) $u \cdot v = v \cdot u$, for all u and v.

(b) $ku \cdot v = u \cdot kv = k(u \cdot v)$, where k is a scalar.

(c) $u \cdot (v + w) = u \cdot v + u \cdot w$.

(d) $u \cdot u = \|u\|^2$, for all u.

(e) The angle θ between u and v is determined by
$$\cos(\theta) = \frac{u \cdot v}{\|u\| \|v\|} .$$

(f) Non-zero vectors u and v are perpendicular if and only if $u \cdot v = 0$.

PROOF: Parts (a), (b), (c) and (d) are straightforward and we ask you for the proofs in the Problems. To prove part (e), refer to Figure 9.8 below.

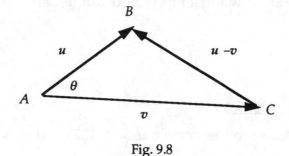

Fig. 9.8

By the Law of Cosines, $\overline{BC}^2 = \overline{AB}^2 + \overline{AC}^2 - 2\,\overline{AC}\,\overline{AB}\cos(\theta)$. In terms of vectors, this means
$$\|u - v\|^2 = \|u\|^2 + \|v\|^2 - 2\|u\|\|v\|\cos(\theta).$$
By part (d), this is equivalent to:
$$(u - v) \cdot (u - v) = u \cdot u + v \cdot v - 2\|u\|\|v\|\cos(\theta)$$
or, by parts (a), (b) and (c)
$$u \cdot u - 2u \cdot v + v \cdot v = u \cdot u + v \cdot v - 2\|u\|\|v\|\cos(\theta).$$
Upon cancelling like terms and solving for $\cos(\theta)$, we get the desired result. Part (f) follows directly from part (e) since two vectors are perpendicular if the angle between them is $\pi/2$. Therefore, $\cos(\pi/2) = \dfrac{u \cdot v}{\|u\|\|v\|} = 0$ from which $u \cdot v = 0$, since neither $\|u\|$ nor $\|v\|$ is 0.

Note that the zero vector $\mathbf{0}$ has no direction, so we can assume that it is perpendicular to *every* vector. This is consistent with Theorem 9.2(f) since $\mathbf{0} \cdot v = 0$ for every v.

Our definition of dot product is not the only one we could have chosen. In a more advanced course, you might see how other dot products can be defined. The only requirements are that parts (a), (b) and (c) of Theorem 9.2 hold and that $u \cdot u \geq 0$ for all u, and $u \cdot u = 0$ if and only if $u = 0$. Once we specify the dot product, then we can define the "length" of a vector by $\|u\| = \sqrt{u \cdot u}$, consistent with part (d). Finally, we can define the cosine of the "angle" between two vectors as in part (e). However, only with the dot product we have defined will the "length" and "angle" correspond to our usual geometric notion of what lengths and angles are. This is a topic for further investigation.

EXERCISES FOR SECTION 9.1:

Exercises 1 through 6 refer to the vectors $u = \langle -4, 7 \rangle$ and $v = \langle 2, 3 \rangle$.

1. Determine the coordinates of:

   (a) $-3u$ (b) $u + v$ (c) $4u - 5v$

2. Determine the length of the vector u.

3. Determine the dot product of the vectors.

4. Find any non-zero vector that is perpendicular to the vector v.

5. Find the angle between u and v.

6. Find a vector parallel to v with a magnitude of 3.

Exercises 7 through 9 refer to the vector $u = \langle 3, b \rangle$.

7. For what value(s) of b will the magnitude of u be 5?

8. Let $v = \langle -12, b \rangle$. For what value(s) of b will u and v be perpendicular?

9. Let $w = \langle 1, 2 \rangle$. For what value(s) of b will $\|u + w\| = \sqrt{32}$?

10. Determine the coordinates of a vector of length 4 that makes an angle of $3\pi/4$ with the x-axis.

11. Determine the coordinates of a vector that goes from the point $(-1, 5)$ towards the point $(3, 3)$.

12. The vector $v = \langle 3, -2 \rangle$ is drawn with its tail at $(1, 4)$. What are the coordinates of its head?

PROBLEMS FOR SECTION 9.1:

1. Prove the second part of Theorem 9.1.

2. Prove parts (a) through (d) of Theorem 9.2.

3. (a) Let $u = \langle t, t + 2 \rangle$ and $v = \langle t + 2, 4 \rangle$. Find all values of t for which u and v are perpendicular.

   (b) Let $u = \langle t, 1 \rangle$ and $v = \langle t + 2, 4 \rangle$. Show that there are no values of t for which u and v are perpendicular.

4. An airplane flies at a constant ground speed of 450 mph due east and encounters a 50 mph wind from the northwest. Find the air speed and direction in which the airplane must fly to maintain its original speed and direction.

5. Let u and v be vectors in the plane. We showed that the angle between the vectors is given by $\cos(\theta) = \dfrac{u \cdot v}{\|u\|\|v\|}$. Use this to prove that $|u \cdot v| \leq \|u\|\|v\|$.

6. Let u and v be vectors of length 1 such that u is perpendicular to v. Let w be any other vector. Show that w can be expressed in the form $w = au + bv$, where $a = u \cdot w$ and $b = v \cdot w$. (The numbers a and b are called the **coordinates of w with respect to u and v**.)

TYU Answers for Section 9.1

   1. $\langle 6, 6\sqrt{3} \rangle$ 2. $\|w\| = 5\sqrt{5}$, $\theta = -63.4°$ or -1.11 radians   3. $w = \langle -8\sqrt{3}, 8 \rangle$
   4. $z = \langle 2\sqrt{3}, -2 \rangle$ 5. -13 6. $b = 3$ 7. $\left\langle \dfrac{1}{\sqrt{26}}, \dfrac{5}{\sqrt{26}} \right\rangle$

9.2 VECTOR FUNCTIONS AND PARAMETRIC EQUATIONS

Let's analyze in more detail the problem of describing the motion of a ball. Suppose we throw the ball from initial height h at an angle θ_0. As it moves, both its horizontal and vertical positions are changing. What we need is some way of studying both quantities at the same time. This is where vectors are useful.

First introduce a coordinate system in which the ground is the x-axis and the y-axis passes through the initial position of the ball. At any given time t, we can represent the position of the ball by a **vector function** $\boldsymbol{r}(t) = \langle x(t), y(t)\rangle$. If we agree to draw the vectors with their tails at the origin, then $x(t)$ and $y(t)$ are the rectangular coordinates of the ball at time t. See Figure 9.9.

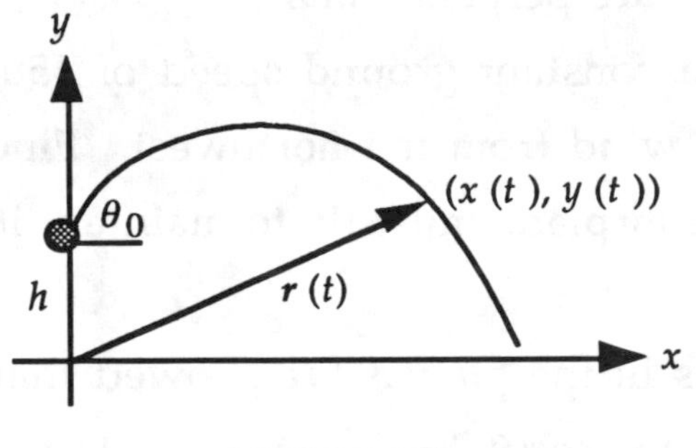

Fig. 9.9

Since the ball starts at height h, then $\boldsymbol{r}(0) = \langle 0, h\rangle$. As the ball travels up towards the maximum height, both $x(t)$ and $y(t)$ are increasing. On the other hand, when the ball is on the way down, $x(t)$ is still increasing, but $y(t)$ is decreasing. We'll explicitly determine $\boldsymbol{r}(t)$ later in this chapter.

□ In general, we can use vector functions to describe curves in the xy-plane. If we draw the vector at any time t with its tail at the origin, then the curve defined by the vector function is the path traversed by the head of the vector. These curves differ from functions of the form $y = f(x)$ that we have studied previously in two respects. First, the curve may or may not be the graph of a function $y = f(x)$ in the usual sense (that is, there may be more than one y-value for a given x). Furthermore, not only do we know what points are on the curve but also at what time the curve passes through these points. This additional information is somewhat like a train schedule: Not only do we know where the train is going but when it will be at each point (at least in theory).

Note: Although in many applications t represents time, this need not be the case. Unless we have a specific reason to think of t as time, we'll just treat it as a variable of which the vector r is a function.

For example, let $r(t) := \langle 2t, t - 1 \rangle$ for $-\infty < t < \infty$. Then $r(0) = \langle 0, -1 \rangle$, $r(1) = \langle 2, 0 \rangle$, $r(2) = \langle 4, 1 \rangle$, etc. We can plot these vectors, obtaining the graph in Figure 9.10(a). It is often more instructive (and less confusing) to plot just the path traversed by the heads of the vectors. This is shown in Figure 9.10(b). Note that we have indicated the direction in which the path is traversed for increasing values of t.

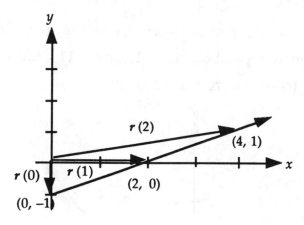

Fig. 9.10(a)

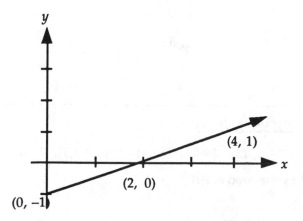

Fig. 9.10(b)

It appears that the curve traversed by $r(t)$ is a straight line. In order to verify that the graph is indeed a straight line, we can try to eliminate t and get an equation for the path in terms of x and y. Since $x = 2t$, then $t = \frac{1}{2}x$. Thus, $y = \frac{1}{2}x - 1$ which is indeed the graph of a straight line. Moreover, since we assume t can take on all real values, then x can take on all real values; hence, we do get the entire line.

EXAMPLE 9.6:

Determine an xy-equation for the curve C represented by the vector function $r(t) := \langle 3t, 9t^2 - 1 \rangle$, for $-\infty < t < \infty$. Sketch the curve, indicating direction of traversal.

Since $9t^2 = (3t)^2 = x^2$, then $y = x^2 - 1$ is the desired equation. The graph of this function is a parabola as in Figure 9.11. Since x increases as t increases, the path is traversed from left to right.

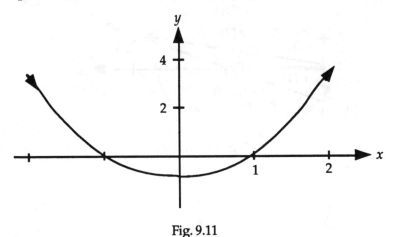

Fig. 9.11

♦

TEST YOUR UNDERSTANDING

1. Let $r(t) := \langle t^3 + t, t^2 \rangle$. Determine $r(-1)$ and $r(3)$. Is the point $(-10, 4)$ on the curve traced by the head of $r(t)$?

2. Let $r(t) := \langle 9t^2 - 1, 3t \rangle$ which is the function in Example 9.6 with the coordinates reversed. Sketch this curve for $-\infty < t < \infty$, indicating the direction of traversal. Write an xy-equation for $r(t)$.

□ There are many different vector functions which trace the same curve. For example, the curve C in Figure 9.11 is traced by the vector function $s(t) := \langle -3t, 9t^2 - 1 \rangle$. (Convince yourself that it is the same curve.) Now, however, x decreases as t increases. Therefore, the curve is traversed from right to left.

The vector function $u(t) := \langle t, t^2 - 1 \rangle$ also traces C, traversed from left to right. Note that $r(0) = u(0) = \langle 0, -1 \rangle$. However, $r(1) = \langle 3, 8 \rangle$ while $u(1) = \langle 1, 0 \rangle$. In fact, $u(3) = \langle 3, 8 \rangle$; hence, u must trace the curve more slowly than r. This suggests that it would be useful to discuss the concept of speed; we shall do so later in this chapter.

The vector function $v(t) := \langle t^2, t^4 - 1 \rangle$ also corresponds to $y = x^2 - 1$ and, hence, we may be tempted to think that v also traces the curve C. However, there is more to it. Since the horizontal component $x = t^2$, then $x \geq 0$ for all t. So the correct xy-equation is $y = x^2 - 1, x \geq 0$ which is just the right half of the parabola. As t goes from $-\infty$ to 0, the head of $v(t)$ comes in from "outer space" along the curve to the point $(0, -1)$, which it reaches when $t = 0$. Then it changes direction and heads back to outer space (as t increases from 0), never to be seen again.

Often curves defined by vector functions are described by writing a pair of equations, one for each component. For example, the vector function v above would be written as $x(t) := t^2$, $y(t) := t^4 - 1$. As t changes, we get a set of ordered pairs $(x(t), y(t))$ which define the curve. There is no underlying notion that the curve is being traced by a "moving vector". The equations are called **parametric equations**; the variable t is called a **parameter**. The two different representations are equivalent. However, in some applications, such as the ball, there is a physical vector quantity (position, velocity, force, etc.) being studied. In this case, the vector function notation is more natural. In other instances, we may have two quantities that depend on some parameter t but don't have an actual interpretation as the components of a vector. If so, we may use the parametric equations definition. We'll see some examples later.

EXAMPLE 9.7:

Suppose $x = \sin(t)$, $y = 2\sin(t)$ are parametric equations of a curve C (that is, C is the curve traced by the vector function $r(t) := \langle \sin(t), 2\sin(t) \rangle$. Determine an xy-equation for C and plot it, indicating the direction of motion.

Clearly, $y = 2x$, which is a line through the origin with a slope of 2. However, since $-1 \leq \sin(t) \leq 1$, then $-1 \leq x \leq 1$. So, we don't get the whole line, only the line segment joining the points $(-1, -2)$ and $(1, 2)$. As t increases, a particle will move back and forth along this segment. See Figure 9.12.

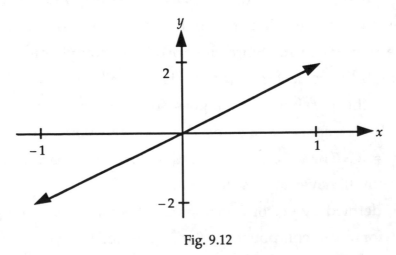

Fig. 9.12

EXAMPLE 9.8:

Let $x = \cos(t), y = \sin(t)$ be parametric equations of a curve C. Find a corresponding xy-equation. Sketch C, being sure to indicate the direction of traversal.

The easiest way to eliminate t is to square both equations and add. (It's okay if you didn't think of this right away--it's a useful trick which you should remember for future problems.) We get

$$x^2 + y^2 = \cos^2(t) + \sin^2(t) = 1.$$

This is the equation of a circle, centered at the origin, with radius of 1, as in Figure 9.13.

Imagine a particle moving around the circle. At $t = 0$, the particle is at the point $(1, 0)$ while at $t = \pi/2$, it is at $(0,1)$. Therefore, the circle is being traversed counter-clockwise. Furthermore, t is the angle between the radius drawn to the point (x, y) and the x-axis.

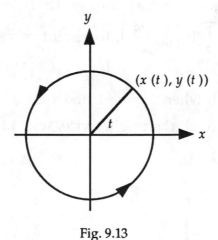

Fig. 9.13

◆

▢ We can use what we learned about sketching curves in Chapter 3 to help us sketch curves represented parametrically. In particular, it may be useful to find the local extrema of both x and y, in terms of t.

EXAMPLE 9.9:

Sketch the curve represented by $x = 1 - t^2$, $y = t^3 - t$, for $-3 \leq t \leq 3$.

By looking at $\frac{dx}{dt} = -2t$, we see that x has a critical point at $t = 0$ which is a local maximum. Thus, x is increasing for $t < 0$ and decreasing for $t > 0$.

By looking at $\frac{dy}{dt} = 3t^2 - 1$, we see that y has two critical points--a local maximum at $t = -\sqrt{\frac{1}{3}}$ and a local minimum at $t = \sqrt{\frac{1}{3}}$. Thus, y is increasing for $t < -\sqrt{\frac{1}{3}}$ and $t > \sqrt{\frac{1}{3}}$ and is decreasing for $-\sqrt{\frac{1}{3}} < t < \sqrt{\frac{1}{3}}$.

We can summarize this in a chart:

	$(-\infty, -\sqrt{1/3}]$	$[-\sqrt{1/3}, 0]$	$[0, \sqrt{1/3}]$	$[\sqrt{1/3}, \infty)$
x	incr.	incr.	decr.	decr.
y	incr.	decr.	decr.	incr.

The point on the curve corresponding to $t = 0$ is $(1, 0)$; the point corresponding to $t = -\sqrt{\frac{1}{3}}$ is $\left(\frac{2}{3}, \frac{-2}{3\sqrt{3}}\right)$; the point corresponding to $t = \sqrt{\frac{1}{3}}$ is $\left(\frac{2}{3}, \frac{2}{3\sqrt{3}}\right)$.

Note also that $x = 0$ when $t = \pm 1$ and that $y = 0$ when $t = 0, \pm 1$. Thus, the curve passes through the origin twice, when $t = 1$ and $t = -1$.

The graph is in Figure 9.14.

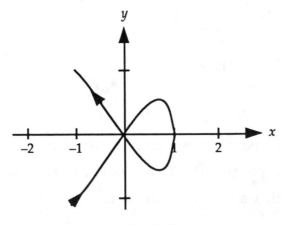

Fig. 9.14

EXAMPLE 9.10:

Sketch the curve represented by $x = e^t + e^{-t}$, $y = e^t - e^{-t}$.

First note that $\frac{dx}{dt} = e^t - e^{-t}$ which is equal to 0 only when $t = 0$. Thus, x has a critical point at $t = 0$. Since $\frac{d^2x}{dt^2} = e^t + e^{-t} > 0$ for all t, then the critical point is a local minimum. The point on the curve corresponding to $t = 0$ is $(2, 0)$.

Furthermore, $\frac{dy}{dt} = e^t + e^{-t} > 0$ for all t. Hence, y is strictly increasing. The graph is in Figure 9.15.

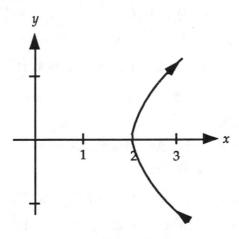

Fig. 9.15

EXERCISES FOR SECTION 9.2:

1. Find an xy-equation for the curve traced by the vector functions or parametric equations given below. Note any domain restrictions.

   (a) $v(t) := \langle 4t,\ 2t^2 + 6 \rangle$ (b) $x = t^3 + 1$, $y = t^2 - 1$

   (c) $x = \sin(t)$, $y = \cos^2(t)$ (d) $r(t) := \langle e^t,\ e^{-2t} \rangle$

   (e) $u(t) := \langle 1/t,\ 1/(t^2 + 1) \rangle$ (f) $x = 2\sin(t)$, $y = 3\cos(t)$

   (g) $r(t) := \langle \sin(2t),\ \cos(2t) \rangle$ (h) $x = \ln(t)$, $y = t^2$

2. Sketch each of the curves in Exercise 1 for $-\infty < t < \infty$. Indicate the direction of traversal.

3. (a) Is $(7, 3)$ on the curve in Exercise 1(b)?

   (b) Is $(0, 1)$ on the curve in Exercise 1(c)?

4. Let $x = t^2 + t$, $y = t^2 - t$ be parametric equations for C. Find a corresponding xy-equation. (Hint: First compute $x + y$, then $x - y$ in terms of t.)

5. Determine a parametric representation for the curve in Exercise 1(f) that is traversed in the opposite direction.

6. Determine the maximum and minimum x- and y-values for each of the following. Then sketch the curve and indicate the direction of traversal.

   (a) $x = 1 - t^2$, $y = t^3 - 3t$ (b) $x = t^4 - 2t^2 + 1$, $y = t^2$

   (c) $x = t - \sin(t)$, $y = 1 - \cos(t)$ (d) $x = t^2 + 4$, $y = (1 - t)^2$

7. Show that the curve $x = e^t + e^{-t}$, $y = e^t - e^{-t}$ in Example 9.10 is equivalent to $x^2 - y^2 = 4$. What kind of curve is this?

PROBLEMS FOR SECTION 9.2:

1. Curve C_1 is given by parametric equations $x = t^2$, $y = 2t^2 + 1$. Curve C_2 is given by $x = t + 1$, $y = t^2 + 3$.

   (a) Determine the points of intersection of C_1 and C_2.

   (b) Assuming t represents time, would particles travelling along C_1 and C_2 collide? Explain.

2. Let C be the curve defined parametrically by $x = \dfrac{1 - t^2}{1 + t^2}$, $y = \dfrac{2t}{1 + t^2}$.

   (a) Show that every point on C is also on the circle $x^2 + y^2 = 1$.

   (b) Describe the motion of a particle along the curve as t increases from 0.

   (c) Is every point on the circle also on C?

3. Determine a vector function that traces a circle of radius 4 centered at $(2, 3)$.

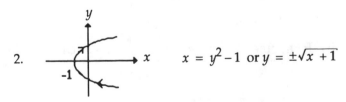

9.3 TANGENT VECTORS, VELOCITY AND ACCELERATION

For scalar functions of the form $y = f(x)$, we defined the derivative $f'(x)$ as the limit of the slope of the secant joining $(x, f(x))$ and $(x + \Delta x, f(x + \Delta x))$ as $\Delta x \to 0$; that is,

$$f'(x) := \lim_{\Delta x \to 0} \frac{f(x + \Delta x) - f(x)}{\Delta x} .$$

Evaluating the derivative at $x = c$ gives the slope of the tangent to the graph of f at the point $(c, f(c))$. We could then use the derivative to describe the direction of the function.

In this section, we will do the same thing for vector functions. Specifically, we will define the derivative $r'(t)$ and interpret it in the context of the direction of the curve traced by $r(t)$.

¤ First, we need to define what we mean by the limit of a vector function. Recall our definition for limit of a scalar function: $\lim_{x \to a} f(x) = L$ if and only if $|f(x) - L|$ can be made arbitrarily close to 0 by taking x sufficiently close to a. For vector functions, we have:

DEFINITION: $\lim_{t \to a} r(t) = w$ if and only if $\|r(t) - w\| \to 0$ as $t \to a$.

By definition, $\|r(t) - w\| = \sqrt{(x(t) - w_1)^2 + (y(t) - w_2)^2}$, where $r(t) = \langle x(t), y(t) \rangle$ and $w = \langle w_1, w_2 \rangle$. Since both terms under the radical sign are always non-negative, then the only way that $\|r(t) - w\|$ can approach 0 is if $x(t)$ approaches w_1 and $y(t)$ approaches w_2. This, in turn, implies that we can compute the limit of a vector function by taking the limit of its coordinates; in other words,

(3) $\lim_{t \to a} \langle x(t), y(t) \rangle = \langle \lim_{t \to a} x(t), \lim_{t \to a} y(t) \rangle$

provided the limits of the individual coordinates exist.

We are now prepared to define the derivative of a vector function.

DEFINITION: The derivative of the vector function $r(t)$ is:

$$r'(t) := \lim_{\Delta t \to 0} \frac{r(t + \Delta t) - r(t)}{\Delta t} \ .$$

Note that $r(t + \Delta t)$ and $r(t)$ are vectors, so $r(t + \Delta t) - r(t)$ is a vector. Since Δt is a scalar, then $\dfrac{r(t + \Delta t) - r(t)}{\Delta t}$ is a vector; hence $r'(t)$ is a vector.

Suppose $r(t) = \langle x(t), y(t) \rangle$. It would be nice if the coordinates of $r'(t)$ were $x'(t)$ and $y'(t)$. The next theorem shows that this is indeed true.

THEOREM 9.3: If $r(t) = \langle x(t), y(t) \rangle$, then $r'(t) = \langle x'(t), y'(t) \rangle$.

PROOF: By definition, $r'(t) := \lim_{\Delta t \to 0} \dfrac{r(t + \Delta t) - r(t)}{\Delta t}$

$$= \lim_{\Delta t \to 0} \frac{\langle x(t + \Delta t), y(t + \Delta t) \rangle - \langle x(t), y(t) \rangle}{\Delta t} \quad \text{by the definition of } r$$

$$= \lim_{\Delta t \to 0} \frac{\langle x(t + \Delta t) - x(t), y(t + \Delta t) - y(t) \rangle}{\Delta t}$$

$$= \lim_{\Delta t \to 0} \left\langle \frac{x(t + \Delta t) - x(t)}{\Delta t}, \frac{y(t + \Delta t) - y(t)}{\Delta t} \right\rangle$$

$$= \left\langle \lim_{\Delta t \to 0} \left(\frac{x(t + \Delta t) - x(t)}{\Delta t} \right), \lim_{\Delta t \to 0} \left(\frac{y(t + \Delta t) - y(t)}{\Delta t} \right) \right\rangle \quad \text{by (3)}$$

$$= \langle x'(t), y'(t) \rangle.$$

TEST YOUR UNDERSTANDING

1. Determine $r'(t)$ if $r(t) := \langle 4t^2, e^{2t} \rangle$.

Many of the rules for differentiation of scalar functions can be adapted to vector functions. For example, the derivative of the sum of two vector functions is equal to the sum of the derivatives. There is a product rule for differentiating the product of a scalar function times a vector function and one for differentiating the dot product of two vector functions. (Of course, there is no quotient rule since we don't define the quotient of vectors.) We will explore some of these rules in the problems at the end of this section.

We can also find antiderivatives of vector functions by finding the antiderivative of each component. For example, if $r(t) := \langle 3t^2, 2t \rangle$, then $\int r(t)\,dt = \langle t^3, t^2 \rangle + c$, where c is a constant vector. Given additional information such as the value of r, for some value of t, we can solve for c.

TEST YOUR UNDERSTANDING

2. Determine $r(t)$ if $r'(t) := \langle e^t, e^{2t} \rangle$, and $r(0) = \langle 2, 5/2 \rangle$.

¤ The next question to consider is, what is the geometric interpretation of $r'(t)$? Figure 9.16 shows the vectors $r(t)$, $r(t + \Delta t)$ and $r(t + \Delta t) - r(t)$.

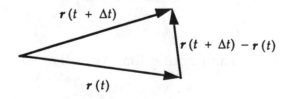

Fig. 9.16

Thus, $r(t + \Delta t) - r(t)$ is a vector in the same direction as the secant line joining the points $(x(t + \Delta t), y(t + \Delta t))$ and $(x(t), y(t))$. Dividing by Δt does not change the direction of a vector (only its magnitude), so $\dfrac{r(t + \Delta t) - r(t)}{\Delta t}$ is also in the same direction as the secant line. By letting $\Delta t \to 0$, the secant line approaches the tangent line and, hence, <u>$r'(t)$ is a vector parallel to the tangent to the curve traced by $r(t)$</u>. Moreover, it points in the direction in which a particle moving along the curve is headed. See Figure 9.17.

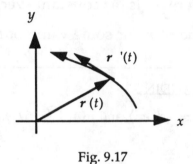

Fig. 9.17

There is a connection between the tangent vector $r'(t)$ and the derivative $\dfrac{dy}{dx}$. Let $\Delta y = y(t + \Delta t) - y(t)$ and $\Delta x = x(t + \Delta t) - x(t)$. Then,

$$\frac{\Delta y}{\Delta x} = \frac{y(t + \Delta t) - y(t)}{x(t + \Delta t) - x(t)} = \frac{\dfrac{y(t + \Delta t) - y(t)}{\Delta t}}{\dfrac{x(t + \Delta t) - x(t)}{\Delta t}} .$$

Upon taking limits as $\Delta t \to 0$ and noting that $\Delta x \to 0$ as $\Delta t \to 0$, we have:

$$\lim_{\Delta t \to 0} \frac{\Delta y}{\Delta x} = \frac{\displaystyle\lim_{\Delta t \to 0} \frac{y(t + \Delta t) - y(t)}{\Delta t}}{\displaystyle\lim_{\Delta t \to 0} \frac{x(t + \Delta t) - x(t)}{\Delta t}} .$$

In other words,

$$\frac{dy}{dx} = \frac{dy/dt}{dx/dt} = \frac{y'(t)}{x'(t)}.$$

Warning: Do not confuse the direction of the curve with the direction in which it is being traversed. Saying that "y is an increasing function of x" still means that, as we move from left to right along the x-axis, the y-values get bigger. This is independent of the direction in which the curve is being traced by the vector.

¤ We showed in Chapter 3 that if $r(t)$ is the position of a particle (moving in one dimension), then $r'(t) = v(t)$ is the instantaneous velocity. The same thing is true here.

THEOREM 9.4: If $r(t)$ is a vector function representing the position of an object at time t, then the tangent vector $v(t) = r'(t)$ is the velocity function.

Moreover, if we define speed to be the magnitude of the velocity, then we have the following:

THEOREM 9.5: The speed of an object moving along the curve traced by the vector function $r(t)$ is given by $v(t) = \|r'(t)\| = \sqrt{\left(\frac{dx}{dt}\right)^2 + \left(\frac{dy}{dt}\right)^2}$.

(The "v" is the Greek letter "nu", as in "What's v with you?")

EXAMPLE 9.11:

Determine the velocity and speed of a particle whose position is given by $r(t) := \langle \cos(t), \sin(t) \rangle$.

By Theorem 9.4, $v(t) := \langle -\sin(t), \cos(t) \rangle$

By Theorem 9.5, $v(t) := \sqrt{\left(\frac{dx}{dt}\right)^2 + \left(\frac{dy}{dt}\right)^2} = \sqrt{(-\sin(t))^2 + (\cos(t))^2}$
$$= \sqrt{\sin^2(t) + \cos^2(t)} = 1. \qquad \blacklozenge$$

Note that in Example 9.11 the speed is constant for all t. This does not usually happen; it is more likely that the speed will vary with time.

EXAMPLE 9.12:

Find the speed of a particle moving along the curve defined parametrically by $x = t^2$, $y = 2t + 1$ at the point $(4, 5)$.

$$v(t) := \sqrt{\left(\frac{dx}{dt}\right)^2 + \left(\frac{dy}{dt}\right)^2} = \sqrt{(2t)^2 + 2^2} = 2\sqrt{t^2 + 1}.$$

The particle is at the point $(4, 5)$ when $t = 2$; hence $v(2) = 2\sqrt{5}$. ◆

EXAMPLE 9.13:

The velocity of a particle is given by $v(t) := \langle 3t^2 + 1, 4t^3 - 3 \rangle$. If the position of the particle at time $t = 1$ is given by the vector $\langle 2, 1 \rangle$, determine its position as a function of time.

Since $v(t) = r'(t)$, then $r(t) = \int v(t)\,dt := \langle t^3 + t, t^4 - 3t \rangle + c$. Therefore, $r(1) = \langle 2, -2 \rangle + c = \langle 2, 1 \rangle$, implying $c = \langle 0, 3 \rangle$. Therefore, $r(t) := \langle t^3 + t, t^4 - 3t + 3 \rangle$. ◆

TEST YOUR UNDERSTANDING

3. What is the speed of the particle moving along the curve in Example 9.12 at the point $(1, -1)$?

4. Determine the velocity, $v(t)$, and speed, $v(t)$, for the vector function $r(t) := \langle e^t, e^{2t} \rangle$.

Now that we have its speed, we can determine how far the particle moves along the curve during the time interval $[a, b]$. We know that if the particle moved in a straight line at constant speed, then its distance would be the product of the speed and the length of the time interval. Since the speed need not be constant in this case, things are not so simple. However, we can recall similar situations in Chapter 6 in which we used Riemann sums and integrals to find the "product" of non-constant quantities (e.g. area = length × variable height; work = variable force × distance, etc.).

Specifically, let's partition the time interval $[a, b]$ into n small sub-intervals of length Δt and let ΔL_j be the length of the segment of the curve traversed by the particle during the time interval $[t_{j-1}, t_j]$. Assume the speed is a constant $v(t_j)$ during the subinterval. Therefore, $\Delta L_j = v(t_j) \Delta t$.

To get the total length of the curve, we add up the lengths of all the little segments and then let $n \to \infty$. That is, $L = \lim\limits_{n \to \infty} \sum\limits_{j=1}^{n} v(t_j) \Delta t$. Using an argument similar to the ones we used in Chapter 6, the limit of the summation defines a definite integral. Therefore:

THEOREM 9.6: The length of the curve traced by the vector function $r(t) = \langle x(t), y(t) \rangle$ over the time interval $[a, b]$ is given by $L = \int_a^b v(t)\, dt$, where $v(t)$ is the speed of the particle at time t.

Note: Theorem 9.6 is valid only if no part of C is retraced as t goes from a to b.

EXAMPLE 9.14:

Find the distance travelled by a particle moving along the curve in Example 9.12 during the time interval $[0, 2]$.

Since $v(t) := 2\sqrt{t^2 + 1}$, then $L = \int_0^2 2\sqrt{t^2 + 1}\, dt$. Using formula #27 from the table of integrals, we have

$$L = t\sqrt{t^2+1} + \ln\left|t + \sqrt{t^2+1}\right| \Big|_{t=0}^{t=2} = 2\sqrt{5} + \ln(2+\sqrt{5}) \approx 5.91 .$$ ◆

TEST YOUR UNDERSTANDING

    5. Write an integral which represents the distance travelled by the particle in TYU 4 during the time interval [0, 3]. Do not evaluate this integral.

ACCELERATION AND CURVATURE

Now that we've talked about velocity and speed, our next task is to talk about **acceleration**. In Chapter 3, we noted that acceleration is the derivative of the velocity. We'll note the same thing here; that is, the acceleration $a(t)$ $= v'(t) = r''(t) = \left\langle \dfrac{d^2x}{dt^2}, \dfrac{d^2y}{dt^2} \right\rangle$.

We can use an argument similar to the one we used for velocity to give a geometrical interpretation of the acceleration vector. Figure 9.18(a) shows the curve defined by $r(t)$ and the tangent vectors $v(t + \Delta t)$ and $v(t)$. In Figure 9.18(b), we translate $v(t + \Delta t)$ so that it shares a tail with $v(t)$ and also include the difference $v(t + \Delta t) - v(t)$. (We've also maginified them a bit for clarity.)

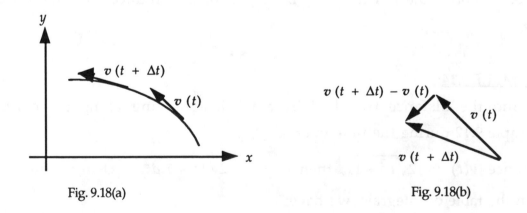

Fig. 9.18(a)   Fig. 9.18(b)

Note that $v(t + \Delta t) - v(t)$ is pointed toward the inside of the curve which means that $a(t)$ will be pointed in that direction as well. Newton's second law of motion says that the force $F = ma$. Since m is a scalar, then F is a vector pointing in the same direction as a. Thus, in our picture, the force must be pointed in the direction that the curve bends which explains why, looked at from another point of view, the curve is bent in that direction.

EXAMPLE 9.15:

Let $r(t) := \langle \cos(t), \sin(t) \rangle$ as in Example 9.11. Show that $a(t)$ is perpendicular to $v(t)$.

$v(t) := \langle -\sin(t), \cos(t) \rangle$ and $a(t) := \langle -\cos(t), -\sin(t) \rangle$. The dot product of these is $v \cdot a = (-\sin(t))(-\cos(t)) + (\cos(t))(-\sin(t)) = 0$. So, the vectors are perpendicular. ◆

It is unusual for the velocity and acceleration vectors to be perpendicular as in Example 9.15. The reason this happens here is that, as we showed in Example 9.11, the speed is constant; that is, $v(t)$ has the same magnitude for all t. In the problems at the end of this section we will ask you to show that the velocity and acceleration vectors are perpendicular whenever the speed is constant.

EXAMPLE 9.16:

Let $r(t) := \langle 3t^2, 4t^2 + 5 \rangle$. Show that $a(t)$ is parallel to $v(t)$.

$v(t) := \langle 6t, 8t \rangle$ and $a(t) := \langle 6, 8 \rangle$. Thus, $v(t) = t\, a(t)$, a scalar multiple of $a(t)$. Hence, they are parallel. ◆

It is equally unusual for the velocity and the acceleration to parallel as in Example 9.16. The reason this happens is that the motion is in a straight line. Notice that if $x(t) := 3t^2$ and $y(t) := 4t^2 + 5$, then $y = \frac{4}{3}x + 5$. However, the speed $v(t) := 10t$ is not constant. In general, if the speed changes but the direction of the velocity remains the same, then the acceleration is parallel to the velocity.

◻ As we said earlier, $a(t) = \langle x''(t), y''(t) \rangle$ so that $x''(t)i$ and $y''(t)j$ are the horizontal and vertical components of $a(t)$. While these are easy to compute, they aren't particularly useful. Imagine that you are driving along a winding road. When you accelerate, a force pushes you back in your seat; when you brake, one throws you forward. As you turn, you are pushed from one side or the other. Thus, the total force acting upon you is the sum of two components, one in the direction of motion and one perpendicular to the direction of motion. Since force is just a scalar multiple of acceleration, then the acceleration $a(t)$ can also be decomposed into two components, one parallel to the velocity vector and one perpendicular to the velocity vector. Let T be a vector of length 1 parallel to $v(t)$ and N be a vector of length 1 obtained by rotating T 90° counterclockwise. (T and N are called the **unit tangent and unit normal** vectors, respectively.) Then we can write

$$a(t) = a_T T + a_N N.$$

The coordinate a_T can be interpreted as a measure of how much the speed is changing while a_N measures how much the direction is changing (i.e., how much the curve is bent).

In Example 9.15, we showed that the velocity and acceleration vectors are perpendicular. Thus, $a(t)$ is parallel to N and perpendicular to T. This means there is no acceleration in the direction of motion (the speed is constant). Thus, the tangential coordinate $a_T = 0$. Conversely, in Example 9.16, we showed that the velocity and acceleration vectors are parallel. The motion is in a straight line so there is no change of direction. This means the normal coordinate $a_N = 0$.

More generally, consider the curve pictured in Figure 9.19. The acceleration $a(t)$ is expressed as the sum of two vectors $a_T T$ and $a_N N$. Note that the tangential component $a_T T$ is in the same direction as T; hence, the coordinate a_T would be positive. Conversely, the normal component $a_N N$ is in the opposite direction as N; hence the coordinate a_N would be negative.

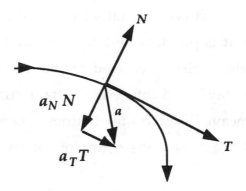

Fig. 9.19

Once T and N are determined, a_T and a_N can be computed rather easily. Although we won't go into the details here, it turns out that $a_T = \dfrac{d\,v}{dt}$, the rate of change of the speed, and a_N is proportional to $[v(t)]^2$ which explains why you have to slow down when you go around a curve, lest you slide off the road.

Now imagine you come to a curve in the road. If the curve is sharp (or tight), then the force pushing you to the side will be much greater than it would be if the curve were gradual. This suggests that it might be useful to quantify the "amount of bending" in a curve. One way to do this is by a number called the **curvature**, denoted by κ (the Greek letter "kappa"). Curvature can be thought of as follows: If your steering wheel is turned to the right, then the curvature is negative; if it is turned to the left, the curvature is positive. The more tightly the wheel is turned, the greater the curvature (in absolute value). Thus, for example, a circle of radius 3 traversed counterclockwise will have a constant, positive curvature while one of radius 3 traversed clockwise will have a negative curvature. Furthermore, a circle of radius 3 has greater curvature than one of radius 5. The curve in Figure 9.19, traversed in the indicated direction, has negative curvature also. It turns out that a_N is proportional to κ which explains why you have to slow down more on sharp curves than on gradual curves. (Actually, $a_N = \kappa v^2$, which is consistent with our earlier statements.) This is a topic for further investigation.

Note that we are using curvature, rather than concavity, to describe how curves are bent. While it is possible to define concavity, it could cause some confusion. For example, a circle centered at the origin, which we agree is always "bent the same way" (and thus has constant curvature) is concave up on the top half and concave down on the bottom. Somehow, this is not very satisfying and we shall not pursue the notion of concavity further here.

SOLUTION OF THE BALL PROBLEM

We are now in a position to solve the problem posed earlier in this chapter of describing the motion of a ball thrown into the air with initial velocity $v_0 = \langle v_0 \cos(\theta_0), v_0 \sin(\theta_0)\rangle$, where $v_0 = \|v_0\|$ is the initial speed and θ_0 is the initial angle. Assuming the only force acting on the ball is gravity, which pulls downward, then the acceleration vector at time t is

$$a(t) := \langle 0, -g\rangle.$$

Integrating both sides gives:

$$v(t) := \langle 0, -gt\rangle + c,$$

where c is a constant vector. Substituting $t = 0$ implies $c = v_0$ so

$$v(t) := \langle 0, -gt\rangle + \langle v_0 \cos(\theta_0), v_0 \sin(\theta_0)\rangle$$
$$= \langle v_0 \cos(\theta_0), -gt + v_0 \sin(\theta_0)\rangle.$$

Integrating once more gives:

$$r(t) := \langle (v_0 \cos(\theta_0))t, -\frac{gt^2}{2} + (v_0 \sin(\theta_0))t\rangle + c.$$

If the object initially is at height h above the ground, then $c = \langle 0, h\rangle$ and, finally,

$$r(t) := \langle (v_0 \cos(\theta_0))t, -\frac{gt^2}{2} + (v_0 \sin(\theta_0))t + h\rangle.$$

In other words, the horizontal position (relative to the starting point) of the object at time t is given by

(4) $x(t) := (v_0 \cos(\theta_0))t,$

and the vertical position (height above the ground) is given by

(5) $\qquad y(t) := -\dfrac{g t^2}{2} + (v_0 \sin(\theta_0))t + h.$

EXAMPLE 9.17:

Suppose the ball is thrown from a height of 3 ft. with initial velocity 64 ft./sec. at an angle of $\pi/6$. How far downrange will the ball travel before hitting the ground and what is the maximum altitude it attains?

We are given $h = 3$, $v_0 = 64$ and $\theta_0 = \pi/6$. Using $g = 32$ ft./sec.^{2} and since $\sin(\pi/6) = 1/2$, we get

$\qquad y(t) := -16t^2 + 32t + 3.$

To find out when the ball hits the ground, set $y(t) = 0$ and solve for t. Using the quadratic formula, we get $t = \dfrac{-32 \pm \sqrt{1216}}{-32}$ which is either 2.09 or – 0.09. We take the positive root of the equation $t = 2.09$.

The distance travelled is $x(2.09) = (2.09)(64)(\cos(\pi/6)) = 115.8$ ft.

The maximum altitude occurs when $y(t)$ is a maximum. Using the techniques of Chapters 3 and 5, we set $y'(t) = 0$. Here $y'(t) := -32t + 32$, so $y'(t) = 0$ when $t = 1$. Convince yourself that this is the global maximum; hence, we conclude that the maximum altitude attained by the ball is $y(1) = 19$ ft. ◆

Although we know the altitude and distance downrange at any time t, we do not know the actual trajectory followed by the object. We can determine this by expressing y explicitly in terms of x.

To do so, simply solve Eq.(4) for t obtaining $t = \dfrac{x}{v_0 \cos(\theta_0)}$. Now substituting in Eq.(5) gives

(6) $\qquad y = ax^2 + bx + h,$

where $a = \dfrac{-g}{2v_0^2\cos^2(\theta_0)} < 0$ and $b = \tan(\theta_0) > 0$. This is a concave downward parabola. The vertex of the parabola--i.e, the maximum height attained by the ball--occurs at $y = h - \dfrac{b^2}{4a} = h + \dfrac{v_0^2\sin^2(\theta_0)}{2g}$. The corresponding x-value is $x = \dfrac{-b}{2a} = \dfrac{v_0^2\sin(\theta_0)\cos(\theta_0)}{g}$.

A graph for the case $h = 25$, $v_0 = 20$, $\theta_0 = \pi/6$ is given in Figure 9.20.

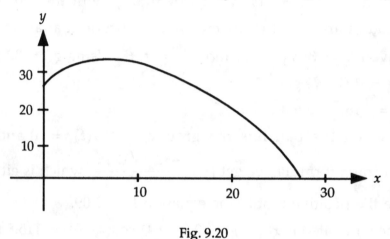

Fig. 9.20

The maximum height is $y = 31.25$ feet occurring when $x \approx 5.4$ ft. Note that $x \approx 28$ when $y = 0$. This means the ball travelled approximately 28 ft. before hitting the ground.

Note that had we just considered Eq.(6) by itself, we would know the trajectory and, consequently, the maximum height and range. We would not, however, be able to tell how long it takes for the ball to hit the ground or at what time the ball is 10 feet off the ground. That information comes from Eqs.(4) and (5).

EXERCISES FOR SECTION 9.3:

1. Let $r(t) := \langle t - \sin(t), 1 - \cos(t) \rangle$. Determine

    (a) $v(t)$ (b) $a(t)$ (c) the speed at $t = \pi/2$

2. Let $r(t) := \langle e^{2t}, e^t \rangle$. Determine the acceleration at time $t = \ln(2)$.

3. A particle moves along the curve defined by $x = t^2 - 4, y = 9 - t^2$.

    (a) Determine the speed of the particle at time t.

    (b) Determine the length of the curve from $(-4, 9)$ to $(5, 0)$.

4. Let $r(t) := \langle t^2, 2 \rangle$. At what time is the speed equal to 6?

5. Determine the length of the curve defined by $x = t^{3/2}$, $y = t$ over the interval $[0, 2]$.

6. Write an integral that can be used to determine the length of the curve defined by $x = 2t + 1, y = t^2$ from $(3, 1)$ to $(7, 9)$. Do not evaluate.

7. Let $r(t) := \langle t^3, t^2 \rangle$. At what time(s) is the magnitude of the acceleration equal to $\sqrt{40}$?

8. Find $r(t)$ if $r'(t) := \langle 2t, 6t^2 \rangle$ and $r(0) = \langle 1, 3 \rangle$.

9. Find $r(t)$ if $r'(t) := \langle e^t, \cos(t) \rangle$ and $r(0) = \langle 2, -4 \rangle$.

10. The speed of a particle travelling along the curve $x = f(t), y = g(t)$ is given by $v(t) := \sqrt{40t^2 + 12t + 1}$. If $f(t) := t^2 + 1$, what is $g(t)$?

11. A ball travels along the curve defined by $x = 30t, y = -16t^2 + 40t$.

    (a) What is the initial height of the ball?

    (b) What is the initial velocity of the ball?

    (c) How far has the ball travelled horizontally the first time it attains a height of 24ft.?

    (d) What is the maximum height attained by the ball?

    (e) What is the (straight line) distance from the initial position of the ball to the highest point it attains?

12. Suppose a golfball is hit from the ground with an initial speed of $v_0 = 100$ ft./sec. at an angle θ_0 such that $\sin(\theta_0) = 4/5$ and, obviously, $\cos(\theta_0) = 3/5$.

    (a) What is the height of the ball when it has moved 30 ft. horizontally?

    (b) At what time does the ball hit the ground and how far has it travelled horizontally at that time?

    (c) What is the maximum height attained by the ball?

    (d) Show that the speed of the ball is given by $v(t) := \sqrt{3600 + (80 - 32t)^2}$.

    (e) Write, but do not evaluate, an integral representing the total distance travelled by the ball.

PROBLEMS FOR SECTION 9.3:

1. (a) Let $r(t) = \langle x(t), y(t) \rangle$ and $u(t) = \langle w(t), z(t) \rangle$ be vector functions. Show that the derivative of the dot product of $r(t)$ and $u(t)$ is given by:

    $$\frac{d}{dt}(r(t) \cdot u(t)) = r(t) \cdot u'(t) + r'(t) \cdot u(t).$$

    (b) Apply the result of (a) to find the derivative of $\langle 3t, t^2 \rangle \cdot \langle t^3 + 1, 4t - 3 \rangle$.

2. In Theorem 9.2(d), we claimed that the dot product of a vector with itself gives the square of the length of the vector. Use this along with the result of Problem 1 above to show that the velocity and acceleration vectors are perpendicular if the speed is constant. [Hint: $(v(t))^2 = v(t) \cdot v(t) = c$, for some constant c.]

3. Joe Slugger thrilled fans at a baseball game by hitting a monumental homerun. It struck the scoreboard 450 feet from home plate at a height of 53 feet. Assume the ball was 3 feet off the ground when initially struck and left the bat at an angle of $\pi/4$.

    (a) Determine, in terms of the initial speed v_0 (which is unknown), the time required for the ball to reach the scoreboard.

    (b) Use the fact that its altitude at that time is 53 feet to find v_0.

    (c) How far would the ball have travelled if it hadn't struck the scoreboard?

4. (a) Show that the curve defined parametrically by $x = f(t)$, $y = g(t)$ has a horizontal tangent whenever $g'(t) = 0$ and $f'(t) \neq 0$ and a vertical tangent whenever $f'(t) = 0$ and $g'(t) \neq 0$.

    (b) Find all horizontal and vertical tangents for the curve $x = t^2 - t + 2$, $y = t^3 - 3t$.

5. In Problem 2 of Section 7.3, we claimed that the horizontal range of a ball thrown with initial speed v_0 at angle θ_0 with the horizontal is given by

    $$R = \frac{v_0^2 \sin(2\theta_0)}{g}.$$

    (a) Prove this result.

    (b) What happens to the range as θ_0 increases from 0 to $\pi/2$?

6. Show that the maximum height of a thrown object increases if either the initial speed v_0 or the angle with the horizontal θ_0 increases. Furthermore, if either $\theta_0 = 0$ or $v_0 = 0$, then the initial height h is the maximum height.

TYU Answers for Section 9.3

1. $r'(t) := \langle 8t, 2e^{2t} \rangle$ 2. $r(t) := \langle e^t + 1, \frac{1}{2}e^{2t} + 2 \rangle$ 3. $v(-1) = 2\sqrt{2}$ 4. $v(t) :=$
$\langle e^t, 2e^{2t} \rangle$, $v(t) := \sqrt{e^{2t} + 4e^{4t}}$ 5. $L = \int_0^3 \sqrt{e^{2t} + 4e^{4t}}\, dt$

9.4 SOME OTHER APPLICATIONS

In this section, we consider two applications that give rise to parametric equations through a system of two first-order differential equations.

RADIOACTIVE DECAY

Suppose a substance X decays radioactively into a substance Y which, in turn, decays into something else. Initially, we start with b grams of X and 0 grams of Y. We would like to determine how much X and Y are present at any time t.

Let $x(t)$ and $y(t)$ represent the number of grams of X and Y, respectively, at time t. We will make two assumptions.

1. The rates of decay of X and Y are proportional to the amounts present. (This is the same assumption we made in Chapter 5 when we discussed exponential growth and decay.)

2. One gram of X decays into one gram of Y.

As we have seen in Chapter 5, assumption 1 implies that

(7) $\dfrac{dx}{dt} = -kx,$

for some positive constant k. The initial condition is $x(0) = b$.

The rate of change of Y has two components. First Y increases because some X is turned into Y. Also, Y decreases because it is decaying into something else. Thus,

(8) $\qquad \dfrac{dy}{dt} = kx - hy,$

where h is another positive constant. Note that assumption 2 means that the k in Eq.(8) is the same as in Eq.(7). The initial condition is $y(0) = 0$.

Intuitively, the amount of X should decrease steadily toward 0 while the amount of Y should increase for a while, then decrease toward 0. We can justify this intuition graphically.

From Eq.(7), it follows that $\dfrac{dx}{dt} < 0$ for all t since, presumably, $x \geq 0$. From Eq.(8), we see that $\dfrac{dy}{dt} > 0$ when $y < \dfrac{k}{h}x$ and $\dfrac{dy}{dt} < 0$ when $y > \dfrac{k}{h}x$. Thus, we can partition the first quadrant of the xy-plane into two regions as shown in Figure 9.21.

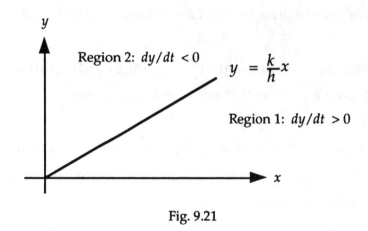

Fig. 9.21

At time $t = 0$, we're at the point $(b, 0)$. This is in Region 1 in which $\dfrac{dy}{dt} > 0$ and $\dfrac{dx}{dt} < 0$. This means that Y increases and X decreases. Once we reach the line $y = \dfrac{k}{h}x$, we cross into Region 2 where Y starts to decrease (X is still decreasing). Thus, the trajectory resembles the one in Figure 9.22.

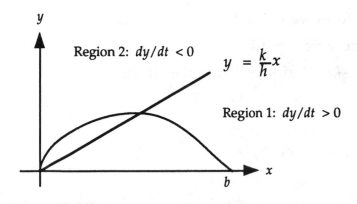

Fig. 9.22

To get an analytical solution, we could first solve Eq. (7), obtaining:

(9) $x(t) := be^{-kt}$.   (Verify.)

Then we could substitute this in Eq. (8) to get:

(10) $\dfrac{dy}{dt} = kbe^{-kt} - hy$.

Although this is a first-order differential equation, it does not separate and, consequently, we cannot solve it with the techniques we've learned so far.

Here's another approach. First differentiate Eq.(8) with respect to t:

(11) $\dfrac{d^2 y}{dt^2} = k\dfrac{dx}{dt} - h\dfrac{dy}{dt}$.

Note that, upon adding Eqs.(7) and (8), we have $\dfrac{dx}{dt} + \dfrac{dy}{dt} = -hy$ or $\dfrac{dx}{dt} = -\dfrac{dy}{dt} - hy$. Substituting in Eq.(11) and rearranging terms gives the second-order differential equation

(12) $\dfrac{d^2y}{dt^2} + (h+k)\dfrac{dy}{dt} + hky = 0$

which is of the form we learned to solve in Chapter 7.

The characteristic equation is $r^2 + (h + k)r + hk = 0$ whose roots are $r = -h$ and $r = -k$. (Verify.) Thus, the general solution of the differential equation is:

(13) $y(t) := c_1 e^{-ht} + c_2 e^{-kt}.$

The initial conditions are $y(0) = 0$ and, from Eq.(8), $y'(0) = kx(0) - hy(0) = kb$. After substituting and solving, we get $c_1 = \dfrac{kb}{k-h}$ and $c_2 = \dfrac{-kb}{k-h}$; hence, the specific solution is:

(14) $y(t) := \dfrac{kb}{k-h} (e^{-ht} - e^{-kt})$

A graph of this function, for the case $h = 2, k = 3, b = 10$ is given in Figure 9.23. Note that, as we surmised, y increases from 0 to a maximum of approximately 4.5, then decreases asymptotically towards 0. In the Problems at the end of the section, we'll ask you to show that the maximum value of y occurs at $t = \ln(1.5) = .4055$ or, more generally, at $t = \dfrac{\ln(k) - \ln(h)}{k-h}$.

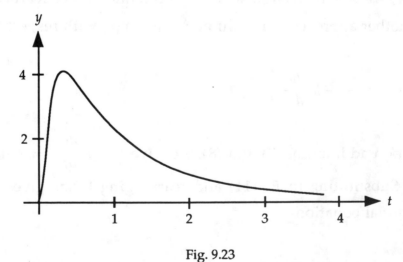

Fig. 9.23

COMBAT MODEL

Suppose two countries, X and Y, are engaged in a battle involving ground troops only. Let $x(t)$ and $y(t)$ be the number of troops for countries X and Y, respectively, at time t. Assume that no reinforcements are available and that the battle is over when one side has no troops left. A very simple model says that *the rate at which troops are lost is proportional to the size of the enemy's forces.*

Whether this model is reasonable is debatable. It certainly makes sense that one country will lose troops faster if the enemy has more troops. What is not clear is whether the rate is proportional to the number of troops, or the square of the number of troops, or the square root, or any other function. This probably depends on a number of factors such as the type of weapons and the troop configuration. For instance, this model is probably most accurate when conventional weapons are used (guns as opposed to weapons of mass destruction such as bombs) and all the troops are "on the front line". Modifications in the model can be made if these assumptions are not valid.

Note: Models of this type were first studied by F. W. Lanchester during World War I and are often referred to as **Lanchester Combat Models**.

Assuming this model is valid, then $x(t)$ and $y(t)$ satisfy the differential equations:

(15) $\qquad \dfrac{dx}{dt} = -ay(t) \quad$ and

(16) $\qquad \dfrac{dy}{dt} = -bx(t)$

where a and b are constants measuring the "effectiveness" or "efficiency" of Y's and X's weapons, respectively. In other words, the bigger a is, the more X troops each Y troop can kill per unit time.

One way to solve this system is to differentiate Eq.(15) with respect to t, obtaining:

$$\frac{d^2x}{dt^2} = -a\frac{dy}{dt}$$

Now substitute Eq.(16), whence

(17) $\quad \dfrac{d^2x}{dt^2} = abx.$

Upon rewriting Eq.(17) as $\dfrac{d^2x}{dt^2} - abx = 0$, we see that it is in the form that we learned to solve in Chapter 7. For convenience, let $k^2 = ab$ (which we can do since a and b are positive.) The characteristic equation is $r^2 - k^2 = 0$, whose roots are $r = \pm k$. Therefore, the general solution is

(18) $\quad x(t) := c_1 e^{kt} + c_2 e^{-kt}.$

It is more convenient to express this solution in terms of hyperbolic functions. Recall from the problems at the end of Chapter 7 and in the hanging cable problem of Chapter 8 that we defined the hyperbolic sine and cosine functions by:

$$\sinh(t) := \frac{e^t - e^{-t}}{2} \quad \text{and} \quad \cosh(t) := \frac{e^t + e^{-t}}{2}.$$

It is easy to see that $\frac{d}{dt}(\sinh(t)) = \cosh(t)$ and $\frac{d}{dt}(\cosh(t)) = \sinh(t)$. Furthermore, an expression of the form in Eq.(18) can be written as:

(19) $\quad x(t) =: C_1 \sinh(kt) + C_2 \cosh(kt)$

for suitable constants C_1 and C_2 (not the same as c_1 and c_2).

In order to find C_1 and C_2, we need initial conditions. Assume X starts with x_0 troops and Y starts with y_0 troops. Then

$$x(0) = x_0 \text{ and } y(0) = y_0.$$

Also, from Eqs. (15) and (16), we have:

$$x'(0) = -ay(0) = -ay_0 \text{ and } y'(0) = -bx(0) = -bx_0.$$

Substituting $t = 0$ in Eq.(19) and noting that $\sinh(0) = 0$ and $\cosh(0) = 1$ gives $C_2 = x_0$. Differentiating Eq.(19) gives

$$\frac{dx}{dt} = kC_1\cosh(kt) + kC_2\sinh(kt).$$

Substituting $t = 0$ here gives $-ay_0 = kC_1$ from which $C_1 = \frac{-ay_0}{k}$ $= -\sqrt{\frac{a}{b}}\, y_0$. Putting this all together gives:

(20) $\quad x(t) := x_0 \cosh(kt) - \sqrt{\frac{a}{b}}\, y_0 \sinh(kt).$

Now we can substitute Eq.(20) into Eq.(16) to obtain:

(21) $\quad \frac{dy}{dt} = -b(x_0 \cosh(kt) - \sqrt{\frac{a}{b}}\, y_0 \sinh(kt))$

$$= -bx_0 \cosh(kt) + ky_0 \sinh(kt).$$

This can be integrated with respect to t to obtain $y(t)$.

(22) $\quad y(t) = \frac{-bx_0}{k} \sinh(kt) + y_0 \cosh(kt)$

$$= -\sqrt{\frac{b}{a}}\, x_0 \sinh(kt) + y_0 \cosh(kt)$$

(You may wish to verify that Eq.(22) satisfies the initial conditions $y(0) = y_0$ and $y'(0) = -bx_0$.)

While Eqs. (20) and (22) give us the solution to our original differential equations, they do not clarify who wins. We know from Eqs. (15) and (16) that both x and y are decreasing functions of t (since both are postive), but they start at different values and decrease at different rates. Therefore it is likely that one of them will hit zero before the other. The situation illustrated in Figure 9.24 shows X starting with a larger army, but losing troops at a greater rate, so that Y wins.

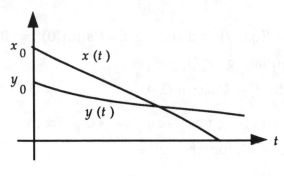

Fig. 9.24

In order to determine who wins, let's eliminate the parameter. Doing so directly from Eqs.(20) and (22) is tedious. A simpler approach is to go back to the original differential equations. Upon dividing Eq.(16) by Eq.(15), we have:

$$\frac{dy}{dx} = \frac{-bx}{-ay} = \frac{bx}{ay}$$

or, upon separating variables,

(23) $ay\, dy = bx\, dx.$

Integrating both sides gives

$$\frac{ay^2}{2} = \frac{bx^2}{2} + c, \text{ or}$$

$$ay^2 - bx^2 = C, \text{ where } C = 2c.$$

Substituting the initial conditions $x(0) = x_0$ and $y(0) = y_0$ implies $C = ay_0^2 - bx_0^2$ and, hence, the solution is:

(21) $ay^2 - bx^2 = ay_0^2 - bx_0^2.$

This is an equation of a hyperbola. If the right side of the equation is positive --which occurs if $\frac{x_0}{y_0} < \sqrt{\frac{a}{b}}$ --then the hyperbola passes through a point on the positive y-axis, implying that country Y will have troops remaining when country X's troops have been annihilated. In other words, Y wins. See Figure 9.25. On the other hand, if $\frac{x_0}{y_0} > \sqrt{\frac{a}{b}}$, then the curve passes through a point on the positive x-axis, meaning that X wins.

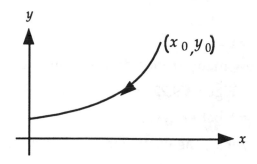

Fig. 9.25

Let $m = \frac{x_0}{y_0} - \sqrt{\frac{a}{b}}$. We have claimed that X wins if $m > 0$ and Y wins if $m < 0$. (Presumably, there is a draw if $m = 0$.) Note that m increases if x_0 increases (meaning X starts with more troops), y_0 decreases (meaning Y starts with fewer troops), a decreases (meaning that Y's troops become less efficient), or b increases (meaning X's troops become more efficient). Intuitively, all of these should make it easier for X to win.

PROBLEMS FOR SECTION 9.4:

1. In the radioactive decay model, verify that the maximum y-value occurs when $t = \frac{\ln(k) - \ln(h)}{k - h}$.

2. (a) Divide Eq.(14) by Eq.(9) to show that $\frac{y(t)}{x(t)} = \frac{k}{k-h}\left(e^{(k-h)t} - 1\right)$.

    (b) Determine $\lim_{t \to \infty} \frac{y(t)}{x(t)}$ and interpret. Note there are two cases: $h < k$ and $h > k$.

3. Suppose each gram of substance Y decays into one gram of some stable substance Z. If $z(t)$ represents the amount of Z at time t, then $\frac{dz}{dt} = hy$. Substitute Eq.(14) into this equation and solve for $z(t)$, given that $z(0) = 0$. Sketch the solution and interpret.

4. Suppose the rate at which country X loses troops is equal to 3 times the number of troops Y has and the rate at which Y loses troops is equal to 5 times the number of troops X has. X starts with 10000 troops and Y starts with 20000 troops.

(a) Assuming the model described in the text applies, determine $x(t)$ and $y(t)$.

(b) Plot $y(t)$ vs. $x(t)$.

(c) Who wins and how many troops do they have left?

5. Draw graphs similar to Figures 9.22 and 9.23 illustrating a victory by X.

6. Suppose X's troops get better weapons that can kill Y's troops twice as efficiently. In other words, the coefficient b is doubled. By how much can X reduce its initial forces and still win?

7. Another variation of the combat model can be described by the differential equations $\frac{dx}{dt} = -axy$, $\frac{dy}{dt} = -bxy$. (This corresponds to the case in which each side uses weapons, such as bombs, capable of killing many enemy troops at one time. Then the rate at which X loses troops not only depends on the number of troops Y has but also on the number X has.)

(a) Divide the two differential equations and solve.

(b) Sketch a few solutions.

(c) Argue that X wins if and only if $\frac{y_0}{x_0} < \frac{b}{a}$.

9.5 THE CYCLOID

There are many interesting problems in geometry which give rise to curves that can be represented parametrically. In this section, we examine one of the more remarkable ones--the cycloid.

Let P be any point on the circumference of a wheel whose radius is r. As the wheel rolls along a flat surface, the point P traces out a path consisting of a sequence of "arches". Part of one arch is shown in Figure 9.26. Let's try to derive an equation of this path.

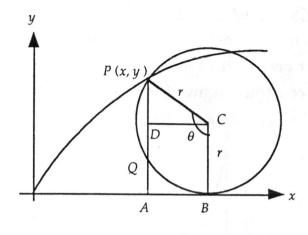

Fig. 9.26

The first thing we need to decide is what parameter to use. Although we frequently use time t as our parameter, here it is convenient to use angle θ as the parameter.

Let $(x(\theta), y(\theta))$ be the coordinates of P. Then

$$x(\theta) = OA = OB - AB = OB - DC \quad \text{and}$$

$$y(\theta) = PA = PD + AD = PD + r.$$

In $\triangle PCD$, $\angle CPD = \pi - \theta$. Therefore,

$$DC = r \sin (\angle CPD) = r \sin (\pi - \theta) = r \sin(\theta) \quad \text{and}$$

$$PD = r \cos (\angle CPD) = r \cos (\pi - \theta) = -r \cos(\theta).$$

Furthermore, OB = length of the arc $\overparen{PQB}$ = $r\theta$.

Putting this all together, we have

$$(25) \qquad x(\theta) := r\theta - r \sin(\theta) = r(\theta - \sin(\theta)) \qquad \text{and}$$

$$(26) \qquad y(\theta) := r - r \cos(\theta) = r(1 - \cos(\theta)).$$

These are the parametric equations of this curve, which we call a **cycloid**.

Mathematicians have studied the cycloid for many years and have discovered many fascinating properties. Two of the most interesting are:

1. <u>THE BRACHISTOCHRONE PROPERTY</u>: Suppose you wanted to travel from point A to point B, where A is above and to the left of B, in the shortest time, subject only to the influence of gravity. It turns out that the way to do this is to construct an inverted cycloid such that A is at the top of one of the arches and B is on the arch. See Figure 9.27.

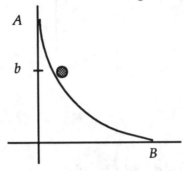

Fig. 9.27

2. <u>THE TAUTOCHRONE PROPERTY</u>: Suppose you let a bead roll down a frictionless inverted cycloid. Then the amount of time it takes for the bead to reach the bottom is independent of where along the cycloid it started. In other words, a bead starting at the top of the cycloid will reach the bottom in the same amount of time as one starting near the bottom.

   While the brachistochrone (Greek for "shortest time") property is hard to prove, the tautochrone (Greek for "equal time") property is considerably easier and we shall prove it here.

STEP 1: The first thing we need to do is derive parametric equations for the inverted cycloid. If we multiply Eq.(26) by −1, we will flip the curve over the x-axis. The first local minimum will be at $(\pi, -2r)$. It will be more convenient if this point is on the x-axis, so we will raise the curve up by adding $2r$ to the y-equation. Thus, the inverted cylcoid can be represented by the equations:

(27) $x = r(\theta - \sin(\theta))$ and

(28) $y = -r(1 - \cos(\theta)) + 2r = r(1 + \cos(\theta))$.

STEP 2: Chop the cycloid into small pieces and let the jth piece join the points $P(x_j, y_j)$ and $Q(x_j + \Delta x, y_j + \Delta y)$. See Figure 9.28. We can approximate the length of this piece by the length of the line segment PQ. Let L_j represent the length of PQ. Then, as we have seen before,

$$L_j^2 = (\Delta x)^2 + (\Delta y)^2 = (\Delta y)^2 \left(1 + \left(\frac{\Delta x}{\Delta y} \right)^2 \right).$$

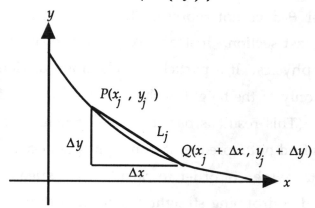

Fig. 9.28

Note that as we move from P to Q, y decreases. Hence, $\Delta y < 0$.

If Δy is small, then

$$\frac{\Delta x}{\Delta y} \approx \frac{dx}{dy} = \frac{dx/d\theta}{dy/d\theta} = \frac{1 - \cos(\theta)}{-\sin(\theta)}.$$

So,

$$L_j^2 \approx (\Delta y)^2 \left(1 + \frac{(1 - \cos(\theta))^2}{\sin^2(\theta)} \right) = (\Delta y)^2 \left(\frac{2(1 - \cos(\theta))}{\sin^2(\theta)} \right)$$

$$= (\Delta y)^2 \left(\frac{2(1 - \cos(\theta))}{1 - \cos^2(\theta)} \right)$$

$$= (\Delta y)^2 \left(\frac{2}{1 + \cos(\theta)} \right) = (\Delta y)^2 \left(\frac{2r}{y_j} \right).$$

Therefore, the length of PQ is approximately

(29) $L_j = -\sqrt{\dfrac{2r}{y_j}}\, \Delta y$.

Note that since Δy is negative, we take the negative square root to make L_j positive.

STEP 3: The next step is to determine the speed of the bead as a function of y. Since the parameter θ does not represent time, we cannot simply calculate the speed as in the last section. Instead, we make use of the following well-known result from physics: If a particle travels along a frictionless track, its speed is a function only of the height of the particle and is independent of the shape of the track. (This result is based on the principle of conservation of energy and you can find out more about it in a physics book.)

If this result is true, then in order to calculate the speed, we may as well assume that the bead is dropping straight down. (In other words, assume the track is vertical.) Then,

$$\frac{d^2 y}{d t^2} = -g$$

whose solution, subject to the initial conditions $y(0) = b$ (the initial height) and $y'(0) = 0$ (the bead is dropped not thrown), is

$$y = -\frac{1}{2}g t^2 + b .$$

Solving for t gives

$$t = \sqrt{\frac{2(b-y)}{g}} .$$

The speed is given by

(30) $v = |y'| = gt = \sqrt{2g\,(b-y)}$.

STEP 4: The time t_j required to travel the jth segment can be obtained by dividing the length by the speed. Assume that the segment is short enough so that the speed can be considered constant v_j. Then,

(31) $\quad t_j = \dfrac{L_j}{V_j} = \dfrac{-\sqrt{\dfrac{2r}{y_j}}}{\sqrt{2g(b-y_j)}} \Delta y = -\sqrt{\dfrac{r}{gy_j(b-y_j)}} \Delta y$.

To get the total time required to travel the entire cycloid from $y = b$ to $y = 0$, we add up the time required to travel each little piece; then let $\Delta y \to 0$. In other words, the total time

(32) $\quad T = \lim_{n \to \infty} \sum_{j=1}^{n} t_j = -\int_b^0 \sqrt{\dfrac{r}{gy(b-y)}}\, dy = \int_0^b \sqrt{\dfrac{r}{gy(b-y)}}\, dy$.

This integral in Eq. (32) can be evaluated by making the substitution $y = bu^2$, $dy = 2bu\, du$. Then

(33) $\quad T = 2\int_0^1 \sqrt{\dfrac{r}{gbu^2(b-bu^2)}}\, bu\, du = 2\sqrt{\dfrac{r}{g}} \int_0^1 \sqrt{\dfrac{1}{1-u^2}}\, du$.

Although we could finish this integral (we leave it for you as a problem), the important fact is that the expression for T is *independent of the initial height b*. Therefore, the time required for the bead to travel the cycloid is the same no matter where it starts!!! (Another fact for the "strange, but true" file.)

PROBLEMS FOR SECTION 9.5:

1. Show that the length of one arch of the cycloid $x = r(\theta - \sin(\theta))$, $y = r(1 - \cos(\theta))$ is $L = 8r$.

2. Complete the integral in Eq.(33) at the end of the last section used to find the total time T for a bead to travel down a cycloid.

3. Suppose a wheel of radius r rolls along a flat table, as in the description of the cycloid. Rather than being on the circumference of the wheel, let P be a point inside the wheel at a distance b from the center. The path P

follows is called a **trochoid**.

(a) Modify the derivation of the equations of the cycloid to show that the trochoid can be defined parametrically by:

$$x = r\theta - b\sin(\theta) \qquad y = r - b\cos(\theta)$$

(b) Sketch the trochoid for the case $r = 2$, $b = 1$.

4. Why is it plausible that travelling on a cycloid will get you from A to B in Figure 9.25 faster than if you travelled in a straight line?

QUESTIONS TO THINK ABOUT

1. Vectors were introduced in this chapter in order to discuss certain physical quantities. What were some of these quantities and what problems with them made the introduction of vectors desirable?

2. Discuss the acceleration of a particle moving on a curve. Include some discussion of the tangential and normal components of acceleration and their physical interpretation.

3. Three different applications of parametric equations were discussed at the end of this chapter: Radioactive decay, the Lanchester combat model and the cycloid. Discuss similarities and differences among these applications. Include some discussion of setting up the models and of solving any auxilliary problems.

PROJECT 9.1

A MODEL OF CELL DIFFUSION

OBJECTIVE: Two cells of equal volume are separated by a permeable membrane through which chemicals can diffuse in both directions. At time $t = 0$, 1 gram of chemical is introduced into cell 1 and allowed to diffuse. Let $x(t) :=$ amount of chemical in cell 1 and $y(t) :=$ amount of chemical in cell 2, at time t. The objective of this project is to derive and solve a system of differential equations for $x(t)$ and $y(t)$ and sketch the solutions.

PROCEDURE:

Part 1: Preliminary observations
  a. What must always be true about $x(t) + y(t)$?
  b. What must be true about $x'(t) + y'(t)$?
  c. Intuitively, what do you think happens to this system after a long time? You might first consider what would happen in the extreme case that no chemical could diffuse back from cell 2 to cell 1. Then what would happen if chemical could diffuse from cell 2 to cell 1, but very slowly? What if it diffuses quickly?

Part 2: Deriving the differential equations
  A simple model of diffusion says that the rate of diffusion from cell 1 into cell 2 is proportional to the amount of chemical in cell 1 and the rate of diffusion from cell 2 into cell 1 is proportional to the amount of chemical in cell 2. In other words, if there are $x(t)$ grams of chemical in cell 1, then the amount chemical that will diffuse to cell 2 during a short time interval Δt is approximately $\alpha x(t)\Delta t$, where α is the diffusion constant.
  a. Let $\Delta x = x(t + \Delta t) - x(t) =$ change in the amount of chemical in cell 1 during the time interval $[t, t + \Delta t]$. Suppose the diffusion constant from cell 1 to cell 2 is α and the constant from cell 2 to cell 1 is β. Argue that $\Delta x \approx -\alpha x(t)\Delta t + \beta y(t)\Delta t$.
  Hint: You must take into account the fact that some chemical is leaving cell 1 to go to cell 2 and some is coming into cell 1 from cell 2.
  b. Divide both sides of the expression above by Δt and let $\Delta t \to 0$, thus obtaining a differential equation for $x(t)$.
  c. Let $\Delta y = y(t + \Delta t) - y(t)$. Derive an approximation similar to the one in 2a for Δy. Repeat step 2b to obtain a differential equation for

$y(t)$. Do your results to 2a and 2b confirm your answer to 1b?

Part 3: The solution

a. Show that $x(t) := \dfrac{\beta}{\alpha + \beta} + \dfrac{\alpha}{\alpha + \beta}e^{-(\alpha + \beta)t}$ and

$$y(t) := \dfrac{\alpha}{\alpha + \beta} - \dfrac{\alpha}{\alpha + \beta}e^{-(\alpha + \beta)t}$$

satisfy the differential equations and that $x(0) = 1$ and $y(0) = 0$.

b. What are $\lim\limits_{t \to \infty} x(t)$ and $\lim\limits_{t \to \infty} y(t)$? What does this mean about the behavior of the system after a long time? Does this support your intuition of Part 1c?

c. Graph $x(t)$ and $y(t)$ as functions of t on the same axes for the case $\alpha = 2, \beta = 3$.

d. Sketch a graph of $y(t)$ vs. $x(t)$; that is, if $r(t) := \langle x(t), y(t) \rangle$, sketch the path traversed by the head of $r(t)$. Indicate the direction of motion.

e. We could have obtained the answer to 3b without knowing 3a as follows: Assume the system really does "settle down" after a while; that is, $\lim\limits_{t \to \infty} x(t)$ and $\lim\limits_{t \to \infty} y(t)$ both exist. Then $\lim\limits_{t \to \infty} x'(t) = \lim\limits_{t \to \infty} y'(t) = 0$. (Why?) Show that, by taking the limit as $t \to \infty$ in the differential equations and using the fact that $x(t) + y(t) = 1$ for all t, you get the answer to 3b.

Part 4: Three cells

Now suppose there are three cells with membranes between cells 1 and 2 and between cells 2 and 3. Let $x(t)$, $y(t)$ and $z(t)$ be the amounts of chemical in cells 1, 2 and 3, respectively. Let α be the diffusion rate from cell 1 to cell 2, β be the diffusion rate from cell 2 to either cell 1 or 3 and γ be the diffusion rate from cell 3 to cell 2. Again assume 1 gram is placed in cell 1 at time $t = 0$.

a. Follow the discussion in Part 2 to show that

$$x'(t) = -\alpha x + \beta y, \quad y'(t) = \alpha x - 2\beta y + \gamma z, \quad z'(t) = \beta y - \gamma z$$

b. Use an argument like the one in 3d to show that

$$\lim\limits_{t \to \infty} x(t) = \dfrac{\beta\gamma}{\alpha\gamma + \beta\gamma + \alpha\beta}, \qquad \lim\limits_{t \to \infty} y(t) = \dfrac{\alpha\gamma}{\alpha\gamma + \beta\gamma + \alpha\beta}$$

$$\lim\limits_{t \to \infty} z(t) = \dfrac{\alpha\beta}{\alpha\gamma + \beta\gamma + \alpha\beta}$$

c. Make a rough sketch of $x(t)$, $y(t)$ and $z(t)$ for the case $\alpha = 2, \beta = 3, \gamma = 1$.

PROJECT 9.2

THE HYPOCYCLOID

OBJECTIVE: In Section 9.5, we studied the cycloid, the curve generated by following the path of a point on the outside of a wheel as it rolls along a flat table. Now suppose P is a point on the perimeter of a wheel of radius b rolling around the inside of a wheel of radius r (where $r > b$). The path traversed by P is called a **hypocycloid**. In this project, we will derive parametric equations for the hypocycloid. Then we will look at a special case when $r = 4b$; the curve generated in this case is called a **hypocycloid of four cusps** for reasons which will become clear when we graph one.

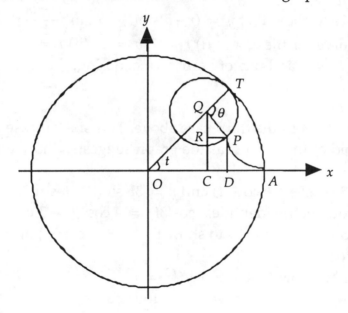

PROCEDURE:

Part 1: Geometrical observations

In the diagram above, point P was initially at A. The small wheel rotated clockwise through an angle θ. The coordinates of P are (x, y). Our goal is to express x and y in terms of t, the angle formed by OQ and the x-axis.

a. Which line segment in the diagram has a length equal to x?

b. Which line segment in the diagram has a length equal to y?

c. Argue that the length of $\overset{\frown}{AT}$ = length of $\overset{\frown}{PT}$.

d. How long is OQ in terms of r and b? (Remember b is the radius of the small circle.)

e. Express angle PQR in terms of t and θ.

Part 2: Deriving the equations

a. Express the length of $\overset{\frown}{PT}$ in terms of b and θ. Express the length of $\overset{\frown}{AT}$ in terms of r and t.

b. Use 2a and 1c to show that $\theta = \frac{rt}{b}$.

c. Express QC and OC in terms of r, b and t.

d. Express QR and PR in terms of r, b and angle PQR.

e. Use 1e to show that $PR = b \cos\left(\frac{r-b}{b}\right)t$ and $QR = b \sin\left(\frac{r-b}{b}\right)t$.

   You may need the fact that $\cos(90° - \alpha) = \sin(\alpha)$ and $\sin(90° - \alpha) = \cos(\alpha)$ for all α.

f. Use 1a and 2e to show that $x = (r - b)\cos(t) + b\cos\left(\frac{r-b}{b}\right)t$.

g. Use 1b and 2e to show that $y = (r - b)\sin(t) - b\sin\left(\frac{r-b}{b}\right)t$.

h. Graph the curve for the cases: (i) $r = 2, b = 1$; (ii) $r = 3, b = 1$; (iii) $r = 4, b = 1$ and one of your own choosing.

Part 3: A special case

a. Suppose $r = 4b$ as in the third case above. This special case is called a **hypocycloid of four cusps**, as the graph suggests. Show that, for this case,
$$x = 3b\cos(t) + b\cos(3t) \text{ and } y = 3b\sin(t) - b\sin(3t).$$

b. Use the trigonometric identities $\cos(3t) = 4\cos^3(t) - 3\cos(t)$ and $\sin(3t) = 3\sin(t) - 4\sin^3(t)$ to show that $x = r\cos^3(t)$ and $y = r\sin^3(t)$.

c. Eliminate t and show that $x^{2/3} + y^{2/3} = r^{2/3}$.

d. Find the length of the hypocycloid of four cusps in terms of r.

PROJECT 9.3

ACCELERATION AND CURVATURE

OBJECTIVE: In Section 9.3, we defined the acceleration vector $a(t) = r''(t)$, where $r(t)$ is the position vector. If $r(t) = \langle x(t), y(t) \rangle$, then $a(t) = \langle x''(t), y''(t) \rangle$; that is, $x''(t)$ and $y''(t)$ are the horizontal and vertical components of $a(t)$. Now imagine that you are driving along a winding road. What you feel as the car twists and turns are forces pushing you forward and back or side to side. This may or may not coincide with north-south and east-west directions. So, what we really want to do is express the acceleration in terms of a component in the direction of the motion (the **tangential component**) and a component perpendicular to the motion (the **normal component**).

As you go around a corner, you experience a force perpendicular to the direction of motion. The magnitude of this force depends on how sharp the corner is. We measure "sharpness" in terms of **curvature** which, as we expect, is related to the normal component of acceleration.

In this project, we'll learn how to compute the components of acceleration and curvature.

PROCEUDRE:

Part 1: A little review
  a. Let $v = \langle a, b \rangle$ and $w = \langle -b, a \rangle$. Show that v and w are perpendicular.
  b. Show that v and w have the same length.
  c. Show that w is the vector one would get by rotating v through $90°$ counterclockwise.
  d. Let $z = \alpha v + \beta w$, where α and β are constants. Show that $\alpha = \frac{z \cdot v}{v \cdot v}$ and $\beta = \frac{z \cdot w}{w \cdot w}$. (This is a generalization of Problem 6 of Section 9.1.)
  e. Show that if v is a unit vector, then $v \cdot v = 1$. (See Theorem 9.2(d).)

Part 2: Unit tangent and unit normal vectors
  Consider the curve traced by the vector function $r(t) = \langle x(t), y(t) \rangle$. Let $v(t) = r'(t)$ be the tangent vector and let $v(t) = \|v(t)\|$ be the speed.
  a. Show that the vector $T(t) = \left\langle \frac{x'(t)}{v(t)}, \frac{y'(t)}{v(t)} \right\rangle$ is a vector of length 1 parallel to $v(t)$. $T(t)$ is called the **unit tangent vector.**

b. Show that the vector $N(t) = \left\langle \dfrac{-y'(t)}{v(t)}, \dfrac{x'(t)}{v(t)} \right\rangle$ is a vector of length 1 obtained by rotating $T(t)$ 90° counterclockwise. $N(t)$ is called the **unit normal vector**.

c. Determine $T(t)$ and $N(t)$ for the circle traced by the vector function $r(t) = \langle 2\cos(t), 2\sin(t) \rangle$.

Part 3: Components of acceleration

Let $a(t) = a_T T(t) + a_N N(t)$, where $T(t)$ and $N(t)$ are defined in Part 2. The numbers a_T and a_N are the **tangential and normal coordinates** of $a(t)$. The vectors $a_T T(t)$ and $a_N N(t)$ are the tangential and normal components. It follows from 1d and 1e that $a_T = a \cdot T$ and $a_N = a \cdot N$ since T and N are unit vectors.

a. Show that $a_T = \dfrac{x'(t)\,x''(t) + y'(t)\,y''(t)}{v(t)}$ and

$a_N = \dfrac{x'(t)\,y''(t) - y'(t)\,x''(t)}{v(t)}$.

b. By differentiating the equation $[x'(t)]^2 + [y'(t)]^2 = [v(t)]^2$ with respect to t, show that $a_T = v'(t)$.

Part 4: Rotating tangent vectors

As a curve $r(t)$ bends around a corner, the unit tangent vector $T(t)$ will rotate. The sharper the corner, the faster T rotates. We might be able to determine how fast T rotates by looking at its derivative, T'. In particular, $\|T'\|$ should be large when T rotates rapidly. It can be shown that since $\|T(t)\| = 1$ for all t, then T and T' are perpendicular. (See Problem 2 of Section 9.3.) Thus, $T' = kN$ for some constant k.

a. Show that $|k| = \|T'\|$.

b. Show that k is positive when T rotates counterclockwise (towards N) and negative when T rotates clockwise.

c. Determine k for the circle in 2c. In which direction is T rotating?

d. Take the dot product of both sides of $T' = kN$ with N to get

$k = T' \cdot N$.

Part 5: Curvature

We could use the constant k from Part 4 to measure how fast T rotates. Unfortunately, doubling the speed at which the curve is traversed doubles k. Hence, this is not a very effective way to measure how much the curve is bent. To overcome this, we divide by the speed. Thus, the curvature is defined by $\kappa(t) = \dfrac{T'(t) \cdot N}{v(t)}$, where $T'(t)$ is the derivative of T with respect to t and $v(t)$ is the speed.

a. Use 2a to show that
$$T'(t) := \left\langle \frac{v(t)\,x''(t) - x'(t)\,v(t)}{[v(t)]^2}, \frac{v(t)\,y''(t) - y'(t)\,v(t)}{[v(t)]^2} \right\rangle.$$

b. Show that $\kappa(t) := \dfrac{x'(t)\,y''(t) - x''(t)\,y'(t)}{[v(t)]^3}$.

c. Use 3a to show that $a_N = \kappa[v(t)]^2$.

d. Let $r(t) := \langle c\cos(t), c\sin(t) \rangle$ be the vector function that traces a circle of radius c. Show that $|\kappa| = 1/c$. Is this reasonable in the context of our intuitive discussion about curvature?

e. Let $r(t) = \langle 3\cos(t), 2\sin(t) \rangle$. Show that $r(t)$ traces out an ellipse. Sketch.

f. Show that the curvature of the function in 5e is
$$\kappa(t) := \frac{6}{\sqrt{(9 - 5\cos^2(t))^3}}.$$

g. For which values of t is the curvature in 5f maximum? minimum? Indicate these points on the graph.

PROJECT 9.4

PREDATOR-PREY MODEL

OBJECTIVE: In Section 9.4, we studied a combat model, in which two countries fight each other in a battle. We derived a criterion for determining which side will win and showed that, except for one special case, the battle ends in a finite amount of time.

In this project, we will study a system consisting of two species, one of which (the predator) eats the other (the prey). There are many examples of this in the real world: birds eat worms, cats eat mice, foxes eat rabbits, etc. We might be inclined to think that once the predator eats all the prey, then there are no prey left, so the predator eventually dies off. In fact, we will show that, under certain assumptions, this does not happen. Rather, the two species can exist forever without being completely wiped out.

PROCEDURE:

Part 1: The model

For concreteness, assume the predators are foxes and the prey are rabbits. Let $F(t) :=$ number of foxes in the population and $R(t) :=$ number of rabbits in the population, at time t. In the absence of foxes, the number of rabbits will increase without bound (assuming there is adequate food for the rabbits). In the absence of rabbits, the foxes will die because they have nothing to eat.

a. Argue that a plausible model is $\frac{dR}{dt} = a_1 R$ when there are no foxes and $\frac{dF}{dt} = -a_2 F$ when there are no rabbits, where a_1 and a_2 are positive constants.

If there is a small number of foxes, the number of rabbits may still increase although not as quickly as if there were no foxes. Once the number of foxes exceeds a certain threshold, the number of rabbits will start to decrease. Similarly, if there is a small number of rabbits, the number of foxes will still decrease but not as quickly as if there were no rabbits. Once the number of rabbits exceeds a certain threshold, the number of foxes will start to increase.

b. Argue that the model $\frac{dR}{dt} = (a_1 - b_1 F)R$, $\frac{dF}{dt} = -(a_2 - b_2 R)F$ is consistent with these assumptions and with the special case described in 1a.

c. How many foxes must there be in order for the rabbit population to decrease? How many rabbits must there be in order for the fox population to increase?

We'll derive an exact solution of this system in Part 4. For now, let's look at the qualitative behavior of the solution.

Part 2: Equilibria and trajectories

An **equilibrium** for a system of differential equations occurs when all the derivatives are equal to 0.

a. Show that the system in 1b has two equilibria: $F = 0, R = 0$ and $F = \frac{a_1}{b_1}, R = \frac{a_2}{b_2}$.

The first of these implies that there are no foxes or rabbits in the system. This isn't terribly interesting, so let's look at the second equilibrium.

b. For each of the four subregions of the first quadrant pictured below, determine the sign of $\frac{dR}{dt}$ and $\frac{dF}{dt}$.

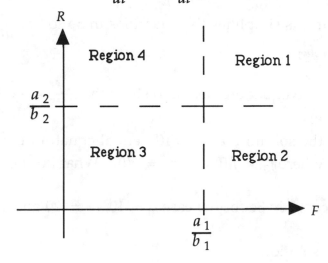

c. Suppose the initial populations are $R(0) = R_0$ and $F(0) = F_0$. Argue that if (F_0, R_0) is in Region 1, then the populations move downward to the right until they reach Region 2. What happens once it hits Region 2?

d. Continue the process in 2c and show that the population cycles clockwise around the equilibrium.

e. We have not shown whether these cycles are closed curves or spiral inward or outward. What are the implications of each of these three possibilities in terms of the population sizes?

Part 3: Stability

In this section, we will show that the equilibrium $\left(\frac{a_1}{b_1}, \frac{a_2}{b_2}\right)$ is **neutrally stable**. This means that, assuming the initial population sizes are close to the equililbrium values, then the cycles are closed curves. (If the cycles spiral outward, we say the equilibrium is **unstable**; if they spiral inward, the equilibrium is **stable**.)

a. Let $r(t) := R(t) - \frac{a_2}{b_2}$ and $f(t) := F(t) - \frac{a_1}{b_1}$. What are the physical interpretations of $r(t)$ and $f(t)$?

b. Note that $\frac{dR}{dt} = \frac{dr}{dt}$ and $\frac{dF}{dt} = \frac{df}{dt}$. Substitute in the differential equations in 1b to show that $\frac{df}{dt} = b_2\left(f + \frac{a_1}{b_1}\right)r$ and

$$\frac{dr}{dt} = -b_1\left(r + \frac{a_2}{b_2}\right)f.$$

c. Assume $|f|$ is much less than $\frac{a_1}{b_1}$ and that $|r|$ is much less than $\frac{a_2}{b_2}$. Show that this simplifies the equations in 3b to get $\frac{df}{dt} = \frac{a_1 b_2}{b_1} r$ and

$$\frac{dr}{dt} = -\frac{a_2 b_1}{b_2} f.$$

d. Divide the two equations above to show that $\frac{df}{dr} = -k\frac{r}{f}$ for some constant k.

e. Show that the solution of this differential equation is $f^2 + kr^2 = f_0^2 + kr_0^2$, where $f_0 = f(0)$ and $r_0 = r(0)$. What kind of curves are these?

f. Sketch the curve in 3e for the case $f_0 = 10$, $r_0 = 20$ and $k = 0.25$.

Part 4: The exact solution

a. Divide the two equations in 1b to eliminate t.

b. Separate variables and show that $\frac{b_2 R - a_2}{R} dR = \frac{a_1 - b_1 F}{F} dF$.

c. Integrate and rearrange to show that $F^{a_1} R^{a_2} = C\, e^{b_2 R}\, e^{b_1 F}$, where C is a constant.

d. Let $p(F) := \frac{F^{a_1}}{e^{b_1 F}}$ and $q(R) := \frac{R^{a_2}}{e^{b_2 R}}$. Show that the maximum value of p occurs when $F = \frac{a_1}{b_1}$ and the maximum value of q occurs when $R = \frac{a_2}{b_2}$. Sketch graphs of p and q.

e. Let $M_F = p(\frac{a_1}{b_1})$ and $M_R = q(\frac{a_2}{b_2})$ be the maximum values of p and q, respectively. Argue that the equation in 4c has no solution if $C > M_F M_R$ and exactly one solution if $C = M_F M_R$.

f. Now let's see what happens if $C < M_F M_R$. Suppose $C = s M_F$, where $0 < s < M_R$. Show that the equation $q(R) = s$ has two solutions R_1 and R_2, where $R_1 < \frac{a_2}{b_2}$ and $R_2 > \frac{a_2}{b_2}$.

g. Argue that if $R < R_1$ or $R > R_2$, then $p(F) > M_F$. Since this is not possible, then the rabbit population can never be less than R_1 or greater than R_2.

It follows that for each R between R_1 and R_2, there are two values of F satisfying the equation in 4c. One of them $F_1 < \frac{a_1}{b_1}$ and the other $F_2 > \frac{a_1}{b_1}$. This, in turn, implies that the solutions near the equilibrium are periodic.

CHAPTER 10

POLAR COORDINATES

10.1 THE POLAR COORDINATE SYSTEM

One of the greatest intellectual achievements of the seventeenth century was the discovery by the astronomer Johannes Kepler of 3 simple laws that accurately describe the motion of planets in the solar system. These laws are:

1. Planets move around the sun in elliptical orbits with the sun at one focus.

2. The radius drawn from the sun to a planet sweeps out equal areas in equal times. In other words, if the planet takes the same time to go from P to Q as it does to go from R to S, then the areas of the two sectors are the same. (See Figure 10.1.)

3. The square of the period of a planet (i.e. the time it takes to revolve once around the sun) is proportional to the cube of its semi-major axis, OA.

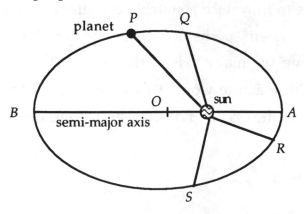

Fig. 10.1

Kepler used observational data to derive these laws, the collection of which took his predecessor Tycho Brahe more than 20 years. Later in that century, Newton used his newfangled calculus and a few facts from his newfangled physics to derive Kepler's laws analytically. This provided evidence for the "correctness" of both Newton's and Kepler's work. Let's develop a general framework in which to look at Newton's remarkable calculation. We'll work out some of the details in Section 10.4.

We need to make some basic assumptions:

1. There is a gravitational attraction between the planet and the sun that keeps the planet in orbit. The magnitude of this force is given by Newton's Universal Law of Gravitation:

$$F = \frac{GMm}{r^2}$$

where G is the universal constant of gravitation (6.67×10^{-11} m^3/kg-sec^2), M is the mass of the sun (2×10^{30} kg), m is the mass of the planet (6×10^{24} kg for earth) and r is the distance from the planet to the sun (on average, about 1.5×10^8 km for earth).

2. The planets themselves are far enough apart and small enough compared to the sun that gravitational attractions between planets can be ignored.

¤   The first task is to introduce a suitable coordinate system. We could use a rectangular (x, y) system, perhaps with the center of the orbit at the origin and the x-axis along the major axis of the orbit. This turns out to be a very awkward system in which to work. To see why, recall that an equation of an ellipse with center at the origin and major axis along the x-axis is

(1) $$\frac{x^2}{a^2} + \frac{y^2}{b^2} = 1$$

where a = semi-major axis and b = semi-minor axis. (We assume $a > b$.) The foci are at $(c, 0)$ and $(-c, 0)$, where $c = \sqrt{a^2 - b^2}$. See Figure 10.2.

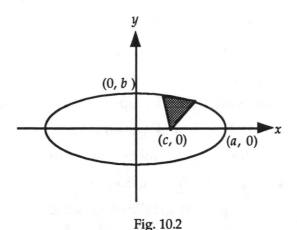

Fig. 10.2

Kepler's Second Law talks about the area of a sector such as the one shaded above. Usually, we talk about finding areas of regions bounded by $y = f(x)$, the x-axis (or, perhaps, another function $y = g(x)$) and vertical lines $x = a$ and $x = b$. This elliptical sector is not of this type--its sides are diagonal, not vertical--and hence, determining the area of this region using the techniques of Chapter 6 is very difficult.

We could shift the coordinate system so that the origin is at one focus of the ellipse since that is where the sun is and all the forces are directed toward the sun. This complicates the equation of the ellipse and does not make the aforementioned area problem appreciably easier.

Another problem with using rectangular coordinates is that they are static. They only describe the path followed by the planet but do not take time into account. In other words, we know "where" but not "when". To remedy this, we might try a parametric representation such as those we encountered in Chapter 9. It is not hard to show that the ellipse in Eq.(1) can be represented by the parametric equations

(2) $x = a \cos(t),\ y = b \sin(t).$

(See Exercise 1(f) in Section 9.2.) Of course, there are many other possibilities and it is not clear which one, if any, actually describes the motion of the planets. Furthermore, the area calculation is no easier.

¤   This suggests that it might be useful to invent another type of coordinate system that might overcome these difficulties.

What properties should this new coordinate system have? It would be convenient if it had a center, like the origin, about which all of the action could take place. That would be the spot at which we'd place the sun. Secondly, the new system should allow us to find areas of sector-like regions (with their points at the origin) more conveniently than rectangular coordinates allow. Also, at least for the Kepler-Newton discussion, the new coordinate system ought to permit a relatively simple description of ellipses and other curves that circle the origin.

Perhaps "circle" is exactly what we want! Imagine drawing the circle on the earth of all points 3400 miles from the North Pole. That circle would go through New York City (more or less). In fact, you could completely describe the position of New York by giving this distance and the city's longitude. So, New York has "North Pole coordinates" (3400, 74° 1' W). Indeed, you could describe any spot on earth similarly: a pair of numbers giving its distance from the pole and its longitude.

Now imagine moving directly up from the North Pole and looking down on the earth. Imagine seeing the lines of longitude and latitude the way they appear on a globe. As you rise higher and higher, the earth (or at least its top half) seems to flatten and become a disc. The lines of latitude become circles centered at the pole and the lines of longitude become rays that start at the pole. In particular, you'll see a special line of longitude or meridian, the one that goes through Greenwich, England from which all longitude is measured.

This scheme is the basis for a different coordinate system, which we call (surprise!) **polar coordinates**. An origin (or **pole**) is selected and an axis (called the **polar axis**) is drawn radiating out from the pole. Typically it is drawn pointing east (to the right) from the pole. Concentric circles of radius 1, 2, 3, ... are drawn around the pole. Rays radiating from the pole at various angles to the polar axis are also drawn. See Figure 10.3.

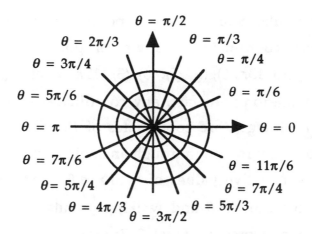

Fig. 10.3

To get the polar coordinates of a point P on the plane, draw a line segment connecting P to the pole O (a line of longitude). Let θ be the angle, measured counter-clockwise in radians, between OP and the polar axis (the Greenwich meridian) and let r be the length of OP (the distance from the pole). The polar coordinates of P are (r, θ).

Note: This convention for measuring θ differs from that used by navigators. They usually measure angles clockwise, with 0^0 being due north.

For example, suppose the polar coordinates of P are $(3, \pi/6)$. To get to P, stand at the pole, facing along the polar axis. Rotate an angle of $\pi/6$ counter-clockwise and walk 3 units out from O. See Figure 10.4.

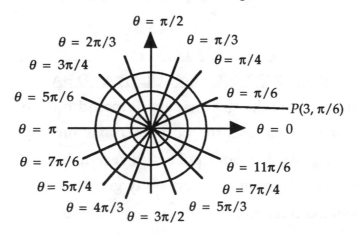

Fig. 10.4

¤   Unlike the rectangular coordinates of a point, which are unique, there are infinitely many polar coordinates for any given point P. The point $(3, \pi/6)$ also has coordinates $(3, 13\pi/6)$, $(3, 25\pi/6)$, $(3, -11\pi/6)$, etc. (Negative values of θ mean clockwise rotation.)   In fact, any coordinates of the form $(3, 2n\pi + \pi/6)$, where n is an integer, are coordinates of P. (Of course, if n is large, you might get quite dizzy rotating through an angle of that magnitude.)

We can also use negative values of r. If $r < 0$, then we get to the point (r, θ) by rotating to an angle θ and walking r units *backwards*. Therefore, the point $(3, \pi/6)$ can be represented by $(-3, 7\pi/6)$.

TEST YOUR UNDERSTANDING

1. (a) Write 2 other sets of polar coordinates with $r = 2$ for the point whose polar coordinates are $(2, 2\pi/5)$.

   (b) Write 2 sets of polar coordinates for the point in (a) with $r = -2$.

2. What are some sets of polar coordinates for the pole?

POLAR TO RECTANGULAR AND BACK

Imagine that a rectangular grid is superimposed on top of the polar grid with the origin at the pole and the positive x-axis on top of the polar axis. Every point on the plane has both polar and rectangular coordinates. Given the polar coordinates of a point, we can easily get the rectangular coordinates. Figure 10.5 shows the relationships among x, y, r and θ.

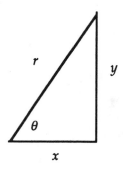

Fig. 10.5

A little elementary trigonometry shows that:

(3) $x = r \cos(\theta)$ and

(4) $y = r \sin(\theta)$.

Thus, given r and θ, we can easily (and uniquely) find x and y.

EXAMPLE 10.1:

Find rectangular coordinates of the point whose polar coordinates are $(2, \frac{3\pi}{4})$.

Since $\cos(\frac{3\pi}{4}) = \frac{-\sqrt{2}}{2}$ and $\sin(\frac{3\pi}{4}) = \frac{\sqrt{2}}{2}$, then $x = 2 \cos(\frac{3\pi}{4}) = -\sqrt{2}$ and $y = 2 \sin(\frac{3\pi}{4}) = \sqrt{2}$ are the desired coordinates.   ♦

- -

TEST YOUR UNDERSTANDING

3. In which quadrant would you find the point whose polar coordinates are:

(a) $(5, 3\pi/4)$ (b) $(-3, 5\pi/3)$ (c) $(7, 4)$ (d) $(-3, 9)$?

4. Determine rectangular coordinates for the point whose polar coordinates are:

(a) $(10, 2\pi/3)$ (b) $(4, 3\pi)$ (c) $(6, \arcsin(1/3))$ (d) $(-6, 3\pi/4)$

The reverse process--finding the polar coordinates given the rectangular coordinates--is trickier. Clearly, r and θ must satisfy

(5) $r^2 = x^2 + y^2$ and

(6) $\tan(\theta) = y/x.$

However, there are two values of r and infinitely many values of θ that satisfy Eqs. (5) and (6) and we must be careful to pick a pair that does indeed represent the given point.

EXAMPLE 10.2:

The rectangular coordinates of P are $(-3, 3)$. Find polar coordinates.

$r^2 = (-3)^2 + 3^2 = 18$, so $r = \pm 3\sqrt{2}$.

$\tan(\theta) = y/x = -1$, so $\theta = 3\pi/4, 7\pi/4, 11\pi/4, 15\pi/4, -\pi/4$, etc.

Since P is in the second quadrant, then if we use $\theta = 3\pi/4$, we must take $r = 3\sqrt{2}$.

Note that if P had coordinates $(3, -3)$, the calculations would be exactly the same. Now, however, P is in the fourth quadrant; thus, if we use $\theta = 3\pi/4$, then we must take $r = -3\sqrt{2}$. Alternatively, we could use $\theta = 7\pi/4$ with $r = 3\sqrt{2}$. ♦

---

5. Determine a set of polar coordinates for the point whose rectangular coordinates

are: (a) $(-2, 2\sqrt{3})$ (b) $(0, -2)$ (c) $(3, 4)$

Throughout this chapter, we will be careful to specify whether a given ordered pair is the polar or rectangular coordinates of a point. Indeed, there is a point on the plane whose *polar* coordinates are $(3, -3)$, where once again we note that θ is measured in radians.

EXERCISES FOR SECTION 10.1:

1. Determine the rectangular coordinates for the points whose polar coordinates are:

(a) $(1, \pi)$ (b) $(3, \pi/4)$ (c) $(4, 2\pi/3)$ (d) $(-2, \pi/6)$

(e) $(3, 3\pi)$ (f) $(6, 2)$ (g) $(5, \arcsin(2/5))$ (h) $(-4, 9\pi/2)$

2. Determine a set of polar coordinates for the points whose rectangular coordinates are:

(a) $(-3, 0)$ (b) $(0, 4)$ (c) $(-1, \sqrt{2})$ (d) $(2, -2)$

3. Find 3 sets of polar coordinates for the points whose rectangular coordinates are:

(a) $(1, 0)$ (b) $(-1, 1)$ (c) $(-2, 2\sqrt{3})$.

4. A point P has polar coordinates $(r, 5\pi/6)$ and rectangular coordinates $(-4, y)$. Find r and y.

5. Find the area of $\triangle OPQ$, where O is the pole and the polar coordinates of P and Q are $(3, \pi/4)$ and $(4, 3\pi/4)$, respectively. How long is side PQ?

6. Determine polar coordinates of the point which is the midpoint of the line segment PQ, where P and Q have polar coordinates $(1, 0)$ and $(1, \pi/2)$.

PROBLEMS FOR SECTION 10.1:

1. (a) Let P and Q have polar coordinates (r_1, θ_1) and (r_2, θ_2), respectively. Derive a formula for the length of the line segment PQ.

(b) Use your formula to find the length of the line joining $(1, 2\pi/3)$ and $(3, \pi/3)$.

Hint: You might want to use the Law of Cosines, which says that in $\triangle ABC$, $c^2 = a^2 + b^2 - 2ab \cos(C)$, where a, b and c are the lengths of the sides of the triangle and C is the angle opposite the side whose length is c.

TYU Answers for Section 10.1

1. (a) $(2, 12\pi/5), (2, -8\pi/5)$ (b) $(-2, 7\pi/5), (-2, 17\pi/5)$ 2. $(0, \theta)$ for any θ

3. (a) Quad. II   (b) Quad. II   (c) Quad. III   (d) Quad. IV   4. (a) $(-5, 5\sqrt{3})$ (b) $(-4, 0)$

(c) $(4\sqrt{2}, 2)$ (d) $(3\sqrt{2}, -3\sqrt{2})$ 5. (a) $(4, 2\pi/3)$ (b) $(2, 3\pi/2)$ (c) $(5, \arcsin(.8))$ or $(5, .927)$

10.2 FUNCTIONS IN POLAR COORDINATES

Remember that one of our hopes for this new coordinate system was that it would make the description of curves that circle the origin (in particular, ellipses) easier to describe. Consider such a curve, shown in Fig. 10.6. Notice that for each value of θ, there is just one value of r such that (r, θ) is on the curve. Thus, we can think of r as a function of θ: $r = f(\theta)$.

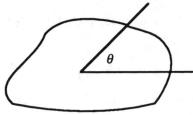

Fig. 10.6

As with vector functions in Chapter 9, we can think of the curve being traced by a particle, or by the head of a vector whose tail is at the origin. The vector interpretation is particularly appropriate since r and θ are the magnitude and direction of the vector pointing from the origin to the point whose polar coordinates are (r, θ). Also, remember we are interested in wedges with points at the origin. We can think of wedges as being swept out by this vector turning through some interval of angles, say $\theta_1 \le \theta \le \theta_2$.

The simplest function is the constant function $r = c$. We actually described this graph in the previous section: All points a fixed distance c units from the pole. In other words, a circle of radius c, centered at the pole.

TEST YOUR UNDERSTANDING

1. What is the graph of $\theta = c$?

Many of the interesting polar graphs involve trigonometric functions. Consider the function $r = \sin(\theta)$. One way to graph this is to make a table of values.

θ	0	$\pi/6$	$\pi/4$	$\pi/3$	$\pi/2$	$2\pi/3$	$3\pi/4$	$5\pi/6$	π
r	0	.5	.71	.86	1	.86	.71	.5	0

If we plot these points, we appear to get a circle of radius 1/2 centered at the point with rectangular coordinates (0, 1/2). See Figure 10.7. Convince yourself that this is the whole picture; had we continued using larger values of θ, we would just retrace the circle.

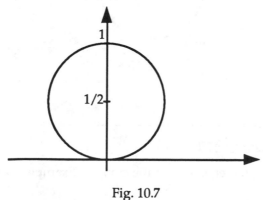

Fig. 10.7

We can verify that the graph is indeed a circle by deriving the equivalent rectangular equation. Since $\sin(\theta) = \frac{y}{r}$, then the equation $r = \sin(\theta)$ is equivalent to $r = \frac{y}{r}$ or, upon multiplying by r, $r^2 = y$. Substituting $r^2 = x^2 + y^2$, we have

$$x^2 + y^2 = y.$$

Upon completing the square, this can be rewritten as

$$x^2 + (y - \frac{1}{2})^2 = 1/4,$$

which is an equation of a circle of radius $\frac{1}{2}$, centered at $(0, \frac{1}{2})$.

EXAMPLE 10.3:

Sketch the graph of $r = 2\cos(\theta)$.

Again, we make a table of values for $0 \le \theta \le \pi$.

θ	0	$\pi/6$	$\pi/4$	$\pi/3$	$\pi/2$	$2\pi/3$	$3\pi/4$	$5\pi/6$	π
r	2	1.73	1.41	1	0	−1	−1.41	−1.73	−2

Being careful to plot the points with negative r-values correctly, we get what again appears to be a circle, this time centered at $(1, 0)$ with a radius of 1. See Figure 10.8.

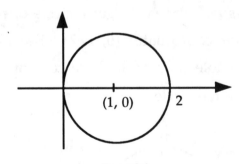

Fig. 10.8

♦

- -

TEST YOUR UNDERSTANDING

2. Derive a rectangular equation for the curve in Example 10.3.

3. (a) Sketch the curve given by $r = \dfrac{1}{\sin(\theta)}$ for $\pi/4 \leq \theta \leq 3\pi/4$.

(b) Derive a rectangular equation for the curve in (a).

- -

In general, analysis of curves in polar coordinates is more difficult than in rectangular coordinates. One reason is that every point on the plane has infinitely many sets of polar coordinates as opposed to a unique set of rectangular coordinates. Also, concepts such as slope, direction and concavity were designed for rectangular coordinates. We will do whatever analysis we can and then make use of the computer to draw graphs.

¤ It will be convenient to build up a list of common polar curves, as we did in Chapter 1 for rectangular curves. We'll do some preliminary analysis first. We can often easily find upper and lower bounds for r. Polar functions often contain trigonometric functions, such as sine and cosine, and we know their smallest and largest values. If that fails, we can use the techniques we learned in Chapters 3 and 5 for maximizing and minimizing functions.

It is also helpful to find all θ for which $r(\theta) = 0$. These correspond to points where the curve passes through the pole. (Remember, the coordinates of the pole are $(0, \theta)$, for any θ.)

We can also look for symmetry. We'll consider two types:

1. If $f(\theta) = f(\pi - \theta)$, for all θ, then the graph is symmetric about the line $\theta = \pi/2$ (the y-axis). For example, consider the function $r = \sin(\theta)$, pictured in Figure 10.7. Since $\sin(\theta) = \sin(\pi - \theta)$ for all θ, then this function is symmetric about the line $\theta = \pi/2$. In general, functions which contain only $\sin(\theta)$ possess this type of symmetry.

2. If $f(\theta) = f(-\theta)$, for all θ, then the graph is symmetric about the polar axis. For example, the function $r = 2\cos(\theta)$ considered in Example 10.3 is symmetric about the polar axis since $\cos(\theta) = \cos(-\theta)$, for all θ. In general, functions which contain only $\cos(\theta)$ possess this type of symmetry.

SOME POLAR FUNCTIONS

1. <u>Rose curve</u>: A function of the form $r = a\,\sin(n\theta)$ or $r = a\,\cos(n\theta)$, for some positive integer n and constant a is called a **rose curve** (we'll see why later). Note that, since $-1 \leq \sin(n\theta) \leq 1$, then $-a \leq r \leq a$, for all θ. For $r = a\,\sin(n\theta)$, note that $r = 0$ whenever $n\theta = k\pi$, for some integer k. For example, suppose $r = \sin(3\theta)$. Then $r = 0$ if $3\theta = 0, \pi, 2\pi, 3\pi, \ldots$; that is, for $\theta = 0, \pi/3, 2\pi/3, \pi, \ldots$.

Graphs of some rose curves are given in Figure 10.9. Notice that the graph of $r = \sin(3\theta)$ has three "leaves", while the graph of $r = \sin(2\theta)$ has four leaves. In the problems at the end of the section, we ask you to determine how many leaves the general rose curve will have.

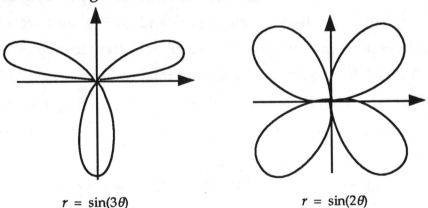

$r = \sin(3\theta)$ $r = \sin(2\theta)$

Fig. 10.9

2. <u>Limaçon</u>: A function of the form $r = a \pm b\,\sin(\theta)$ or $r = a \pm b\,\cos(\theta)$, for some constants a and b, is called a **limaçon** (pronounced "lee-mah-sohn" and is the French word for "snail"). Consider the case $r = a - b\,\sin(\theta)$, where a and b are positive. Since $-1 \leq \sin(\theta) \leq 1$, then $a - b \leq r \leq$

$a + b$. Depending on the values of a and b, the curve may or may not pass through the pole. Notice that $r = 0$ when $\sin(\theta) = \frac{a}{b}$ which can happen only if $\frac{a}{b} \leq 1$. If $a \leq b$, then $\frac{a}{b} \leq 1$ so there is some value of θ for which $\sin(\theta) = \frac{a}{b}$. Thus, the curve passes through the pole. (If $a < b$, then it actually passes through twice since there are 2 "distinct" values of θ for which $\sin(\theta) = \frac{a}{b}$.) However, if $a > b$, then $\frac{a}{b} > 1$, so there is no such θ; that is, the curve does not pass through the pole.

As with the rose curves, limaçons involving $\sin(\theta)$ are symmetric about the line $\theta = \pi/2$, while those involving $\cos(\theta)$ are symmetric about the polar axis.

The special case of the limaçon when $a = b$ is called a **cardioid**. The cardioid passes through the pole only once, thus causing the graph to resemble a heart (hence the name "cardioid").

Some limaçons and a cardioid are shown in Figure 10.10.

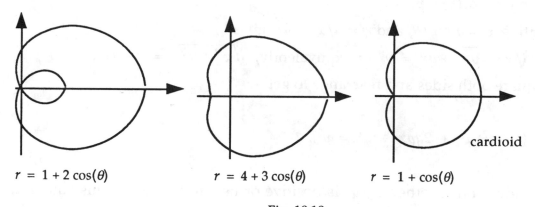

$r = 1 + 2\cos(\theta)$ $r = 4 + 3\cos(\theta)$ $r = 1 + \cos(\theta)$ cardioid

Fig. 10.10

3. <u>Spiral</u>: The function $r = a\theta$, where a is a constant, is called a **spiral**. Clearly, if $a > 0$, then r increases as θ increases. Note that, as always, θ must be measured in radians. The graph of this function, for $0 < \theta < 2\pi$ and $a = 1$, is given in Figure 10.11.

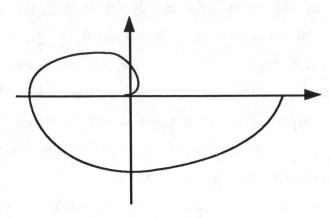

Fig. 10.11

4. <u>The Conic Sections</u>: Let $r = \dfrac{p}{1 + q\,\cos(\theta)}$. Here, rather than directly graphing the function, we'll transform it into rectangular coordinates and discover that these curves are already known to us. First, cross-multiply, obtaining

$$r + rq\,\cos(\theta) = p.$$

Substituting $x = r\,\cos(\theta)$ and $r = \sqrt{x^2 + y^2}$ gives

$$\sqrt{x^2 + y^2} + qx = p \quad \text{or, equivalently,} \quad \sqrt{x^2 + y^2} = p - qx.$$

Now square both sides and rearrange to get

$$(1 - q^2)\,x^2 + 2qpx + y^2 = p^2.$$

Depending on whether $1 - q^2$ is positive or negative or zero, this equation represents an ellipse, a hyperbola or a parabola, that is, a **conic section**. The number q in this equation is called the **eccentricity** of the conic. For example, if $q = 0$, we have (not surprisingly) a circle with radius $|p|$ and center at the origin. As q increases from zero toward 1, the figure becomes an ever more eccentric ellipse with major axis along the x-axis until, when $q = 1$, it becomes the parabola $2px + y^2 = p^2$, again with axis of symmetry along the x-axis. When $q > 1$, the figure is a hyperbola, once more with its axis along the x-axis. Of course you will be gratified to learn that, in every case, *a focus of the conic section is at the origin*. This is a topic for further exploration.

There are many other interesting curves which result from polar functions. In all but the simplest cases, we won't be able to do much analysis to tell us what the graph will look like; instead, we will rely on a computer or graphing calculator to graph the curves for us. There are some examples in the exercises and problems at the end of this section.

<u>EXERCISES FOR SECTION 10.2</u>:

1. Graph each of the following polar curves:

   (a) $r = 4$ (b) $r = 6\sin(\theta)$ (c) $r = \sin(\theta) + \cos(\theta)$

   (d) $r = 2 + \cos(\theta)$ (e) $r = 3 - 3\sin(\theta)$ (f) $r = 4\sin(3\theta)$

2. Discuss the symmetry of each of the curves in Exercise 1.

3. Determine a rectangular equation for the curve whose polar equation is:

   (a) $r = \sin(\theta) + \cos(\theta)$ (b) $r = 3\sec(\theta)$ (c) $r = \dfrac{1}{1 + \cos(\theta)}$

4. Determine the polar coordinates of the points of intersection of:

   (a) $r = 2$ and $r = 4\sin(\theta)$ (b) $r = 1 + \sin(\theta)$ and $r = 2\sin(\theta)$

   (c) $r = \sin(\theta)$ and $r = \cos(\theta)$

   In all cases, it might help to draw pictures first.

5. For what values of a will $r = 4$ and $r = a\cos(\theta)$ have:

   (a) no points in common   (b) one point in common   (c) two points in common.

6. Use your computer or graphing calculator to graph:

   (a) $r = 1 - \sin(2\theta)$ (b) $r = \sin^2(\theta)$ (c) $r = e^{\cos(2\theta)} - 1.5\cos(4\theta)$

7. Identify the following conic sections. Then use your computer or graphing calculator to graph them.

   (a) $r = \dfrac{1}{1 - \cos(\theta)}$ (b) $r = \dfrac{2}{2 + \cos(\theta)}$ (c) $r = \dfrac{1}{1 - 2\cos(\theta)}$

8. Determine the range of r-values, the values of θ for which $r = 0$ and the symmetry for the function $r = a\cos(n\theta)$.

PROBLEMS FOR SECTION 10.2:

1. Show that the function $r = 2a \sin(\theta) + 2b \cos(\theta)$ always represents a circle. Express the coordinates (rectangular) of the center and the radius in terms of a and b.

2. Use the computer to graph rose curves of the form $r = \sin(n\theta)$, for $n = 4, 5$ and 6. What conclusions can you draw about the number of leaves?

3. Consider the polar equation $r = \dfrac{1}{1 + a \cos(\theta)}$, where a is a constant.

   (a) Use the computer to graph this function for the cases $a = 0, a = .25$, $a = .5, a = .75$ and $a = 1$. Describe what happens to the curves as a increases from 0 to 1.

   (b) Use the computer to graph this function for the cases $a = 1.25, a = 1.5, a = 2$. Describe what happens to the curves as a increases from 1 to 2.

1. A line through the pole at an angle θ with the horizontal. 2. $(x - 1)^2 + y^2 = 1$

3. (a) Horizontal line from $(\sqrt{2}, 1)$ to $(-\sqrt{2}, 1)$. (b) $y = 1, -\sqrt{2} \le x \le \sqrt{2}$

10.3 AREA IN POLAR COORDINATES

One motivation for introducing polar coordinates was to overcome the difficulty imposed by rectangular coordinates in calculating the area of a sector of a planetary orbit. Such a sector is bounded by an ellipse and two lines through the pole (sun).

This suggests that it might be useful to consider the more general region R bounded by the polar curve $r = f(\theta)$, and the lines $\theta = \alpha$ and $\theta = \beta$. See Figure 10.12.

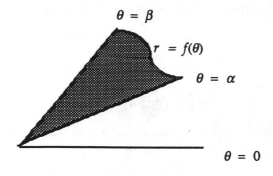

$\theta = \beta$

$r = f(\theta)$

$\theta = \alpha$

$\theta = 0$

Fig. 10.12

¤ Recall that in rectangular coordinates, we approximated the area of the region bounded by $y = f(x)$, the x-axis and the lines $x = a$ and $x = b$ by partitioning the interval $[a, b]$ into n equal parts of length $\Delta x = \dfrac{b-a}{n}$, constructing rectangles and adding up their areas (a Riemann sum). Specifically, we let $\Delta A_j = $ area of jth rectangle $= f(x_j)\,\Delta x$. Then the total area A was approximately $\displaystyle\sum_{j=1}^{n} f(x_j)\,\Delta x$. To get the exact area of R, we took the limit of this Riemann sum as $n \to \infty$; that is, $A = \displaystyle\lim_{n \to \infty} \sum_{j=1}^{n} f(x_j)\,\Delta x$.

We will do something similar here. Partition the "sector" defined by the lines $\theta = \alpha$ and $\theta = \beta$ into n "subsectors", each with central angle $\Delta\theta = \dfrac{\beta - \alpha}{n}$. This divides R into "pizza slices". Consider the jth slice, bounded by the lines $\theta = \theta_j$, $\theta = \theta_{j+1}$ and the curve $r = f(\theta)$. See Figure 10.13.

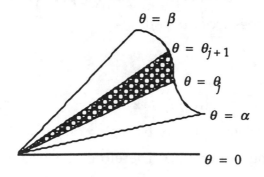

$\theta = \beta$

$\theta = \theta_{j+1}$

$\theta = \theta_j$

$\theta = \alpha$

$\theta = 0$

Fig. 10.13

If the curve were a circle, then the area of the sector would be proportional to the angle $\Delta\theta$; that is,

$$\frac{\text{Area of sector}}{\text{Area of circle}} = \frac{\Delta\theta}{2\pi} .$$

Since the area of the circle is πr^2, then the area of the sector is $\frac{1}{2}r^2\Delta\theta$. For small $\Delta\theta$, we can use this to approximate ΔA_j = the area of the jth slice. Specifically,

$$\Delta A_j \approx \frac{1}{2}r_j^2\Delta\theta ,$$

where $r_j = f(\theta_j)$.

Therefore, the total area of R is approximately

$$A \approx \sum_{j=1}^{n} \frac{1}{2}r_j^2\Delta\theta = \sum_{j=1}^{n} \frac{1}{2}[f(\theta_j)]^2\Delta\theta ,$$

which is a Riemann sum for the function $g(\theta) = \frac{1}{2}[f(\theta)]^2$. To get the exact area, we let $n \to \infty$. As we know from Chapter 6, this converts the summation into an integral. Thus, we have:

THEOREM 10.1: The area of the region bounded by the polar curve $r = f(\theta)$, and the rays $\theta = \alpha$ and $\theta = \beta$ is given by $A = \int_{\alpha}^{\beta} \frac{1}{2}(f(\theta))^2 d\theta$.

The most difficult part of using Theorem. 10.1 is finding the limits of integration. A sketch is often helpful. Imagine that the region is being "swept out" by the radius vector from the pole (as opposed to just tracing the curve). It is important to make sure that no part of the region is swept out more than once as θ goes from α to β.

EXAMPLE 10.4:

Find the area inside the circle $r = 2\sin(\theta)$.

The entire circle is swept out by using values of θ between 0 and π. (Verify this by drawing the graph.) Therefore, the area is given by

$$A = \frac{1}{2}\int_0^\pi (2\sin(\theta))^2\,d\theta = 2\int_0^\pi \sin^2(\theta)\,d\theta$$

$$= \theta - \sin(\theta)\cos(\theta)\Big|_{\theta=0}^{\theta=\pi} = \pi.$$

◆

EXAMPLE 10.5:

Find the area of the "half-moon" region in the first quadrant swept out by the spiral $r = \theta$ between $\theta = 0$ and $\theta = \pi/2$. (See Figure 10.11.)

$$A = \frac{1}{2}\int_0^{\pi/2} r^2\,d\theta = \frac{1}{2}\int_0^{\pi/2} \theta^2\,d\theta = \frac{\pi^3}{48}.$$

◆

EXAMPLE 10.6:

Find the area of the region insided the cardioid $r = 1 - \sin(\theta)$, as shown in Figure 10.14.

The entire cardioid is swept out by using values of θ between 0 and 2π. (Again, verify this.) Therefore,

$$A = \frac{1}{2}\int_0^{2\pi} (1 - \sin(\theta))^2\,d\theta = \frac{1}{2}\int_0^{2\pi} (1 - 2\sin(\theta) + \sin^2(\theta))\,d\theta$$

$$= \frac{1}{2}\left[\theta + 2\cos(\theta) + \frac{\theta}{2} - \frac{\sin(\theta)\cos(\theta)}{2}\right]\Bigg|_{\theta=0}^{\theta=2\pi} = \frac{3\pi}{2}.$$

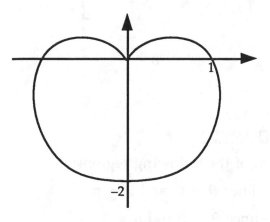

Fig. 10.14

◆

EXAMPLE 10.7:

Find the area of the inner loop of the limaçon $r = 1 - 2\cos(\theta)$ as shown in Figure 10.15.

The tricky part about this problem is finding the limits of integration. When $\theta = 0$, $r = -1$. This is the furthest point on the inner loop. As θ increases to $\pi/3$, r increases towards 0, which completes the bottom half of the inner loop. Integrating from 0 to $\pi/3$ will therefore give us half the desired area. Hence, the area of the inner loop is given by

$$A = 2\left(\frac{1}{2}\right)\int_0^{\pi/3} (1 - 2\cos(\theta))^2 \, d\theta = \int_0^{\pi/3} \left(1 - 4\cos(\theta) + 4\cos^2(\theta)\right) d\theta$$

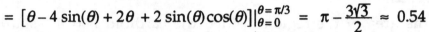

$$= \left[\theta - 4\sin(\theta) + 2\theta + 2\sin(\theta)\cos(\theta)\right]\Big|_{\theta=0}^{\theta=\pi/3} = \pi - \frac{3\sqrt{3}}{2} \approx 0.54$$

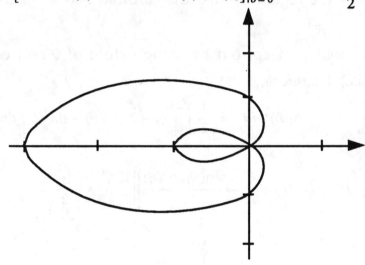

Fig. 10.15

♦

EXERCISES FOR SECTION 10.3:

1. Find the area of each of the following regions:

    (a) $r = 2\theta$, and the lines $\theta = 0$ and $\theta = \pi$

    (b) $r = e^\theta$, and the lines $\theta = 0$ and $\theta = 1$

    (c) inside the circle $r = \cos(\theta) + \sin(\theta)$

    (d) one leaf of the rose $r = \sin(2\theta)$

(e) inside the limaçon $r = 2 - \sin(\theta)$

(f) the inner loop of the limaçon $r = 2 + 4\sin(\theta)$

(g) the triangle bounded by $r = 5\sec(\theta)$, the lines $\theta = \pi/4$ and $\theta = -\pi/4$

2. Find the area of the region inside the circle $r = 2\sin(\theta)$ and outside the circle $r = \sin(\theta)$.

PROBLEMS FOR SECTION 10.3:

1. Determine the area of the region *between* the loops of the limaçon $r = 1 + 2\cos(\theta)$.

    Hint: Be very careful about the limits of integration. As θ increases from 0 to $2\pi/3$, r decreases from 3 to 0. In doing so, the radius sweeps out half of the limaçon, including the inner loop.

2. A troop of soldiers is located at point P. There is a trench running north-south at a distance of b yards from P. The soldier spread out in all directions from P and head towards the trench. Once they get to the trench, they cross it and continue c more yards in the same direction. Show that the final position of the soldiers can be described by the polar curve $r = c + b\sec(\theta)$. This curve is known as the **Conchoid of Nicomedes**.

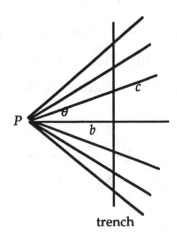

trench

10.4 KEPLER'S LAWS OF PLANETARY MOTION

In Section 10.1, we outlined the problem of describing the motion of the planets. After realizing the shortcomings of using a rectangular coordinate system to describe this motion, we introduced polar coordinates. In Section 10.2, we looked at polar curves and in Section 10.3, we derived a method for calculating areas of regions of the type described by Kepler's Laws. Now we can put it all together and look at Newton's justification of Kepler's theories.

The first thing we have to talk about is acceleration. (After all, acceleration is proportional to force and forces play a big role in Newton's physics.) Recall Chapter 9 where we talked about the acceleration of a particle whose path was given by the vector function $r(t) = \langle x(t), y(t) \rangle$. The acceleration vector is $a(t) = r''(t) = \langle x''(t), y''(t) \rangle$. We noted that while the horizontal and vertical components of the acceleration are easy to compute, they aren't very useful. We said it was more interesting to talk about a tangential component of acceleration (in the direction of the velocity vector) and a normal component (perpendicular to the velocity vector). The tangential component determines how much the speed of the particle changes (in fact, it is the derivative of the speed); the normal component determines how much its direction changes.

We need to do something similar here, only this time we will determine the **radial acceleration** (in the direction of r) and the **angular acceleration** (in a direction perpendicular to r). See Figure 10.16.

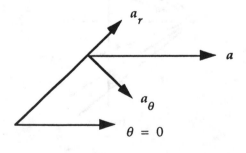

Fig. 10.16

After a mess of algebra and calculus from which we will spare you, it can be shown that the radial and angular components of the acceleration are given by:

(7) $\qquad a_r = \dfrac{d^2 r}{dt^2} - r \left(\dfrac{d\theta}{dt}\right)^2 \quad$ and .

(8) $\qquad a_\theta = 2 \dfrac{dr}{dt} \dfrac{d\theta}{dt} + r \dfrac{d^2 \theta}{dt^2}$

Keep in mind throughout this discussion that both r and θ are functions of t.

◻ Our first assumption was that the only force acting on the planet was a gravitational attraction to the sun, which is in the radial direction. There are no other forces; in particular, there are no forces in the angular direction and, since according to Newton, force is proportional to acceleration, the angular component of the acceleration must be 0. Therefore,

(9) $\qquad 2 \dfrac{dr}{dt} \dfrac{d\theta}{dt} + r \dfrac{d^2 \theta}{dt^2} = 0.$

This is a second order differential equation containing the derivatives of two different functions. While we can't solve for $r(t)$ and $\theta(t)$ explicitly, we can derive a simpler relationship that $r(t)$ and $\theta(t)$ must satisfy. First, multiply Eq.(9) by r, obtaining:

(10) $\qquad 2r \dfrac{dr}{dt} \dfrac{d\theta}{dt} + r^2 \dfrac{d^2 \theta}{dt^2} = 0.$

After a bit of thought, you might recognize the left-hand side of Eq.(10) as $\dfrac{d}{dt}\left[r^2 \dfrac{d\theta}{dt}\right]$ and, hence, Eq.(10) can be rewritten as:

(11) $\qquad \dfrac{d}{dt}\left[r^2 \dfrac{d\theta}{dt}\right] = 0.$

Upon integrating both sides of Eq.(11) with respect to t, we see that any functions $r(t)$ and $\theta(t)$ which satisfy Eq. (9) must also satisfy the relationship

(12) $$r^2 \frac{d\theta}{dt} = k,$$

where k is a constant.

Now consider the area A of the region swept out by the radius during an arbitrary time interval $[a, b]$. We know from Theorem 10.1 that $A = \frac{1}{2} \int_{\alpha}^{\beta} r^2 \, d\theta$, where $\theta(a) = \alpha$ and $\theta(b) = \beta$. But from Eq. (12), $r^2 \, d\theta = k \, dt$, so:

$$A = \frac{1}{2} \int_{a}^{b} k \, dt = \frac{1}{2} k(b - a).$$

Now, $b - a$ is the length of time it takes for θ to go from α to β. Therefore, the area depends only on the *length* of the time interval and not on the specific times involved; e.g., the area swept out during the interval $[4, 7]$ is the same as the area swept out during the interval $[10, 13]$ since the intervals are the same length.

Hence, we have proved that <u>if the only force acting on the planet is directed toward the sun, then Kepler's second law is valid.</u>

◻ The next task is to prove Kepler's first law. In order to do so, we use Newton's observation that gravitational force (which is in the direction of r) is inversely proportional to the square of the radius. In other words,

$$F_r = ma_r = \frac{-GMm}{r^2}.$$

(The minus sign is needed because the force is directed in towards the sun, the negative direction for r.)

Upon substituting for a_r from Eq. (7) and dividing by m, we see that $r(t)$ and $\theta(t)$ must also satisfy the differential equation:

(13) $\quad \dfrac{d^2r}{dt^2} - r\left(\dfrac{d\theta}{dt}\right)^2 = \dfrac{-h}{r^2}$

where $h = GM$, as in Newton's Universal Law of Gravitation.

The first step is to use Eq. (12) to write this equation strictly in terms of r. This gives

$$\dfrac{d^2r}{dt^2} - \dfrac{k^2}{r^3} = \dfrac{-h}{r^2} \quad \text{or, equivalently,}$$

(14) $\quad r^3 \dfrac{d^2r}{dt^2} + hr = k^2.$

Notice that Eq. (14) is a non-linear, second-order differential equation for which we have no direct method of solving. Instead, we will see if a conic section satisfies it.

Let

(15) $\quad r = \dfrac{p}{1 + cp \, \cos(\theta)}$

where $p = \dfrac{k^2}{h}$ and c is an arbitrary constant. Then,

(16) $\quad \dfrac{dr}{dt} = \dfrac{cp^2 \sin(\theta)}{(1 + cp \, \cos(\theta))^2} \dfrac{d\theta}{dt} = cr^2 \sin(\theta) \dfrac{d\theta}{dt} = ck \sin(\theta),$

from Eq. (12). Differentiating once more gives

(17) $\quad \dfrac{d^2r}{dt^2} = ck \, \cos(\theta) \dfrac{d\theta}{dt} = \dfrac{ck^2 \cos(\theta)}{r^2},$

again using Eq. (12).

Thus, $r^3 \dfrac{d^2 r}{dt^2} + hr = rck^2 \cos(\theta) + hr = rh(cp\ \cos(\theta) + 1) = \dfrac{rhp}{r} = hp$

$= k^2$ and the given function is, indeed, a solution of the differential equation (14).

We know from Section 10.2 that Eq.(15) represents a conic section in which the eccentricity is cp. Depending on whether $1 - (cp)^2$ is positive, negative or zero, we have an ellipse, a hyperbola or a parabola. If we're talking about planets, the orbit must be closed (they don't fly away), so the equation must be that of an ellipse. Hence, Kepler's first law is proven.

Note that we are not claiming that functions of the type given by Eq.(15) are the only solutions to Eq.(14). There may be others (and, indeed, there are). See Problem 1 at the end of this section.

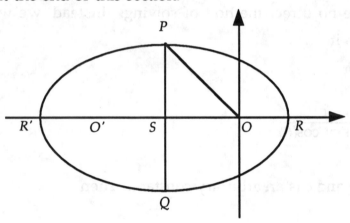

Fig. 10.17

⌑ To prove Kepler's third law, let $a = SR$ be the length of the semi-major axis and $b = SP$ be the length of the semi-minor axis as seen in Figure 10.17. Note that $OR = r(0) = \dfrac{p}{1+cp}$ and $OR' = r(\pi) = \dfrac{p}{1-cp}$. Thus, $a = \frac{1}{2}[r(0)+r(\pi)] = \dfrac{p}{1-c^2p^2}$.

The defining property of ellipses is that for any point X on the ellipse, $OX + O'X = 2a$. In particular, let $X = P$ and note that $OP = O'P$ by symmetry. We have $OP + O'P = 2OP = 2a$. Thus, $OP = a$. Furthermore, $OS = a - r(0)$. By the Pythagorean Theorem,

$$b^2 = (SP)^2 = (OP)^2 - (OS)^2 = a^2 - (a - r(0))^2 = 2ar(0) - r(0)^2$$

$$= \left(\frac{2p}{1 - c^2 p^2}\right)\left(\frac{p}{1 + cp}\right) - \left(\frac{p}{1 + cp}\right)^2 = \frac{p^2}{1 - c^2 p^2}.$$

Hence, $b = \dfrac{p}{\sqrt{1 - c^2 p^2}} = \sqrt{pa}$.

It is well-known (see Problem 3 at the end of this section) that the area of an ellipse is $A = \pi ab = \pi \sqrt{p}\, a^{3/2}$. Since Kepler's second law says that area is swept out at a constant rate k per unit time, it follows that $A = kT$, where T is the period of the orbit--that is, the time it takes for the planet to complete one revolution around the sun.

Therefore, $kT = \pi \sqrt{p}\, a^{3/2}$. Upon squaring both sides, we find that T^2 is proportional to a^3, which is Kepler's third law.

EXERCISES FOR SECTION 10.4:

1. Planet X has a period of 1 year and a semi-major axis of 25 million miles. If Planet Y has a semi-major axis of 50 million miles, what is its period?

2. A planet moves from point P to point Q in its orbit in 30 days and moves from Q to point R in 60 days. If the sun is at point O (one of the foci), what is the ratio of the area of sector QOR to sector POQ?

PROBLEMS FOR SECTION 10.4:

1. Show that the function $r = r_0$, where r_0 is a constant satisfies Eq.(14). What kind of curve does this represent? Express r_0 in terms of h and k.

2. A particle moves along the circle whose polar equation is $r = \sin(\theta)$.

   (a) Show that $\dfrac{dr}{dt} = \cos(\theta)\dfrac{d\theta}{dt}$ and $\dfrac{d^2 r}{dt^2} = -\sin(\theta)\left(\dfrac{d\theta}{dt}\right)^2 + \cos(\theta)\dfrac{d^2\theta}{dt^2}$.

   (b) Use Eq.(7) and (8) to show that the radial and angular components of acceleration are given by $a_r = -2\sin(\theta)\left(\dfrac{d\theta}{dt}\right)^2 + \cos(\theta)\dfrac{d^2\theta}{dt^2}$ and $a_\theta = 2\cos(\theta)\left(\dfrac{d\theta}{dt}\right)^2 + \sin(\theta)\dfrac{d^2\theta}{dt^2}$.

(c) Suppose the particle moves at constant angular velocity; that is, $\frac{d\theta}{dt} =$
k. Show that $a_r = -2k^2 \sin(\theta)$ and $a_\theta = 2k^2 \cos(\theta)$.

(d) Notice that the entire circle is traced for $0 \leq \theta \leq \pi$. Show that $a_r \leq 0$
for all θ in this interval. Does this make sense?

3. Show that the area enclosed by the ellipse $\frac{x^2}{a^2} + \frac{y^2}{b^2} = 1$ is πab.

QUESTIONS TO THINK ABOUT

1. Discuss Kepler's Laws of Planetary Motion, including their origin and their nature. Are scientific laws presented in this form today?

2. Discuss Newton's Laws of Motion and of Gravitation. Contrast their style to that of Keplers' Laws. What is the significance of the differences between them?

3. Why would Newton attempt to derive Kepler's Laws from his own? Imagine yourself in the late 17th century trying to promote a newfangled mathematics and newfangled physics.

4. Discuss the differences and relationships between polar and rectangular coordinates. Under what circumstances is one system preferable to the other?

SOME PROBLEMS IN POLAR COORDINATES

OBJECTIVE: There are some problems, such as finding the slope of the tangent to a curve and the length of a curve, that we can solve when the curves are defined in rectangular coordinates. Now we look at how to solve these problems, and a few others, for curves defined in polar coordinates.

PROCEDURE:

Part 1: Tangent lines

Let $r = f(\theta)$ define a curve C in polar coordinates. We know that rectangular coordinates are related to polar coordinates according to the formulas $x = r\cos(\theta)$, $y = r\sin(\theta)$. Therefore, C can be defined parametrically by $x = f(\theta)\cos(\theta)$, $y = f(\theta)\sin(\theta)$. For example, the four-leaf rose $r = \sin(2\theta)$ is equivalent to the parametric equations $x = \sin(2\theta)\cos(\theta)$, $y = \sin(2\theta)\sin(\theta)$.

a. Starting with $x = f(\theta)\cos(\theta)$, $y = f(\theta)\sin(\theta)$, find $\dfrac{dx}{d\theta}$ and $\dfrac{dy}{d\theta}$.

b. The slope of the tangent line is $\dfrac{dy}{dx}$. Use your answers to 1a to show that $\dfrac{dy}{dx} = \dfrac{f'(\theta)\sin(\theta) + f(\theta)\cos(\theta)}{f'(\theta)\cos(\theta) - f(\theta)\sin(\theta)}$.

c. Find $\dfrac{dy}{dx}$ for the four-leaf rose $r = \sin(2\theta)$.

d. Write an equation (in rectangular coordinates) for the line tangent to $r = \sin(2\theta)$ at $\theta = \pi/4$.

e. Write an equation for the line tangent to $r = 1 + \cos(\theta)$ at $\theta = \pi/2$.

f. Show that the graph of $r = e^{a\theta}$ has a vertical tangent line when $\tan(\theta) = a$.

Part 2: More about tangents

Let P be a point on the polar curve $r = f(\theta)$. Draw a line tangent to the curve at P. Let ϕ (a Greek letter pronounced "fee" or "figh", but never "fo" or "fum") be the angle between the radius OP and the tangent, measured counterclockwise. It can be shown that $\tan(\phi) = f(\theta)/f'(\theta)$.

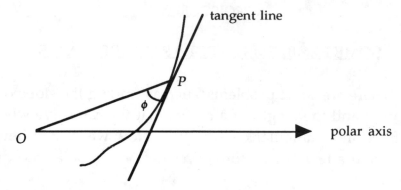

a. Determine ϕ in terms of θ for the circle $r = a \sin(\theta)$.

b. Show that ϕ is constant (independent of θ) for the curve $r = e^{a\theta}$.

c. Show that the radius is perpendicular to the tangent if $f'(\theta) = 0$.

Part 3: Polar subtangents and subnormals

Let P be a point on the polar curve $r = f(\theta)$. The line perpendicular to OP at O and the line tangent to the curve at P intersect at T. PN is perpendicular to PT. (See diagram.) Segment ON is called the **polar subnormal** and segment OT is the **polar subtangent**.

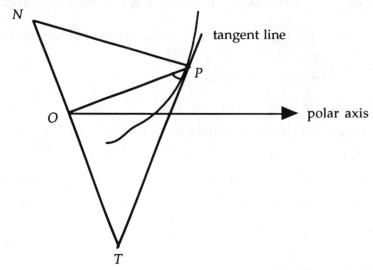

a. Show that the length of $ON = dr/d\theta$ and the length of $OT = \dfrac{r^2}{dr/d\theta}$. (Hint: Angle OPT = angle PNO and use Part 2.)

b. Find the length of the polar subtangent and polar subnormal for the spiral $r = a\theta$.

c. Show that the length of the polar subtangent for the curve $r = a/\theta$ is a constant, independent of θ.

Part 4: Arc length

We showed in Chapter 9 (Theorem 9.6) that the length of the curve defined parametrically by $x = x(t)$, $y = y(t)$ for $a \le t \le b$ is

$$L = \int_a^b \sqrt{\left(\frac{dx}{dt}\right)^2 + \left(\frac{dy}{dt}\right)^2}\, dt$$

a. Use the results of 1a and this theorem to show that, in polar coordinates, the length of the curve $r = f(\theta)$, $\alpha \le \theta \le \beta$ is

$$L = \int_\alpha^\beta \sqrt{(f(\theta))^2 + (f'(\theta))^2}\, d\theta \,.$$

b. Use this formula to find the length of the circle $r = 2\sin(\theta)$. Confirm your result using geometry.

c. Write an integral that can be used to find the length of one loop of the four-leaf rose $r = \sin(2\theta)$.

d. Find the length of the cardioid $r = 1 + \cos(\theta)$. To evaluate the integral, you will need the fact that $1 + \cos(\theta) = 2\cos^2\left(\frac{\theta}{2}\right)$.

Index

We ask your indulgence using this index. In some cases, editing after the index was created has moved a referent to a near-by page. If you cannot find the term you were seeking on the page listed in the index, try the previous and succeeding several pages.

Page references that begin with the letter "p" refer to the projects at the ends of chapters. For example, the page reference "p6.3" refers to Project 6.3; that is the third project at the end of Chapter 6.